WAR BENEATH
THE SEA

WAR BENEATH THE SEA

Submarine Conflict During World War II

PETER PADFIELD

NEW ENGLAND INSTITUTE
OF TECHNOLOGY
LEARNING RESOURCES CENTER

John Wiley & Sons, Inc.
New York • Chichester • Brisbane • Toronto • Singapore

TO JOHN L. STEVENS
one-time submariner, RNR
Altor, Upstart, Otway, Unbending,
doctor: *Mayflower II*,
who failed to return from his last voyage in *Slyboots*

Copyright © 1995 by Peter Padfield
Published by John Wiley & Sons, Inc.

Library of Congress Cataloging-in-Publication Data

Padfield, Peter.
   War beneath the sea : submarine conflict during World War II /
Peter Padfield.
     p. cm.
   Includes bibliographical references and index.
   ISBN 0-471-14624-2 (cloth : alk. paper)
   1. World War, 1939–1945—Naval operations—Submarine. I. Title.
D780.P33 1996
940.54'51—dc20   95-46299

Printed in the United States of America

10 9 8 7 6 5 4 3 2 1

CONTENTS

ILLUSTRATIONS

(between pages 272 and 273)

NMM – National Maritime Museum, Greenwich
IWM – Imperial War Museum, Lambeth
RNSM – Royal Navy Submarine Museum, Gosport
USNA – United States National Archives, Washington DC
BA – Bundesarchiv, Koblenz

PREFACE

First I should like to thank David Roberts, whose original idea this book was, and Grant McIntyre for much support while I was working on it.

The demands of narrative and readability, not to say time and translation, have forced me to limit the scope of the book to the major campaigns of the major submarine services, German, American, British and Japanese, giving indications only of the parts played by the Italian, French, Russian, Dutch, Greek, Polish and Norwegian services. Thus the book is by no means encyclopaedic. I have attempted rather to illumine the decisive and the typical as well as the heroic, to catch mood and feeling as well as follow the strategic, tactical and technological developments.

To an extent the availability of archive material has played a part in shaping the book: the German archives are readily accessible, the Japanese have been largely destroyed. For Japanese operations I have relied greatly on the findings of the US Naval Technical Missions to Japan after the war and the works of W.J. Holmes, an intelligence officer at Pearl Harbor throughout the war, subsequently historian of the underwater campaigns in the Pacific. For all that, the German U-boat campaign was the most potentially decisive aspect of submarine operations in the Second World War, and I make no apology for the space devoted to it. The US submarine campaign had equal potential, but in the event the service was only one of three unstoppable US naval arms. For US submarine operations I owe a debt to W.J. Holmes for his *Undersea Victory* and *Double-edged Secrets* and to Clay Blair Jnr. for his detailed history, *Silent Victory*.

I am deeply in debt to Peter Hansen, a wartime U-boat officer of enquiring mind and wide horizons, who has gone to great trouble explaining both material and psychological factors in U-boat service under Dönitz, and submarine matters in general, and has allowed me to quote passages from his letters to me. Similarly I should like to thank two distinguished wartime submariners, Vice-Admiral Sir Ian McGeoch for his detailed answers to my queries and for allowing me to quote from them and from other papers and letters and his recent memoir, *An Affair of Chances*, published by the Imperial War Museum; and Captain Edward L.

vii

Beach, USN, for his great help and enthusiasm and for permission to quote from his epic *Submarine!*, published by Henry Holt, and his article entitled 'Radar and Submarines in World War II' published in *Defense Electronics*.

I had many conversations about the higher direction of the war with the late, greatly missed Lieutenant-General Sir Ian Jacob, military secretary to Churchill's War Cabinet, and will ever be grateful for his encouragement, help and wisdom. The opinions expressed in this book are mine, however, not necessarily his.

I should like to thank Gus Britton of the Royal Navy Submarine Museum, Gosport, for his help, generously given, and for permission to quote from a letter he wrote home from the *Uproar* in the Mediterranean, previously quoted in Richard Compton-Hall's *The Underwater War 1939-1945*, published by Blandford Press. And I am extremely grateful to Commander William King, RN, for permission to quote extracts from his classic individual account of his own submarine war, *The Stick and the Stars*, published by Hutchinson in 1958.

Fred Lake and Bridget Spiers of the naval section of the Ministry of Defence Library were most helpful in pointing me to material, and Alan Francis and Robert Coppock of the Naval Historical Branch were, as ever, immensely knowledgeable and ready with help and advice. Paul Kemp and Ian Carter guided me through the vast photographic archive at the Imperial War Museum, and I should like to record my debt to their help and expert knowledge. I am particularly excited by the astonishing, hitherto unknown pictures of the capture of *U110* which Paul Kemp was able to provide. My editor, Gail Pirkis, has been an indefatigable support, for whose care with the text I am most grateful. I should also like to acknowledge my debt to the excellent Suffolk County Library interlending service.

Finally I would like to thank the following for permission to reproduce quotations: Lothar-Günther Buchheim, *The Boat* and *U-Boat War*, HarperCollins; Herbert A. Werner, *Iron Coffins*, Arthur Barker; Nicholas Monsarrat, *Three Corvettes*, Cassell; W.J. Holmes, *Undersea Victory*, Doubleday; Edward Young, *One of Our Submarines*, Hart-Davis; Peter Cremer, *U-Boat Commander*, Bodley Head; I.J. Galantin, *Take Her Deep*, Unwin Hyman; and Heinz Schaeffer, *U-Boat 977*, William Kimber. And I should like to thank Rear-Admiral J.R. Hill, editor of *The Naval Review*, for permission to quote from the late Patrick Beesley's article, 'The Operational Intelligence Centre N.I.D. 1939-1945'.

I apologize if by oversight I have omitted anyone.

ABBREVIATIONS

asdic	Allied Submarine Detection Investigation Committee
ASV	British aircraft radar; ASVII metric wavelength; ASVIII centimetric wavelength
ASW	anti-submarine warfare
B-Dienst	*Funkbeobachtungsdienst*, German radio monitoring and decrypting service
BdU	*Befehlshaber der U-boote*; chief of the U-boat arm
Bletchley	Bletchley Park, British radio decryption station
Cast	US Navy Code and Signals Section, Corregidor
Cdr.	Commander
Cinclant	Commander-in-Chief Atlantic Fleet
CO	Commanding officer, or captain of a submarine
Cominch	Commander-in-Chief US Fleet
Comsubaf	Commander Submarines Asiatic Fleet
Comsubpac	Commander Submarines Pacific Fleet
DA	director angle; the aim-off required to hit a moving target
DF	radio direction-finder; apparatus to find the bearing of a transmitting radio
DSEA	Davis Submerged Escape Apparatus
D.T. Gerät	early camouflage name for German asdic
Enigma	cipher machine used by German armed services, 'M' for the *Kriegsmarine*
ERA	engine room artificer; in RN submarines the chief engineer
exec.	executive officer, US Navy, the senior officer below the CO; equivalent to RN first lieutenant
FAT	*Fläschenabsuch* (or *Federapparat*) *Torpedo*; an anti-convoy torpedo that travelled a set course for a set distance, then turned and steered back
FdU	*Führer der U-boote*; up to 1939 chief of the U-boat arm; subsequently theatre U-boat chief
FK	*Fregattenkapitän*
FLAK	*Fliegerabwehrkanone*, anti-aircraft gun
Frupac	Fleet Radio Unit Pacific

Fu MB	*Funkmessbeobachtung*; radar detector
GC & CS	Government Code and Cipher School, Bletchley Park
HF/DF or Huff Duff	high-frequency direction-finder
Hypo	US Navy Code and Signals Section, Pearl Harbor
Kapitän	*Kapitän zur See*
KK	*Korvettenkapitän*
KLt.	*Kapitänleutnant*
LI	*Leitender Ingenieur*, chief engineer of a U-boat
Lt.	Lieutenant
Lt.	*Leutnant zur See*
Lt.-Cdr.	Lieutenant-Commander
LUT	*Lagenunabhängiger Torpedo*; an improved FAT anti-convoy torpedo
MAD	Magnetic Airborne Detector
MOMP	mid-ocean meeting point
Negat	US Navy Code and Signals Section, Washington
ObdM	*Oberbefehlshaber der Kriegsmarine*; supreme commander, German Navy
OIC	Operational Intelligence Centre, British Admiralty
OLt.	*Oberleutnant zur See*
PPI	plan position indicator
Sonar	US and now universal term for asdic
SST	sub-sonic transmission; signalling through water by means of asdic/sonar
TBS	talk between ships radio telephone
TBT	torpedo-bearing transmitter; US submarine night-sight apparatus for surface attack
TDC	torpedo data computer; electro-mechanical torpedo fire-control computer in US fleet submarines
U-boat	anglicization of *U-boot*, short for *Unterseeboot*; submarine
Ultra	Allied signals intelligence from decrypts of top-level Axis ciphers
UZO	*Überwasserzieloptik*; U-boat's night-sight apparatus for surface attack
Wabo	*Wasserbomb*; depth charge

1st Lt.   1st Lieutenant, RN (second in command of submarine)

1WO   1st watch officer, U-boat (second in command of submarine); equivalent to RN first lieutenant and USN executive officer

2WO   2nd watch officer, U-boat

Ranks

RN, USN, IJN		*Kriegsmarine*	
Midshipman/Ensign		*Fähnrich zur See*	
Lieutenant	Lt.	*Leutnant zur See*	Lt.
		Oberleutnant zur See	OLt.
Lieutenant Commander	Lt.-Cdr.	*Kapitänleutnant*	KLt.
Commander	Cdr.	*Korvettenkapitän*	KK.
		Fregattenkapitän	FK.
Captain	Captain	*Kapitän zur See*	Kap.z.S.

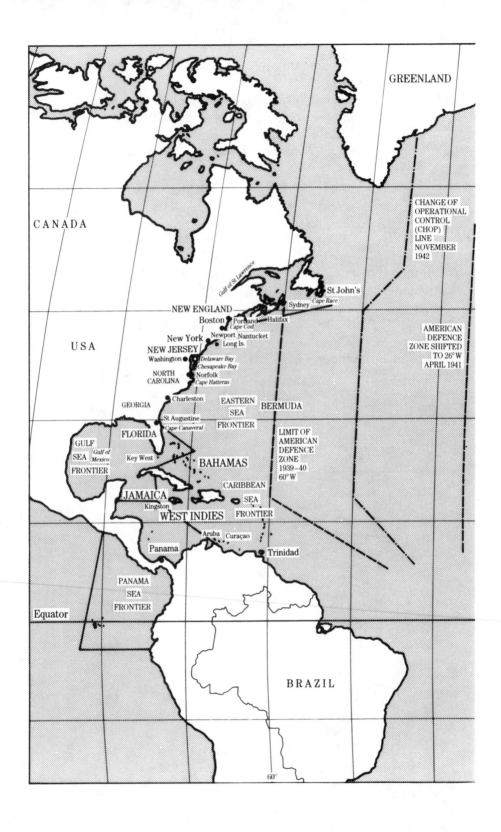

GREENLAND

CANADA

CHANGE OF
OPERATIONAL
CONTROL
(CHOP)
LINE
NOVEMBER
1942

Gulf of St Lawrence

St John's
Cape Race
Sydney

NEW ENGLAND
Boston Portland Halifax
Cape Cod

USA

New York Newport Nantucket
NEW JERSEY Long Is.

Washington Delaware Bay
Chesapeake Bay
NORTH Norfolk
CAROLINA *Cape Hatteras*

AMERICAN
DEFENCE
ZONE SHIFTED
TO 26°W
APRIL 1941

GEORGIA Charleston

EASTERN
SEA
FRONTIER

BERMUDA

St Augustine
Cape Canaveral
FLORIDA

LIMIT OF
AMERICAN
DEFENCE
ZONE
1939–40
60°W

GULF
SEA *Gulf of
Mexico*
FRONTIER Key West

BAHAMAS

JAMAICA
Kingston
WEST INDIES

CARIBBEAN
SEA
FRONTIER

Aruba Curaçao
Panama Trinidad

PANAMA
SEA
FRONTIER

Equator

BRAZIL

60°

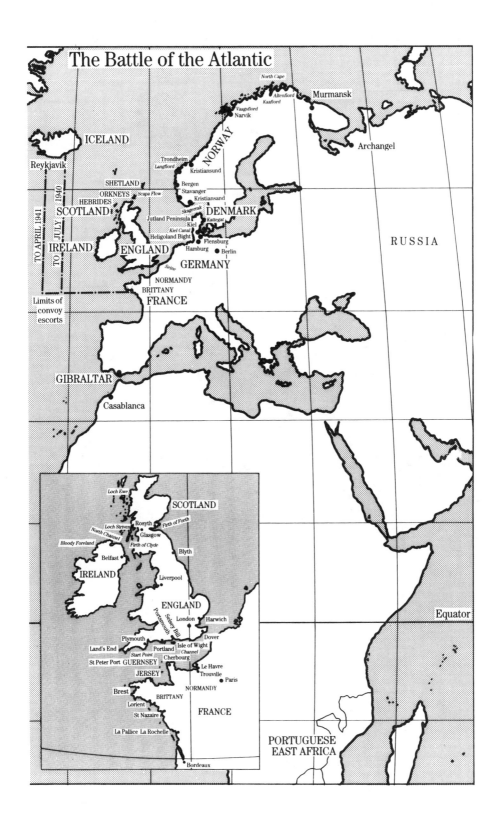

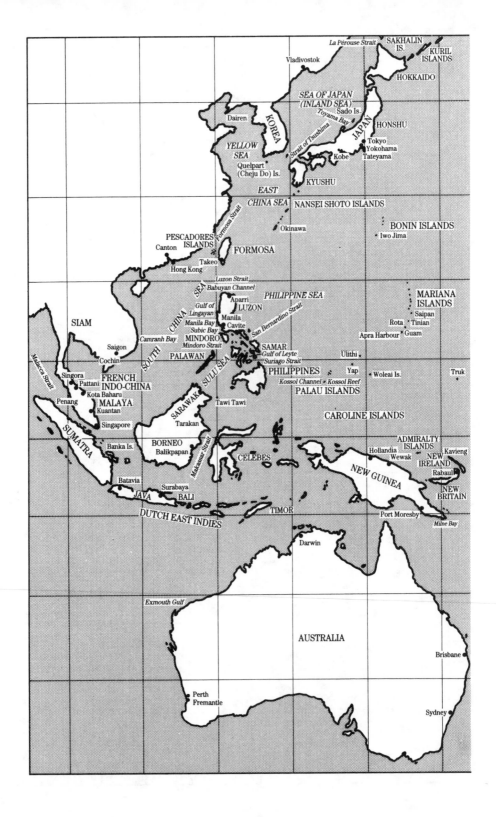

The Pacific War

Midway Is.

French Frigate Shoal

Pearl Harbor
Honolulu Kahoolawe
HAWAII
HAWAIIAN ISLANDS

Wake Is.

Johnston Is.

Kwajalein **MARSHALL ISLANDS**
Majuro

Makin
GILBERT ISLANDS Tarawa

Bougainville
SOLOMON ISLANDS
Buin Florida Is./Tulagi **ELLICE ISLANDS**
The Slot Malaita
Savo Is. Indispensable Strait
Cape Esperance
Guadalcanal

ESPIRITU SANTO
NEW HEBRIDES **FIJI ISLANDS**

NEW CALEDONIA

NEW ZEALAND

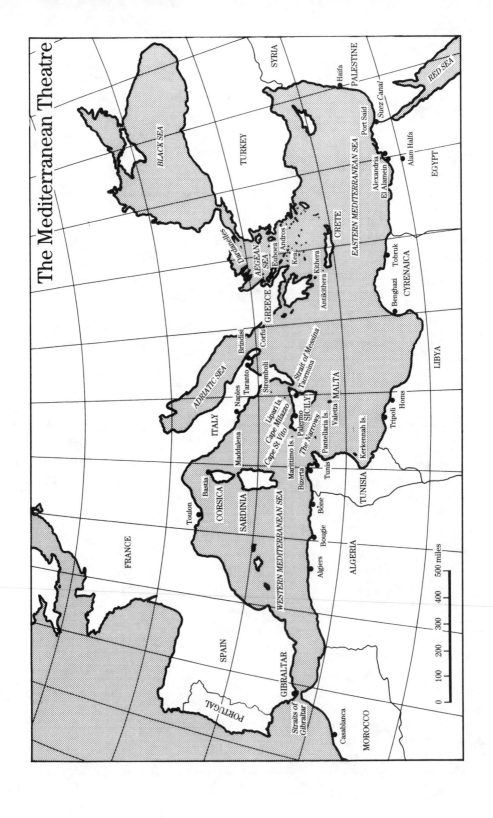

The Mediterranean Theatre

PRELUDE

THE 13,581-TON DONALDSON Atlantic liner *Athenia* departed Glasgow at midday on 1 September 1939, shortly after Hitler had announced to his startled people and the world that German forces were in action against Polish troops on the border. While the British and French governments sought an agreed response she called at Belfast and Liverpool, sailing finally on the 2nd for Montreal with 1,103 passengers, among them Jewish refugees who had fled Nazi Germany at the eleventh hour, and 300 United States citizens. In Canada she was to be fitted with guns for service as an armed merchant cruiser. Following Admiralty instructions to avoid normal shipping lanes, after leaving the North Channel between Ireland and the western capes of Scotland she steered well to the north of her usual westerly course across the Atlantic.

At eleven the following morning, 3 September, Great Britain honoured her treaty obligation to Poland by declaring war on Germany, and shortly afterwards a message, 'Total Germany', went out from the Admiralty to the fleet. The signal was intercepted by the German Radio Intelligence Service, *B-Dienst*. Within minutes copies were with the supreme commander of the *Kriegsmarine*, Admiral Erich Raeder, presiding over his morning staff conference at the *Seekriegsleitung* in Berlin, and the *Führer der U-boote* (chief of the U-boat arm), Kapitän Karl Dönitz, likewise at his morning conference, although at the far less impressive U-boat headquarters in a timber barrack hut at Sengwarden on the outskirts of Wilhelmshaven. Both were deeply shocked. Hitler had assured Raeder he would isolate the Polish campaign; they need not expect war in the west until at least 1943–4 when the great surface fleet they planned, and an expanded U-boat arm would be ready to challenge the Royal Navy. At present both were woefully unprepared. '*Mein Gott!*' Dönitz exclaimed, '*Also wieder Krieg gegen England!*' – 'So it's war against England again!'

Despite his profound dismay the news was not unexpected. Preparations had been made; since 24 August Dönitz's small force of ocean-going U-boats, twenty-one all told, had sortied and traversed the North Sea in secret. They lay waiting to the west of the British Isles and down the Atlantic coast of Europe as far as the Straits of Gibraltar. Their COs had instructions, in case of war,

1

to operate against merchant shipping according to the *Prisenord-nung* (Prize Regulations), thus to stop and search merchantmen and ensure all passengers and crew were in lifeboats within safe reach of land before sinking a vessel. Now they were informed by radio that they were at war with Great Britain, and early that afternoon Dönitz sent a further message instructing them to act against merchant shipping in accordance with the operations order, thus under the *Prisenordnung*.

One of the COs receiving this message was OLt. Fritz-Julius Lemp of *U30*. A rather plump-cheeked 26-year-old with an open, informal manner, he had gained his men's respect through competence rather than overt demonstrations of discipline; indeed his casual style was regarded by more ambitious colleagues as bordering on laziness – if that were possible in the taut service Dönitz ran. Certainly routine bored him. He took short cuts if he could and was apt to make sudden decisions without discussion. His officers found him somewhat quick-tempered and unpredictable in mood. They had no doubts about his ability, though, and his men trusted and liked him very much. After two weeks at sea there was little to distinguish him from them save his battered officer's peaked cap and once white cap cover.

By chance *U30* lay directly on the evasive route the *Athenia* had chosen. At some time in the early evening – exactly when will never be known since after his return to base Lemp was instructed to tear out the relevant log book pages – smoke was sighted above the horizon to the east. Called to the bridge, Lemp pointed *U30* towards the smudge. The bearing remained constant over the bow as the tips of the steamer's mastheads rose above the wavy rim of ocean practically in line, confirming she was heading directly towards him.

'*Auf Gefechtsstationen!*' he called, and hit the alarm button.

The lookouts leaped for the open hatch to the conning tower as bells shrilled through the compartments below, and slid down the ladder and through the hatch beneath to the next ladder into the control room one by one, sliding and thudding to the deck plates and moving aside quickly before the next one crashed down. The officer of the watch followed, and after him Lemp lowered himself through the hatch, lifting the cover and swinging it shut above his head as he stepped down the rungs, then spinning the horizontal handwheel that secured it in its seating.

Way below the chief engineer (LI) who would dive the boat had already reached the control room; two of the bridge lookouts were seated near him next to one another facing the hydrophone controls against the starboard side. Other sailors and machinists were scrambling to their stations, and reports were coming through the speaker system from the engine and bow compartments: the air induction and exhaust valves for the diesels had been closed, the fuel switched off, the engines declutched; aft of them in the motor compartment, the electric motors had been started and were driving the propeller shafts.

The LI focused his attention on the battery of lights, handwheels and levers on the port side known as the *Weihnachtsbaum* – the Christmas tree. When all lights were green he would know that every opening in the pressure hull was shut and secure. As the last light changed he started the familiar sequence of orders to open the vents of the main ballast tanks in succession from forward aft. The sailors and machinists standing by the red or grey-green levers pulled them from the side and down, using their full body weight; others turned handwheels. Sea water flooded in from the bottoms of the tanks, and the air which had provided the boat with buoyancy was forced from the vents at the top in a continuous roar. The LI turned his attention to the hydroplane indicators before the two seated 'planesmen to starboard. The after indicator showed a 5° inclination, the forward indicator hard a-dive. Already the deck plates had taken a perceptible bow-down angle. The pointer of the depth gauge above had begun to move around its circular dial. The LI shifted his eyes to the finer scale Papenberg indicator whose water column was rising past the depth gradations.

In less than half a minute the conning tower had slipped beneath the surface. In place of the blast of escaping air there was silence, broken only by the whirr of fans and from far aft the soft hum of the electric motors. The LI gave quiet instructions to the planesmen, levelling the boat out of her dive, and to the leading hand on the compressed air distributor panel. The hiss of the high-pressure air could be heard as water was expelled from the trim and negative buoyancy tanks. Satisfied he had the boat in hand and perfectly balanced, he took a step towards the open hatch to the conning tower and called to Lemp above, *'Boot ist eingependelt, Herr Oberleutnant!'*

'Auf Seerohrtiefe!' Lemp replied without ceremony, and as the LI ordered the hydroplanes set to rise to take the boat up 20 feet or so to periscope depth, he swung himself on to the metal bicycle-type seat straddling the attack periscope housing abaft the hatch opening. Unlike the system in other navies, the eyepiece on German attack periscopes did not move up or down with the shaft, but remained at a fixed height so that the CO, once seated, never

moved from his position. Foot pedals allowed him to train the whole apparatus on which he was seated; a lever at his left hand allowed him to raise or lower the shaft of the periscope, a knob at his right hand controlled the vertical angle of the upper prism. Lemp leant his forehead into the rubber cushioning around the eyepiece and moved the lever actuating the hoist motor. The oiled hiss of the shaft gliding up was reassuringly familiar. He had done this so many times in practice. Yet this time it was real. He was gripped by a sudden emptiness.

Dark gave way to ever lighter green in his eyepiece, and suddenly he saw sunlight and beads of water rolling from the upper glass. A translucent wave washed over, leaving more droplets. As they cleared he adjusted the knob in his right hand and pressed down on his left foot pedal until he had the steamer clear in view and centred against the crosswires and range graticule. She was still hull down, but he could see her tall funnel streaming smoke and the front of her wide bridge structure brilliant white in the westering sun. Her masts were still almost in line. She was steering a steady course towards him. He trained round, scanning the horizon for any other vessels which might have appeared since they had dived. There was nothing.

What now possessed Lemp will never be known for he did not survive the war. Those very few of his crew who did survive have told how he had immediately leapt to the conclusion that she was a troop transport, and ordered the four bow tubes made ready for torpedo attack. The belated official explanation was that he mistook her for an armed merchant cruiser, but this was a standard justification for naval mistakes. There were absolutely no indications for either assumption, rather the reverse. She was well into the Atlantic, some 250 miles north-west of northern Ireland, steering a steady westerly course. Most passengers were at dinner as she closed and none were about the decks, but their absence from view gave no reason to suspect she had been converted from the passenger liner she obviously was into a naval auxiliary. And it is hard to understand why at the start of war she should have been carrying troops away from the British Isles across the Atlantic. The simplest explanation for Lemp's mistake is that she presented him with a tempting target on a course which might have been designed for him to attack, and in his precipitate way he convinced himself she was what he wanted her to be.

He called out her bearing, range and his estimate of the very small angle between her course and his line of sight to the 1st watch officer (1WO) just behind him at the fire-control calculator, and instructed the helmsman, the only other person in the cramped space of the tower, to alter course to starboard. He would move further from the target's track, then swing back to fire, aiming with the whole boat, the torpedoes' gyro compasses set to zero. With the speed at which the liner was approaching there was little time for overmuch calculation. Deciding on a spread of only two torpedoes in the first instance, he gave the order to make ready tubes 1 and 2.

The torpedo petty officer in the bow compartment repeated the order, reporting moments later, 'Rohr eins fertig! Rohr zwei fertig!

Raising the periscope more cautiously as the liner neared, her bridge touched with the pink of the setting sun, the paintwork of her bows rippling with reflections from the white foam swelling down her side, Lemp called his final observations from 1,000 yards range shortly after 21.40 German time, which was two hours ahead of the *Athenia*'s time. The 1WO confirmed the aim-off angle.

'Rohr eins,' Lemp said quietly down the speaking tube, 'Los!' and he pressed the firing button. It was 21.42.[1]

'Los!' The response came back from the torpedo petty officer in the bow compartment as he hit the brass hand-firing lever beside No. 1 tube, the back-up in case the electric firing failed.

The boat gave a slight lurch as the torpedo was ejected, and all hands felt a sensation in their eardrums as the compressed air which had launched it was sucked back into the hull to prevent an eruption on the surface giving away their position. The LI gave a brief order to the machinist manning the flood valve of the forward trimming tank, who wrenched his handwheel round, admitting water to compensate for the weight lost. From the sound room just forward of the control room the hydrophone operator, listening to the torpedo's propellers, reported it running normally, 'Torpedo läuft regulär!'

The 1WO in the tower with Lemp had pressed the button of his stop-watch as the 'eel' left the tube, and was counting the seconds softly; as he reached eight Lemp fired the second tube. Nothing happened. The torpedo petty officer in the bow compartment hit the hand-firing lever a second time; still nothing happened. He hit it again repeatedly, but the torpedo refused to move. It was a *Rohrstecker*, stuck fast in the tube.

In the *Athenia* neither the bridge watch nor the forward lookout had sighted Lemp's periscope as it poked up briefly through the waves during the approach, and they did not see the torpedo racing in from their port beam since it was powered by an electric motor and left no tell-tale air bubbles in its track. It struck aft of mid-length at the after end of the engine room, the force of its detonation destroying part of the bulkhead between that compartment and a boiler room astern of it, rising through the stairwell above that led up from the Third and Tourist Class dining-saloon, wrecking it and trapping all the diners inside in semi-darkness as the ship's lights went out. A deluge of sea water raised by the explosion crashed back on the boat deck. The stink of high explosive wafted through open cabin windows.

The master, Captain Cook, was at dinner in the First Class saloon. By the time he reached the bridge the liner was already taking a list to port. He instructed the radio officer to send an SOS, and the chief officer to sound 'Abandon ship!' As sailors began throwing off the gripes from the lifeboats and the passengers swarming out on deck were shepherded to muster stations, those on the port side saw the sinister green-grey shape of a U-boat's conning tower rising from the sea only 800 yards off the quarter, grey-clad figures emerging and climbing down as the bow and long foredeck appeared, streaming white water. The figures gathered by the deck gun, whose barrel trained round towards the liner; a burst of smoke and a sharp report heralded the first shell which passed harmlessly overhead. Another followed, dense smoke blowing back to shroud the conning tower so that only the forward section of the submarine's deck and a short length of the after deck could be seen on either side of it. Watching in horrified fascination, passengers and crew saw the shark-nosed bow dip into the waves and disappear. As the smoke dispersed it was evident that the U-boat had submerged again.

Lemp had realized the full extent of his mistake when he saw women and children coming out on deck. He had attempted to shoot away the wireless aerial and radio room aft of the bridge, but had thought better of it when his own radio man picked up the liner's distress calls. What feelings of mingled triumph and dismay jostled in his mind? He was evidently at a loss. He cruised at periscope depth, steering up past the liner's bows and across to her starboard side as she listed further to port and slowly settled. The sounds of the sea rushing into her broken hull and bulkheads and fittings buckling and rending before the pressure carried plainly through the short space of water, as did the shrieks of women and children from the Third and Tourist dining-saloon trapped in the stairwell lobby as the water rose about them. The shocking noises were magnified for the sound man as he listened through his hydrophone earphones.

All the boats were filled and lowered safely except one, which fell from the davits straight to the water, and nearly all who got away from the liner were rescued by ships responding to her SOS calls. Lemp had gone by then. Having cruised submerged around the lifeboats in the gathering darkness, he had made off when his radio operator reported two British destroyers on their way to the scene with other ships. He did not report the sinking by radio.

Of the *Athenia*'s total complement of 1,418 passengers and crew, 118 were lost, most either killed in the torpedo explosion or trapped in the after stairwell lobby; among them were 69 women and 16 children, 22 of them citizens of the United States of America.[2]

Shock waves radiated around the world. The sinking recalled the *Lusitania*, likewise torpedoed without warning in the First World War, and seemed to presage a similarly ruthless U-boat campaign against neutrals and civilians.

1

Submarines and Submariners

THE SUBMARINE WAS a subversive force. Its ability to hide within the element on which the battlefleet held sway threatened the great ships, the theory and practice of their employment, above all the admirals who had risen in their service; during the 1920s and 1930s these held power and patronage, not simply in the Royal Navy where, for reasons of proud historic supremacy and incipient decline, it might have been expected, but also in those younger, thrusting navies of the United States, Nazi Germany and Imperial Japan who looked to seize the trident. All these in the years leading to the Second World War cleaved to orthodoxy.

The articles of faith had been set down from 1890 by an American naval officer, Alfred Thayer Mahan, in a series of works extracting the principles of sea power from history – actually a period of history practically confined to the centuries of British naval ascendancy. Mahan placed the battlefleet at the core of naval strategy. By defeating the enemy battlefleet or bottling it up in port, the dominant fleet established 'command' of the oceans; and by blockading, that is throwing a cordon around the enemy's coast, strangled his trade and brought him low. At the opposite pole to this strategy, and generally practised by the weaker naval power, was commerce-raiding, known after its French exponents as *guerre de course*. According to the doctrine this would never prevail over the superior battlefleet power.

The experience of the First World War appeared to confirm the theory. The British Grand Fleet had met the German High Seas Fleet off Jutland and driven it home, whence it had seldom ventured again, while the Royal Naval blockade had reduced the German population to near-starvation, anarchy and revolution. In the meantime, the German submarine or U-boat *guerre de course* had been contained.

Yet it had been a close-run thing. In April 1917 the British government had looked at defeat. That month, in which the United States entered the war against Germany, the Anglophile Admiral William Sims, despatched to liaise with the Admiralty in London, was horrified when shown the figures of merchant shipping losses: 536,000 tons sunk in February, 603,000 tons in

March, 900,000 tons predicted for the current month. His dismay was heightened by a talk with the First Sea Lord, Sir John Jellicoe.

'It is impossible for us to go on with the war if losses like this continue,' Jellicoe told him.

'It looks as though the Germans are winning the war,' Sims replied.

'They will win unless we can stop these losses – and stop them soon.'

When Sims questioned him about a solution, he said that at present they could see absolutely none.[1]

Towards the end of the month Jellicoe, believing the government had not grasped the full gravity of the situation, wrote a memo to his civilian chief, the First Lord of the Admiralty, suggesting that it was necessary to bring home to the War Cabinet 'the very serious nature of the naval position':

> We are carrying on the war ... as if we had the absolute command of the sea, whereas we have not such command or anything approaching it. It is quite true that we are masters of the situation so far as surface ships are concerned, but it must be realised – and realised at once – that this will be quite useless if the enemy's submarines paralyse, as they do now, our lines of communication.[2]

He went on to suggest saving shipping space for the import of foodstuffs by withdrawing entirely from the Salonika campaign, and cutting down ruthlessly on all imports not essential to the life of the country,

> but even with all this we shall be very hard put to it unless the United States help to the utmost of their ability ... Without some such relief as I have indicated – and that given immediately – the Navy will fail in its responsibilities to the country and the country itself will suffer starvation.[3]

This crisis in the naval war did not disprove the doctrine of battlefleet command since the Admiralty had brought it on itself by misunderstanding and thus disregarding the simplest, time-honoured response to *guerre de course*: convoying merchant ships instead of allowing them to sail independently while attempting to hunt the raiders. Mahan himself had written:

> the result of the convoy system ... warrants the inference that, when properly systematised and applied, it will have more success as a defensive measure than hunting for individual marauders – a process which, even when most thoroughly planned, still resembles looking for a needle in a haystack.[4]

In desperation, and in response to more thoughtful officers in the fleet, at the eleventh hour the Admiralty introduced convoys for oceanic trade. Almost at once the shipping haemorrhage eased. It should have been a lesson: at the height of the campaign that April there were on average less than 50 of Germany's 128 operational U-boats at sea at any time.[5] It was this handful of comparatively inexpensive war machines which had come within an ace of sinking the most powerful naval and trading empire, aided not simply by her maritime allies, France, Italy, Japan and finally the United States, but also by the shipping and shipyards of neutrals. After the convoy system was instituted it was American yards building ships faster than the U-boats could sink them that allowed the Allies to transport sufficient materials and troops to win the Continental war.

In November 1918, as Germany's acceptance of the armistice conditions became known, one of the U-boat COs, OLt. Karl Dönitz, who had been captured after his boat surfaced out of control while he was attacking a convoy, was held aboard a British cruiser off Gibraltar. He was watching scenes of jubilation in nearby ships with a bitter heart, when he found the cruiser's captain approaching. Dönitz gestured at the ensigns flying from the armada of ships in the roads, British, American, French and Japanese, and asked the Britisher if he could take any pleasure from a victory attained with the whole world as allies.

'Yes, it's very curious,' the Captain replied thoughtfully.[6]

A submarine was a thick-skinned steel cylinder tapering at both ends, designed to withstand enormous pressure at depth. Buoyancy chambers termed main ballast tanks, fitted in most cases as lozenge-shaped bulges outside this pressure hull on either side, kept the cylinder just afloat. An outer steel 'casing' liberally pierced with openings to let the sea flood in and out provided a sharp bow, a faired stern and a narrow deck atop the cylinder; only a few feet above the sea, this was washed in any weather like a half-tide rock. About midway along its length rose a low structure enclosing another small pressure chamber called the conning tower, accessible from the pressure hull via a circular hatch and allowing access to the bridge above it by another small, pressure-tight hatch.

To submerge, the diesel engines which drove the craft on the surface, sucking air in through ducts from the tower structure, were shut down, and electric motors which took their power from massed batteries and consequently used no air were coupled to the propeller shafts. Buoyancy was destroyed by opening valves in the main ballast tanks, allowing the trapped air to be forced out by sea water rushing in; and horizontal fins, termed hydroplanes or just planes, projecting either side at bow and stern were angled against the water flow caused by the boat's progress to impel the bows down. Approaching the required depth as shown on a gauge in the control room below the conning tower, the diving officer attempted to balance the boat in a state of neutral buoyancy, 'catching a trim' in which they neither descended further nor rose. He did this by adjusting the volume of water in auxiliary tanks at bow and stern, and either side at mid-length, flooding or pumping out, aiming to poise the submarine so perfectly that she swam on an even keel weighing precisely the same as the space of sea she occupied, completely at one with her element and floating firm and free as an airship in the air. It was an art attained by minute attention to the detail of prior consumption of stores and fuel, and by much experience. Sea water is seldom homogenous; a boat passing into a layer of different temperature or salinity, and hence density, becomes suddenly less or more buoyant, dropping fast or refusing to descend through the layer until more tank spaces have been flooded; when going deep the pressure hull would be so squeezed between the ribs by the weight above that it occupied less space and the boat had to be lightened by pumping out tanks to compensate. Most vigilance was required at the extremes: going very deep the boat might plunge below the point at which the hull could withstand the pressure; near the surface at periscope depth she might porpoise up to break surface in sight of the enemy.

Submerged, a submarine stole along at walking pace or less, either to conserve her batteries which could not be recharged by diesels until she surfaced again or, when hunted, to make as little engine and propeller noise as possible. With both sets of batteries 'grouped up' in parallel she might make twice a fast walking speed, 8 or 9 knots, but only for some two hours at most before the batteries ran dangerously low. This was her shortcoming: while she had great range and speed on the surface, once submerged she lost mobility by comparison even with the slowest tramp steamer. Against a battle squadron she could not hope to get within range for attack unless already lying in ambush very close to its track. For this reason the submarine was held to be 'a weapon of position and surprise'.

Once her presence was detected and she became the hunted her submerged endurance was limited by the amount of air within the pressure hull, which of course was all the crew had to breathe; as they exhaled it became progressively degraded with carbon dioxide, after twenty-four hours or so reaching dangerous and finally fatal levels. Headaches and dizziness were common in operational submarines, but they were accepted among the other discomforts of an exacting life; remarkably little was known of the speed of deterioration of air. It was, for example, not appreciated that when the carbon dioxide content reaches 4 per cent thinking becomes difficult and decisions increasingly irrational; by 10 per cent extreme distress is felt, followed soon after by unconsciousness; at over 20 per cent the mixture is lethal.[7] No doubt this was not realized, and air purifiers were not installed – although in the German service individual carbon dioxide filter masks with neckstraps were provided – since before the advent of radar a submarine could usually surface at night to renew her air while remaining invisible. That indeed was the usual operational routine: to lurk submerged on the lookout for targets by day, coming up after nightfall to recharge the batteries, refresh the air and perhaps cruise to another position.

The submarine's main armament was provided by torpedoes, each a miniature submarine in itself with a fuel tank and motor driving contra-rotating propellers, a depth mechanism actuating hydroplanes to maintain a set depth, and a gyro compass linked to a rudder to maintain a set course. At the forward end a warhead of high explosive was detonated by a mechanism firing on contact or when disturbed by the magnetic field of the target ship. These auto-piloted cylinders, known as fish or in the German service as eels, were housed in tubes projecting forward from the fore end of the pressure hull and often aft from the after end as well. In some classes two or more tubes were housed externally beneath the casing, but unlike the internal tubes from the pressure hull whose reloads were stowed in the fore and after compartments, external tubes could not be reloaded until return to base.

While devastating when they hit the soft underpart of a ship or exploded beneath her, torpedoes were neither as accurate as shells from guns, nor for several reasons could they be 'spotted' on to the target. They were launched from their tubes – after these had been opened to the sea – set to steer a collision course to a point ahead of the target ship, ideally at or near a right angle to her track. Whether they hit depended largely on whether the relative motion problem had been solved correctly, which before radar meant how accurately the target's course and speed had been estimated. The most certain data available was the target's bearing read from a graduated ring around the periscope. Range was obtained by reading the angle between the waterline and the masthead or bridge of the target, either from simple graduations of minutes of arc or by a split-image rangefinder built into the periscope optics. Using the height of the mast or whatever feature had been taken, the angle was converted into range by a sliding scale. Since in most cases the masthead heights had to be estimated from the assumed size or class of the target ship, usually a difficult judgement to make from quick periscope observations, and since there was a tendency to overestimate size, ranges were often exaggerated. In addition the observer made an estimate of the angle between the target ship's heading and his own line of sight, known as 'the angle on the bow'; this too was often overestimated. Speed was deduced from a count of the propeller revolutions audible through the submarine's listening apparatus, the distance of the second bow wave from the stem, or simply from the type of vessel and experience. With this data a plot was started incorporating both the target's and the submarine's own movements; updated by subsequent observations as the attack developed, the plot provided increasingly refined estimates which were fed into computing devices of greater or less mechanical ingenuity according to the nationality of the submarine. In British and Japanese navies the firing solution was expressed as an aim-off or director angle (DA) ahead of the target, in the US and German navies as a torpedo-course setting. Finally, a salvo of two or usually more torpedoes was fired with an interval of several seconds between each; this was to avoid upsetting the trim with such a sudden release of weight as would result from the simultaneous discharge of all tubes, and to allow for errors in the estimated data or the steering of the torpedoes themselves. In the British service, where it was assumed that at least three hits would be required to sink a modern capital ship, COs were trained to fire a 'massed salvo' of all torpedoes – usually six – at 5-second intervals, so spreading the salvo along the target and its track. In the American and German services particularly, where the torpedoes themselves could be set to run the desired course, 'spread' was often achieved by firing a 'fan' with a small angle between each torpedo.

Few attacks were as straightforward as this description might imply: the target was generally steering a zigzag pattern; surface and air escorts were often present to force the submarine into evasive alterations during the approach. The periscope could be used only sparingly, the more so the calmer the sea, lest the feather of its wake were spotted by lookouts; and between observations the submarine CO had to retain a mental picture of the developing situation, continuously updating calculations of time, speed and distance in his head as he attempted to manoeuvre into position to catch the DA at the optimum time when the torpedoes would run in on a broad angle to the enemy's track. There were other situations when snap judgements had to be made on a single observation or while the submarine was turning with nothing but the CO's experience and and eye to guide him. It was sometimes said that a successful CO needed a sportsman's eye. Like most generalizations about submarine COs, this can be disproved by individual example: David Wanklyn, for instance, the highest-scoring British ace, did not shine at ball games.

Some British COs appear to have dispensed with overmuch calculation: John Stevens, the very successful CO of *Unruffled* in the Mediterranean, remarked, 'I say if the target's worth firing at, give him the lot [a full salvo] and, anyway, the DA is always ten degrees.'[8] It is not possible to compare the results of this cavalier approach statistically with those of American or German COs who relied on fire-control computers generating continuous solutions since the three services operated in very different conditions and, particularly with the Americans, the percentage of hits was depressed by torpedo failures. All that can be deduced from the figures is that all navies had a few COs who consistently outhit the average, and at the other end of the scale a few who seldom hit anything. The qualities the aces showed were aggression, determination, imperturbability in attack, and painstaking attention to training. To a greater extent than in any other type of warship, officers and crew were simple extensions of the CO's will. When he attacked submerged, he alone saw the enemy – apart from some US submarines where the executive officer took the periscope – and it was the CO's coolness, resolve and daring, or his timidity, exhaustion and nervous fatigue, that decided the course of the action.

The submarine, more than any other warship, was designed and operated as what would now be called a weapon system. Except in the US service, no concessions were made to the comfort or even the convenience of the crew. They were carried merely to serve the system, fitting in the spaces around the reload torpedoes and stores for the voyage, in most cases sharing bunks, 'hot bunking' with a shipmate from another watch and sleeping on unchanged sheets that became dirtier by the day. They were unable to bathe or shower, scarcely to wash hands and face, and frequently could not get dry after a wet spell on watch. There was often a queue for the fiendishly complex WC in the heads, and even that could not be used when submerged below about 70 feet because of the exterior pressure. Thereafter they were obliged to relieve themselves in buckets and empty bottles whose smell mixed with the confined, humid odour of diesel oil, past cooking, unwashed bodies, chlorine and stale bilges which permeated every area. They were forced to eat hashes of tinned food and dehydrated vegetables after the fresh provisions ran out, could not take proper exercise, could not even walk on the deck casing lest an enemy aircraft were sighted and the boat had to make an emergency dive; and when submerged for any length of time they were subject to nausea, splitting headaches and, if the mind were allowed to dwell on it, incipient claustrophobia. Paradoxically, the sheer frightfulness of conditions and the sense of vulnerability, and hence of mutual responsibility, engendered comradeship across barriers of rank which in turn ensured high morale, probably higher than in any other class of warship, irrespective of nationality. It depended, however, on a good CO; this meant above all an officer who, whatever his qualities or faults, the men felt they could trust.

It was a young man's game. In the British service an officer was judged too old for operational command at 35. The US service began the war with COs for fleet submarines nearer 40 than 35 but many proved over-cautious, which may have had more to do with unrealistic peacetime training than with age; they were soon replaced by younger officers whose aggression, helped by radar, was largely responsible for the devastating campaign which severed Japan from its external supplies. By the last year of the war most US submarine COs were in their early thirties, many not yet 30. In the German service a more dramatic decline in the age of COs was due to the loss of men in the Atlantic and the simultaneous expansion of the U-boat fleet; in the later years many German COs were under 25; youngest of all was Hans Hess, who was 21 when he took command of U995 in 1944.

Who in sound mind volunteered for the hazards of such an unnatural life? Before the war sufficient came forward in all navies, and it was only necessary to draft a few, mostly specialist ratings. Some would insist they joined for the extra allowance paid for service in submarines, or because they needed the extra money to get married. There were other powerful inducements: for officers, especially, responsibility and command came much earlier than in the surface fleet; for all hands there was the special camaraderie and informality of the close life aboard, and a different kind of discipline, maintained more by competence and self-respect than by mere rank. In a submarine more than in any other type of vessel each member of the crew was vital to the team; a mistake by any one person might lead to disaster. It was in every sense a close fraternity with all the certainties and reassurance of such, bonded by shared trials, miseries, unique hazards and proficiency in overcoming them. In every navy the submarine service was a club apart with a particular *esprit de corps*, attracting the bright and non-conformist seeking escape from the hierarchy and meaningless apple-polishing of a big-ship navy in peacetime. The future German aces, Prien, Schepke and Kretschmer, were of this type, as was the American submarine CO Ignatius Galantin, who wrote of his two years' battleship service after graduating from the Naval Academy: 'I became increasingly restive . . . I wanted to be free of the dull, repetitious, institutionalised life of the battleship navy, and to be part of a more personalised, more modern and flexible sea arm.'[9]

As Galantin hints, the submarine was exciting as a new weapon at the forefront of naval technology and strategy. On the other hand it had retained from the first war the aura of clandestine, piratical operations by such COs as Martin Dunbar Nasmith, who had forced the nets, minefields and powerful currents of the Dardanelles to attack Turkish transports for Gallipoli in the Sea of Marmora; Max Horton, whose exploits in the Baltic had led the Germans to put a price on his head; and from the other camp Lothar von Arnauld de la Perière, 'ace of aces', whose record of ships and tonnage sunk remains unbeaten, and Dönitz's first CO, Walter Forstmann, who stands only a little below Arnauld in the record book.

One of the distinguished band of British submariners (now Vice-Admiral Sir) Ian McGeoch has listed his reasons for volunteering:

> I was a dedicated small boat sailor, and navigator in offshore racing yachts; I was keen to get the early command which submarine service offered; I was engaged to be married, so that the extra six shillings per diem was an attraction; and I had read most of the accounts of the operations of British submarines in WW1.[10]

In both Germany and Japan, where youthful idealism was harnessed to a martial ethic, the submarine arms were deliberately raised to élites, their image enhanced by propaganda; in Germany posters depicted dashing U-boat heroes sailing under streaming pennants towards the enemy. Despite this, during the war both Germany and Japan, while attempting to maintain the fiction of an all-volunteer service, resorted increasingly to drafting suitable young men from the surface fleet, as indeed happened in Great Britain and America. But even when drafted, by no means all measured up to the physical and temperamental demands of submarine life. In all navies the submarine branch remained an élite of fit, stable young men from which temperamental misfits and those not prepared to pull their weight were very quickly weeded, or weeded themselves.

2

Towards the Second World War

THE SUBMARINE DID not change between the wars; it simply developed in small ways from its forerunners in the first war, yet there were distinct differences between the national fleets. These had less to do with differing national requirements than with a shared misunderstanding of the role and strategic potential of the weapon by the gunnery admirals at the top, aggravated by the distorting effects on design of naval limitation treaties.

The Royal Navy's policy can only be described as one of wilful blindness. As guardians of the greatest merchant fleet and volume of external trade, and an empire bound by sea routes, British admirals had recognized the danger of the submarine from its beginnings, and wanted to outlaw it. Nevertheless, they had taken care to develop the arm, if only to be able to devise counter-measures. After the shocking experience of April 1917 when it had seemed their worst fears were about to be realized, the policy became a parody. At the Washington Conference of 1922, called by the United States to prevent a naval building race, the British delegation sought to have submarines banned; when this failed they persuaded the other delegates to sign a declaration not to use them, as U-boats had been used, for an unrestricted war on merchant shipping – although this section was never ratified by France.

The Washington Treaty formalized the end of Great Britain's naval supremacy. It had been implicit from at least the turn of the century with the growth of Germany, the United States and Japan as industrial and naval powers. The colossal debt run up in the First World War finally ended any possibility of Britain maintaining a world-wide navy able to take on all comers; in her weakened condition she could not have matched the United States alone in a building competition. She had no option but to agree to an American limitation proposal whereby the United States, Great Britain and Japan – since the defeat of Germany the three major naval powers – accepted a ratio of 5:5:3 in capital ship tonnage. This faced her with the prospect – in the early 1920s apparently remote – of finding herself inferior to Japan in the Far East if challenged at the same time by an enemy in the Atlantic or the Mediterranean; logically she could now deploy the arguments of the lesser battlefleet powers, France and Italy, who were building submarines intended to whittle down a larger enemy fleet to a size at which their own might meet it in battle.

It would be unreasonable to expect that admirals nurtured in a period of British supremacy on a Nelsonic legend of offence and success against all odds would or could have adapted their attitude to such very different conditions. In any case, baulked in their aim of abolishing beastly submarines, they experimented with eccentric ideas for equipping them with heavy guns or seaplanes, or building huge submersible 'cruisers', meanwhile protecting capital ships with underwater anti-torpedo 'bulges' and developing a submarine detection system pioneered in 1917 by the Allied Submarine Detection Investigation Committee. The apparatus, known from the acronym of the committee as asdic, sent out pulses of ultra-sonic sound waves in a cone-shaped beam which could be trained in any direction under water; echoes reflected back from dense objects were picked up and the time elapsed since transmission of the pulse converted into range. Thus not only could submarines be discovered up to a mile or so away, but their range and bearing could also be plotted, though not their depth in the early stages of an attack. In theory the apparatus could be used by submarines themselves to locate and attack surface ships from below periscope depth; as it was also developed as a discreet means of underwater communication known as SST (sub-sonic transmission), it was fitted in both destroyers and submarines. Besides asdic, all sub-marines were fitted with arrays of listening heads termed hydro-phones to detect the presence and bearing of other vessels from their engine and propeller noise.

Despite the sense of security derived from asdic, and presumably also from the Washington Treaty outlawing unrestricted war on merchant ships, the Sea Lords and the British government con-tinued to press for the abolition of submarines at the London Naval Conferences of both 1932 and 1935, without success; indeed by the latter meeting Japan had withdrawn from international limitations of any kind, and Germany, formerly prevented from possessing submarines by the terms of the Versailles Treaty, had launched a new U-boat arm. The first London Treaty did, however, set limits for the western navies, who agreed not to exceed Great Britain's total submarine tonnage of 52,700, nor to build individual boats over 2,000 tons (standard surface) displacement.

Meanwhile the Admiralty had ordered two distinct new types, both revealing an obsession with battlefleet doctrine: one of these, the O class, followed by improved versions, Ps and Rs, was intended to hold the ring on the outbreak of war with Japan – by this time considered more than a possibility – until units of the fleet in the Mediterranean or home waters could reach the Far East. The other, River class, marked a revival of the concept of submarines sufficiently fast to work with the battlefleet. The original attempts at this idea during the first war had resulted in a disastrous, steam-powered K class. The idea was fundamentally misconceived: a few hours on a tactical board would have shown that once submerged on contact with the enemy, the chances of the boats working into a favourable position for torpedo attack would have been remote. This was all the more surprising considering the general view of the submarine as a weapon of position and surprise.

In the final years of peace a new type was designed to replace the O, P and R classes, which suffered many technical problems, not least a tendency, which would prove fatal in war, to leak oil from external tanks. Although international limitation was dead before the first of the new boats was laid down, the specifications were drawn up before the 1935 London Naval Conference, when the Admiralty hoped – if they failed to ban submarines altogether – at least to reduce the total tonnage allowed each country to 45,000 tons. Hence, instead of specifying boats of comparable size and speed to the classes they were to replace, or building up to the 2,000-ton individual limit, the Admiralty opted for a boat of 1,000 tons. The figure was picked chiefly, it seems, to obtain a greater number of boats within the overall tonnage limit they hoped to negotiate. In such a negative spirit the T class was born. The boats had one very positive feature, a bow salvo of ten torpedoes. Six tubes opened from the forward end of the pressure hull, two from a bulbous casing above and two more faced forward under a raised deck at mid-length. This gave the boats the most powerful forward battery of any submarine in the world, at least in theory; the intention was to increase the chances of scoring a sufficient number of hits to sink a highly compartmented modern capital ship. However, the four external tubes could not be reloaded at sea, nor could their torpedoes be inspected and serviced; consequently they were not so dependable as those in the internal tubes, especially over a long patrol. Moreover, the bulge of deck casing necessary to accommodate the forward external tubes caused difficulties with trim and raised a visible bow wave at periscope depth. To correct these faults in a second series laid down after the outbreak of war, the external bow tubes were moved 7 feet aft and the bow casing was fined down. And to give the boats greater flexibility in attack, a single external torpedo tube was added beneath the casing at the stern, and the two tubes at either side amidships were turned to face aft. This still left a powerful bow salvo of eight torpedoes but it did nothing to mitigate the inherent disadvantages of external tubes. Nor did it improve the shape of the casing, whose undulation over the external tubes created considerable 'drag', adversely affecting the underwater speed.

To avoid the technical problems that had plagued their predecessors, the machinery of the T class was designed for simplicity, reliability and ease of maintenance rather than outstanding performance, a decision that proved itself in the war. Nevertheless, by choosing an arbitrary tonnage figure half the permitted size the Admiralty had sacrificed range, habitability in the tropical seas for which the class was intended, weight of armament and surface speed – which in any case they regarded as unimportant in a weapon of position: maximum speed was scarcely over 15 knots, and only six reload torpedoes were carried. As it turned out this perverse policy did not have the dire effects it deserved: the Ts were chiefly employed in the Mediterranean, where their comparatively small size, quick diving time, ruggedness and handiness under water suited the conditions; they only wanted speed to be ideal.

The other new type to emerge just before the outbreak of war was the U class. Designed as unarmed boats to train surface forces in anti-submarine work and to provide young officers with their first command, these were under 550 tons standard surface displacement. With war imminent, they were equipped with four internal and two external bow torpedo tubes, but the bulbous casing this necessitated produced the same problems as experienced with the T-class boats, and when a full salvo was fired it proved scarcely possible to prevent the bow broaching the surface. In consequence, after the first three boats the external tubes were omitted; the bulbous bow casing was retained nevertheless in six boats of a second series laid down after the outbreak of war – including what was to become the most famous of all British submarines, *Upholder* – and this made them difficult to hold to a trim at periscope depth. The later boats without the raised bow casing were beautiful to handle.

The U-class boats were the first British submarines to employ diesel-electric drive, as pioneered in the US service since the 1920s. The main diesels drove generators which supplied current to electric motors coupled to the two propeller shafts, or of course charged the batteries which supplied power to the motors for submerged running. The system provided a degree of flexibility both for the internal design and for operation. The boats were intended to make 7 knots submerged and 12 knots on the surface, but few reached that speed and they were by far the slowest boats, apart from midgets, used by any navy in the war. They could get under the surface in under 20 seconds, however, faster than any other submarine, and in the war they proved well suited to the confined waters of the Mediterranean.

Besides these two classes which emerged in the nick of time, an earlier S class designed for patrol work in the North Sea also proved a success in action. The original series laid down in the early 1930s were of 670 tons standard surface displacement and had six bow torpedo tubes and six reload torpedoes. An improved series laid down after the outbreak of war were of 715 tons and were equipped with an additional single torpedo tube at the stern. Like the T and U classes, the S-class boats were deficient in speed, making only 14 knots on the surface. All three types mounted a small calibre quick-firing gun forward of the conning tower for surface action.

Most peacetime exercises with submarines were necessarily unrealistic. Night surface attack was not practised since against battle groups, virtually the only targets foreseen, the risk of collision with darkened screening destroyers was too great. By day, practice torpedoes were seldom actually discharged in a massed salvo; instead the number of probable hits – if any – was determined by analysis of the CO's estimates of target course, speed and range as signalled when he made his dummy attack. One of his chief concerns on these occasions was to make the approach to effective range, some 1,000 yards, without being detected by the asdic-equipped escorts, to which end he tried to keep bows on to the nearest vessel in the screen. This natural preoccupation with asdic appears to have diverted attention from the highly sensitive hydrophone arrays developed by the Germans for anti-submarine craft, and it was only as a result of war experience that the need for complete silence in boats in contact with the enemy was realized.

Regarded in the surface fleet chiefly as 'clockwork mice' to train fleet destroyers in submarine detection, inhibited by the artificial conditions of peacetime exercises and too often dogged by mechanical troubles, the submarines' positive potential was seriously neglected. And so little were the exigencies of real war patrols imagined that it was to take the loss of several boats in the first months of the war before notes based on First World War experience were hurriedly compiled and issued as guidance for patrolling at night. In the Mediterranean and the Far East flotilla commanders exercised their boats as mobile patrol groups, using flag signals, radio and asdic to manoeuvre, often in close order on the surface, and practised exciting close-range gun-layers' firing. As developed in the 4th Submarine Flotilla in China, this involved each boat putting ten rounds into a 10-foot square target at 600 yards range in a minute, starting with the boat invisible below the surface and ending with it once again submerged. The gunnery officer attached to the flotilla between 1936 and 1938 has described this remarkable evolution:

> they'd approach putting their periscope up and down and they'd get the range and the speed of the target, and they'd get within 600 yards, then say 'Stand by for gun action!' . . . all the gun's crew would be ready in the conning tower [or gun tower just forward], then . . . they'd pop up. And while the conning tower [and gun tower] was still under water they'd open the hatch, and the air pressure blew the gun's crew out. They'd fire their ten rounds and they'd all scramble back again, and I'm not exaggerating when I say they invariably got full marks by getting ten shots in this target and disappearing within a minute. And it was all done by the gunlayer . . . they knew exactly what they were going to do – the bearing would be green nine oh – they'd got this on the periscope – the range would be 600 yards, and as soon as they got there they'd just open fire.[1]

It was huge fun and an excellent drill for keeping the crews on their toes, but it was hardly preparation for war against fast enemy fleets. Thoughtful young officers pressed for more realistic training. Lt. Ian McGeoch, serving in the fleet submarine *Clyde* in the Mediterranean, submitted a paper to the flotilla staff arguing that they should practise firing torpedoes at night. He was convinced that the submarine's small silhouette gave it an advantage in night surface attack, and pointed out that in any case unless they did try night firing they would never find out if their night torpedo sights were any good. He had not seen the night-sights in the *Clyde* used.[2] Nothing came of the proposal; British night-sights remained crude by comparison with others, especially those of the Germans.

Torpedo and gun fire control was similarly neglected. The Royal Navy had led the way in developing computers for gunnery fire control before the First World War, but no such drive went into torpedo firing. The CO had only the navigator's plot and a multi-disc calculator known as the Is-Was as aids to determine the director angle he should allow. The Is-Was was upgraded into a mechanical submarine torpedo director, known as the fruit machine, but still this only provided solutions valid for the instant of observation; it did not produce a running picture of the attack, as a machine adapted from the surface navy's gunnery fire-control table might have done, and as US and German torpedo fire-control computers did. These latter also set the gyro compasses of the individual torpedoes which took up the set course after being launched from their tubes. British torpedoes had no such angling device; as in the first war, COs aimed the whole submarine along the firing track. Cdr. William King described this in his classic account of one man's submarine war, *The Stick and the Stars*:

> To fire . . . you had to point the submarine like a bow and arrow. It needed a virtuoso to do it well, and in mock attacks I had learnt how often I lacked brilliance . . . If war came – would I be any good? . . . for the artistry required to attack with a submarine was not to be acquired by merely trying hard.[3]

British submarines had another disadvantage in attack: their periscopes were made not of steel but of bronze – in order not to affect the magnetic compass in the conning tower – and hence could not bear the same unsupported length as the steel periscopes fitted in the submarines of other navies, who perhaps placed more faith in gyro compasses. The periscope depth being shallower by as much as 10 to 16 feet, British boats were more subject to surface swell, hence more difficult to control and more liable to break surface at critical moments in an attack. Solicitude for the magnetic compass also cost British submarines diving depth since conning towers were likewise built of bronze, which added extra weight by comparison with steel construction, and this was paid for by thinner plating for the pressure hull, little over half an inch compared with three-quarters to seven-eighths of an inch in German and US boats.

The Royal Navy's dismissive attitude to its submarine arm was only exceeded by its neglect of the necessary protection for merchant shipping against submarine – and indeed air – attack. Undoubtedly faith in asdic played its part. By 1935, when the prospect of a new German U-boat arm had become reality, the Admiralty was confident that asdic had 'virtually extinguished the submarine menace'.[4] And in 1937 the departing First Lord, Sir Samuel Hoare, reassured the House of Commons that 'the submarine is no longer a danger to the security of the British Empire'.[5] Yet asdic had a maximum range in reasonable conditions of 2,500 yards (1¼ miles), much less than the range of torpedoes, and average range actually achieved by asdic was just over half this, 1,300 yards.[6] Moreover, the instrument went blind within 200 yards or so of a submerged submarine, allowing submarine COs to move aside from the track in the vital final moments of the approach and while the stern-launched depth-charges sank to the level at which they had been set to explode. Development of ahead-thrown charges which would reduce the effect of this blind period was halted by financial constraints.

But apart from these technical considerations, where were the vessels which were to carry asdic and depth-charges to protect ocean-going merchant convoys? There were none. Destroyers, the submarine's chief enemy, had been designed to protect the battlefleet and deliver massed torpedo attacks on the enemy fleet at the next 'Jutland' against the Japanese; they lacked the necessary endurance. The former First Sea Lord, Jellicoe, had warned after the first war and again in a book published in 1932 that fast ocean escorts could not be improvized hurriedly; yet this is what the Admiralty proposed, and what finally they were forced into doing too late. Moreover, no exercises in the protection of slow convoys of merchant ships took place during the inter-war years.[7]

Another fatal flaw in the Admiralty's asdic-induced complacency was the assumption that enemy submarines would only deliver submerged attacks; for asdic was powerless to detect a submarine on the surface. In 1918 half the U-boat attacks on merchant shipping – in the Mediterranean over half – had been made on the surface at night.[8] Furthermore, as has been noted, thinking British submariners advocated night attack. In 1938, after his failure to move the Mediterranean submarine staff, Lt. McGeoch wrote a paper – which in the event he was not allowed to publish – attempting to demonstrate the offensive value of the modern submarine; it contained a short section on the submarine's 'very important tactical capability . . . [for] surface night attack'.[9] The new German U-boat arm was trained from the start in night surface attack, and in early 1939 its inspirational commander, Kapitän Karl Dönitz, published a book in Berlin obligingly describing the submarine's advantages in night surface attack.[10]

Correlli Barnett, in his account of the Royal Navy in the Second World War, has deemed the Admiralty's neglect until too late of 'the enormous operational and quantitative problems' of setting up a convoy system of defence against U-boats their most serious failure of judgement in the inter-war years; he lays the blame on 'the want of organised, scientifically conducted operational research. No such department was set up by the Admiralty until 1942.'[11] More surprisingly, even naval staff histories stopped short of the final years of the first war and the near-fatal unrestricted U-boat campaign. This was because the Treasury clamped down on further research and writing in 1925. Whether senior Admiralty civil servants connived at this because, as D.W. Waters has argued, they regarded well-informed naval officers as a threat to their own indispensability in policy-making is not for debate here; what is clear is that no Admiralty official or naval officer between the wars had either data or analysis on which to base a strategy of trade protection in the submarine era. Such statistics as were available were buried in the generally uninformative fifth volume of the official *History of Naval Operations*, and in two volumes of the official Air Ministry history – aircraft having been a vital factor in anti-submarine warfare – which latter were not published until 1934 and 1937.

In view of the terrifyingly narrow margin by which Great Britain had avoided defeat at the hands of U-boats in 1917 it seems scarcely credible that no systematic examination and analysis of the U-boat campaign was carried out between the wars, but such was the case.[12] No doubt the failure, which itself has never been properly explained, had many causes, among them perhaps the final triumph of the Royal Navy erasing the memory of catastrophe, perhaps the specialized training or indoctrination of naval officers from a very early age, certainly the Admiralty's reluctant, haphazard and tardy development of modern staff work; as the historian H.P. Willmott has put it, 'the interwar RN . . . lacked the institutional structure and the sympathy to accommodate those [with first war experience] who might have provided it with a knowledge and understanding of ASW [anti-submarine warfare]'.[13]

In mitigation Willmott has pointed out that the inter-war years were dominated by economic retrenchment – he might have added that the sentiment of peace prevailed throughout the land – and there was no enemy in view: 'The threats posed by Germany in general and U-boats in particular emerged very late indeed, not until 1938–39', and 'any attempts to have built up British anti-submarine forces before the last couple of years prior to the outbreak of war would have been for both the nation and the navy financially irresponsible and strategically irrelevant.'[14] This leaves out of account the threat posed to British Far Eastern shipping by Japan through the 1930s, and the concessions made to the new German U-boat arm in the Anglo-German Naval Treaty of 1935.

However that may be, it is undeniable that the Admiralty as an organization shrugged off the most humiliating reverse in its history and simply lost the anti-submarine lessons of 1917–18. The causes surely run deeper than reason. Ultimately, so little thought was invested in trade protection not because so little money was available, as it was, nor because there was no immediate enemy on the doorstep, although there was, nor, as Paul Kennedy has argued,[15] because the Admiralty necessarily lacked the gift of prophecy – although they might perhaps have employed the gift of imagination – but simply because merchant shipping lacked glamour or promotion prospects. Much the same went for submarines. Naval officers rose, as in all large organizations, by aggressive ambition, ability, social compatibility and adaptability to the aims of the service, not usually through independent or unorthodox thought; indeed the service's aversion to cerebral activity was as legendary as its assumption of supremacy. Officers showing a bent for technical innovation or historical or lateral thought were too often written off as theorists, in the jargon 'x-chasers' trying to 'blind [their seniors] with science'. Not that the proud heirs of Nelson did much worse in trade protection than their counterparts in other major navies, indeed they eventually did better. Yet understandable in human and organizational terms, the failures of the inter-war Boards of Admiralty were so grave in their consequences and so potentially disastrous that they merit the judgement made by Vice-Admiral Sir Peter Gretton, one of the most distinguished escort commanders of the war: 'We were criminally unprepared for the Battle of the Atlantic in 1939.'[16] In effect the country was left wide open to defeat by submarine blockade, a defeat from which it was only saved by science in the shape of radar, the folly of its principal enemy, the productive power of its principal ally and the ingenuity and resolve of unorthodox officers bypassed for promotion.

The United States Navy was as focused on the next great fleet battle, also against the Japanese, as the Royal Navy. It was similarly heedless of the lessons of the first war U-boat campaign, and when impelled into the second war at the end of 1941 even disregarded the lessons the Royal Navy had been relearning painfully since 1939. Nevertheless, in the design of submarines the US Navy did very much better.

They had sought a submarine fast enough to work tactically with the battlefleet since before the first war; a prototype had been authorized in 1914, but delays in design and construction held up her completion until 1920, by which date she was obsolescent. Standard 800-ton S-class submarines in service proved far too small and unreliable to work with the fleet over the vast distances of the Pacific, and consequently another design of 'fleet' boat, designated V1, was laid down. The three boats of this class were of some 2,000 tons surface displacement and borrowed several features, although not the overall concept, from U-boats obtained as prizes of victory in the war; however, when commissioned between 1924 and 1925 they proved a disappointment in practically every department. Following them the US Navy had a brief fling with very large submarines of 2,700 tons, the first for minelaying, the next two as submersible 'cruisers', each mounting two 6-inch guns. Before they were completed, dissatisfaction within the submarine arm about the performance of the S class and the new fleet boats, and the slow pace and apparent misdirection of development led to the formation of the Submarine Officers' Conference. Designed as a forum for discussion, the Conference brought together serving officers and technical experts from the Bureaux of Construction and Engineering to provide precisely the sort of thinking and co-ordinating body that the Royal Navy's submarine arm so conspicuously lacked. Results were immediate: out went the idea of fleet submarines and the flirtation with great size, and in their place came the concept of a moderate-sized boat for independent offensive operations, what would later be called a patrol submarine with the emphasis on manoeuvrability, habitability, reliability of machinery and economy in mass production.[17]

The result was a 1,500-ton boat, *V7*, later named the *Dolphin*. After her there was a brief regression to a class of smaller boats modelled on the first war German U-cruiser, *U135*, but in retrospect the *Dolphin* can be seen as the first in the true line of evolution of the formidable submarines which fought the Pacific war. They were developed through a series of similar classes from 1933 when the new United States President, Franklin D. Roosevelt, presided over a naval expansion programme designed for the twin purposes of responding to Japanese military aggression in east Asia and mass unemployment at home. The Submarine Officers' Conference was the essential mechanism through which development was guided; and if there was a single officer whose contribution was vital it was Cdr. Charles Lockwood, first as a representative of serving submariners while commanding a division of the latest boats, and from 1938 as Chairman of the Conference.

By 1939 the type had evolved. The *Tambor* class laid down that year incorporated practically every feature, bar radar, of the mature US wartime submarine. Of almost 1,500 tons surface displacement, they had the high, flat-sided, shark's-nose bow – derived from first war U-boats – the long sweep of deck in a straight line to the stern, and the low conning-tower structure placed rather forward of mid-length that distinguished all later fleet submarines, as they continued to be called despite the changed emphasis to independent operations. Powered by four diesel engines serving as generators to supply power to electric motors driving the twin propeller shafts, they could make 20 knots on the surface, or could cruise 11,000 miles at 10 knots. They were armed with twenty-four torpedoes for six bow and four stern tubes and mounted one 3-inch gun designed for high-angle or surface fire. They were painted black overall.

The superiority of these boats to the British T class designed at about the same time for the same area of operations against the same enemy was so marked as to render them a different species altogether. The extra 500 tons displacement allowed an advantage of at least 5 knots top surface speed, over 6,000 miles range at cruising speed and a payload of twenty-four instead of sixteen torpedoes, although the British boats, as noted, had the heavier initial salvo. Internally the crew accommodation, including a well-equipped galley, a separate mess room with mess tables apart from the sleeping quarters, and showers in the heads, was of a standard impossible to obtain on the smaller British boats. They also enjoyed air-conditioning. Older naval officers sniffed at 'hotel accommodation', but air-conditioning was a practical measure, not a luxury. Without it the temperature in a submerged boat quickly rose over 100° F and, with 100 per cent humidity causing the cold outer plating to sweat copious streams, the electrical machinery especially suffered and became liable to faults. The effects on health and alertness were if anything more dangerous, particularly if extended over a long war patrol in enemy waters where most of the days had to be spent submerged. Although the air-conditioning neither absorbed excess carbon dioxide nor added oxygen to the depleted atmosphere, it did filter out grease and other impurities which contributed to the headaches and nausea suffered below and helped to prevent heat exhaustion.

As mentioned, US boats had the great advantage of an advanced electro-mechanical torpedo data computer, or TDC, which provided a continuous display of the relative positions of target and submarine, together with a running solution to the torpedo angle problem, and in addition kept the gyro compasses of each torpedo in its tube set to this continually changing course, allowing the CO to fire at any time from any heading he happened to be steering. Fleet boats were also fitted with ultra-sonic transducer echo-receiver instruments like the British asdic; in the US service this was known as sonar; the sonar head was usually mounted on a retractable shaft poking down below the forward torpedo room, and it occasionally suffered from inadvertent grounding.

These large fleet submarines provided the US Navy with an awesomely effective submersible fighting ship; and while it was inferior to the German U-boat in specific areas, particularly optics, diesels and pressure-hull construction for deep diving, in the wide ocean spaces for which it was designed the US fleet submarine outmatched other powers' boats as once Dreadnought battleships had outmatched pre-Dreadnoughts. Besides their evident advantages in performance, they were mechanically reliable – after initial engine failures had been remedied – and proved astonishingly robust under depth-charge attack, the result not only of pressure-hull design and construction, but also of painstaking testing of individual components by underwater explosion, redesigning where weaknesses were exposed. In diving time they almost equalled the smaller British T class; with the help of a down-express tank kept flooded while on the surface, fleet boats could submerge to periscope depth in 35 seconds. Once down, they handled well and had a submerged maximum speed of 10 knots, almost equal to the top surface speed of the British U class.

There were several other factors contributing to the US Navy's success in out-designing other powers. The Submarine Officers' Conference has been mentioned and was obviously vital. The lack of class differentiation between engineer and executive officers, who shared a common entry and grounding at the Naval Academy – a system the great British First Sea Lord, 'Jacky' Fisher, had tried to establish in the Royal Navy before the first war – played a part. Underpinning the whole effort was the industrial and technologically buoyancy of the country: the US Navy's advantage over the Imperial Japanese Navy and the Royal Navy in this respect was most marked in electrical and radio engineering, perhaps accounting for their lead in fire-control computers.[18] In diesel engineering, a field in which they had lagged at the start, the US Navy worked in partnership with companies producing lightweight diesels for the railroads and, gradually assuming the role of 'catalyst, planner and director' came eventually to drive US locomotive engine development for the benefit of the submarine arm.[19]

With hindsight it appears that in the fleet submarine the US Navy had by 1939 a potential war winner which needed only to be produced in sufficient numbers and deployed scientifically against Japan's weakest link, its merchant shipping, to strangle that island empire's ambitions in short time before the immense human and material toll of the greater Pacific war, certainly before the atom bomb. That this was not realized was due to strategic, tactical and technological failures.

The strategic error which the US shared with all major navies was of course an obsession with battleships and the great fleet battle for command of the sea. This was enshrined from before the first war in Plan Orange for war against Japan; after the decisive fleet battle, the US Navy would blockade the Japanese islands much as the Royal Navy had blockaded its enemies during its centuries of supremacy. Had there been a proper analysis in the light of the first war U-boat campaign against British merchant shipping, it would have been noted that Japan was even more dependent on imports by sea than Great Britain, that her merchant fleet was substantially smaller, that over 50 per cent of the oil on which her armed forces moved was imported, and 40 per cent of her foreign trade was carried in foreign ships; that she had no conceivable ally who could have made up the deficiencies; in short, she could be brought to her knees fairly quickly with comparatively little expense by an unrestricted submarine campaign. But such use of submarines against merchant shipping had been outlawed by treaty, to which the United States was a signatory, and doubtless this attitude counted, despite the nature of warfare and the enemy, who was unlikely to abide by treaty restrictions of any kind. However, the fact that the United States had signed the treaty was a symptom of her view of the submarine as a menace in enemy hands rather than an asset in her own. In any event the analysis was never made; there was no lateral leap of imagination from the North Atlantic to the Pacific, and the option of a submarine campaign against merchant shipping was never considered.

The second failure lay in the training of submarine COs. This was due partly to the US Navy's lack of recent battle experience, as can be seen by comparison with the training methods of all other major submarine forces; it was also due to the battlefleet doctrine whereby only battleships, battlecruisers and aircraft-carriers were deemed proper targets for submarine torpedoes or, in exceptional circumstances by special order, cruisers. In exercises submarines attacked high-speed targets screened by both aircraft and sonar-equipped destroyers; COs who were detected in their approach – and assumed to have been caught and sunk – were reprimanded. In the Asiatic Submarine Squadron COs were threatened with instant dismissal from command if their periscopes were sighted during exercises. This led to habits of extreme caution and the practice, when air patrols were present, of attacking blind from well below periscope depth using only data supplied by sonar; since this did not provide sufficiently accurate bearings or ranges, the chances of hitting in a sonar attack were small indeed. Neither night surface nor group tactics were practised, a state of affairs which quite remarkably persisted even after 1940 when U-boats in the Atlantic demonstrated their devastating effects. So far as group tactics went, the neglect can again be put down to caution, the fear that the radio signalling necessary would reveal their position to the enemy. And COs received no training in attacking either merchant convoys or single supply ships.

Apart from the over-caution instilled, COs were judged, as in most navies in peacetime, more by their regard for the regulations, paperwork, good discipline and bright ships than by the less measurable qualities needed in war, especially in submarines. Thus too many US submarine COs when faced with the real test were found wanting in aggression and confidence in their weapon; by the end of the first year of the Pacific war almost a third of those who held command at the start had been relieved as inadequate.[20]

Finally, there were truly shocking and, in the eyes of veteran submariners today, unforgivable faults in the torpedoes. These went uncorrected for far too long into the war. The most notorious case was the magnetic torpedo exploder which was supposed to be triggered by the magnetic field of the target ship while the torpedo passed a few feet beneath the hull. It was a response to the anti-torpedo compartmentalization of modern capital ships below the waterline, and a way of ensuring that the whole force of the explosion was vented on the target to break its back instead of partly dissipating upwards outside the hull. The new exploder was developed in the utmost secrecy at the Newport, Rhode Island, Torpedo Station of the Bureau of Ordnance, after which trials were conducted with dummy warheads against a cruiser in equatorial latitudes off South America. The submarine officer overseeing the development, Lt.-Cdr. Ralph Christie, tried to obtain an old hulk to use for trials with live warheads but failed; production of the exploders was started on the strength of the dummy run results, which were judged a success, without a single live test taking place. The new exploders were then stored in such secrecy that not even submariners knew of their existence until the outbreak of the Pacific war. Subsequent reports of failures in action did not persuade the experts at Newport that anything could be wrong, and eventually officers in the Pacific had to take matters into their own hands. Since the conventional contact exploder also misfired when it struck the target at the prescribed large angle, US submarines fought the first year to eighteen months of the war under a handicap the more sapping for being continually denied by the Bureau specialists.

These failures in grand strategy, training and main armament cancelled out the design advantages of US fleet submarines at the beginning of the Pacific war and it was some time before the boats began to reveal their devastating potential. Mistakes are inevitable in any sphere; in war they are shown up quickly. The most surprising aspect of the American mistakes was the time taken by fleet and submarine force commanders to correct them, but this, too, was probably a symptom of pre-war battlefleet doctrine which underestimated the weapon.

The Japanese made mistakes of a more fundamental kind which could never be corrected. Their cardinal error was to go to war with the United States. Rational officers like Admiral Isoroku Yamamoto, who as Commander-in-Chief of the Combined Fleet devised and executed the attack on Pearl Harbor, knew it was a war they could not win, and made his opposition plain up to the time the fateful decision was taken in 1941.[21] On the other hand, the war had been inevitable for many years before 1941; indeed the service had been developed in conformity with a single plan for waging it, each unit of the fleet designed not so much as a type which might be employed in a variety of roles according to circumstance, but as a piece to fill a specific slot in the overall strategy against the Anglo-Americans in the Pacific. It represented a distinctly un-naval cast of thought more appropriate to the military. But in part the Imperial Navy's rigidity was a response to the impossible task it had been set, the containment of the two leading naval powers, Great Britain and the United States, the latter at the cutting edge of new technology and with a gross national product over ten times that of Japan. Such a task necessarily concentrated minds and resources; there were no margins for compromise or alternatives. But if the core of the plan devised proved mistaken or outmoded by technology, as it did, or if the enemy reacted in unexpected ways, the whole structure was bound to collapse and the over-specialized units, unfit for other roles, would inevitably flounder.

The fault was especially marked in submarine design and employment. Apart from a few medium, RO types for coastal and harbour defence, Japan's entire submarine force was developed for action against the enemy's capital units, first to find them far from Japan, and then to attack and lame or destroy them while they steamed towards imperial waters, finally to join the battlefleet in action against those remnants which entered the perimeter where the decisive battle was to be fought. It was the strategy of attrition adopted by all the weaker battlefleet powers, adapted to the great distances and island groups of the Pacific.

Three types of large submarine were evolved to fulfil the strategy: a scouting type equipped with a seaplane to extend the range of reconnaissance; a headquarters or flagship type, also equipped with a seaplane, but with accommodation for a group commander and extra communication facilities; and an attack type with eight bow torpedo tubes leading from two compartments one above the other, and on the after casing fittings for securing a two-man midget submarine to be launched in the decisive fleet battle.

All these classes were larger and faster than US fleet submarines; the headquarters type, A1, was almost 2,500 tons standard surface displacement – over 4,000 tons submerged – and was thus 1,000 tons larger than the US *Tambor* class, 372 feet in length against the *Tambor*'s 307 feet, with a beam of over 31 feet against the *Tambor*'s 27 feet. The scouting and attack types, B1 and C1, had a standard surface displacement of 2,200 tons and a length of 356 feet. All were capable of over 23 knots on the surface, 8 knots submerged, and had a range of 14,000 miles or over at a cruising speed of 16 knots. This vast range was dictated by the aim of finding the enemy force as far away as the west coast of America and the exit of the Panama Canal; and the high surface speed was to enable the boats to outrun the enemy fleet at its normal cruising speed, concentrate ahead to attack, and afterwards race ahead again for a second attack.

Such was the final pre-war evolution of the various I, or large fleet types; they were laid down in what was known as the Third Replenishment Plan of 1936 after Japan had publicly repudiated all naval limitations, and were completed in a crash programme in 1940-1. The same plan included the giant battleships *Yamato* and *Musashi*, designed to outrange the largest US battleships and overpower them with heavier broadsides in the decisive battle, and at the other extreme Type A midget submarines to be deployed from both mother ships and attack submarines in this decisive battle.

The midgets looked like outsize torpedoes, 78 feet long by 6 feet in diameter with two normal torpedo tubes, one above the other, projecting from the bow, and a small conning tower with a short, protruding periscope about mid-length. A single electric motor was designed to drive them at 23 knots on the surface and because of their streamlined, pencil shape, at the astonishing speed of 19 knots under water for a maximum distance of 18 miles. Their two-man crews would be virtually volunteers for suicide as there was no generator to recharge the batteries, and the chances of being picked up in the midst of a fleet action were remote.

Like all other units, they were designed not simply for a specific role, but for a specific tactic. In the decisive battle they were to be launched ahead of the enemy fleet – now supposed to be reduced from its original size by at least 30 per cent by submarine and aircraft attrition during the passage from its west coast or Hawaiian base – while a fast surface force attacked from the flank with massed torpedoes. The enemy, in turning from this flank attack to parallel the torpedo tracks, would present its broadsides to torpedoes from the midgets and attack submarines which had launched them from ahead of its original course. Into the mayhem thus created would plunge salvoes of 3,200lb. shells from the *Yamato* and *Musashi* standing off some 14 miles, outside effective US gun range. It was a meticulous concept. Nothing resembling it was to occur or ever seem likely.

Besides the new large classes completed in 1940 and 1941 were the former types from which they had evolved: attack boats only slightly larger than US fleet submarines with similar performance, scouting types of about 2,000 tons with great range and twin cylindrical hangars abaft the conning tower – one containing the seaplane's wings, the other its fuselage and floats – and earlier 'cruiser' types without aircraft developed from German first war U-cruisers, and mounting two 5.5-inch guns.

In designing submarines like chess pieces to be moved according to a predetermined plan, the Japanese pressed them into roles for which they were unsuited and failed to develop them as well as the Americans did for the role to which they were suited. The most striking examples of misplaced ingenuity were the scouting submarines. It was clear that the small, collapsible seaplanes they carried were less effective than carrier- or land-based reconnaissance aircraft, and equally clear that the time the submarine had to spend on the surface while the seaplane was assembled and launched, and afterwards recovered, endangered the boat itself. Yet the need to extend vision in enemy waters outside the range of even their carrier aircraft outweighed these considerations, for the overall strategy demanded the attrition of the enemy fleet far away from Japan. In this and other ways both payload and rapid diving were sacrificed. The latest scouting and headquarters types had six bow tubes and carried seventeen and eighteen torpedoes respectively; some earlier large boats carried as few as fourteen torpedoes, fewer even than the British T-class boats of less than half their size. The latest attack type had eight bow tubes and carried twenty torpedoes. Yet the smaller and handier US fleet submarines had six bow and four stern tubes, allowing greater flexibility in attack, and carried a total of twenty-four torpedoes. The two-man midget submarines were another example of an over-ingenious solution since they lacked the endurance or conning facilities needed to play any useful part in a fleet action on the high seas.

Besides basic conceptual errors, the backwardness especially of the Japanese electrical and communications industries by comparison with the United States condemned their sonar, and later radar, fire-control, radio and, when fitted, air-conditioning and cooling systems to inferiority. Prickly heat and heat exhaustion became usual during the war in Japanese submarines operating in tropical waters, as did equipment failure due to condensation and design faults. A Japanese wartime publication categorized a cooling system which kept the air temperature down to 88°F (31°C) as efficient, as indeed it was by comparison with that in another boat of the same class where the temperature over a short patrol of only sixteen days averaged nearly 99°F (37°C). Not surprisingly, 'almost all [the crew] were afflicted with prickly heat. Furthermore fatigue among the crew was great.'[22] The harsh attitude towards enlisted men in the Japanese services ensured that habitability came last in the design specifications, and it appears from comments in a US technical appraisal at the end of the war that sanitation was equally disregarded: 'any American who boarded or passed to leeward of a surrendered Japanese submarine before the Japanese were forced to clean it up, will agree that it is a wonder they were able to do even as well as they did'.[23] On the other hand, standards of cleanliness in US fleet submarines were unusually high.

The torpedo fire-control system in the Japanese I type submarines, while not in the same class as the US torpedo data computer, was in advance of the British system. Like the British fruit machine it was simply an angle solver whose solutions were valid for the instant of observation; it could not provide a running picture. It did, however, allow for angled firing. The data – torpedo speed and desired angular spread (plus or minus 10°), target range, speed (plotted), angle on the bow (estimated), and own speed – were cranked in manually, while the target's relative bearing was transmitted automatically from the periscope, although this too could be fed in by hand. The firing solution was expressed as an angle relative to the submarine's heading, up to 120° left or right. This angle, corrected for spread, was conveyed to pointers beside the torpedo tubes by four electric transmitters built into the angle solver, each transmitter serving two tubes. The gyro compasses in the individual torpedoes were then set manually by matching the pointers.

As in other navies, the Japanese submarine force was officered and manned by an élite of volunteers, chosen for fitness and temperament. It was trained for virtually its only task, attacking heavily screened US battle squadrons, in exercises so dangerously realistic that they claimed several boats and crews. Much was expected from the force; success in the decisive battle was believed to depend on the submarines' campaign of attrition beforehand. The submariners believed they would be successful. Morale was high: as one admiral expressed it, there was 'a feeling of almost supernatural skill in the competence with which our submarines carried out their attacks in training and on manoeuvres'.[24] The force entered the Pacific war in the belief that its craft, equipment, men and methods were superior to those in any other navy.[25] In 1945 a US Navy technical investigation team came to a different conclusion: 'the Japanese submarine force, like the Japanese Navy and the nation as a whole, was completely outclassed in all fields of warfare, material, scientific and personnel, and was incapable of the war it undertook'.[26]

This assessment was wrong in at least one respect: Japanese torpedoes were far superior to those of the United States and indeed any other navy in speed, range, size of warhead and, most important, reliability. But this merely serves to highlight the Japanese failure. Their submarines were larger and the latest ones several knots faster than US fleet boats, and their main weapon, the torpedo, was much more powerful and reliable, yet when it came to war, apart from one purple patch in the Solomons campaign in the late summer of 1942, they were to disappoint. In large measure this was due to the US lead in radar and signals intelligence, and the weight of US industry translated into air power, but the Imperial Navy contributed: the pre-war obsession with the decisive battle and the consequent over-specialization in design and training had stifled initiative from top to bottom. In war even the number of torpedoes to be fired was laid down in orders: full salvoes were permitted only against capital units – aircraft-carriers and battleships; three torpedoes were allowed against cruisers, but against destroyers or merchantmen only one.[27] The chances of hitting with a single torpedo outside a range of about 1,000 yards were slight. These priorities were never changed except for specific commerce-raiding missions in the Indian Ocean; US supply convoys across the Pacific were never subjected to sustained attack. Valuable targets were passed up because they did not belong to the force or category specified in the mission orders. Lessons were not learned, or if learned not acted upon because the necessary staff organization did not exist.[28] Eventually, from the over-rational rigidity of the war plan the navy, like the nation, passed to pure irrationality.

Thus Japan came full circle: the war had begun irrationally as an expression of the values of a military caste stunted by its own myths and driven by the dynamic of territorial expansion. Ostensibly the Western powers were attacked for two reasons. First, Japanese conquests in mainland Asia, begun in 1931, could not be sustained or carried to completion without seizing the oil, rice and metals of the Dutch East Indies and the rubber of Malaya. Second, in June 1940 the US Congress voted $4 million for a 'two-ocean navy' which would increase the ratio of US fleet preponderance over the Imperial Navy from 10:7 in 1940–1 to 10:3 by 1944. This was too great a superiority to overcome even with the navy's war plan; it was necessary to strike before it materialized, and while Great Britain was fully occupied against Germany in the Atlantic and Mediterranean. Neither the army nor the navy were certain of success; the navy was sure only that they could not win a protracted war.[29] Yamamoto told the Prime Minister, Prince Konoye, in September 1941 that if ordered to fight, he would 'run wild considerably for the first six months or a year; but I have utterly no confidence in the second and third years [sic]'.[30] The decision to strike south against Britain and America was imposed by the army on the navy and the civilian government in a spirit of reckless overconfidence bred from Japan's recent history of success and easy conquest in Asia, and the belief common to military castes that 'fighting spirit' was decisive in battle: 'confidence in certain victory', 'loyalty to the Emperor', 'willingness to sacrifice one's life for the country', all would, it was believed, overcome the mere material advantages of the enemy.[31]

The navy, while relatively more rational in the upper ranks than the army, was imbued with the same spirit. The over-elaborate planning of the 1930s did not amount to a reasoned strategy, rather, as H.P. Willmott has recognized, a substitute for one:[32] knowing they could not sustain, let alone win a protracted war against the United States, it was an assertion that the American will to fight could be broken by a demonstration of Japanese martial prowess.[33] The 'decisive battle' was not, as in the Western dogma, to achieve control of the sea, but to demonstrate the superiority of Japanese fighting spirit over *matériel* and force the enemy to the negotiating table. No plans were made for a long campaign. Although the war was supposedly being fought for the oil and supplies of the Dutch Indies, which had to be carried by sea, no positive steps were taken either to protect these vital transports or to attack the enemy's supply lines as he moved west across the Pacific. There was no comprehensive plan for convoy, nor a building programme for convoy escorts.[34] In 1945, Cdr. Sogawa, formerly of the Naval General Staff, told his US interrogators that before the war it had been estimated that 360 large escorts would be needed for their long lines of communication:

> The Navy postponed building additional escort vessels, so when the war started we had old destroyers, a few minesweepers and such craft assigned to this duty under the various fleet commanders and commanders of naval bases. At that time there was no unified control of escort, and these various commanders did the best they could with the means at their disposal.[35]

As for severing the enemy's even longer lines of communication, there were no plans; as noted, merchant shipping was assigned the lowest priority as a target for the submarine force, which was designed and trained exclusively for attacking capital ships.

Although similar neglect of the trade and supply war has been noted in both the Royal and US Navies, neither carried it to such extremes, nor planned to take on such overwhelming naval odds – nor, when it came to the test, failed to adapt. The Imperial Japanese Navy failed miserably, the causes of its failure lying deeper than inadequate technological and industrial resources. They were to be found in the habits of mind of a neo-feudal people indoctrinated with a belief in its superiority and divine mission in the world and taught absolute obedience to the Emperor and State in an education system that denied free enquiry and was designed to inculcate the martial virtues, willingness to die as the supreme consummation of 'loyalty to the Emperor and love of country'.[36]

The Greater Japanese Empire has been described by one Japanese scholar, Saburo Ienaga, who lived through it, in terms parodying militaristic excess as 'a Kafkaesque state dedicated to the abuse of human rights'.[37] The navy was both a part of the system and a contributor. Officers and men were subjected to as harsh a regime as their counterparts in the army. Cruelty was both a training device and a means of so charging the men with suppressed anger and hatred they would explode in action against the enemy; the 'skilful' commander used calculated brutality to mould his men into a fierce fighting unit.[38] Atrocities against enemy prisoners and civilians were natural side effects. While the submarine arm of the Imperial Navy cannot equal the record of horror left by the Japanese army during its fifteen-year rampage of conquest, it became feared for its brutality towards survivors. This and, towards the end, its descent to suicide tactics were a consequence of the Japanese social system; so too were its irrational strategy and its failure to adapt to the searching demands of war with an advanced industrial power. It proved, in the words of the US Navy investigation team already cited, 'incapable of the war it undertook'.[39]

The German navy also suffered from the irrationality of a martial culture, the values of the Prussian military parodied in the Nazi state. Its submariners were to pay the highest price: of the 40,000 officers and men who entered the arm over 30,000 were lost, their average life expectancy at the end no more than two war patrols. The men, known ironically as *Pairs* (Lords) were not brutalized but rather were pampered between missions as a valued élite, and they fought an unimaginably stoic, brave and on the whole clean war with no more brutal exceptions than disfigured the record of Royal Navy or US submariners.

The first war U-boats had been superbly engineered; they were surrendered after the armistice and distributed among the victor nations, who took them apart and borrowed heavily from their pre-eminent technology in their own subsequent designs. It is no exaggeration to say that German engineers and designers provided a technical platform from which all navies of the victorious alliance, which included Japan, continued their development between the wars; Japan indeed had direct assistance from German engineers and constructors, which resulted among other classes in their first 2,000-ton 'cruiser' scouting types.[40] The Germans themselves were denied submarines – as also naval aircraft – by the terms of the Versailles Treaty. This did not prevent them continuing clandestine development. A small U-boat office was concealed at first within the Mines and Torpedo Inspectorate at Kiel, later in a department of the Naval High Command in Berlin. They assembled, analysed and evaluated wartime U-boat records, and advised on the numbers and types needed to fulfil the navy's war plan, which throughout the 1920s was based on a Franco-Polish alliance against them. Here, the argument against giant submarines was won as much by analysis of war experience as by theoretical principle; and it is noteworthy that it was here, alone among the submarine staffs of the major navies, that the war lessons of night surface and group attack were kept alive. Meanwhile, a design office was set up under cover of a naval engineering company in Holland to draw up plans and oversee the construction of submarines ordered by foreign nations, the Argentine, Finland, Turkey and Spain. German officers, engineers and constructors went abroad for training on these boats, while at home the suppliers of specialized equipment, Zeiss for periscopes, MAN for diesels, Anschütz for gyro compasses, Lorenz for radio equipment, Askania for underwater sound gear, and numerous other precision suppliers were able to continue design and development work under the noses of Allied armaments inspection teams.[41]

By the early 1930s, when German statesmen were seeking to throw off the shackles of Versailles by dividing the wartime allies, Great Britain and France, and calling for equality of treatment with the victor powers, the navy had worked out a building programme designed to meet the possibility of war with France and Poland in 1938. Rejecting the Versailles limitations, this secret *Umbau*, or reconstruction, plan provided for an aircraft-carrier, nine squadrons of naval aircraft and three half-flotillas of U-boats, sixteen in total. It was adopted by the Defence Minister in 1932, before the Nazi seizure of power, and that year also saw approval for the first training course for future U-boat officers and engineers, as opposed to the previous occasional training aboard foreign submarines designed by the clandestine German firm in Holland. It was conducted under cover of the *U-bootsabwehr*, or Anti-submarine School, by a wartime U-boat CO, Werner Fürbringer, who had since trained German crews aboard two boats delivered to the Turkish Navy, and subsequently stayed on in Turkey to run the submarine school there.[42] Again it is noteworthy that Fürbringer included both night and day surface attack in his course.[43] The officers chosen for instruction were 25-year-old *Oberleutnants*.

When Hitler came to power in 1933 he adopted the *Umbau* plan in its entirety, but prohibited any start on U-boat building until the political situation permitted. He was as determined as his predecessors to split France from Great Britain, in which cause he intended doing nothing which might appear to threaten the Royal Navy or the British Empire. His initial success was astonishing: by June 1935 he had persuaded a gullible British government and Admiralty staff to sign a bilateral naval treaty allowing the German navy to build up to 35 per cent of Royal Naval tonnage in most classes, 45 per cent in submarine tonnage, and in view of the comparatively small number of British submarines, up to 100 per cent in submarine tonnage should the situation in future warrant it. By this time France and Soviet Russia had been forced together by renascent German militarism, and the navy's *Umbau* programme had been upgraded to meet a war against a Franco-Russian coalition; the U-boat total was increased to seventy-two.

This number was to be made up of small 250-ton boats – Type II – for use in securing the Baltic and the vital iron-ore trade from Sweden against Russian or French naval forces, and also as boats which could be built rapidly for training purposes; and 750-tonners – Type I – for use against the French Navy and troop transports in the Mediterranean and North Atlantic. Both classes had been evolved from first war U-boat designs via the submarines built under cover for Finland and Spain, now modified for the German war plan; the most interesting modification was a reduction in size of conning tower to diminish the surfaced silhouette,[44] another indication of the importance attached to night surface attack. However, in the light of the naval treaty with Great Britain it was decided to obtain a greater number of boats within the tonnage limit by moving to a 550–600-ton ocean-going type instead of the 750-tonner; this evolved from final developments in first war U-boat design via one of the boats built for Finland in the late 1920s.[45] It was designated Type VII. Thus, as with the British T class of the same date, an arbitrary element had been introduced into the specifications by treaty considerations. Like the T class, the Type VII proved a great success, by the test of numbers built the most successful submarine ever. Like the T class it was intended not for *guerre de course*, but for action against warships – in this case French blockading forces. Nevertheless, it came to play the chief part in the Battle of the Atlantic against merchant shipping and largely determined the limits of strategy.

Hitler had given the order to begin U-boat construction before the agreement with Great Britain was concluded, and the first of the Type II 250-tonners was launched only four days after the treaty was signed in June 1935; earlier the same month FK Karl Dönitz had been chosen to command the new flotilla. There is no record of why he was selected; he had served in U-boats in the first war, but so had over fifty other officers of suitable rank on the active list. It is possible he had been groomed for the task by the clandestine U-boat staff: two of his post-war appointments had been with torpedo boats practising tactics similar to those of surfaced U-boats – finding the enemy by day, holding on to him at the limits of visibility and closing in gradually with dusk to deliver the attack under cover of darkness. His second torpedo boat appointment had been as chief of a half-flotilla; the excellent reports on him by his flotilla chief had been countersigned by one of the leading lights in clandestine U-boat development.[46] Whatever the truth, it is clear from a paper he wrote just before taking command of the U-boat flotilla at the end of September 1935 that he was fully informed of the war plan against France and Russia, and took the staff view of the U-boat's function:

> In a war against an enemy who is not dependent on overseas supplies as a vital necessity, the task of our U-boats, in contrast to the world war, will not be the trade war, for which the U-boat in consequence of its low speed is little suited. The U-boat will be placed in a stationary position as close as possible before the enemy harbours at the focal point of traffic. Attack target, the enemy warships and troop transports.[47]

Thus as he took up his post Dönitz, whose name will ever be associated with the most sustained, bitter and wide-ranging attack on merchantmen in history, echoed the British Admiralty view of the submarine as a weapon of position and surprise for use primarily against enemy warships.

By the end of the year a new staff appreciation of the strategic situation concluded that the 550–600-ton Type VII U-boat lacked the range or armament capacity to fulfil its function in the western Mediterranean; consequently a much enlarged version of the discarded 750-ton Type I was hurriedly extrapolated and a batch ordered to take up the small amount of tonnage remaining below the 45 per cent limit.[48] These were designated Type IX; the first eight were launched between the spring of 1938 and August 1939.

The German U-boat arm thus entered the war with two ocean-going classes, Type VII and Type IX. The majority of the boats which fought the early, successful phases of the Atlantic battle were enlarged versions of the Type VII, designated VIIB and VIIC, of over 750 tons surface displacement with a top speed above 17 knots – 8 knots submerged – and a range of 6,500 miles at 12 knots. They had four bow torpedo tubes and one stern tube, and carried from eleven to fourteen torpedoes. The larger Type IXs were of over 1,000 tons surface displacement, could make above 18 knots and had a range of more than 8,000 miles at 12 knots, increased later in the war in Type IXCs to 11,000 miles; they had four bow and two stern tubes, and carried twenty-two torpedoes. Owing to the shortage of boats Dönitz used them for a long time with Type VIIs in group convoy actions in the North Atlantic, but they took a longer time to dive, could not go so deep and proved more susceptible to faults and damage, and he eventually withdrew them to operate, usually singly, in more distant waters.

Both classes had considerable speed and range advantages over the latest British S, T and U classes, and greater versatility provided by the stern tubes; they lacked only the potentially devastating initial ten-torpedo bow salvo of the Ts and the extraordinary sprightliness in diving of the Us. Neither were, of course, in the same class as the 1,500-ton US fleet submarines or the even larger Japanese boats so far as speed or range were concerned; nor did they compare in habitability with the US fleet boats, for they were designed, like all German warships, as functional weapons; officers and the 'Lords' had to find what space and comfort they could.

One of the few common factors in the evolution of these very different national types was that all were designed for action against enemy capital units; yet all found their true role in *guerre de course*, except the Japanese boats which were allowed little chance.

The U-boats enjoyed an advantage in optics and torpedo fire-control over the others. The Zeiss 7 × 50 lookout binoculars were lighter and generally more waterproof than those provided in other navies; and the attack periscopes were of a more sophisticated design, as already described, with an eyepiece at a fixed height and on the trunk below it a folding-seat attachment on which the CO sat, controlling the movements of the 'scope with foot pedals and hand controls. The surface-attack rangefinder binoculars, or *Überwasserzieloptik* – UZO for short – which were carried up from below and fixed atop a special UZO-post at the fore part of the bridge before a night attack were, prior to radar, immeasurably superior to the surface-attack instruments in other submarine arms. As the attack officer trained the UZO on the target the bearing was transmitted automatically to the fire-control computer, or *Vorhaltrechner* – literally aim-off calculator – in the conning tower below. This was an electro-mechanical analogue device like the American torpedo data computer; when set with target data and connected to the U-boat's gyro compass and the UZO, or the periscope bearing ring in a submerged attack, it provided the torpedo firing angle as a running solution and transmitted it via a spigot to the gyros of individual torpedoes in the tubes; these could then be fired whatever course was steered, providing it was within 90° – or later during the war 135° – of the torpedo setting. Later models had the edge over the US TDC because, once the speed and course of an enemy force or convoy had been ascertained, the *Vorhaltrechner* could be fed data on up to five separate targets within the force; it would hold these, transmitting different gyro angles to different torpedoes, which could then be fired one after the other within seconds at the five separate targets. It was this facility which helped to make U-boat night surface attacks on convoys so devastating.[49] U-boat pressure-hull construction was also superior to that in other navies, allowing German COs to dive deeper than any others when evading depth-charge attack.

The weak links in the U-boats' otherwise superb technology were the torpedoes. A new type powered by batteries was developed through German-owned firms in Sweden during the period of clandestine U-boat activity. Although lacking both the speed and range of conventional torpedoes driven by compressed air, the electric types did not emit the tell-tale bubbles which could alert the target ship and reveal the bearing of the firing boat to anti-submarine craft; a new type of combined electrical contact and magnetic influence exploder – the Pi1 – was also developed, but the Torpedo Inspectorate failed to put these potentially advanced weapons through adequate tests. As a result, in the early years of the war U-boat COs were to experience all the problems that plagued the Americans in the Pacific.

In training and the evolution of tactics the new U-boat arm soon outstripped other submarine forces. This was due in part to the U-boat staff, who had researched and preserved the lessons of the first war, but in the main it was the result of the leadership of Karl Dönitz, who enthused his young crews with his own transparent commitment and zeal, and inspired them with confidence in their weapons and themselves. After the first year the fleet commander reported that Dönitz's 'indefatigable work and personal instruction' had raised his new flotilla to a state of war readiness within six months; and he added, 'Attention must be paid to the fact that in his burning ardour he does not demand too much from his physical strength.'[50] Years later one of the young officers under training recalled that time: 'Mondays to Fridays eight attack exercises under water by day and six attack exercises on the surface by night. That was the upper limit of our physical and nervous capacity.'[51]

Apart from night surface attack on the precise lines practised in his former torpedo boat commands, the chief development for which Dönitz is remembered and always claimed credit is the group or *Rudel* (wolfpack) attack. Mutual co-operation between two or three boats had been practised in the later stages of the first war, indeed Dönitz himself had taken part in one such attempt although his partner had not shown up. During the period of clandestine development after the war several papers filed by the U-boat staff pointed to the need for U-boats to work together in future, chiefly to extend the search area;[52] this was made practicable by tremendous strides in radio technology allowing boats to transmit and receive signals over great distances, even when submerged to periscope depth.

Dönitz's pack tactics evolved from exercises with boats formed in patrol line for reconnaissance; the first boat sighting the enemy was required to signal to others and attack, whereupon the others would close his position and follow in. Later reconnaissance groups were supplemented by 'attack' groups under the command of a group leader who received instructions from an overall controller ashore at U-boat Command.[53] Dönitz's papers leave no doubt that these tactics were evolved for use against Russian and French warships in the Baltic and Mediterranean; apart from the necessity of extending the very small search area of a single boat, they were designed to overwhelm the enemy defences or, as he liked to put it, to oppose a concentration of the enemy with a concentration of U-boats. For as in the submarine arms of all other navies, asdic was a cause of great anxiety. In his memoirs Dönitz stated that his officers were so indoctrinated with respect for asdic during their U-boat training course that they expected to fire torpedoes from outside detection range, 3,000 yards or so; he, however, felt that asdic was unproved and probably overrated, and encouraged his men to attack close in where the chances of hitting were so much greater.[54] This was certainly how U-boats achieved their early successes.

His emphasis on the need for groups to search and attack led Dönitz to advocate an increase in the number of boats rather than in their size; asked at the end of 1936 for his views on future construction, he suggested the smallest type suitable for the Mediterranean, which he expected to be the centre of gravity of the next U-boat war, in order to obtain the maximum number. Meanwhile, over-age admirals at the *Seekriegsleitung* in Berlin, unduly impressed by great French and Japanese aircraft-carrying submarines, were advocating similar types; and contracts for monster, four-gun cruiser U-boats – numbered *U112–U115* – were actually handed out. It took two years for the MAN company's engineers to convince these officers that diesels of a size to drive such craft at the speed specified could not be built. In the meantime, because of the small tonnage quota for submarines and the great hole the cruiser U-boats made in it, construction of the smaller classes Dönitz wanted had been held up. In this sense the Anglo-German Naval Agreement did serve the British Admiralty's purpose; at all events Dönitz entered the war with far fewer U-boats than he might otherwise have had.

During 1937 it became apparent to Hitler as it had always been to Raeder and the Naval Staff, that Great Britain might not stand idly by while he established German hegemony of the continent of Europe; he called for naval expansion aimed against Great Britain, hitherto a forbidden topic. Raeder's staff produced a memorandum arguing that Britain's strengths were her battlefleet, which Germany could never hope to match, and her commanding position across Germany's exits to the sea; her weakness lay in her dependence on overseas communications: consequently 'The sea war [against Britain] is the battle over economic and military communications.'[55]

The concept was developed into a building programme termed the Z Plan, providing for fast, long-range armoured and light cruisers designed for commerce war in the Atlantic, and a heavy battle squadron with aircraft-carriers to support the cruisers' breakout through the Royal Naval blockade. U-boats were accorded a fairly low priority: it was felt they would have limited effect under the Washington rules – the *Prisenordnung* – whereby merchant ships had to be stopped and searched, and could not be sunk before the crew and passengers had taken to the lifeboats within safe reach of land. Besides, the naval staff had great faith in asdic, and assuming that merchant convoys would be escorted some distance into the Atlantic believed that approaching U-boats would infallibly be detected. The Z Plan therefore called for a gradual expansion of the U-boat arm to 174 by the end of 1945; of these 100 were to be Type VIIs, 44 Type IXs, 60 the small coastal Type IIs and the remaining few large minelayers and artillery 'cruisers' and 'fleet' types envisaged for operations with surface raiders.[56]

Dönitz disagreed fundamentally with the staff attitude; he believed U-boats were the only craft capable of getting through, or more accurately under, the Royal Navy's blockade, and were besides far cheaper and quicker to build than the great gunned warships proposed in the programme. After a wargame in early 1939 during which he set U-boat packs against British Atlantic convoys in the assumed conditions of 1943 – the date before which Hitler had promised Raeder there would be no war against England – he concluded that he required 90 continuously operational boats in the Atlantic; allowing for time in port and transit, 'at least 300 of these types [VII and IX] are necessary for successful operations'.[57] After the war he was to claim that with these 300 boats he could have brought Great Britain to her knees; the claim has been repeated in too many books. The wargame had shown nothing of the kind; indeed it had resulted in almost complete failure for the U-boats. Dönitz had probably chosen the figure 300 as larger than the Z Plan total, but not so much larger as to rule it out altogether. It hardly needs saying that if the German U-boat arm had approached this strength it would have triggered alarms and counter-activity at the Admiralty in London; consequently the claim is impossible to substantiate.

At the time he was conducting the wargame a book he had written entitled *Die U-bootswaffe* (*The U-boat Arm*) was published in Berlin. British naval intelligence missed it. Had they obtained a copy they would have found that the chief of the German U-boat arm believed that 'the destruction of enemy trade, the attack on the enemy sea communications is the proper purpose of sea warfare',[58] and would have learned that he had trained his boats in surface attack by night, using them literally as torpedo boats and relying on the U-boat's small silhouette to achieve complete surprise. More interestingly, perhaps, they might have gleaned from the heroic style and extreme Nazi views expressed that if this man were to lead his boats in war with Great Britain the Royal Navy would be facing a dangerous, indeed fanatical enemy. But they did not obtain a copy until 1942, by which time these points had been made.

Dönitz's great strengths as an inspirational leader were to become his weaknesses in his conduct of the war at sea, particularly in the final years: he saw only his own goals, disregarding obstacles or the probable reactions of others. This was apparent even before the outbreak of war. After the autumn manoeuvres of 1938 during which his boats carried out successful night surface attacks, a young officer in his headquarters ship, the cruiser *Königsberg*, pointed out to him that radar would soon make it difficult if not impossible for U-boats to approach undetected on the surface. He was in a position to know since the *Königsberg* was being used to test a prototype fire-control radar which was already able to detect objects as small as harbour buoys. Years later the officer, Otto Kohler, told the author Jak Mallmann Showell that his remark had been followed by an icy silence; then the U-boat officers around Dönitz had begun to argue against the point he had raised. Outnumbered, he had withdrawn.[59]

During the fleet's spring cruise the following year, 1939, Dönitz carried out a practice attack by fifteen boats disposed in four groups ahead of the track of a 'convoy' represented by two ships and an escort. The exercise was highly successful: those boats sighting the convoy kept touch in exemplary fashion, calling up the others by signal, until by the end of the exercise the 'convoy', which sustained innumerable dummy attacks, was surrounded by thirteen U-boats. Despite the artificial conditions, Dönitz's conclusions were unequivocal: 'The simple principle of fighting a convoy of several steamers with several U-boats is correct. The summoning of the U-boats was under the conditions of the exercise successful. The convoy would have been destroyed.' He dismissed the argument that the amount of signalling necessary in such attacks would allow the enemy to locate the attacking boats by wireless direction-finding (DF), for he doubted the accuracy of this equipment; in any case, he suggested, the attacks would take place outside the range of any coastal aircraft which could be called up to protect the convoy.

A few days earlier Werner Fürbringer had written a memorandum stating that a U-boat campaign against England depended on making the boats asdic-immune, all attempts at which had so far proved unsuccessful. Until this could be done there was no point in even beginning a U-boat war against trade, and 'to commit the valuable U-boat crews [to such a war] would be irresponsible'. He had gone on to argue that air forces would be necessary to destroy the convoy escorts, and in war the tasks of the navy and the naval air arm would be so interwoven that 'they must be welded into unity by the outbreak of war if heavy failures are not to result'.[60] Shown this paper, Dönitz doubted the usefulness of naval aircraft in the open Atlantic, and while agreeing that the asdic-immune boat had not yet been developed, he was confident that it would be in the foreseeable future. His views remained unchanged: U-boats alone would be able to break through the Royal Navy's blockade; U-boats in concentration would beat the concentration of ships in convoy, as he had just successfully demonstrated in the Bay of Biscay.[61]

Thus all the factors which were eventually to render his U-boat campaign impossible – radar, wireless direction-finding, escorting aircraft, asdic-equipped surface escorts – had been recognized and pointed out to Dönitz before the outbreak of war; that he chose to ignore them is understandable in view of his character and the superb tactical machine he had developed, and may appear justified by events; that he continued to ignore them after they had become grim reality was a result of the Nazi system of command and the atmosphere of unquestioning obedience, sycophancy, fear of punishment and silence that it fostered. Under these conditions his single-mindedness was allowed, indeed encouraged to become obsessive; no one dared oppose him.

It is interesting that before the war both the Germans and the Japanese attempted to develop submarines with high underwater speeds which, if successful, would have revolutionized undersea warfare. The German project was initiated by an engineer, Professor Helmuth Walter, who conceived the idea of storing oxyyen in the form of hydrogen peroxide (H_2O_2) to enable a steam turbine to be driven under water without depleting the air in the boat. He convinced the naval construction staff, who in early 1934 commissioned him to develop the concept. By 1940 he had built the first prototype, a small fish-shaped craft of 80 tons, designated V80, which achieved just over 28 knots in submerged tests in the Gulf of Danzig. Scaling up to an operational boat introduced complications, however, which slowed further development. The Japanese aimed for the same goal by increasing the battery capacity and the power of the electric motors and, like Walter, streamlining the hull. A 200-ton prototype was completed in the summer of 1938, concealed under the designation No. 71, and achieved over 21 knots in submerged trials. After extensive testing she was scrapped, and the concept was not resurrected during the war until too late to be of use.

The other naval powers, France, Italy and the Soviet Union, had numerically stronger submarine arms at the outbreak of war in 1939 than the major navies described, but for various reasons none played a significant role in the decisive campaigns.

France, while protesting her need for submarines to compensate for the smaller battlefleet tonnage allotted her at Washington, had built large, ocean-going classes evidently designed for *guerre de course*, and planned a class of seven giant boats which could scarcely have been intended for anything else. Only one of these was built, named *Surcouf* after a notorious St Malo privateer who had wreaked havoc among British shipping in the early nineteenth century. She was completed in 1931, and at well over 3,000 tons surface displacement was by some margin the largest submarine in the world until her loss early in 1942. However, she was plagued with mechanical troubles. Her principal twin 8-inch guns were positioned in an insufficiently watertight turret on the fore casing, she took a dangerously long time to submerge to periscope depth and she proved very difficult to trim once down; in addition the seaplane with which she was equipped could only be eased from its hangar and hoisted out, and afterwards recovered, in a flat calm.[62] Her design was too ambitious to be practical; indeed, she was useless for war and sailed on her last cruise, which was to end in circumstances which have never been clearly established,[63] chiefly as a symbol for General de Gaulle's Free French forces. Several of her smaller sisters also hoisted Free French colours and fought alongside the Allies, chiefly in the Mediterranean, but also in the North Sea. The most successful of these was the *Rubis*; making repeated patrols off the Norwegian coast under successive brave and skilful COs, her deadly eggs were to account for fifteen merchant vessels of altogether 26,000 tons and eight small naval auxiliaries.

Italy's substantial submarine force was designed and trained for action in the Mediterranean against the British fleet, but the possibility of larger boats operating in the Atlantic and Indian Oceans was agreed in talks between the Chiefs of Naval Staff, Admiral Domenico Cavagnari and Raeder, in June 1939 shortly after Hitler and Mussolini had signed the 'Pact of Steel'.[64] With large, very visible superstructures accommodating galleys and washrooms, lacking surface speed to shadow and attack by night, slow in diving and clumsy in manoeuvre, they proved ill-suited to oceanic warfare and Dönitz, who controlled them operationally, came to despair of them. In fact their record, while poor in comparison to that of the German U-boats, was better than the dismissive comments in his war diary imply. The greater number of Italian submarines remained in the Mediterranean, where they were poorly directed, and accomplished little. It was only in the design and operation of human torpedoes that the Italian under-water forces made a real impact on the war.

These craft were conceived and developed by two engineer sub-lieutenants named Tesei and Toschi inspired by the success of two first war Italian officers who had developed a piloted, torpedo-like craft with which they penetrated the defences of Pola harbour and sank the Austrian flagship late in 1918. Tesei and Toschi proposed to do the same to British warships in their Mediterranean bases, with a massed surprise attack on the outbreak of war. Only in this way, they believed, could Italy with her small industrial capacity hope to prevail against Great Britain. Both were ardent patriots; Tesei's letters reveal a spiritual sense of mission.[65] Despite the favourable precedent, the naval staff showed no interest, but the two persevered, building a prototype in their own time from materials procured at the submarine yard. In 1935, six years after their original proposal, Mussolini's invasion of Abyssinia caused a sudden deterioration in relations with Great Britain, even the threat of war. The two officers again put forward their plan and the following year demonstrated the submersible craft they had built. It was similar in size and shape to a torpedo, but was driven by an old lift motor powered by electric batteries, and made about 3 knots under water. The two officers, clad in waterproof rubber suits and wearing masks and breathing apparatus, rode it behind a curved plastic screen to deflect the water stream, the foremost 'pilot' steering and keeping trim by means of luminous instruments. In action it was proposed that they should be provided with cutting gear to penetrate net defences and a detachable delayed-fuse warhead to attach magnetically to the underwater hull of an enemy.

After the demonstration the scheme was officially taken up in a division for special operations termed Group H, but the naval staff failed to give it sufficient support and the young officers' vision of simultaneous surprise attacks on the British fleet bases at Gibraltar, Malta and Alexandria with 100 of the craft at the outbreak of hostilities came to nothing. Later they demonstrated in the most convincing manner what might have been achieved. The victim, the Royal Navy, paid them the compliment of taking the idea a step further.

The Soviet Navy began building new classes of submarines from the late 1920s modelled on earlier Tsarist or British boats, and aided by German technical assistance during a period of clandestine service co-operation. Subsequently they purchased designs from the undercover German firm in Holland, and produced a modern class of 800 tons, with a speed of over 19 knots, following this in the late 1930s with the potentially formidable K class of 1,500 tons, armed with ten torpedo tubes and capable of 22 knots.

By the time Hitler attacked in the summer of 1941 they possessed a numerically large submarine arm, at least on paper, of over 200 boats, mostly small or medium types for coastal defence and operations in the Baltic and Black Seas in support of the Red Army. However, they were dispersed in four widely separated fleets – Northern, Baltic, Black Sea and Pacific – and seem to have been poorly maintained and to have lacked modern communications, sonar or even apparently torpedo fire-control knowledge or equipment.[66] Above all they suffered from the inhibiting presence of political commissars and a total lack of direction from their shore commands, who provided no intelligence of the enemy. In the one area where they might have made a significant contribution to the war, the Baltic – the U-boats' training ground and a vital lifeline for the German armaments industry – they were shut out with minefields and extensive multiple net barriers between Estonia and Finland, and so harried by anti-submarine forces that they accomplished little.

So it was that the vital undersea campaigns which affected the fate of armies and the outcome of the world war were to be fought in the Atlantic, the Mediterranean and the Pacific by the submarines of Germany, Great Britain and the United States of America.

3

War

DÖNITZ WAS RECALLED from holiday on 15 August 1939 during
the period of tension before Hitler's intended assault on Poland.
Although the campaign was to be presented as a response to Polish
aggression, the naval and U-boat staff had laid plans reflecting the
possibility that Great Britain would honour her recent treaty
obligations to Poland. Twelve Type VII boats were to sail northabout around Scotland to take up individual waiting stations
across the north- and south-western approaches to the British Isles,
while five of the larger Type IXs, taking a similar route, were to
press on southwards to billets off the Iberian peninsula and the
Straits of Gibraltar; fourteen of the smaller coastal Type II boats
were to take station in the southern North Sea and Channel, a few
in the Baltic and approaches. Ten more boats were to follow when
ready.[1] This comprised all the operational submarines available
to U-boat Command. The decision to send them all out, leaving
no reserves to fill their places when they had to return, had been
taken by the Naval Staff in Berlin, not by Dönitz.

As they sailed over the following days he saw each off personally, commenting afterwards in his war diary on 'the very confident attitude of the crews'. He went on to confide his frustration
at the quite insufficient numbers for a war against Great Britain:

> My plans have all been restricted by lack of boats . . . In order to occupy
> the positions [around the British Isles] without a break I would need a
> further 43 boats and an additional 43 boats which as experience shows
> would be in dock for overhaul. Thus for a war of some length 130 U-boats
> would be necessary; even then I would have no reserves . . . Also there
> are not enough boats for the Atlantic and remote sea areas. Therefore the
> minimum requirement to be aimed at is 300 boats.[2]

Hitler's strategy was to isolate the Polish campaign. If this were
not possible, he still hoped for a short war in the east followed
by a swift peace in the west. Consequently he wanted nothing
done which might provoke Great Britain's genuine enmity; hence
Dönitz's orders to his COs, if it came to war in the west, were to
operate against merchant shipping strictly in accordance with the
Prize Regulations. While this negated the U-boats' advantages of
stealth and surprise, and laid the boats open to danger on the

surface, Dönitz believed it would take some time for the British to organize their defences and sail convoys. Meanwhile ships would be proceeding independently; 'the important thing is to catch these single ships at once', he noted in his war diary. He intended to direct operations by radio from U-boat headquarters but nevertheless sent two of the Atlantic boats out with senior officers who could assume local tactical control should he decide to call the boats from their separate areas and concentrate them in two groups, north and south,[3] for the pack tactics in which he had been training the force, explaining in his war diary on 26 August, 'U-boat warfare must at all times be concentrated against merchant shipping.'

On the evening of 31 August Raeder sent a message to all boats informing them that hostilities against Poland would commence at 04.45, 1 September; 'Attitude of Western powers still uncertain'.[4] Great Britain's position was clarified on the morning of 3 September, and early the same evening Raeder informed the boats in the Atlantic that France considered herself at war with Germany from 17.00, but they were to take no hostile action against French merchant shipping except in self-defence. 'This order means that according to the Prize Law French ships and goods must be released.'[5]

Three hours later Lemp in *U30* sighted the *Athenia* approaching, and at 21.42 his torpedo detonated in her port side, wounding her mortally. As the news burst in the world press next morning Dönitz had the orders to the boats checked, noting in his war diary, 'It is inconceivable they could have been misinterpreted'. Nonetheless he sent another message that afternoon again calling the COs' attention to the Prize Regulations. Neither he nor the Naval Staff in Berlin were animated by humanitarian or international legal considerations; they intended, if the war with the Western powers continued, to move by stages to an unrestricted campaign of the type waged by U-boats in the first war. A staff paper dated 'beginning of September 1939' makes this clear:

> With the expected general arming of enemy merchantmen a situation will develop allowing the sinking without warning of all enemy merchantmen which, because of the release of armed merchantmen into the category of military targets, will be unobjectionable in international law . . .[6]

It is clear from the paper that international legal considerations were judged important simply for their effect on the most powerful neutral, the United States of America, whose 'neutrality statute takes account of a possible special treatment for armed merchant-

1.Aufstellung: Spannungszeit bis 15·9·1939

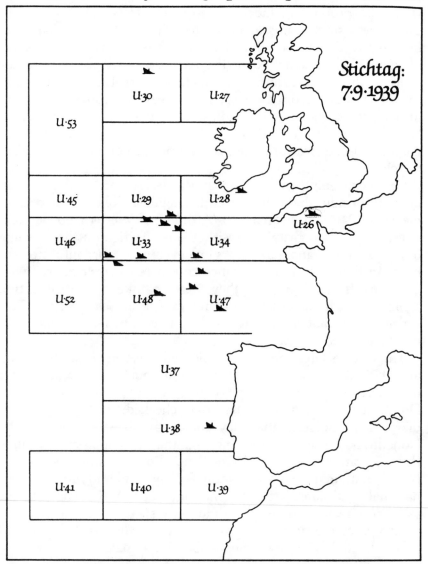

German chart showing areas of operation allocated to the Atlantic U-boats from the period of tension (*Spannungszeit*) in late August through to early September 1939, and the positions of their victims after the outbreak of war. Note *U30*'s victim approximately 250 miles north-west of Ireland – the *Athenia*.

men'. U-boat strategy was designed not to annoy the United States, and in the immediate context to facilitate peace with Great Britain and France after the conquest of Poland by driving a wedge between them, hence Raeder's orders to take no action against French merchant shipping. Later that night, such was the international furore aroused by the *Athenia*'s sinking, Raeder sent out another message to all boats: 'By order of the Führer no hostile action of any kind is to be taken for the present against passenger ships, even passenger ships in convoy.'[7]

No definition of 'passenger ships' was given, a significant omission suggesting the confusion into which Lemp's action had thrown the Naval Staff. Meanwhile Joseph Goebbels, Hitler's Minister for Public Enlightenment and Propaganda, began a campaign to confuse the world's press, accusing Churchill of ordering the liner's sinking in order to bring America into the war.[8] He was so successful that a small section of the US press was unsure of the real cause of the *Athenia*'s loss until the evidence was produced after the war.

At the British Admiralty preparations for the introduction of convoy were lent an added urgency. The first east coast convoy sailed on 6 September from the Thames to the Forth, and the following day the first ocean-going convoys sailed from the Thames down the Channel, and from Liverpool through the Irish Sea; a week later homeward convoys were started from Halifax, Nova Scotia, Kingston, Jamaica, and Freetown, Sierra Leone, and at the end of the month from Gibraltar. These comprised ships in the 9- to 15-knot speed range; slower or faster vessels still sailed independently, directed in the immediate approaches to the British Isles along so-called 'controlled routes', which were patrolled by groups of anti-submarine vessels[9] – a throwback to a system which had proved ineffective wherever tried in the first war. And such was the shortage and short range of escorts that even the convoys were only escorted to or from points 200 miles west of the Irish coast or southwards to just below Ushant in the Bay of Biscay, and similar short distances from the Canadian coast. When the escorts left at their cut-off points these ships too dispersed to make their way individually to their separate destinations. It was to be almost two years before transatlantic convoys could be escorted the whole way across.

In the meantime the U-boats waiting off the south-western approaches picked off single ships. *U-47*, commanded by KLt. Günther Prien, shortly to enter legend and become the earliest of a new school of aces, was first to score under Prize Regulations.

Patrolling off Biscay in the early morning of 5 September, he sighted a small freighter approaching and dived to observe her. She proved to be the Cunarder *Bosnia*, 2,400 tons. He allowed her to pass, then surfaced on her quarter and fired a shot across her bows. She turned away, attempting escape and signalling SSS for submarine attack, and it took six shells which started fires in her cargo of sulphur to stop her. Prien closed as the crew took to the boats and, seeing an injured man in one, had a glass of brandy sent up for him. By this time another steamer was approaching. Finding she was a neutral Norwegian Prien asked her captain to take the *Bosnia*'s crew aboard. Then, having discharged his duties under the Regulations to the full, he gave the furiously burning *Bosnia* the *coup de grâce* with a torpedo. Over the next two days he stopped and sank two more small British cargo vessels[10] before being recalled by Dönitz, who did not want all boats returning at the same time with none to replace them on station.[11]

Lemp, after his initial blunder, took the greatest care to abide by the Regulations. On 4 September he allowed the liner *Duchess of Bedford* to pass without molestation, and when on the 11th he stopped the freighter *Blair Logie*, he saw the crew into the boats before sinking her, supplied them with schnapps and cigarettes, and stayed with them all night, firing red distress signals, only leaving at dawn when an American ship came up. Two days later he stopped the freighter *Fanad Head* and put a party aboard to search her. They were still aboard, foraging for food, when Lemp was surprised by two Skua aircraft from the carrier *Ark Royal*, operating as part of a U-boat 'hunting group' – another strategy which had proved ineffective in the first war. Lemp made a rapid decision and put a torpedo into the freighter before diving. Both Skuas, coming in too low as the boat submerged, were brought down by the blast of their own bombs; Lemp surfaced and took both pilots aboard as prisoners of war. *U30* had suffered only superficial damage to her bows and two torpedo tubes, but one of the boarding party had been seriously wounded in the freighter. Lemp sent a signal to U-boat Command requesting permission to call at Reykjavik to land the man. Dönitz agreed.[12]

The day of this attack, 14 September, KLt. Gerhard Glattes, commanding the Type IX *U39*, was west of the Hebrides on his way home northabout around Scotland after recall by Dönitz, when he found himself in the track of the *Ark Royal*'s group. He was able to manoeuvre into position within 900 yards of the carrier and fire a salvo. Two torpedoes exploded prematurely just short of the target and another passed astern, whereupon the destroyers of the group located the boat by asdic and blew her to the surface with well-placed depth-charges; her crew scrambled out before she sank, the first U-boat loss of the war and a portent of the potency of asdic-fitted destroyers, trained and working together as a team. While this success might suggest that hunting groups were a useful way of deploying scarce anti-submarine resources, it was the U-boat which found the group and revealed her presence by attacking, not the other way about; and it had been a close call for the carrier, only saved perhaps by the premature detonations. Dönitz did not find out about these until much later.

Next day the first of the recalled boats arrived home, Prien's *U-47*, *U-46* and in the evening *U45* berthing in Kiel, the Type IX *U-37* in Wilhelmshaven. Of the four only Prien had scored. Continuing the tradition of the first war he flew three small white pennants from his partly raised periscope, each sewn with figures denoting the tonnage of one of his victims. Tantalizingly for Dönitz, who wondered whether he had recalled the boats too soon, the first sighting of a convoy had come in earlier that day: *U31* off the Bristol Channel had reported the ships steering westwards, and she was keeping contact. Dönitz ordered the nearest three boats to the position, *U-34*, *U29* and *U53*. He desperately wanted to prove his boats and the tactic of group attack in action against a convoy; a week earlier he had confided to the war diary his dream of 'a great success – e.g. wiping out an entire convoy'.[13] Now he wrote of the boats he had ordered in:

> Perhaps they have a chance. I have hammered it into commanders again and again that they must not let such chances pass . . . if only more boats were out now! Nevertheless I still think it was correct to recall the boats. Without them there would be a total lack of boats by the beginning of October.
>
> The practical disposition of the boats of the next series, with which the annihilation of a convoy must be achieved, is under constant consideration.[14]

Next day, 16 September, *U-31*, still shadowing the convoy she had reported, moved ahead and submerging in its track fired two torpedoes at the 6,000-ton freighter *Aviemore*. Both hit and she went down with twenty-three of her crew, the first loss from a convoy. The same day *U26* came upon the ships, but the three boats Dönitz had ordered up could not find them and the mass attack he longed for never materialized. However, the following evening, one of the three, *U29*, chanced upon a second U-boat hunting group, the aircraft-carrier *Courageous* and two destroyers;

two other destroyers had parted temporarily on a rescue mission. *U29*'s CO, OLt. Otto Schuhart, who had already sunk two tankers and a tug, thought at first that he was too far off track; then the carrier turned towards him as she came into the wind to fly on her aircraft, and he was able to move into position to fire a salvo from inside 3,000 yards. He heard two hits before he went deep to avoid the destroyer counter-attack. The rending sounds of the carrier sinking were overlaid by the explosion of patterns of depth-charges as he crawled away below.

'A wonderful success!' Dönitz wrote in his war diary next day after the BBC had announced the loss of the carrier and over 500 of her crew; and as yet unaware of the fact or manner of the destruction of *U39* in rather similar circumstances, 'a further confirmation that the British countermeasures are not as effective as they claim'.[15]

Two more boats arrived home that day: *U48* had not scored; *U38* under KLt. Heinrich Liebe with Wolfgang Lüth as his 1WO, both future aces, had sunk two large ships, the second a tanker whose crew they had taken from a sea of burning oil and transferred into a passing American tanker.

Despite these successes, which in the first two weeks of war amounted to twenty-five British merchantmen[16] and one major warship, Dönitz had too few boats to do much more than alert the Admiralty to the seriousness of their problem. By 20 September there were only four boats on station and by the 22nd two of these had started for home, leaving only two in the Atlantic approaches. Besides this, the reports of the returning COs revealed too many torpedo failures, particularly premature explosions and duds when a boat's own hydrophones picked up the metallic clink of the torpedo striking the target's hull, with no explosion resulting. Both conventional and electric torpedoes were detonating after running for only 250 yards, in one case so soon after leaving the tube that the U-boat's bows had been damaged. The Torpedo Inspectorate were at a loss for an answer.[17] Dönitz was also concerned about the dangers to which his boats exposed themselves when operating under the Prize Regulations; in particular it seemed that British aircraft were appearing on the scene after ships sent out the distress call for submarine attack, and he asked the Naval Staff, Berlin, for a ruling on whether ships using their radios in this way might be considered part of the enemy anti-submarine network and sunk immediately. On the 24th he received permission to issue orders to this effect.[18] Specific steps towards an unrestricted U-boat campaign had been under consideration in Berlin for some time;

on the 18th Raeder had told Dönitz he intended declaring an 'unrestricted' zone around the British Isles, but he wanted to start with British ships only, not neutrals. Dönitz had replied that it was usually impossible for a U-boat lying in wait to identify the nationality of a ship in time to attack without warning; in any case the British would probably start sailing their own ships under neutral flags. The project was dropped.[19]

On 27 September U30 returned to Wilhelmshaven with one engine out of action due to a design fault common to all Type VIIA boats. Dönitz was waiting on the quay. Lemp made his report, adding afterwards in a low voice that he had something else to say: he had sunk the *Athenia*; he had thought she was a troop transport.

'You've certainly landed yourself in a thick stew, Lemp,' Dönitz apparently replied. 'I shall have to bring you before a court martial. In the meantime you must swear your men to the strictest silence.'

In the event Raeder decided against a court martial, it seems because of the adverse publicity it would cause, but instructed Dönitz to have the pages recording the incident stripped from the boat's log. Dönitz also omitted any mention in his own war diary, crediting U30 only with the *Blair Logie* and *Fanad Head*, 'Total 9,699 tons'.[20] Dönitz concentrated on essentials and tended to disregard details. In this and at least one other similar case later in the war when he ordered log-book pages removed he omitted to ensure that the relevant pages of the torpedo and artillery logs were similarly torn out and faked.[21] Lemp's torpedo log went the rounds of Torpedo Command in the normal way, and he was soon being called 'Athenia Lemp' by a wide circle of officers.

By the date of U30's return there were no boats on station in the Atlantic or the North Sea; all had returned home or were on their way; two had been destroyed. Besides U39, U27 had been found and sunk on 20 September by an armada of asdic-fitted destroyers sent from the Home Fleet after she had been reported stopping and sinking fishing vessels off the northern end of the Hebrides. Dönitz presumed both boats lost. He was nonetheless satisfied with results thus far: forty-one merchantmen totalling an estimated 150,000 tons or more had been sunk by his boats; others, although he did not know the numbers, had fallen victim to mines laid by U-boats.[22] He was convinced that, if only the building programme could be accelerated sufficiently, he had a potentially decisive weapon to reverse the decision of the first war. As one of his adjutants recalled later, he could not forget the Royal Navy's 'hunger blockade' of Germany.[23] He was passionately determined to humble England.

On the 28th, Hitler, fresh from the triumph of the Polish campaign, visited the Sengwarden headquarters; Dönitz treated him to a highly optimistic exposition of the potential of his boats, pointing to their 'actual and psychological effect over a wide area' and the 'huge strides in U-boat communications' which allowed him to meet a concentration of ships in convoy with a concentration of U-boats.

'After analysis of all questions concerning the U-boat war,' he said grandly, 'I have arrived at the conviction that in them [U-boats] we possess a means of striking England decisively at her weakest point.'

However, he continued, this meant having enough boats, and again he gave the magic number, 'at least 300', adding that even more had to be built to cover losses which, on first war experience, would be between 5 and 10 per cent. He concluded, 'On the basis of this number of boats I believe the U-boat arm can achieve decisive [durchschlagenden] success.'[24]

From the modest timber barrack which served as his headquarters, Dönitz accompanied Hitler and his entourage of high-ranking naval and army officers to the U-boat dock to inspect the rust-streaked boats and bearded crews who had just returned, thence to the officers' mess, where the young COs and even younger watch officers, cleanshaven and spruce in number one uniforms, were not reticent in retailing their experiences at the 'front'. As Hitler's naval adjutant wrote later, 'the Führer carried back to Berlin an excellent impression of the leadership of the U-boat arm as well as of the liveliness and spirit of the crews.'[25]

Since the start of hostilities Dönitz had been pondering an operation against the Royal Navy's main fleet base at Scapa Flow in the Orkneys north of Scotland. It had been attempted twice by U-boats in the first war without success, and both boats had been lost. However, having received a report that the underwater defences in the eastern passages to the anchorage had been neglected, he had instructed the CO of U16 to reconnoitre, and asked the Luftwaffe to fly a photographic mission over the Flow. After studying the resulting photographs he had concluded that there was an 18-yard gap between blockships sunk in the northernmost of the eastern entrances which would just be negotiable by a U-boat on the surface at slack water. This indicated a night operation. The hazards were formidable, not least the navigation, but if successful it would provide the spectacular exploit he craved for his U-boat arm. He had his senior staff officer, KLt. Victor Oehrn, draw up a detailed plan, and on Sunday, 1 October, summoned Günther Prien, the CO of *U16* and Prien's flotilla chief, to a meeting aboard the submarine tender *Weichsel*, which he was using as a headquarters ship.

Prien was three months short of his thirty-second birthday, older than the normal run of U-boat COs since he had entered the navy late after serving in the merchant service and gaining a Master's certificate. He was keen, capable, very assured and a convinced Nazi, had indeed been a member of the Party for a period before joining the navy. Dönitz, as mentioned, had extreme Nazi views. Prien was one of his favourite COs. When he arrived Dönitz showed him the aerial photographs to compare with the chart of Scapa Flow, and outlined the plan worked up for the night of 13/14 October when both periods of slack water fell in the dark hours and the moon would be new. After a full discussion he told Prien not to make up his mind about the mission at once, but to think it over, and report back to him on Tuesday. Prien was back on Monday; his answer was 'Yes', as of course Dönitz had known it would be. He swore him to secrecy; not even his officers and crew should know their destination before they sailed.

The following Sunday morning, 8 October, Prien took *U47* from her berth in Kiel and through the Kaiser Wilhelm canal into the North Sea, making speed on the surface at night, submerging by day. The British Home Fleet had sailed meanwhile to hunt a German surface force believed to be attempting a breakout into the Atlantic, but actually, and equally unbeknown to Dönitz, trying to entice the British heavy ships into the southern North Sea. After an abortive search the Home Fleet put back into Loch Ewe on the west coast of Scotland – since Scapa Flow's defences were known to be dangerously incomplete – and only a few ships returned to the Flow. Most of these dispersed during the next few days, leaving the old battleship *Royal Oak*, the old seaplane-carrier *Pegasus* and the new heavy cruiser *Belfast* as the only large ships when *U47* arrived off the eastern side of the islands surrounding the base on the 12th.

Thus far Prien had kept the mission secret; now he told the crew what he intended, adding in the hush greeting the news that anyone who did not want to take part was free to leave. He surfaced that evening to check his position with visual bearings, ventilate the boat and charge the batteries, then submerged again before dawn to spend the daylight hours of the 13th resting on the bottom. During this tense period journals and comics passed around between the men as they rested. In one was a cartoon depiction of a bull with its head down, about to charge, smoke issuing from its nostrils. They would remember this on the return trip and paint a similar bull on the fore end of the conning tower;[26] and U47 would wear it as her symbol and badge of pride until her end. All boats had removed the numbers on their conning towers at the outbreak of war; COs had devices of their own choosing painted on instead.

Surfacing in the evening and opening the conning-tower hatch, Prien was startled to see the northern sky illuminated with the dramatic light of the aurora borealis, a phenomenon Victor Oehrn had not taken into account. Despite doubts about entering in such brilliant visibility, he set course for the southern cape of the main island enfolding the northern flow, diving when a steamer was sighted soon after 23.00, surfacing twenty-five minutes later and continuing the run-in trimmed down to reduce the boat's silhouette. He had prepared himself by learning by heart all the features of the approach from the chart and was thankful he had done so, for the tide was running with them and the boat was swept towards the narrow channel between Lamb Holm and the main island at astonishing speed. As the submarine entered the channel hugging the northern shore the stream caught her stern, twisting it to port; at the same time Prien saw the anchor cable of the northernmost blockship, which he intended leaving to port, stretching down at 45° ahead. He called for starboard helm, then feeling the boat grounding he had the remaining tanks blown and quickly ordered port helm to swing the stern away from the cable. They caught it nonetheless, well aft, and scraped along until suddenly they were free and inside the Flow. It was 00.27.

The whole expanse of water enclosed by islands was lit as if by moonlight, and the fleet anchorage ahead was plainly empty. Casting about, Prien made out ships and masts against the land in the north-eastern corner and steered along the northerly trend of the shore towards them. By the time he neared, shortly before 01.00, the aurora borealis had faded and the night was black, but he had recognized furthest from the shore what he believed were two capital ships, the *Royal Oak* and beyond her the *Repulse*, actually the seaplane-carrier *Pegasus*. He determined to divide his first salvo between the two.

As he began the attack run, his 1WO, Engelbert Endrass, later to become an ace in his own right, strained through the night-sights atop the UZO-post at the shadow targets; at 3,000 yards Prien gave him permission to fire, and he pulled the lever to send the first torpedo on its way, confirming it with a call down the voice-pipe to the control panel. After a short interval he fired the next, and the next, *'Los! . . . Los! . . . Los! . . .'* The last torpedo jammed in its tube, but three were reported running straight. Captain and 1WO stared at the second hands of their watches as the time lengthened. The Flow was quiet, the two ships and lines of destroyers closer inshore asleep.

Three and a half minutes passed, then the sound of a detonation carried across the water, just one. It seemed to come from the further ship. Prien swung *U47* around to fire the single stern tube. Below in the narrow space of the forward torpedo compartment the hands urgently manhandled reloads into two of the empty tubes. In the *Royal Oak*, whose company had been rocked awake by the dull thump of an explosion from right forward, officers tried to establish its location and source. They concluded that combustible material in the forward store must have exploded spontaneously.

Prien took *U47* round again to head for the battleship he believed they had missed; as the tube-ready lights glowed on the control panel, Endrass made the final checks, then pulled the firing lever three times in succession. Less than twenty minutes after the initial salvo three more eels drove towards the *Royal Oak*. Again the officers on the bridge counted the seconds.

The first explosion sounded after three minutes. The next two, as both following torpedoes hit in quick succession, were lost in a rumbling concussion of detonations growing into a thunderous roar as the cordite in a main armament magazine detonated. Water stood up like a wall, bursts of fire flickering through it, blue, red, orange, yellow, whiting out the sky, and intersected by rocketing shadows as large parts of the stricken ship were hurled high, only to descend and throw up more coloured fountains in the water.[27] Gradually the tumult subsided, the broken hull rolling over and settling. Prien called down through the open hatches, 'She's finished!'

There was a moment of quiet in the boat then yells of triumph from every throat merged into 'a single animal cry in which the frightful tension of the past 24 hours released itself'.[28] Prien shouted down for silence.

By now the destroyers beyond had come to life with signalling lights, and car headlights had become visible ashore. Prien steered south on the surface and threaded his way past the blockships off Lamb Holm on a falling tide while guard boats and destroyers chased about the Flow in a vain search. It had been a bold operation, conducted with exemplary coolness and judgement, marred only by the absence of the fleet; the *Royal Oak* was too slow and ill-protected to engage modern capital ships and her end was less serious than the loss of 833 trained officers and men who perished with her. It was, nonetheless, a moral and propaganda triumph of the first order and appropriately, when *U47* nosed back to her berth to the strains of a band on the 17th, both Raeder and Dönitz headed the considerable welcoming committee. Prien, now and forever 'the Bull of Scapa Flow', and all his crew were decorated with the Iron Cross; later, after a wash and a shave ashore, they were flown to Berlin by aircraft of Hitler's flight. They were already heroes throughout the country and when, next morning, they attempted to march across the Wilhelmplatz to the Reich Chancellery to be received by Hitler, the hysteria of the crowd was such that the police had to rescue them. Hitler shook hands with each and made a short speech harking back to his time in the trenches in the first war, after which he presented Prien with the Knight's Cross, then the highest order of the Iron Cross.

After lunch the crew was paraded for a press conference; the American correspondent William Shirer noted Prien as 'clean cut, cocky, a fanatical Nazi and obviously capable'.[29] Dönitz, who had been promoted to *Konteradmiral* on 1 October, was now stepped up to *Befehlshaber* (Commander-in-Chief) from *Führer der U-boote*, from FdU to BdU.

Of more lasting significance that October were the inexorable, planned moves towards an unrestricted U-boat war which had begun with instructions to sink ships using their radios. Early in the month the Prize Regulations were withdrawn in the North Sea and the approaches to the Baltic, and boats were given permission to attack without warning merchantmen seen to be armed or listed as armed or, in the waters around the British Isles and out to 15°W (the cut-off point for convoy escorts), ships steaming without lights at night. Later this was extended to any ship identified as an enemy, and through October and November Hitler progressively lifted the prohibition on attacking passenger ships, providing they were clearly identified as belonging to the enemy.

Simultaneously Dönitz issued new standing orders to his COs prohibiting them from putting boarding parties aboard ships and forbidding gun action; ships were to be sunk with torpedoes only. This was in response to a worrying increase in U-boats feared lost, which he put down to their vulnerability on the surface, both to aircraft and to British merchantmen themselves which had been fitted with guns and instructed to try and ram when they saw a U-boat. In fact, of the six boats he listed as definitely, probably or possibly lost before issuing these orders, four had been accounted for by destroyers, two by mines. The difficulty of discovering exactly how his boats met their end was something Dönitz was never to overcome; the British took care not to help.

U-boat COs interpreted their release from restrictions liberally, as they were undoubtedly intended to, since at the same time German propaganda to neutral countries was seeking to create an impression that it was suicidally dangerous to trade with Great Britain. On 24 November this was spelled out in an official warning from the German government: the safety of neutral ships in the waters around the British Isles and the French coast could no longer be taken for granted. That month the Anti-Submarine Warfare Division of the Admiralty commented:

> By the beginning of November the Germans showed by their conduct they had abandoned all pretence of observing those rules of international law that relate to sea warfare. Neutral ships as well as British have been torpedoed without warning and fairways along which merchant ships pass have been strewed with mines ...[30]

At the end of November or beginning of December Dönitz issued a new order to his COs which emphasized the abandonment of Prize Regulations in the starkest terms:

> Rescue no one and take no one with you. Have no care for the ships' boats. Weather conditions and the proximity of land are of no account. Care only for your own boat and strive to achieve the next success as soon as possible! We must be hard in this war. The enemy started the war in order to destroy us, therefore nothing else matters.[31]

It seems from comments in his war diary that this order, too, was prompted chiefly by concern for the dangers his boats ran on the surface. Too many COs appeared to him to be putting consideration for survivors above the safety of their boat or the accomplishment of their mission. This is confirmed in British accounts; thus when *U41* under KK Adolf Mugler sank the SS *Darino* off Biscay in November, the ship's chief officer and eleven surviving crew members were pulled aboard the U-boat; the chief officer recounted later:

> When he picked us up the captain said he could only take 12 survivors altogether, as any excess of this would have upset the boat's trim. We were told that on one occasion before this they had seven men on board from an enemy ship ... We were taken below, our clothes were taken off and

we were put into bunks; some of the men on the submarine turned out of their bunks for us to use . . .[32]

After ten hours Mugler had stopped an Italian ship bound for England and transferred the *Darino*'s men to her. It is evident from other accounts that while few COs went to these lengths many showed their victims the comradeship of the sea by passing over bottles of spirits, or cigarettes, or cans of fresh water if the lifeboat's water tanks were foul, and continued to do so after Dönitz's order.[33]

Despite his satisfaction that the boats were now free to deploy their strength as weapons of stealth and surprise, Dönitz was intensely frustrated by lack of numbers. The early losses had not been made good by new boats and consequently he had even fewer boats than at the outbreak of war. Rather than spread these thinly in a cordon, he concentrated them in areas of natural traffic convergence in the south-western approaches to the British Isles and off the Straits of Gibraltar, for as he made clear in his war diary at the beginning of October, he still had his eyes fixed on a 'great success' against a convoy: 'Aim must be to find convoys and concentrate the few available boats to destroy them.'[34] He continued to send out a senior officer in one of the boats in each area, who would 'if necessary take over control of convoy operations'. But as in the first war convoys were difficult to find and the vast majority of ships sunk were sailing independently.

The nearest to pack attacks came in mid-October when three boats were successfully directed on to a homeward convoy in the western approaches; U45 under KLt. Alexander Gehlhaar sank three ships in quick succession on the morning of 14 October, and U48, commanded by the future ace KLt. Herbert Schultze, sank another. Three days later Schultze found a second homeward convoy and shadowed, while the senior officer Dönitz had sent out in U37, KLt. Werner Hartmann, directed U46 in to the attack; Hartmann kept U37 out of the action in order to retain an overview, thus of the three boats in position only U48 and U46 under KLt. Herbert Sohler took an active part. These sank four ships between them before shore-based aircraft forced them under and the remainder of the convoy escaped. Despite the small number of boats engaged Dönitz felt that 'the attack as a whole proved a success, showing that co-operation between U-boats is a practical proposition'.

His greatest problem at this time, apart from numbers of boats, was torpedo failure. After the many premature detonations reported from the first patrols, he had banned use of the new magnetic pistol. Now came reports of contact exploders failing. The explanation seemed to be provided on 20 October, when the chief of the Torpedo Inspectorate told him by phone he had discovered that both conventional and electric torpedoes were running 2 metres below their set depth. Dönitz immediately issued orders that settings were to be 2 metres less than the draft of the target ship. Since the minimum setting in an Atlantic swell was 4 metres – lest the torpedo broach the surface – vessels with a draft of less than about 6 metres could not now be attacked; this included destroyers and other escorts. Three days later he attended a conference with the chiefs of the Torpedo Inspectorate, Trials and Experimental Divisions, which served merely to increase his disillusion; he was told that torpedoes were subject to greater depth variations than hitherto assumed, and the cause of the premature explosions had still not been established. After more reports of failures at close range at the end of the month he noted in his war diary: 'There is now no doubt that the T[orpedo] I[nspectorate] themselves do not understand the situation . . . At least 30 per cent of all torpedoes are duds . . .'[35] Later analysis suggested that 40.9 per cent of unsuccessful shots were caused by torpedo failure.[36]

Early in November an adaptation of the magnetic pistol Pi(a-b) was issued to operational boats, but it was not long before further reports of failures and premature detonations were coming in. Dönitz sent the details to the Torpedo Inspectorate for analysis. They refused to believe the pistol was at fault, blaming the COs' inaccuracy. 'I can no longer accept this explanation', Dönitz recorded in his war diary;[37] his scepticism was confirmed by tests in January 1940, and on the 21st he wrote:

The fact that its main weapon, the torpedo, has to a large extent proved useless in operations has been the greatest difficulty with which the U-boat arm has had to contend since the beginning of the war, and has had a most serious effect on results . . . at least 300,000 tons which might have been sunk can be reckoned to have been lost due to torpedo failure . . . The faith of the commanders and crews in the torpedo is seriously shaken . . . I will continue as before to use all my influence, despite setbacks, to maintain the attacking spirit of the U-boat arm.[38]

The number of ships sunk rose nonetheless through January and February 1940 as COs, unrestrained by any requirement to establish a vessel's nationality before attacking, and driven by intense competition to enter the ranks of the new aces like Prien and Schultze, picked off independent ships and stragglers from convoys. Increasingly they attacked on the surface at night. The Admiralty Anti-Submarine Warfare Division noted that ships lost to night attack had risen from about 33 per cent of all losses the previous October to 58 per cent in February, and commented: 'The great advantage of such a method is that the U-boat can escape at speed on the surface.'[39] They might have added that asdic could not detect a surfaced submarine. COs returning to base frequently could not name the ships whose estimated tonnage they displayed on their victory pennants. When *U44* under KLt. Ludwig Mathes berthed on 9 February with eight pennants totalling 38,266 tons, the highest total in any patrol thus far, she listed only three names amongst her victims; the others were described as 'darkened ships', 'steamer in convoy', 'armed steamer' and 'steamer without markings'.[40]

On 24 February Herbert Schultze brought *U48* in to Kiel after a minelaying patrol flying four pennants for ships sunk by torpedo totalling 34,930 tons. This brought his aggregate over four patrols up to sixteen ships, by his estimate totalling 114,510 tons, and established him as the leading ace, the first to reach the 100,000-ton mark. The following month he was awarded the Knight's Cross of the Iron Cross, which became the invariable distinction for those who reached 100,000 tons.

In February the handful of boats on station at any one time sank forty-five ships, more than had been accounted for the previous September by the entire U-boat arm and a fearful warning of what Dönitz might achieve should the numbers promised by the U-boat building programme ever come into service. The Admiralty Anti-Submarine Warfare Division took comfort, however, from the success of the convoy system: 'Out of 164 ships sunk during the first six months [to the end of Feurary] only seven were in convoys escorted by anti-submarine vessels' – this despite most convoys sailing with only two escorts, frequently only one. 'It would appear, therefore, the U-boat has a marked antipathy against attacking convoys, preferring lone neutrals and stragglers.'[41] This, of course, was the reverse of the truth, so far as Dönitz was concerned; the relative immunity of the convoys was a result of the extreme difficulty of finding them with so few boats and little if any co-operation from Göring's Luftwaffe.

Conversely, British forces had found it difficult, because of the extremely short range of asdic, to detect U-boats. But the Anti-Submarine Warfare Division was able to find satisfaction in the fact that 'the first six months of the war have shown that if the position of a U-boat is revealed close to anti-submarine vessels the chances of its destruction are high'.[42] To the end of February no less than fifteen U-boats had been destroyed – over 25 per cent of Dönitz's force on the outbreak of war – and of those ten had been sunk by or as a result of depth-charge attack by destroyers or other anti-submarine vessels. This went some way to justify the Admiralty's pre-war faith in asdic, but the main problem remained the dearth of escorts in which to fit asdic. Trawlers and steam yachts had been pressed into extemporized service, but still the numbers were wholly inadequate and none had the range for ocean convoys. Three escort destroyers of an emergency programme were launched in December 1939, and the first of a new type of ocean-going escort based on whale-catchers slid down the ways towards the end of January 1940; she was named *Gladiolus*, harbinger of what came to be called the Flower-class corvettes, without which, as the official British naval historian, Stephen Roskill, has commented, it is difficult to see how Great Britain could have survived.[43]

That was for the future: in March relative peace settled over the oceanic trade routes as Dönitz was instructed to prepare his force for screening operations during a planned seaborne invasion of Norway and Denmark.

The British submarine force had so far failed to achieve either the actual or the psychological impact of the U-boats. There were fewer of them, at the start only eighteen operational boats in home waters. But chiefly they lacked a role and a single-minded operational leader; their pre-war training had been deficient, and since it was not in Great Britain's interest as a nation depending on sea lifelines to encourage Hitler to break the Prize Regulations, they were debarred from acting without warning against merchant ships, indeed were not even allowed to sink them unless they could make arrangements for the safety of the crew.[44]

The main strength of the British submarine force was concentrated at Singapore against the Japanese threat; other boats were in the Mediterranean and Atlantic. The most powerful force at home was the 2nd Flotilla at Dundee on the east coast of Scotland, comprising eight S-class boats, three of the new and larger T-class with their powerful ten-tube salvo and three fleet submarines – two old O-class and the rather newer, larger and faster *Thames*. Further south on the east coast of England at Blyth above Newcastle was the 6th Flotilla with three small, new U-class boats and one even smaller, ancient H. During October 1939 both flotillas were concentrated at Rosyth on the Forth, while later a 3rd Flotilla was created far to the south on the East Anglian coast at Harwich with four S-class and three minelaying boats withdrawn from the Mediterranean.

On the outbreak of war the boats had been despatched to patrol areas off the Dutch and German North Sea coasts and to south-west Norway off the entrance to the Baltic; they were a part of the declared naval 'blockade' of Germany, but undoubtedly their primary duty, certainly off Norway, was to act as scouts and report the breakout of German fleet units and surface commerce-raiders. Their orders stated that no favourable opportunity for attacking enemy warships should be neglected, but there was a proviso that this should not interfere with 'the primary object', that of acting as the eyes of the fleet.[45] This was of course in line with the Admiralty's pre-war downgrading of all units to little more than ancillaries of the fleet, which was seen as the queen on the strategic board. The contrast with Dönitz's standing orders, admittedly in the different context of a trade war, could hardly have been more striking. Dönitz demanded attack:

> In the first line attack, always keep attacking; do not allow yourself to be shaken off; should the boat be forced away or under water for a time, search in the general direction of the convoy to regain touch, advance again! Attack![46]

The boats from the 2nd Flotilla off Norway had been stationed at 12-mile intervals as extensions of the reconnaissance area of the Coastal Command of the Royal Air Force, whose obsolescent Anson aircraft operating from Scotland could not quite reach the Norwegian coast. The very narrow separation of the boats' patrol areas in terms of submarine navigation in poor weather, together with the tragic failure of a recognition signal and signal lamp at a critical moment on the night of 10 September, led to the first submarine loss of the war when *Triton*, after challenging three times, torpedoed and sank her flotilla sister *Oxley*. Only the *Oxley*'s CO and one of the bridge lookouts survived the destruction of the boat. Four nights later there was a near repeat of the disaster with two other boats on the patrol line; fortunately the torpedo missed.

A week later the Coastal Command Ansons were replaced with modern Lockheed Hudsons bought from America, whose range easily extended to Norway, and the submarine patrols were moved south into the Skagerrak, off the Jutland peninsula and in the Heligoland Bight; at the same time their orders were amended to make the primary object 'to attack enemy war vessels'.[47]

The only enemy encountered were aircraft and trawlers or other small anti-submarine vessels listening with hydrophones since the German version of asdic, known by the camouflage name *D.T. Gerät*, was as yet too large to be fitted in any vessel smaller than a light cruiser. More constant enemies were the elements. Cdr. William King has described the endurance required for these patrols in or close to enemy waters in that first autumn and winter of the war.[48] He was then a lieutenant in command of the S-class *Snapper* in the 3rd Flotilla operating out of Harwich after recall from the Mediterranean. On his first patrol it blew a gale incessantly for a fortnight, piling up the shallow, sand-sluicing seas of his billet off the Dutch coast into precipitous ridges of blown water. It was necessary to keep these on the beam since driving into head seas might hold up an emergency dive for vital seconds; the resulting continuous waterlogged rolling sapped all hands mentally as much as physically, and the clamorous din and vibration of the main engines, and the ever-present smell of diesel oil, reduced many to that utter misery known only to the desperately seasick.

Even when submerged during daylight hours it was seldom possible to go deep enough to avoid all wave movement lest they hit the shallow bottom and knock off the asdic dome projecting below the hull. This was vital to their function since in those high, steep seas they were unable to maintain periscope depth; instead of a visual watch they could only listen for the beat of engines through the water. King himself was so anxious about the possibility of scraping the bottom that he was unable to sleep during the day in order to make up for sleepless hours at night on the surface. The extreme difficulties of navigation gave every cause for anxiety. In the first light of dawn he and his navigator would wedge themselves against the sides of the bridge, shielding their sextants from the salt wind, but they were seldom granted even a glimpse of stars through the wild grey overcast above, and had to plot their track for the most part by de'd reckoning.

Eventually the inevitable happened: they made a wrong estimate of the tidal drift and struck ground one dark night with an onshore gale driving them further in; every comber lifted the boat as it passed beneath, then dropped her shockingly on the bottom as it foamed away. King had been alerted by an unguarded light ashore moments before they struck and had ordered the helm hard over to point her seawards. Now, shutting off the diesels, he rang the electric motors full ahead each time he sensed the boat begin to lift on a wave, stopping them as she was dropped with a crash to the ground. He feared she would be pounded to destruction, but gradually as he coaxed her away the bumps became less frequent and when dawn broke, revealing the breakers white against the shallows, she ceased to ground. She was free.

Some days later, still on patrol despite a wrecked asdic dome, they were ordered to intercept reported enemy ships. This meant a passage on the surface heading into the seas. The wind had moderated somewhat by then and the overcast had broken into low, driven clouds through which the sun shone, glistening on white wave caps. Recognizing that conditions were ideal for air attack from behind cloud, King stayed on the bridge to keep the lookouts alert. His apprehensions were justified. 'Aircraft, green thirty, low and close!' the Coxswain cried.

'Dive! Dive! Dive!' King called before spotting the plane himself. The officer of the watch pressed the klaxon; the lookouts leaped for the hatch and threw themselves down the vertical ladders into the control room, those above bruising those beneath them. As CO, King was last to leave the bridge; he glimpsed a sea lifting the bows and holding them up for agonizing seconds when they should have been dipping before he scrambled down the hatch, swinging the lid shut over his head and clipping it. As the conning tower slid beneath the surface the aircraft's bomb burst just above; a moment later the bows punched the seabed below with an equally loud crash. Fortunately neither concussion did more than shock the crew temporarily and cause superficial damage, and they were able to extricate themselves and creep away.

After surfacing, the wireless operator picked up a signal from a Coastal Command aircraft reporting the destruction of a U-boat in the position and at the time of the attack on *Snapper*. This was far from the only instance of British submarines being attacked by friendly air patrols; fortunately the anti-submarine bombs which Coastal Command aircraft then carried were useless.

This was another symptom of the loss of the lessons of the first war fight against U-boats by both Admiralty and Air Ministry between the wars, and of the perfunctory interest either great service had shown in the protection of the country's shipping lifeline, or merchant sailors. In the summer of 1937, after a protracted inter-service struggle, the Admiralty had regained from the Air Ministry full control over its fleet air arm, though not over the land-based squadrons provided for reconnaissance and trade protection around the coasts and approaches to the British Isles. These remained, with Bomber and Fighter Command, as one of the three divisions of the Royal Air Force. The best the navy could manage was an agreement whereby Coastal Command co-operated with the navy on maritime reconnaissance and shipping protection. It was an unsatisfactory compromise. Since air marshals were preoccupied with the fighter defence of the country, and were otherwise as dedicated to 'strategic bombing' as admirals to a decisive fleet action, Coastal Command was from the start deprived of resources; its few obsolescent aircraft, trained primarily for reconnaissance to spot raiders or merchantmen breaking the naval blockade of Germany, lacked striking power, and until after the outbreak of war their crews had no training in the protection of shipping or action against U-boats.[49] Their anti-submarine bombs had been taken into service in 1931 without testing, and were aimed by eye without a bomb sight; consequently pilots often came in too low and, as described earlier, were a greater danger to themselves than the U-boats they attacked; not only were the bombs unpredictable, they were harmless outside 6 to 8 feet of a submarine's pressure hull. In eighty-five attacks made in the first eight months of the war only one U-boat was sunk.[50]

Despite this dismal record and proposals since before the war to modify depth-charges for use from aircraft, neither the Admiralty nor the Air Ministry took action; it was left to the C-in-C, Coastal Command, to push through his own trials, as a result of which modified depth-charges were introduced on a small scale in the summer of 1940; but it was not until the spring of 1941 that an effective model was brought into general use.[51] Until then U-boats sighted on passage by aircraft were alarmed and forced to dive, but were seldom even damaged.

King and his crew were not alone in passing their comfortless patrol without sight of a target. The first British submarine success did not come until two and a half months after the outbreak of war, and that only when the CO of the *Sturgeon*, annoyed by anti-submarine trawlers lying listening along his billet in the Skagerrak, sank one of them, as he explained, to keep them on the move and reduce the effectiveness of their hydrophones. It was to prove an unfortunate precedent, as will appear.

Next, Lt.-Cdr. Edward Bickford lifted the service with an outstanding patrol in the *Salmon*. He was one of the brightest of a band of young officers who before the war had pleaded for more realistic training, for the most part vainly, although Captain Philip Ruck-Keene had provided a shining exception to the general rule when in command of the 1st Submarine Flotilla in the Mediterranean. Patrolling to the west of the Skagerrak on 4 December, Bickford sighted through the periscope what he took to be a box floating on the water, but shortly identified as the distant conning tower of a U-boat steering north – in fact *U36* under KLt. Wilhelm Fröhlich outward bound to her patrol area. He was unable to close the track, but fired a salvo at long range, and was rewarded after four and a half minutes of suspense by the sight of a great flash and debris flying 200 feet into the air. He surfaced and closed to look for survivors, but there were only pieces of timber, lifebelts, slicks of oil fuel and one dead sailor floating in the wrack. Amazingly, however, four members of the crew had survived and were picked up later by fishing boats.

Eight days later, again submerged but deeper this time since Bickford had just sighted an aircraft, the engines of a large vessel were detected on the hydrophones. Going up to periscope depth he was met with the incredible sight of the 40,000-ton German transatlantic liner *Bremen*, which he had travelled on as a passenger before the war, on course to cross his stern at about a mile. Repressing the urge to fire at so seductive a target, he surfaced for gun action and flashed the international signal X for her to stop, intending, if she took no notice, to fire a warning shot across her bows; if that failed to halt her he was entitled under international law to fire on her. He had no sooner given orders for the warning shot after making X five times than a Dornier aircraft escorting the liner was sighted, and he had to dive. By the time he came up to periscope depth the *Bremen* had steamed beyond range.[52] She was returning to Germany from the Soviet port of Murmansk, where her master had been waiting for the longer, darker nights before risking the passage through the North Sea.

Next morning Bickford was equally amazed to see through his periscope what he took to be the main battle strength of the German fleet escorted by light cruisers. The main body – in fact a squadron of destroyers returning from a minelaying mission off the River Tyne – was too far distant, but he fired a salvo at long range at the nearer cruisers, seeing hits on both the *Nürnberg* and the *Leipzig* before diving and lying quietly on the bottom for the anticipated counter-attack. This developed quickly and lasted two hours, the destroyers dropping depth-charges indiscriminately; on two occasions they passed right over the *Salmon* without detecting her. Neither cruiser sank, but the *Nürnberg* was out of action for five months, and the *Leipzig* never returned to operational service.

Bickford returned to Harwich to a rapturous welcome from a country starved of good news, and received promotion to Commander and the DSO. His flotilla captain characterized the patrol as an epic, 'an example to submarine officers for all time'. The sight of the *Bremen* remained very much on Bickford's mind. He confessed to his great friend and flotilla messmate, King, how much he had wanted to attack her: 'I just itched to torpedo her without surfacing – talk about *temptation*.'[53]

In early January 1940 three British submarines were lost in quick succession in the Heligoland Bight, two at least after trying to emulate the *Sturgeon's* feat of sinking a listening anti-submarine trawler; instead they gave themselves away and in the shallow waters paid the price. The celebrated first war submarine CO, now Vice-Admiral Sir Max Horton, had just been appointed Flag Officer Submarines. He and his staff spent days examining possible causes of these losses without arriving at any conclusion; but no more submarines were sent into the Bight.

Horton had a deserved reputation for drive and ruthlessness. He had accepted the post on condition he would be allowed a free hand, and he immediately created a new headquarters in a block of flats called Northways at Swiss Cottage, North London, far enough from the Admiralty to allow independence, close enough for his staff to have day-to-day contact with the naval staff and intelligence divisions. At Northways he brought together the administrative branches of the submarine arm and operational control of submarines in home waters and the Atlantic, under the overall command of the C-in-C Home Fleet; the Mediterranean and Far Eastern flotillas came under their own theatre C-in-C. Horton had an instinctive appreciation of the vital importance of the air in all naval and submarine operations and from the first established an intimate co-operation with Coastal Command Headquarters at Northwood, only 15 miles from Northways. He also established personal bonds with his home flotillas, making frequent visits and inspiring the men with his fighting spirit; as one officer recalled, 'In a few months his personality had pervaded the whole of the submarine flotillas and their morale rose to the top and stayed there all the war . . . Few realised what a great man he really was.'[54] His inspiration extended to Polish and French submarines serving under British control, and when later that year General de Gaulle established the Free French Forces, their submarines carried in their wardroom a portrait of Horton beside that of their leader.

Meanwhile patrols continued through an icy winter, and another detail that had escaped attention in exercises before the war was brought into cruel prominence: the provision of watchkeeping gear suitable for prolonged vigils in bad weather. While U-boat men harvesting unsuspecting merchantmen in the Atlantic weathered storms in grey-green, felt-lined leather long coats and trousers, long-brimmed sou'westers, oilskins, rubber leggings and cork-soled boots, British lookouts fought the numbing cold and wet of the North Sea wrapped in a variety of scarves and balaclava helmets produced by knitting circles in the villages of England, topped with regulation sou'westers and oilskins that were not designed for the lashing rain and spray about a submarine's open bridge. Once wet, the clothes could never be properly dried for the atmosphere below was too heavy with moisture; the hull plates dripped, shoes grew mould, woollens took on a damp, foul smell.

Despite an extreme shortage of permissible targets, the strain of continuous vigilance as patrol succeeded patrol, silently evading anti-submarine forces, diving to avoid aircraft, aware of the ever-present possibility of straying into German minefields, had a cumulative effect, especially on COs, who could never forget their absolute responsibility for the boat and her entire complement. But lack of success was as wearying as danger and cold, clammy discomfort. King came to hate his grey-green slot of sea off the Dutch islands.

All was changed by the German invasion of Norway and Denmark. By coincidence at the same date in early April 1940 the Admiralty planned to mine Norwegian coastal waters to block the inshore route by which Swedish iron ore, vital for German armaments, was shipped from the port of Narvik down to the Skagerrak and Germany. There was another motive. It was hoped that the action would provoke Hitler into attempting an invasion of Norway, so providing a pretext for pre-emptive British landings to secure Narvik and the Swedish orefields themselves; in anticipation of such a German response Horton sent all available submarines to reinforce the patrols off the Skagerrak and southern Norway. Dönitz had already disposed his entire operational force of thirty U-boats, half off Norway to screen the invasion, half in Scottish waters to intercept the British fleet if it emerged to interfere; the scene was set for both sides' submarines to operate in textbook conditions.

The score was opened by a Polish submarine, *Orzel*, under Cdr. J. Grudzinski, which had made an adventurous escape from the Baltic early in the war and was now operating for the Allies from Rosyth. Shortly before noon on 8 April off Kristiansand in the Skagerrak she sighted the 5,200-ton German transport *Rio de Janeiro* lined with troops, and torpedoed and sank her. Soldiers rescued by a Norwegian destroyer and fishermen revealed that they were on their way to Bergen 'to protect it from the British'.[55] Much information indicating that a German invasion of Scandinavia might be under way had already reached Naval Intelligence from a variety of sources, and this report might have confirmed it, but so strong was the presumption that the Germans would only risk invasion after being provoked by the mining operation that the report was discounted, as were others from submarines in the Skagerrak. The opportunity to launch pre-emptive landings was missed.

Meanwhile, the greater part of the German invasion forces bound for Narvik, Trondheim, Bergen and Stavanger had steamed past the British submarines on patrol during the previous two nights, undetected in the darkness; early the following morning, 9 April, the landings began, supported by the Luftwaffe, and achieved complete surprise. At the same time German army units moved up to occupy Denmark.

Later that afternoon the light cruiser *Karlsruhe*, leader of a small force which had landed troops to occupy Kristiansand on the southern corner of Norway, began her return voyage with accompanying destroyers across the Skagerrak. The force was sighted approaching at a favourable angle for attack by the submarine *Truant*; her CO, Lt.-Cdr. C.H. Hutchinson, was lining the cruiser up, waiting for a broad-angle shot, when the ships zigzagged away, leaving *Truant* trailing behind. He determined on a long shot nonetheless and, rapidly adjusting his target data, came round to unleash a full salvo of ten torpedoes at spaced intervals along the *Karlsruhe*'s track. As the torpedoes closed on their converging course their wakes were sighted by lookouts and the cruiser was swung to parallel them, but such was the number in the salvo and the fine judgement with which they had been spread it was impossible to evade them all; one struck astern, wrecking the rudder and screws, and opening the hull and after compartments to an inflow which the damage party was powerless to control.

The destroyers heeled as they came about to follow the torpedoes back along their course while Hutchinson took the *Truant* down. All hands waited silently, anticipating the pounding to come. The sound of high-revolution propellers carried through the water. Hutchinson gave a quiet helm order to try and move the boat further off the line as she crept away at dead slow on depleted batteries; she had been submerged since dawn. The swish-swish-swish-ing sounds increased in volume, reaching a sibilant intensity overhead, and then started to diminish. The hands braced themselves, imagining canisters of high explosive sinking through the water above. The click of the first charge as it reached its depth setting was audible, followed on the instant by the concussion and tremendous roar of the explosion. The boat shivered like a live thing. A second followed; and one after another the rest of the pattern detonated, beating pressure waves against the hull like giant hammers, reverberating thunderously through the compartments where those not on duty tried to rest, holding to some solid fixture, feigning unconcern as the submarine rocked and the bunk or floor plates beneath them jumped. Dust and flakes of paint fluttered in the close, already stale air. Damage reports began to come in to the control room from the engine and motor compartments.

The water was relatively deep and Hutchinson was able to take her down to 300 feet, where they sat out successive attacks, speaking when necessary in whispers, careful not to make the slightest sound which might be detected on hydrophones, finding it increasingly difficult to breathe as leaks had been started in the air system used for blowing tanks, and the pressure inside the boat was rising, augmenting the effects of carbon dioxide build-up. After nearly three hours, when all seemed quiet above, Hutchinson took the boat up to periscope depth, only to see the silhouettes of another anti-submarine group waiting. He eased her down again. Ninety minutes later he came up and found the enemy had gone. He surfaced, opening the conning tower, his feet held from below by the coxswain against a gale sweeping up around him, until at last he could gulp in the deliciously keen night wind. They had been submerged for nineteen hours. Some distance away the *Karlsruhe* had sunk.[56]

Meanwhile, in the War Cabinet in London the decision had been taken to lift the rules against sinking merchant ships without warning in those areas which German supply traffic for the invasion had to pass, off the Danish peninsula, in the Kattegat and Skagerrak, and within ten miles of the south coast of Norway. By chance, as this signal was broadcast to the submarines, a large, unescorted German freighter in the Kattegat was being stalked by Lt.-Cdr. J.E. Slaughter in the *Sunfish*. He was practising a dummy attack when he received a message from the radio operator that a signal had just come in from headquarters about the rules for attacking merchantmen, and was being decoded. The words were called to him at the periscope as they were made out. He ordered the bow tubes brought to the ready, and finally, as the meaning became unambiguous, sent the first torpedo of the salvo on its way – to be rewarded soon afterwards with the thump of an explosion.[57] Slaughter's was not the first merchantman sunk by a British submarine; in March Lt.-Cdr. G.C. Phillips in the *Ursula* had torpedoed a 6,000-ton ore-carrier in the Kattegat under the Prize Regulations after ensuring all the crew were in boats, and on 8 April, shortly after the *Orzel* sank the troop transport *Rio de Janeiro*, Lt.-Cdr. A.G.L. Searle in the *Trident*, near her in the Skagerrak, had sunk an 8,000-ton tanker.

The evening after Slaughter's instant response to the lifting of restrictions Lt.-Cdr. E.F. Pizey in the *Triton* fired a salvo across a supply convoy in the Skagerrak and sank two sizeable freighters and a smaller vessel, after which he was forced down and depth-charged heavily but none too accurately by the escorts; he managed to draw away when they fastened on to the submarine in the next billet, *Spearfish* under Lt.-Cdr. J. H. Forbes, transferring the attack to her. It was probably this that King described hearing from the *Snapper* 12 miles away. 'The noise seemed appalling beyond belief. It was rather like hearing a friend being flogged at school.'[58] Later, he realized the sounds must have been reflected in some way from the seabed, for he seldom heard anything as loud again. Forbes escaped after three hours and surfaced in the dark for a much-needed influx of fresh air. Soon afterwards a white wave was sighted thrown up by a vessel travelling at speed, then the silhouette of a large warship – in fact the pocket battleship *Lützow*, formerly the *Deutschland* – returning from supporting landings in Oslo. Forbes fired his full salvo of six torpedoes by eye at the fast-moving target, scoring one hit right astern which crippled and nearly sank her. She was towed back to Kiel with her after end hanging down and scraping the bottom, but it was a year before she re-entered service.

Despite these early successes, triumphs of the spirit of the submarine arm over every pre-war deficiency in vision, design and training, conditions became progressively more difficult. As the nights shortened in those high latitudes the boats had less and less time on the surface in which to recharge batteries, while by day the clear waters around Norway allowed them to be seen by aircraft patrols as far down as 90 feet below the surface.[59] And since by that date the German radio interception service *B-Dienst* was able to read between a third and a half of all messages picked up in the British naval cipher,[60] boats making reports or receiving positional instructions from Horton were often found and attacked by air or surface anti-submarine forces. Three boats were sunk and one laying mines in the Kattegat was captured after being so damaged she could only move in circles on the surface. Another was sunk after a collision with a Norwegian merchantman.

Nonetheless, during April and the first week in May, after which most boats were redeployed off the Heligoland Bight and Dutch coast to meet an anticipated German assault on the Low Countries, British submarines sank eighteen merchantmen totalling over 60,000 tons, one light cruiser, one U-boat and a gunnery training ship, and severely damaged a pocket battleship, while submarine-laid mines accounted for five small merchantmen and seven mine-sweeping or anti-submarine trawlers.[61]

Among these statistics were three ships sent to the bottom by the *Snapper*, the first a small tanker, the other two from separate convoys.[62] The second convoy appeared out of a dawn mist while King was still recharging his batteries on the surface. Reckoning he would not have time to dive to fire from periscope depth without being seen and forced deep, King decided on a snap salvo from the surface. With no time to calculate a DA and only the crude Admiralty night-sight with which to aim he remembered an old saw whereby the aim-off was given by the width of a hand at arm's length for a slow-moving target, two hands for a fast-moving target. This was a slow convoy. Pointing the boat ahead of the nearest ship, and stationing himself at the fore end of the bridge with his arm held out straight towards the bow, he waited until the target's stem nudged the side of his fist, then called 'Fire!' down the voicepipe, spreading his three remaining torpedoes by launching them at 7-second intervals afterwards. Before the first could reach the target, escorts sighted the submarine and he called 'Dive! Dive! Dive!'

He was about to follow his watch officer down the hatch when he saw a column of water rise up the side of the target ship; it was followed immediately by the thump of the explosion. A few seconds later, as he clipped the conning-tower hatch shut above his head, there was a second thump, shaking the boat, a third when he reached the bottom of the ladder in the control room, and moments later a fourth. There was little time to enjoy the success before depth-charges were exploding in the water, fortunately not too close as he crept away at 120 feet.[63]

When *Snapper* returned to Harwich every ship in harbour was lined with sailors to cheer her home, caps swinging up as their hurrahs sounded across the water. After the high tension of the patrol it was an intensely moving moment.

In contrast to the British boats, the U-boats achieved little in the Norwegian campaign. The conditions might have been designed for them as the British War Cabinet, unbalanced by the surprise the German invasion had achieved, reacted too late and blundered into widely dispersed landings from Narvik in the far north to Namsos and Andalsnes on either flank of Trondheim in the centre, providing numerous thinly protected targets including cruisers and battleships which steamed close in to provide supporting fire. Had the boats which Dönitz had positioned in groups off the principal ports been able to take advantage of the situation the Royal Navy would surely have suffered devastating losses. In the event the torpedo failures which had plagued them from the beginning robbed them of certain successes.

From the first days of the campaign reports of premature explosions and unexplained misses began to come in to U-boat Command. Two aces, Prien in *U47* and Schultze in *U48*, whom Dönitz had placed in what he believed was the most important and endangered area off Narvik, were among those worst affected: between 10 and 16 April these two reported failures against two cruisers, the battleship *Warspite*, two destroyers and, inside the Vaagsfiord to the north of Narvik, a 'solid wall' of anchored troop transports, cruisers and destroyers, the nearest only 750 yards distant; this last from Prien. So little impression did his torpedoes make that the British ships were not aware they had been targets. It was midnight, practically the only period of darkness in this high latitude, and Prien surfaced, determined on a second salvo with no mistakes. He made a thorough check with his 1WO of all fire-control data and torpedo settings, then launched four torpedoes aimed through the night-sight at the motionless ships. They waited, counting the seconds, until past the running time one torpedo exploded against the cliffs and brought the inlet to life. Prien turned his boat to withdraw, but ran aground and was fortunate to work her off close by a patrol and make his escape. Three days later, on his way home in the open sea about the latitude of Namsos just north of Trondheim, he chanced upon the *Warspite* and was able to approach within 900 yards before firing his last two torpedoes; again there was no result until one torpedo exploded at the end of its run, alerting the battleship's escorting destroyers, who subjected him to prolonged counter-attacks.[64]

By this time COs had lost all confidence in their weapons. Many like Prien had placed themselves in the utmost hazard from asdic-fitted British escorts in the almost constant daylight of the far north; five boats had paid the ultimate price. The despair of the survivors may be imagined. Prien himself told Dönitz he could not be expected to fight with a wooden rifle. For Dönitz it was too much; he vented his frustration and anger in his war diary: 'All operational and tactical questions are again and again coloured by the intolerable state of the torpedo arm. The problem of where to operate the boats depends not only on the usual conditions but in every case the question has to be considered, "Will the torpedo work?"'[65]

Two days before, on 17 April, the chief of the Torpedo Directorate and his assistants had visited him to discuss the problems. The meeting was as disconcerting as the others he had endured with these people since the start of the war; he learned that new pistols with four- instead of five-bladed arming propellers had been issued to some boats without adequate trial, and 'due to an oversight' 10 per cent of these could be expected to fail to arm the detonator. Improvements were already in hand. Further, the hydrographer had advised that magnetic influence, resulting in premature detonations, must be expected in the fiords, although not in the open sea unless there were hitherto undiscovered layers of ore below the seabed. Finally, sufficient depth-keeping experiments had not yet been made to arrive at a conclusive judgement, but the chief of the Inspectorate so distrusted the torpedoes' depth-keeping that he strongly advised against relying on impact firing, as Dönitz had again instructed his commanders to do, and suggested a return to magnetic setting.[66]

After the meeting Dönitz had issued his COs with a new set of instructions which were, as he put it in the war diary, 'so complicated that I would never give them to operational boats except in the present circumstances'.

The failures continued. On the 19th Dönitz recorded that of twenty-two shots fired in the previous few days in Zone 0, north of latitude 62°36'N, at least nine had exploded prematurely, detonating others from the same salvo or causing them to miss. 'The Navy', he wrote despairingly, 'has no torpedo which can be used in the area north of 62°30'.' He had already instructed the boats off Narvik to leave the fiords; now he withdrew the boats from the Trondheim area to more southerly, safer billets.[67]

> That the BdU has to burden himself with wearing discussions and investigations into the causes of duds – and struggle to correct them – is an absurdity. (So long, however, as these bodies [the Torpedo Inspectorate and Experimental Department] limp along behind with their measures I am thrown back on my own resources.)[68]

On the 22nd he was asked by the Naval Staff in Berlin if he could return U-boats to Narvik to operate against the transports reinforcing and supplying the beachhead the British had established. He refused. At the end of the month he reported to Raeder in Berlin on the problems his boats had suffered, chiefly the torpedo failures, but also enemy asdic, and emphasized that a counter to asdic was urgent and essential for the future success of U-boat warfare. He asked that the best sonic technicians, chemists and physicists be employed to develop one. His conclusion on the campaign as a whole was unequivocal: 'Torpedo failures cheated the boats of sure successes.'[69] This cannot be doubted. The distinguished submariner Vice-Admiral Sir Arthur Hezlet has concluded from the logs that in twenty attacks on major British warships, four on the *Warspite* alone, and ten against transports, torpedo failures robbed the U-boats of 'almost certain success against the *Warspite*, seven cruisers, seven destroyers and five transports'.[70]

The Norwegian campaign was from the British angle a strategic and political disaster; although Narvik was eventually captured with the aid of French and Polish troops, German possession of the country to the south, together with overwhelming air superiority, forced evacuation as soon as the railway, power and harbour installations for the iron-ore traffic had been destroyed. The material losses Dönitz's boats might have inflicted with adequate torpedoes would have affected the outcome of the battle for Narvik; whether the political and moral effects would have changed the course of the whole war is arguable. Yet combined with the losses the Luftwaffe did inflict on the Royal Navy and the loss of another aircraft-carrier to the guns of the *Scharnhorst* during the campaign, the sinking of a battleship and several cruisers by U-boats would have dented the Royal Navy's aura of ascendancy, and perhaps inspired German commanders to bolder strategies. That is jumping too far ahead of facts. What is certain is that during the campaign U-boats claimed just one supply ship and one submarine, the *Thistle*, sunk off the south-west corner of Norway by the small coastal boat *U4* under OLt. Havro von Klodt-Heydenfeld the day after the German landings. Otherwise, during the whole of April they sank only five merchantmen in the North Sea,[71] by far the smallest monthly total since the outbreak of war.

Raeder had ordered an investigation of the torpedo scandal, and on 15 May Dönitz heard the preliminary findings from Professor Cornelius, who had worked on torpedo development during the inter-war period; 'The facts are worse than could have been expected,' Dönitz recorded afterwards in the war diary:

I have been told that the functioning of the AZ [contact setting] was considered as proved in peacetime after only two not even faultless shots.

Such working methods can only be described as criminal. The numerous
defects of the torpedoes were only suspected little by little by the BdU on
the basis of practical operational experience ... In all cases the torpedo
technicians either denied the possibility of a failure or else attributed it
now to one cause, now to another. In all cases a basic defect was in fact
finally discovered.[72]

The result, he went on, was 'staggering'. After twenty years'
work in peacetime they should have had a better torpedo than was
used in the first war; instead, apart from the splashless discharge
and the elimination of the wake of bubbles, 'there is nothing right
with our torpedoes'. He concluded: 'I do not believe that ever in
the history of war can soldiers have been sent out against the
enemy with such a useless weapon.'

A few, but by no means the chief causes of failure had been
discovered and were being corrected. It was not until January 1942
that the reason for erratic depth-keeping was found – air of a
higher than atmospheric pressure was leaking into the depth-
keeping chamber of the torpedoes from the interior of the boats.
High pressure inside a boat was caused in several ways: the air
used to launch torpedoes was sucked back inside the hull to give
a 'splashless' discharge; leaks in the compressed-air system and, on
occasions after long submergence, the deliberate release of oxygen
to counter carbon dioxide build-up might all contribute.

The anomalies in the magnetic setting took longer to identify,
and it was early 1943 before results with an improved pistol, Pi2,
were considered satisfactory.[73] Meanwhile, in May 1940 Dönitz
determined to abandon magnetic firing and demanded that the
very simple British contact pistol, as discovered in torpedoes from
the submarine captured circling helplessly in the Kattegat, be
copied as quickly as possible. Even when properly armed, the German pistols were failing if they hit at anything less than a 45°
angle. Until a satisfactory contact pistol was ready he determined
not to risk the boats in operations on the high seas.[74]

These torpedo failures, which cost the U-boat arm so much in
terms of lost opportunities, perhaps even providing the margin by
which Great Britain weathered the disasters of the early phases of
the war, were not due simply to peacetime theory giving way to
the exigencies of action; the erratic depth-keeping had been shown
up in 1936 and 1937 during the Spanish Civil War, and confirmed
by trials in 1938 set up expressly to examine that experience. Yet
nothing had been done.[75]

4

Wolfpacks

THE GERMAN OCCUPATION of Norway and Denmark was followed
in May by the invasion of France and the Low Countries. By early
June Hitler's Axis partner, Mussolini, had been persuaded by the
Wehrmacht's irresistible advance to bring Italy into the war against
the western Allies. By midsummer Holland and Belgium had been
overrun and France broken; the terms of the armistice she signed
on 22 June conceded German occupation of the north and west of
the country. Thus in little over three months Hitler had acquired
the entire coastline skirting the British Isles from the North Cape
of Norway through Denmark, the Low Countries and the French
Channel coast to Ushant, and even southwards around Biscay to
the Spanish border, outflanking Britain and providing a spring-
board for the oceanic strategy Raeder craved. Dönitz lost no
time in establishing U-boat bases in Norway and on the Biscay
coast. In the Mediterranean the Italian navy, which included over
100 operational submarines, threatened the three British bases,
Gibraltar, Malta and Alexandria, from which the Royal Navy
commanded the southern flank of Europe and the direct route to
the Indian and Far Eastern empires.

For Britain, bar miracles, the war was lost. Few in the country
were prepared to recognize the fact, least of all the new Prime
Minister, Winston Churchill, propelled into office by the disaster in
Norway. Determined to enlist the United States in the struggle, he
roused the nation and empire to extraordinary heights of defiance.
The immediate threat was the invasion of England. While Hurri-
canes and Spitfires of the Royal Air Force disputed the Luftwaffe's
attempt to gain control of the air over the Channel and south-
eastern England, Coastal Command aircraft flew constant reconnaissance missions to detect the shipping concentrations that would
presage invasion. In clear weather they were vulnerable to German
fighters, in thick weather they could see little; submarines were sent
as additional scouts off the enemy-held coasts from Norway down
to the Channel, their orders to report directly they sighted invasion
forces, then attack. The second part was thought optimistic by COs:
they were bound to be sighted as soon as they surfaced to report;
they would be lucky to finish the signal before being destroyed.

During their vigils submerged off an enemy-held coast, submarine crews were at 'watch diving', two hours on, four off, with just enough hands to keep the boat to her course and set depth and to operate the periscope and hydrophones, the rest sleeping or reading, or possibly before the fug became too noxious playing the game of Ludo known in the Royal Navy as 'Uckers' – but for the most part sleeping, conserving the air.

For the officer of the watch at the periscope two hours was as long as concentration could be maintained:

'Up periscope!'

The hand at the control panel operated a lever starting the periscope motor; the bronze column leading into a deep well below the deck plates of the control room began to slide upwards with a quiet, hissing sound, its wire hoist moving down past it. As the lower end of the column rose above the deck plates, the officer bent to grasp the closed bar handles either side, snapping them open to form a right angle with the shaft, leaning his forehead into the rubber cushion of the eyepiece and rising with it as the upper lens broke through the heaving surface some 30 feet above. When the lens had cleared he began to shuffle round, turning the periscope as he scanned horizon and sky above, the brilliant picture obscured from time to time as waves passed over the lens, leaving it blurred with bubbles and water for moments before it drained. After sweeping a full circle, he snapped the grip in his right hand a half turn towards him for high-power setting; the view narrowed and closed. He trained round again, more slowly this time, searching for the tip of a mast beyond the waving edge of sea or tell-tale smudges of smoke against the sky, but this time turning only through a sector of 90° before snapping the setting back to low power and making another cautionary all-round sweep.

'Down periscope!' He closed the handles up against the shaft as it began its descent.

In *Snapper* and other boats King commanded, orders and responses were given in whispers when in enemy waters lest the sounds should be picked up by enemy hydrophone operators. Probably few COs went to such lengths, but all orders were given in low tones and unnecessary noise avoided. When the watch officer next ordered the periscope up he repeated the previous drill, but searched another 90° sector in high power.

So it went, the routine varied every half hour by the need to take bearings ashore to 'fix' the boat's position on the chart over the tiny chart table in the corner of the control room. And it was necessary to maintain a good trim throughout to allow the planesmen sitting together at the fore and after hydroplane controls to keep the boat to a steady 30 feet, neither submerging the periscope, nor projecting it so high above the surface that it might be seen by watchers ashore or in the air. As Cdr. Edward Young, at that time a young lieutenant, put it in his reminiscences, an efficient periscope watch demanded continual exercise of the imagination; it was necessary to keep thinking all the time, 'at this very moment an enemy vessel may be approaching just beyond the horizon . . .';[1] for after a long period with nothing to view save the same circle of empty waves and sky with perhaps occasional sea birds, it was too easy to relax and cease to believe in the imminence of danger, or a target.

For those boats patrolling off the Norwegian coast in these tense summer months when fate was being decided in the air above southern England it was an especially harrowing time. There were no hours of complete darkness in which to surface in safety to recharge batteries and revitalize the poisonous air below. The sea was clear and enemy aircraft seemed to be constantly overhead. It was not guessed at the time, but as in the Norwegian campaign their presence was frequently the result of the boats' own reports, or signals sent to them from submarine headquarters, intercepted and deciphered by *B-Dienst*. In August the Admiralty changed the naval code and cipher, reducing *B-Dienst*'s success for a time, but the codebreakers gradually worked themselves back in.[2]

After being sighted by an air patrol and probably attacked, often with depth-charges, with which German anti-submarine aircraft were now equipped, a boat could expect surface anti-submarine forces to arrive on the scene to take up the hunt. Later, having lain low, the crew gasping the depleted air into wracked lungs, they would surface into the half glow of the midnight sun, exposed and vulnerable. The stress sculpted itself in half-moon ridges across the fingernails of many officers and petty officers and all COs; each ridge denoted the period spent on patrol.[3] Even in port crews were at instant readiness for the anticipated invasion. The COs, who at sea suffered the loneliness of absolute responsibility, became taut with tiredness and strain. As through July one boat after another failed to return, Bickford's *Salmon* amongst them, and in early August Forbes' *Spearfish*, the deep sense of loss in their small, tight-bound community was mixed with fatalism about their own chances of survival.

The same thing happened in the Mediterranean. By the time Italy declared war on 10 June a dozen submarines had been recalled from the Far East to form two half-flotillas based on Alexandria and Malta. The majority were older fleet boats of the O, P and R classes which had been trained in mobile patrolling for action against the Japanese fleet. They had large surface silhouettes and comparatively slow diving times of 40 seconds or more; they were also noisy and plagued with a fatal tendency to leak fuel oil. Three were lost within a fortnight, two more in July, with only a scouting success to show for their operations. Alastair Mars, first lieutenant of the *Perseus*, which joined the flotilla at Alexandria in early August, described after the war the 'paralysing situation' they met. He ascribed the initial losses as much to inexperience and lack of caution among the young COs, and to complacency and lack of imagination in their training, as to material factors; moreover, the hard lessons learned in home waters since the start of the war had not been disseminated.[4]

With hindsight it is also apparent that these large and ageing boats were misused by the Mediterranean staff. They were sent to patrol in the vicinity of Italian naval bases with warships as priority targets. This was a natural response to the threat posed by the Italian fleet, especially in the light of pre-war doctrine and the impossible restrictions of the Prize Regulations which still applied to British submarines sinking merchant ships outside the North Sea; so the softer supply traffic to Italian troops in North Africa was not molested; moreover, the boats patrolled confined waters as clear on calm days as those of Norway, under skies held by the Italian Air Force.

Because the submarine arm was so small each loss was, as Mars wrote, a personal matter for all submariners. 'Both officers and men not only knew their contemporaries in the sunken submarines, but had at least an acquaintance with many others, both senior and junior.' Each loss was a sadness which he likened to the grief felt for a brother.[5]

The Italian submarine force, so impressive on paper, with 116 operational boats in nine bases, suffered even more heavily after one notable success, the sinking of a light cruiser on the second day after Italy's entry. Due in large measure to signals intelligence alerting the Royal Navy to their patrol areas, six of the fifty boats deployed in the Mediterranean and four of eight in the Red Sea or Persian Gulf had been destroyed or captured by the end of June. The 1939 agreement with Raeder whereby the larger boats would operate in support of the German oceanic campaign had been confirmed a week before Mussolini's entry into the war, and the first three ran the gauntlet of the Straits of Gibraltar in June but sank nothing outside.

By contrast with the unhappy situation of British and Italian submarines, the smaller number of operational U-boats began to experience what came to be known as the first 'glückliche' (fortunate) time. After the revelations of torpedo inadequacy in May, Dönitz had sent out his first staff officer, KLt. Victor Oehrn, on a proving cruise in *U37*. Oehrn fired four duds, then enjoyed a remarkable string of perfect detonations with the contact settings he was using, and returned to Wilhelmshaven on 9 June to bands and flowers, his bridge decorated with ten victory pennants totalling 43,000 ton – an estimate which, remarkably, was increased by post-war research to over 50,000 tons hit, although one 9,500-ton victim, the *Dunster Grange*, made port.[6] With such a boost to morale Dönitz sent out almost half his twenty-nine operational boats – fewer than at the outbreak war since the building programme had not made good the twenty-four losses suffered to date. Hardly had these arrived in their patrol areas off the Spanish peninsula and the western approaches to the English Channel than *B-Dienst* supplied U-boat Command with information on two convoys. One consisted of three large passenger liners, including the *Queen Mary*, carrying 26,000 Australian and New Zealand troops, and escorted by the battlecruiser *Hood*, an aircraft-carrier and cruisers, making northwards from Sierra Leone after rounding the Cape from Australia. The other was a very slow transatlantic convoy from Halifax, Nova Scotia, steering east for its rendezvous with escorts at 17°W. Dönitz formed a group of six boats to meet the slow convoy with Günther Prien in *U47* 'in tactical command if necessary', ordering them to positions through which the convoy was due to pass at midday on 16 June, the day before the rendezvous. On the assumption of good weather, Dönitz disposed five of these boats to cover an area 90 to 100 miles either side of the convoy's track, and the sixth boat on the track to the east of them.

So it is to be expected with certainty that two boats will make contact on 16 June even if the convoy passes the posts of the outer boats. If no contact is made on 16 June the boats have orders to surround the rendezvous in attacking positions at 06.30, 17 June.[7]

B-Dienst had not supplied him with details of the course or position of the fast liner convoy from Australia, but he judged that the activity of his U-boats off Finisterre would probably force it further from the coast than the usual track at about 12°W; he therefore disposed the five boats he had off Spain in widely separated positions to the west of the twelfth meridian with KK Hans Rösing in *U48* in tactical command should they make contact. All boats in both groups were ordered to keep radio silence and attack only valuable targets before this.

In the event both convoys were missed; Dönitz had never known the route of the liners, and the rendezvous position of the Halifax convoy was shifted south after reports of U-boats in the western approaches. Nonetheless, during that month the boats found and sank over forty independently routed ships and eight sailing in weakly protected convoys, achieving with Oehrn's victims fifty-eight ships totalling 284,113 tons, by far the highest monthly total of the war to date; Prien himself claimed a record of ten ships amounting to 66,587 tons. Losses caused by surface raiders, the Luftwaffe and mines raised the total June sinkings to 140 ships of 585,496 tons, a staggering figure reminiscent of the first war U-boat campaign which rang alarm bells through the Admiralty and War Cabinet.

While Prien returned northabout around Scotland to Kiel, Lemp, who had been sent to reinforce his group the day before the Halifax convoy was expected, was ordered to Lorient on the Biscay coast to rearm and provision; he took U30 in on 7 July, the first boat to use the port. He was soon followed by others, and on 2 August Lorient became a fully operational base as the facilities of the former French naval dockyard were brought into service for overhauls and refits. This placed the Atlantic boats close on the flank of the shipping converging on the English Channel and, by eliminating the long outward and return journeys around the north of Scotland, gave them almost an extra fortnight in the operational area. The British responded by routing ships and convoys in to home waters by the North Channel between Northern Ireland and Scotland, forcing the boats to follow them into those latitudes; despite this they still gained many extra days on patrol.

The unrestricted campaign Dönitz had been waging since before the turn of the year was formalized on 15 August 1940 when Hitler decreed the 'blockade of Great Britain', a form of words considered less provocative to neutrals than 'unrestricted warfare', although to be valid in international law it had to be effective, and Dönitz had far too few boats for that. At the same time neutrals were warned that any ship entering the war zone ran the risk of destruction. This was scarcely news: the neutrals had lost over 100,000 tons of shipping during the last two months alone.[8] It may be an indication of the importance Dönitz attached to the decree that the operational boats were not informed until the 17th.[9]

In the meantime a new ace, KK Otto Kretschmer, had made his name, and been adopted by the German propaganda media, not that he played that part as they might have wished; he was known to his fellows as 'Silent Otto'. He was 'an unusually quiet, well-formed character, yet with inner strength', to quote from his service report, 'very likeable, unassuming, well-mannered in behaviour and demeanour'.[10] Twenty-eight years old, the son of a primary schoolmaster, he had passed his final school exams, the Abitur, at the early age of 17 and had spent the next year in England studying literature and English at Exeter University, afterwards travelling in France and Italy until, old enough to compete for naval officer entry, he had gained a place in the class of 1930. Six years later he had been posted to the infant U-boat arm and, after service off Spain in one of the first Type VII boats during the Spanish Civil War, was given his own boat, the small Type IIB *U23*. He was still in command of her at the outbreak of war, and during the next six months made eight patrols to the east coast of Britain and the Scottish Isles, sinking six mainly small merchantmen totalling almost 21,000 tons and a destroyer escorting a Norwegian convoy. He would have sunk more had he not suffered the usual torpedo failures, chiefly premature detonations; his own estimate of the failure rate was 50 per cent, little above that suggested by post-war research.[11]

Unlike the rather cocky Prien, Kretschmer was popular with fellow officers and his crew who, according to his fleet commander's report, were able 'to see beyond his reserve and recognise his true value'.[12] His seniors were impressed with his 'exceptional ability' as an operational commander, and his confident, thoughtful, intensely thorough approach to his profession had already marked him out for the highest posts in the service.

In April 1940 he had been stepped up to command an ocean-going boat, the Type VIIB *U99*. After regulation working-up exercises in the Baltic, repeating emergency dives until the boat could disappear beneath the waves in under 30 seconds, practising submerged attacks, or target practice on the surface, running engine trials, until each man responded automatically to every anticipated situation and knew without thinking every switch, lever or valve wheel he had to operate, as in older days sailors knew every rope in the dark, in June he took her from Kiel on her first war patrol. He was soon back, damaged by friendly air attack; when he sailed again it was technically *U99*'s second war patrol. He made the normal northabout passage into the Atlantic where he sank seven merchantmen totalling almost 23,000 tons, afterwards putting in to Lorient.

Sailing again in the last week in July, he headed for the southwestern approaches to Ireland; there he sank the 13,200-ton liner *Auckland Star*, and continuing north two days later accounted for two cargo liners of 7,300 and 5,500 tons, and the next day, 31 July, a 6,300-ton liner in an outward-bound convoy. Forced down by the escorts, he shadowed as he had been trained, over the edge of the horizon by day, closing at dusk, for three days until the escorts turned back for home, then attacked and torpedoed three tankers in succession. He assumed they went down, but the compartmentalization of tanker hulls made them difficult vessels to sink, especially when in ballast, and these three all succeeded in limping home. Two days later he sank a 7,200-ton freighter from a homeward-bound convoy, bringing his total for the cruise by his own estimate, which included the three tankers, to 65,137 tons and his overall total since the start of the war to over the magic 100,000-ton mark. He was notified that he had been awarded the Knight's Cross, and on his return to Lorient the presentation was made personally by Grand Admiral Raeder.

Kretschmer was the fifth U-boat ace to achieve this distinction after Prien, Schultze, Schuhart and KLt. Wilhelm Rollmann, CO of *U34*. Before the end of the month Lemp and KLt. Heinrich Liebe had joined the select group; more were to follow in September and October as Dönitz at last achieved his ambition of directing several boats simultaneously on to convoys.

The great difficulty had always been to find convoys in time to form a group in position to attack. Since he had so few boats he pleaded with Göring for long-range reconnaissance aircraft to operate from western France in conjunction with U-boat Command. There were no such aircraft, and as staff officers had pointed out before the war,[13] neither aircraft nor the navigation and communication skills involved in tactical co-operation between air and submarine forces could be hastily extemporized. Besides, Göring was immersed in the attempt to subjugate the Royal Air Force prior to the invasion of England. Dönitz had to negotiate with the local Luftwaffe commander at Brest for the services of a handful of Dornier 17s and 18s; but their low range and small fighting capacity in relation to British air patrols precluded operation where they were most needed off the North Channel.[14] In the event their lack of training in shipping reconnaissance rendered them useless. Meanwhile British Coastal Command aircraft, while unable to destroy the boats Dönitz disposed across the shipping lanes converging on the North Channel, harried them and forced them under sufficiently often to hamper their movements. Dönitz spread them further in to the Atlantic in an east–west disposition. This allowed greater freedom of movement and, although it reduced the chances of sightings, gave them the opportunity, should they pick up homeward convoys, of following them for a longer time before air patrols forced them under.

However, it was *B-Dienst* which provided the information for the first successful group action. On 28 August they deciphered the rendezvous position at which the homeward slow convoy SC2 from Sydney, Nova Scotia, had been directed to meet its escorts; this was 200 miles into the Atlantic on the latitude of the Hebrides. Dönitz ordered four boats there, one to take position at the rendezvous point itself, the others disposed 'in quarterline astern of it [south-easterly]' to cover 'a certain depth ... and a total breadth of 40 miles'.[15] Again, all boats were ordered to keep radio silence before contact was made, but in contrast to earlier attempts at group attack no senior officer was instructed to assume tactical control. It had been decided that since a command boat needed to keep out of the action lest she be driven deep and prevented either from receiving signals or sending instructions, control could best be exercised from ashore by U-boat Command itself; once in contact each CO was to attack as best he could without attempting to co-ordinate his movements with any other boats.

The SC2 convoy was picked up by KLt. Hans-Gerrit von Stockhausen in *U65* somewhat to the east of the rendezvous after the escorts had joined. These sighted and forced him deep while the merchantmen passed, but such was the shortage of escort vessels, due now to the need to concentrate light forces in the east and south against the threatened invasion, that they were soon obliged to rejoin the convoy. Von Stockhausen surfaced, hastened after them in a rising gale, regained touch and reported in exemplary fashion. The signals enabled another of the group, Prien in *U47*, to home in on the convoy that night, and he attacked on the surface in wild conditions just before dawn on the 7th, sinking three ships before Coastal Command flying boats arrived with the light and forced both him and von Stockhausen down. The boats surfaced afterwards, made their best speed in the direction the convoy had taken, regained touch, reported position, course and speed, ran round ahead unseen at the limit of visibility and shadowed as they had been trained. Their signals brought in two new boats, not members of the original group, KLt. Günter Kuhnke in *U28* and Kretschmer in *U99*. Attacking that night in appalling conditions Kretschmer failed, but Prien and Kuhnke each sank one ship.

It was not the annihilation Dönitz craved – only five ships out of fifty-three in the convoy had been sunk – but he was encouraged that the principles of shadowing and reporting, and directing other boats to the scene had been proved; a greater success had only been prevented by the wild weather.[16] He directed Prien, who had only one torpedo left, to take up position to the west of 23°W as weather-reporting boat, sending reports twice a day as required by Berlin, chiefly for the Luftwaffe planners. It was a task heartily disliked by U-boat COs and crews, and naturally it irked Dönitz, but Göring insisted and Hitler backed him.

The following week the next slow convoy from Nova Scotia, SC3, was sighted by KLt. Heinrich Bleichrodt who had succeeded Rösing in command of *U48*; he made a devastating lone attack on the surface, sinking four merchantmen, one after gun action at close range, and an escorting sloop. Next, on 20 September, Prien, still on station as weather-reporter, sighted a fast convoy from Canada, HX72, reported and shadowed. Dönitz directed the six boats he had in the area towards the track.

That same evening 700 miles eastward, close to the North Channel, OLt. Wolfgang Lüth, who had brought the small Type II *U138* from Kiel northabout around the Hebrides, sighted through his periscope an outward-bound convoy, OB216, steaming towards him on a westerly course. There was no escort ahead and with cautious use of his periscope he was able to manouevre inside the columns without being seen. Picking two ships, he fired one torpedo at each from inside 500 yards range. The first ship, *Boka*, shortly blew up; the second, *New Sevilla*, struck on the port quarter, heeled wildly, then righting herself began to settle by the stern. At the sound of the first explosion the sloop *Scarborough*, stationed on the starboard flank of the convoy, turned away 90° to starboard firing starshell illuminant. The new whale-catcher type corvette *Arabis* on the port flank also turned away from the convoy as current practice demanded to search for the U-boat outside the columns, and the ancient first war destroyer *Vanquisher*, stationed astern, hauled out to port after the *Arabis*. The convoy itself began a ponderous emergency turn to starboard, apart from one ship at the rear which turned to port. Lüth meanwhile was lining up another target for his third and last bow tube, while forward his torpedo hands began reloading; their movements upset the trim of the little craft to such an extent that the engineer controlling the depth had to organize all spare hands as movable ballast, sending them scurrying back and forth through the confined spaces to keep the boat on an even keel at periscope depth. Six minutes after the first torpedo had left its tube, Lüth fired the third, hitting his target, the *Empire Adventure*, at mid-length. The *Arabis* away to port began dropping depth-charges indiscriminately. Lüth let the ships sail away in confusion, the three escorts quartering the empty sea a long way off, while his men heaved and guided the reloads into the empty tubes. Half an hour later he surfaced and set off in the dark at full speed after the convoy; catching up in the early hours of the 21st, he sank a fourth ship, the *City of Simla*, before disengaging and, with all torpedoes spent, set course for Lorient.[17]

The same morning of 21 September, Bleichrodt in *U48* came up with Prien's convoy, HX72, and sank two ships before taking over as shadower. During the day Kretschmer and a rising ace KLt. Joachim Schepke in *U100* and von Stockhausen in *U65* also came up with the convoy, and after dark Schepke and Kretschmer made devastating attacks on the surface, hitting another nine ships, seven of which sank. The next morning escorts reached the convoy, forcing the boats away.

Kretschmer had been much struck the previous day by the sight of a tiny raft alone in the ocean with a single man in underclothes clutching an oar sticking up as a mast, flying a white shirt in the wind. He now steered back along the track to try and find him. He was successful and took the man aboard *U99*, restoring him with dry clothes, blankets and a hot drink followed by a glass of brandy; later he transferred him into the lifeboat of another of the victims together with food and fresh water, and gave the officer in charge of the boat the course to steer for the Irish coast. This was not an isolated gesture. On earlier cruises, after sinking unescorted ships sailing independently, he had handed down bottles of brandy or rum and blankets into the boats and shouted a course to steer.

For Dönitz the action against HX72 seemed further confirmation that his methods had been right. 'This inward-bound convoy was attacked altogether by five boats which were originally up to 380 miles away from the point of first sighting', he wrote in his war diary. He attributed their success to early interception while the escort was weak, correct procedure by the shadowing boats, and fair weather, concluding: 'Actions in the last few days have shown that the principles established in peacetime for the use of radio in the presence of the enemy and the training of the U-boats in attack on convoys were correct.'[18]

More dramatic confirmation came the following month. Having rearmed and provisioned in Lorient, or in a few cases Brest or St Nazaire, now also serving as bases, a wave of boats was sent out to form a line west of Rockall beyond the point where convoys met their homeward escorts and spread roughly 60 miles apart, as

Dönitz put it 'about twice the range of maximum visibility' to cover a wide area. At first, storms and fog prevented them concentrating on the only convoy sighted, then the weather changed, and on the night of 16 October with the moon shining from a clear sky lookouts on the bridge of *U48* sighted shadows at the edge of the gently heaving ocean. They were ships of the slow convoy SC7 steering easterly from Sydney, Nova Scotia, escorted by the same sloop, *Scarborough*, whose captain had never suspected Wolfgang Lüth's presence inside the columns of his former charges, together with one other sloop and a corvette; as with convoy OB216 they were stationed on either flank and astern. They had not worked together before and at night their sole means of communication with each other was by none too reliable radio.

Bleichrodt in *U48* kept the nearest column of merchantmen under observation, plotting course and speed, then reported to U-boat Command and shortly before midnight closed and torpedoed a 9,500-ton tanker and two smaller freighters, one of which remained afloat. The convoy made an emergency turn to starboard while the escorts wheeled outwards firing starshell, then searched vainly. With daylight on the 17th a Coastal Command flying boat arrived and spotted *U48* shadowing, forcing her down. The sloops steamed up to search the area where she had dived, continuing for so long that Bleichrodt lost the convoy, as did the *Scarborough*, which maintained the hunt throughout that day. Meanwhile, Liebe in *U38* made contact with the convoy and took over as shadower, allowing Dönitz to direct five boats to form a line ahead. Liebe made two attacks that night, but his single victim was kept afloat by a cargo of timber and he was driven off by the escorts. He regained touch later and continued shadowing and reporting.

By noon next day the boats Dönitz had directed across the track were patrolling a line less than 50 miles to the east of the convoy, but it soon appeared from Liebe's reports that the ships would pass 30 miles north of the northernmost boat. Accordingly, at 15.30 Dönitz cancelled the line, instructing the boats to operate on *U38*'s reports. They steered north-easterly and shortly before 18.00 KLt. Fritz Frauenheim in *U101* sighted an escort and, astern of her, the smoke of many ships. He reported by radio and signalled by light to Kretschmer 2 miles south of him. Soon afterwards Kretschmer himself saw the warship and the smoke over the horizon on his bow; as masts and funnels appeared he turned easterly to gain bearing ahead. The weather was clear, the sea ruffled by a gentle breeze, and after twilight faded into night a full moon shone between light clouds. Somewhere unseen the 'other COs were racing into position, Frauenheim in *U101*, Schepke in *U100*, KLt. Karl-Heinz Moehle in *U123*, and in *U46* Prien's former 1WO KLt. Engelbert Endrass, now an ace in his own right.

By 20.15 the trap was sprung. The escorts had been reinforced but the grey shapes of the submarines, trimmed low, were not seen as the first fan of torpedoes was launched from outside the starboard column. A detonation within the convoy provoked the escorts into independent life, wheeling and firing starshell, which made little impression against the light sky. The U-boat COs probed the gaps they left, each 1WO lining up a sharp image of a merchantman across the illuminated hairline of his night-sight, pulling the lever to launch the eel. Detonation followed detonation; fountains of water illumined by flame rose above the dark sides of ships which slowed, falling behind others as they settled lower in the water, their crews scrambling to launch lifeboats; some, loaded with steel ingots, went down within minutes, taking the men with them.

Kretschmer missed with his first shot from outside the starboard column and, swinging to bring his stern tube to bear, fired at a freighter from 700 yards. He saw the water column and bright flash of the explosion just forward of mid-length, and within 20 seconds the vessel had disappeared. The ships seemed to have lost cohesion now; each appeared to be zigzagging independently. After another miss with a bow tube, he decided to cut out the gyro-angle transmitter to the torpedoes from the fire-control computer and aim with the boat. As he came in again he realized he had been sighted; a ship had fired a rocket and was turning towards him at speed to ram. He altered away and outran her. Later he steered back and attacked near the tail of the columns missing his target but hitting a larger vessel nearly 2,000 yards off. He saw the flash of the explosion abreast the foremast and soon her bows had sunk beneath the surface. After reloading he came in again and hit a freighter he estimated as 6,000 tons; a second explosion followed immediately, sending up a high column of flame from bow to bridge topped by smoke rising 600 feet against the silver-blue luminescence of the sky. She was the Cardiff tramp *Fiscus* of 4,800 tons; the detonation tore her in two, each half rolling over separately, glowing with green flames, and sinking within minutes, taking all but one of her thirty-nine crew down.

While manoeuvring for his next target Kretschmer saw three escorts approaching in line abreast; he swung away, ringing up emergency full speed on the diesels, and soon outdistanced them. Returning afterwards, he attacked from astern again, describing

it afterwards in his log: 'Torpedoes from the other boats are constantly heard exploding. The destroyers [in reality sloops and
corvettes] do not know how to help and occupy themselves by
continually firing star shells, which are of little effect in the bright
moonlight . . .'[19]

During the next two and a half hours he expended his seven
remaining torpedoes from ranges of between 700 and 1,000 yards,
seeing four hits and hearing another far off after a running time of
seven minutes. The last was fired just before 04.00 on 19 October;
he waited near the victim as she dropped astern lest she failed to
sink and he had to finish her off with gunfire. Instead, unbeknown
to him, Moehle approached from her other side and fired into her;
as shells began landing near U99, thinking it must be one of the
escorts, Kretschmer turned away and set course for the return
voyage. It was 05.00. The convoy had suffered a massacre. Broken,
burning ships, lifeboats, rafts, bodies in lifejackets, floating debris
and slicks of oil bobbed and rolled in long swathes to westward.
Reporting to U-boat Command, Kretschmer claimed seven ships,
Frauenheim eight, Moehle five, Endrass four and Schepke three
which, with the three claimed earlier by Bleichrodt, brought the
total to thirty vessels of 196,000 tons.[20] It was an overestimate;
several of the torn vessels remained afloat, but of the thirty-
five which had sailed from Sydney, only fifteen reached their
destination.

While Kretschmer, Frauenheim and Moehle, torpedoes spent,
steered for Biscay, Prien, who was trying to reach the scene of the
action, ran into another homeward convoy 250 miles off Bloody
Foreland at the north-western tip of Ireland, HX79 from Halifax.
Dönitz directed the remaining boats to it. They came up the same
evening, 19 October. Conditions were little changed; a bright
moon shone on light clouds and a calm sea; the ranks of ships were
silhouetted against a luminous sky, and despite a stronger escort
of a destroyer, two sloops, two corvettes, four armed trawlers
and the Dutch submarine O14, the previous night's scenes were
re-enacted. From just after 21.15 until 03.00 next morning, 20
October, the night was rent by explosions, the shimmering sea
brightened by the flash of torpedo detonations, starshell from
the escorts, the white-hot explosion of tanker cargoes, shooting,
searing flames from oil. Prien claimed eight ships of 50,000 tons,
Endrass three of 26,000 tons, Schepke three of 19,600 tons, Liebe
two and Bleichrodt one, in total seventeen ships of 113,000 tons.[21]
Again this was an overestimate; several damaged ships reached
port, and the true figures were twelve ships of 75,069 tons.[22] It

was a stunning achievement nonetheless, and not a single U-boat had been lost or damaged in either action; indeed none had been lost since August. Dönitz was naturally jubilant: 'Therefore by joint attack in the last three days 7 U-boats with [altogether] 300 men in the crews have sunk 47 ships totalling about 310,000 tons. A colossal success.'[23]

Again he drew the conclusion that the development of his tactics and training since 1935, 'to oppose the concentration in convoys with a concentration of U-boat attack', had been correct. Such actions were only possible with COs and crews who had been thoroughly trained in these tactics, he went on; and while recognizing that future successes on this scale might be denied by fog, bad weather or other circumstances, he nevertheless judged that the determining factor would always be the ability of the CO. In this and his other conclusions Dönitz gave no sign of realizing that the humiliated, now thoroughly alarmed enemy might develop answers to the problem of screening merchantmen against wolf-packs; understandably, in view of the extreme paucity of boats, his chief concern was for more:

The possibility of such operations will arise more frequently the more boats are in the operations area and the greater the probability of fastening on the convoys with more eyes, i.e. more boats.

Further, more boats mean that after such attacks England's traffic lanes will not immediately become free because, as today, almost all boats must return after using up all their torpedoes.[24]

By this time a base had been established at Bordeaux for the promised Italian Atlantic Flotilla. The first three boats had arrived in early September 1940, since when a further ten had joined them. Making the passage of the Straits of Gibraltar through RN patrols and against currents had been a considerable feat, for which they were not credited by Dönitz – nor by most subsequent historians. A further eight were on their way, and these, too, were to make the transit of the Straits safely.

The flotilla commander, Rear-Admiral Angelo Perona, was responsible for administration and discipline, but the boats came under the operational control of U-boat Command. Realizing that they were 'sadly wanting in war experience', Dönitz had sent the first batches to develop their skills off the Azores where the weather was generally better and anti-submarine activity minimal.[25] Results had been meagre, a total of nine ships sunk up to 15 October, all by different submarines.[26] Nevertheless, such was his need to increase the number of 'eyes' to sight convoys, towards the end of October

he ordered them up to the western approaches to the North Channel; at the same time he demanded the fastest possible turn-around time for his own boats returning from patrol. By 1 November six Italian boats and four German, including *U99*, were on station in the patrol area.[27]

Meanwhile, he lost the first of the new breed of aces, OLt. Hans Jenisch in *U32*. Jenisch had been awarded the Knight's Cross on 10 October; on the 26th he had torpedoed and sunk the 42,300-ton liner *Empress of Britain* under tow after being bombed and set on fire 70 miles off Bloody Foreland. Four days later *U32* was caught by two destroyers and subjected to sustained depth-charging.

The experience has often been described from the German side: the sound of propellers somewhere above increasing in volume, the metallic chirp of the asdic beam audible not only through the hydrophones but throughout the boat as it bounces off the hull, its regular interval shortening as the hunter nears; the crew remaining still and silent, feet clad only in socks, bracing themselves against a solid fixture as the weep-weeping propeller noise reaches maximum intensity overhead; and the silent wait, anticipation building until, as Lothar Günther Buchheim has observed, the hull of the boat becomes like the skin of the men inside, the smallest noise like a touch on a nerve.[28] 'The man who says he wasn't scared, he's a liar', commented a former crew member of *U123* after the war. 'The difference was that in a U-boat you couldn't show your fear.'[29] The slick of the first *Wasserbomb*, or *Wabo*, reaching its depth-setting, followed by the hammer blow of the explosion rocking the boat, is succeeded by others one after another, thundering through the close compartments. 'When the charges start to explode,' Lüth wrote, 'everyone looks to the officers.'[30] The CO's expression especially is studied by all nearby in the control room, his confidence or nonchalant pretence communicating itself to the crew as the boat shudders, electrics short, lights flicker out, instrument glasses smash, gauges fail and hand-held flashlights probe the darkness, lighting flakes of paint and cork and dust shaking in the eerie glow; and the first quiet damage reports come in to the control room.

U32 suffered a close fourteen-charge pattern which left her without lighting or any electrics, her valves jammed, the compressed air lead junction fractured and air leaking into the boat, raising the pressure. Leaks in the stern glands and after compartment unsettled the trim. She descended, taking a steep angle by the stern; Jenisch ordered the hands forward to balance her and had all tanks blown. She rose to the surface, still with her stern well down, in sight of the destroyers, and he considered diving

again, but the compressed air they would need to bring her up afterwards was exhausted, so he ordered 'Abandon ship!' Those valves which could be turned were opened to scuttle her as the crew scrambled up the conning-tower ladder and down the side.

British interrogators were not unduly impressed with their first ace. While 'determined, possibly obstinate ... unquestionably brave and cool-headed', he was rated 'personally an uninteresting and not very intelligent human being'. All *U32*'s officers with the exception of the engineer were found to be 'remarkably sensitive to anything which might be construed as a slight on their dignity as officers' and, while reasonably polite to British officers, 'behaved somewhat arrogantly to NCOs and men when they thought they could do so with impunity', an attitude which had not been so evident among officers captured earlier in the war. They were also utterly convinced of the inevitability of German victory, and the run of German successes appeared 'to have established Hitler in their minds not merely as a god, but as the only God'.[31]

Such, at the height of success, was the spirit and sense of worth pervading the very young officers of this élite arm that Dönitz had forged.

At the British Admiralty even those directly involved with countering the U-boat campaign had been caught by surprise by the devastating new tactic of group attack; in September shipping losses had risen to almost 300,000 tons sunk by U-boats alone, in October to over 350,000 tons. The forgotten lessons of the first war about the use of aircraft and the likelihood of night surface attack had been relearned long since, together with the new lesson that U-boats on the surface could not be detected by asdic and could outrun all escorts save destroyers. It was now apparent that Dönitz had taken advantage of advances in radio communications to perfect a system of mass attack. The tactic had been analysed by the Anti-Submarine Warfare Division. It is interesting that, like the Germans later, they failed to realize that the enemy was reading signals, and attributed the U-boats' initial contacts only to reports from long-range aircraft or other U-boats, or sighting smoke.

The U-boat gains contact with the convoy during the day ... and then proceeds to shadow at visual distance on the bow or beam. When darkness has fallen the U-boat, trimmed down on the surface, closes the convoy broad on its bow. She keeps a very careful watch for the escorts and endeavours to pass astern of those stationed on the bow of the convoy. The attack is pressed home as close as the U-boat captain dares and it is possible that in some cases a firing range of about 600 yards has been achieved. Having reached a firing position on the beam of the convoy most U-boats increase to full speed, fire a salvo of four torpedoes, turn away, still at full speed, firing stern tubes if fitted, and retire as rapidly as possible in the direction considered safest . . . No U-boat has yet been known to make attacks at intervals of less than an hour . . .[32]

This was certainly the tactic in which U-boat COs had been trained and which many, perhaps the majority, still used, but Lüth, Kretschmer and probably others of the high-scoring aces, aided by the gyro-angling facilities of the *Vorhaltrechner*, were now firing single torpedoes at each target from close range.

The Anti-Submarine Warfare Division recommended increasing the separation of the columns within convoys from 3 to 5 cables (600 yards to half a mile) to reduce the theoretical chances of a salvo hitting more than one ship; and increasing the number of escorts, stationing them in line ahead at 3,000-yard intervals on either wing with instructions in the event of attack to 'turn 90 degrees outwards and proceed at full speed for a distance of ten miles from the convoy firing star shells to illuminate the area' in an attempt to sight and force down the U-boats, when they could be detected by asdic.[33] Other recommendations were of more importance: they concerned a type of radar, known as ASV developed for shipboard use, and the need to train escorts as a group:

To achieve initial detection before the enemy can develop his attack [at night] we are pressing on with the fitting of ASV to our escort vessels as rapidly as it can be done. The first ships so fitted are already at sea, but experiencing teething troubles with this new device. No effort is being spared to clear up these difficulties and it is hoped that ASV will soon become effective and its use by our escort vessels universal.

It will be realised however that successful action against U-boats by night calls for a quick appreciation by the senior officer and for greatly developed teamwork by the ships under his command . . . this it is hoped is being achieved by forming ships into groups, each under its own leader, each working as a team and sharing a common training . . .

Air escort to our convoys can be of immense value. The main burden of work which should fall on the air is keeping down submarines who may be shadowing outside visibility distance in daylight, and in locating U-boats that may appear in darkness. This vast undertaking calls for use of ASV in aircraft, and this is being developed at the highest priority . . .[34]

Besides ASV, which at this date was a primitive 1½-metre wavelength device unable to detect a U-boat beyond 2 or 3 miles in favourable conditions, both surface escorts and aircraft were being fitted as rapidly as possible with radio telephone sets which would allow constant inter-communication.[35]

These measures emanating from the Division, represented at weekly Trade Protection meetings at the Admiralty, were approved at the highest level by the Defence Committee chaired by Churchill himself. But although the Admiralty had the answers, the means were not yet to hand. More escorts were made available, now the danger of invasion had receded with the summer weather, by the release of flotillas from the south and east coasts, but the improvement and manufacture of ASV sets in the quantities required and against the higher priority accorded airborne interception sets for night fighters, took many months. As Correlli Barnett has observed, there was 'a disharmony between [Britain's] scientific genius and industrial backwardness'.[36] The same applied to the aircraft desperately needed by Coastal Command. Air Force chiefs monopolized production for their own ends, as impervious to naval arguments as Göring was to those of Raeder and Dönitz; the dogmas of Bomber Command especially seized Churchill's imagination beyond even the threat to the island's shipping lifelines. Coastal Command continued to be furnished with aircraft discarded from the more important task of taking the war to German cities. To this unscientific offensive countless ships and sailors were to be needlessly sacrificed. For the air was the key to the U-boat problem. Once forced below the surface by aircraft ranging wide over convoys a boat was immobilized, unable to attack or shadow or proceed towards a convoy reported by others; it was not necessary to destroy it. This was understood at the Anti-Submarine Warfare Division; it was to take over two years and a greater crisis before the Air Ministry 'bombers' were forced to yield a little of their grip on strategy.

In the meantime, while scientists wrestled with the problems of sea 'clutter' and reverse echoes bedevilling the first ASV sets fitted in escorts, the Trade Division of the Admiralty could only try to route convoys around U-boat patrols. The attempt was made possible by the Operational Intelligence Centre (OIC), a unique organization representing one of the undoubted success stories of the pre-war Royal Navy. The centre had been set up in 1937 to collect and correlate intelligence from all sources worldwide and distribute it on an immediate basis to those needing it for current operations. One of its specialized sections located in a complex of rooms in a sub-basement of the Admiralty was devoted to enemy submarines. This Submarine Tracking Room was fed with reports of U-boat sightings from Coastal Command aircraft or ships, SSS signals and fixes obtained by the Direction Finding (DF) Section, which plotted the bearings of U-boats' wireless transmissions picked up by DF stations located at seven widely separated sites, from the Shetland Islands north of Scotland to Land's End at the south-western tip of the British Isles, and also at Gibraltar. These were later supplemented by new stations in Iceland and the Azores. The accuracy of the fixes depended on atmospheric conditions and the skill of the operators, but with a good spread of bearings from the majority of sites a transmitting boat could be located to within about 25 miles.

The signals themselves could not be decrypted; the German naval Enigma machine cipher had resisted attack by the crypto-graphers of the Government Code and Cipher School (GC & CS) at Bletchley Park, Hertfordshire, but study of the patterns of calls, known later as traffic analysis, had identified certain routine signals: a short signal made by all U-boats at 10°W after departing a French base to notify U-boat Command that they had crossed Biscay safely and were on their way to the patrol area, sighting, shadowing and weather reports, and long end-of-patrol messages indicating a boat was on its way home, could all be recognized.[37] In addition a lesser code, christened by Bletchley Park 'Dockyard', was being read currently. Used for signals to and from shipyards, patrol boats, minesweepers and other auxiliaries, decrypts gave the submarine plotters precise knowledge of when and where the small vessels used for escorting U-boats in and out of their bases either left outward-bound boats or met those coming home, and enabled the Section to build up a picture of the numbers training in the Baltic, in dockyard hands or en route to or from operations.

The Trade Division's Movements Section in an adjacent room worked closely with the Submarine Tracking Room to divert con-voys away from and around areas where a boat or boats had been plotted, while a complex of direct telephone and teleprinter lines spreading out from the OIC to naval home commands, and Fighter, Bomber and Coastal Command Headquarters, with radio links to force commanders at sea, enabled air or surface patrols to be directed towards boats whose positions had been established.

At this period in November 1940 a minor revolution in method was in train. The chief of the Submarine Tracking Room, Pay-master Captain Ernest Thring, a veteran of the first war naval intelligence centre, Room 40, was superbly sceptical and cautious in his assessments and generally refused to try and predict a U-boat's future movements. His assistant, Rodger Winn, a barrister in his late thirties who had joined him in August 1939, believed fervently that the attempt should be made, arguing that if they did no more than beat the law of averages by 1 per cent they would achieve something. At the end of the year Winn succeeded Thring as leader of the tracking team and carried his theory into practice. Each U-boat, identified with a double-lettered tab, was advanced on the great plotting table representing the Atlantic at a speed corresponding to a U-boat's daily average along a track predicted for it by the latitude in which it had made its short signal at 10°W, or by other factors; every U-boat sighting or DF fix or reported attack was linked to the most likely boat on the plot, which was then moved to that position. As one of Winn's team, Patrick Beesley, wrote:

> This could not be more than intelligent guesswork, and we were frequently caught out by an incident occurring hundreds of miles away from the nearest U-boat tab on our plot. Nevertheless, it did mean that the plot bore some relation to reality, with at least the right number of boats at sea, on patrol or outward- or homeward-bound.[38]

Dönitz was playing a similar guessing game at a new headquarters in a small château at Kerneval, near the mouth of the River Scorff serving Lorient. He had transferred his staff there in November after a brief move to Paris. At nine sharp every morning he would step into his operations room, where his chief of staff, Kapitän Eberhardt Godt, waited with the officers of his team before a great wall-chart of the Atlantic. U-boats were marked on it by blue-numbered flags, whose positions had been brought up to date during the previous hour, convoys by red flags. Having studied the latest signals and heard reports from the first and second staff officers, Dönitz would listen to the third staff officer on enemy shipping, almost exclusively convoy intelligence from decrypts supplied by B-Dienst. After further reports from two other officers on the small team, Dönitz and Godt would study the chart, pondering the dispositions to be ordered. Despite B-Dienst's frequent successes, the last-minute evasive routing practised by the Trade Division of the Admiralty to Winn's plots increasingly cancelled out their efforts.

Adding to Dönitz's frustrations was the realization that the Italian submarines were not and never could be brought up to German standards. Their design limitations have been mentioned: their superstructures were too large, their surface speed too low and they took too long to dive. Above all their officers had not been trained in the U-boat tactics of shadowing and attacking by night. While the few operational U-boats sank thirty ships during November, an almost equal number of Italian boats sank just two. By the beginning of December 1940 Dönitz despaired of them:

> I did at least hope they would contribute a better reconnaissance of the operations area. In actual fact, during the whole time I have not received one single enemy report from them on which I could take action . . . They have never managed to maintain contact even for a very short time. During the period in which German boats sank 260,000 tons the Italian successes in the same area amounted to 12,800 tons . . . I am not at all sure that their presence in the operational area of the German boats, the way they let themselves be sighted, their radio traffic, their clumsy attacks, do not do us more harm than good . . .[39]

Unable to attack unnoticed or remain unseen, incapable of understanding the principles of hauling ahead of a slower enemy, or shadowing and reporting, and with 'no idea' of how to attack on the surface at night, the Italians were, he concluded, simply insufficiently hard and determined for the type of warfare taking place in the Atlantic, and their personal conduct lacked discipline: 'in view of all this, I am forced to detail the German boats without regard to the Italian boats'.[40]

In addition, the weather had turned against him. November had begun with promise: Kretschmer had sunk two large liners converted to armed merchant cruisers and a freighter, and two days later torpedoed a 7,000-ton tanker laden with crude oil which blew apart in the middle of a convoy with a roar and pillar of flame that split the night. This last had brought his aggregate of sinkings as calculated by U-boat Command to over 217,000 tons, and he had been awarded the Oak Leaves to his Knight's Cross. *U99*'s return to Lorient with a band on the quay and pretty girls distributing bouquets of flowers had been filmed and shown on newsreels throughout Germany, as had Kretschmer's subsequent visit to the Reich Chancellery in Berlin to receive the Oak Leaves from Hitler himself; he was the second U-boat commander after Prien to win this distinction, only the sixth recipient in the German armed forces as a whole.

For the rest of November gales swept the Atlantic, raising great seas. Driving rain or sleet, or fog, further decreased the chances of sighting and, once sighted, holding targets. From the low bridges of the four to eight boats on patrol at any one period in the heaving wastes west of the North Channel, vision was practically confined to the sweep of wild, spume-veined slopes up the ridges of water towering above, their translucent green crests torn to foam and spray. The boats climbed, hanging for moments at the top with views over further blown hills, before plunging down, propellers racing as the stern rose, seas surging green over the deck casing, cascading around the conning tower, streaming, hissing white from every aperture. The officer of the watch and four lookouts, one for each quadrant of the compass, achingly wet beneath their double-knotted sou'westers and oilskins, boots squelching sea water, faces stung raw by the slap of salt spray, brows, faces, lips, beards caked with salt, hands numb around their binoculars, wedged themselves between periscope standards and bridge plating. They were secured against being washed overboard by steel safety harnesses clipped to the structure, but again and again as seas broke above them they had to crouch below the protection of the bridge plating, clinging with all their strength against the pull of the water beating down and swirling around them waist-deep, filling their boots; as it fell away they raised their heads and almost without thought brought the binoculars to their eyes, attempting to steady them against the frenzied wind.

> No captain of a steamer has seen anything like this. We do not look down onto the sea, but up out of it, enveloped in water like swimmers. Whenever we are pulled down into its valleys, we have to stretch our heads up and back; we see with the eyes of the sea . . .[41]

There was little more comfort for the watch below; braced against the motion and buckled into their bunks, or swinging in hammocks from side to side as the boat screwed and seesawed, they could scarcely sleep, but dozed, feeling the slam and judder of the hull, hearing the beat of waves and wash and gurgle of the seas over the casing through their twilight consciousness. Those on duty held on to solid fixtures, or when moving groped from support to support. Nothing could be cooked. Humidity caused condensation to stream in rivulets down the inside of the hull plating and drop from pipes and cables overhead. Everything felt wet and slimy to the touch. Bread grew soggy, fresh food rotted; clothes, when men were roused to go on watch, were damp and clammy. Leather grew mildew, paper became limp or dissolved altogether. To gain a respite from the unending, wearying motion to cook and eat or just to rest it was necessary to take the boat down over 160 feet.

For both sides the sea demanded more attention than the enemy, whom they scarcely saw. It was a relief to the British. Nicholas Monsarrat, a young reserve officer in one of the new whale-catcher escorts, better known as the Flower-class corvettes, whose violent motion in any sea was as uncomfortable and dangerous for the unwary as the oscillations of a U-boat, described that winter of 1940 and his dislike of fine weather and 'everything that made sea-going easy and pleasant'. To get the convoys through they craved storms:

> It was odd to look forward, on setting out, to the chance of a gale – anyone who really wants the North Atlantic to do its worst in winter should be qualifying for a lunatic asylum – but that was what it amounted to ... It made it infinitely harder to hang on to the convoy, it turned zigzagging into tip and run in the dark, but it was harder still for the submarines to trail us, and that weighed more than all the hardship and the intolerable strain that bad weather brings.[42]

In its November report the Anti-Submarine Warfare Division noted that for the first time since the intensification of the U-boat campaign monthly sinkings had fallen appreciably, and were comparable to the total for the second month of the war; this they ascribed to the success of evasive routing.[43] Gales continued throughout December and on into January 1941; winds of force 7 or above were recorded on fifty-two out of the ninety-two days of the three winter months, and after the beginning of December no convoy was attacked until the end of January. The destruction of independents and stragglers continued; monthly sinkings averaged 162,000 tons, not much more than half the average for the summer and autumn.

The U-boats made their way back to Biscay singly at the end of their solitary patrols. Dönitz could watch them from the long *salon* windows of the château at Kerneval as they passed up-river, their once green-grey paint streaked with rust, white *Siegeswimpel* – victory pennants – flying from a slightly raised periscope, officers crowding the bridge, a white cap cover distinguishing the CO, the crew drawn up along the deck casing below in salt-encrusted leathers bleached a dirty grey, hirsute and white-faced with gaunt cheeks and eyes shadowed with the fatigue of constant motion and strain. They could look forward to a welcoming reception at their berth in Lorient, the greetings of comrades and, after the flotilla commander had come aboard for the perfunctory formal inspection, smiles and kisses from nurses handing out flowers, or perhaps girls from the town *établissements* welcoming back their customers. Afterwards there were letters from home, and the great home-coming celebration with quantities of the good, fresh Brittany food they had missed for weeks, champagne and as much German beer as they could swallow. Later there would be time to soak in the first bath since they had sailed and feel the accumulated grime and odours dissolve; and afterwards the luxury of laundered white sheets.

Dönitz did his utmost for his front-line crews. For those going on leave there was a special express train known as the BdU *Zug* to Bremen and Hamburg via Nantes and Paris. For the others rest hostels had been set up at Quiberon and other coastal resorts away from the activity of the base. Country châteaux or hotels were requisitioned for the officers. With a very favourable exchange rate for the franc and their pay almost doubled by U-boat pay and additional diving allowances, all hands could afford to unwind in style, and did so. Release from the tensions of patrol, the natural exuberance of young men and the sense, carefully fostered by Dönitz and the *Propaganda Kompanie*, of being an élite within the élite of the conquering German nation, led to nights of wild indulgence.

Officers might visit Paris, where they could watch the noon parade of the German guards regiment down the Champs-Elysées, but rarely did. Most would stroll around stores stocked with luxuries which had not been seen for years under the war economy in Germany, and in the evenings drink in the sophistication of the bars and cabarets of Montmartre – perhaps hear Edith Piaf singing *La Vie en Rose*. Many would end up at the Schéhérazade, 3 rue de Liège, in the Pigalle *quartier* which was owned and staffed by White Russian émigrés, and boasted a Russian cabaret and soulful Russian music; it had become a favourite rendezvous from the earliest days in France, and remains the subject of legend and nostalgic reminiscence among old U-boat comrades.[44] Some officers, overspent and under the influence of too much champagne, signed IOUs and asked for the bills to be sent to Dönitz at Kerneval.

> Such probably unenforceable charges were paid promptly, and the officer in question ribbed and reprimanded in a gentle way the next time he showed his face at U-boat Command. On such occasions Dönitz actually did display a certain tolerance, and even sense of humour ...[45]

Lorient was the 'port of aces'; young COs looked up to the veterans, who were already legends, Prien 'the Bull of Scapa', Kretschmer 'the Tonnage King', Schepke of film-star good looks, and emulated their conscious sang-froid, determined to rival them during coming patrols. The scenes in the Bar Royal at the Hotel Majestic in La Baule, near St Nazaire, as inebriation began to efface the boundaries between the 'Old Salts' and the 'Young Turks' in the opening of Lothar-Günther Buchheim's epic, *Das Boot*, have been execrated by U-boat veterans as gross exaggeration; yet they contain the core of truth; these were young officers, even the 'Old Salts', under the double stress of glorification in press, radio and newsreels as the Führer's shining knights, while at sea bearing the entire responsibility for the safety of their boat and crews, and for scoring. Small wonder if the 'Old Salt' Thomsen leaped to his feet sending glasses flying when the telephone rang at the Bar Royal, recalling to his befuddled mind the alarm bells at sea.[46]

Signs of the intolerable pressures, which would play a large part in the loss of several aces, and the strain on officers and men caused by Dönitz's determination to turn each of his few boats around in the shortest possible time were already apparent to the British Anti-Submarine Warfare Division. Shortly after the loss of Hans Jenisch's boat, U31 had suffered a similar fate. Interrogation of her crew revealed many who were 'nervously and physically exhausted'; officers frankly admitted that U-boat warfare was affecting their nerves. The men expressed particular dissatisfaction at the minimum time allowed in port for essential repairs before they were sent to sea again. The interrogators concluded that 'the whole crew had recently been worked beyond their capacity and junior ratings reduced to a state of sullen apathy'. All remained convinced, nevertheless, that Germany would win the war: 'some men sadly said that as P.O.W.'s they would miss the first days of rejoicing over final victory'.[47]

Both Prien and Kretschmer sailed for a much-trumpeted 'spring offensive' towards the end of February 1941. Dönitz had come to suspect that convoys were being re-routed further north, and had shifted the operations area to correspond. By 1 March Prien's U47, Kretschmer's U99 and two other boats were cruising to the south of Iceland between 59° and 62°N, and four others were on their way. One of their victims that day was the Esso tanker Cadillac. The torpedo that hit her ignited her cargo, which spilled out through the torn tanks, spreading the flames to the surrounding sea. By the time the one boat to get away had cast off from the side it was surrounded by a wall of flame radiating unbearable heat and making it hard for the crew to breathe, impossible to see anything beyond. The second mate, one of only four badly burned survivors, later recounted the tragedy:

> most of the men in the boat jumped into the water with the oars. They
> were nearly mad with the heat and pain and some were calling out and

others were praying, they did not know what they were doing. There was about a foot of water in the bottom of the boat, so I lay down at the bottom where I found it was slightly more easy to breathe, and after a few minutes I heard someone . . . say 'We are getting out of it'. There was only five of us left in the boat, we found the oars . . . and somehow managed to pull clear of the flames . . .[48]

Six days later, in the evening, Prien's lookouts sighted smoke from an outward-bound convoy. He reported and shadowed while Dönitz ordered up Kretschmer, KK Joachim Matz in *U70* and KK Hans Eckermann in *UA*, originally built for Turkey. The two destroyers and two corvettes of the escort under Captain J.M. Rowland were well trained as a group, and when Prien and Eckermann attacked in the early hours of the next morning, 7 March, both were detected and driven deep. *UA* was so seriously damaged by depth-charging that Eckermann could only lie low, then set course back for Biscay, which he eventually reached. Meanwhile, Matz had come up and attacked, and after him, shortly before dawn, Kretschmer weaved past the escorts and fired a salvo at the 20,000-ton whale-oil tanker *Terje Viken*. Matz, a new CO, had missed with a salvo of three and was lining her up for another shot when two of Kretschmer's torpedoes exploded in the tanker's side, blowing her apart. Both COs then made successful submerged attacks on two other ships from very close range in the first grey light of day. The Dutch tanker *Mijdrecht*, falling back out of station to rescue the crew of Matz's victim, was herself hit by a torpedo, but while she still had way her bridge watch sighted the feather of wake behind *U70*'s periscope off the starboard bow, and she turned to ram. Matz was unable to evade her. The tanker struck his boat, rolling it on its side as she passed over, still making some 7 knots. Matz blew tanks, intending to escape on the surface, but when he got up to the bridge he saw corvettes approaching and dived again. He was subjected to a devastatingly accurate pattern of depth-charges which wrecked the interior of the boat and forced him to the surface where he barely had time to get the crew off before *U70* sank.[49]

Prien, who was lagging some way astern from his earlier encounter, chased during the day and found the convoy again that evening, homing in on hydrophone bearings of the massed engine and propeller noises. He reported and shortly after midnight took advantage of a rain squall to close. Both destroyers of the escort were fitted with an improved but still primitive mark of radar called Type 286, and it seems that he was detected as he tried to cut in astern of them, for one of the destroyers, *Verity*, fired starshell, forcing him to dive. He went deep and survived five hours of hunting by asdic before surfacing; why he came up will never be known, but he appeared a short distance from Rowland's destroyer, *Wolverine*, which turned to ram. Prien dived again; *Wolverine* raced over the area of disturbed water and dropped a pattern of charges set for shallow depth, followed by *Verity*, which dropped another ten-charge pattern. Rowland was turning back for another run when oil was seen on the surface and the hydrophone operator reported 'a loud clattering sound like crockery breaking'; shortly afterwards *U47* rose up for a moment from the sea, disappearing almost immediately as if out of control. *Wolverine* ran over the spot and dropped another shallow pattern. The party watching from her stern as the explosion boiled up from the wake saw beneath the water an eerie red-orange glow lasting by some accounts a full 10 seconds before fading. Afterwards pieces of wreck bobbed to the surface, briefly marking the spot where Germany's most renowned U-boat ace and all his crew had met a fiery end.

The British had no idea whom they had accounted for, but took comfort from the performance of the trained escort group which had beaten off the pack and destroyed two U-boats for the loss of two ships sunk, two damaged.[50]

Lemp had been away from the Atlantic since the previous autumn when he had been posted to command a new Type IXB boat, *U110*, completing at Bremen. He had taken two of his former officers from *U30* with him and most of his petty officers, but the majority of the ratings were new and raw, as was his 1WO, Dietrich Loewe, a cousin of his from a landed family of Mecklenburg, whose bullying behaviour, in contrast to Lemp's quiet competence, had, according to later interrogation reports, made him extremely unpopular during the trials and exercises in the Baltic. Lemp, who would have liked to take his dog to sea with him, had had a terrier puppy painted on the conning tower of *U30*, and *U110* now bore the same device.

On 9 March, the day after Prien's loss, Lemp departed Kiel and, after traversing the Kiel Canal, took the usual route northwards to the Norwegian coast to avoid the Dover mine barrage, thence west to the Fair Isle Channel between the Orkneys and Shetlands north of Scotland, passing through on the 13th and continuing west-north-westerly. Soon after midday on the 14th when south of Iceland he sighted the smoke of an inward-bound convoy, reported and shadowed. This was HX112 from Halifax, fifty ships escorted by the unusually powerful and well-trained 5th Escort Group under Captain Donald Macintyre. Dönitz ordered up the other boats in the area, including Kretschmer's *U99*.

Lemp continued shadowing, for the most part on the surface, through the 14th and the daylight hours of the 15th. He then closed after dark and evaded the escorts to penetrate inside the convoy, picking targets from the first column for his bow torpedoes at 600 yards, turning and firing from the stern tube as a tanker in the second column passed at 100 yards. The tanker exploded with a blast which shook the boat bodily, the flames illuminating her 'as if in a spotlight';[51] seeing two destroyers outside the convoy turn towards him, Lemp made an emergency dive. He was not located in the asdic search that followed, but fell far astern and lost the convoy for a while. In the meantime, Kretschmer had arrived and he took over the shadowing and reporting role through the 16th.

After dark, while the escorts were engaged with other boats that Dönitz had directed across the convoy's track, Kretschmer closed and made the most devastating attack of his career from inside the columns of merchantmen, leaving four tankers ablaze and two freighters sinking – by his estimate 59,000 tons, bringing his total for the voyage to a record 86,000 tons. One of the tankers remained afloat and made port five days later; nevertheless, the total was over 61,000 tons, his highest ever.[52]

The boat occupying the attention of part of the escort during this lethal virtuoso display in the early hours of 17 March was *U100*. Schepke had arrived the previous evening and been forced down, then located by asdic in Macintyre's own destroyer, *Walker*, and depth-charged. The destroyer *Vanoc* had joined Macintyre shortly afterwards and made a second attack. She was turning to resume station when her radar operator reported a contact 1,000 yards to starboard, and as the wheel was put over the grey shadow of a U-boat was seen 10° on the bow heading from port to starboard.

Schepke had been forced to surface by the damage sustained in the depth-charge attacks. Now he found the diesels would not start; the fuel lines had been ruptured. Still shaken by the under-water pounding and with the destroyer closing fast, her high, white bow wave clearly visible, he was momentarily so distracted he ordered astern on the starboard electric motor instead of ahead to try and align himself along the enemy's track. As the boat swung towards a broader angle with the track, he thought for an instant that the destroyer would pass astern, then realized this was unlikely and shouted down the hatch to the crew to abandon ship. They seized life belts and ran up the ladders, some even jumping aft to man the 20-mm machine gun on the platform abaft the bridge. It was too late even for that defiance. The destroyer came on at full speed, her bows smashing through the ballast tanks, striking the pressure hull squarely abreast the conning tower, driving in and indenting the tower itself. Schepke was crushed between the side of the bridge and a periscope standard and killed instantly. The *Vanoc* was brought up all standing. As the wreck of *U100* slipped beneath the surface survivors were left struggling in the water; her CO's remains and the crew who had not had time to climb up from below were carried down with her.[53]

There now occurred two remarkable coincidences: Kretschmer, having expended all his torpedoes within the convoy, withdrew to resume his shadowing towards the very spot where *U100*'s survivors were climbing scrambling nets lowered over the side of the *Vanoc*, and the *Walker* was circling her to provide cover against possible U-boat attack. The *Walker*'s crest was a horseshoe open end downwards; Kretschmer had a horseshoe painted on the front of his conning tower, open end upwards.

Kretschmer himself was below when the bridge watch sighted the *Walker*; his standing orders in these circumstances were to turn away and run, showing the smallest possible silhouette. It appears, however, that a lookout's negligence had allowed the boat to approach too close, for the watch officer immediately sounded the alarm and dived.[54] Shortly afterwards, the *Walker*'s asdic operator reported a contact close to the *Vanoc*, which was still rescuing survivors. He was so confident it was a U-boat that Macintyre attacked and six minutes later, 03.43 in the morning of the 17th, dropped a pattern of six depth-charges set from 100 to 150 feet. *U99* was then at three times this depth, 390 feet, according to the account given later to British interrogators; however that may be, the explosions put the steering gear and electric motors out of action and started leaks aft which caused the stern to sink. The boat went down to over 450 feet before Kretschmer ordered the tanks blown, intending to try and escape on the surface. He came up 1,000 yards astern of the *Vanoc*, directly between her and the *Walker*, so that for a brief period neither destroyer could open fire without endangering the other. *Vanoc* illuminated the boat by searchlight and went ahead, leaving the remaining survivors of *U100* in the water, and at 03.54 both she and the *Walker* opened fire.

By this time it was evident to Kretschmer that his boat was sinking by the stern; he called the crew up from below to abandon ship and instructed his senior radio operator to signal in clear: '*U99. Zwei Zerstoerer. Wasserbomben. 53,000 BRT versenkt. Gefangenschaft. Heil! Kretschmer.*'[55] Because of damage and damp in the circuits the signal was not powerful enough to reach German shore stations. However, *U37* nearby did pick it up, and later, after hearing U-boat Command calling *U99* vainly, she relayed it: '*U99*; Two destroyers. Depth-charges. 53,000 tons sunk. Captured. Heil! Kretschmer.'

As the destroyers' 4-inch shells and tracer from lighter guns snicked by, raising waterspouts around the boat, Kretschmer flashed a message by signal lamp to the *Walker*, 'Captain to Captain. Please save my men drifting in your direction. We are sunking [*sic*].' Macintyre ordered firing to cease and as the destroyers' guns fell silent turned bows on to the U-boat in case she still had fight in her, and approached cautiously to windward, ordering a boat away to attempt to board.

In *U99* the engineer, KLt. (Ing.) Schroeder, had blown the after ballast tanks to raise her stern. Kretschmer, seeing the preparations to lower a boat from the *Walker*, became alarmed they might board, whereupon Schroeder volunteered to go below again to vent the after tanks. As the valves were opened admitting the sea and the stern dipped, Kretschmer called to him down the hatch to come up; he never reappeared. The crew washed off the after deck into the water heard his shouts as the boat sank, the sea lapping up the sides of the tower, over the bridge where Kretschmer stood alone, and pouring green down the open hatch. Moments later Kretschmer was floating, feeling the icy cold of the water. He swam around to make sure that none of his crew remained at the scene, then struck out towards the *Walker* whose port searchlights illuminated her side, his men scrambling up her nets and ropes. By the time he reached the nets himself he was so chilled he could scarcely hold on. Seeing his plight a British sailor climbed down and pulled him aboard. He was the last. Of his crew, all but Schroeder and two ratings had been rescued.[56]

The 'spring offensive' had cost Dönitz three of his highest-scoring aces in little over a week. To those who knew him best the depth of his emotion was betrayed by a sterner than usual reserve and aloofness. Although the remaining aces and 'Young Turks' continued to vie for honour and fame, it would never be quite the same again. Apart from one brief period of easy pickings off the US east coast early the following year, the Atlantic battle would become ever grimmer, ever more costly in boats and young lives. And the number of ships sunk per U-boat at sea, which had peaked at over five during the moonlight pack attacks of October the previous year, had sunk to half that figure and was destined to continue falling away as the numbers of boats increased. The high days and especially nights of the solo aces were over. It was to become a costly battle of attrition.

This is evident in retrospect. It was not at all evident to Dönitz at the time. U-boat production had increased from an average of two or three boats a month in early 1940 to nine, and although he still had fewer boats on patrol than in September 1939, over eighty new boats were training in the Baltic, and he could look forward to a rapid expansion of the operational force in the coming months and, by extrapolation of the sinking figures, to 'decisive' victory.

Otto Kretschmer gave his British interrogators the impression of being 'a quiet, deliberate man . . . [who] looked more like a student than a U-boat captain . . . His whole demeanour was calm and quiet, and he seemed anxious to be friendly.'[57] He told them he made no elaborate plans for attacking convoys, but felt confident he could take advantage of 'whatever the passing moment offered'. He also admitted he had been weary of the war for some time, and latterly had found no satisfaction in sinking ship after ship.

His crew gave the British the impression of 'having obtained a higher degree of co-operation and of having worked better together than other U-boat crews interrogated in recent months. The senior petty officers were more experienced', and there were fewer new and green youngsters amongst the ratings. Also 'for the first time in this war' the men made no criticism of their officers; indeed all expressed great loyalty towards and admiration for Kretschmer himself. They had, however, been spoiled by their heroic image:

> The crew of U99 had an exaggerated idea of their importance and dignity; these inflated opinions were no doubt due to the extraordinary degree of public adulation to which they had become accustomed. Special aeroplanes and bouquets at railway stations had long since become part of their daily lives ashore.[58]

The British organization to defeat the U-boats had grown to formidable proportions, at least on paper. At its peak was the Battle of the Atlantic Committee, known usually as the Atlantic Committee. It convened for the first time on 19 March 1941, two days after the destruction of Kretschmer's and Schepke's boats, and met every week until May, then fortnightly. It comprised the War Cabinet, representatives of concerned ministries such as Food, Supply, Transport and Shipping, and from its third meeting onwards the First Sea Lord, Admiral Sir Dudley Pound, and the chief of Coastal Command, Air Marshal Sir Frederick Bowhill, together with staff officers from the three services; Churchill himself took the chair. Despite its title, however, the subjects discussed were, in W.J.R. Gardner's words, 'almost entirely concerned with shipping and imports, with virtually no time devoted to the conduct of the battle or the provision and development of weapons for the campaign'.[59] The repair of merchant shipping and the rate of imports received the most attention, and Gardner has suggested that the name by which it was first known, the Import Executive, would have been more appropriate.

There appears to have been little or no effective liaison between those in the Anti-Submarine Warfare Division and Western Approaches Command, who were actually directing the battle, and the Committee or its chairman. A fortnight before the first meeting Churchill had issued a directive headed 'The Battle of the Atlantic'; it began, 'We must take the offensive against the U-boat ... the U-boat at sea must be hunted, the U-boat in the building yard or in dock must be bombed ...'[60] The second part of the exhortation was proper, the first so general as to obscure the real issue, which was the protection of shipping, convoys in particular. Submariners and the Anti-Submarine Warfare Division knew that this could best be done in the vicinity of the convoy from the air. Churchill did not. The suspicion is that even if Pound had presented the case with sufficient force and intellectual rigour Churchill would not have listened. He had a predeliction, indeed a lust for the offensive, and the Air Staff, still as convinced of the potentially 'decisive' effects of bombing German industries and industrial workers as Dönitz was of cutting Britain's supply lines with more U-boats, had his ear: they possessed the only force able to take the offensive to the enemy nation.[61]

That month Dr Fritz Todt, Hitler's Minister for Armaments and chief of the Todt Construction Organization, visited Dönitz at Kerneval to discuss the construction of roofed-in, bomb-proof U-boat pens at Lorient and other bases established in Biscay. When shortly afterwards work was begun on the foundations, Bomber Command might have destroyed them with relative ease, indeed should have done so had Churchill's directive been followed. Instead, through 1941 at Lorient and La Pallice, near La Rochelle, Todt was allowed to raise them into giant reinforced concrete bunkers of a thickness impervious to any known bomb, and by the summer of 1942 at St Nazaire and Brest, where they can be seen today. Some time after their completion Bomber Command began to lay waste the surrounding port areas; the U-boats lay refitting in perfect safety within their shelters.

While the Air Staff failed to support a maritime air strategy when it conflicted with their own goals, or to provide the modern, long-range aircraft desperately needed to fight U-boats in the

Atlantic, the Admiralty had won a concession which Raeder and Dönitz could never gain from Göring: in February, Coastal Command had been placed under the operational, though not direct, control of the Admiralty. On a day-to-day basis this meant that the C-in-Cs of the naval command areas stated requirements which the chiefs of the respective Coastal Command Groups did their best to translate into orders to their squadrons. In the most vital area the Admiral Commanding Western Approaches and the Air Vice-Marshal Commanding No. 15 Group Coastal Command covering much the same section had adjoining, interconnecting offices in a subterranean, bomb-proof joint headquarters beneath Derby House, Liverpool, known as the Citadel. Both looked out through a common glass wall to the Operations Room where a huge wall-chart of the Atlantic twice room height displayed every convoy, escort group, independent naval unit, air patrol, rescue tug and U-boat report; it duplicated the Trade and Submarine Tracking Room plots in the OIC in London, now moved to a bomb-proof underground headquarters close by the Admiralty, also known as the Citadel, and was connected to them by direct telephone and teleprinter links.[62]

The system had been so successful in routing convoys around known or suspected U-boat patrol lines – or, given the very few boats Dönitz deployed, appeared to have been so successful – that Dönitz was convinced the positions of his patrols were being given away to the enemy by spies. He had taken ever stricter precautions to prevent his operations room chart from being seen by anyone outside his small staff, and had stopped sending daily position reports to Naval Headquarters West and other naval and Luftwaffe commands.[63] Yet the predictions, or 'working hypotheses' on which Rodger Winn based his plot in the Submarine Tracking Room were in many cases no more than educated guesswork. What was needed to evade the greater number of boats anticipated in the summer and autumn was a break into the U-boat cipher. This had proved virtually impossible except for brief periods after the capture of tables of daily settings ('keys') for the Enigma machines on which the signals were enciphered at U-boat Command and deciphered in the boats, or vice versa.

The U-boat Enigma M-3 machines used three rotors with an alphabet ring and twenty-six brass contacts around the circumference, each contact wired to a lettered key like that of a typewriter. Each rotor turned between similar but fixed plates with corresponding contacts wired to small bulbs beneath different letters on a panel which provided the encipherment; the letter illumined was the encrypted equivalent of the letter pressed on the keyboard. Each time a key was pressed, the first rotor turned by one contact, so changing the encipherment path, and after making a complete rotation of twenty-six turns, the second rotor was moved on by one contact, again changing all the pathways; when the second rotor had completed one turn – thus after 26 × 26, or 676 letters – the third rotor moved on by one contact, altering the pathways to the encipherment panel yet again. Consequently it was 17,576 (26^3) letters before the same encipherment pattern was repeated. The wiring pathways were further varied by inserting pairs of plugs into lettered sockets in a switchboard below the keyboard.

The daily 'keys' listed the three rotors to be used out of a possible eight and their order from left to right in the machine, their starting positions as shown by the letter on their alphabet ring appearing in an indicator hole in the machine, and the switchboard plug settings. Having set up the machine, the operator at U-boat Command had to follow an extraordinarily complex and lengthy procedure involving the arbitrary selection of 'indicator' groups and random letters, and the encipherment of pairs of letters from combinations of these by reference to bigram tables listed for the day, to establish a message key. The three letters of this key were pressed out on the keyboard, their illumined equivalents noted on the cipher letter panel, and the rotors then reset so that these enciphered key letters showed in their indicator holes. The machine was now ready for the message, and the operator could begin encrypting by noting on his encipherment form each letter illumined as he pressed out the plain text.[64] When complete the encrypted message was signalled to the boats, whose radio operators, having set up their Enigma machines using the same daily 'keys', went through the process in reverse, pressing in the cipher text and noting the plain-text letters as they were illumined on the panel.

British Naval Intelligence had been thinking up schemes to capture German naval tables of 'keys' from the first days of the war, and recently escort-vessel commanders had been instructed to attempt to retrieve secret material by sending boarding parties to U-boats forced to surface. Guidance sheets had been issued with such phrases as 'Boot hoch halten sonst wird keiner gerettet!' – 'Keep the boat afloat or no one will be rescued!' – and 'Papiere behalten sonst schiesse ich!' – 'Hold on to those papers [don't throw them overboard] otherwise I shoot!'[65] The first partial success had come in early March 1941 when the German naval chart overlaid with the grid used instead of latitude and longitude for signalling position, and the Enigma 'key' tables for February, were captured from the armed trawler *Krebs* during a raid on the Lofoten Islands off northern Norway. While a powerful team of naval cryptanalysts working in Hut 8 in the grounds of Bletchley Park advanced their methods and knowledge of the naval cipher by reading traffic intercepted in February, plans were made to capture one of the lone and vulnerable weather ships that the German navy stationed in far northern waters. A young traffic analyst, F.H. (now Sir Harry) Hinsley, had suggested the idea after noting that weather reports were enciphered on Enigma. On 7 May the weather ship *München* was captured and the officer from the OIC with the boarding party retrieved the short weather signals cipher and the tables of 'keys' for June.[66] The day before these were delivered to Hut 8 more valuable material was captured from *U110*.

Lemp had regained convoy HX112 after being forced down by escorts in the early hours of 16 March, and had been present during Kretschmer's attacks that night and early morning of the 17th.[67] Afterwards he had lost the convoy and, following seven days of uneventful cruising, had turned for home, reaching Lorient on the 29th. He sailed again on 15 April, taking a young member of the *Propaganda Kompanie*, Helmut Ecke, aboard to record impressions of U-boat life. On the 27th, west of Ireland, he fired a single torpedo at a French freighter sailing independently, sinking her. Afterwards he rescued a survivor, reunited him with others in one of the ship's lifeboats and passed down a bottle of spirits. He was then ordered progressively further north and west as Dönitz probed for an area beyond Coastal Command air patrols and the cut-off point for convoy escorts. On 5 May he and other boats south of Iceland were ordered to intercept an outward-bound convoy assembled off the Hebrides. Two days later the convoy, OB318, ran into one of the boats. Her sighting report was plotted in the Submarine Tracking Room and, although not decrypted, passed on to the escort commander, who succeeded in shaking her off by turning north.

The convoy was still steering north-westerly under the powerful protection of both the 6th and the 3rd Escort Group – the latter having joined that afternoon from Reykjavik, which had come into service as a naval refuelling base the previous month – when it ran into KLt. Herbert Kuppisch's *U94*. Kuppisch reported and during the light evening worked into position ahead, then submerged and manoeuvred beneath the surrounding escorts and into the columns of merchantmen, as Lüth and many other U-boat commanders were now doing in the belief that they could hide from asdic in a ship's wake. He was detected briefly by the asdic operator in the destroyer *Bulldog* commanded by the senior officer of the escort, Cdr. A.J. Baker Cresswell, stationed ahead of the starboard columns. In an attempt to regain asdic contact Baker Cresswell turned 80° and steamed back through his charges. He had reached the last ships and must have been close to *U94* when her torpedoes exploded in the rear ships of the fourth and fifth columns away on his starboard beam. He turned again to hunt the boat inside the next column to starboard, but the convoy passed over *U94* and a few minutes later the sloop *Rochester*, closing the two victims who had fallen astern, sighted her periscope and forced her down. Immediatedly afterwards the destroyer *Amazon*, which had steamed back through the convoy from a position ahead of the port columns, located her by asdic and attacked; she was followed by the *Rochester* and soon joined by the *Bulldog*, Baker Cresswell controlling the hunt by radio telephone. His subsequent report indicated how new this facility was:

> Communication between *Bulldog* and *Amazon* was excellent and never failed during the four hours' hunt. It took some time to get *Rochester* on the air, but once established, communication was good. The advantages of good R/T communications are undoubtedly very great. Not only did the hunt work smoothly on account of each ship knowing what the others were doing . . . but it was also possible to give orders to the escort of the rapidly disappearing convoy at the same time.[68]

Although *U94* suffered damage to her hydroplanes under repeated depth-charge attack, Kuppisch succeeded in escaping. Dönitz moved the other boats further across the convoy's new track, and at 18.15 the following evening, 8 May, Lemp's lookouts sighted the ships' smoke on the port bow. He closed during the night but the moon was too bright and the escorts too numerous for him to risk an attack, and he shadowed from 15 miles off the starboard bow while Dönitz redirected the other boats in the light of his reports. At dawn on the 9th, OLt. Adalbert Schnee in *U201* found him; after exchanging recognition signals, the two COs closed and conferred by signal lamp, *U110*'s guest correspondent, Helmut Ecke, filming the meeting.

There are two versions of what passed between Lemp and Schnee. The story obtained by British interrogators afterwards was that Schnee was anxious to attack at once and Lemp agreed, against the advice of his long-serving chief quartermaster who informed him that they were approaching 32°W, as far west as any U-boat had yet attacked a convoy, and the escorts would soon be leaving. He was right. Baker Cresswell was due to take his group back to Reykjavik that afternoon. The other, German, version is that Schnee thought they should follow the convoy until nightfall, then make a surface attack; by then the escorts would probably have left. Lemp, however, did not have a great deal of fuel left and wanted to get rid of his remaining torpedoes and return to base rather than proceed further west. He therefore decided on an immediate submerged attack; he would go in first, Schnee following in about thirty minutes.[69] This version is the more plausible, especially as Lemp was the senior CO and daytime submerged attacks on convoys were rare at this period. However that may be, this was one of the very few occasions that U-boat COs were able to co-ordinate an attack.

Lemp spent the rest of the morning gaining position ahead on the starboard wing of the convoy, then he closed. At 11.37 he dived to make his attack run diagonally between the escort ahead of the starboard column of merchantmen and the escort off the starboard wing. Unlike Kuppisch, he did not penetrate the convoy, but while still 800 yards outside fired three electric torpedoes from his bow tubes at three different targets he had selected, the first at one minute before noon. Counting the seconds, he heard the thud of their detonations at the correct intervals, one after the other.

Baker Cresswell, on the bridge of the *Bulldog* stationed ahead of the centre of the convoy, also heard the explosions and water columns rise from the leading ship of the starboard wing column and, moments later, the leading ship of the third column from starboard. The first detonation was seen from the corvette *Aubretia*, zigzagging independently abreast the third ship in the starboard column, and an instant later the second ship in the column, off her bow, was struck. Lemp had scored with every shot. At about the same time, or moments before the explosions, a report of hydrophone effect from a torpedo's propellers to starboard reached the *Aubretia*'s bridge. Lt.-Cdr. Vivian Funge Smith, RNVR, increased speed to 13 knots and came round towards the bearing. He was still turning when his asdic operator reported a contact on 335° distance 1,000 yards, then lost it. Funge Smith steadied on 340° and stopped engines to maximize asdic reception. A minute later, at 12.04, a periscope was sighted 20° on the starboard bow,

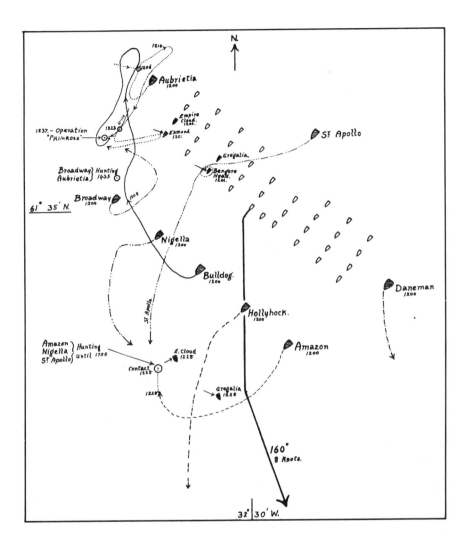

U-boat attacks on OB3 – 9 May 1941: diagram enclosed with 'Report of Proceedings' of the 3rd Escort Group. 'Primrose' is *U110*; 'contact' at 12.28 to the south of 'Primrose' is *U201*.

moving to starboard. He rang the engines to full speed and came round to cut across the U-boat's track on a collision course.

It appears that Lemp's concentration may have been momentarily diverted. He had aimed his fourth bow torpedo at what he believed to be a 15,000-ton whale factory ship, but it had misfired, and his 1WO, the bullying Loewe, had started an argument about it with the engineer. When Lemp next swung the periscope round he saw the corvette steering straight for him. He dived, ordering the crew forward to increase the angle of descent. They were going down rapidly when the *Aubretia*'s charges, set to 100 and 225 feet, began exploding, wrecking the depth gauges and causing other minor damages. In the stillness after the detonations, as the corvette's propeller noises grew more distant, then stopped, the sound man reported two other 'destroyers' approaching. These were the *Broadway*, originally stationed ahead of the starboard wing column of merchantmen, and Baker Cresswell's *Bulldog*, from ahead of the centre. The swishing noise of the propellers neared and they heard the sharp ping of asdic pulses ringing off the hull plates; shortly afterwards another pattern of charges began exploding, but further from them, as the *Broadway* attacked. An emergency and probably inaccurate depth gauge showed 95 metres (311 feet). Lemp, seemingly unconcerned by the hunt above, gave quite orders to the helmsman as the hydrophone operator reported the enemy's movements.

Five minutes later they recognized their first attacker's propeller from astern as she came in for a second run, and the unnerving chirping sound of asdic in contact, and braced themselves, looking upwards after the propeller noises passed as if able to see through the skin of the boat and the sea to the charges tumbling towards them. The first 'click' of a depth trigger was followed by a stupendous detonation, described afterwards by Helmut Ecke as 'far louder and more terrifying than anything he had heard on the western front'.[70] The boat, slammed by the pressure wave, jerked like a live creature; lights went out, glass shattered, fittings clattered to the deck. In the dark the men gripped their supports as succeeding charges erupted around them like rolling thunder, seizing and shaking the boat bodily. By the time the full pattern of ten charges had burst, the electric panel was wrecked; the starboard electric motor had cut out, hydroplanes and rudder were inoperable, water was forcing in to a tank somewhere aft and the stern was sinking; formerly abutting deck plates in the control room were squeezed by pressure into an overlap position, and somewhere a battery had cracked; the first alarming hints of chlorine were evident to the nostrils. As the boat took an ever steeper angle by the stern the men scrambled in panic up the slope towards the bow. Helmut Ecke was among them; reaching the control room he found himself confronted by Loewe who drew his attention in the blue glow of the emergency lighting to 'the terrified faces of the unhappy crew', and suggested he might observe something he could record in one of his propaganda articles.[71]

Lemp meanwhile ordered all tanks blown. The order could not be carried out; the wheel controlling the blowing system had been snapped off by the contortions to which the hull had been subjected; it was found on the deck plates. Lemp and the engineer must have known they had reached the end. The ocean floor was over 2 miles below; even if by some miracle the boat did not sink below the level at which frames and the pressure hull itself would buckle and implode, unless they could get her to the surface they would be poisoned by the battery gases. Lemp gave no indication of alarm; all his men spoke afterwards of his unshakeable calm.[72]

As they struggled to regain trim the boat began to heave in an odd way as if feeling a surface swell, and shortly before 12.35, eleven minutes after the last charge had gone off, she started to roll and pitch. Somehow she had found her own way to the surface. It may be that the concussion that had snapped off the control wheel had at the same time turned it fractionally, releasing air slowly to the tanks. Lemp dashed up the ladder and without pausing to vent the pressure which had built up inside the boat, unclipped and raised the hatch; a gale of dust and small debris blew up past him.

Baker Cresswell saw the conning tower emerge 800 yards off his port beam. He ordered his guns' crews to open fire and swung the destroyer round towards the U-boat as it surfaced, intending to ram. The *Broadway*, which had been in asdic contact and was coming in for her second depth-charge run, did the same; the *Aubretia*, which had caused all the damage, had broken off to rescue survivors from the torpedoed merchantmen. For Lemp on the bridge a moment's glance was enough to indicate the hopelessness of the situation. He called down the hatch to the crew to take lifejackets and abandon ship, and to the LI to open the vents to admit the sea. Men scrambled up the ladder to the hum of 4.7-inch, 3-inch and pom-pom shells and a fusillade of machine-gun and small-arms fire from both approaching destroyers, tearing the nearby sea or ringing against the plates of the conning tower. Most men jumped straight from the bridge into the waves 15 feet below.

Lemp stood by the hatch hustling up those willing to brave the fire, and urging them to jump.

When Baker Cresswell saw the crew abandoning the U-boat so precipitately it flashed upon him that instead of sinking her he might be able to capture her and perhaps retrieve the cipher material and other papers. Instructing the *Broadway* not to ram, he ordered the cease-fire with his heavier guns, stopped engines and called away an armed whaler's crew, detailing a young sub-lieutenant, David Balme, to lead the boarding party. The *Broadway*, meanwhile, had approached so close to *U110* on her attack run that as she turned aside she grazed a stern hydroplane, which ripped through her port forward fuel tank, letting oil spill into the sea.[73] This near miss may have been crucial in preserving the Enigma machine, its rotors and cipher 'keys'. The 2WO and radio petty officers responsible for destroying them in an emergency and throwing the secret papers overboard in loaded bags had been so stunned by their ordeal in the depths and the sounds of gunfire after surfacing that they had done nothing, and when Lemp began to shout more urgently down the hatch, 'Out! Out! The destroyer is going to ram us!'[74] those still sheltering below scrambled up with no other thought than to avoid being trapped and carried down in a sinking boat.

It is probable that Lemp and any other officers on the bridge with him jumped into the sea as the destroyer's bows neared; several of the crew saw him swimming afterwards, and while in the water he asked both Loewe and the engineer about the 2WO, who had only recently recovered from illness. There seems no doubt that he and perhaps one of his petty officers started swimming back to *U110* after it became apparent that the *Broadway* had not struck and the U-boat showed no signs of sinking.

In his official report Baker Cresswell described seeing 'two men [who] appeared to be manning the submarine's forward gun' – this after the whaler under Balme had left the destroyer's side – whereupon 'Fire was again opened by Lewis gun and two or three men were hit. My object was to keep the crew rattled.'[75] By this time the *Bulldog* was lying stopped 100 yards to windward of the U-boat, whose crew by the same account 'already appeared dazed and uncertain what to do'. It is highly unlikely that anyone would or could have taken on two destroyers with the boat's deck gun; apart from any other considerations the ammunition had to be passed up from below through the conning tower. It is equally unlikely that Baker Cresswell could not see precisely what the 'two men [who] appeared to be manning . . . the gun' were doing from only 100 yards away. Had Lemp and a petty officer managed to use the swell to scramble up on the low after ballast tanks and work their way towards the forward hatch? This had been opened and some of the crew had escaped through it. Did Baker Cresswell order fire from the Lewis gun to prevent them getting below to scuttle the boat or destroy whatever secret material had not been disposed of? In view of the vital importance of the capture this would have been a necessary and legitimate act of war. All that is certain is that Lemp, having been seen swimming and talking to his officers in the water, did not survive. The British reports are silent on the manner of his end; and the German officers and men, who were picked up by the *Aubretia's* boats, taken to the corvette and bundled below so rapidly they did not even know their submarine had been boarded, evidently did not witness the death of their CO.

Post-war German historians assume that Lemp tried to swim back to his boat when he saw it was not sinking and was shot before he got there.[76] Some British post-war accounts suggest that he may have committed suicide after seeing his boat boarded and realizing he had failed to destroy the secret papers. The German version seems more plausible, particularly in the light of the complete lack of information or surmise about the manner of his end in any of the official reports by the British officers concerned. It is improbable now that the whole truth will ever be known.

Instead of taking his whaler around to leeward in a seamanlike manner, Balme was so concerned about the U-boat sinking or being scuttled before he could board, he ran straight aboard from to windward, the boat riding up over the ballast tanks on a wave and jamming between the conning tower and deck rails on the port side, where it was subsequently smashed. Balme, who was carrying a large service revolver, holstered it to climb the conning tower; he was followed by his armed party. Arriving at the bridge, he found the hatch shut. This was so unexpected in an apparently hastily abandoned submarine that he wondered if some of the crew were waiting below. It took nerve to open it. Peering down he saw the conning tower was empty but the hatch below into the control room was also closed. He climbed down the ladder with a heightened sense of unease – why should anyone close both hatches on a submarine they were abandoning? He unscrewed the locking wheel of the lower hatch. There was no burst of fire as he opened it. The control room seemed empty and eerily silent, lit by the blue emergency bulbs. He went down. The hatches in the bulkheads fore and aft were open; there was no sign of life:

> The U-boat had obviously been abandoned in great haste as books and gear were strewn about the place. A chain of men was formed to pass up all books, charts etc. As speed was essential owing to the possibility of the U-boat sinking (although dry throughout) I gave orders to send up ALL books except obviously reading books ...
>
> Meanwhile the telegraphist went to the W/T office, just forward of Control Room on starboard side. This was in perfect condition, apparently no attempt having been made to destroy books or apparatus. Here were found C.B.'s, Signal Logs, Pay Books and general correspondence, looking as if this room had been used as ship's office. Also the coding machine was found here, plugged in as though it was in actual use when abandoned. The general appearance of this machine being that of a typewriter, the telegraphist pressed the keys and finding the results peculiar sent it up the hatch ...[77]

The books, documents and charts, and the Enigma M-3 machine and its accessories were transferred to the *Bulldog* in a boat Baker Cresswell had sent to replace Balme's whaler, while little over a mile to the south the destroyer *Amazon* and two other escorts dropped depth-charges over *U201*. Schnee had come in almost exactly half an hour after Lemp's first shot, and had torpedoed a fourth freighter when he was detected by asdic and counter-attacked. He eventually escaped from the hunt which lasted until nearly 18.00 that evening.

U110 was down by the stern and listing 15° to port with 'a slight bubbling noise' audible from outside the pressure hull on the port side aft, but she was considered seaworthy; Baker Cresswell had a line passed from the destroyer, recalled all hands, and at 18.30 began towing her towards Iceland. During the night the wind got up, raising a lumpy sea, and at 11.00 the following morning the U-boat's stern suddenly sank, leaving the bow standing up vertically out of the water; as that slipped away the tow line was cut.

Baker Cresswell was bitterly disappointed at being robbed of his prize, but it was probably a fortunate accident: had he succeeded in bringing her in, the fact must have leaked to the enemy. As it was the capture of 'Primrose', as she was codenamed, and her priceless documents was one of the best-kept secrets of the war. Not even the German prisoners knew their boat had been boarded, indeed interrogation revealed 'they were confident that the U-boat had sunk before we could reach it. There was not the least suspicion in their minds that we had boarded it'.[78] Had any of them had any idea Dönitz would have been informed within months through the medium of the 'Ireland code' by which messages were sent in apparently innocent letters home, using the initial letters of every fifth or tenth word.

Dönitz and the German code and cipher experts who advised him never guessed that the British had managed to seize a working Enigma machine with all its rotors and ancillary equipment, the tables of 'keys' for April and June – since they were printed in water-soluble ink the May tables were probably destroyed accidentally during transfer to the *Bulldog* – the short signal code-book, 'For Officers Only' coding tables, the 'indicators' and 'bigram' books for preparing message keys, a radio logbook, instruction manuals, secret grid charts of the Atlantic, charts of the minefree approaches, channels and routes for the Biscay coast, and a wealth of other valuable material. Bletchley Park was able to read all U-boat traffic in June as rapidly as Dönitz or the boats themselves, and after the capture of another lone weather ship at the end of that month all July traffic. The speed of deciphering fell in August, but the insights the naval cryptanalysts gained from Balme's haul allowed them to crack most U-boat signals for the rest of the year. It was probably the most valuable capture of the war with the most direct effect on the Atlantic battle; it has been compared to a major victory at sea, indeed King George VI, when presenting Balme with a DSO at Buckingham Palace, told him that the action in which he had won the decoration was the most important single action of the war at sea.[79]

The first practical result was the destruction of the tanker and supply ship net established for the battleship *Bismarck*, surface raiders and long-distance U-boats that Dönitz had sent into the South Atlantic. So complete was this destruction that Dönitz decided he could no longer rely on surface tankers to replenish his boats, but must build tanker and supply U-boats, so-called 'Milchkuhe' – 'milch cows'.

Although not in the very highest rank of aces, Lemp died a hero and had one of the U-boat men's rest camps near Lorient named after him. He would have been remembered differently had his cardinal error become known; undoubtedly the insights the British gained into the German naval cipher and the routes and channels used by the boats from the Biscay bases cost the lives of hundreds, probably thousands of U-boat men and others. Yet given the terror all the officers and men had experienced in the depths – as Herbert Werner puts it in another context, 'that one death that every sub-mariner pictures a thousand times' – the fierce crossfire they ran into directly they came up, and the threat of imminent annihilation under the bows of the *Broadway*, it is evident they were in a state of shock, overwhelmed by events. Balme's view of their neglect was simple: 'obviously . . . they thought the U-boat was certain to sink at once'. And he reported that the demolition charges had been set.[80] Whatever the explanation, Lemp, possibly alone, attempted to rectify his error.

The other officers, all of whom survived, told their interrogators of their 'tremendous admiration' for their CO, as did the petty officers and crew. It appeared, however, that Loewe was detested by the men and considered both 'brainless and inefficient', while the junior watch officer was 'so unreliable his subordinates could not trust him to carry out any important observation or calculation properly'. Only the LI was well regarded. Morale was found to be high, but the interrogators gained the impression that there was real difficulty in manning the boats since many had been drafted into the submarine arm without option.[81]

As for the Type IX boat herself, Balme recorded his impressions in his report for Baker Cresswell:

> She was new and a fine ship both in the strength of the hull, in the fittings and instruments and general interior construction. Absolutely nothing 'ersatz' about her . . . Spotlessly clean throughout. Ward Room finished off in light varnished woodwork and all cupboards were numbered with corresponding keys to fit . . . In W/Room there were several sets of writing paper and envelopes, well printed and illustrated reading books, cards, dice and the usual art studies. Bunks were one on top of another both in officers' and crew's spaces . . .[82]
>
> Plenty of tinned ham, corned beef and 3 sacks of potatoes in Control Room; also luxuries such as beer, cigars, Players cigarettes (German printing on packets) and a plate of shrimps were all found in the W[ard] Room. Magnificent galley forward of the W[ard] Room . . .[83]

5

Mediterranean Centre

SINCE THE NORWEGIAN campaign in April 1940 British submarines as a whole had not distinguished themselves. They had been misused escorting Atlantic convoys; others patrolling off Norway had been forced so far from the coast by Luftwaffe and anti-submarine patrols, and in summer by long hours of daylight which prevented them surfacing, they had neither damaged enemy coastal traffic nor reported or intercepted the surface raiders which had broken out from time to time into the Atlantic. When two of the major raiders, *Scharnhorst* and *Gneisenau*, put in to Brest all the boats which could be mustered, including a high proportion too small, cranky or obsolete for the task, had been sent to maintain a blockade, termed an 'iron ring', around the port. They had orders not to attack U-boats lest they sink one of their own by mistake, and accomplished nothing.

In the Mediterranean their misapplication had more serious consequences. The early deployment against the Italian fleet and restrictions against attacking merchantmen without first warning, and then ensuring the safety of the crew were continued too long, the latter for its political effect on neutrals; the boats were only allowed to conduct 'unrestricted' war on merchantmen within 30 miles of the Italian or Italian-held Libyan coasts, where the defence was at its strongest. As a result, tankers supplying vital oil from Black Sea ports, and troop transports and supply ships for Italian forces in North Africa aiming for Egypt and the Suez Canal, and from October Italian forces invading Greece, were barely touched. Up to the end of 1940 Mediterranean submarines had sunk just nine ships and one Italian submarine for the loss of nine of their own number, a wholly insupportable exchange rate.

New submarines were sent to replace the losses, among them from the turn of the year a number of small U-class boats. These were based at Malta, whose position between Italy and the Libyan ports was ideal for striking at supply traffic for the Italian North African forces. Early in February 1941 the zone for 'unrestricted' submarine warfare was widened considerably to include all waters south of the latitude of Malta itself; any merchantman encountered here could be deemed an enemy transport and sunk on sight.

Results continued to be disappointing, however. There were isolated successes, but through February and March a German armoured division under General Erwin Rommel and half a million tons of equipment and stores to shore up the Axis partner in North Africa were carried across the central Mediterranean with little loss; only six of the hundred transports used were sunk. And of a total 220,000 tons of Axis supply shipping to Libya during those two months only 20,000 tons failed to reach its destination.[1] In part this was due to the comparatively few modern boats at Malta, six Us and three Ts – four surviving older boats being transferred to Alexandria as the Us arrived – in part to lack of signals intelligence on the sailing dates and routes of enemy convoys. Bletchley Park had been able to read Italian naval signals on Italy's entry into the war, but the cipher had since been changed to a system based on a Swedish encrypting machine, and this had not been broken.[2]

The lack of sustained successes by the Malta-based boats was also due to the extraordinarily low surface speed of the U class, 10½ knots at best for most despite the designed speed of 12 knots,[3] and the small number of torpedoes they carried; combined with an acute shortage of torpedoes at Malta this resulted in COs restricting themselves for the most part to two-torpedo salvoes. The primitive British night-sights, the almost equally primitive fruit machine for computing the director angle, and the inexperience of the COs on their early patrols were all contributory factors. A prime example was Lt.-Cdr. David Wanklyn of *Upholder*: his first four patrols resulted in just one hit which damaged but did not sink a transport. It is significant that this came from a submerged attack at 900 yards range. In two earlier night attacks on this first patrol he had been unable to approach closer than 2,500 and 3,000 yards because of lack of speed on the surface. In addition he had greatly over-estimated his targets' speed. In his final attack on his first patrol he had fired from 4,000 yards.[4] He exceeded even this extreme range during his fourth patrol in early April. The commander of the 1st Submarine Flotilla at Alexandria, to which Malta-based boats were attached, had stipulated that no torpedoes were to be fired at ranges over 2,500 yards unless at especially valuable targets, but Wanklyn fired one salvo at a merchantman at 6,400 yards.[5] This drew a stinging comment from Alexandria. Wanklyn's chief at Malta, Cdr. G.W.G. Simpson, who had been his CO in a submarine before the war, knew him thoroughly and respected his sterling competence, but agonized over whether 'such a poor shot could be kept in command'. Simpson, known as 'Shrimp' because of his short but robust frame, in effect told Wanklyn he had just one more patrol to prove he could score.[6]

On 21 April Wanklyn sailed on his fifth patrol for the coast of Tunisia, finding his first target, a laden merchantman, on the afternoon of the 25th. A heavy swell made it extremely difficult, as always, to hold a trim at periscope depth, but maintaining sufficient speed to control the boat with hydroplanes, he closed to 700 yards before firing two torpedoes. After an anxious wait the explosion was felt as much as heard; many of *Upholder's* light bulbs were shattered. Next, ordered to the shallows off Kerkenah, where a destroyer and supply ship were grounded after a surface action, he took *Upholder* alongside the merchantman by moonlight, sent up a boarding party and left her ablaze; he was unable either to approach or fire at the shallower-draught destroyer higher up the shoal. The crowning point of the patrol came on the morning of 1 May with an attack on a small convoy escorted by four destroyers; choosing two merchantmen as their profiles overlapped, he hit both, sinking the larger one of 7,300 tons and returning in the evening to finish off the smaller with his last two torpedoes. The intervening counter-attack by destroyers had not been accurate; at this date the Italians had no asdic and their anti-submarine craft hunted solely with passive hydrophones.

The British equivalent of the victory pennants flown by U-boats on return to base was a black flag bearing a white skull and crossbones – the pirate Jolly Roger of popular legend – sewn with white bars or stars to represent the boat's successes with torpedoes or guns respectively. The custom had been started by the present Flag Officer Submarines, Max Horton, when in command of the submarine *E9* in the opening weeks of the First War. He had sunk the light cruiser *Hela* inside the Heligoland Bight and returned to Harwich flying the Jolly Roger from his periscope, no doubt an ironic reference to the conventional naval view of submariners as pirates. On his second patrol he had sunk a destroyer and returned flying two Jolly Rogers.

Not all British COs followed the practice of flying the Jolly Roger, but it was generally adopted in the Mediterranean, particularly at Malta, where the pirate flags, each 12 × 18 inches, were soon being embroidered by nuns. Probably no one was more relieved than 'Shrimp' Simpson when *Upholder* returned from her fifth patrol flying the skull and crossbones with four bars over a German ensign taken from the boarded merchantman, and the hands lined on the casing wearing German helmets from the same source. The following week Wanklyn wrote to one of his brothers saying he had just returned from 'a most successful patrol' and had 'at last been recommended for a decoration – so here's hoping'.[7] Over the following months David Wanklyn, known in the fraternity as 'Wanks', went on to accumulate the highest aggregate of tonnage sunk by any British submarine CO in the war.

He shared several characteristics with the leading German ace Otto Kretschmer, chiefly single-minded dedication in his approach to his profession, painstaking attention to detail and strict maintenance of discipline; as one of his junior officers recalled, 'he never set out to be popular with anybody'.[8] He too was a quiet, deliberate man, not given to outward show, who was trusted implicitly by both officers and men. It is also a curious coincidence that the building number of the U-class boat which he took over at the Vickers Armstrong Barrow yard and later rode to immortality as *Upholder*, was 99, the same number as Kretschmer's U-boat. Comparisons cannot be pushed too far. Wanklyn was an Englishman of his time and class, not representative but recognizable.

As a boy he had been shy and quiet, earning the nickname 'Mouse' within his family; the shyness had been marked at the Royal Naval College, Dartmouth, where he had worked hard in class, passing out top in five subjects but not distinguishing himself particularly at games. His favourite pursuits were angling and shooting, which he had learned with his father in the country around the home the family moved to in Wigtownshire, West Scotland, when he was 8. During the depression years his father had run into debt, and in 1931 had died suddenly, leaving Wanklyn's mother practically penniless. Although it was usual for young naval officers to be subsidized by their parents, Wanklyn somehow managed to reverse the situation, saving some of his meagre sub-lieutenant's pay to help his mother in the first desperate year of her widowhood,[9] a feat which can only have hardened him and driven him deeper into himself. One contemporary looking back fifty years later remembered 'a strangely solitary character'; making all allowance for the effects of hindsight, 'I do think we recognised he was a strong character in his quiet way'.[10]

It was probably not so much the extra six shillings a day – although in his family circumstances that must have been an inducement – as escape from the gregarious, institutionalized round of big-ship service life, so alien to his temperament, that led him to the submarine branch, where more than any other he might walk his own path. After passing the training course at HMS *Dolphin*, Gosport, near Portsmouth, in the summer of 1933, he joined his first boat in September as fourth hand, the most junior officer, responsible for navigation and signals. By 1935 he had risen to first lieutenant, the executive officer – 'Jimmy' to the crew, 'Number One' to the officers – and had begun to establish a reputation for discipline combined with excellent relations with his men; sometimes hard cases were deliberately transferred to his boat to be brought into line. The wife of one of his crew at that time believed it was 'his naturalness that made him so popular' and, confirming a point made in many other recollections, added, 'he actually did get on better with us [the men and their wives] than he did with the officers'.[11]

In 1938 Wanklyn married in Malta, afterwards honeymooning at the fashionable resort of Taormina on the Strait of Messina, Sicily. Typically, with war obviously just around the corner, he spent the train journey along the Sicilian coast on the lookout for features he might report. Later that year came the posting as first lieutenant to 'Shrimp' Simpson's *Porpoise* and the forging of that mutual respect that was to sustain him during his first desperately disappointing wartime patrols in *Upholder*.

Photographs from 1941 show him as tall with an almost patriarchal dark beard, gaunt cheeks and rather wide-apart eyes with a direct, even artless gaze. His biographer, Jim Allaway, has described his appearance in profile as 'hawkishly intent; face on oddly vulnerable'.[12] He was seldom seen without a briar pipe in his mouth even when the boat was submerged and he was sucking on a cold stem; he had a habit of stroking his beard when thinking. Such in essence was the intensely reserved, able but very vulnerable man, so different from many of his more clubbable, boisterous and flamboyant fellow submarine officers, who was soon to establish himself as the leading ace of the Malta flotilla.

He sailed for his sixth patrol on 15 May, in his first attack south of the Strait of Messina exceeding even his previous long-range shooting by firing at a small, escorted convoy from 7,000 yards, without result. A few days later he made another long-range attack, hitting and damaging a tanker; then in the late evening of 24 May some distance off the south-eastern corner of Sicily his lookouts sighted against the darkening western sky the silhouette of a huge liner. As other large passenger liners appeared steering southwards with escorting destroyers it became evident that this was a troop convoy for North Africa, steaming at an estimated 20 knots. A high swell was running, making periscope observation difficult, but there was still too much light for a surface attack. Wanklyn closed the track submerged, soon losing sight of the destroyers zigzagging ahead and on the wing of his target, and unable to detect them on the sound apparatus because it was out of action. As he was swinging the periscope on his final observation prior to firing he saw a white bow wave and the sharp shadow of a destroyer heading for the boat, and took her down just in time. Rising afterwards to periscope depth astern of the destroyer and rapidly re-working his angles, he fired a full salvo of four torpedoes at one of the troopships, then went down again, counting the seconds. At the correct time two dull thumps were heard, and the hands in the control room saw their CO's bearded face break into a grin of pleasure.

The counter-attack began shortly afterwards. Wanklyn stood in the corner of the control room, his first lieutenant (now Captain) M.L.C. Crawford recalled, listening to the sounds of the destroyers' propellers clearly audible throughout the submarine, stroking his beard as he gave quiet orders to the helmsman, 'and it was just the general air of reassurance he generated that impressed the chaps more than anything'.[13] Explosions of patterns of charges were interspersed with strange popping, creaking and scraping noises as the liner settled and collapsed internally. Wanklyn gave a running commentary on the sounds to calm the men, one of whom confessed years later that he couldn't stop his legs from shaking, although he hadn't let anyone see.[14] They counted thirty-seven depth-charges, the last four uncomfortably close. Despite Wanklyn's nonchalant example one man broke, dashing to the lower conning-tower hatch and attempting to release the clips before he was restrained and held.

Returning to the surface after the destroyers left two hours later, the first thing noticed as Wanklyn, followed by the bridge watch, emerged into the night air was the smell of oil fuel from the liner which had gone down. She was the Conte Rosso of almost 18,000 tons and had been carrying 3,000 Italian soldiers, more than 1,200 of whom were lost.

Simpson rested Wanklyn for most of June, sending a relief CO to take out Upholder for her next patrol. 'Shrimp' Simpson occupies a place in British submarine lore alongside his legendary protégés in the Malta boats, recognized formally in September as the 10th Flotilla, although still under the operational control of Alexandria. Absolutely dedicated to his boats and their young COs and crews, he possessed indestructible energy and optimism and a fighting spirit recognizing no obstacles, a living example of the Royal Navy's tradition that 'there is nothing the Navy cannot do'. His taut, often caustic manner was complemented by a twinkling humour and kindliness which united his small unit in a bond reminiscent of Nelson's 'band of brothers' in the Mediterranean almost a century and a half before.

His base was a former quarantine hospital, the Lazaretto, built of sandstone blocks on a small island in the harbour north of Grand Harbour, Valetta, and connected by causeway to the suburb of Sliema. After his arrival in January Simpson had set Maltese workmen, assisted by officers and men between patrols, to excavate bomb-proof tunnels in the sandstone at the rear of the Lazaretto. Later he installed workshops and a sick-bay there. The offices, wardroom mess and other facilities, traditionally provided in the British service by a depot or 'mother' ship, were on the ground floor of the building, whose south walls were bounded by a sleeve of water in which the submarines, painted a vivid cobalt blue for Mediterranean conditions, were moored to buoys or tied up alongside. Officers' rooms were on the floor above, opening on to a wide common veranda overlooking the boats.

Soon after Simpson's arrival Malta had come under sustained assault from the Italian Air Force and Luftwaffe *Fliegerkorps* X stationed in Sicily. Raids around the clock had made Grand Harbour untenable as a fleet base and virtually cut off supplies by sea; when in late March a convoy had been sneaked in it was attacked after berthing. Simpson had taken care not to draw attention to the whereabouts of his headquarters, and thus far had not lost a boat. His minute staff, extemporizing from stores left in the naval dockyard, converting destroyers' torpedoes for use in submarines, retreating to the tunnelled shelters at the sound of the air-raid alarm, somehow kept the force operational. In the circumstances, and considering the limitations in the boats' speed and armament, their comparative lack of success in cutting the Axis supply lines was perhaps less remarkable than their ability to operate at all. William King called at Malta that summer in a new command, *Trusty, en route* to the 1st Flotilla at Alexandria; his *Snapper* had not returned from patrol when he was on leave. 'What a fighter!' he wrote of Simpson, and ascribed the spirit he maintained in his command to his 'fundamental, burning toughness'.[15]

By the time Wanklyn was rested that June, another CO of very different temperament had begun to build a reputation: Lt.-Cdr. E. P. Tomkinson, 'Tommo', had arrived in *Urge* at the end of April having sunk a blockade-running tanker of over 10,500 tons in Biscay on his way out. He was a powerful man physically and in force of personality, with an easy-going, open manner and friendly expression. Before the war he had been Navy golf champion. Ian

McGeoch, who took passage with him to Malta as a relief CO, described him as 'one of the best officers of his seniority',[16] an opinion undoubtedly shared by the Malta officers. He had the self-confidence to oppose Simpson if he felt him wrong, even to refuse to sail on patrol if he was not certain of his boat's or his own readiness. Simpson found his forthright opinions a valuable check on his own decisions.

On his first patrol in May Tomkinson attacked one of the small convoys typical of the Italian supply run, four transports escorted by five destroyers, the leaders dropping single depth-charges at irregular intervals to warn off submarines. Alerted by the sound of the charges, Tomkinson was able to approach submerged to 500 yards before firing four torpedoes, sinking a 5,000-ton tanker and damaging a transport. The boat was so close when the transport was hit that the lights were shattered and the crew in the forward compartment thrown flat. He had to take the boat down fast as he saw the rear destroyer approaching, and went to 278 feet, 28 feet over the theoretical limit, during the depth-charging that followed; he had not increased speed to counteract the descent with the hydroplanes lest the noise were picked up on the destroyers' listening apparatus.

Tomkinson's next patrol was uneventful, but on his third mission at the end of June he landed commandos on the coast of Sicily, who blew up a train near Taormina, Wanklyn's honeymoon resort, and later he sank a 7,000-ton freighter.

It was about this time that the natural rivalry between COs was animated by a pictorial scoreboard put up in the Lazaretto wardroom, showing opposite each boat's name little diagrams of sinking ships together with their tonnage. *Utmost* under Lt.-Cdr. R.D. Cayley, who had arrived in January at the same time as Wanklyn, but had 'got his eye in' long before him, Tomkinson's *Urge*, and Wanklyn's *Upholder* were top scorers, their very different COs a celebrated trio in that close community. Altogether there were eight Us operating from Malta that summer; ten had arrived from England, but two had been lost, probably to mines which the Italians had sown liberally off their waters and the approaches to the North African ports.

With this small number of boats only about four could be on patrol at any one time, and despite the comparatively confined area of sea through which the Axis supply traffic had to pass and the obvious focal points forced by geography, sightings were rare; because of the slow speed of the boat, actions were even rarer. Alastair Mars, later in command of the *Unbroken* in the

Mediterranean, has written of the 'tedium of endless patrolling, a tedium accentuated by harsh living conditions and an exacting routine, in which few obtain more than a couple of hours sleep at a time'.[17]

Living quarters were as uncomfortable as those in Type VII U-boats: twenty seamen and stokers were confined in the closest proximity in the forward compartment, or 'fore ends', with the four reload torpedoes and most of the provisions for the three-week cruise, heavy weather gear, seaboots and woollens. A small table in the centre served for their messing and any card or board games they played. There were no bunks. To move about the space it was necessary to crouch below the close-packed hammocks in which they slept; as described by Signalman Gus Britton in a letter home from the *Uproar*:

> In one corner there is a washbasin, and to use it you have to squeeze behind the tail of a torpedo and put a hand either side of the coxswain's hammock. Potatoes and cabbages are piled in one corner, and as it is as damp as Eastney Beach, after six days there is a horrible smell of rotting vegetables.[18]

He was not complaining, he assured his family; he really loved submarines and 'wouldn't swop it for anything', sentiments which, however much designed to reassure anxious relatives, expressed the special comradeship bred in the cramped, noisome quarters of all submarines. In the summer, when it was usually necessary because of long hours of daylight and the expectation of air-craft patrols to submerge at dawn and remain below for eighteen hours or so, conditions became barely tolerable as the temperature increased and the air deteriorated. By evening all hands would be sweating freely and struggling for every breath. Signalman Britton described in his letter the blessed relief felt at night when the order came for 'diving stations', then some ten minutes later 'Blow one and six!'; the boat would shudder with the rush of air into the tanks:

> I am at the bottom of the ladder in the darkened Control Room, and sing out the depth which I can see on the gauge – 25 feet – 20 – 15 – 10 – 5; and then the captain opens the hatch and up rushes all the foul air just like a London fog and if I don't hang on I would go up with it as well. Beautiful, marvellous air . . .

A doctor who made a patrol in *Upright* described the 'fore ends' as permanently damp from condensation, the cork-based deck-covering (Corticene) completely sodden, and the hammocks likewise never dry. 'Bad weather has a noticeably depressing effect on the ship's company as sleep becomes impossible, and even the old hands are seasick.'[19] He suggested that twelve days at sea was the maximum compatible with any degree of efficiency.

It was hardly better for the petty officers and engine-room artificers (ERAs) in cramped messes just aft of the 'fore ends', or for the four officers in an equally tight wardroom forward of the control room and separated from the ERAs by the galley. If in bad weather the officer on the bridge became soaked, he remained in wet clothes for the remainder of the patrol; there were no drying facilities and the atmosphere below was heavy with moisture. The film-maker and war correspondent Anthony Kimmins, who made a patrol with Wanklyn in *Upholder*, describing the experience as being 'cooped up in a steel tube about the size of a London tube [train]', remarked on the amazing amount of time spent sleeping, 'largely because of the lack of oxygen when submerged'. He went on:

> There is, of course, no exercise to be had in the terribly cramped quarters, and during the twenty-four hours you will probably move only a few paces – and yet you are always hungry and, oddly enough, by the end of a patrol you have probably lost weight.[20]

Although there were desperate food shortages in Malta, the best of available provisions were kept for the submariners and the crews of the few fighter aeroplanes, the only other offensive force on the island. At sea, meals came chiefly from tins, tinned herrings in tomato sauce one day, tinned sardines another, tinned pilchards another, interspersed with traditional hashes prepared by the rating, seldom a trained cook, who presided in the galley; cheese 'oosh' was a favourite, 'train smash', a mix of tinned bacon, tomato and dried scrambled egg, another. The coxswain, the senior petty officer in British submarines responsible to the first lieutenant for the discipline of the crew and the cleanliness of the interior, and for provisioning, was also in charge of the traditional daily issue of one-eighth of a pint of rum to each man.

It is scarcely surprising that health suffered in these conditions; and the close proximity in which the men lived and the lack of any bathing or shower facilities led to periodic outbreaks of the itching skin infestation, scabies, and bodylice known as 'crabs' or 'mobile blackheads'. Simpson's staff tried to ensure that each crew had at least ten days' break ashore between patrols, and arranged rest camps for the men away from the capital and the continuous bombing. For the officers there were Saturday night dances at the Sliema Club, invitations to stay with the Governor at his palatial residence, walks in the countryside, beach parties, the ward-room bar and traditional wildly boisterous after-dinner horseplay indulged in with added abandon as a discharge from the accumulated tension of patrols.

As Wanklyn and Tomkinson and Cayley laid the foundations of their reputations in the central Mediterranean in that high, nervous summer of 1941 when the war seemed poised on Hitler's will, a CO of very different stamp began a series of spectacular patrols in the eastern Mediterranean. Lt.-Cdr. Anthony Miers of the new T-class *Torbay* has been described by Alastair Mars as 'a turbulent friend and implacable foe';[21] the words were no doubt carefully chosen. Others knew him as cocksure and self-willed to the point of arrogance, boorish and bullying.[22] Vice-Admiral Sir Hugh Mackenzie, who as a junior officer before the war had served with Miers as first lieutenant, and later during the war as a fellow CO in the 1st Submarine Flotilla in the Mediterranean, and who remained a friend through his later life, has written of his reputation for 'resolute, bold, determined and decisive action, and great honesty of purpose, whether on duty or off'.[23] The American Admiral Ignatius Galatin, who knew him later in the war in the Pacific, has written of him recently as 'a very likeable and fun-loving companion, who had not outgrown his days in the Royal Navy Gunroom'.[24] Miers' son has described him as 'a colourful and passionate man'.[25] He was also a very physical man: as a young officer he had been court-martialled for striking a rating; later, as British liaison officer to the US submarine arm in the Pacific, he would challenge the American officers in the mess to wrestle, and floor every one until he met his match in Lt. Benjamin Jarvis, executive officer of the *Sailfish*, formerly a footballer and wrestler at the Naval Academy.[26] 'Crap' Miers, as he was known, was neither an easy nor a generally popular officer. He was brave to the point of recklessnesss, but how many submarine COs navigating the mine-strewn, dangerously clear waters of the Mediterranean were not brave?

He brought the *Torbay* in to Alexandria on 13 May with Paul Chapman, a young officer who had just passed his twenty-first birthday and put up his second gold stripe, as first lieutenant. Chapman had joined as fourth hand a few months earlier after Miers had sacked the original fourth hand. Later, while working up the new boat, Miers had sacked the third hand. After the first patrol as escort to a North Atlantic convoy, and while half the officers and crew were travelling home on leave, the *Torbay* had been ordered at short notice to join the 'iron ring' around the *Scharnhorst* and *Gneisenau* at Brest; Chapman, as acting first lieutenant at the time, had sailed as such with a scratch replacement crew and two young officers as third and fourth hands. Miers had nursed him in his new responsibilities and, confirmed in his judgement of the young man's competence and sharp mind, had made the position permanent when the boat had been ordered urgently from Biscay to the Mediterranean. He thus commanded probably the youngest wardroom of officers in any submarine anywhere at that stage of the war. As for the half-crew left behind in England, many arrived in Alexandria in another submarine a few months after *Torbay* and were offered the chance of returning to Miers' command; they elected to stay where they were.[27]

In the weeks preceding *Torbay's* arrival the Mediterranean fleet based at Alexandria had suffered crippling losses and damage from enemy air attack while engaged in evacuating British and Commonwealth forces, first from Greece, where they had been sent to aid that country, against the Italian invasion, then from Crete. The submarines of the 1st Flotilla, now consisting of five new Ts, six of the older and larger boats and a number of Greek submarines, had been disposed against the intervention of enemy surface forces, or on special rescue, commando or supply operations. Apart from successful minelaying by the *Rorqual* they had made little impact.

Miers was sent to the Aegean to intercept the traffic from the Black Sea via the Dardanelles. After the war his first lieutenant described how Miers always made an intense study of all available information about any area to which he was sent. In this case his research suggested that, owing to the strong currents and layers of water of different density caused by the outflow from the Black Sea into the Mediterranean, the approaches to the Dardanelles were untenable by submarines. Miers told Chapman they would go there; 'We will say that *Torbay* "tenned" it.'[28]

They sailed on 28 May; on 1 June between the islands of Andros and Euboea on the main shipping route between the Dardanelles and southern Greece they sighted one of the local coasting caiques the Germans used for troop transport and supplies. Miers sent the crew to diving stations and, as he closed, 'gun action stations'. The gunlayer, briefed on the target, climbed the ladder in the gun tower forward of the conning tower, followed by his trainer and the two loading numbers, and waited just below the upper hatch. Within 1,000 yards of the caique Miers, taking a final look at her through the attack periscope, called out her range and bearing and gave the order to surface when ready. Chapman had the mid-length main ballast tanks blown, the fore hydroplanes set at hard-a-dive to counterbalance the emptying tanks and hold her down, then ordered, 'Surface!' The planes were reversed and numbers one and six ballast tanks at the ends were blown. The boat took an upward inclination and lifted fast. At 20 feet the control-room messenger began to call the depth; the gunlayer released one clip from the hatch above his head. Miers, who had climbed the ladder from the control room, did the same with the upper conning-tower hatch. As 10 feet was called both released the second clips; the hatches blew open and gunlayer and CO, steadying themselves against the pressure venting up around them and preventing the sea coming down green, climbed out virtually into the water cascading from the superstructure. Within seconds the gunlayer had fixed the sights which he had carried up with him, the trainer had wheeled the barrel to the target bearing and the first 4-inch shell had been rammed home, the breech closed and locked. On the bridge the watch officer and four lookouts had followed Miers up and were at their stations as the first round went off; below, the ammunition numbers passed up shells from the magazine while Chapman had Q tanks flooded. These small tanks on either side at mid-length were normally empty when the boat was submerged. They were flooded to increase depth quickly or, when the boat was surfaced, to assist rapid diving. But in this case the caique, evidently carrying explosives, blew up with a violent detonation on the fifth round.

Two days later off the Turkish coast they sank a second caique loaded with drums of oil, again by gun action, then moved up off the entrance to the Dardanelles, keeping outside neutral Turkish waters. The information on currents and layers of density proved only too accurate. Submerged with just enough way to make the hydroplanes effective, the officer of the watch needed to take bearings every fifteen minutes to discover in which direction the boat was being carried; when going deep a 'feather bed' layer of denser water was encountered which was impossible to penetrate until some five tons of sea had been let into the auxiliary ballast tanks at bow and stern. Coming up from below, the opposite applied; the auxiliary tanks had to be pumped out. Since this took ten minutes Miers avoided going deep unless absolutely necessary.

On 6 June, after observing much neutral traffic which they were not allowed to touch, since the 'sink at sight' zone did not extend to the Aegean, they identified a Vichy French tanker making for the Dardanelles and the Black Sea; Miers ran in to attack. At the last moment the tanker made a radical turn which left him trailing. He moved right astern and swung round to fire a single torpedo directly up her wake; it hit, wrecking her propeller and rudder, but she remained afloat and, lacking any power of motion, dropped anchor. Miers hit her with a second torpedo. Still she wouldn't sink. He waited until after dark, then brought the submarine alongside, bridge Lewis guns at the ready, and sent a boarding party up over the side. She was deserted, but the engine room was flooded and they were unable to open the valves to scuttle her. Instead they parted the anchor cable with a demolition charge, so casting her adrift. Two days later she was sighted again, this time under tow. Miers fired a third torpedo but it merely frightened the tug away. Finally, after diving and lying low for an Italian destroyer which appeared, they found her again and put forty shells into her waterline. Even this failed to sink her, but she drifted away and was never salvaged.

The same morning, 10 June, a small convoy escorted by two Italian destroyers was sighted heading for the Dardanelles. Miers manoeuvred to attack the leading merchantman, but as the angle came on found himself close off the bow of a destroyer; he let her pass, had the firing solution re-worked for the second merchant-man and fired a salvo of three torpedoes, going deep immediately. They heard two sharp explosions, too soon for the torpedoes to have reached their targets, and wondered that the Italians had been so quick with their counter-attack. Presently the sound of fast propellers heralded the start of the real attack with patterns of charges; under this first test the crew remained, as Miers reported, perfectly steady.[29]

Miers had been warned by signal from Alexandria to expect an Italian tanker to leave the Dardanelles on or about the 10th. This may have been signals intelligence: Bletchley Park had begun to break into the Italian naval cipher that month. Once the hunt had ceased Miers came up to periscope depth, sighted the laden tanker leaving as expected, and torpedoed her, after which he was again attacked by a destroyer, soon joined by two anti-submarine boats. His technique when hunted differed from that of most COs; he never dived below about 80 feet – whether or not there was, as in this case, a 'feather-bed' layer – believing that the submarine's frame and vulnerable hatch and other openings were in a better condition to resist the shock waves from depth-charges when not already under extreme pressure at maximum depth; further that he could more easily come up to periscope depth to review the position from 80 feet. By shutting off all auxiliary motors and maintaining the lowest speed compatible with holding trim, he hoped to remain undetectable by the Italian passive listening devices; so indeed it proved, particularly off the Dardanelles, where the layers of water of different temperature and salinity refracted any sounds that might have been picked up.

The laden Italian tanker sank and Miers began the return passage, sinking a supply caique next day by ramming her after allowing the Greek crew to take to their boat, and the following day, 12 June, destroying by gunfire a schooner carrying troops and munitions. He arrived back at the depot ship, *Medway*, to the plaudits of the Captain Submarines, who had been alerted as much by enemy distress signals as by *Torbay*'s own reports of the havoc she had created. He was able to tell Miers that he had sunk one of the two destroyers escorting the convoy he had attacked, but not the merchantman, which accounted for the two detonations heard so soon after firing the salvo. In all, the *Torbay*'s first Mediterranean patrol had accounted for one destroyer, two tankers, a schooner and three supply caiques; as the Captain Submarines expressed it, 'A brilliantly conducted patrol'.[30] Undoubtedly Miers' resolution in maintaining station in such difficult navigational conditions at the mouth of the Dardanelles had brought the opportunities which he had used to such effect.

Torbay sailed for her second Mediterranean patrol, also in the Aegean, on 28 June, carrying two young soldiers from the Special Boat Section at Alexandria equipped with a wooden-framed canvas canoe known as a folbot. It was hoped they would extend the range of the submarine's disruptive activities. Following much the same track as before to the shipping lane off the south-eastern capes of Greece, on 2 July in the passage between the island of Kea (Keos) and the mainland they sighted a convoy of two merchantmen escorted by two destroyers. Despite a flat calm Miers made his attack run undiscovered and fired a salvo of three torpedoes at the leading merchant ship, then waited for the second ship to reach the chosen firing angle and launched a second salvo of three. The first ship was hit and sank, but the second, alerted by her fate, altered away before the torpedoes of the second salvo reached her, escaping while the destroyers counter-attacked. Two days later, while lurking 50 miles to the north-east between Andros and Euboea where Miers had sunk his first caique on the previous patrol, a caique and a schooner were sighted, both flying a swastika ensign and carrying German troops. Miers stalked them and surfaced for gun action, sinking both vessels and subsequently using two Lewis guns from the bridge to ensure that no soldiers survived;

as Chapman put it in his later account: 'everything and everybody was destroyed by one sort of gunfire or another'.[31]

They moved southwards and late the following evening sighted the large bridge structure of an Italian submarine close in to the south shore of the island of Mykoni (Mikonos). Plotting soon established that she was travelling westwards, and Miers started the attack. Chapman ensured the boat was well trimmed down by the head so that when the bows rose after the discharge of a full salvo he would not have to flood Q tanks, the normal method of compensating for the loss of weight before the automatic inboard venting system of flooding the tubes and a small inboard venting tank took effect; flooding the Q tanks would take the boat down below periscope depth for a while, which would not have pleased Miers. At about 1,500 yards Miers fired a salvo of six torpedoes launched at eight-second intervals across the Italian's track; the hydroplanes set at hard-a-dive prevented the bows from rising above the surface. After the correct time they heard two detonations, then the enemy submarine was ripped apart by an explosion whose shock waves were so violent they destroyed the *Torbay*'s navigation lights.

Moving south-westward to the Kithira Channel between the islands of Kithira below the extending fingers of the Greek Peloponnese and Antikithera off the western end of Crete, they destroyed another schooner by gunfire. Then in the very early moonlit hours of the next morning, 9 July, they saw four caiques and another schooner steering northwards; as it turned out these were carrying, in addition to petrol, ammunition and food supplies, Bavarian mountain troops going on leave from the Crete garrison. *Torbay* surfaced for gun action against the nearest caique, destroyed her and all aboard with the 4-inch, Lewis and Bren guns, and steered towards the next. The skipper of this vessel, a young German named Ehlebracht, was naturally startled as the submarine appeared suddenly out of the night and opened fire, and he jumped over the side with some of the crew and soldiers. Those remaining aboard raised their arms in surrender, and someone called out, 'Captain is Greek. We surrender!'

By this time the *Torbay* was running short of ammunition, so Miers called away a boarding party to sink her with demolition charges and brought the submarine alongside. One of the Special Boat Section commandos, Corporal George Bremner, was leading the boarding party over when he saw a German about to lob a grenade, and shot him with his Bren gun; the fourth hand, Sub-Lt. David Verschoyle-Campbell, shot another who raised a rifle.

While the charges were being set in the caique Bremner rounded up and disarmed seven of the Germans, then shepherded them back to the submarine and removed some of their caps and insignia for identification, after which he asked Miers' permission to take them below. Miers refused, shouting furiously that submarines never took prisoners. Bremner went to look for a raft or float for them, and failing to find one, went below. Exactly what happened next is not clear; the German skipper, Ehlebracht, who was still in the water, reported afterwards that the men aboard the caique, including two sailors and the engineer, were ordered into a rubber dinghy. In the *Torbay*'s log it is stated that all aboard the caique were forced to launch and jump into a large rubber float. Whether the soldiers aboard the *Torbay* were also ordered into the float is not apparent. When Bremner asked afterwards what had happened to his prisoners he was told simply that they had been shot in the water; no mention was made of a raft or float.

It seems possible that Miers had them thrown into the sea and told Corporal Jim Sherwood of the Special Boat Section, and then Chapman, to shoot them; both refused and he ordered another crew member to shoot them, threatening to shoot the man if he did not obey. When his blood was up Miers seems to have resorted to such threats: on a later patrol he threatened to shoot Bremner after the commando had refused to paddle to the shore in his folbot in a gale. Unlike Bremner on that occasion, the signal-man ordered to shoot the soldiers in the water did not call his captain's bluff. According to Ehlebracht's report, fire was opened on the rubber dinghy, killing two sailors and seriously wounding the engineer and one soldier, after which the submarine 'circled twice around the troops swimming in the water and used machine gun fire in an attempt to bring them together. I foiled this by ordering them to swim apart.'[32] After the *Torbay* had made off to chase the other targets, only one of which escaped her, Ehlebracht and a few other survivors of the slaughter clung to the wreck of the caique, which remained afloat, and were later sighted and rescued.

Miers made no attempt in his patrol report or log to conceal his actions: 'Submarine cast off', the log recorded, 'and with the Lewis gun accounted for the soldiers in the rubber raft to prevent them regaining their ship . . .' And when he returned to base after sinking an escorted tanker off the island of Kea, bringing his aggregate for the patrol to one Italian submarine – the *Jantina* – one freighter, one tanker and seven local motor sailing troop and supply transports, together with an unknown number of soldiers, he was warmly congratulated by both the Captain Submarines and the C-in-C Mediterranean Fleet, Admiral Sir Andrew Cunningham; the former passed Miers' recommendations for decorations to London, the latter commented, 'A brilliantly conducted patrol. Lieutenant Commander Miers is an outstanding commanding officer.'[33] Neither, it appears, reprimanded Miers or cautioned him in any way for disregarding both the Royal Navy's Nelsonic tradition of magnanimity in victory and the provisions of the Hague Convention for the treatment of prisoners. The reason may be that after the battle for Crete, which had cost the Royal Navy dear and during which German dive-bomber pilots had strafed British survivors in the water, an unofficial policy of no quarter had been encouraged or at the least condoned in the Mediterranean.

That is speculation, but reports reaching German Naval High Command of survivors being shot in the water during the Crete campaign in the spring of 1941 support such an interpretation. In the period from 20 to 23 May, that is after the *Torbay* had arrived in the Mediterranean and immediately before her first patrol, there were reports of attacks on eight separate motor sailers or transports to Crete, and one convoy during which British surface forces were alleged to have machine-gunned survivors in the water. There was also a report of an unnamed British submarine attacking the motor sailer *Osia Paraskivi* on 12 May, the day before *Torbay's* arrival in Alexandria; after allowing the surviving Greek crew into the lifeboat the submarine had fired 'aimed shots from close range' at a German officer and three soldiers who had jumped from the vessel into the water 'until all four had been hit and had gone under'.[34] It was natural and common for survivors to imagine that shots hitting the water nearby had been aimed at them personally. Nonetheless, the detail in many of the reports reaching Berlin was specific.

British actions between 20 and 23 May had been aimed at preventing seaborne landings on Crete and consequently troops had been the target; if the reports were correct – and their validity has not been tested – soldiers were shot in the water to prevent their rescue and subsequent employment against the British and Commonwealth troops defending Crete. In such a case it might appear that Miers, choleric as he was, was merely acting in the spirit of other officers at Alexandria. However that may be, it is impossible to imagine Wanklyn or Tomkinson shooting men in the water in cold blood, impossible to imagine it of William King, now in command of *Trusty* in the Mediterranean; arriving at Alexandria later that summer 'tired to the bone' from the accumulated tensions of patrols since the outbreak of war, he knew he 'hated killing. I hated sinking, burning and drowning . . . I desperately wanted to cease hunting ships. I also wanted to cease being hunted myself.'[35]

When Miers' report reached Admiral Horton in London, the Flag Officer Submarines was concerned about German reprisals, and wrote to the Board of Admiralty: 'As far as I am aware, the enemy has not made a habit of firing on personnel in the water or on rafts even when such personnel were members of the fighting services; since the incidents referred to in *Torbay's* report, he may feel justified in doing so.'[36] The Admiralty wrote a strong letter to Miers instructing him not to repeat the practices of his last patrol.

In the Atlantic, from whichever side one viewed it the battle seemed to be swinging the way of the Germans. U-boat production had been lifted from an average of three a month the previous summer to over fifteen, and was scheduled to rise to twenty a month, far in excess of losses. There were in June 1941 over 130 operational boats; by the end of the year at projected rates the figure would be near 250. However, Raeder's staff was playing a professional long game; only about a third of the boats were available to Dönitz for operations; a third were attached to training schools to produce the necessary officers and men for the hugely expanded fleet anticipated, a third were working up in the Baltic. This meant that the number at sea at any one time seldom exceeded thirty. Of these several were on passage out or home, and others were working in the South Atlantic off the West African coast, probing for and finding weak spots in the defensive system, and thus forcing the British to disperse and dilute the escorts in the North Atlantic, the centre of gravity of the campaign.

The Italian Atlantic Flotilla at their Bordeaux base, known by the abbreviation 'Betasom', was twenty-six strong by the end of June. Thirty-one boats had made the passage through the Straits of Gibraltar and five had since been lost. Still, despite attempts to train their crews to German standards in the Baltic, despite taking their COs on Atlantic war patrols in U-boats and improving the boats' own characteristics, most importantly by reducing the height and length of their huge bridge structures, they remained by German standards ineffective, especially against convoys. In the last three months of 1940 they had sunk thirteen of thirty-eight independent ships encountered, none from convoys, and a further twenty-four in the six months to the end of June 1941.[37] This score over nine months was less than the average monthly total for the U-boats. Dönitz had written them off entirely: 'Despite the efforts to raise their performance through constant influence ... they remain uniformly unsatisfactory. They see nothing, report nothing, or too late, their tactical ability is likewise nil ...'[38]

This was an over-reaction born of impatience and a refusal to acknowledge the different characteristics of the Italian boats. He had assigned them an area off the south-western approaches to the English Channel where they could not interfere with his own boats, now working far to the north and west between Iceland and Greenland. Nonetheless, by the end of the year Dönitz could look forward to more than double the number of German boats; with longer reconnaissance lines he could expect to find more convoys; and with a greater number of boats to attack in packs he could wreak greater destruction.

The British were looking at the same picture. Naval Intelligence estimates of the numbers of U-boats in service and being commissioned each month were remarkably accurate.[39] Even with the moderate numbers of boats operating in the spring and early summer of 1941 total shipping losses from all causes, including surface raiders, aircraft and mines, had averaged well over half a million tons a month; in May U-boats had accounted for over 325,000 tons of the total 511,000 tons sunk.[40] Extrapolating these figures for the next six months and augmenting them for the projected increases in numbers of boats Dönitz would be able to deploy, the Joint Planning Staff concluded that by the end of the year, at the most conservative estimate, the merchant fleet would have lost a further 4 to 5 million tons. Since British and Commonwealth shipyards could not produce more than a million tons a year, and the United States, to whom Britain had turned for assistance, must take at least eighteen months before any mass building programme could become effective – or so it was believed – the situation appeared mortally dangerous. Already on their projected figures of losses the planners anticipated a deficit by year's end of 7 million tons of raw materials and other imports, 2 million tons of food and over 300,000 tons of oil imports. While these could be made good from existing stocks, it could not be more than a short-term expedient; the planners concluded that it was 'only by a reduction of the rate of loss that a real margin of safety can be achieved'.[41] Although not expressed in the stark terms Jellicoe had used in April 1917, the inference was the same: unless the number of sinkings could be reduced, Germany would win the war.

To those in the Anti-Submarine Warfare Division, on Churchill's Atlantic Committee, in the Submarine Tracking Room and in the Citadel below Derby House, Liverpool, where day-to-day convoy operations were controlled, the situation did not appear so hopeless. The threat was not underestimated, but it was felt that measures to meet it were understood and had begun to coalesce. The use of Reykjavik in Iceland from May as a mid-ocean base, together with a remarkable expansion in the Royal Canadian Navy and the completion of numbers of escort destroyers and corvettes under the War Emergency Building programme had at last made it possible to provide escorts the whole way across the Atlantic for homeward convoys and, from July, for outward convoys. Canadian escort groups based at St John's, Newfoundland, took the ships on the first leg from Sydney or Halifax, Nova Scotia, to a mid-ocean meeting point (MOMP) at about 35°W; thence British escort groups from Iceland took them to about 18°W, where they were met by escorts from Western Approaches Command for the final leg home – and in the reverse order for outward convoys. Moreover, by basing Coastal Command aircraft in Iceland, air cover had been extended further west than the extreme range from British airfields; Canadian Air Force planes covered the approaches to Newfoundland almost as far as Greenland.

This still left an 'air gap' in mid-Atlantic of 300 miles either side of the MOMP at 35°W, the precise area in which Dönitz was now concentrating his groups. There were two solutions to this problem: either to provide each convoy with its own air cover by converting merchantmen to auxiliary carriers, meanwhile building small escort-carriers for the longer term, and/or buying American Liberator aircraft, which alone had the range to close the air gap from shore bases. The Admiralty had already converted merchant-men to fly fighter aircraft for the defence of convoys against Luftwaffe attack in home waters and around Biscay to Gibraltar; in May the Atlantic Committee recognized the value of similar auxiliaries to provide anti-submarine patrols around convoys, and six escort-carriers were ordered from American yards. It was not a sufficiently urgent response, particularly as Admiralty and Coastal Command requests for long-range aircraft and especially very long-range, or VLR, US Liberators continued to come up against Bomber Command's obsessive, unscientific, indeed lunatic conviction that they could defeat Germany virtually on their own by saturation bombing of industrial cities – a euphemism for terrorizing German industrial workers and depriving them of homes. That they were allowed to prevail may have been due in part to intellectual weakness at the top of the Admiralty, but was mainly the result of Churchill's predilection for offence over defence. As he presided over both the War Cabinet and the Atlantic Committee, it needed only his word to change priorities. That word did not come until almost too late; it could be argued that if Hitler had not invaded Russia that June, it would indeed have come too late.

This is not hindsight: as noted, the lessons of the first war about the value of aircraft in the defence of merchant shipping had been forgotten, but the same lesson learnt through bitter experience during the first months of this second war was now being expressed by those officers closest to the anti-U-boat campaign; they were disregarded. It was a remarkable failure of the staff machine. Indeed, the joint planners predicted catastrophic destruction of merchant tonnage over the next six months, which if continued must lead to shortages of fuel and raw materials and eventually, as increasing numbers of U-boats concentrated on dwindling shipping resources, to actual hunger with all its political effects. This was also the warning that Hitler's deputy, Rudolf Hess, brought to Great Britain when he flew across with peace proposals that May. Against the scale and apparent imminence of this threat the Atlantic Committee's response was frivolously complaisant.

Behind the scenes, British scientists, forging ahead of their counterparts in Germany, had pioneered the tools necessary to render obsolete current designs of submarine and wolfpack tactics. The early radar sets have been mentioned; the potential of radar had since been revolutionized by the development of very short, centimetric wave-length sets providing far better definition at greater ranges. The British electrical industry had been unable to mass-produce the advanced components, which had been put out to US firms, but once again Bomber Command had prevailed in the struggle for resources: priority had been given to an airborne centimetric radar designed to allow bombers to find their targets through cloud and black-out. However, the prototype of a centimetric set for use at sea had been developed at the Admiralty Signal School, and in shipboard trials in April this had proved capable of detecting surfaced submarines beyond 4,000 yards range. The tool to counter the surfaced U-boat was to hand, but production difficulties were such that by the end of 1941 only fifty escorts had been provided with the new sets, christened Type 271.[42] Similarly a high-frequency direction-finder, HF/DF or, as it became known, Huff Duff, on which the shortest U-boat radio transmission left a trace on a screen from which the bearing of the transmitting boat could be ascertained, had been developed for use in escorts, but was not yet available in sufficient quantities to make an impact.

Of the advances that were to have the greatest effect that summer, the most important was the breaking of the U-boat Enigma ciphers following the capture of Lemp's *U110*; armed with knowledge of the position of every U-boat at sea, and where Dönitz was directing his patrol lines, Derby House succeeded in routing the vast majority of convoys around them. Allied with this was a simple triumph for scientific analysis: the discovery that slower independently routed ships were at much greater risk than faster ones led to an increase from 13 to 15 knots as the speed above which ships could be sailed independently.

The question of whether Dönitz, aided by Luftwaffe attacks on home waters shipping and ports, could have brought Great Britain to terms during 1941 can never be answered; the statistical projection of losses over the first six months, augmented by the increase in numbers of operational boats over the final months suggest that he could have done so; the authors of the history of British wartime intelligence suggest that 'it was only by the narrowest of margins that . . . the U-boat campaign failed to be decisive during 1941'.[43]

However, such a conclusion takes no account of the increasingly effective Allied defensive measures, nor of the remarkable concentration of minds which must have been forced by imminent defeat; it is difficult to imagine Bomber Command's arguments continuing to prevail had the War Cabinet and the Atlantic Committee faced the prospect of actual hunger. In the event, on 22 June Hitler launched his assault on Russia; the centre of German effort, particularly Luftwaffe effort, shifted decisively east. Merchant shipping losses to air attack fell; so did losses to U-boats because of evasive routing, the higher speed of ships sailing independently and Hitler's diversion of a dozen of the precious operational boats to the Baltic and Arctic to aid the eastern campaign. These found no targets. The tonnage lost from all causes in July and August fell to a third of that lost to U-boats alone in May and June.

The war also spread westwards that summer. From the beginning, the US President, Franklin D. Roosevelt, had recognized Great Britain as the front line in the defence of America against Hitler's 'regime of force and aggression'.[44] Since the American people as a whole had not and still did not perceive the threat and were not prepared for direct intervention, he had to move with caution to aid Great Britain. In March 1941 his Lease-Lend Bill which would turn US industry into the arsenal for Britain's fight had passed into law, and fifty mothballed First World War destroyers were made available to the Royal Navy in exchange for bases in Newfoundland,

Bermuda and the West Indies. In April, anxious that Britain might be forced out of the war by the U-boat attack on trade even before lease-lend could become effective, he took a bolder step. Doubting that Congress was ready to agree to the US Navy convoying trans-atlantic trade, he extended the boundaries of the so-called Pan-American Security Zone patrolled by the US Navy as far east towards Great Britain as possible. As described by his Secretary for War, Henry Stimson: 'We had the Atlas out and by drawing a line midway between the westernmost bulge of Africa and the easternmost bulge of Brazil, we found that the median line between the continents was at about longitude 25 . . .'[45]

The line was fixed at 26°W, over 1,000 miles east of the original limit of the Pan-American Security Zone in the North Atlantic. Roosevelt would not go so far as to sanction the escort of convoys within this area by units of the US Atlantic fleet; they were merely to patrol or follow the convoys and warn them of U-boats or enemy surface raiders. Even this complicated the U-boats' task and threatened incidents with US warships; Roosevelt undoubtedly hoped these would harden American public opinion. In May the US Navy established a base at Argentia on the south-east coast of Newfoundland and in July US Marines relieved the British garrison at Reykjavik, Iceland. In August the United States' com-mitment to the struggle by all means short of war was symbolized in a meeting between Roosevelt and Churchill at Argentia, and a joint declaration of intent called the Atlantic Charter.

Roosevelt was also looking west. Imperial Japan, like Nazi Germany a rigidly controlled nation schooled in an exaggerated military ethic and sense of national superiority, and similarly engaged on a career of conquest and expansion, had reached a critical stage. Further advance signified conflict with the United States, Great Britain and the Dutch East Indies. Not to advance meant the negation of her aims for a defensible Greater East Asian Co-Prosperity Sphere, a euphemism for an empire of helot peoples. Instead, she would face gradual decline to a third-class power dependent on the United States. The reasons were her lack of strategic raw materials, especially oil, and the United States' vast economic superiority, presently being projected into naval ascen-dancy. A so-called Two-Ocean Navy Act passed by Congress the previous summer, largely in response to Japanese expansion, threatened to reduce the Japanese Navy from the current 75 per cent to 50 per cent of US naval strength within two years, and to a mere 30 per cent by 1944.[46] Time was against Japan. To com-plete her conquests on the mainland and in the western Pacific, so putting herself in a strategic position to resist the United States, she needed to control the oil and raw materials of the Dutch East Indies and British Malaya; but to gain these she had to strike south before she had achieved security *vis-à-vis* the United States. And because the United States could not afford to allow her to gain her objectives, and in any case had bases and forces in the Philippines astride her route south, she had to risk war against America. Victory in such a war was scarcely conceivable, despite a decade spent planning and building for it; but to delay was to place herself at an ever-increasing disadvantage in relation to the US Navy. The problem was not capable of rational solution; as at other such times in history the chief actors went through their parts in a trance induced by fate.

During the mid-1930s US cryptanalysts had broken the Japanese Foreign Office rotor machine cipher, which they had christened Red, and had since broken a new machine cipher employing stepping switches in place of rotors, christened Purple, which the Japanese had introduced after 1939 – a feat at least equal to Bletchley Park's break into the German Enigma ciphers. The US-educated Japanese Foreign Minister, Yosuke Matsuoka, knew this but for his own reasons kept the knowledge to himself.[47] He was a man of infinite subtlety, but the suspicion must be that he supported that faction, based in the army, which pressed for a strike north against Russia rather than south against the Anglo-Americans and Dutch.

Thus it was that Roosevelt learned in mid-July 1941 that the Japanese intended occupying the bulge of Vichy French Indo-China facing the South China Sea, there to build bases which would threaten the main British Far Eastern naval base at Singapore and the Dutch Indies. He called a Cabinet meeting which decided on drastic sanctions, and when on 25 July, after negotiations with the Vichy French government, the Japanese army arrived in Saigon, Roosevelt froze all Japanese assets in the United States and announced an oil and trade embargo to take effect from the end of the month; Great Britain and the Dutch Indies followed suit. Without oil the Japanese war machine could not function. The Japanese embarked on a twin policy of simultaneously negotiating and preparing for war with the United States. Since they knew their negotiating conditions would not be acceptable there was little doubt about the result; nor had Roosevelt or his Cabinet and naval and military chiefs much doubt; the only questions were when and where the assault would come.

One of the most persistent and courageous Japanese opponents of war with the United States, noted earlier, was Admiral Isoroku Yamamoto, Commander-in-Chief of the Combined Fleet. He maintained his opposition throughout that summer, but argued that if war were chosen it was essential at the outset to knock out the Pacific fleet at Pearl Harbor; otherwise Japan had no chance at all. After a convincing table-top demonstration of his plan before a select group at the Naval Staff College in the second week in August, he began final preparations and training for the surprise strike. Besides aircraft from the carrier force, this involved long-range submarines both in a reconnaissance role and as transports for those two-man midget submarines which had been developed for the decisive fleet encounter; the midgets were to penetrate the US naval base and attack the capital ships at the same time as the carrier aircraft struck.

One of the U-boats searching the Atlantic that summer of 1941 for convoys that seldom materialized was OLt. Ottokar Paulssen's *U557*. Aboard her for his first war patrol was a young *Fähnrich*, or midshipman, Herbert Werner, who was to survive the war and write what is surely the classic, if on occasions factually muddled account of one man's U-boat battle in the Atlantic, *Die Eisernen Särge (Iron Coffins)*. The new Type VIIC boat had departed Kiel on 13 May; as she reached the open sea after passing through the Kiel Canal, Werner had to adapt to the rocking motion, ducking his head when he moved lest he bang it against pipes or ducts and handwheels, walking gently, riding with the boat. At night, wedged into a narrow upper bunk in the petty officers' mess after a four-hour bridge watch, he was kept awake by the rhythmic knocking of the diesels from aft, the hiss and splash of waves along the side plates nearby, and turbulent thoughts of sailing against the enemy.

They sank only one ship on this first voyage, a lone freighter encountered while rounding the Shetland Isles north of Scotland after the passage up the North Sea. Diverted to a patrol line to intercept British forces chasing the *Bismarck* after she had broken into the Atlantic and sunk HMS *Hood*, then to rescue survivors after the German battleship herself had been destroyed, *U557* arrived too late for either task. In early June she was directed back to the northern convoy lanes and patrolled in fog banks east of Newfoundland without sight of a ship. As her fuel ran low she was ordered to meet the German tanker *Belchen* off the southern point of Greenland. She made the rendezvous, replenished her tanks and tinned food in company with *U109* and *U93*, and was cruising away southwards when the boom of gunfire was heard over the horizon astern. Paulssen suspected that the tanker had been discovered by the enemy, and next morning they intercepted a radio signal from *U93* reporting the *Belchen* sunk by British warships.[48] Though they could not know it, the tanker was just one of the supply network destroyed as a result of the finds in Lemp's *U110*.

During the following weeks they were ordered to successive grid squares as part of patrol lines searching for convoys, but saw nothing. As noted, the possibility of a leak in security at U-boat Command had occurred to Dönitz in April when the British Submarine Tracking Room team had been able to produce little more than DF fixes and 'working hypotheses' as a basis for evasive routing. But at this stage in late June Dönitz was inclined to think the convoys were breaking through his lines under cover of the frequent fogs off the Newfoundland banks 'possibly assisted by some long-range location apparatus'.[49] The solution would have been to spread his boats further west off the Canadian and northern American ports of departure, but he was not permitted to operate west of 50°W because of the sensitive situation with the United States, who must on no account be given an excuse to swing from 'neutral' hostility to open war. He decided to leave the Newfoundland area and disperse the eighteen boats he had in the North Atlantic in a loose disposition south-east of Greenland.[50]

The same day, 20 June, KLt. Rolf Mützelburg in *U203* sighted the US battleship *Texas* in the area prescribed by the German Naval Staff as the 'blockade' zone, and manoeuvred to attack – in vain, as his periscope was sighted. Apprised of the episode, Dönitz signalled all boats that by order of the Führer any incidents with the United States were to be avoided; in the light of the US 'lease-lend' destroyers, he continued:

> Until further notice attacks on warships within and outside the blockade zone may only be made on cruisers, battleships and aircraft carriers and only if these are definitely recognised as enemy. Warships proceeding without lights at night are not to be assumed as necessarily enemy.[51]

On 22 June Hitler launched the German armies and Luftwaffe into the vast spaces of Russia. The news stunned and excited Werner and the crew of *U557*. Early the next day they were directed to a convoy less than 200 miles east of their position, which was steering east at 10 knots. They drove towards it on the surface at full speed throughout the day and that night, passing through its estimated position without a sight or sound, and continuing the search the next day. They had practically given up hope when, shortly after 21.30 there was a yell down the conning-tower hatch, 'Captain to the bridge! Shadows ahead!'[52]

Racing up the ladders wearing red-tinted glasses to shade his eyes from the lights inside the boat, so easing adaptation to the darkness falling outside, Paulssen soon realized they had run into the stern of the convoy, and ordered battle stations. Werner dashed up to the bridge. As his eyes adjusted to the dusk he made out the indistinct low shape of an escort to starboard. Paulssen manoeuvred away, leaving her on the quarter, and eased up astern of the columns of merchantmen, reducing to their speed and following, while the 1WO, OLt. Kern, who had fixed the binocular night-sights on the UZO-post, chose his targets and called the data down the speaking tube to the officer at the *Vorhaltrechner* in the conning tower. Below, the radio man enciphered a report to U-boat Command, detailing the convoy position, course and speed. For Werner, on the bridge watch, it was unforgettable: cruising at 10 knots within 300 yards of the nearest, unsuspecting enemies and choosing which was to die.

They had no means of knowing, but this was HX133 from Halifax, Nova Scotia, protected by a Royal Canadian Navy escort group of four corvettes led by the destroyer *Ottawa*. It was the first convoy to be located positively since the end of May, and Dönitz had ten U-boats in contact or closing. Their sighting reports were intercepted and deciphered by Bletchley Park, and additional escorts sailing from Iceland to meet an outward-bound convoy were re-directed to reinforce the *Ottawa*'s group.

U557 was detected while she trailed checking target data. Paulssen had just given Kern permission to fire when Werner saw the narrow shadow of a warship, then another beside it approaching from astern, pale foam at their bows. He held silent, not wishing to disturb Kern's aim, then, unable to contain himself, reported them. Paulssen turned and saw the two escorts heading straight for the boat. He ordered Kern to fire, an unmistakeable note of urgency in his voice.

Directly Kern had launched the torpedoes Paulssen ordered the tube doors shut and rang full ahead both engines three times for emergency speed. The noise of the diesels intensified; starshells began bursting overhead and parachute flares hung, lighting the scene. Werner, waiting for detonations which never came, saw besides the two escorts astern, another on the beam converging from behind a column of merchantmen. Caught between them Paulssen ordered an emergency dive. The bridge watch leaped for the hatch and tumbled down as the alarm bell shrilled through the boat and the hands scrambled to diving stations. Orders and responses followed in quick succession as if at a particularly urgent drill: 'Air vents open – one, two, three, five! Flood valves open! Diesel air valve closed! Diesel exhaust valves closed! Diesels shut down and disengaged . . .'

It seemed to Werner they had scarcely dipped below the surface when they were lifted and hurled off course by a thunderous explosion astern, followed by four more close eruptions as they descended out of control in the darkness. The emergency lamps came on and he saw the needle of the depth gauge swing from 125 rapidly round to 180 metres (590 feet) before the LI arrested the descent. Damage reports were coming into the control room: a leak in the diesel compartment, the starboard electric motor out of action, the rudder jammed. Above they could hear the thrashing, swishing noise of propellers as a destroyer came in for a second run, the hateful chirp of its asdic ringing through the hull. Paulssen ordered half ahead on the port motor to move the boat aside from the track but the next spread of three charges seemed to burst right above the conning tower, whipping the boat, setting up eerie moans in the hull, jerking the deck plates beneath their feet, shattering dial glasses, dislodging movable objects and sending them flying, pressing the boat deeper. Waiting in comparative silence after the detonations, they were heartened by two more distant thuds from the direction in which the convoy had been moving; their comrades had arrived.

The escorts left shortly after two further, less accurate attacks. This was due to the inexperience of the Canadian group, newly formed with many of the crew raw and not provided with the latest equipment supplied to Royal Naval ships. It was probably the destroyer *Ottawa* which had dropped the first two devastating patterns; she had located a U-boat by asdic and attacked, then ordered the corvettes with her to continue the hunt while she rejoined the convoy. Misreading the lamp signal, the corvettes had broken off too and followed her.[53] At all events *U557* was left alone, and after two hours surfaced in an empty ocean.

It was soon apparent that the damage inflicted was too serious for emergency repairs at sea: the starboard motor had been unseated, the shaft bent, and one of the after ballast tanks torn open. Paulssen reported to U-boat Command and set course for Biscay. The crew were in high spirits, their ordeal in the depths pushed aside by the prospect of leave. *U557* arrived in Lorient on 10 July flying a single victory pennant indicating 7,000 tons.

After what had been in effect a double patrol lasting eight weeks, the sights and smells of the land in bright summer sunshine were dreamlike in their beauty. Among the military and naval uniforms in the reception committee lining the quay were nurses from the hospital holding bunches of flowers; a military band played the boat alongside, comrades shouted greetings, the girls smiled. When the gangplank had been secured the acting flotilla chief, KK Heinz Fischer, stepped aboard, returning Paulssen's salute, shaking hands and congratulating him on promotion to *Kapitänleutnant*; afterwards Fischer turned to the white-faced, hollow-eyed and bearded men lined on the battered and rust-marked fore casing and shook each by the hand; the girls followed, distributing flowers.

The dreamlike impression was heightened when they stepped ashore, for the land itself seemed to dip and sway beneath their feet. They walked unsteadily to the former French Naval Préfecture, where the tables were set with white cloths and gleaming cutlery and glass for the home-coming feast; champagne and fresh lobster were followed by ample courses of such food as they had only dreamed of for two months. Paulssen made a speech recounting their experiences; a short, stocky man with fair hair, blue, twinkling eyes and a forthright manner, he seemed to Werner and no doubt all whom he had brought so calmly through *U557*'s first patrol the beau ideal of a U-boat CO. Afterwards their mail was brought to them. They devoured it in rapt silence, and then, provided with German beer, sang their release from confinement and ever-present tension.

It was a far cry from the usually quiet return of British submarines to base. The U-boat men were lauded and treated as the élite they were, the brief Brittany idylls of wine and girls and sun fitting rewards for the self-discipline and monotony, broken by stunning periods of mortal hazard, which they endured in the Atlantic.

U557 sailed again in early August 1941. After weeks of fruitless search, in the evening of the 27th, streamers of smoke from many funnels were sighted above the horizon. They were from OS4, only the fourth convoy to Freetown, Sierra Leone, to be provided with continuous escort. Finding the ships were heading towards him, Paulssen submerged to periscope depth. The throb of propellers, at first audible only to the sound man at the hydrophones, could soon be heard throughout the boat, and as it grew louder the high-pitched pings of an escort's asdic began to strike the plating, ringing through the hull before escaping and spreading out. Forced deep and losing bearing, Paulssen decided to wait for darkness and attack the convoy from astern.

He surfaced shortly before 23.00 into a black, moonless night and high seas. Shadows of ships loomed ahead and he entered the columns undetected, instructing Kern at the night-sight to fire one eel at each target he chose, taking the largest and furthest ship first, the nearest last. Training his sight at each in turn, Kern called out the angle, speed and range down the speaking tube, repeating the process again and again to check and refine the data, until at 23.40 Paulssen gave permission to fire and he launched the torpedoes in succession. Within seconds four from the bow and one from the single stern tube were speeding on their way, each turning to a different, pre-set gyro course to a collision point ahead of its own target ship.

The first explosion erupted on the starboard bow, the second, third and then a fourth from the port side, the detonations compressing the air and shaking the boat. Flames leapt high, illuminating the tense faces on the bridge, while starshell arched skywards from other parts of the convoy. Already the ships had begun an emergency turn. Pieces of debris hurled from the explosions in the nearest target rained down, raising splashes in the sea nearby, impelling those on the bridge to crouch behind the plating.

Three of the ships hit appeared to sink within minutes. *U557*, still undetected, followed in the wake of the shadows, while below, the radio operator enciphered a message to U-boat Command, and the torpedo party in the fore compartment sweated on the chain hoists to lift the greased reload eels, and heaved and guided them into the empty tubes. When all were loaded and Paulssen was closing for a second run a message was received from U-boat Command instructing him not to attack, but to shadow and transmit beacon signals. Cursing, he slowed and eased away to seek a safe distance, at which point he was detected by an escort. Ringing the telegraphs three times for extra full speed on both hammering diesels, Paulssen tried to escape on the surface, heading into the high seas, but was forced into an emergency dive as the escorts gained. Over the scrum of the bridge watch hurling themselves down the ladders, he bellowed to the LI below to take her down to 170 metres (558 feet), and with the waves closing around the tower ordered a hard turn on the helm to reverse the course.

As the first destroyer swished overhead *U557* was heading in the opposite direction below, diving steeply, and the first pattern of charges did little damage beyond knocking out the lighting. At 600 feet the LI caught and balanced her. Paulssen gave quiet orders for silent running, and with the auxiliary machinery shut down, the motors turning at low speed, the boat whispered through the depths, all hands focused on the sounds above, the hum of turbines and swish-swish-swishing propellers and the high ping of the asdic 'that penetrated the steel plates and struck every man's heart'.[54]

They survived two further depth-charge runs, protected, Werner concluded, by the high seas on the surface and their extreme depth. He was surely right. U-boat prisoners of war had given away by loose talk that their boats could go down to 200 metres (656 feet) but British naval intelligence had refused to believe it.[55]

British complacency was to be destroyed by a U-boat which fell into their hands that same day, 27 August. The new Type VIIC *U570* under KLt. Hans Rahmlow was only four days out of Trondheim on her first war patrol when she had the extraordinary ill-fortune to come up immediately under a Coastal Command Hudson; the aircraft had been in the periscope blind spot overhead when Rahmlow gave the order to surface. The pilot, Sqdn. Ldr. J.H. Thompson, dropped depth-charges, which exploded close either side and so shocked Rahmlow that he surrendered. Seeing white flags displayed from the bridge Thompson called for naval assistance and stayed with the U-boat. He was relieved after some hours by a Coastal Command Catalina which continued the vigil through the evening until naval vessels began to arrive shortly before midnight. Despite high seas Lt. H.B. Campbell managed to board the U-boat the following morning, after which she was towed, this time successfully, to Iceland.

Although the Enigma cipher machine and most keys and other secret papers had been thrown overboard, British technical teams made significant discoveries, among them the workings of her GE-7 electric torpedoes and the fact that previous U-boat survivors had not exaggerated when they spoke of going down over 600 feet. It was not for some time, however, that depth-charge settings were adjusted accordingly. *U570* eventually entered British service as HMS/M *Graph*; meanwhile the unfortunate Rahmlow had an unenviable time in a prisoner-of-war camp, where he was ostracized by his fellows.

Besides the deep-diving superiority of the Type VII U-boat, Werner's account of the convoy action on the day of *U570*'s surrender illustrates the all-round supremacy of the type over the British U and S classes of roughly comparable size and the much larger British Ts. The extraordinarily long range at which Wanklyn and other U-class COs had to fire because of the low speed of their boats, and thus the number of torpedoes they had to expend in 'spreads' to try and ensure a hit, and the time all British COs had to take between targets in order to calculate a new DA – unless they simply fired by eye on the turn – indicate how comprehensively British submarines were outclassed.

When *U557* returned to Lorient she flew only four victory pennants, all from the one convoy action; in total her victims aggregated 20,400 tons. She was, nonetheless, one of the most successful of the returning boats. Sinkings in August had dropped to a mere 80,000 tons, 14,000 tons less than July, which had seen the lowest figure since the torpedo crisis of the spring of 1940. Wolfgang Lüth, now an established ace with the Knight's Cross, commanding a Type IXA boat, *U43*, who had sailed from Lorient shortly before Paulssen, had a more typical cruise: he returned after six weeks south of Greenland without a single victory pennant, a unique experience for him. So well had the convoys been routed around the patrol lines that practically his only sightings had been US warships, which he was not allowed to touch.

A fortnight before his return OLt. Georg-Werner Fraatz, commanding *U652*, had been provoked into attacking one. In the early morning of 4 September, while patrolling south-west of Iceland, Fraatz had been forced to dive by a Coastal Command aircraft. Unbeknown to him the aircraft flew on towards an approaching US destroyer, *Greer, en route* for Reykjavik with mail, supplies and personnel for the US garrison in Iceland. Calling her by signal lamp, the aircraft informed her of the U-boat's presence 10 miles ahead. This put the destroyer's captain, Lt.-Cdr. Laurence Frost, in a dilemma. His orders were simply to 'trail and report', not to attack German submarines, and they did not provide for combined operations with British aircraft. However, he steered to the position indicated, slowed to improve reception for his sonar, the US version of asdic, and soon detected and held the U-boat in the beam as Fraatz manoeuvred at low speed below.

The aircraft stood by for over an hour and then, with fuel running low, signalled the *Greer* to ask if she was going to attack. Frost replied in the negative, whereupon the aircraft flew ahead of the destroyer and dropped four depth-charges before making off for base. The charges exploded some distance from *U652*, but Fraatz assumed they must have been dropped by the destroyer. He had no means of knowing she was American; he had viewed her through the periscope and identified her from bows-on as a four-funnelled US destroyer of the type transferred to the Royal Navy under 'Lease-Lend'. After three more hours of listening to the relentless ping of her sonar he decided to attack, but missed with two torpedoes, after which Frost, released from his passive role, dropped a pattern of eight charges, the first shots fired by the Americans in the war. They caused some minor damage, but failed to harm the boat seriously, and later in the afternoon Fraatz succeeded in creeping away. Frost broke off the attack in the early evening.[56]

This was precisely the type of incident Roosevelt had been angling for when he extended the Pan-American Security Zone and sent US forces to garrison Iceland, precisely the type of incident that was bound to occur. He made full use of it in a speech to the nation on 11 September, categorizing the U-boat's attack on the *Greer* as 'piracy, legally and morally', and, together with German attacks on US merchant ships, evidence of a 'Nazi design to abolish the freedom of the seas and to acquire absolute control and domination of the seas for themselves'. Describing the U-boats and German surface raiders as 'the rattlesnakes of the Atlantic ... a menace to the free pathways of the high seas ... a challenge to our sovereignty', he promised that US warships would no longer wait for Axis U-boats and raiders to strike first, but would hence-forth 'protect all merchant ships – not only American ships but ships of any flag' sailing in the Pan-American Security Zone; and he warned that German or Italian warships or submarines entering the zone – now extending two-thirds of the way across the Atlantic – did so at their own peril.[57]

This was tantamount to a declaration of war against the Axis powers in the Atlantic, particularly the U-boats, and both Dönitz and Raeder appealed to Hitler for a relaxation of the decree against attacking US warships. Hitler, still wishing to keep the United States formally out of the war until he had settled affairs in the east, insisted the decree remain in force; incidents with the United States were to be avoided at all costs. It was of course impossible. The US Atlantic Fleet had now begun to act in concert with the Royal Navy in the protection of multi-national convoys as far as Icelandic waters, and was receiving daily reports of the positions of U-boats in the Atlantic derived from the Admiralty Submarine Tracking Room plot.

The following month there were two serious incidents: on 17 October, the *Kearney*, one of a division of four US destroyers sent to reinforce a Canadian escort group fighting off a 'wolfpack' south-west of Iceland, was damaged by a torpedo from *U568*, under KLt. Joachim Preuss, and eleven sailors were killed, twenty-four injured, the first US casualties of the war. At the end of the month, the *Reuben James*, one of five US destroyers escorting a fast convoy from Halifax, was torpedoed by the ace KLt. Erich Topp in *U522*. The explosion detonated the forward magazine and the ship was blown apart; she was the first US warship lost during the war; all her officers and over 100 of her crew went down with her.

These affronts and the loss of American lives helped Roosevelt in his campaign to move public opinion towards direct intervention against Hitler, and in the short term to push a bill through Congress revising the US Neutrality Act in order to allow US merchantmen into the war zone, thus increasing the tonnage available to supply Great Britain with the food and manufactures she needed to continue the struggle. The revision, which also allowed the arming of US merchant ships, was finally passed on 13 November.

Meanwhile, the US industrialist Henry Kaiser, a man of protean conception, had initiated and organized a novel programme of rapid ship-building by prefabricating sections and welding them together on the ways. Termed 'Liberty ships' in line with Roosevelt's propaganda, they were very simple 10,500-ton freighters with a speed of 11 knots based on an English design of 1879 from Newcastle upon Tyne. The first was launched in September. By the end of 1941 thirty-five had been completed, but as the programme gathered pace in 1942 they were to be constructed at the rate of over sixty – thus more than 600,000 tons – a month, and even more rapidly the following year, rendering Dönitz's task of cutting transatlantic supplies virtually impossible.

Dönitz was not yet aware of this potential, nor could he have foreseen it: ships could not be produced at anything approaching this rate by conventional means. The figures of ships sunk had risen in September and October, chiefly as a result of the greater number of operational boats, and he was more concerned with direct orders from Hitler, passed through Raeder, diverting the greater part of his boats to unproductive areas, most to the Mediterranean where there were few merchantmen to sink since British trade to and from the Far East and supplies for the North African army went the long way around the Cape. Other boats were transferred on Hitler's direct orders to the equally unproductive waters off northern Norway. He complained that the diversions would mean the practical end of 'U-boat warfare' by mid-November, repeating his argument that success was only possible with large numbers of boats in the reconnaissance lines to find convoys; it was necessary to concentrate resources.[58] There is no doubt he was right.

His pleas were disregarded; by the end of November his remaining boats were ordered to the Mediterranean or the approaches to Gibraltar. With them, it is plain in retrospect, went any prospect of winning the race against time and US ship construction. Hitler's decrees, prompted chiefly by concern for his Axis partner in the Mediterranean, had removed any possibility of victory in the Atlantic battle. Dönitz expressed his extreme frustration in the names he gave his packs for their final forays between Iceland and

Greenland: *Schlagetot, Mordbrenner, Reisswolf* – 'Strike dead', 'Incendiary', 'Tearing wolf'.

He was equally frustrated by the continuing failure of the boats in his carefully formed patrol lines to sight convoys. Although reconnaissance lines sweeping the convoy routes should in theory have been more successful than a loose disposition of individual boats, the contrary had proved to be the case; as he recorded in his war diary on 19 November, 'individual boats find convoys, but with one exception convoys have never been found by a patrol line unless there was a previous report from an individual boat'. The reason, he went on, was not yet clear:

> Chance alone it cannot be – chance does not always fall on one side, and experience extends over almost ¾ of a year. A likely explanation would be that the English, from some source or other, obtain knowledge of our concentrated dispositions and avoid them, thereby running into boats proceeding singly.[59]

As for possible ways in which the enemy might obtain their information, he had already taken all possible steps to avoid disclosure of U-boat positions by spying or treason; the possibility of a break in the U-boat cipher had been discounted time after time by the expert cryptologists, and a recent extended investigation led by the signals expert Rear-Admiral Erhard Märtens had led to the same conclusion. Mathematically, the Enigma M-3 cipher was safe.[60] Moreover, even if the enemy had captured some papers, so it was argued, the safeguards built into the procedure for establishing the message key meant that besides the tables of rotor settings, which were changed each month, they would also need the indicators' list and bigram tables, which were also changed from time to time.[61] The idea that the enemy could have seized all three elements of the cipher system as well as the eight different rotors, and could continue to do so each month as the tables were changed was rejected. This response of the cryptologists and communications branch of the Naval Staff showed some lack of imagination; they failed to envisage the scale of effort the British would put into seizing the keys, or the speed and sophistication of the machines they would develop to crack new settings, or the possibility of access via more easily readable codes like 'Dockyard' duplicating some messages, or by the recognition of often repeated forms of signal. No doubt they also suffered from the experts' disease of infallibility which had afflicted the torpedo department earlier, and was to show up again in the US Navy's torpedo establishment. However, while the possibility of a breaking of the

Enigma ciphers continued to be vigorously denied in Berlin, neither Dönitz nor his own small signals staff were satisfied.[62] It was no doubt a result of their scepticism that development was started on a fourth, very thin rotor which could be fitted into existing machines in parallel with the three normal rotors.

Other possible ways in which the British might discover the dispositions of the patrol lines, Dönitz noted in his war diary, were by a combination of radio traffic and reports of sightings by high-flying aircraft, or by some location gear such as radar. In the absence of any clear information as to how it was done, he decided to ask for an experienced officer from *B-Dienst* to be posted to U-boat Command to help investigate the problem. In the mean-time, he kept all patrol lines on the move to make it more difficult for the enemy to avoid them.[63]

Post-war analysis has led the U-boat historian, Dr Jürgen Rohwer, to the conclusion that during the second half of 1941 – since Bletchley's breaking of the U-boat ciphers – as many as 300 merchant ships were saved by the evasive routing of convoys around Dönitz's patrol lines. Since this period appears to Rohwer to be the turning point when Dönitz lost his 'race with time', he has placed Ultra, as the decrypts were codenamed, at the head of the factors which decided the outcome of the Atlantic battle; the deduction is surely too simple and one-dimensional, since it leaves out of account any Anglo-American reactions to crisis.[64]

The diversion of U-boats to the Mediterranean was in response to increasing disruption of the Axis supply lines to North Africa, in particular by the Malta-based submarines. Bletchley Park had succeeded in breaking the Italian naval cipher towards the end of June; the first current intelligence from this source had been sent to Simpson on 23 June, detailing a convoy of four large liners sailing from Naples to Tripoli with Italian troops. On that occasion Simpson had sent Wanklyn out in *Upholder* at short notice to intercept, but he had failed to sight them. On 10 July, Bletchley Park had broken the July settings, and from that date traffic was read with little delay;[65] a priceless stream of Ultra information flowed to the Mediterranean commands and enabled submarines to be directed to targets and even spread on patrol lines across the track of convoys.

It was a Bletchley decrypt that led to the biggest single coup against the supply line. On 17 September Simpson learned that three of the great Italian liners Wanklyn had missed in June – and missed again after another Ultra decrypt in August – were about to sail from Taranto for Tripoli with German *Afrika Korps* troops for the Axis combined force, now under Rommel's supreme command and known as *Panzerarmee Afrika*. He called an immediate conference of five COs at Malta – Wanklyn of *Upholder*, Tomkinson of *Urge*, who on his last patrol had hit and damaged the 23,600-ton liner *Duilio*, Lt.-Cdr. E.A. Woodward of *Unbeaten*, Lt. Wraith of *Upright*, who had recently sunk an Italian destroyer, and Lt. Arthur Hezlet, a spare commander for *Ursula*.

After outlining the intelligence, without revealing its source, Simpson detailed dispositions to intercept the convoy in the dark of the following early morning off the coast of Libya: *Upright*, *Upholder* and *Unbeaten* to spread 10 miles apart 60 miles northeast of Khoms (Homs), 55 miles east of Tripoli, where experience had shown the Italian convoys made their landfall, *Ursula* and *Urge* closer inshore to the west to tackle whatever got through the first line in the early light. Owing to the slow speed of the Us they would have to leave within the hour to be in their billets by the time the convoy came through. However, Simpson concluded, if anyone felt too exhausted now was the time to say so. Tomkinson asked to be counted out, saying he had little faith in plans devised suddenly on signals which had just come in, and Simpson agreed at once; in his autobiography written after the war, Simpson said that he knew Tomkinson would have been the first to volunteer had he been feeling well and rested; 'obviously he was tired and on edge and had the guts to say so'.[66] The other four hurried to their boats while the crews were rounded up from their quarters and the bars of Sliema. One of *Upholder*'s leading seamen recalled much later that after they had left harbour Wanklyn told them they were 'on a tricky job – it's a big troop movement for Libya, and you know our army are having a rough time of it now. We've got to stop them at all costs,' whereupon they had looked at one another, thinking 'Oh God!'[67]

The boats reached their billets by midnight and trimmed down with only their conning towers above the surface, spray from rolling seas blowing across the bridges, drenching the watch. Three hours later the shapes of big ships were sighted from *Unbeaten*, steering to pass her to the north. Woodward tried to report to Wanklyn, senior officer of the group, using his asdic in its SST role as underwater signalling apparatus, but failed to make contact. He then attempted to get through by wireless. It took half an hour before he succeeded. Wanklyn had scarcely climbed to *Upholder*'s bridge in response before the shadows appeared, bulky against the light of a low moon with the squat shapes of destroyers ahead and on the wing. Wanklyn rang up full speed, 10½ knots, and with the gyro out of action, steered a converging course by magnetic compass. The speed of the convoy would prevent him gaining position ahead or even approaching close on the bow; he had no option but to take an opportunist long shot using the very rudimentary night-sighting apparatus.

The liners were formed in two columns; he waited until two of the silhouettes presented a continuous, overlapping target, then began firing a salvo spread by eye. The range was about 5,000 yards; the magnetic compass card was swinging, the boat's head yawing from side to side in the seas, and he had to catch the moment to fire, making allowance for the degree of swing during the time-lag before the torpedo left the tube. In utilizing the yawing movement of the boat, he altered the normal pattern of spread, aiming first at the bow of the leading ship, next at the stern of the rear ship before putting two torpedoes between them at mid-length of the double target.

When all were on their way the officer of the watch, Crawford, began clearing the bridge for diving. Wanklyn looked round and asked where they were all going. 'I thought we were about to dive, Sir,' he replied. Wanklyn hesitated for a moment, then agreed. Crawford had the impression he was keen to stay up and watch the results.[68]

As it turned out, the usual counter-attack did not develop. One of the torpedoes wrecked the propellers of the 19,400-ton liner *Oceania*, stopping her, another tore a hole in her sister *Neptunia*'s side, causing her to list and settle; the third liner, *Vulcania*, steamed away to the west at speed with two destroyers while the other destroyers began rescuing the troops from the sinking *Neptunia*. The *Upholder*'s tubes were reloaded and, as dawn broke, she closed the stationary *Oceania* from the east, up-sun, to finish her off. Unbeknown to Wanklyn, Woodward was also closing her in *Unbeaten*. The third submarine in the group, *Upright*, had steered south to gain bearing ahead of the convoy and was now, as a result of Wanklyn's successful shooting and the *Vulcania*'s alteration to a westerly course, far out of position.

As Wanklyn approached the *Oceania* he was forced deep by a screening destroyer and ran on under the surface beyond the liner before turning and rising to periscope depth. To the east Woodward in *Unbeaten* was making his final periscope observations of the liner before firing when she erupted with the explosions of two of Wanklyn's torpedoes. She went down inside eight minutes, the sound of her internal bulkheads collapsing before the inrush of the sea clearly audible to the submarine crews. Meanwhile in *Ursula*, positioned to the west, Hezlet had sighted the *Vulcania* at long range and fired a full salvo but, underestimating her speed, missed astern.

On his return after this brilliantly successful action, christened later within the flotilla as 'the Battle of Bottoms Up', Wanklyn appeared dejected. Asked why, he replied that it had only been luck as he had fired by eye. The Captain Submarines at Alexandria in his report preferred to call it 'devastating accuracy at 5,000 yards in poor light and with his ship yawing badly . . .'[69]

Even before this action, which cost the *Panzerarmee Afrika* 5,000, mostly German troops besides two irreplaceable liners, concern over the disruption and losses on the supply routes to North Africa had caused Hitler to offer his Italian ally twenty U-boats; it made little tactical sense since the greater part of the damage was being caused by Malta-based aircraft and submarines, and although submarines were successful from time to time in destroying their own kind they were more successful at sinking merchantmen. Raeder had managed to dissuade Hitler earlier, but as the Mediterranean situation deteriorated through the summer he had been forced to order the despatch of U-boats to prop up their ally.

The real problem with the continuing losses was that Italy could neither draw on much neutral shipping nor build fast enough to replace the tonnage destroyed. As in the Atlantic, the Mediterranean battle, and with it the outcome of the North African campaign, appeared to be turning on merchant tonnage. The Chief of the German Naval Staff in Italy pointed this out to Raeder on 9 September, warning of an imminent, very severe supply crisis. The most dangerous British force in the Mediterranean, he stated, were the submarines, especially those operating from Malta. Raeder's response was to submit that the Italians should be supplied with anti-submarine vessels, asdic – now operational in small craft and known as *Funk Mess Gerät* – and German technicians to instruct them in its use and maintenance, but it was not until November that Hitler gave his approval for this. In the meantime, the attrition continued; in September submarines sank eleven ships of over 60,000 tons, in October six of nearly 16,000 tons, while over the same two months aircraft sank nineteen ships of over 50,000 tons; together with minefields, the British thus accounted for 145,000 tons and destroyed practically 25 per cent by weight of all supplies for North Africa during the period.

Early in November the Malta striking forces were augmented

by a small squadron of two light cruisers and two destroyers, designated Force K. They sailed on 8 November on intelligence of an important convoy of seven supply ships bound for Tripoli, gained contact in the early hours of the 9th and, despite an Italian close escort of six destroyers covered by two heavy cruisers with four more destroyers, sank all the merchantmen and one destroyer for no loss. Sailing again later in the month they destroyed a convoy of two ships carrying aviation fuel to Benghazi for the Luftwaffe. Together with another fifteen supply ships sunk by submarine and aircraft, these devastating sorties brought the total sunk in November to over 75,000 tons. Although this was less than the September figure fewer ships had sailed, and it represented a loss of 30 per cent of those that had; as a result, only 30,000 tons of supplies were landed, chiefly in Tripoli, less than half the monthly requirement of the *Panzerarmee*.[70] Meanwhile, a British land offensive threatened Rommel's supply lines over the desert, and on 4 December he ordered a general retreat.

The apparent cause and effect in the Mediterranean supply battle was not as simple as it appears. In a study of Rommel's logistical difficulties Martin van Crefeld has demonstrated convincingly that the *Panzerarmee* had been in an untenable position from the time in April when, disregarding Hitler's orders and most professional advice, Rommel had made a lightning advance from Sirte across Cyrenaica to Sollum just over the Egyptian border. This advance had extended his land supply line from the major disembarkation port of Tripoli to 1,000 miles – 400 miles more than the German armies in the east had to go to reach Moscow. He had acquired the port of Benghazi, but not Tobruk, which he had bypassed and invested. However, Benghazi was vulnerable to attack from British aircraft based in Egypt, as a result of which the Italians had continued to direct most supply convoys to Tripoli.

Since there was no railway, fuel, provisions, ammunition and men had to be moved 1,000 miles to the front in 2-ton trucks, of which Rommel never had sufficient, and which probably consumed well over a third of all the fuel landed for his forces.[71] It was here on land that the bottlenecks built up. It is significant that his complaints about shortages had started in May; by June, during which month a record 125,000 tons of supplies had been landed in North Africa, he was 'living from hand to mouth'.[72]

Through the autumn, while convoy losses had been at their highest, an average of 72,000 tons of supplies had still been landed each month – 2,000 tons a month more than the *Panzerarmee*'s consumption. Supplies reaching North Africa only fell below requirements in November, due chiefly it seems to Italian shortages of fuel for convoy escorts. At the same time the British offensive had begun, bringing the inadequate land supply columns under sustained attack from aircraft and armoured cars, and finally forcing Rommel to acknowledge his impossible situation.[73]

This is not to suggest that the attrition at sea had failed; the alarm of the German Naval Staff in Italy is sufficient evidence of the serious threat posed by the boats of the 10th Flotilla especially; but it was the combination of all arms on land, sea and particularly in the air, combined with Rommel's greatly overstretched supply lines, that doomed his first thrust for Alexandria and the Suez canal.

The achievements of the 10th Flotilla had been accompanied by a series of losses. The chief danger at that time before the Italians had asdic was from the multitude of mines sown in the shallow approaches to the harbours and focal points of the convoy routes. One of the most dangerous barriers for the Malta boats lay in the Narrows between Sicily and Tunisia. To negotiate them they always followed exactly the same route which had been pioneered by Cayley in the *Utmost* after Simpson had asked for a volunteer in late July. This involved sailing from Malta by night north-westerly to arrive at Cape San Marco on the southern shore of Sicily 40 miles from the western end of the island at dawn, there obtaining an accurate 'fix' by shore bearings before diving to 150 feet beneath the mines and steering 300° for 55 miles, adjusting speed to surface at dusk 10 miles south-west of the island of Marittimo.[74]

In April and May, *Usk* and *Undaunted* had been lost, probably to mines, *Union* in July to depth-charges from a particularly successful Italian anti-submarine torpedo boat, *Circe*, and in August *P32* and *P33*, both U-class boats, failed to return, both probably, one certainly sunk by mines. These latter had been sent to patrol areas respectively north-east and west of Tripoli. Hezlet, relieving the Malta flotilla veteran Lt. A.F. Collett, in command of *Unique*, had taken up a billet between theirs on 18 August and signalled with asdic in its SST role to let them know his position. Only Lt. D.A.B. Abdy in *P32* replied. That afternoon Abdy sighted a convoy approaching the swept channel through the minefield across the harbour, and took his boat down to 60 feet, steering beneath the mines with the intention of reaching the channel ahead of the ships. As he began planing up to periscope depth at the other side of the minefield the boat was lifted and shaken by a thunderous detonation from forward which blew the watertight door to the fore ends shut and hurled all hands to the deck. The lighting cut out, and the boat began plunging downwards out of control.

She came to rest on the bottom at 210 feet where it soon became apparent that the forward watertight door was jammed, the forward compartment flooded and the torpedo party drowned if not killed by the blast. There was no response to tapping on the bulkhead. All attempts to shift the boat from the seabed proving fruitless, Abdy gave the order to abandon ship. Each man donned a Davis Submerged Escape Apparatus (DSEA) set, combining oxygen breathing apparatus with a buoyancy bag, and mustered in the narrow aisle between the two diesel engines. The escape hatch was above the forward end of this passage just aft of the watertight door into the control room.

There were twenty-five officers and men, including Abdy. Feeling that this was too many to escape from the single hatch at such a depth, he asked who would join him in an attempt from the conning-tower hatch. The coxswain and ERA volunteered, whereupon these three went into the control room, shutting the watertight door behind them and leaving the first lieutenant to organize the escape of the rest of the crew from the engine-room escape hatch.

The method was to lower a flexible twill tube or 'trunk' from the hatchway to form an extension of the hatch down to just above deck level, then to open the flood valves, allowing sea water into the compartment until the air inside was compressed to the same pressure as the water outside, thus preventing further ingress; the bottom of the twill trunk was then under water. The first man would duck under, enter the trunk, climb the ladder to the hatch and open it, so allowing the sea in to fill the trunk. Afterwards the men would duck below the water one by one to enter the trunk and, with the aid of their inflated buoyancy bag, float up through the open hatch to the surface.

This was not possible in the conning tower since the hatch was not fitted with an escape trunk. After opening the vent to admit the sea to the control room the three men could only line up on the ladder, the ERA at the top just beneath the hatch, the coxswain next, Abdy at the bottom, to wait until the pressure had equalized. The ERA then released the two clips, opened the hatch and, as the sea poured in, disappeared upwards through the opening. The other two followed and rose successfully to the surface, where they found him dead. He may have hit his head on the crosspiece joining the two periscope standards; he may have succumbed to the effects of the pressurized nitrogen in his system expanding during his rapid ascent into lower water pressures; but how had Abdy and the coxswain escaped without also falling victim to 'the bends'? At all events, these two waited for the men from the engine-room party to appear. No one came up. After a while they realized they were the only survivors.

Much later, they were picked up by a boat sent out from Tripoli after the naval authorities had been alerted by a patrolling aircraft whose crew had flown over to investigate the 60-foot high column of water raised by the explosion. They had reported seeing two survivors and two corpses, suggesting that at least one of the engine-room party had come to the surface. It is perhaps possible, however, that one of the corpses had emerged from the hole blown by the mine in the forward compartment. If so it may be that the men in the engine room had been unable to open the escape hatch because it was bolted from the outside with so-called 'salvage clips'. These were designed to prevent the hatch lifting if compressed air were pumped into a submarine during a salvage operation; they were not designed to be secured when a boat went out to sea, but it seems that some COs, alarmed by accounts of hatches jumping under depth-charge attack, did have them secured. Subsequently, P32's coxswain told a committee of enquiry that he had realized afterwards, when he had time to collect himself, why no one had escaped from the engine room: 'the salvage clips. They were only fitted before that patrol . . . and they must have slipped everyone's memory in the crisis of the moment'.[75] It is more likely that the men in the engine room, who would have had a slightly lengthier wait while rigging the twill trunk, simply succumbed to carbon-dioxide poisoning or, if they used their breathing apparatus, oxygen poisoning. The submarine had been submerged all morning and the effects of the carbon-dioxide build-up in the atmosphere would have been increased seven-fold by the increasing air pressure as the compartment was flooded.[76] Whatever the truth, Abdy and his coxswain were the only men to survive from thirteen U-class submarines lost in the Mediterranean during the war, and their escape was made from a hitherto unequalled depth.

Two days later, Hezlet in *Unique*, the only survivor of the three boats off Tripoli, was alerted to the approach of a convoy by the distant thud of depth-charges as the escorts warned off submarines in the usual manner; he manoeuvred into position off the entrance to the swept channel to such good effect that he was able to fire a full salvo at 600 yards at the leading transport in the port column. *Unique's* bows nearly broke surface after the discharge, and flooding to compensate took her straight down to 60 feet, but

Hezlet had the satisfaction of hearing three distinct detonations, soon followed by breaking-up noises as the ship sank; she was the 11,700-ton liner *Esperia*.

In this vital supply battle the 10th Flotilla was assisted by boats from the 1st Flotilla at Alexandria or the 8th at Gibraltar. Among these, especially at Gibraltar, were many Dutch boats, described by Alastair Mars who was in the Mediterranean at the time, as showing 'remarkable skill and tenacity'.[77] There were also some Free French and Greek boats, and others manned by Polish crews. It was in truth an allied effort. Unfortunately, the shore direction from the three bases, under the overall command of the C-in-C Mediterranean, Admiral Sir Andrew Cunningham, entirely lacked focus. For long periods the small U-class boats from Malta maintained the battle against the main Axis supply lines to North Africa on their own.

With the arrival of the first two batches of U-boats in the Mediterranean in early November the underwater war ignited afresh. On the 13th, KLt. Friedrich Guggenberger in *U81* made a submerged attack on the carrier *Ark Royal*, which was returning to Gibraltar after flying off aircraft to reinforce Malta, hitting her with one torpedo which proved mortal; and on the 25th, KLt. Hans-Dietrich von Tiesenhausen in *U331* penetrated the destroyer screen surrounding the 1st Battle Squadron, the *Queen Elizabeth*, *Barham* and *Valiant*, and put three torpedoes into the side of the *Barham*. The battleship rolled over almost on her beam ends, then blew up. When the dense cloud of yellowish-black smoke cleared she had disappeared; 861 of her complement were lost with her.

Meanwhile, a third wave of Type VII boats had been ordered from Biscay to pass through the Straits of Gibraltar, among them Paulssen's *U557*. Herbert Werner was not aboard her, having been transferred for further training to the U-boat Training Division at Gotenhafen (Gdingen). The posting had been a blow, the end of 'the wonderful camaraderie that had united men and officers', and in saying his goodbyes Werner had noticed traces of moisture in several eyes.[78] It was the last time he was ever to see the comrades with whom he had shared a fiery initiation as a warrior. He was not with them off the British base at Alexandria on the night of 14/15 December, when *U557* torpedoed and sank the cruiser *Galatea* which was already damaged, nor on the 16th when that archetypal U-boat CO, Paulssen, and his officers and men made their last dive together after being rammed and depth-charged by the Italian torpedo boat *Orione*, which mistook her for an enemy.

As in the Atlantic, so in the more difficult conditions of the

Mediterranean U-boat success pointed up the undistinguished record of Italian submarines as a whole. On 19 December, however, Italian Underwater Special Forces – *Motoscafi Sommergibile*, or MAS – based at La Spezia, went some way to redress the balance. The development by two engineer lieutenants, Tesei and Toschi, of a two-man human torpedo, *Silura a lente corsa*, or SLC – commonly called a 'pig' by the crews – and their proposals for using the weapons in mass attacks on the British Mediterranean fleet bases have already been discussed.[79] Lack of support had deprived them of the numbers of craft necessary to achieve this vision, but after the outbreak of war they had attempted small-scale penetrations with the very few craft at their disposal. After early disappointments against Alexandria and Gibraltar when the mother submarines were sunk or the 'pigs' went to the bottom out of control, Tesei had taken part in an assault on Grand Harbour, Valetta, towards the end of July 1941. He had the vital role of cutting the boom and anti-submarine net to allow a force of fast motor boats towing other craft packed with explosives to penetrate the harbour. Technical difficulties with one of the SLCs delayed the run in towards the net and, in order to achieve the breakthrough in time before dawn broke, Tesei decided to go in on his own craft and place a charge with an instantaneous fuse to destroy the boom. He did so at 04.45 on the morning of 26 July, sacrificing himself for his idea. However, the assault force had long been under surveillance by Malta radar and the boats were blown out of the water by gunfire from the forts as they approached, the remnants destroyed by Hurricane aircraft.

Two months later the weapon Tesei developed scored its first success. In the early hours of 20 September three SLCs were launched from the submarine *Scire* off Algeciras. The crews, clad in rubber suits with masks and breathing apparatus, riding astride their craft with just heads and upper bodies above the surface, steered east across the bay towards the rock fortress of Gibraltar. Two of the pilots dived under tankers at anchor in the bay to attach magnetic charges with delayed fuses; the third continued to the harbour mouth. Diving below the boom, he and his number two eased their mount and themselves through the large mesh of the anti-submarine net, afterwards surfacing inside and steering for a tanker tied up alongside the detached mole scarcely 200 yards away, diving as they approached and nosing along the hull plates. After attaching their 660-lb charge by the bilge keel, they left by the same route and, like the two other crews, scuttled their craft in the bay, then swam ashore at Algeciras and made their way to a safe house established before the operation. Two hours afterwards, at 08.45, Gibraltar was alerted by explosions in the three ships; all were so seriously damaged as to be out of service for some months.

This exploit was quite eclipsed by the next MAS operation directed against the main fleet base at Alexandria. Again three SLCs were carried to the launching point by the submarine *Scire*, which negotiated the protective minefield submerged and surfaced late on the evening of 18 December less than a mile from the approach to the harbour. The three pilots submerged their craft and set off, fortunate to reach the boom across the entrance at the same time as two British warships, which they followed in without having to negotiate or cut the anti-submarine netting. The pilots then steered for individual targets, the leader, Cdr. Count Luigi de la Penne, making for the battleship *Valiant*, the other two for the battleship *Queen Elizabeth* and a supply tanker lying close to her. They reached the ships unseen and attached their charges although de la Penne, whose number two had parted with the craft after trouble with his breathing apparatus, simply dropped his charge on the shallow bottom a few feet beneath the *Valiant*'s keel. He then scuttled his 'pig' and joined his crewman clinging to a buoy. Both were sighted, taken prisoner and interrogated, but gave nothing away.

Later in the morning when the incident was reported to Admiral Cunningham aboard the *Queen Elizabeth*, he gave instructions for the frogmen to be confined below the waterline in the *Valiant*. As the time approached for the fuses to detonate de la Penne sent a message to the captain to say his ship would blow up in five minutes. The two were brought on deck, and shortly afterwards the charges went off, first under the tanker, seriously damaging a destroyer alongside her as well, then beneath the two battleships, which settled to rest on the bottom, their upper decks above the surface. They were brought to an even keel and over the following weeks the shattering success de la Penne and his band had achieved was hidden from Axis intelligence by a deception of normality, the emission of smoke from the funnels and the performance of all the ordinary rituals of ships in commission. In fact, the British Mediterranean battlefleet had been removed from the board. Cunningham was left with only light cruisers, some destroyers and the submarines to hold the middle sea, apart from the independent Force H at Gibraltar comprising one small old carrier and an ancient battleship.

The 10th Flotilla at Malta, despite the low speed of the Us, played its part in the underwater violence erupting against surface warships in the Mediterranean during these last months of 1941. In November, Wanklyn in *Upholder* had sunk a destroyer, Cayley in *Utmost* had severely damaged the 7,800-ton Italian cruiser *Ducca d'Abruzzi*, and on 14 December Tomkinson in *Urge* had torpedoed the 35,000-ton Italian battleship *Vittorio Veneto* while she was making a zigzag course northwards through the Strait of Messina, heavily escorted by destroyers, torpedo boats and aircraft. The great ship was out of action for some months. Tomkinson, who already had a DSO and Bar, had at his own request been awarded two years' seniority in place of a second Bar.

Three days before his feat Wanklyn had been awarded the Victoria Cross, the highest British decoration for gallantry, for his earlier successes; this was only the seventh VC awarded to the navy in the war, the first to a submarine officer. Simpson recorded in his memoirs how Tomkinson, 'a gay personality with a gentle nature, who hated war and despised its rewards', had been pleased for Wanklyn, saying he had earned it and it suited him and made him so happy. 'But, sir,' he had added, 'if you want to know what medal would make me most happy, it's one they haven't struck yet – the End of the War medal.'[80]

The end was a long way off: on 7 December 1941 Admiral Yamamoto had realized his plan for a surprise attack on the US fleet base at Pearl Harbor; the conflict had widened to the Pacific and four days later, Hitler had declared war on the United States, bringing America into the Atlantic battle.

Simpson gathered all his boats back at base for Christmas that year, allowing his surviving veterans to come together for a brief space. It was a gathering whose like would not be seen again. These few had learned to use their small craft to such effect that they had tilted the balance of the war in North Africa and, as a direct consequence, in the Atlantic; for since the successes of the first wave of U-boats transferred to offset their depredations from Malta, the German Naval Staff had been persuaded to make the Mediterranean the centre of gravity for U-boat operations, depriving Dönitz of boats for his Atlantic tonnage war.[81] Considering the backwardness of the U class in performance and technology, particularly by comparison with the Type VII U-boat, it had been an extraordinary feat, a triumph of character and the offensive tradition of the Royal Navy over mere *matériel*. It had also been very dangerous and was about to become more so as the anti-submarine vessels, asdic and German technicians that Raeder was making available to the Italians came into service. Of the very young, consciously insouciant 'band of brothers' who celebrated Christmas together in Malta that year, only two were to live to see another.[82]

6

America at War

THE UNSURPASSED FEATS of US cryptanalysts against the Japanese diplomatic cipher allowed American service chiefs a unique insight into the Japanese course to war. Top-level military and naval ciphers, however, were not read so comprehensively, and the details of the impending Japanese attack were not clear; in particular the carrier air attack on Pearl Harbor in the Hawaiian islands was, despite several indications, not anticipated either by the US Navy Code and Signals Section in Washington – codenamed 'Negat' – or its main centres in the Pacific, 'Hypo' at Pearl Harbor itself and 'Cast' at Corregidor, a rock island in Manila Bay, the Philippines.

As noted, the Pearl Harbor strike was planned by Admiral Yamamoto, the C-in-C of the Combined Fleet, who had been and remained strongly opposed to war with the United States, but who insisted that if it was to be war, the US Pacific Fleet had to be knocked out at the outset. Thus while a 'Southern' expeditionary force sortied towards the end of November 1941 for the invasion of the Philippines, British Malaya and Borneo as staging posts for the conquest of the main British Far Eastern fleet base at Singapore and the oil-producing regions of the Dutch East Indies, the Combined Fleet's main carrier strike force – *Kido Butai* – with a support force headed by two battleships and two heavy cruisers, steered through the empty northern Pacific for the Hawaiian islands, preserving complete radio silence. This force was preceded by three of the new Type B1 2,000-ton scouting submarines, each carrying a seaplane in a hangar forward of the conning tower to warn of vessels in the path of the fleet, and after the strike to attack any enemy forces which might emerge to engage the *Kido Butai*.

Meanwhile, an advance force of fleet submarines had sailed to take up station in Hawaiian waters. Submarines were, as mentioned, accorded an important place in the overall Japanese strategy in the Pacific. Apart from their scouting role, they were expected to contribute to the attrition of enemy capital units before the 'decisive fleet battle' was accepted in the western Pacific. The Chief of Staff, Naval General Staff, Vice-Admiral Shigeru Fukutome, stated after the war that he expected the submarines in the Pearl Harbor striking force to inflict more damage over a longer period than the fleet aircraft attacks, which would necessarily be of short duration.[1] He and indeed the Japanese naval officer corps as a whole believed Japanese submarines to be the best in the world, and expected much from them.[2]

Thirty of the large and long-range I class were organized under the command of Vice-Admiral Mitsumi Shimizu as the Sixth (Submarine) Fleet in three squadrons, each commanded by a rear-admiral, and it was these boats which had departed to take up stations around Oahu – the island in which Pearl Harbor is situated – in the hours preceding the scheduled attack: to the north, the direction from which the carrier strike would come, the huge headquarters Type A1 *I9* with the 1st Submarine Squadron commander aboard, and three of the newest 2,000-ton B1 Type scouting boats were spread in separate patrol sectors; their task was to attack ships escaping from Pearl Harbor northwards, or any force moving out for a counter-attack on the *Kido Butai*. The other new boats of the 1st Squadron, five Type C1 attack boats of the same size and speed as the B1s, designated for this operation the Special Attack Group, took position to the south of the island off Pearl Harbor itself; each carried, clamped to the long after casing, one of the very speedy Type A two-man submarines designed for the decisive fleet battle. They would be launched before the air strike to penetrate the harbour and attack the capital ships with their two torpedoes each, so increasing the confusion as the fleet aircraft attacked. They had rendezvous positions for recovery by the mother submarine after the battle, but this was scarcely more than a formality to cover the fact that theirs was virtually a suicide mission. The somewhat smaller, slower and older boats of the 2nd and 3rd Squadrons of the Sixth Fleet completed a ring around the island, twenty-eight boats in all; the remaining two boats were on reconnaissance missions to the Aleutians in the north and the US islands of the South Pacific.

The glow of light from Pearl Harbor and the neon signs of Waikiki Beach were plainly visible across the water as the five boats of the Special Attack Group carrying the two-man submarines lay on the surface 8 miles off the entrance buoy on the night of 6 December 1941. The very young sub-lieutenants in command of the midgets had arranged their few possessions for forwarding home, written their final letters to their parents, prayed at the small shrine in the mother submarine and composed their minds for the mission ahead; there was no higher honour than to sacrifice one's life for one's country. At about midnight they reported to the submarine CO on the bridge, then climbed down and, with an equally young crew member, entered their tiny craft, closed off the communicating hatches, checked batteries and instruments, and gave the signal that they were ready to proceed. The holding clamps were released. The mother submarines dived, leaving the five midgets floating, turning for the entrance channel to the fleet base.

At 03.42 on the morning of the 7th lookouts aboard a US minesweeper on patrol 2 miles off the entrance buoy sighted a periscope; the young reserve officer in command called the Inshore Patrol destroyer USS *Ward* by signal light, and she began a search. Nothing was seen for two and a half hours, then a patrolling aircraft sighted the periscope again, or a different one in the wake of a barge towed by a repair ship making for the harbour; the midget evidently intended passing through the gate in the anti-submarine netting as it was opened for the ship. The aircraft dropped a smoke pot which enabled the *Ward* nearby to spot the craft, and she opened fire, the first shots of the Pacific war, hitting with her second salvo of 4-inch shells. The little submarine disappeared and the *Ward*, passing over the spot, dropped depth-charges. At 06.54 she reported the attack by radio, the first report of hostile activity to reach the base, and when twenty minutes later the decoded message was handed to the duty officer, another destroyer, USS *Monaghan*, was ordered to put out to assist her. The *Monaghan* was under way, still inside the harbour, when at 07.55 the first wave of Japanese carrier aircraft appeared and began dropping bombs over the moored lines of the Pacific Fleet battleships. Surprise was complete.

In the meantime, another of the midget submarines had passed through the gate in the nets which had been negligently left open after the entry of the minesweeper patrol almost three hours earlier. Having with utmost skill negotiated the long channel to the inner harbour, she was now lining up to attack a moored seaplane tender inside. The periscope was spotted from the tender, which opened fire and hoisted a flag signal. Alerted, the CO of the *Monaghan* turned towards the midget as she fired her first torpedo. Seeing the destroyer coming, the captain swung his craft round and launched his second torpedo at her. It missed, as the first had missed the tender. Moments later, the *Monaghan's* stem struck and crushed the tiny craft, running her over and leaving her sinking.

Another of the midgets had a faulty compass and ran aground on a reef outside the harbour. Her CO, Sub-Lt. Kazuo Sakamaki, managed to work her off, but choking chlorine fumes from cracked battery cells began to fill the craft, and he had no option but to beach her. In the attempt he grounded on another reef. He set the demolition charges, and with his crewman began to swim for land, which he alone reached. Next day he suffered the ignominy of becoming the first prisoner of war in the Pacific campaign; he refused to answer his interrogators, only demanding to be shot.

Neither of the other midgets fared any better; one was almost certainly, the other possibly sunk by destroyer depth-charge attacks outside the harbour. Despite the courage and commitment of the young crews this weapon, from which so much had been hoped, achieved nothing. Of the ten crew members, nine were later deified and had their names inscribed on a special memorial shrine to midget submariners erected at the Naval Academy at Etajima; only Sakamaki was omitted.[3]

The fleet submarines ringing Oahu were also a disappointment. They sank five merchant ships over the following days, and sighted and chased one US carrier group, but scored no hits; in return one submarine was lost to the carrier's aircraft. Afterwards the 1st Submarine Squadron was directed to the US west coast, where the boats sank another five merchantmen. The 2nd and 3rd Squadrons remained on patrol off or near Pearl Harbor without further success and on their way home individual boats bombarded American and British islands. Since the range-finding method was to plot their own position on the chart then measure the distance to the target these were useless exercises, serving only to assist that section of Combat Intelligence at Pearl Harbor which was keeping track of enemy vessels by monitoring radio transmissions.

The 4th and 5th Submarine Squadrons, composed of twelve older I-class fleet submarines built between the mid-1920s and the early 1930s, and two 900-ton RO-class boats, did not form part of the Sixth (Submarine) Fleet, but came under the Combined Fleet of Admiral Yamamoto. For the opening strikes they were assigned to the Southern Force in support of the invasion of Malaya and the Philippines; they were to reconnoitre the British fleet base at Singapore and the landing areas, and protect the invasion shipping. In the latter role they were spread on a patrol line to the east of the Malay peninsula about midway between Singapore and the initial landings on the Siam/Malay isthmus 500 miles north of the British base.

On news of the landings on 8 December, Admiral Sir Tom Phillips, commander of the British Battle Squadron, *Prince of Wales* and *Repulse*, the only capital units of the Royal Navy in the Far East, sailed from Singapore to strike at the transports and supply shipping. Early in the afternoon of 9 December his force reached the Japanese submarine patrol line and was sighted by

165. Upon her report that two capital ships were heading north, an air search was ordered, the 22nd Air Flotilla was held back from an intended raid on Singapore, and the main support group battle squadron was ordered to intercept.

Later that afternoon the British force was sighted by aircraft from the cruisers *Kinu*, flagship of the 4th Submarine Squadron, and *Kumano*; seeing the aircraft Phillips decided to break off his operation since his main defensive weapon, surprise, was lost. He altered course westerly as if making for the landings at Singora (now Songkhla), then after dark when his shadowers had left, turned south. Soon after midnight, however, he received a message reporting another Japanese landing at Kuantan, under 150 miles south-west of him. Calculating that he had deceived his enemies and would be able to achieve surprise, he altered course for the spot. Unfortunately at 02.20 he almost overran *158* of the 4th Submarine Squadron, which fired a salvo of five torpedoes at the speeding ships. All missed, but on the strength of her report that the battle squadron was now heading southerly the 22nd Air Flotilla was launched from Saigon before dawn. Not expecting to find the British force close in to the coast the aircraft missed it on the outward flight, but as they turned for home a reconnaissance plane on the last leg of its patrol sighted Phillips' ships; ten minutes later the first wave of high-level bombers attacked, followed by sixteen torpedo planes which swooped to within 100 feet of the waves to launch their weapons from 1,700 yards, hitting and crippling the *Prince of Wales*. Subjected to repeated mass attacks, both she and the *Repulse* succumbed within two hours, the first capital ships to be sunk by air attack while under way in the open sea.[4]

At Pearl Harbor six of the eight moored battleships of the US Pacific Fleet had been wrecked, sunk or seriously damaged by the strike aircraft of the *Kido Butai*; the cream of the Japanese submarine force had contributed nothing to this annihilation of American battlefleet power in the Pacific and had failed to damage the carrier *Enterprise* after sighting her and giving chase. Now land-based air forces had extinguished the only British capital ships in the theatre; submarines had provided the vital sighting reports, but the one boat with the opportunity to attack had missed and two squadrons disposed to protect the transports had played no part in the destruction of the main threat.

US submarines made an equally inauspicious start. There were forty-four fleet boats attached to the Pacific and Asiatic Fleets based on Pearl Harbor and Cavite Naval Station, Manila, respectively, together with eighteen of the medium S boats that had proved inadequate in pre-war exercises for long-range oceanic war; these latter were disposed between Manila, San Diego and Panama. As with British practice, the boats were directed by an area submarine commander under the supreme command of the fleet C-in-C; there was no overall submarine force operational commander. Thus the boats based on Pearl Harbor under the Commander Submarines Pacific Fleet (Comsubpac), Rear-Admiral Thomas Withers, acted independently of those based on Manila under the Commander Submarines Asiatic Fleet (Comsubaf), Captain John Wilkes.

Twelve of the very latest *Tambor*-class fleet boats of 1,500 tons surface displacement, 20 knots surface speed, with six bow and four stern torpedo tubes, together with six of the old prototype fleet boats of the V class and three fleet boats commissioned between 1936 and 1937, were based at Pearl Harbor. However, the main submarine strength of twenty-three fleet boats and six medium S boats was based at Manila in the Philippines; in a reverse image of Japanese plans and expectations, these boats, and US Army aircraft, were to provide the chief attack weapon to hold the Philippines against the anticipated invasion forces until the Pacific Fleet could fight its way westward from Pearl Harbor. As with Japanese submarines, their primary targets were to be enemy capital units, battleships, battlecruisers and aircraft-carriers; they had not been trained to attack slower, more lightly escorted merchant ships and transports; nor had they been trained to attack on the surface at night; they had no night-sights, and as yet no radar.

There were no British submarines in the area. Although the Royal Navy's main submarine strength had once been stationed and trained for use against the Japanese fleet, all the boats of the China submarine flotilla had been sent back to the Mediterranean on Italy's entry into the war. The British C-in-C China took seven Dutch submarines under his command in early December, and there were a further eight Dutch boats, either obsolescent or refitting, in Surabaya, Java. However, despite earlier American-British-Chinese-Dutch (ABCD) staff talks, no Allied command structure or system of co-operation had been worked out; there was not even a common signal book. The US C-in-C Asiatic Fleet, Admiral T.C. Hart, had to plan the defence of the Philippines with his own resources alone. His surface force of a few cruisers and destroyers could not face the Japanese fleet so he dispersed them southwards to preserve them from air attack. His submarine commander, Wilkes, having issued the hitherto secret Mark VI magnetic exploders for torpedoes to all fleet boats, divided the submarines three ways: seven were sent to patrol areas off the Japanese advanced bases from Formosa to Camranh Bay and Cochin in French Indo-China, there to scout and attack communication lines; twelve, including the Ss, were disposed around Luzon, the main island of the Philippines, against the anticipated invasion; and a main strike force of eight boats was held back in Cavite, together with two under repair, ready to be sent out once the main invasion force had been located. On 9 December, however, after a Japanese air attack on Clark Field airbase, north of Manila, had crippled US air power in the area and made it impossible to rely on aerial reconnaissance to detect the approaching forces, this reserve force was sent out to augment the patrols around Luzon.

After the assault on Pearl Harbor the order had gone out to 'execute unrestricted air and submarine warfare' against the Japanese, but the briefings the submarine COs received before they sailed for patrol enjoined extreme caution. Wilkes' operations officer directed them not to go out to try and win the Congressional Medal of Honor: 'The submarines are all we have left. Your crews are more valuable than anything else. Bring them back!'5 While understandable in the light of total American inferiority in the area, this reinforced the cautious attitudes induced in training, now heightened by uncertainties about the nature and efficiency of Japanese submarine detection devices.

The first minor Japanese invasion force sailed between the sparse patrols off the north coast of Luzon to land at Aparri on 10 December. Three days later Lt.-Cdr. Frederick Warder arrived in the fleet boat *Seawolf* and found a destroyer patrolling outside Aparri Bay pinging with a sonar echo-ranging device; it was an unpleasant surprise, suggesting that the Japanese were probably not behind the US Navy in submarine detection techniques. Whatever briefing Warder had received before sailing, he was not by nature cautious; he was a fighter, idolized by his crew, whose exploits were to earn him the nickname 'Fearless Freddie'. Next morning he crept into the bay submerged and, sighting a seaplane tender at anchor, approached and fired his full bow salvo of four torpedoes at just inside 2 miles range; for a motionless target this was close enough to ensure a hit. All missed. He swung round and fired his four stern tubes at 4,500 yards on his way out towards the entrance; this time he saw a small column of water rise up against the tender's side, but there was no accompanying explosion. Some months later, when Hypo at Pearl Harbor went back through earlier Japanese intercepted signals, it was learned that *Seawolf*'s magnetic torpedoes had run under the tender and one had hit the side, all without exploding.[6]

Lt.-Cdr. Tyrrell Jacobs of the *Sargo* off Camranh Bay, French Indo-China, had an equally frustrating experience that day. Sighting a lone 4,000-ton freighter, he fired a single torpedo fitted with a Mark VI magnetic exploder from 1,000 yards, only to hear and feel a thunderous detonation after 18 seconds, before the torpedo was halfway to the target. After discussions with his officers he concluded that possibly the Japanese had learned of the secret exploders and had fitted their ships with some device to detonate them at a safe distance. Jacobs had spent two years as a postgraduate student in ordnance engineering at the Naval Academy and had completed a course in torpedoes; he thus had the knowledge and confidence to have all the new exploders removed, de-activated and replaced with contact exploders. This did not end his problems. In his next attack ten days later on Christmas Eve, with a salvo of three torpedoes spread for two freighters in line ahead at 1,000 yards range, all missed, perhaps due to the ships turning to evade, for his periscope was sighted as he fired. He swung round and launched two of his stern torpedoes at the nearest ship from 1,800 yards. Both missed, as did his next two aimed some hours later at the rear ship of another two-ship line from 900 yards.

Jacobs felt a mixture of bewilderment and doubt about his own performance against such apparently simple targets at optimum ranges, together with anxiety about the effects on his crew should the failures continue. Suspecting the gyro angling might be at fault, on his next attack run, again at a column of two unescorted freighters, he made his approach for a zero gyro angle, took the greatest care in checking that his periscope data agreed with the TDC readings, and had his executive officer – equivalent to the first lieutenant in British submarines – take the periscope after him each time to make independent observations. When certain that all data tallied he fired two torpedoes at the leading ship from 1,200 yards and, as the rear ship steamed up to the firing line, another two from 1,000 yards, all with zero gyro angle. All missed. Evidently something was very wrong with the torpedoes. Concluding that they must be running under their set depth, he had the depth-steering mechanism adjusted on all remaining stock. On his next attack, however, on a lone, slow-moving tanker he again failed to hit. His frustration and strain may be imagined. He broke radio silence to inform Wilkes of the thirteen torpedoes he had expended in vain, and his belief that they must be running deeper than set.[7]

Meanwhile, on 21 December the main Japanese invasion force had made its approach to Luzon from the north-west and steamed into the Gulf of Lingayen, long recognized as the most likely landing point since it offered a flat and easy march southwards to Manila. The force had been detected from its multiple smoke columns way over the horizon by the *Stingray* patrolling to seaward of the Gulf, and the submarine's CO had turned towards the enemy; but seeing numerous escorts and hearing the ping of sonar – as much of an unwelcome shock to him as it had been to Warder the previous week – he had sheered off northerly, as he reported to base, to clear the echo-ranging. He was ordered to attack, but he made no opportunity that day, and next morning, finding a destroyer nearby, he went deep and evaded. By the time he came up to periscope depth again the sea was empty. The landings were under way inside the Gulf.

On receiving his report, Wilkes had ordered four fleet and two S boats from adjacent billets to enter the Gulf and attack. First to arrive in the early morning of 22 December was *S38* commanded by a former Naval Academy football star and boxer, Lt. Wreford Chapple. He made his way in without sighting any hostile craft, possibly because in the darkness, with no shore lights or visible navigational features, he passed over the reef barring the western side of the bay, thus bypassing Japanese patrols off the entrance channel to the east. Submerging before dawn, he made his way further in and, as the sun came up, sighted a column of four transports with two destroyers ahead on either bow and an inner screen of patrol boats stacked high with depth-charges, moving slowly towards the landing area. He started an attack run at dead slow to prevent his periscope leaving a visible trace as he raised it cautiously at intervals. Among the many modern devices the S boats lacked were a TDC or automatic gyro angling; the only fire-control calculator was the disc slide-rule known as the 'Is-Was', but in this instance it hardly mattered: the small convoy was moving at barely 5 knots. He ordered the torpedoes' depth set to 12 feet to travel beneath the shallow-draft screening boats and had all four bow tubes brought to the ready. The moment came to raise the periscope for the final observation before firing. As related by another submariner, who must have had it from Chapple: 'The palms of his hands were wet and the back of his throat was dry. Radiating from his stomach was a feeling of emptiness. It transmitted tangible weakness in his knees. He felt as though he was about to vomit.'[8]

His torpedo officer operating the 'Is-Was' confirmed the periscope angle, in Royal Naval terms, the DA, as 12°. Chapple found himself intensely annoyed by his calm tone, as if at target practice. This was real. He ordered, 'Up periscope!', hearing with surprise that his own voice sounded equally calm. With the chief of the boat, equivalent to the coxswain in the Royal Navy, he set the graduated periscope ring to 12°, then bent his knees and reached down to grip the handles as they rose from the well below, snapping them down and apart and pressing his forehead into the rubber cushion around the eyepiece, rising with it. He found the routine reassuring. The darkness of the reflected water grew a lighter and lighter green; suddenly there was sunlight and a wave was clearing from the lens to reveal the bows of the leading transport moving towards the graduated crosswire.

'Stand by one!'

His order was repeated by the telephone talker nearby in the crowded control room. As the funnel of the transport moved on to the crosswire Chapple gave the order, 'Fire one!' The chief of the boat pushed the firing key and started his stopwatch; moments afterwards they felt the familiar lurch and heard the grunt of compressed air as the torpedo left the tube. This was not an occasion to linger while the other transports moved up slowly into the firing line. Chapple ordered left rudder and fired two, three and four tubes on the swing at roughly 15-second intervals as the periscope crosswire passed in turn across the second, third and fourth transports, lined with soldiers ready to disembark. After the last one left the tube he had the boat taken down to 100 feet. The first torpedo's running time to reach the target passed without a sound as they descended, then the second and third and fourth. All had missed.

Disappointment was eclipsed by the sound man's report of high-speed screws to starboard; they became only too audible throughout the boat as a destroyer approached and rumbled overhead, her sonar pinging off the hull, but she did not detect them and dropped no charges. Distant explosions suggested the boats of the inner screen were dropping their charges indiscriminately around the convoy. Chapple reasoned that the transports must have been special shallow-draft vessels which his torpedoes had underrun. When the tubes had been reloaded he had the depth settings adjusted to 9 feet.

Creeping further up the Gulf towards the landing area and rising to periscope depth, he sighted an armada of vessels, and steered towards a large transport at anchor and encircled by another screen of patrol boats. Making a cautious approach on her beam to within 500 yards, he fired two torpedoes, watching as the wakes headed straight towards the target; after 30 seconds a column of white water erupted up her side, followed closely by the blast of the explosion and, as he ordered the boat down to 80 feet, a second booming detonation.

This time they heard two destroyers hunting them with sonar. Chapple steered slowly away, unable to go below 80 feet because of the shallowness of the water so far up the bay; he was fortunate not to be detected, especially so when the boat ran on to a rising mud incline and slid up it until the depth gauge was showing only 47 feet, when at last it was realized why all efforts to keep her trimmed down were failing. They stopped and lay there for the rest of the day with the top of the periscope shears only just below the surface, motors and all auxiliary machinery shut down, the men moving about the boat, if strictly necessary, in bare feet, exchanging information in whispers, listening to the destroyers searching, while from time to time small craft churned the water just above. Leaks in the stern glands and pneumatic control systems contributed to a build-up of pressure in the ever fouler atmosphere. It was as tight a situation as any submariner might have imagined in his worst moments.

After dark, when the destroyers' sonar could no longer be heard, Chapple reversed slowly off the mud and crept away to the west side of the bay where he felt it safe to surface. He was unable to complete recharging the batteries that night, so took the boat down at first light to spend another day on the bottom, coming up and finishing the charging after dark. At dawn on their third day inside the Gulf, he submerged and set off again for the main channel, soon sighting a column of six transports on their way out towards the entrance. He had barely begun an attack run when the boat was shaken by an explosion close by; guessing it was a bomb or bombs from an aircraft which had seen their shadow beneath the surface, he took the boat down to 90 feet and once again steered slowly away, rigged for silent running, as patrol boats hunted nearby dropping patterns of charges. He made the comparative safety of the unfrequented west side of the bay again and lay low.

Surfacing after dark, he had just given orders to ventilate the interior when an accumulation of hydrogen in the after battery exploded, injuring three men, one fatally. After this tragedy, which left the boat with only half her battery capacity, he received a radio message from Wilkes ordering him to return to base. He was not reluctant to comply, and started northwards on the surface to clear the reef barring the western bay, submerging as patrolling destroyers were sighted, only to be detected later by another patrol with sonar. He attempted to escape submerged over the reef, but scraped and grounded so many times that eventually, having lost his pursuers, he came up and ran for it on the surface. By then it was early afternoon. Fortune favoured him; in about two and a half hours at the boat's best speed, little over 12 knots, he crossed the reef undetected and was able to submerge and set course southwards for Manila.[9]

Of the other boats Wilkes had ordered into the Gulf, *S40* under Lt.-Cdr. Nicholas Lucker Jr. made a submerged approach and came upon a group of transports near the entrance. He fired a full salvo at one of them, but missed – or probably underran. More seriously, his exec. lost the trim, allowing the bows to break surface. One of the escorting destroyers headed for the boat as he went deep, and he was fortunate to escape with a severe shaking as a pattern of depth-charges detonated close above. On surfacing after dark it was found that most of the after casing had been blown away. Wilkes ordered the boat back to base.

None of the four fleet boats sent in succeeded in getting through the patrols across the entrance. Lt.-Cdr. Eugene McKinney in the *Salmon* made a spirited attempt to speed through on the surface by night, but was seen and chased. He fired two torpedoes at one destroyer from 2,500 yards, missing, and as he was being over-taken from right astern launched a third at his pursuer's bows straight down her track. He saw an explosion and believed he had sunk her; he was then forced to dive by another approaching destroyer which subjected him to repeated depth-charge attacks over several hours, preventing him from making any further pro-gress into the Gulf. Next day he was recalled to base. On his return he was credited with sinking a destroyer, but Japanese records do not bear this out. Possibly the explosion he saw was a premature detonation.[10]

The other three fleet boats approached submerged, two trying without success to torpedo destroyers they found patrolling out-side; all were picked up by sonar and depth-charged with varying degrees of accuracy, which deterred them from further attempts. With hindsight, in the light of Chapple's experiences with his smaller boat and the faults in the torpedoes, it was probably as well. Nonetheless, it seems from the record that, in common with the CO of the *Stingray*, who had evaded the sonar pulses of the invasion force, and hence the force itself on its way to the Gulf, the COs of the fleet boats failed to match the standards of resolve and aggression demanded by war and exemplified by the deter-mined actions of Chapple and Warder.

It is hardly surprising that this was so. Peacetime service requirements emphasizing discipline and drill did not necessarily select for leaders in the exacting conditions of real submarine warfare when lone COs could rationalize the need to withdraw, uninhibited by the presence of consorts or of officers who had their own periscope view of the situation. Not only did US submariners' training exaggerate caution; it also failed to instil the tenacity required simply to patrol for any length of time under war conditions. One CO returning from his failed attempt to penetrate the Gulf of Lingayen reported that his crew had been aboard under trying conditions since 8 December, 'and an opportunity to rest and relax in the sunshine is rapidly becoming imperative for the maintenance of good health, morale and efficiency'.[11] His was a fleet boat with air-conditioning, refrigerated food, separate messroom and washing facilities, and two-bunk cabins termed staterooms for officers and petty officers, all of which would have been the envy of the submariners of any other navy, indeed of their own S boat crews. On the other hand, no navy has ever been able to select in peace for the mix of qualities required in war, especially in the submarine service, where aggression needs to be tempered by calculation of the odds, cold-blooded courage by a steady brain for the mathematics of attack, and imagination to seize the opportunity and the determination to see it through by the judgement and moral courage to resist mere recklessness.

Only war can weed for these and the other qualities needed, and in all navies the aces were a select band. It appears, however, that US training and promotion methods, together with lack of previous submarine battle experience, and perhaps the American outlook on life, combined at the beginning to cause a higher proportion of unsatisfactory submarine COs than were found in the other major navies at the start of war; by the end of the first year no fewer than 40 out of 135 Pacific and Asiatic Fleet submarine COs had been relieved before time, chiefly for lack of aggression.[12] But the torpedo failures cannot be omitted from the equation: repeated misses were bound to lower morale, as they had among Dönitz's U-boat COs; conversely had those shots which missed been seen to hit and explode, as a high proportion should have done with efficient torpedoes, confidence and with it aggression must surely have increased.

In the event, the combination of torpedo failure and caution shading to extreme caution on the part of several COs deprived the Asiatic Fleet submarines of the successes that had been predicted. The main Japanese invasion force was scarcely touched; Chapple's 5,500-ton transport in the Gulf of Lingayen and an

865-ton freighter sunk by the *Seal* on its way to the Gulf were the only losses they suffered. Elsewhere four ships were sunk by Asiatic Fleet submarines during December, although many more were claimed; a few were claimed from pure sonar attack without periscope observation. The Pearl Harbor boats did no better in the defence of Wake Island from invasion or during patrols off Japan and the Japanese island bases. By the end of December the forty-four fleet and six S boats of the Pacific and Asiatic Fleets had between them sunk only ten enemy ships totalling 43,600 tons.[13]

The few Dutch submarines under British control made no more impression on the tide of the Japanese advance. Although before the war Singora had been considered the most likely landing area for an invasion of the Malay peninsula and the Royal Navy had as much advance warning of the impending strike as the Americans, no Dutch boats were positioned to intercept. When on 12 December Cdr. A.J. Bussemaker arrived off Patani, near Singora, in *O16* he attacked four transports and believed he had sunk them all; Japanese records reveal damage to one transport and an army auxiliary. On the same day Lt.-Cdr. H.C.J. Coumou of *KXIII* attacked a transport off the landing beach at Kota Baharu further south on the Malay peninsula, and the following day a 3,500-ton tanker; Japanese records suggest that only the tanker was damaged. Later in the month, as the Japanese landed in Sarawak, Cdr. van Well Groeneveld of *KXIV* attacked a convoy at the same time as naval aircraft, damaging three freighters and sinking one, and on 25 December Lt.-Cdr. L.J. Jarman of *KXVI* sank a destroyer. He was counter-attacked and sunk, the first Allied submarine to be destroyed by Japanese depth-charges, although the previous week the *O20* had been sunk by gunfire after depth-charges had forced her into an attempt to escape on the surface. Two other Dutch submarines were lost during December, *O16* on her return voyage to mines laid by the Japanese east of Singapore, and *KXVII* probably to the same minefield, although possibly to a torpedo from *I66* of the Combined Fleet's 5th Submarine Squadron, which claimed to have sunk an enemy submarine at this time.[14] The loss of four boats from the small Dutch force was a heavy price to pay for the minimal damage they caused.

The failure of Allied submarines to make any impact on the Japanese fleet or impede the progress of their invasion forces was due more to torpedo faults and the inexperience of COs than to

Japanese anti-submarine forces. The sonar patrols certainly deterred several US COs, and the Japanese equipment was at this early stage as good as that of the Americans or British, but they had failed to solve the mathematical problem of where to drop depth-charges or what depth to set them to explode, and appeared not even to realize that these were problems since they were seldom persistent in attack and assumed a 'kill' on the flimsiest of evidence.[15] Chapple's escape from shallow and restricted waters deep inside the Gulf of Lingayen is an example of poor Japanese techniques in ideal hunting conditions.

The Japanese had also, like the Royal Navy before the war, failed to build escorts to protect supply shipping on the long and, as their advance progressed, ever-lengthening lines of communication. Each year the Naval Staff officer responsible for shipping protection had submitted a plan for ocean escort and an estimate of the numbers of vessels needed. However, fleet warships for the grand plan had priority and the escorts were never built; at the outbreak of war old destroyers, minesweepers and other auxiliaries had to be converted for the purpose, and there were never enough of them.[16] As a consequence much shipping was sailed in small, unescorted groups; interestingly this was not simply to improve the chances of rescue from ships which might be sunk, but because the British had found it successful in the first war, and somewhere the fact had been noted.[17]

Besides lacking escorts, the Japanese had no overall shipping protection organization nor any standard communication plan or escort doctrine; convoys and their protection were a matter for the authorities responsible for the ships concerned, whether Navy, Army or Munitions Ministry, and area naval commands. Nor was there an overall shipping directorate to apportion tonnage. Although the Japanese people and war economy relied on imports, and the nation had gone to war ostensibly to secure the raw materials of South-East Asia, only those vessels actually controlled by the civilian shipping ministry carried imports. The liners and freighters controlled by the armed services returned empty from their invasion and supply missions.[18] This extraordinary neglect of merchant shipping was but another symptom of Japan's extreme martial culture.

On the Allied side it must be accounted a major failure of imagination that the US Naval Staff did not mount a systematic attempt to cut off Japan from her distant supplies of oil and other vital materials and foodstuffs at an early stage. The failure began before the outbreak of war when the U-boats' successes might have prompted some radical rethinking of the naval war plan against

Japan; for what was the war but a continuation of the peacetime embargo on oil and raw materials for Japan? The failure of the US Naval Staff, as of the Royal Naval and indeed the Imperial Japanese Naval Staffs, derived from the current orthodoxies of the 'decisive fleet battle' and Mahan's strictures on *guerre de course* as ineffective. In this sense officers in the thinking departments had perhaps read or unconsciously absorbed too much naval history. In another sense, as has been noted, the attack and defence of merchant shipping was simply not as stimulating to the tactical mind or the fighting spirit as the clash of great battlefleets, and was not a suitable specialization for ambitious officers, indeed it was beneath their notice. Japanese destroyer captains were contemptuous of convoy duty; their mission was torpedo and night attack in a fleet action. And so far as US submariners were concerned, merchant ships had been virtually off limits as targets since the Washington declaration against unrestricted submarine warfare.

The unrestricted air and submarine warfare declared after the strike on Pearl Harbor made it possible to review the role of the submarines. This could not have been expected in the immediate emergency; the fact that it never occurred, or only partially occurred after immense expenditure of blood, must lie ultimately to the account of the C-in-C, and from March 1942 Chief of Naval Operations US Fleet, Admiral Ernest King.

King was the archetype of a forcible American who had risen by ability, ruthless strength of character, arrogant self-confidence and ambition. He had been born to a Scottish immigrant father and an English immigrant mother. His father had worked his way up to foreman in a railway repair workshop at Loraine on the shore of Lake Erie, near Cleveland, Ohio. At school King proved highly intelligent, possessing a first-class memory and natural leadership qualities. His interest in the navy had been aroused by a magazine article and his father had encouraged him, since the Naval Academy offered higher education at State expense. After cramming for the competitive examination, he had won a place in 1897, graduating four years later, fourth in his year, but more important having achieved the top leadership position of Battalion Commander.

A good-looking and apparently supremely assured young officer, his promise was recognized early in his sea-going career despite bouts of wild drinking and womanizing and, on occasions when he felt his superiors to be wrong, insubordinate plain-speaking. That his contentiousness was more emotional than reasoned is suggested by the fact that he crossed and was relieved of one post by Captain William Sims, one of the leaders of reform in the early twentieth-century Navy, who was open to rational argument, indeed encouraged it. When America entered the First World War King was on the staff of the Vice-Admiral commanding the Battleship Force of the US Atlantic Fleet. As such he attended high-level conferences with British flag officers and Ministers and went to sea aboard Royal Naval ships. His biographer does not dwell on this formative period, but it seems that he acquired a strong Anglophobia at this time, induced perhaps by the US Fleet's junior role and what he probably saw as the condescension of British officers.

His early career coincided with a great expansion in the size and national importance of the US Navy, and a revolution in its *matériel*, as submarines, torpedoes and aircraft were developed to challenge gunned surface ships. Consciously aiming for the very top, King trained in the new branches: as a captain of 41 he entered the course at the Submarine School, New London, and although he never took the qualifying exams, he subsequently commanded a division of four S-class boats and afterwards the submarine base itself. Later, approaching his fiftieth birthday, he learned to fly, obtained his wings and, after a spell in command of the air base at Norfolk, Virginia, was appointed captain of the magnificent new carrier, *Lexington*. Earlier he had served as executive officer of the Naval Engineering Experimental Station. He combined these experiences at the forefront of the new navy with wide reading in military history and biography, and contributed articles to the thinking officers' journal, the *Naval Institute Proceedings*. His first essay, replete with stringent criticisms of naval conservatism, had won the annual prize; a later essay enjoined naval officers not to allow their minds to stagnate: 'Go to the Naval War College. Read. Think. Write.'[19]

His service record, high intelligence and an awesome reputation for sparing neither himself nor his subordinates in pursuit of the highest standards, appeared to fit him for the top post to which he had always aspired. He looked the part; as described by the US naval historian Samuel Eliot Morison, he was 'tall and spare and taut with piercing brown eyes, a powerful Roman nose and deeply cleft chin'; Morison added that 'he was more feared than loved'.[20] But it is as difficult in peace to pick an admiral to command fleets in war as it is to spot the future ace submariners. King, who as C-in-C of the three US fleets – Atlantic, Pacific and Asiatic – and Chief of Naval Operations combined, became the most powerful admiral in the world, was a poor choice.

Overlooked in his selection was his failure throughout his career to delegate or consult. His desire to control, manifest as a school-boy, had grown unchecked, no doubt because of his intelligence, prodigious memory and powerful personality.[21] Yet for all his wide reading in naval history – which in any case had practically nothing to say about such fundamental changes as had occurred in naval technology, and thus in strategy and tactics in his own lifetime – he was not a seeker after truth so much as an exponent of the truth as he knew it. In this respect he was no more rational than his Japanese opponents.

A discerning Englishman, Colonel Sir Ian Jacob, military secretary to Churchill's War Cabinet, found King a difficult man to assess, confiding to his diary after one meeting that the admiral seemed 'to wear a protective covering of horn' and gave the impression of being 'exceedingly narrow-minded, and to be always on the lookout for slights. He is secretive, and I should say treats his staff stiffly and at times tyrannically.'[22] Here Sir Ian had put his finger on King's weakness and perhaps the ultimate reason for flawed US naval policies: King's career as a senior officer had demonstrated that he was unable to use a staff except as an executive instrument for his own ideas, unable to resist abuse of subordinates, and practically impervious to argument. As Morison remarked, if anyone tried to argue with King beyond a certain point 'a characteristic bleak look came over his countenance as a signal that his mind was made up'.[23]

As C-in-C US Fleet (Cominch), King's first priorities in the Pacific were surely correct: to secure communications with the Hawaiian islands and with Australia. US supply shipping was organized in convoys routed to evade Japanese submarines from the start. It was but a step to reverse the viewpoint and realize the extreme vulnerability of Japanese strategic supplies. This was soon appreciated, but King never adapted the organization or the priorities of the submarines accordingly: individual forces remained attached to their own areas, serving the area commanders' needs.

The Asiatic fleet boats were withdrawn from Cavite at the end of December 1941 to the Dutch naval base at Surabaya, Java, and in January 1942 were spread off the staging posts for the next Japanese southward thrust to Borneo. They arrived too late to intercept the invasion forces and sank only one small freighter, while Japanese anti-submarine forces claimed their first victim, the fleet boat *Shark*; earlier in December a fleet boat under repair at Cavite had been lost in the first Japanese air attack on the base. Singapore fell on 15 February, whereupon the majority of surviving Dutch submarines from Surabaya, together with two British T-class boats which had been sent out from the Mediterranean, fell back on Trincomalee, Ceylon. The US fleet submarines did no better against the continuing Japanese advance to Java, Bali and Timor in February and were withdrawn to Exmouth Gulf and Fremantle, Western Australia. In place of Allied co-operation in the east, responsibilities were now divided: the Royal Navy was assigned the Indian Ocean, Malaya and Sumatra, the US Navy the whole of the Pacific including Australia and New Zealand.

Wilkes, who set up his Australian headquarters at Perth in March, was instructed by King to act against Japanese supply lines in the East Indies and South China Sea, and to send his S boats to Brisbane on the east coast of Australia, where another submarine base was established under Captain Ralph Christie, the officer who had overseen the development of the new magnetic exploder for torpedoes. King reinforced Christie with a division of S boats from the Atlantic, bringing his force up to eleven; they were to patrol off Darwin against an anticipated invasion of Australia. Meanwhile the Pearl Harbor boats under Withers continued to patrol off Japan and the main Japanese naval bases in the Caroline and Marshall Islands.

The unchanged division of the fleet submarines in two independent commands patrolling separate areas resulted in both forces covering the main enemy fleet bases in their theatre with only a small number of boats. Instead of a decision to mount a unified campaign with the maximum numbers available, probing for weak points in the enemy's supply lines – as Dönitz had done since the start of the European war over two years before – the American submarines were spread out in an indiscriminate and piecemeal way, usually in the most heavily patrolled areas, and were frequently directed to attack fleet units whose movements were detected by direction-finding or decrypts, for US cryptanalysts had begun to break into the main Japanese naval cipher. Moreover, the dividing line between the two commands passed through the main highway for supply traffic to Japan, the Luzon Strait between the northern Philippines and Formosa; as a result this prime hunting-ground distant from enemy patrols was a sensitive area for submarine operations, and Wilkes never employed his boats there for fear they might attack or be attacked by boats from the other command. The Asiatic boats were also diverted on supply or evacuation runs for General MacArthur's army, and at the end of March 1942 King assigned overall command of naval forces in the southwest Pacific to MacArthur, thus placing the Asiatic submarines under the general's ultimate control, with consequent further diversions. It is small wonder they achieved few sinkings.

King made similar mistakes with Nimitz's surface forces, dispersing the carriers, which were already inferior to the *Kido Butai*, for unnecessary minor raids. At the same time, on the eastern seaboard he presided over an American defeat of far greater significance than Pearl Harbor.

The Japanese strikes on the Anglo-American position in the Far East and the Pacific had been greeted with rapturous enthusiasm at Hitler's headquarters and in the high commands of the German armed services, not least the navy; even before Hitler had fulfilled his pledge to Japan to declare war on the United States, Raeder gained permission to release the U-boats from all restrictions against attacking US ships in 'the so-called Pan-American Security Zone'. For Dönitz the whole east coast of America was suddenly open to attack:

> [This is] an area in which the assembly of ships at the few points of departure for Atlantic convoys takes place in single-ship traffic. Here, therefore, is an opportunity to get at enemy trade in conditions which have been absent for a long time [elsewhere]. Further, there can scarcely be any question of practised patrols in the American coastal area, at least of patrols used to U-boats. The attempt must be made as quickly as possible to utilise these advantages, which will disappear in foreseeable time, and to 'beat the drum' [*einem Paukenschlag auszuholen*] along the American coast.[24]

This diary entry for 9 December 1941 is an interesting commentary on the difficulties the U-boats now faced from the strengthened and experienced British and Canadian escort groups in the North Atlantic. Two years earlier he had written, 'Aim must be to find convoys and concentrate the few available boats to destroy them';[25] now he was only anxious to strike at single ships before they too were organized into convoys.

It was 2,400 miles from the Brittany bases to the shipping assembly point off Halifax, Nova Scotia, over 3,000 miles to New York. As the German refuelling ships in the North Atlantic had all been sunk, only the larger Type IX U-boats with ranges up to 11,000 miles – or 13,500 miles at a slower cruising speed of 10 knots – would be able to complete the round voyage and operate for a reasonable time off the North American coast. Dönitz requested twelve of these for the operation. The Naval Staff in Berlin, either wedded to the Mediterranean as the decisive theatre, or perhaps jealous of the 'war of the *Kapitänleutnants*' as they sometimes slightingly called Dönitz's campaign, refused to release six boats patrolling to the west of Gibraltar.[26] This left only six Type IXs available, and since one could not be made ready in time, the final count was five.

Dönitz called the COs to his office as their boats were refitted beneath the shelter of the giant concrete bunkers at Lorient, and instructed them to prepare for a long cruise. He did not tell them where they were going because of his stringent, indeed paranoid security precautions; each would receive a sealed envelope from the flotilla commander on departure, to be opened when they reached 20°W. As they approached the operations area, further details would be signalled. They would act independently, not as a group, but to achieve surprise all would begin operations on the same day; the date would be signalled to them by radio. While *en route* they were not to give away their position by radio signals or by attacking ships unless they were positive the target was at least 10,000 tons. Finally he told them he had named the mission *Operation Paukenschlag*, literally a bang or roll on the kettledrums.[27]

The first boat, *U125*, commanded KLt. Ulrich Folkers, departed on 18 December. Every available space was crammed with tins of food, sacks or nets of fresh bread, vegetables and potatoes, with sausages and hams hung from the clusters of deckhead piping. The next boat, *U123* under KLt. Reinhard Hardegen, sailed on 23 December, sent off poignantly with a Christmas carol from the band on the quay. After dropping the escorts beyond the swept channel, the COs put their crews through emergency dives until they could get under the surface in 35 seconds.

On the evening of 24 December, Hardegen, no doubt Folkers too, submerged to celebrate Christmas. A tree had been erected in the control room and decorated with electric candles; other trees were distributed in the different crew compartments. Hardegen read St Luke's account of the birth of Christ to the hands gathered amongst the hanging sausages in the control room, after which they dispersed and the duty messmen came round with Christmas pancakes and stew, followed by fruit, cakes and glasses of wine punch, a surprising treat in a boat commanded by Hardegen, who never allowed his crew alcohol at sea. A traditional *Knecht*

Ruprecht – St Nicholas's servant – handed out presents provided by an infantry battalion which had adopted the boat, together with Christmas mail from home, then they sang familiar carols to the accompaniment of an accordion from the control room: '*In Bethlehem geboren ist uns ein Kinderlein . . .*'[28]

On Christmas Day the third *Paukenschlag* boat, KK Richard Zapp's *U66*, departed Lorient, and Hardegen's *U123*, reaching 10°W, made the statutory short signal to notify U-boat Command that she had passed safely across Biscay.

The signal was intercepted by the British 'Y' or listening service, and passed to Bletchley Park, from there to the Submarine Tracking Room in the underground Citadel in London, where a double-letter tab representing Hardegen's boat was pinned on the main plotting table at 10°W. The tab for Folker's boat was further west, having been advanced at a rate corresponding to a 10-knot cruising speed.

In succeeding days, first the tab for Zapp's *U66*, and later those for the two final *Paukenschlag* boats, *U109* under KLt. Heinrich 'Ajax' Bleichrodt and *U130* under KK Ernst Kals, joined the first two on the table, thereafter following them on a steady progression westward.

On 27 December, the day the last two boats departed Lorient, *U123* reached 20°W. Hardegen opened his safe and drew out the blue envelope containing his orders. He discovered that he was to operate off New York harbour, starting on a day to be designated, after which he was to pursue targets down the coast as far as Cape Hatteras, North Carolina. U-boat Command had been unable to obtain charts, pilot books or sailing directions for the area; all he was supplied with for navigation were a small-scale chart of the North American seaboard upon which different sea areas had been designated with boldly inked Roman numerals, and two tourist guidebooks of New York, one containing a folded map in a pocket, showing the city and outlying shoreline and the ship channel out to the Ambrose Light. Folkers, who was to operate off New Jersey, had found much the same in his envelope two days before. Zapp, opening his on the 29th, discovered he was to operate off Cape Hatteras, and at the end of the month Bleichrodt and Kals found themselves assigned respectively to Halifax, Nova Scotia, and the mouth of the Gulf of St Lawrence.

Two day later *B-Dienst* intercepted a message from a Greek steamer, the *Dimitrios Inglessis* east of Newfoundland, which had a damaged rudder and was requesting assistance. It was passed to U-boat Command, where it was noted that *U123* should have reached a position near the crippled ship. In the early hours of 2 January 1942, Dönitz had the information signalled to Hardegen and gave him permission to attack if he was within 150 miles. Hardegen set course for the position. Later that day the Naval Staff in Berlin released four new Type IX boats originally allotted to the Gibraltar area for use on the US coast and Dönitz sent them out that week with the sixth boat of the original group, to follow the five *Paukenschlag* boats as a second wave on the US coast.

Meanwhile, Dönitz's message to *U123* had been intercepted by the 'Y' service, and Bletchley's decrypt reached the Submarine Tracking Room in the Citadel that night, 2/3 January. Next morning Rodger Winn's assistant, Patrick Beesley, cabled Ottawa, alerting the Canadian Navy to *U123*'s presence. Since Dönitz was now disguising his navigational grid squares with an additional encipherment that Bletchley had not yet broken, Beesley also requested the exact position of the *Dimitrios Inglessis*. When this came it proved to be somewhat south of *U123*'s hypothetical position on the plotting table. Winn gave Beesley permission to shift the tab down to within a 150-mile radius of the Greek steamer's position.

By this time Hardegen was even further south. He had reached the steamer in the night, but finding two destroyers in attendance had withdrawn, an uncharacteristic decision from a CO who had proved himself several times in resolute attacks on convoys and was about to show himself tenacious and daring to the point of recklessness. He passed south-westerly off Nova Scotia and the New England coast, running into heavy storms on the 9th, 600 miles east of the Massachusetts coast.

Seas tumbled green and icy over the bridge watch as the boat rose towards the crests, the long, flat bow casing rearing high before plunging towards the next trough. Snow mixed with driving spume whited out the view, stinging the exposed cheeks of the lookouts, penetrating inside their oilskins and scarves and already soaking leathers.

That afternoon all five *Paukenschlag* boats received an 'Officers Only' signal from U-boat Command. It instructed each CO to occupy a different area, denoted by one of the Roman numerals superscribed on their charts, and ordered the three who were to operate off the United States coast to be sure of reaching their area by 13 January. It concluded that the five boats would form Group *Paukenschlag*. The decrypted signal was in Patrick Beesley's hands in the Submarine Tracking Room on the morning of the 10th. The plotting table was now showing a group of Type VII boats moving into position off Newfoundland, the first five Type IXs already in or approaching Canadian waters, and a further five Type IXs following across the Atlantic. Beesley handed Winn the *Paukenschlag* transcript. It was the first time Dönitz had used Roman numerals to designate patrol areas, which suggested they represented something different, perhaps coastal zones, Winn thought. And since three of the five, including Hardegen's *U123*, had been instructed to be on station by the 13th, three days hence, it was evident that any zones they were making for were considerably further south than their present positions off the Canadian or New England seaboard; Winn estimated three days' travel from Hardegen's presumed position could take him as far as Delaware Bay below New Jersey; he decided to use this as a 'working hypothesis' for advancing the tabs of the three leading *Paukenschlag* boats.

The following afternoon, *U123*'s lookouts sighted smoke on the starboard bow. Hardegen was called, and altered towards it, soon raising the distinctive masts and funnel of a Blue Funnel liner steering a north-easterly course towards them. With the aid of a merchant ship recognition volume, he identified her as a 10,000-tonner – she was in reality 9,067 tons – and resolved to sink her. He shadowed from the edge of visibility, closing at dusk on a converging course. The liner was steering a zigzag without lights and it took some time before the 1WO, OLt. Rudolf Hoffmann, was satisfied he knew her course. After Hardegen had given permission to fire, he called his final estimates down the speaking tube to the 2WO at the *Vorhaltrechner* in the conning tower. The response came back, '*Folgen!*', indicating that the data tallied with the computer readings and the aiming solution was transmitting to the selected torpedo, as confirmed by a second '*Folgen!*' from the torpedo petty officer in the forward compartment. '*Los!*' Hoffmann pulled the firing lever, and began counting the seconds of the estimated running time to the target.

She was the *Cyclops, en route* from the Panama Canal to Halifax to join a homeward convoy; she had loaded in the Far East and, in addition to her normal crew, was carrying 100 Chinese seamen to augment the pool of sailors for British ships. The torpedo struck on her starboard side between the two after holds, opening both to the sea, and as the radio operator sent a distress signal, the captain ordered 'Abandon ship!' The distress signal was picked up aboard *U123*, and Hardegen, who had directed the gun's crew to shoot away the liner's radio office, gave the order to cease fire and, steering across his victim's bows, had Hoffmann put a second torpedo into her port side at close range. Her boats had pulled away by this time but the captain and officers were still searching for anyone left aboard. They leaped into the sea as the ship began breaking up beneath them, and swam to a life-raft. The following day 60 of her total complement of 179 were rescued; the others had been killed in the explosions or had died from exposure.[29]

The *Cyclops'* distress signal, intercepted by the British 'Y' service, confirmed Winn's hypothesis precisely, and he composed a confident situation report detailing 'a heavy concentration of U-boats off the North American seaboard from New York to Cape Race [Newfoundland]'. One group was already in position off Cape Race and St John's, he went on; another group of five, 'apparently approaching the American coast between New York and Portland [Maine]', would 'reach their attacking positions by January 13th'; five others were advancing towards one or other of these groups, and a further five were also advancing westerly, in total twenty-one U-boats.[30]

The report was sent to US Navy headquarters – Main Navy, Washington – as had been the practice since US ships had first become engaged in convoying in the western Atlantic the previous summer; it was addressed to King as Cominch. Thence a copy went to the Combined Operations and Intelligence Center, where Rear-Admiral Frank Leighton presided over a situation chart similar to that in the Citadel in London. He amended his chart in line with the information and sent a message to the headquarters of Atlantic Command, Western Atlantic Escort Command and the Atlantic Coastal Frontier Commands warning of a large U-boat concentration off the Canadian and north-east US coasts, and the presence of 'three or four U-boats near 40°N 65°W'; this was 500 miles due east of the New Jersey coastline. He added that the *Cyclops* had been torpedoed in 41°51'N, 63°48'W[31] – 500 miles east of Cape Cod.

The area affected was the North Atlantic Coastal Frontier stretching from Maine on the Canadian border down to North Carolina, and commanded by Rear-Admiral Adolphus 'Dolly' Andrews from a headquarters in New York City. In common with every other major navy, the United States Navy had neglected to address the protection of merchant shipping in its building programme before the war and lacked sufficient escorts; those destroyers not required by the fleet or previously despatched to Great Britain under lease-lend, or more recently to the Pacific, had been assigned to Atlantic convoy duty. Andrews had none under his control to defend his length of coastline, only a motley collection of seven Coast Guard cutters, three patrol boats commissioned in 1919, four timber-hulled submarine chasers, two gunboats commissioned in 1905 and four converted yachts. None had the speed of a U-boat on the surface, and most were so mechanically unreliable as to be next to useless, especially in the present stormy conditions.[32] The aircraft available were no better adapted for anti-submarine work: although 100 were based at naval air stations along the coast, most were trainers or scouts capable only of short inshore patrols; for sustained reconnaissance and attack out to sea Andrews had to rely on Army Air Force bombers whose crews had not been trained for the work.

Without adequate means to protect shipping Andrews had taken the commonsense, unscientific and unhistorical view that it would be wrong to organize convoys; for once discovered they would provide multiple targets for a U-boat or boats, whereas ships sailing independently could only be sunk one at a time. This revealed ignorance of British experience in the first war and of the statistics of losses in the current Atlantic battle: both showed that convoys – especially if routed evasively – were found far less often than ships sailing independently and providing a continuing stream of targets spread out along the shipping lanes. In any case by 12 January, the date on which Andrews received the message warning him of three or four U-boats about to enter his domain, he had taken no steps to safeguard shipping in any of the ways suggested by British experience in two wars; with the warning in hand he failed to show even common prudence. Merchant ships continued to steam independently along the coast exactly as they had in peace, following their normal tracks around known landfall points along routes marked with flashing buoys and lighthouses, and showing steaming lights after dark. He took no action to alter this situation.

The delay caused Hardegen by his attack on the *Cyclops*, together with storms and head seas, prevented him reaching his station by the 13th. Folkers and Zapp were also held up by storms, and Kals in *U130* was the only CO to strike on the day Dönitz had decreed for the opening of *Paukenschlag*; he torpedoed two smallish freighters at the mouth of the Gulf of St Lawrence.

Late that night Hardegen sighted the loom of the light at Montauk Point at the extreme easterly tip of Long Island, and soon after midnight local time, thus on the 14th, his lookouts saw the lights of a ship approaching from fine on the bow. He swung away to gain distance off her track while Hoffmann set up the night-sight binoculars and began gathering data on her course and speed. It was soon apparent that she was a large tanker unaware of danger, since she was steering a straight course at 10 knots, and had made no attempt to black out or even dim her lights. Hoffmann hit her with one of two torpedoes fired from 800 yards, its detonation sending a column of flame high above her masthead. Her distress calls revealed her as the *Norness*, a 9,500-ton Norwegian tanker. While her crew abandoned her, Hardegen manoeuvred for a stern shot and Hoffmann hit her again. She remained afloat, and it took two more torpedoes, one of which missed or went deep, before she started settling by the stern, coming to rest eventually on the shallow bottom with her bows pointing up above the surface.

The bows and one of her lifeboats and a raft were spotted next morning by a naval patrol plane, and a destroyer of the Atlantic Convoy Escort Command exercising off Newport, Rhode Island, was ordered to the scene; she picked up the survivors early that afternoon. The *Norness*'s distress call, which had reported hitting a mine, had not been noted by any shore station, and this was the first the naval authorities knew of a U-boat operating close inshore. Still no action was taken. There were twenty-five Atlantic Convoy Escort Command destroyers spread between Maine, Boston, Newport, New York and Norfolk, Virginia, seven of them in New York to escort an Atlantic troop convoy gathering there, but neither Andrews nor the escort force commander appear to have considered deploying any of them to hunt down the U-boat operating off Long Island, and perhaps the other U-boats of which both admirals had been warned by Leighton at Combined Operations and Intelligence. Nor did Cominch – King – bang their heads together.

Hardegen spent the daylight hours of the 14th 100 feet down on the bottom off Long Island, alerted from time to time by the sound of thrashing screws as ships entered or cleared New York. He surfaced as darkness fell and steered in, as he thought for the Ambrose Light and the ship channel, but sheered off urgently as the depth fell and he saw lines of surf ahead, and beyond them sand dunes, a hotel and lights against a background of dark trees. Probing cautiously along the shoreline with nothing but his tourist guide map to help him, he gradually closed the lights of Rockaway Beach and Coney Island beyond, and on his port bow the low, dark spit of Sandy Hook. Ahead the massed lights of Brooklyn and Manhattan lit the sky. He had been to New York on a round-the-world cruise as a cadet, and could imagine the skyscrapers he could not see, the neon signs in Times Square, the shows on Broadway, and the bars and crowds. He found the sensation unbelievably moving; 'for the first time in this war a German soldier looked out upon the coast of the U.S.A.'[33]

He waited below the narrows off Sandy Hook, hoping a ship would come out. When none did he turned and was steering back towards the open ocean when a lookout reported a vessel following. She was silhouetted against the glow of light from the city beyond, another tanker, steering a steady easterly course. Hardegen altered round towards her, and at 750 yards range Hoffmann fired a single torpedo, hitting her below the bridge. Red and yellow flame shot skywards, criss-crossed with dark shapes of flying debris, lighting the rapt faces watching from the U-boat's bridge. As the blazing vessel slowed, Hardegen steered in and Hoffmann hit her with a second torpedo whose detonation broke her back. Fireballs arched into the sea as she sank stern first and, like the *Norness*, settled on the bottom with her bows above the surface pointing skywards. She was the 6,700-ton British tanker *Coimbra*; of her crew of thirty-six only six survived the explosions and subsequent inferno, all burned or wounded.[34]

Hardegen steered away southwards along the New Jersey shore-line as the Coast Guard, alerted by residents on Long Island, began a rescue operation. By this time, the early hours of 15 January, a further six destroyers had joined the seven assembled in New York to escort the troop convoy, but again none of the admirals variously responsible for the area and the escorts, nor their superiors appear to have thought of detaching any destroyers to hunt down the U-boat or boats which had so brazenly left two calling cards on their doorstep, nor even of postponing the sailing of the convoy.

Hardegen submerged at dawn and spent the daylight hours of the 15th on the bottom. When he surfaced at dusk a lookout spotted a dark speck high against the western sky and called out. 'Alaaarm!' Hardegen cried, and hit the alarm button. Alone on the bridge for moments as the lookouts leaped for the hatch and crashed down the ladders, he saw the aircraft turn towards the boat. He swung himself down the hatch, pulling the cover shut, and spun the locking wheel. In the control room the LI, conducting the urgent drill that was now second nature, ordered all spare hands to the bow. They scampered down the central aisle and through the small openings in the bulkheads in hunched posture. The deck began to tilt. The depth-gauge pointer moved around the dial and the water column rose up the Papenberg. It reached 10 metres (32 feet) when they heard the detonations of four bombs some way away to starboard.

After a while trimmed deep Hardegen returned to periscope depth. A careful search all round through the sky periscope revealed nothing, and he surfaced and set course southwards for a new patrol area off the New Jersey coast. Two nights later he sank a small freighter, the *San Jose* of 1,900 tons. He then steered south for Cape Hatteras as his orders directed.

This was the area assigned to Zapp in *U66*. He had just arrived after a stormy passage, and the following night, 75 miles to seaward of the Cape, he claimed his first victim, a 6,600-ton loaded tanker bound for New York. Hardegen saw the brilliant flash of the hits above the horizon as he headed southwards off the string of islands and shoals fringing the coast of North Carolina; moments later came the thump of two explosions. Of the tanker's crew of thirty-five, only thirteen survived the blazing fires which spread over the sea as she sank.

The following night, remaining close inshore in the shipping lane, whose flashing light buoys had still neither been removed nor extinguished, Hardegen sank a 4,500-ton freighter. Continuing towards Cape Hatteras, at midnight he saw the lights of a ship ahead on the same course and rang up full speed to overtake. He was still gaining bearing when Zapp, 70 miles to seaward, torpedoed an 8,000-ton Canadian National liner, the *Lady Hawkins*; she heeled and went down so rapidly that only three lifeboats could be launched; of these only one was found later. The 71 survivors crowded in it were all who were saved from 321 passengers and crew. A few minutes after she had disappeared Hardegen, having achieved a position ahead of his target at extraordinarily close range, inside 300 yards of her track, gave Hoffmann permission to fire. There was no difficulty with target data: the vessel, a 5,000-ton freighter steaming with dimmed lights, was silhouetted clearly against a glow of illuminations from beaches beyond. The detonation as the torpedoes hit was felt physically by the bridge watch, who were soon ducking below the plating as flying debris hurtled into the sea about the boat. The ship took an immediate list which prevented any boats being launched, and soon rolled over on her beam ends. Of her crew of forty-seven, only three were later rescued.

Remaining in the shipping lane just to the north of Cape Hatteras, Hardegen and the bridge watch were astonished to see, three hours before dawn, a cluster of ships steaming south towards them, their navigation and deck lights clearly distinguishable against the night and the glow of lights ashore. There were only two torpedoes left now, and Hardegen decided to slip into the traffic just astern of the leading ship, disable her with gunfire, then wheel round to attack the following ships with his last torpedoes, trusting that surprise would prevent any return fire.

The leading ship proved to be another tanker. He moved into her wake a quarter of a mile astern, increased speed to catch her and opened fire from inside 250 yards, hitting the bridge structure and starting fires aft while passing up the port side. Leaving her as she slowed, he swung northward to find that the other ships had switched off their lights and were fleeing. One was still coming south, however, and as she passed at 500 yards Hoffmann hit her with one of the remaining torpedoes. Her crew launched a lifeboat and pulled away as she settled. Hardegen turned and steered back to the tanker he had crippled, and whose distress call his radio man had picked up; she was the 8,200-ton *Malay* out of Philadelphia. Small fires still glowed through portholes in the after accommodation as he approached, but she was under way again and had turned to steer northwards. Hoffmann fired the last torpedo at a range of 400 metres (435 yards), hitting her aft of the mainmast. The spectacular fires they had come to anticipate from previous experience did not break out this time since she was in ballast; in the event her empty tanks kept her afloat and she managed to reach Hampton Roads under her own steam, demonstrating again how difficult it was to sink tankers in ballast.

With all his torpedoes spent, Hardegen set course for home by way of Bermuda. He arrived off the British island on the 22nd and cruised along the coast that night, noting towns, harbours and navigation lights and buoys as brightly lit as they had been on the US coast. Three days later in mid-Atlantic a small freighter was sighted; Hardegen submerged in her track and surfaced for gun action inside 500 yards. She was armed with a deck gun aft and a machine gun on the bridge, and put up a determined resistance before *U123*'s shells destroyed both positions and set the vessel ablaze, after which the surviving crew launched the lee lifeboat and abandoned ship. Closing, Hardegen learned she was the British Royal Mail steamer *Culebra*, 3,000 tons, out of Liverpool and steering for Bermuda after losing her convoy in a gale a fortnight earlier. Finding the boat full of water and the only bailer holed, Hardegen had buckets passed down to the men, as well as bread, sausages, tinned food and a knife with which to open the tins. He considered them worthy opponents, in his log paying tribute to the 'astonishing coolness' with which they had kept firing despite continued hits around them: 'they held out and did not leave their stations'.[35] The boat did not weather a gale which sprang up the following day, and consequently there were no survivors from the steamer's complement of forty-five.[36]

Hardegen sank one more ship by gunfire on the way home, a 9,000-ton Norwegian tanker, which also put up a stout resistance with machine guns. Afterwards he chased a nearby neutral and brought her back to save those in the water. This final victim raised the total sinkings for the cruise by his own reckoning to ten ships aggregating 66,000 tons. Since the tanker holed off Cape Hatteras had made port, the total was actually nine ships of 53,164 tons.[37] It was a prodigious tally nonetheless, the result not simply of boldness and resolution, but also of great professionalism, fully justifying the Knight's Cross conferred on him shortly after he had signalled his results to U-boat Command. Dönitz notified him of the award by radio.

While Hardegen was returning, the other *Paukenschlag* boats maintained the assault: Zapp off Cape Hatteras sank another four ships between 22 and 24 January; Kals in *U130*, taking advantage of Dönitz's dispensation to change stations, cruised south from the wintry seas off the St Lawrence and between the 21st and 27th sank five more ships off the US east coast between Nantucket and Hatteras. Bleichrodt in *U109*, after sinking a freighter off Nova Scotia, also came south and sank four more vessels including an 11,000-ton tanker between the US coast and Bermuda, while the first of the second wave of boats, *U106*, opened her account off Cape Charles, Virginia, on the final day of January. The only *Paukenschlag* CO to disappoint was Folkers of *U125*. Although he began operations in much the same area as Hardegen, off the New Jersey coast and the approaches to New York, he suffered a series of misses or failures and did not score until 27 January 70 miles off the coast of Virginia. This was his only success apart from two ships damaged, and on his return to Lorient towards the end of February he was received somewhat coldly; Dönitz entered a rare criticism in the war diary. The gap between his performance and that of Hardegen was indeed remarkable, pointing up once again the importance of the CO's quality in all submarine operations. It is interesting, however, that despite his poor start Folkers went on to success and eventually won the Knight's Cross himself.

Dönitz had every reason to be gratified by the results of his American probe: between them the five *Paukenschlag* boats had sunk by their own reckoning twenty-eight ships totalling almost 200,000 tons – by post-war reckoning, twenty-seven aggregating 165,267 tons[38] – without loss and with only superficial damage. In the United States, meanwhile, Rear-Admiral Andrews and Main

Navy, Washington, instead of reacting to popular alarm with positive measures, fell back on official secrecy and lies: naval spokesmen claimed that a number of U-boats operating off the east coast would 'never enjoy the return portion of their voyage', and people were requested to make secrecy their personal anti-submarine weapon; anyone who might have seen a U-boat captured or destroyed was enjoined to keep silent.[39]

U123 returned to Lorient on 7 February flying ten white victory pennants, the fore end of the conning tower decorated with two depictions of the Knight's Cross – one for her previous CO, Moehle, who had won his in the first *'glückliche Zeit'* – together with a large kettledrum and sticks and the figure '224,805', the aggregate tonnage claimed by both COs during the boat's career. A military band on the quay played the *Englandlied* as Hardegen, distinguished from the other unshaven officers on the bridge by his red beard and white cap cover, brought her slowly alongside. Dönitz, foremost amongst the large and enthusiastic welcoming crowd, stepped aboard directly the timber gangplank had been secured and, after returning Hardegen's salute and shaking him by the hand, hung the Knight's Cross around his neck. Much later, after the customary homecoming feast and speeches, he listened to Hardegen's report, writing afterwards in his war diary that the expectation of finding much single-ship traffic, unskilled ship-handling, and little sea and air anti-submarine protection had been fulfilled to such a degree that conditions could only be described as practically those of peacetime: 'The commander ... had such an abundance of opportunities for attack that he could not by any means utilise them all: there were at times up to ten ships in sight, sailing with lights burning on peacetime courses.'[40]

Already Dönitz's second wave of five Type IX boats was taking advantage of the easy pickings, and a third wave of another five Type IXs was on its way further south to the Dutch West Indies oil ports of Aruba and Curaçao, and Trinidad, focal point for shipping to and from South America; a further two were making for the coast of Florida. And such was the enthusiasm at U-boat Command and among COs themselves that he was allowing even Type VII boats to cruise southwards from Canadian waters and despatching others from Biscay ports direct to the US seaboard crammed with extra provisions and spare parts, and carrying additional fuel in auxiliary or fresh-water tanks. By cruising at slow speed on one engine these were able to extend their normal range and spend two or three weeks in the new hunting-grounds. One of the first, *U96* under KLt. Heinrich Lehmann Willenbrock, had departed St Nazaire at the end of January and would not return until 23 March, an outstanding feat of endurance in such cramped, confined and noisome conditions, and the sternest test of leadership; she flew five victory pennants aggregating over 25,000 tons.

Rodger Winn and with him Admiral Leighton at Combined Operations and Intelligence, Washington – whose efforts King despised and ignored – had no means of knowing the precise destination of all these boats, for on 1 February U-boat Command had switched to new cipher keys using the thin fourth rotor developed for the Enigma machines. Immediately the cryptographers at Bletchley Park were shut out and Winn was forced back to his guessing game of the 'working hypothesis', a situation which was to last until the end of the year. It made little or no difference: wherever U-boats struck along the US coast, the Gulf of Mexico or the Caribbean, there was no defence.

Despite the long lead-in time provided by the Pan-American Security Zone and the US Navy's convoy escort work in the western Atlantic, despite the shocks of January, no effective anti-submarine measures had been taken. Andrews still presided over the eastern seaboard, his area now extended down to Charlestown, South Carolina, and renamed the Eastern Sea Frontier, without an adequate force to defend it. The ships and aircraft he and the commanders of the Gulf (of Mexico), Caribbean and Panama Sea Frontiers needed were still commanded by the C-in-C Atlantic Fleet – Cinclant – whose flagship was frequently at sea and who in any case had no co-ordinated Operations and Intelligence such as Leighton might have provided from Washington had his department been brought into play. The copies of Rodger Winn's weekly U-boat situation reports that Leighton had circulated to all Atlantic commands had, it is clear, been ignored, a symptom of the contempt for intelligence officers shared by navy chiefs.

Above all, 'Dolly' Andrews, a rather conceited 'gun club' admiral who had served in several high political liaison posts, entirely lacked the perspective on anti-commerce war that might have come from naval historical analysis or recent, hard-won British experience. That experience had been freely and fully provided to the US Chief of Naval Intelligence the previous year, and the British First Sea Lord, Admiral Pound, had been in Washington in discussion with US Admirals from immediately after Hitler's declaration of war in early December 1941 until 17 January 1942, some days after the start of *Paukenschlag*.[41] He was a sick man, but it is hard to believe that he failed to mention the vital importance of convoy to defeat the U-boats which were bound to appear on the US coast – unless of course he thought this lesson self-evident from all the experience of the war. Yet no coastal convoys had been organized. Without convoys, when Andrews managed to obtain Atlantic escort destroyers on an emergency, short-term loan basis he could only use them to patrol the shipping lanes, the least effective method of finding, deterring, impeding or destroying U-boats, as proved time and again by British experience. Even more astonishing in retrospect is that no attempt had been made to black out the city, resort and beach lights against which coastal shipping stood up like a passing shadow show for U-boats to seaward; and lighthouses and buoys still flashed to guide the enemy in to the shipping lanes, although some had been dimmed.

Meanwhile Churchill, alarmed by the shipping carnage, but retaining a perception of anti-submarine warfare more appropriate to the cavalry officer he once was, had persuaded Roosevelt to try U-boat decays known as 'Q ships'. They had been used by the Royal Navy with a modicum of success in the First World War, and had since been given unwarranted publicity. King and the Chief of Naval Operations, still a separate office, had seized on this desperate plan, and two old 3,000-ton freighters and a trawler had been taken in hand for conversion and arming. Once again this was directly contrary to British experience in the present war. The Royal Navy had fitted out eight decoy ships in the early months and stationed them on the Atlantic shipping routes and western approaches to the Channel. Two had been sunk; none had even sighted a U-boat. An Inquiry in December 1940 had revealed their complete uselessness, and their further operation had been abandoned. That the US Navy resurrected the idea is a symptom of the lack of communication between King, who distrusted and disliked the Royal Navy, and Pound, who was not intellituallly suited to bridge the gap in culture or experience, although he was one of the few British officers King did trust.

As a result of the faults in command structure, the lack of understanding and imagination, and the rejection of British experience gained in the crucible of war, the massacre of merchant shipping and sailors along the eastern seaboard was to continue through the spring and early summer. Coastal residents, hearing their windows shaken by the detonation of torpedoes, would stare out at the bright funeral pyres of tankers; oil slicks would tar sand beaches; bodies of hideously charred or drowned seamen would be washed up among oiled seabirds and floating wrack at high tide.

On 19 February, the third wave of Type IXs struck in the

Caribbean, finding the same peacetime conditions; by the end of the month they had sunk thirty-three ships of an aggregate 107,000 tons, nearly half of them tankers, while the boats on the US coast had sunk thirty-one ships of almost 200,000 tons.[42] The Italian Atlantic Flotilla contributed with their highest ever tally in the waters around Bermuda and southwards to Brazil, sinking twenty-one ships of a total 125,534 tons between February and the beginning of April, for a very brief space equalling the tonnage per sea day recorded by the U-boats.[43] Lt.-Cdr. Emilio Olivieri of the *Calvi*, operating in the shipping lane around the bulge of Brazil, was responsible for five of this total.

US Navy spokesmen meanwhile discouraged rumour and press and radio reports of the losses lest they aid the enemy, spread alarm and dismay, and damage the war effort; already merchant sailors were leaving the sea and even jumping ship in home ports.

It has been argued that the Allies were fortunate that Dönitz's change to the four-rotor cipher coincided with this second U-boat 'happy time', or as it was termed, mostly it seems by Propaganda Kompanie people, *'die goldene Zeit'*. For had Dönitz still been concentrating his major effort against Atlantic convoys he would soon have realized that they were not able to evade his patrols as effectively as before the cipher change, and would surely have concluded that the British had been reading his earlier signals. As it was, this was hidden from him by the easy plunder of ships sailing independently by free-ranging, single U-boats. It may be that the disaster in US waters preserved the priceless secret of Ultra.[44]

Hardegen sailed on a second cruise to the US coast on 2 March. This time his orders were to steer directly for Norfolk at the mouth of Chesapeake Bay and operate from there down to his earlier and most abundant hunting-ground off Cape Hatteras. On passage he encountered two tankers sailing independently, the first American, the second British, and sent both to the bottom with torpedoes, aided in the British case by gunfire. The survivors of the US crew took to rafts, but none was ever found, and the British seamen perished to a man in a blazing sea of flames which *U123*'s men referred to ever after as the *Tankerfackel*, or tanker torch.

Two days later, on 26 March, still over 300 miles short of the coast of Virginia, Hardegen's lookouts sighted clouds of smoke over the horizon as if from a convoy. On closer approach the murk proved to be coming from a single, smallish freighter steering a zigzag course south-westerly. After dark Hardegen closed on the surface and fired a single torpedo from 650 yards which hit below the bridge. The vessel began losing way and sent out radio submarine distress signals, 'SSS', revealing herself as the *Carolyn*, while her boats were lowered and manned. Hardegen called the gun's crew to stations and approached her from astern, moving towards her starboard quarter. As he did so she began to gather way again, coming round to starboard as if to close him. He called for emergency full speed. Moments later sections of the freighter's bulwarks and the sides of a structure abaft her funnel fell away to reveal 4-inch and machine guns, which opened fire, and the Stars and Stripes was run up her mast. Hardegen swung away, the bridge watch crouching as bullets zipped and clanged against the casing and tower. A shell pierced the bridge plating and ripped open the thigh of a young *Fähnrich*, exploding and shattering the bone. He was lowered carefully down the hatch and Hardegen, confident by that time that he had outrun immediate danger, soon followed him down to apply a tourniquet. Afterwards he ordered diving stations and had the boat trimmed at periscope depth. All hands, including Hardegen, were boiling with fury at the 'U-boat trap', and there were calls to mete out to the crew of the *Carolyn* what they had intended for them.

From Hardegen's account in his log, he attacked submerged as the decoy stopped to pick up her lifeboat party, hitting her with another torpedo in the engine room, after which she listed and settled by the bows. He waited at periscope depth as her surviving crew took to the boats and her stern rose, exposing rudder and screw. An hour and twenty minutes later, while he was moving away from the scene, he saw her rent by internal explosions as if fires had reached her magazines. Calling down to find out how the wounded *Fähnrich* was faring, he was told he was dead. The same night he read the burial service as the lad's body, wrapped in canvas and weighted, was committed to the deep in the traditional manner.

There is no testimony from the USS *Atik*, alias SS *Carolyn*, and given the anger felt by Hardegen and all aboard *U123*, aggravated by the death of the young man, a question mark must hang over this official account, as over the British official account of Lemp's death while attempting to regain his command, *U110*, the previous year. The *Atik's* original SSS signals had been picked up in New York, but such was the secrecy surrounding her operation they had not been recognized for what they were until the following morning. Air and sea searches were then launched, but could find no sign of the ship or her boats, or any survivors. Her sister decoy had also picked up her signals and had steered immediately for the position given, 260 miles west of her own position north of

Bermuda, but by the time she reached the area a gale had blown up, rising over the next day, and she too found no traces. Her captain concluded that 'in view of the state of the wind and sea, all hands perished'.[45]

An alternative possibility was raised by a US admiral after the war, who wondered whether perhaps U123 had surfaced after torpedoing the 'U-boat trap' for the second time, and 'liquidated all survivors to assuage the curious German sense of justice'.[46] There is no evidence to support this speculation, merely questions raised by Hardegen's log account. As for the other decoy ships, neither they nor three further conversions were any more successful than their British antecedents.

Having accounted for three ships and three entire complements, Hardegen reached his patrol area off Cape Hatteras on 30 March, finding many more aircraft patrols than before, and patrol boats cruising the shipping lane. He missed with his first attack when the torpedo ran off course, and missed again a night later against a tanker, but brought her to by gunfire and set her alight, forcing the crew to abandon ship. He then had to dive for a patrol boat approaching at speed to ram; she dropped one depth-charge as he crept away.

A radio signal from U-boat Command had extended his patrol area southwards as far as Key West, and he now steered south, on 8 April torpedoing and sinking two loaded US tankers and a small freighter off the coast of Georgia. Continuing southwards, past the brightly lit beaches and amusement parks of northern Florida, he reached St Augustine and on 10 April torpedoed another laden tanker steering northwards. The tremendous detonation and blinding fire column drew crowds of spectators to the beach as he closed and shelled her from close range, igniting spilled oil on the sea as the hull settled and grounded on the shallow bottom. Aircraft from the naval air station at Jacksonville were soon overhead, guided by the bright flames, and they dropped flares to try and locate the U-boat. Twenty-nine of the tanker's crew were rescued by their light.

That afternoon the US destroyer *Dahlgren*, cruising northwards along the Florida coast, had been ordered to search for a U-boat in the St Augustine area. She arrived after the tanker had gone down, but while the air search continued. Hardegen was manoeuvring on the surface to attack a southbound steamer when he saw her suspiciously low shadow; soon afterwards U123 was illumined by an aircraft flare, and Hardegen was forced into an emergency dive by another aircraft; the bows ploughed into the sea bed at only

20 metres (66 feet). No bombs followed, but as Hardegen turned south-easterly to make for deeper water the sound of a destroyer's propellers became plainly audible throughout the boat, growing in volume and passing directly overhead. Moments afterwards, six depth-charges detonated thunderously close, convulsing the boat, throwing the hands about, and cutting out the motors and main lighting.

Hardegen waited on the shallow bottom listening as the destroyer turned and came back towards them. In his mind he had already given up the boat, imagining that even if this enemy did not destroy them, it must call up consorts and aircraft, and in such shallow water they could not escape. He ordered preparations for destroying the Enigma rotors and tables and for setting the scuttling charges, and had the word passed in whispers for all hands to don escape gear and make their way quietly to the control room. The swish-swish-swish of the propellers neared, and again passed overhead; the men tightened their grip on whatever part of the structure they were holding, bracing themselves for the ordeal. No explosions followed, nor on the next sweep, after which the propeller sounds grew fainter and faded.

The *Dahlgren* was not equipped with sonar. She had not been certain of her target; nor had she called up any patrol boats or aircraft. Hardegen was soon able to surface and have the damage repaired. He continued southwards and two nights later, on 12/13 April in sight of Cape Canaveral Light, launched his last torpedo at a northbound freighter, sinking her. He then called the gun's crew up and attacked what he took to be a northbound tanker, in fact a 4,500-ton phosphate carrier, holing her side until she too went down. In both cases the majority of the crew got away safely in boats.

Hardegen set course homewards in high spirits, reporting to U-boat Command in verse of the seven tankers, one 'U-boat trap' and two freighters for whom 'the hour had struck . . . sunk by the *Paukenschläger'.*[47] Three of the tankers were, however, refloated and repaired, and one had not been a tanker at all; his actual total was three tankers, three freighters and a Q ship totalling just under 38,000 tons sunk, and three tankers aggregating 24,000 tons sunk or damaged but saved. These successes were achieved despite a partial convoy system that Andrews had instituted from 1 April, whereby groups of ships moved by day under escort of miscellaneous patrol boats, Coast Guard cutters and converted yachts manned by volunteers, sheltering at night in protected anchorages.

Also on 1 April the Secretary of the Navy had claimed twenty-eight U-boats 'sunk or presumed sunk' in American waters. In reality it was not until the night of 14/15 April, two nights after Hardegen had set course homewards, that the first was accounted for. The US destroyer *Roper*, on patrol off the coast of North Carolina, detected the Type VII *U85* with a primitive early radar on the surface at under 1½ miles on the bow and charged, forcing her under and dropping eleven depth-charges ahead of the boiling foam of her dive; one or more of these wrecked her. Almost a month later *U352* was sunk, also off North Carolina, by depth-charges dropped from a Coast Guard cutter on passage, which had located her with hydrophones. These were the only losses before a true convoy system was introduced on the east coast in mid-May, five months after the *Paukenschlag* attack.

By then Dönitz, who had moved his headquarters back to Paris after a British commando raid on St Nazaire at the end of March had exposed the vulnerability of U-boat Command itself, had switched the focus of attack further south to the Caribbean, Gulf (of Mexico) and Panama Sea Frontiers. The first U-tankers laid down after it had become apparent that the U-boat arm could not rely on surface supply ships were now in commission; classed Type XIV and known as *Milchkuhe* – milch cows – they were little larger than Type IX's, but of shorter, fuller hull form and reduced engine size, allowing the carriage of 430 tons of fuel oil, together with supplies of tinned provisions and four torpedoes stowed externally. Stationed in the open Atlantic out of range of aircraft or between Bermuda and the West Indies, they allowed Type VIIs to refuel and operate in these distant waters without the need for the time-wasting stratagems employed earlier to bring them to the US coast. And since Bletchley Park had been blacked out by the fourth rotor, the Allies had no means of knowing their where-abouts and knocking them out.

One of the first Type VIIs to refuel from a *Milchkuh* was *U333*, commanded by KLt. Peter Cremer, who after the war wrote a graphic description of his experiences. He arrived on the coast of Florida on 4 May, thankful to find the shipping channel marked out for him with buoys as in peacetime. As darkness fell he sur-faced to an astonishing scene and allowed his men up to the bridge one at a time to share it while breathing in the scented air from the holiday paradise. After blacked-out Europe it seemed a dif-ferent world. The buoys winked; powerful rays from the Jupiter Inlet Lighthouse circled repeatedly seawards; beams from car head-lights followed one another along the coast roads past illumined frontages and neon signs of hotels whose names could be read through glasses, and further down the coast Miami and its suburbs cast an incandescent glow on the underside of the night clouds. 'Before this sea of light, against this footlight glare of a carefree new world, were passing the silhouettes of ships recognizable in every detail and sharp as outlines in a sales catalogue.'[48]

Two months earlier, on 4 March, a meeting of members of the US petroleum industry, concerned at the rapid depletion of tanker tonnage, had recommended suppression of shore lights. Five days afterwards King had made the same request to Andrews. Over a month later Andrews had ordered coastal lights and neon signs extinguished, as had the Governor of Florida after Hardegen's second pyrotechnic cruise off his state. Virtually nothing had changed though. As Cremer was to comment after the war, the holiday season had begun; too much money was at stake; tourism prevailed over the national strategic interest and the lives of merchant sailors. And despite Andrews' partial convoy system, stragglers and independents still steamed up and down the coast by night, advertising their approach by chattering on the radio, parading themselves against the bright shoreline like targets in a shooting gallery. Cremer and three other U-boat COs working off Florida independently at this time, KLts. Reinhard Suhren of *U564*, Robert Gysae of *U98* and 'Ajax' Bleichrodt on a second patrol in *U109*, picked them off one by one; none of them, Cremer commented, had imagined it would be so easy.[49]

Cremer eventually had to pay for his copybook practice, which included two tankers of 11,000 and over 13,000 tons respectively. As Hardegen had noted, many more patrol craft had been gathered, and on the night of 6 April, as Cremer was waiting at periscope depth to ambush another approaching steamer, he saw a Coast Guard cutter closing him at speed. The sound man had already reported the ping of its sonar and high-pitched beat of its propellers, so different from the deeper throb of the merchantman. Cremer ordered 20 metres (65 feet), but the boat had not reached that depth before the first well-placed charge detonated, forcing her stern down and crippling the hydroplanes. With the bows threatening to broach the surface the engineer flooded the compensating tank forward, which took her straight down to the sea bed at 30 metres (98 feet). Lying there motionless, they were subjected to repeated close depth-charges whose shock waves, transferred through the hull plates, hit the men like punches in the pit of the stomach; in the pauses between, while the propeller sounds swished away and then turned to close again, they heard the ping of the sonar against the hull, increasing as the cutter neared into 'a brief pattering noise like rain drops on a tin roof'.[50] This first vessel was soon joined in the attack by another patrol boat, then by a destroyer. Under the combined onslaught *U333*'s fuel tanks began to leak, vents became unseated, allowing sea water to weep in to the hull, gauge glasses shattered and instruments worked loose from the bulkheads. Cremer realized they had to find deeper water; eventually, by trimming to near neutral buoyancy and creeping over the bottom, he succeeded in slipping gradually down to 60 metres (196 feet).

After fifteen hours above them, the hunters left, but another destroyer arrived, assisted as Cremer learned after the war, by an aircraft which marked their position by dropping a smoke float on the oil slick they were trailing. The pounding continued. In their confined steel tube, with the atmosphere becoming ever more depleted, temperature and humidity rising inexorably, all sense of time was lost. By the following evening, breathing in long gasps, bathed in sweat, Cremer knew they could stay down no longer. At 22.00 he surfaced in the darkness; coming up with only the conning tower above the surface, he found the destroyer about a mile away. He turned slowly on the electric motors until he presented the smallest possible silhouette, and crept away. It was the narrowest of narrow escapes. With the damage the boat had sustained he could only set course homewards. Nonetheless, he managed to sink another independent steamer on the way, and arrived back at La Pallice towards the end of the month; a few days later he was awarded the Knight's Cross.

The successes of Cremer and his fellow COs off Florida could not conceal from Dönitz that opportunities on the US coast generally were fading; he had always known it would only be a matter of time before the defence was tightened. The reports he was now receiving from boats lying off the coast suggested a temporary cessation of traffic. This was no doubt due to Andrews' partial convoy system which, as in all historical examples, had the effect of creating great spaces of empty sea between sailings. 'Most of the sinkings this month', Dönitz noted in his war diary on 17 May, 'have been in the Caribbean.'[51] So it continued, for the convoy system only extended as far south as the Florida Keys. By the end of the month forty-eight ships sailing independently and aggregating over 200,000 tons had been sunk in the Caribbean, and a further twenty-six of over 150,000 tons in the Gulf of Mexico. Again, a large proportion were tankers.[52]

From the beginning of the American campaign Dönitz had felt

intense frustration at the Naval Staff in Berlin for diverting his boats
to less productive areas, first because of the strategic importance
accorded the Mediterranean, then because Hitler, fearing an Allied
invasion of Norway, had termed this the 'zone of destiny' to be
defended by all naval force; after which they had ordered twenty
U-boats to be deployed in Norwegian waters. These diversions had
cost Dönitz thousands of tons of easy targets off America; moreover, the Naval Staff constantly raised the argument that his boats
would be better employed for strategic aims, principally sinking
supply shipping bound for the British Isles and the North African
campaign. On 15 April he had been provoked into his clearest
statement of aim:

1) The shipping of the enemy powers is one great whole. It is therefore
in this connection immaterial where a ship is sunk – it must still in the
final analysis be replaced by a new ship . . .

2) . . . I am therefore of the opinion, a) that tonnage must be taken where
it can be destroyed most rationally – in regard to making the best use
of the boats – and 'most cheaply' – in regard to losses [of our
boats] – because it is incomparably more important that sinkings are
actually achieved than that they are reduced by making them in a
prescribed area . . .[53]

On 15 May he visited Hitler's East Prussian headquarters,
Wolfschanze, near Rastenburg, in company with Raeder, and
repeated this view to the Führer in his most assured and optimistic
manner. In support of the argument he claimed that from the start
of the American campaign until 10 May his boats off the eastern
seaboard had sunk 303 ships of a total 2,015,252 tons without loss.
And he continued:

'U-boat operations in American waters are also correct from the
viewpoint that the sinkings of the U-boat war are a race with
merchant ship construction. Her shipbuilding industry lies in the
eastern States. Shipbuilding and its allied industries depend essentially on oil fuel. The chief American oil-producing area is the Gulf
of Mexico. Consequently the greater part of American tanker
tonnage is employed in coastal traffic from the oil-producing areas
to the industrial areas. In the period mentioned 112 tankers totalling 927,000 tons have been knocked out, of which some two-
thirds was American supply tonnage. With every tanker knocked
out the Americans not only lose the ship for transporting oil, but
experience immediate damage to ship construction.'

From all this he concluded that these were especially valuable
sinkings. Why, it should be asked, was there no American Dönitz

in the US submarine arm or in the staff at Main Navy to put a similar case for interdicting Japanese tanker traffic? The answer probably lies in the American service's lack of recent war experience and the consequent rigidity of the command structure. Seniority alone counted.

Dönitz went on to state that on US ship construction forecasts it would be necessary to sink 700,000 tons of ships a month. 'But we are already sinking this 700,000 tons a month – by we I mean German, Italian and Japanese U-boats, aircraft, surface ships and mines.' Moreover, he went on, his experts believed the American production forecasts were unattainable and that the maximum they could build would be about 5 million tons in 1942 – in which case they had only to sink some 400,000–500,000 tons a month. Anything more would cut into the enemy's total tonnage.

The situation in the American theatre would change one day, he suggested; already there were signs that the Americans were making every endeavour to master their great losses. However, their forces were as yet inexperienced and not a serious threat; American fliers saw nothing, and their destroyers and patrol craft maintained too high a speed and were not tenacious enough in attacks. And he quoted figures of the tonnage sunk per U-boat per day at sea, rising from 209 in January to 412 in April, to back his intention to continue operations in American waters. When the prospects there fell off, he explained, he intended to resume operations against the North Atlantic convoys with the greater part of his force. He believed this would be easier than before because of the far larger number of boats now in service. 'Formerly the most difficult part of this battle was in locating [the convoys].'[54]

Greater numbers of boats had, of course, been his watchword from the beginning. Now he was receiving them. Monthly production figures had risen to over twenty. At the beginning of May, 292 U-boats had been in commission; by June the number would be well over 300, although of these only 128 would be available for operations, the remainder undergoing trials or serving for training.[55] It was not therefore the 300 operational boats he had believed necessary at the beginning of the war, but there can be no doubt from his submission to Hitler and from his war diary entries that he was now confident the U-boat arm could swing the war against the Western powers virtually on its own, leaving the army to conquer Eastern Europe; he was burning to prove it.

The worried members of the US petroleum industry would have agreed with his arguments about tanker losses, as indeed would the Allied governments and service chiefs. The following month the US General Marshall wrote to King to say that the losses to U-boats off the eastern seaboard now threatened the entire war effort, and he feared 'another month or so of this' would so cripple their means of transport they would be unable to bring US forces to bear against the enemy.[56] King replied that the situation was not hopeless: 'if all shipping can be brought under escort and air cover our losses will be reduced to an acceptable figure'. He added that escort, by which he meant convoy, was the only way of handling the U-boat menace. 'The so-called patrol and hunting operations have time and again proved futile.'[57]

Besides coming round to this conviction, King had been persuaded to set up a Submarine Tracking Room identical to that in London. Rodger Winn was the catalyst. The Director of Anti-Submarine Warfare and the Lords of Admiralty, horrified that ships which had been safely convoyed across the North Atlantic were falling easy prey to U-boats in American waters, had despatched Winn to Washington in a desperate effort to induce the US naval authorities to adopt the measures they had been pressing on them for so long. After days of discouraging interviews Winn finally gained admission to King's Chief of Staff, Rear-Admiral Richard Edwards, a submariner. Deploying his arguments skilfully as the barrister he was in civilian life, and not hesitating to point out that British as well as American ships were being sunk in great numbers off the American coast, Winn convinced Edwards of the importance of basing convoy routing and the distribution of escort forces on forecasts of U-boat movements. Edwards arranged for him to see King the same afternoon, when Winn repeated the performance. The great man, unaccustomed to such brutal directness from officers, let alone a British 'hostilities only' captain, was also won over.[58] Afterwards he had a retired US lieutenant-commander, Kenneth Knowles, sent to London to study Winn's methods. Returning to Washington, Knowles set up an Atlantic plot at Main Navy which exchanged all information with, and ran in parallel to Winn's Tracking Room, thus giving the commanders of both Allied powers an identical, shared intelligence picture, which was soon extended to the Royal Canadian Navy by means of an identical plot in Ottawa. Knowles was an outstanding success who went on to win King's complete confidence.[59]

There can be no question that the huge loss of merchant tonnage in US and Central American waters, commencing with *Paukenschlag* and continuing unabated until an interlocking convoy system was finally extended to the Caribbean and Gulf areas in July and early August, was a disaster of infinitely greater magnitude than the more dramatic loss of slow and ageing battle-ships from the Japanese strike on Pearl Harbor, indeed it has been termed 'America's worst ever defeat at sea'.[60] The loss of life briefly sketched in a few incidents in these pages has been esti-mated at not less than 5,000 sailors, the loss of ships at well over 400, exceeding 2 million aggregate tons, the loss of raw materials and the setback to US war production incalculable. It was the result of the US Navy's years of concentration on another theatre and an obsolete strategy – the Pacific and the decisive battlefleet action. The Japanese threat had blinded the thinking and opera-tional departments to the vulnerability of shipping in the western Atlantic. The destruction caused there by a few German U-boats in the first war had been forgotten. British experience in the current war had not been transferred. When the potential threat was realized in the *Paukenschlag* boats, the reaction had been arthritic. The excuses made at the time and since concerned lack of escort craft. Yet when Hardegen ran in to Sandy Hook there were seven Atlantic convoy escort destroyers in New York, and by the follow-ing day thirteen. The true causes lay in lack of imagination or forethought, the rigidities imposed by a peacetime system of pro-motion by seniority, confusion caused by civilians hastily enrolled in service departments, and arrant disregard of British warnings.

King's role in this will always be debated. Before assuming supreme command King had been C-in-C Atlantic Fleet, responsi-ble for the escort of shipping between North America and Iceland. He was familiar with the potential threat, the deficiencies in the numbers of escort vessels and the divided command structure. On being appointed US fleet commander, his immediate priorities had lain in the Pacific, and new destroyers of the type so desperately needed for escort in the western Atlantic had been despatched for escort duties in the Pacific. This was a natural response, but he appears to have given little thought to the vulnerability of the eastern seaboard. He placed a building programme for 250 destroyer escorts at the top of the priority list for manpower and materials, but established no centralized command structure or shipping defence system for the Atlantic, rejected British expe-rience, adopted the failed strategies of shipping lane patrols, search missions and Q–ships – admittedly Churchill's suggestion through Roosevelt – and left the separate commanders of escort forces and coastal frontiers to their own devices, or as he would have phrased it, encouraged them to exercise 'the initiative of the subordinate'. Amateur pilots and yachtsmen who volunteered to fill the service deficiencies in aircraft and patrol vessels had been allowed to create chaos at the expense of US taxpayers who met the bills for their fuel, supplies and repairs. The simplest measures of radio silence and coastal blackouts had not been taken. Justified criticism and calls for action had been buried with admonitions to silence and downright lies.

There must always be a time-lag before peacetime systems and habits adapt to the shock of real war. Yet the US Navy had had ample lead-in time, and an ample chance to study the U-boat problem and to co-operate in the countermeasures adopted by the Royal and Royal Canadian Navies. They had also had plenty of warning of the approach of the *Paukenschlag* boats. King was Cominch before the start of the débâcle, and from March Chief of Naval Operations as well. The buck stopped with him – or should have done so.[61]

The British faced an equally critical onslaught in the Mediterranean. The success of the Malta submarine, air and surface forces against the Axis supply ships and transports to North Africa had provoked Hitler into moving an air corps of modern, front-line aircraft from Russia to Sicily with orders to neutralize the island fortress. Since January 1942 they had been bombing around the clock almost daily. In February parachute mines dropped on the 10th Flotilla base at Manoel Island had wrecked the barracks and one end of the old Lazaretto headquarters. Simpson had extemporized new quarters for himself and a few officers in a disused oil tank with duckboards stretching between stinking pools of oil and water. Most officers slept in double-tiered bunks in the tunnels hewn from rock beneath the rear of the Lazaretto building.

The raids had intensified in March. Direct hits on submarines in the creek had caused Simpson to order all boats in harbour to spend the daylight hours on the bottom, aggravating the already serious difficulties of maintenance and provision. The crews, who ashore off duty spent much of their time in shelters, and were even machine-gunned from the air while swimming at rest camps provided on the coast, could gain little respite from the tensions of patrol.

By April the surface and air strike forces operating from the island had been suppressed, prompting the question of whether the submarines could continue to operate. The naval dockyards and great swathes of the surrounding city had been reduced to rubble, and the civilian population was close to starvation as supply convoys had been unable to get through the aerial blockade. Four submarines had been sunk in the harbour, others damaged even while lying on the bottom. Off the approaches, new minefields laid by German E-boats could not be swept as most of the mine-sweepers had been sunk; the few remaining were strafed constantly by Messerschmitts. Outside, the enemy coasts and convoy lanes were more dangerous since Italian escorts had now been fitted with the asdics Raeder had agreed to make available the previous year.

Wanklyn was possibly a victim of the new anti-submarine exper-tise. He took *Upholder* out on 6 April for what was to be her last patrol before returning to England. Since arriving at Malta fifteen months before, he had made twenty-three patrols, the last to the Adriatic off Brindisi, where he had sunk the Italian submarine *Tricheco* before being ordered to a patrol line off Taranto. He had asked for the Brindisi area again for his final mission, but Simpson, noting the tiredness which continual strain had etched in his crew, and fearing that Wanklyn might be tempted into too bold a parting exploit in this heavily protected area, had sent him to the quieter coast of Tunisia on a special mission to land Arab agents. After completing the task Wanklyn kept a rendezvous with the *Unbeaten* to transfer the Special Commando officer, Captain Wilson, who had been in charge of the agents. The *Unbeaten* was returning to England and Wanklyn gave Wilson a letter he had written to his wife the previous evening, 10 April; this said nothing of the devastation of the island fortress, but described the orange blossom in full bloom, and the mass of colour in the gardens, and enjoined her to count the days until he returned to England: 'they are not so many. Only 59.'[62]

The following day Simpson received intelligence of a supply convoy sailing from Taranto, and ordered Wanklyn to take station north of Tripoli in a line with Tomkinson in *Urge* and Lt. Hugh Mackenzie of the 1st Flotilla at Alexandria in *Thrasher*. Both these reached their positions on the 13th, but could not contact the *Upholder*. On the next afternoon an Italian aircraft escorting a convoy well to the north-east of the patrol line sighted a submarine and dropped a smoke float to mark her position for the surface escorts. The large torpedo boat *Pegaso*, which had completed an asdic refresher course only two days previously, detected the sub-merged submarine immediately with her apparatus and attacked, dropping a single pattern of charges. Afterwards, finding the echo had disappeared, she returned to the convoy.[63]

The *Upholder* had not been seen or heard since transferring Captain Wilson to the *Unbeaten*, and was not heard from again. Although the *Pegaso's* attack was made 100 miles from the position

Wanklyn had been ordered to take, and although *Upholder* had not responded to *Urge* and *Thrasher* the day before, this attack on 14 April is held as the most likely cause of her loss. It is also possible that she struck one of the mines with which the approaches to Tripoli were sown. It is doubtful if her end will ever be known with certainty; like many other boats, she simply failed to return.[64]

The loss of this famous submarine and her CO was felt throughout the service as a shock comparable to that felt in the U-boat arm after the loss of Prien the previous year, and as in Prien's case the official announcement was withheld for some weeks. Wanklyn's fellow COs were devastated. In that close community his name had acquired a legendary quality; he had seemed invincible. Arthur Hezlet recalled forty-five years afterwards how the loss had affected him more than any other incident in the war.[65] Simpson wrote to Wanklyn's wife to say he had lost a friend and adviser whom he believed he knew better than his brother.[66] The Admiralty communiqué, when it appeared, was a remarkable panegyric:

> Such was the standard of skill and daring set by Lieutenant Commander Wanklyn and the officers and men under him that they and their ship became an inspiration not only to their own flotilla, but to the Fleet of which it was a part and to Malta, where for so long HMS *Upholder* was based. The ship and her company are gone, but the example and the inspiration remain.[67]

Wanklyn was the top-scoring British submarine ace of the war. His total sinkings amounted to fifteen transports or supply vessels, four others damaged – altogether 119,000 tons – two submarines, one damaged, two destroyers, an armed trawler and damage to a cruiser.[68] The tonnage count was low by the standards of the U-boat aces, but taking into account the inferiority of his instrument, with its extraordinarily slow surface speed and its primitive fire-control and night-sighting apparatus, it was an outstanding record, comparable to that of Kretschmer. And his personal qualities, as Simpson noted them in his letter to Wanklyn's wife, – 'modesty, ability, determination, courage and character' – had impressed his fellows as much as his record.

On 15 April the Governor of Malta announced that His Majesty the King had awarded the George Cross, the highest civilian award for gallantry, to the island fortress. It was a fitting distinction. Over 1,000 civilians had been killed, 10,000 houses wrecked, and a further 20,000 damaged in the constant air raids, and over 100 churches had been destroyed. Many people were living permanently in shelters or in the catacombs in a state of semi-starvation; disease caused by malnutrition and squalor was spreading. 'Never for a moment did they flinch,' Simpson wrote after the war. 'It was the discipline of the people in these circumstances that remains to me the miracle of Malta'.[69]

At the beginning of April Churchill had appealed to Roosevelt for help in preserving the island. On 20 April, two days after the *Upholder* had been posted missing, presumed lost, the US aircraft-carrier *Wasp*, having sailed through the Straits of Gibraltar, flew off forty-seven Spitfires to the island's airfields. They had scarcely landed before the Luftwaffe attacked, and over the next three days most of the new arrivals were wrecked or disabled, a high proportion while on the ground. Simpson, who had already received instructions from Horton to evacuate his flotilla, finally made the decision to leave. By now his force had been reduced to only five boats; they left one by one for Alexandria in the final days of April and early May.

Tomkinson in *Urge* failed to reach his destination. His end will never be known with certainty: *Urge* may have been sunk by Italian aircraft while attacking a supply ship by gunfire on 29 April, or she may have run into one of the mines sown by aircraft and E-boats in the approaches to Malta. It was another grievous blow for Simpson and the submarine service. 'Tommo' had been second only to 'Wanks' among the Malta aces, having sunk or damaged 52,600 tons of supply shipping, sunk one cruiser, damaged another and put the battleship *Vittorio Veneto* out of action for two critical months. Ian McGeoch, who had taken passage in *Urge* to Malta the previous year, recalls Tomkinson, like Wanklyn, as 'a verray parfit gentil knight', who should, in his view, have been awarded the Victoria Cross, 'preferably before he was lost'.[70]

As the four remaining Us of the 10th Flotilla were arriving in the eastern Mediterranean the most successful of the 1st Flotilla boats at Alexandria, Miers's *Torbay*, departed the station on passage home. Miers had added to his reputation for daring during his ninth patrol from the base in early March. Sighting an escorted convoy of four large troopships making northward up the Corfu Channel between that island and the Greek mainland, and assuming they might anchor in Corfu Roads that night, he had followed them in after dark 20 miles up the channel and, having charged his batteries, entered the anchorage. Despite a nearly full moon he had been unable to make out the ships and had waited for dawn, several times forced to dive or avoid approaching patrol craft. With the light it had become apparent that the convoy had passed straight through the channel without anchoring, but two supply ships, estimated as 5,000 and 8,000 tons, and a single destroyer were in the roads. Closing submerged, Miers had fired two torpedoes at each, hitting and sinking both merchantmen, but probably underrunning the destroyer.

He had anticipated that retiring after the attack would be the most dangerous part, but it had proved surprisingly easy as the destroyer and patrol craft hunted the shorter and easier northern exit to the anchorage, dropping forty depth-charges, while he steered out as he had entered by the longer southern route. By noon he had reached the southern end of the island and open sea. On top of his previous patrols, this 'calculated act of most conspicuous bravery'[71] brought Miers the award of the VC.

As the *Torbay* sailed from the depot ship at Alexandria for her return home, officers and men of the Mediterranean fleet manned the ships' sides and the casings of the submarines of the 1st Flotilla and those few who had arrived from the 10th Flotilla to give her a rousing send-off. A month later, in early June, she reached the English Channel and made the final leg of her journey in company with the *Unbeaten* carrying Captain Wilson. Approaching the entrance to Portsmouth, Miers had *Torbay*'s Jolly Roger hoisted above captured German and Italian ensigns; it displayed twelve bars for merchantmen, one each for a destroyer, a submarine and a minesweeper, crossed cannon with nineteen stars for schooners and caiques sunk by gunfire, and several daggers for special operations.

By this time the British situation in the Mediterranean seemed critical. The onslaught Hitler had ordered on Malta had fulfilled its purpose, depriving the base of striking forces and enabling Axis convoys from Italy to run to North Africa practically unscathed; during April a mere 1 per cent of reinforcements and supplies had failed to reach their destination; moreover, a large proportion had been unloaded at Benghazi, which Rommel had retaken at the end of January. Thus replenished, reinforced to the strength of ten divisions, and holding a good port 200 miles further east than his original jumping-off point the previous year, at the end of May Rommel had made a second dash for Alexandria and the Canal. He had captured Tobruk within a month, then struck across Egypt, overruning the British advanced airfields and so tightening the Axis grip on the central Mediterranean and making it virtually impossible for the British fleet to run supply convoys through to Malta from the east. While the British and Commonwealth army dug in at El Alamein only 60 miles to the west of Alexandria, the ships of the fleet were dispersed to Port Said and the Suez Canal, or northwards up the Levantine coast; the submarines of the 1st and 10th Flotillas, the main strength of which had been used earlier in the month in a vain attempt to shield a supply convoy for Malta from the Italian fleet, were sent to Haifa on the coast of Palestine. On the voyage their depot ship, *Medway*, loaded with spare torpedoes and equipment, was sunk by *U372* under KLt. Heinz Neumann. But if the British situation appeared desperate at this juncture, Rommel's was equally in the balance: once again he had extended his land lines beyond the capacity of the supply columns from his major ports.

With Alexandria evacuated and British forces at Alamein drawing supplies overland, U-boats which had been preying on the coastwise shipping formerly used to supply the British forces were withdrawn to the western Mediterranean to operate against any attempt to run supply convoys to Malta through the Straits of Gibraltar. Over the past six months they had accounted for two cruisers and twelve supply vessels, but five boats had been lost and a further two in the western Mediterranean. In the same period seven Italian submarines had been destroyed – two by aircraft patrols in the western basin and five off Sicily or in the Adriatic, four of them remarkably by 10th Flotilla submarines and one by a T-class boat of the 1st Flotilla.

In the Pacific, meanwhile, the irresistible first stage of the Japanese advance had brought them to New Guinea, and they had occupied the important bases of Rabaul and Kavieng in the Bismarck archipelago at the north-eastern end of that island. There they had been checked, in large measure because of succesess by the US Navy cryptanalysts, which had evened the balance for America's vastly outnumbered naval forces. The initial break into the main Japanese naval cipher had been made at Cast, the Code and Signals Section at Corregidor, Manila Bay, but after the evacuation of the Philippines base in February 1942 the attack had been continued at Negat in Washington and Hypo at Pearl Harbor, where the team under the Navy's most skilled codebreaker, Lt.-Cdr. Joseph Rochefort, worked literally around the clock, Rochefort himself and his principal assistants seldom leaving their workplace in the basement below the navy's waterfront headquarters. Their target was not a machine cipher, but a code of five-digit groups encrypted by subtracting other five-digit groups obtained in sequence from a list of 100,000 randomly selected five-digit numbers. The addressees, provided with identical lists of numbers, had only to know at which point to enter the columns to be able to recover the code by reversing the process, adding the numbers in sequence to the cipher groups. By April 1942, 85 per cent of this two-stage code was being read at Hypo, and although the code for the Japanese geographical grid had not been broken, a combination of traffic analysis, cryptanalysis and radio direction-finding enabled Rochefort to provide the C-in-C Pacific, Admiral Chester Nimitz, with a remarkably accurate picture of Japanese movements and intentions.

This information had allowed Nimitz to surprise invasion forces sailing for Port Moresby, New Guinea, and Tulagi in the Solomons group in early May and, at the Battle of the Coral Sea, to administer the first check to the Japanese run of success. In addition, the product of cryptanalysis, which was also known as Ultra in the US services, had allowed US submarine force commanders to direct boats to valuable targets. It was a mixed blessing at this stage since the most valuable targets were the Japanese carriers and battleships which so outnumbered those available to Nimitz, but which because of their speed were the most difficult prey for submarines. Thus after the Coral Sea battle a number of boats were ordered to patrol lines across the homeward track of the damaged carrier *Shokaku*, but failed to hit her. Despite this diversion and despite many eccentric torpedoes, US submarines had shown in May what they might do. During that month they had sunk twenty-one merchantmen totalling over 100,000 tons, a 9,000-ton seaplane-carrier – the largest warship the Japanese had lost to date – two large I-class submarines, a repair ship and a minelayer.

The unofficial liaison between the cryptanalysts and Submarine Command at Pearl Harbor was a former submariner on Rochefort's team, Cdr. W.J. Holmes. Long after the war he described the Intelligence contribution to the Pacific campaign and the extraordinary sensitivity of his role in providing Ultra for the submarines. The anxiety that the Japanese might become suspicious that their signals were being read, and hence change their codes and throw them into the dark once more, had made him realize the weight of responsibility Rochefort had assumed when permitting him to pass the information.[72]

The cryptanalysts' most important single contribution to the war at sea had been made during the latter part of May when the team, working against the clock without respite, uncovered the Japanese plans and order of battle for the next great thrust, a wide pincer attack on the Aleutians in the north and Midway Island in the central Pacific, designed to lure the Americans into the decisive fleet battle. The plan was devised by Yamamoto's Combined Fleet Staff in opposition to the Naval General Headquarters Staff, which had intended the occupation of the chain of islands across the line of communications from the United States to Australia, so creating a defensive barrier behind which Japan could exploit her conquests. The Combined Fleet Staff plan was typically over-elaborate; more important, it split the Japanese forces involved in the northern, diversionary, attack far from the *Kido Butai* and other main groups assigned to the invasion of Midway, thereby removing any chance of mutual support. Since two of the most modern Japanese fleet carriers were out of action, the *Shokaku* from damage received in the Coral Sea, and the *Zuikaku* from the loss of most of her trained aircrew in the same battle, this was a sign of hubris.[73] Nimitz, presented by Rochefort with details of the plan, was able to concentrate his three remaining carriers against the *Kido Butai*, now only four fleet carriers under Vice-Admiral Nagumo, and achieve the surprise the Japanese planners had intended for their own forces.

Submarines were given a prominent role in both sides' planning, as indeed they had been at the Battle of the Coral Sea, although without results in that case. The Japanese Sixth (Submarine) Fleet had been reorganized under a new commander, Vice-Admiral the Marquis Teruhisa Komatsu, of the Imperial inner circle. He had despatched ten of the most modern I-class boats on commerce-raiding missions to the Indian Ocean and off eastern Australia as the Germans had been urging; and for a force not trained for commerce war they achieved good results.[74] His 1st Squadron, reduced under the new organization to five boats, was sent on reconnaissance and patrol in the northern operation against the Aleutians. Four rather older fleet boats of his 3rd Squadron together with seven fleet boats of the Combined Fleet's 5th Submarine Squadron were given patrol and rescue duties in the Midway operation. They were to form a north–south patrol line 200 to 400 miles north of French Frigate Shoal, almost halfway between Pearl Harbor and Midway, in order to report and attack US task forces as they sallied from the fleet base to meet the invasion forces. In addition, three 1,400-ton minelaying submarines now attached to the Sixth Fleet were despatched to French Frigate Shoal, two loaded with 40 tons of aviation spirit and 12 tons of oil each to service flying boats that would meet them at the shoal and make a reconnaissance of Pearl Harbor before the Midway strike. There were also eight Type A midget submarines intended for the fleet action on board a converted seaplane-carrier sailing with the Midway invasion fleet.

The Japanese arrangements were nullified by the pressure of the timetable forced by the planners on the submarine force, already suffering from constant employment, but chiefly by Nimitz's intelligence of the moves. Yamamoto's order detailing the Japanese dispositions went out on 20 May; on the 25th Rochefort personally delivered the signal 90 per cent decrypted to Nimitz, who was in any case aware that Midway was the probable target of Japanese preparations. When the I-class refuelling submarines reached French Frigate Shoal on 26 May they found US seaplane tenders there. Consequently the Japanese flying boats were unable to make their rendezvous and unable to fly a reconnaissance of Pearl Harbor to locate the US carriers. The boats of the Japanese 3rd and 5th Submarine Squadrons were supposed to reach their positions to the north of French Frigate Shoal by 1 June, but did not straggle into place until the 3rd. By then Nimitz's carriers, divided into two groups, the *Enterprise* and *Hornet*, Task Force 16, under Rear-Admiral R.A. Spruance, and the *Yorktown*, Task Force 17, under the overall commander of the carriers, Rear-Admiral F.J. Fletcher, had sailed from Pearl Harbor well past the Japanese scouting line into a waiting position 300 miles north-east of Midway.

The Pearl Harbor submarines were now commanded by Rear-Admiral R.H. English, who had relieved Withers routinely on 14 May. The problem of disposing the boats, designated Task Force 7 for the operation, was complicated by the number of separate invasion, carrier-strike and covering forces in the complex Japanese plan, and by ignorance of the positions conveyed in the Japanese signals. Probably acting on Nimitz's instructions, English deployed the majority as Task Group 7.1 in arcs to the west of Midway, three 200 miles from the island on bearings from west-south-west to north-west, six 150 miles out on bearings from south-west to north, and two with a roving commission from 50 to 150 miles out, north-west and north. Three boats designated Task Group 7.2 were placed 420 miles east of Midway and 200 miles north of French Frigate Shoal, in fact just to the west of the Japanese submarine patrol line; they were to provide support for the main Task Group 7.1, or for the US carriers if they should be forced to retreat. A further four boats, Task Group 7.3, were placed 300 miles north of Pearl Harbor to guard against the possibility of a Japanese feint strike on the fleet base itself.

These eighteen fleet boats were all that were available from

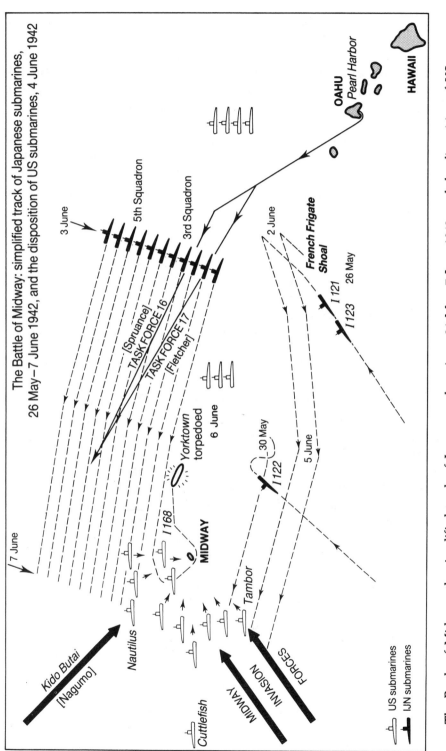

The Battle of Midway: the simplified track of Japanese submarines, 26 May–7 June 1942, and the disposition of US submarines, 4 June

the twenty-nine under English's command: two were in dockyard hands, the others on distant patrol. The majority of these were ordered to return via Midway if they had sufficient fuel and torpedoes and one, *Cuttlefish*, was directed to a position 700 miles west of the island, where Rochefort correctly anticipated enemy activity. The disposition of the main group, 7.1 – whether by English or Nimitz himself is unclear – has been criticized as being too close to Midway, for most boats were inside the distance at which the *Kido Butai* would launch its strike on the island; had they been grouped further to the west they might have had a chance of sighting and attacking the Japanese carriers before they reached their attack position.[75]

Yamamoto's northern strikes against the Aleutians were to be met by ten S boats from Dutch Harbor towards the eastern end of the island chain. In the event these were stationed close by their base and on 3 June the Japanese made unopposed landings on Attu and Kiska islands far to the west.

The main thrust at Midway began early on the morning of 4 June. The *Kido Butai* approached to within almost 150 miles north-west of Midway, and Nagumo launched his air strike against the island at 04.45. During the next hour first the planes, then the force itself were sighted by US patrol aircraft. On receipt of the first positional report Fletcher sent Spruance of Task Force 16 with the carriers *Enterprise* and *Hornet* south-westerly towards the enemy, following with his own carrier *Yorktown* after recovering his patrol planes. An hour later, shortly after 07.00, Spruance launched his torpedo planes and dive-bombers against the Japanese force. It has been called 'one of the most brilliant pieces of operational judge-ment of the Pacific war',[76] timed to hit the enemy carriers at their most vulnerable when they were flying on, refuelling and rearming the planes returning from the Midway strike. A quarter of an hour later, English signalled to his submarines of Task Group 7.1 to give them the position of the enemy, but it was another two hours before he ordered them to attack. Only the three most northerly boats on the 150-mile arc were in a position to do so; all were forced down by aircraft and only one, the *Nautilus*, under Lt.-Cdr. W.H. Brockman, succeeded in closing.

Brockman had started out submerged on his own initiative long before English's signals, working directly from the reports of the US patrol planes intercepted by his radio operator, which by his calculation placed the enemy force inside the northern edge of his 20° patrol sector. At 07.10, while the planes were taking off from the *Enterprise* and *Hornet* far to his east, he saw smoke ahead through his periscope and dark bursts of anti-aircraft fire against the sky as a first wave of torpedo aircraft from Midway Island attacked the Japanese carriers. He pressed on submerged. Forty-five minutes later he made out masts and shortly afterwards the shape of one of the two battleships with Nagumo's force, together with a cruiser and two destroyer escorts which he took to be cruisers on either bow. He had been spotted by a plane, however. His periscope was strafed and one of the destroyers turned towards him, sonar pinging, forcing him deep and dropping patterns of charges as she swished overhead.

The *Nautilus* was an old boat, laid down as a cruiser submarine in 1927 when US designs had been in flux; 1,000 tons larger than the evolved fleet submarine and armed with two 6-inch guns, she had been modernized in 1941 with new engines, fire control and four additional torpedo tubes, two in the superstructure forward of the bridge, two beneath the after casing. The concussion of the destroyer's depth-charges now triggered the motor of a torpedo in one of these new external tubes and it made a 'hot run' inside the tube, sounding like a waste-grinder, propellers spinning, venting steam and exhaust gases which bubbled to the surface. Despite these tell-tale signs the destroyer failed to drop charges accurately, or they were not set to the boat's depth of 90 feet, and at 08.25 Brockman was able to ease up cautiously to periscope depth again. The sight that met his eyes was astonishing. He was surrounded by warships, all apparently circling away at speed to avoid him; in fact most were probably manoeuvring to evade attacking air-craft from Midway, the fifth wave from the island airstrip. The battleship, in fact the *Kirishima*, was 4,500 yards off his port bow, her yards decorated with flag hoists. She fired her starboard batteries, apparently at his periscope, then turned away. Brock-man set up an attack solution and fired two torpedoes after her; one failed to start and the *Kirishima* evaded the other as Brockman was forced deep again by a destroyer. This time he went to 150 feet as depth-charge explosions thundered above.

It was 08.25. Nagumo had just received his first report of what appeared to be a carrier accompanying an enemy force which had been reported an hour earlier. He was having to make a critical decision: either to recover his Midway strike planes, now only minutes away on the return flight to the carriers, or to leave them in the air while launching an immediate strike with those planes already armed against just this unexpected eventuality of an enemy surface force in the vicinity. Probably there was no correct answer. He had been ill-served by his reconnaissance, by his orders and by his staff: elements of the Midway strike had been despatched from all four carriers instead of reserving two ready for the possible anti-ship strike. Yamamoto had also failed him by preserving radio silence rather than passing on intelligence from signals traffic analysis suggesting that a US submarine had sighted the invasion force and a US carrier force was at sea in the vicinity of Midway. Now Nagumo, against the strong advice of his second-in-command, made the decision to fly on the returning aircraft; several were damaged, all were short of fuel and undoubtedly many would be lost if they had to wait while he flew off a strike against the US carrier. Moreover, such a strike would lack air cover since his fighters, having decimated five waves of attackers from Midway and prevented them from making a single hit on his ships, were reaching the end of their fuel endurance.

When Brockman, judging he had evaded the destroyer, came up to periscope depth again, he saw one of the Japanese carriers eight miles distant, the first enemy carrier he had yet seen, speeding south-easterly on a converging course. He had no time to prepare an attack, for a cruiser was heading straight for him. He fired a single torpedo, forcing her to evade, but she turned and came back, and once again he went deep, hearing depth-charges exploding above. The cruiser was actually one of the screen destroyers. While she attacked, the Japanese carriers flew on their returning planes, then turned north-easterly at high speed for the enemy force, arming and refuelling for a strike on the US carrier. After a while the destroyer followed to rejoin the screen. When Brockman came up to periscope depth at 10.00 the sea was empty.

Meanwhile, as a result of Nagumo's change of course, the *Hornet's* dive-bombers and fighters had failed to find him, but her torpedo planes had sighted his smoke and attacked shortly before 09.30. It was a most gallant suicide run without fighter cover and fourteen of the fifteen planes were shot down before even reaching launching positions. They were followed by torpedo planes from the *Enterprise* and finally from the *Yorktown*, but no hits were scored and only six of forty-one planes from the three carriers survived. The Japanese carriers were still weaving to avoid the last torpedoes, which had proved as erratic as those from US sub-marines, when shortly after 10.20 thirty-two dive-bombers from the *Enterprise* arrived overhead, followed within minutes by seventeen from the *Yorktown*. The Japanese fighters had been drawn down practically to sea level by the torpedo planes; look-outs on the ships had been distracted from the upper sky by the low-level threat and dog fights, and there was no radar. High above, the bombers achieved complete surprise. Moreover, the flight decks of the carriers were crowded with planes armed, fuelled and ready to take off within minutes for the strike on the US carrier force; and bombs, torpedoes, fuel lines and bowsers were still spread about the lifts and hangar decks below. The ships were gigantic incendiary machines primed to detonate, and within minutes of the alarming scream of the US bombers hurtling vertically down upon them – the first intimation the Japanese had of their presence – the *Kaga*, the flagship *Akagi*, and the *Soryu* had been turned into exploding, blazing furnaces, the pilots already in their cockpits for take-off burned alive in curtains of flame. Only the *Hiryu*, which had become separated to the north of the other three carriers, escaped. The *Kido Butai*, which only five minutes earlier had dominated the Pacific, was no more; a shocked Admiral Nagumo was led almost forcibly from *Akagi*'s smoke-shrouded bridge to transfer his flag.

This seismic turning-point in the Pacific war may be termed a miracle. At the very least it was an extraordinary turn of fortune that the dive-bombers from the two US carriers met over Nagumo's force. The planes from *Enterprise* had taken off some time before those from *Yorktown*, and had been in the air for over three hours trying to find the enemy; they had expended well over half their fuel, could not expect to make it back to their carrier, and had only come upon their target by adopting the course of a lone Japanese destroyer which the flight leader, Lt.-Cdr. C. Wade McClusky, had assumed might be heading towards the enemy force. This was the destroyer that had been hunting the *Nautilus*; she had indeed been heading back to rejoin her screen. Had Brockman not used his initiative early that morning; had he not persisted where two of his fellow COs failed; had the *Enterprise* flight not continued the search beyond the point of safe return; and had McClusky not made his inspired surmise, the seventeen bombers from the *Yorktown* would have found themselves alone above the target; it is doubtful if they could have struck out all three enemy carriers. And had one or two carriers survived with the *Hiryu* to launch the strike aircraft already lined up on the flight decks the outcome at Midway might have been different and possibly disastrous for the United States. That such a historic moment should turn on such a chain of small chances gives cause for thought.

Brockman was too far south to observe the strike to which he had unwittingly contributed, but at 10.29 he saw through his periscope smoke clouds gathering over the horizon. He had no means of knowing they were from the burning carriers, but he altered towards them and, still submerged, continued on his lone and dogged mission.

Some way beyond the smoke the single remaining Japanese carrier, the *Hiryu*, launched her dive-bombers and six covering Zero fighters for the strike against the *Yorktown*, still the only US carrier reported. They reached their target at noon and, despite being mauled by fighters, hit her with three bombs, stopping her dead and starting fires.

By this time Brockman had made out the blazing hull of a carrier, which he identified wrongly as the *Soryu*, beneath the nearest smoke pall, and had increased to two-thirds speed, about 4 knots, to close her. It took him almost two hours to come within 2,700 yards, then he fired four carefully aimed torpedoes at the stationary target, watching the wakes running straight and true before he was yet again forced deep by a destroyer. As patterns of charges exploded he went to 300 feet, the maximum test depth of the boat. He believed he had sunk the *Soryu* and was so credited on his return, and awarded the Navy Cross for his courage and persistence. After the war it emerged that the carrier he attacked was the *Kaga*, and three of the torpedoes were observed by survivors aboard: two had missed and one had struck amidships, but the warhead had shattered and fallen away, whereupon some of the crew in the water had used the body of the weapon to keep themselves afloat.

The undamaged *Hiryu*, meanwhile, had launched a second strike of torpedo aircraft against the *Yorktown*, now under command again with her damage under control; at 14.42 one group succeeded in pressing in within 500 yards of her port side and hitting the carrier with two torpedoes, which stopped her again and caused such an alarming list that she was abandoned – prematurely as it turned out. At almost the same moment US aircraft searching for the *Hiryu* found her and reported, and three-quarters of an hour later Spruance launched a powerful dive-bomber strike from the *Hornet* and the *Enterprise*, including several of *Yorktown*'s group, which delivered a terrible retribution shortly after 17.00, leaving the *Hiryu*, like the other Japanese fleet carriers, a blazing hulk. By the following evening all four had gone down and Yamamoto, who had called off the invasion of Midway early that morning, was retiring.

Despite Brockman's persistence, submarines had contributed nothing to this most devastating and complete reversal of fortunes in naval history. The decisive input had come from Rochefort;

Spruance had made the battle-winning decision, Yamamoto and Nagumo the fatal mistakes, but fleet aircraft had shown their superiority to submarines both as scouts and as weapon systems, confirming the lessons of the European war and accurately reflecting the relationship between these two new dimensions of naval power at this stage of their development. As suggested, if this point, now surely obvious after the failure of English's Task Group 7.1, had been grasped by the US naval staff, the submarines might have been concentrated under one force commander and deployed, like Dönitz's, for the all-out *guerre de course* for which they were ideally suited, and to which Japan, despite hurried organization of an 'Escort Fleet' that spring, was peculiarly vulnerable. This strategy was never applied.

The strong force of Japanese submarines had failed as comprehensively as the American boats to affect the outcome at Midway. There was, however, one destructive finale to be provided by *I168* under Lt.-Cdr. Yahachi Tanabe. *I168* was a fleet boat of 1,400 tons surface displacement, 23 knots surface speed, commissioned in 1934, now with others of her class in the Sixth Fleet's 3rd Submarine Squadron. Delayed by repairs, Tanabe had taken her out after the other boats which were to take part in the patrol line north of French Frigate Shoal, with orders to reconnoitre Midway Island. He had done so at periscope depth for three days in late May and early June, reporting intense American air activity with an average of 90 to 100 flights from the island airstrip each day and reconnaissance planes spending most of the daylight hours in the air – suggesting they were patrolling out to 700 miles or so.[77] Taken together with the American activity at French Frigate Shoal reported by the refuelling submarines and the conclusions from traffic analysis that a US submarine had sighted the invasion force and US carriers were to the north of Midway, as they were, Tanabe's report of such round-the-clock activity at Midway itself should have rung loud alarm bells for Japanese Intelligence; that it did not was due to the divisions in the Japanese command organization and Intelligence staff, in part perhaps to victory-induced hubris; undoubtedly, the serious Intelligence failure played almost as large a part as the brilliant feats of Rochefort's team at Pearl Harbor in the American victory against all material odds.

In the immediate aftermath of the loss of the Japanese carriers, before Yamamoto had decided to call off the Midway operation, the *I168* and four heavy cruisers were ordered to proceed to the island and bombard, a futile employment for the submarine with her single 3.9-inch gun, lacking an accurate rangefinder. No sooner had she fired her first round at 01.30 on the morning of 5 June than the alerted shore batteries came to life with searchlights and a return barrage that forced Tanabe to take her down, after which he was chased off by destroyers. He was then ordered to seek out the damaged US carrier north-east of Midway.

The US submarines of Task Group 7.1 had meanwhile been ordered to close Midway on their original bearings from the island to act against the anticipated invasion fleet. In the process the *Tambor*, while still 90 miles out, sighted the Japanese heavy cruisers on their way to bombard; in the darkness she could not identify them, and merely signalled a report of 'unidentified ships' and shadowed. Forty minutes later, at 02.55, Yamamoto at last abandoned his intention to proceed with the Midway operation, and the orders to the cruisers were countermanded; they turned to retire westward. At 03.42 a sharp lookout sighted the shape of the US submarine, still shadowing. The flagship flashed the signal for an emergency turn down the line, but it was not seen by the last cruiser, *Mogami*, which as the turn was executed ploughed into the port quarter of her next ahead, *Mikuma*, starting fires and so damaging both ships that they had to reduce to 12 knots.

With first light the *Tambor*, still in contact, recognized the enemy for what they were, but had to dive and was unable to work into position ahead to attack. At 06.00 she sent a report to base, as a result of which dive-bombers from Midway and Spruance's carriers sank the *Mikuma* and reduced the *Mogami* to a blazing shambles; she remained afloat nonetheless, and somehow limped back to the Japanese base at Truk in the Caroline Islands.

Throughout that day, Tanabe in *I168* made his way submerged towards the reported position of the crippled US carrier, continuing after dark at his best speed on the surface. Destroyers from the *Yorktown*'s own task force, also heading towards the carrier with a party selected from her crew to re-board and prepare her for towing to Pearl Harbor, reached her before him. Indeed, it was not until after daylight at 05.30 the following morning, 6 June, that Tanabe made out the mastheads of the group 11 miles to the east. He continued towards them on the surface until, judging he might be seen, he dived and began the slow submerged approach. Checking the position at intervals through the periscope he found the carrier was under tow with one destroyer alongside – in fact the *Hammann*, providing power for the party aboard to pump out flooded compartments and transfer bunker oil to counteract the list. Five other destroyers were screening her at about a mile radius, and the whole knot of vessels was moving south-easterly at 3 knots.

He decided that to be certain of hitting he must penetrate the screen and come within 1,500 yards of the carrier. It was an excruciating, drawn-out approach that took all morning. As the sun climbed towards its zenith, heat built up with the tension inside the boat. Eventually, nearing the group, Tanabe raised the periscope ever more cautiously at longer intervals. The destroyers' sonar pulses were audible through the hydrophones, but as they closed shortly before noon, then passed beneath the screen, the pulses suddenly ceased, deflected perhaps by a thermal gradient. Tanabe was mystified, but trying to keep his voice light and even told his crew it appeared the Americans had interrupted their war for lunch; now was the chance to hit them hard while they ate.[78]

He ran on deep until he judged he had reached his chosen position 1,500 yards on the carrier's beam, but when he came up to periscope depth found he was half that distance off her quarter. Lowering the periscope, he altered round to starboard and ran diagonally away to gain distance before turning back to make the final observation. It was not until 13.30 that he fired the first of four torpedoes aimed to strike the carrier at mid-length below her side armour with a spread of only 2° to concentrate the punch. Two ran straight and exploded opposite the hits made by the Hiryu's torpedo planes, destroying what remained of the Yorktown's mid-length compartmentalization; one ran shallow, hitting the Hammann and breaking her back with the detonation; one veered away erratically and missed.

Tanabe's intention after the attack was to hide deep under the carrier, but he had 1,200 yards to run and the destroyers, combing the visible tracks of the torpedoes, detected him before he could find this cover. The Hammann had sunk by then and two destroyers were rescuing survivors; the other three took turns to pound I168, shaking the boat with pattern after accurate pattern of charges that cut the lighting, caused leaks in both outer and inner doors of No. 1 torpedo tube and cracked cells in the forward batteries, which began to release chlorine gas. The power was cut while electricians, working by torchlight in the darkness, struggled to isolate the damaged jars. Without motors or pumps the boat sank to her test depth of 75 metres (246 feet) and continued sinking with a stern-down angle of 20°. Compressed air was expended in an attempt to keep her up and hold a trim; even so the electricians had to be supported against the angle by other crewmen as they worked.

After nearly two hours the task was completed, the main switches closed again, the motors started, and Tanabe began to creep away from the propeller noises above. But there was little power left in the intact batteries after the long submerged approach that morning, and little compressed air in the cylinders. Nor could they use the pumps to get rid of the water leaking in through the damaged tube doors lest the noise alert their hunters. And the depleted atmosphere inside the boat was poisoned by chlorine fumes. Though it was still daylight, Tanabe had no option but to surface. He came up at 16.45, having managed to move 5 miles away from the destroyers. It would not have been enough had he not been mistaken at first for another US destroyer joining, and he was granted a few vital minutes in which to recharge batteries and replenish his air before the Americans realized their mistake and chased. He emitted smoke to try and obscure their fire control, but as shells began to straddle the boat he dived again, reversing course immediately to underrun his pursuers on a reciprocal course, hoping their speed would affect sonar reception, as it did. He was not detected, and after dark the destroyers left the scene. It was believed the submarine must have sunk due to damage caused in the initial depth-charging.

Tanabe came up at 20.45 and set course homewards on the surface. Astern of him the sea rose inexorably inside the *Yorktown*'s hull, breaking down bulkheads, flooding more areas, drawing the great ship from under the parties still working to save her. Finally she had to be abandoned for the second time, and in the early hours of the next morning she lurched over to port and lay on her beam ends for some minutes, revealing the destruction wrought by *I168*'s torpedoes before she sank.

For this exploit, which he was fortunate to survive, Tanabe became a national hero, justifiably the first Japanese submarine ace.

Like the surface fleet itself, the Japanese midget submarines had not come within striking distance of the enemy. The type had, however, scored its first successes a few days before. The setting was Diego Suarez harbour on the north-eastern tip of the Indian Ocean island of Madagascar, the chief victim the British battleship *Ramillies*, flagship of a British expeditionary force which had seized the area from the Vichy French in early May in order to prevent it falling into the hands of the Japanese; it was strategically situated on the British supply route for the Middle East via the Cape of Good Hope.

The seaplane from *I10*, the A1 headquarters submarine leading the Indian Ocean group of the 8th Submarine Squadron, had spotted the battleship at anchor in the harbour during a reconnaissance flight on the evening of 29 May. The same night the group assembled 10 miles off the narrow entrance to Diego Suarez Bay and midgets were launched from *I16* and *I20* but not from the third mother submarine *I18*, whose craft suffered engine failure. The two small submersibles set out on their lonely one-way mission some time after midnight. What happened to *I16's* craft will never be known, but *I20's*, piloted by Lt. Saburo Akeida with Petty Officer Masamai Takemoto as his No. 2, successfully negotiated the reef-strewn passage into the Bay and, no doubt hiding for much of the daylight of the 30th, crossed to the inner harbour to a firing position off the port side of the *Ramillies* that evening. At 20.25 Akeida's first torpedo struck the battleship just forward of her foremost turret and, notwithstanding a protective 'torpedo bulge' outside the hull proper, opened both forward magazines and shell rooms to flooding. Some minutes later Akeida fired his second and only other torpedo at a 7,000-ton British tanker anchored nearby, hitting and sinking her. The *Ramillies* was patched up over the next three days, then sailed for Durban, where she was given further repairs to enable her to sail home for a complete refit.

The midget was near the end of its battery endurance by the time Akeida fired, and with no means of recharging he beached her and set off with Takemoto on foot. They were later discovered and surrounded. Rather than surrender, they shot themselves, or each other. The details of their exploit were lost with them, but the bare facts speak for skill and determination of a very high order. And since the *Ramillies* was out of action for the best part of a year, it could be said that theirs was a remarkably economical use of force. There were to be few other successes, however, and since such training, skill and courage were not limitless assets, even in such a martial culture as Japan's, it was ultimately an illogical employment of young men to send them to certain death or captivity, and only explicable in terms of the warrior ethic and the desperate sense of industrial inferiority which forced the doctrine of attrition of the enemy battlefleet before the 'decisive battle'.

The other group from the 8th Submarine Squadron operating off the coast of Australia made a similar attack on Sydney harbour the following night, 31 May. The seaplane from the flagship, *I21*, reported a battleship and other warships inside, and three midgets were launched from their mother submarines late in the afternoon 7 miles from Sydney Heads. They set off as the light was fading and two succeeded in passing through an open boom defence; the other became entangled in the nets and her CO, unable to extricate the craft, set the scuttling charge, blowing himself and his No. 2 up with the boat. One of the two craft which penetrated the harbour was sighted and brought under fire from the US heavy cruiser *Chicago*, which *I21's* reconnaissance plane had mistaken for a battleship. She dived and later fired both torpedoes at the cruiser, outlined against the lights ashore. Both missed, one running harmlessly aground without exploding, the other passing under a Dutch submarine berthed alongside an old harbour ferry serving as an accommodation ship, hitting and sinking the ferry with the loss of eighteen lives. The midget was lost on her way out. The third so damaged herself against obstructions that her torpedoes refused to leave the tubes and after being depth-charged her crew scuttled her within the harbour; both the CO and his No. 2 shot themselves after opening the valves.[79]

After these midget operations both submarine groups carried out more or less conventional campaigns against merchant shipping, adding to a reputation for cruelty established with the first sinking of merchantmen at the beginning of the year when survivors had been shot in the water and crowded lifeboats rammed at speed and split apart.[80] Not all Japanese COs acted in this way, indeed there was at least one recorded occasion when survivors from a British ship were given food and water and navigation advice,[81] but Japanese barbarity towards survivors was sufficiently common to make their submarines particularly feared and hated by sailors of all nationalities. As mentioned, this was a natural result of the deliberately cruel naval training methods by which 'skilful' COs built up such a potential of repressed hate and anger in their subordinates for transfer to the enemy in action; they also vented it on prisoners, civilians and helpless maritime survivors. As Saburo Ienaga has put it: 'Individuals whose own dignity and manhood had been so cruelly violated [in training] would hardly refrain from doing the same to defenceless persons under their control'.[82] This was the other face of the superhuman devotion and self-sacrifice displayed by the young crews of the midget submarines especially.

At US submarine headquarters at Pearl Harbor, where it was felt the boats had not performed well at Midway, there was a cull of older COs; they were replaced by generally younger men, although English could not go so far as some urged by appointing those too junior to have been infected by ultra-cautious pre-war training methods. English also pressed for permission to build an advanced submarine base at Midway to reduce the distance to the patrol areas. A refitting and re-supply facility was approved which was to cut the round voyage to Japanese waters by over 2,000 miles.

However, results from the war against Japanese supplies were as poor in June as the submarines' Midway performance, in the whole Pacific theatre a mere half dozen sinkings, less than the individual scores of some U-boats in the Gulf of Mexico and Caribbean. COs placed much blame on faulty torpedoes and malfunctioning exploders; they were undoubtedly right, as a long series of later tests was to prove, but English's staff sought reasons in the COs' own performances. W.J. Holmes, who saw it at first hand and later helped bring the truth to light with decrypts of Japanese reports of US torpedoes exploding prematurely, hitting and failing to explode or underrunning, has described how staff 'endorsements' – or comments on the COs' patrol reports – reflected the Staff Torpedo Officer's curious concept that he was 'an apologist for the torpedo', with the duty of explaining away rather than investigating reported defects.[83]

The faults were taken more seriously in the South West Pacific Command where Rear-Admiral Charles Lockwood had relieved Wilkes towards the end of May. As mentioned earlier, Lockwood had been, as a member and from 1938 Chairman of the Submarine Officers' Conference, one of the leading influences in the evolution of the US fleet submarine. Arriving at Perth he had found an overwhelming sense of gloom. By nature an optimist, he was also, as Admiral Galantin has expressed it, 'a great example of "loyalty down"', whose trust in his officers drew their 'wholehearted support and admiration';[84] indeed his remains a legendary name in the US Submarine Service. He took the COs' complaints seriously, set up an informal inquiry into the Command's disappointing results in the defence of the Philippines and subsequently, and concluded that the causes embraced poor tactical dispositions, 'bad torpedo performance, in that they evidently ran much too deep and had numerous prematures', and 'lack of understanding of aggressiveness'.[85] He put this in a letter to a submarine colleague, King's Chief of Staff, Rear-Admiral Richard Edwards. He also carried out several test firings of torpedoes against vertically stretched fishing nets, proving to his own satisfaction that the standard Mark XIV torpedoes ran on average 11 feet deeper than set; after which he issued instructions to subtract 11 feet from depth settings in future attacks.

In Washington, meanwhile, Edwards had set up an analysis of past torpedo attacks. The conclusion was that there should have been approximately 100 per cent more hits than there had been;

as a result King instructed the Bureau of Ordnance to re-check their data. After a series of tests at Newport in July, the Bureau, which had resisted all previous criticisms of the torpedoes in much the same way as English's staff by blaming the COs for poor aiming, conceded that the Mark XIV ran 10 feet deeper than set. Lockwood and English, but probably few of their submarine officers, now believed that the problem had been solved; by adjusting the depth setting, both magnetic and contact firing pistols would function as designed. But this was only the beginning.

While Lockwood was instrumental in starting the long process that would eventually lead to the solution of the torpedo problem, neither he nor English, nor Christie at Brisbane, improved on the strategic or tactical thinking of their predecessors. They were of course hampered by coming under supreme commanders in their own area who required submarine co-operation in fleet or special missions; but in their normal operations they continued to send boats to obvious, heavily defended base areas or diverted them on Ultra information to fast, strongly escorted capital ship targets. Lockwood and English most conspicuously failed to co-ordinate a joint strategy to strangle Japanese supplies of oil and other strategic materials either at source in the former Dutch Indies or at the 'choke points' in the Luzon Strait and East China Sea. It was not their task to formulate overall strategy; nor could they alter the divided command structure, which led to each theatre commander fighting his own corner, generally against the others. Again the buck stopped with King and his submariner deputy, Edwards, who did nothing.

In strategic terms, the American submarine effort in the Pacific remained ill thought-out, disjointed and essentially unscientific. It showed in the poor results achieved that summer: the majority of patrols recorded no sinkings; the average was less than half a ship sunk per patrol.

7

The Turn of Fortune

AFTER MIDWAY IT was apparent to the upper tier of the Japanese government that the war was lost. It will be recalled that her industrial capacity was barely a tenth of that of the United States and that the pre-war US naval building programme threatened to reduce the Imperial Japanese Navy to less than a third of the US Navy's strength by 1944. Japan's only slim hope of victory over her giant adversary had lain in knocking out the US Pacific Fleet quickly at the start of hostilities, as Yamamoto had argued successfully before the strike on Pearl Harbor and again before the attack on Midway, both of which had been designed solely for that purpose. Instead the American carriers had escaped, the American construction programme had been augmented and accelerated, and now over half of the carriers of the *Kido Butai* and a far greater proportion of its aircraft and trained pilots had been lost. The gamble had undoubtedly failed. Hirohito may not have admitted it was so, but he and his closest advisers knew it with the rational side of their minds; Yamamoto had, of course, predicted it and could only wait for the remainder of his prediction to come true. The Japanese people and armed forces were not told. On 10 June, Tokyo radio announced a great naval victory in which 2 US carriers and 120 aircraft had been destroyed for the loss of only 1 Japanese carrier and 35 aircraft. Instructions were issued for the Midway wounded to be returned under the tightest security to Yokosuka Naval Hospital, there to be held without outside contact.[1]

Before putting out the serious peace feelers which would, they knew, become necessary, Hirohito and his advisers decided to build up their bargaining position by consolidating and extending their grasp on New Guinea and the islands east of Australia; the Naval General Headquarters Staff plan to secure the chain from the Solomons to Fiji to disrupt communications between the United States and Australia and serve as outposts in the defence of the new empire acquired in the south has been mentioned. A force was put ashore on the north coast of New Guinea to march overland to Port Moresby, key to northern Australia, and engineers and labourers were sent to build an airstrip on Guadalcanal in the southern Solomons, 20 miles across a strait from the group capital, Tulagi, which had been occupied at the time of the Battle of the Coral Sea.

The strategic importance of the Solomons had not been lost on the Americans, and on 7 August 1942, 11,000 men of the US 1st Marine Division were landed at Guadalcanal and Tulagi, covered by a carrier task force. The half-complete airstrip was abandoned before their advance, but the defenders of Tulagi gave the Americans their first experience of Japanese fanatic resistance to the last man. The Imperial government reacted to news of the invasion by gathering together an army from the former Midway invasion forces and garrisons on the conquered islands to drive the Americans from the Solomons; so began the long drawn-out contest for the hitherto practically unknown island of Guadalcanal, which was to etch itself bloodily into United States history and legend.

Meanwhile, on the night of the American landings, Admiral Gunichi Mikawa, commander of the misnamed 8th Carrier Division of cruisers at Rabaul, New Britain, 550 miles north-west of Guadalcanal, had embarked all the troops and sailors he could muster on six transports and despatched them with a destroyer escort to reinforce the Guadalcanal garrison. Soon after leaving, the force was sighted by the US submarine S35, patrolling off the southern exit to the channel between New Britain and the neighbouring New Ireland. Her CO submerged and set up an attack on the largest freighter, diving below her accompanying destroyer and while deep firing two torpedoes. Both hit, perhaps the only example of a completely successful sonar attack as exercised by US submarines before the war and attempted unsuccessfully many times in the opening months. The freighter went down with the loss of 300 troops, and since she was carrying the key elements of the force, the others turned back for Rabaul.

The next night Mikawa led his cruisers to attack the US invasion fleet, still offloading supplies on the beaches of Guadalcanal. He surprised two separate divisions of the covering force of one Australian and four US cruisers out of heavy rain squalls near Savo Island off the north-western cape of Guadalcanal in the early hours of 9 August, reducing all but one to riven, blazing hulks. Instead of following up this devastating victory by carrying on to destroy his real target, the almost defenceless transports at their anchorage less than 20 miles to his east, Mikawa withdrew. For the Americans ashore, most of whose supplies were still in the transports, it was a remarkable deliverance.

The following morning, four of the victorious cruisers were returning to base when, off New Ireland, they practically ran over

S44 under Lt.-Cdr. John R. Moore. He managed to move 700 yards off their track as they approached and, lacking a TDC, aimed his boat to fire a salvo of four torpedoes at the second ship in the starboard column. All hit, detonating with a thunderous series of explosions as Moore took his boat deep. The victim, the heavy cruiser *Kako*, of nearly 9,000 tons, settled rapidly with loud, rumbling, bursting and hissing noises 'more terrifying to the crew', Moore recounted, 'than the actual depth charges that followed. It sounded as if great chains were being dragged across the hull.'[2] The *Kako* was the first major warship to be sunk by a US submarine, although several had been claimed.

Despite these timely feats by boats in exactly the right position at the right time, the S-class submarines working from Brisbane had very few successes and were proving manifestly unsuitable for the tropical conditions of their patrol area. They lacked air-conditioning – apart from Moore's *S44*, which had an extemporized arrangement bought privately and fitted by the crew – and the heat and humidity had debilitating effects. To the tensions of patrol in the heavily defended waters near Rabaul were added the miseries of prickly heat, skin ulcers, constant sweating and fatigue; and headaches and nausea from the foul air were too frequently augmented by the frustrations of machinery breakdowns as the moisture in the atmosphere below, condensing and dripping from metal, affected the electrics. Not the least impressive point about Moore's exploit was the fact that in the previous 180 days since he and his crew had arrived in Brisbane from Panama they had spent 127 days at sea.[3]

The Japanese submariners, whose boats also lacked air-conditioning or humidity control, suffered the same torments. These were hardly worse, though, than the savage conditions under which they had been trained and which no doubt they expected in their élite service. For the Americans there was an alternative: before the end of August it had been decided that the Brisbane S boats would be sent home to be re-deployed in more suitable areas, their place to be taken in what had now become the centre of gravity of the Pacific war by faster, more powerful and habitable modern fleet boats from Lockwood's command at Fremantle. This reduced the number of boats available to operate against Japanese supply shipping from the conquered Dutch and British colonies; and since Nimitz instructed English at Pearl Harbor to send boats to patrol off Truk in the Caroline Islands, the Japanese naval base and staging-post for the Solomons campaign, the number of boats operating against merchant shipping in the waters off Japan was also much reduced. This run-down in what Dönitz would have termed the 'tonnage war' was not matched by gains in the struggle for the Solomons; a carrier and a battleship were both damaged off Truk on 28 August – the first capital ships to be hit effectively by US submarines – but otherwise Japanese fleet movements and the transport of troops and supplies for Guadalcanal were scarcely affected.

Japanese submarines were similarly sucked into the cauldron of the Solomons. In the first days Admiral Mikawa had concentrated five boats under his own command, the newly formed Eighth (Submarine) Fleet, in Indispensable Strait between Tulagi and the neighbouring island of Malaita with orders to attack the enemy anchorages at Guadalcanal and Tulagi and bombard the landing operations. Three of these boats were the minelaying-refuelling types which had been sent to French Frigate Shoal before the Midway operation; two were 700-ton RO boats not dissimilar to the US S class. Forced down by US aircraft and anti-submarine surface patrols, they had practically no effect on the vital reinforcement and supply battle, which was decided by air and surface forces.

The pattern was established early. The Americans soon completed the Japanese airstrip, which they named Henderson Field, and by day US aircraft from the strip held the skies, covering the landing of troops and supplies. At dusk, as the planes landed, a force of Japanese destroyers, christened by US Marines the 'Tokyo Express', was already heading at high speed for the passage known as 'The Slot' between the islands. Arriving off Guadalcanal at about midnight, they would bombard the airfield or fight off US forces in murderous, close-range duels before retiring to land troops on the Japanese-held western end of the island. By first light, as US planes took off again, they would already be withdrawing. In these high-speed, twisting jousts, often at point-blank range, which lit the night skies with lethal fireworks and explosions, leaving crippled ships burning like beacons in the seas between the islands, submarines exerted no influence. One of Mikawa's RO boats sank an American transport but was itself sunk before the end of the month by destroyer depth-charge attack, as was one of the minelaying boats.

In the meantime, six of the large Japanese modern B1 scouting submarines of the 1st Squadron, Sixth (Submarine) Fleet, together with their A1 headquarters boat, had been switched from an intended commerce-raiding foray in the Indian Ocean and rushed to take station south-east of the Solomons across the route of the US transports from Espiritu Santo in the New Hebrides, where the Americans had earlier established a base for the anticipated struggle for the islands. Other large scouting boats of the 3rd Submarine Squadron were taken from commerce-raiding operations in Australian waters to join them until there were sixteen boats disposed in two cordons across the line of US communications: an inner cordon just south of the Solomons and an outer cordon 200 miles south of them. The boats, disposed at 30-mile intervals, patrolled their line at right angles to the expected track of the enemy, launching float planes at dawn to extend coverage on either flank. Although they came under the command of a rear-admiral in the Squadron headquarters submarine they were neither trained nor expected to operate, like Dönitz's packs, as attacking groups; indeed on occasions when contact with the enemy was made, the submarines concerned seemed either to attack without signalling, or signalled to the fleet C-in-C rather than their squadron commander.[4]

On the first occasion, on 31 August, *I26* sighted the carrier *Saratoga* and attacked, firing a full salvo of six torpedoes before making an emergency dive in the face of a screening destroyer which had seen the tracks and was heading for the source; the destroyer was so close as *I26* went down that she scraped her. The *Saratoga*, which had only recently returned to the fleet after repairs to torpedo damage from *I6* south-east of Pearl Harbor in January, took one of the torpedoes aft and had to spend another three months in dock.

On 15 September *I19* under Cdr. Taikachi Kinashi scored an even more important success with what has been called 'probably the most effective torpedo salvo in submarine history'.[5] Two US carrier task groups, deployed to cover a convoy of transports carrying the 7th Marine Regiment and its stores to Guadalcanal, ran into his patrol line in the early afternoon of 15 September. He was in the way of the *Wasp*'s group and, penetrating the screening destroyers to within 500 yards of the carrier, unleashed a full salvo of six torpedoes at her. Three struck with terrible effect, starting uncontrollable fires which soon consumed the ship, forcing her abandonment; three missed, but such was the range of the Japanese oxygen-paraffin torpedoes that they sped on beyond Kinashi's horizon – had he still been at periscope depth – and into the *Hornet*'s task group over 5 miles away. One struck the new battleship, *North Carolina*, another hit the destroyer *O'Brien* on the bow. The battleship was able to continue the operation, but she then withdrew to Pearl Harbor for repairs. The gutted hulk of the *Wasp* had to be sunk by torpedoes from one of her own destroyers that night. The *O'Brien*, after temporary local repairs, foundered on her way to America for a thorough refit. However, of at least equal importance, the convoy carrying the 7th Marine Regiment passed safely through the patrol lines to Guadalcanal to land the Marines and the vital supplies.

These achievements of Sixth Fleet submarines against capital units seemed to make up for past disappointments – relieved hitherto only by Tanabe's destruction of the crippled carrier *Yorktown* – and showed that submarines might still fulfil the hopes placed in them before the war. Further boats from the Sixth Fleet were sent to the area, including the Type C1 attack submarines carrying midgets, but the remarkable exploits of those fifteen days between late August and mid-September were not to be repeated. In October, *I176*, now under Tanabe, damaged the heavy cruiser *Chester*, which had to return to the United States for repairs; in November, *I26*, which had damaged the *Saratoga* in August, hit the cruiser *Juneau* while she was retiring damaged from a furious night action off Guadalcanal; she blew up and sank almost instantly. About 200 survivors left in the waters were abandoned by the other, damaged, ships of the force and over the next few days the great majority were eaten alive by sharks; only 10 of the crew of over 600 were eventually rescued.[6]

The isolated Japanese successes against warships were of far less significance for the Solomons campaign than the submarines' continued failure to disrupt the American transport and supply convoys. Two operations to launch midgets from their mother submarines off the Guadalcanal anchorage in November each claimed a supply ship for the loss of eight midgets and their courageous young crews, but the American supply run was never seriously affected.

US submarines continued to be similarly ineffectual against Japanese reinforcements and supply lines. Defective torpedoes were less to blame than strategy. Despite Midway the US fleet remained vastly inferior to the Japanese, hence the priority targets for submarines, as handed down from Admiral King in Washington, remained capital units. And both English in Pearl Harbor and Christie in Brisbane continued to direct their boats to patrol areas off the main Japanese fleet and advanced bases, where they faced strong air and surface anti-submarine patrols, Palau and Truk to the east of the Philippines, Rabaul and Kavieng off the eastern tip of New Guinea. Moreover, they continued to divert them to fast warship targets on Ultra intelligence passed by Holmes from the cryptanalysts of what had been Hypo, now renamed 'Frupac' – Fleet Radio Unit Pacific. There was no shortage of such intelligence. Besides Mikawa's forces operating from Rabaul, the six Japanese carriers remaining after Midway, together with two battleships and four heavy cruisers reorganized under Admiral Nagumo into a strike force named the Third Carrier Division, were in the area contesting American air supremacy. The US submarines directed towards them made frequent sightings and several attacks, but after the two hits on 28 August they failed to make any more.

Through October and November more of Pearl Harbor's most modern fleet submarines were transferred on Nimitz's orders to Brisbane by way of patrols off Truk. This brought to an end for the time being English's already reduced campaign against commerce in Japanese waters, and raised Christie's command to the most powerful US submarine force in the Pacific. It did not affect the Solomons campaign. The controlling factor remained the Wildcat fighters and dive-bombers from Henderson Field, Guadalcanal, which continued to restrict Japanese supplies and reinforcements to what could be dropped during the nocturnal forays of the 'Tokyo Express' down 'The Slot'. This was insufficient for the 30,000 or more Japanese troops on Guadalcanal. By the end of October, after mounting a supreme offensive which failed to dislodge the US Marines from their trenches, the Japanese were desperately hungry, and in their weakened state great numbers were falling away to disease.

During the first week in November two battalions of fresh troops from the 38th Division transported from the conquered Dutch Indies were landed as reinforcements in the usual way by light forces under Rear-Admiral Raizo Tanaka – dubbed by the Marines 'Tenacious Tanaka of the Tokyo Express'. The following week a large operation was mounted to land the remaining 17,000 troops of the division, and their equipment and supplies. They were embarked on eleven transports to sail behind a powerful detachment of the Third Carrier Division headed by the two battleships, whose aim was to destroy Henderson Field and the aircraft on the ground in a night bombardment, then cover daytime landings from the transports.

They were met off Guadalcanal in the early hours of 13 November by a US cruiser force which suffered desperate losses in the ensuing battle – including the *Juneau*, victim of *I26* the following morning – but mortally wounded one Japanese battleship and prevented the intended bombing of the airfield. As a result aircraft were able to fly, and over the following days they sank all the transports. A few of the surviving troops were put ashore off Cape

Esperance; the majority were returned in destroyers to Rabaul. The vital provisions were lost. Meanwhile, the heavy units of both sides met in another incandescent night action in the narrow waters between the islands and the second Japanese battleship joined the scores of holed, burnt and broken hulls lying on the bed of what was christened Ironbottom Sound.

Submarines had played no part in these critical battles. Seven US transports with reinforcements and stores had come safely through the Japanese submarine patrols just prior to the series of actions off Guadalcanal, and it was the aircraft from Henderson Field, not US submarines, which had destroyed the Japanese transports and finally won the supply battle. The air battles during the campaign had also set the seal on Japan's ultimate defeat; against the United States' vastly greater production of aircraft, Nagumo's losses of carrier planes and trained pilots over the Solomons left Japan permanently and progressively inferior in the air.

When news of the latest failure to fight reinforcements through to Guadalcanal reached Tokyo on 16 November, the Emperor decreed that the submarines of Komatsu's Sixth Fleet should be adapted to run in supplies.[7] The submarine and squadron commanders of this élite fighting force were entirely opposed to becoming 'pack mules' for the army, as no doubt was Komatsu himself, but he told them it was an Imperial command that the troops on Guadalcanal were to be supplied at all cost, after which 'no further dissentient voices were heard'.[8]

Trials were already under way at the home base at Yokosuka. The skipper of the old boat RO31, Lt.-Cdr. Mochitsura Hashimoto, recalled after the war how he had been ordered to experiment by firing bags of rice from his torpedo tubes; the bags burst and he had to try with biscuit tins, then with torpedo-shaped wooden containers, but all were broken up by the launching impulse. The solution eventually adopted was to pack the rice in rubber bags which were secured on deck and at the landing area manhandled into boats; when it became apparent that sea water was penetrating the rubber these were exchanged for steel drums secured with devices that could be released from inside the submarine when it was too dangerous for the boat to surface; the drums floated up for collection by the troops ashore. Later, so-called 'freight tubes' were developed. These resembled shallow landing craft with a deck on which up to 2 tons could be lashed; powered by two torpedoes they had a range of over 2 miles at 3 knots, and were steered by a single man at a tiller; these too could be launched from inside while the submarine remained submerged. The guns and reload torpedoes of boats adapted in this way were often removed to provide more space for the stores.[9]

The first supply run from Buin, Bougainville, the northernmost island in the Solomons chain, was made by the ace Yahachi Tanabe. During December the numbers built up until by the new year, 1943, there were twenty boats on the run, one departing every two days, alternating with Tanaka's destroyers, also stripped of some of their armament so that supplies could be piled high on their decks. In this way a proportion of the Japanese force on Guadalcanal was kept barely alive until in early February the tireless Tanaka evacuated over a third of them under cover of a brilliant deception operation staged by the Japanese fleet; some 21,000 emaciated corpses were found later by the Americans. Thousands were never discovered.[10]

Yamamoto had known for some time that his pre-war prophecy had come true, and more precisely than he could have imagined. He had indeed 'run wild for six months' – up to the battle of Midway – 'or a year' – until the decision to evacuate Guadalcanal. Now he had 'utterly no confidence in the second and third years'.[11] He wrote to a friend shortly after the evacuation: 'I do not know what to do next. Nor am I happy about facing my officers and men who have fought so hard without fear of death.'[12]

It was also in practice the end of the submarine fleet as an effective attack or commerce-raiding force, for it appears that the conversion of the Sixth Fleet boats into supply freighters lowered the hitherto splendid morale of the crews.[13] It certainly caused losses as these large boats manoeuvred close in to the reef- and rock-strewn shallows patrolled by fast motor-torpedo PT boats. Two were lost each month from November 1942 to January 1943. The last was the 2,000-ton *I1* which was detected by two 600-ton converted trawlers of the Royal New Zealand Navy, *Kiwi* and *Moa*, as she was about to surface off the landing point on Guadalcanal at dusk on 29 January. She tried to go deep, but was depth-charged and so damaged that her CO had no option but to surface and fight it out with his gun. The two trawlers opened fire as the great submarine emerged from the sea, sweeping the gun's crew and bridge party while they closed to ram.

As recounted by Hashimoto, who was not present and must have heard it from one of the survivors or even at third hand, the first lieutenant and the navigator both collected swords and rushed up to the bridge, where the No. 1, finding no sign of the CO and seeing the gun's crew wiped out, called up the reserve gun's crew. The navigator, an expert swordsman, saw one of the enemy vessels which had rammed them alongside on the port quarter and dashed down along the after casing and tried to leap aboard; the rail was too high and he was left hanging by one hand, waving his sword in the other, as the craft separated. During the ensuing fire-fight, with the trawlers' searchlights illuminating the submarine, blinding the gun's crew, *I1*'s conning tower was repeatedly hit and holed. Turning for the shore, the large boat grounded and took a heavy list to port. Many of those below were able to climb out and into the water but several were trapped by the inflow of the sea down the perforated tower.

The first lieutenant eventually reached land and collected fifty of his men to join the troops waiting for supplies.[14] By then the responsible petty officers had had time to take the current code-books and bury or destroy them, but later US divers on the wreck recovered a priceless haul of secret documents including code addi-tions about to come into effect. The cryptographers at Frupac had been in the dark through the summer and autumn since the Japanese had changed the five-digit code in June and again in August, but they were beginning to work themselves back when the material from the *I1* arrived to accelerate their efforts. Part of a Japanese chart also found in the Solomons and overlaid with the secret grid for referencing positions, hitherto unbroken, allowed them to work out the grid system for the entire Pacific and gave them greater mastery of enemy signals than ever before.[15]

All major navies used their submarines at one time or another for supplying beleaguered garrisons, evacuating personnel and landing or supplying agents and saboteurs. But for Japan in retreat after the struggle for Guadalcanal the supply and reinforcement of isolated garrisons and their subsequent evacuation became a stan-dard, almost principal task.[16] This was the chief reason why they contributed little more in the offensive role for which they had been designed, or the commerce-raiding role to which Komatsu had intended to transfer them when he had taken command of the Sixth Fleet. There were not enough to go round. The Japanese boats were also overtaken by American technology, principally radar and cryptanalysis, which revealed their every movement. It is little wonder if morale declined.

In the Mediterranean in 1942 the supply battle was being fought as fiercely, and again the clinching factor was air power. After the disastrous loss of the Spitfires flown in to Malta in April 1942 from the US carrier *Wasp*, a second reinforcement by the *Wasp* and *Eagle* in May had proved successful; the new Spitfires had repulsed mass Axis air attacks on 10 May, shooting down over twenty enemy planes and damaging, possibly destroying, twice that number for the loss of only three of their own.[17]

In June, after Rommel's offensive had brought him the port of Tobruk, Hitler had cancelled a planned air- and sea-borne invasion of Malta in favour of concentrating all resources through Tobruk for the drive into Egypt for the Suez Canal. His decision seems to have been prompted not simply by the Luftwaffe's failure to gain air control over the island fortress, but also by a belief that Egypt was ripe for revolution, and perhaps more by distrust of his Italian partners, particularly their navy, which he suspected might fail the troops after they had gained the island. The Italians, for their part, had prepared their plans for invading Malta expressly to prevent Rommel making his dash for Egypt. Seven of the ten divisions of the *Panzerarmee* were Italian, and their Supreme Headquarters Staff foresaw only disaster if Rommel overstretched his land lines again. They were right.

For Malta, Hitler's decision had been a turning-point. His failure to invade is generally regarded as a blunder, although it has been argued that the island had become less a strategic asset than a hostage to the enemy to be held at enormous cost for reasons of prestige and pride.[18] However the prestige had been significant, and the depredations of forces from the base of sufficiently vital strategic importance for Hitler to order its elimination. Had the other Mediterranean submarine flotillas been augmented and concentrated with the 10th Flotilla boats in a single-minded assault on Axis supply shipping to North Africa, the strategic importance of the base remaining in British hands would have been even more apparent. This was clear to at least one young submarine CO at the time. Standing by a new S-class boat at Chatham, he wrote a letter to *The Times* in July under the pseudonym 'Naval Officer':

> Let us therefore reconsider the offensive value of the submarine to us at a time when we are deeply concerned about its value to the enemy. Its primary strategic quality is the ability to act unsupported at great distances from a base and in waters under enemy control; tactically it is a means of achieving surprise with that most powerful weapon, the torpedo. Operating singly or in packs, aided by aircraft and aiding them, submarines could cripple the Axis supply line to Libya. Have we built shelters for our submarines in Malta, as the Germans have for theirs in St. Nazaire?[19]

Whatever notice the publication of this letter may have received at the Admiralty or in the War Cabinet, the Mediterranean flotillas were not concentrated under a single command against Rommel's supplies. Nonetheless, as Axis pressure on Malta eased towards the end of July, 'Shrimp' Simpson returned to the old Lazaretto base, followed by the four surviving boats from the 10th Flotilla, which were soon joined by new U-class boats from home. Their immediate tasks were defensive. The island had been reduced by air and sea blockade practically to starvation, and stocks of fuel were dangerously low. Some of the large, older submarines of the O, P and R classes, and the River-class *Clyde*, which had been adapted as tanker and supply boats with half their batteries removed, ran what was termed a 'Magic Carpet' service from Alexandria with the majority of their tanks and even ballast tanks filled with aviation spirit, and every available space crammed with ammunition and provisions. They could not make up all the island's needs and in early August a convoy of fourteen merchantmen sailed from the Clyde with an extraordinarily powerful covering force of three carriers, two battleships and seven cruisers, together with screening destroyers in a supply operation codenamed 'Pedestal'. Six of the 10th Flotilla's eight submarines were disposed on an east–west patrol line south of the island of Pantellaria in the Narrows between Sicily and the Tunisian coast to shield the convoy from enemy surface forces on the final leg to Malta after the heavy ships of the escort had turned back for home. A seventh was directed to a billet off the north coast of Sicily, west of the naval base of Palermo, the eighth and last available boat to Cape Milazzo by the northern entrance to the Strait of Messina; this latter was *P42*, a newcomer to the flotilla, commanded by Lt. Alastair Mars.

The convoy and its heavy escort, together with a further carrier, *Furious*, which was to fly off thirty-eight Spitfires to Malta to replace losses, passed through the Straits of Gibraltar in fog in the early hours of 10 August. The following morning it was picked up by enemy reconnaissance aircraft and shortly after noon, as the *Furious* began flying off her Spitfires, the ships were sighted by *U73* under OLt. Helmut Rosenbaum. He penetrated the destroyer screen without detection, allowed the columns of merchantmen past and set up an attack on the carrier *Eagle* astern and to starboard of the formation, firing a full salvo at close range. All four torpedoes hit, tearing a tremendous gash in her port side, and she sank in eight minutes. That evening, after the *Furious* had completed her fly-off and turned back for the Straits, German bombers and torpedo planes attacked the convoy, but failed to hit, and repeated their attack the following morning, 12 August. The main

air attacks from bases in southern Sardinia came that early afternoon and evening; one merchantman was damaged in the morning
wave and in the first of the evening attacks the carrier *Indomitable*
was put out of action by three direct hits on her flight deck, and
one destroyer was so damaged she had to be sunk. After this,
the covering force of heavy ships turned back for the Straits as
planned, leaving four cruisers and the destroyers to shepherd the
merchantmen through the Narrows between Sicily and the north-
eastern corner of Tunisia, and so on the final leg to Malta.

Two groups of a total of thirteen Italian submarines were waiting across their track before the mined shallows of the Skerki
Bank north of Tunis. An hour later, at 20.00, as the merchantmen
were closing from four columns into two to follow minesweeping
destroyers, the escort flagship, another cruiser and the tanker *Ohio*
were all struck by torpedoes from the *Axum* under Lt. Renato
Ferrini; this was the most devastating single blow by Italian
submarines during the war – apart from the Underwater Special
Forces strike on the *Queen Elizabeth* and *Valiant* in Alexandria
harbour – particularly as the flagship, which had to turn back for
Gibraltar, and the other cruiser, which had to be sunk, were the
only escorts equipped to direct the Malta fighter aircraft by radio.
At first it was not clear whether the explosions had been caused
by mines or torpedoes, but as the convoy altered southerly to
evade the danger another wave of German bombers and torpedo
planes struck, catching the ships in a confused jumble without
fighter cover. Two merchantmen were sunk, another damaged.
They had scarcely re-formed when they ran into the second group
of Italian submarines, and a third cruiser was hit forward by a
torpedo from the *Alagi* under Lt. Sergio Puccini; her damage was
contained and she remained with the convoy. The *Alagi* also
torpedoed a merchantman and the *Bronzo* under Lt. Cesare
Buldrini sank another merchantman already damaged by air
attack.

The surviving ships rounded Cape Bon at midnight and steered
southerly, hugging the Tunisian coast, when they were beset by
German and Italian torpedo boats which disabled a fourth cruiser
and sank four more of the merchant ships and damaged another.
The cruiser's captain, unable to get under way by daylight and
close in to the shore, made the hard decision to scuttle her. Shortly
after dawn, as the surviving ships, now covered by Beaufighter
patrols from Malta, passed south of the line of 10th Flotilla submarines, they were attacked by another wave of German bombers;
despite the Beaufighters one merchantman was sunk and the

tanker *Ohio* received further damage from a crashing Stuka. A second, smaller wave of bombers came in three hours later, setting one merchantman ablaze and stopping the *Ohio* and another merchantman.

After this, Spitfires from Malta took the remaining ships under their wings and escorted them to safety for the remainder of the passage. But of the fourteen merchantmen which had left the Clyde only three sailed into Grand Harbour, Valetta, that afternoon. The following morning a fourth with a gaping hole in her bows limped in stern first. Finally, on the morning of 15 August, the crippled *Ohio*, which had been defended throughout the daylight hours by relays of Spitfires, was towed in, decks awash, lashed between two destroyers. To get these five survivors of the original convoy, including the *Ohio* with her vital cargo of fuel, through the danger zone south of the Sicilian airfields the Malta Beaufighters and Spitfires had flown 407 sorties,[20] while the operation as a whole had cost the Royal Navy casualties more appropriate to a fleet action: one carrier, two cruisers and a destroyer sunk, a second carrier and two other cruisers heavily damaged, against enemy losses of two Italian submarines – one sunk by a destroyer escorting the *Furious* after she had turned back – and a significant number of German and Italian aircraft.

Of the 10th Flotilla submarines, only one sighted an enemy. This was Alastair Mars' *P42* (later named the *Unbroken*) which had been ordered to patrol from 2 miles (by day) to 4 miles (by night) off Cape Milazzo, west of the northern entrance to the Strait of Messina. At his briefing Mars had suggested that this was such an obvious focal point it was doubtful if any enemy force would pass near, and was so close to the lighthouse he would probably be detected. Simpson had told him that the position had been ordered by the Admiralty and could not be altered.[21]

Mars was detected on his first day in the billet, 10 April, and subjected to attacks in which no less than seventy depth-charges were dropped, fortunately inaccurately, as he crawled seawards. He was now in an unenviable situation: it was obviously useless to return to his station since the enemy had been alerted and would avoid the Cape, yet he had already challenged his orders and they had been confirmed emphatically.

Before sailing he had studied all past patrol reports from submarines in the area and had discovered that Tomkinson and Cayley had each sunk an Italian cruiser within sight of the active volcano Stromboli, 30 miles to the north of his station, and that Cdr. Wilfred Woods in the *Triumph* had damaged another cruiser in that vicinity. With Nelsonic disregard of orders, he now reassigned himself a new station 12 miles south-west of Stromboli, selecting a position in the Lipari Islands which appeared likely to be a focal point between three passages through the group.

He spent the daylight hours of 11 and 12 August anxiously in his chosen position at periscope depth without sighting anything, but early the next morning the reward for his preparation and moral toughness was heralded by the throbbing of numerous pro-pellers, after which a squadron of four cruisers in line ahead flanked by destroyers and overflown by anti-submarine seaplanes appeared, heading straight for him. He steered southwards to move off their track and at the same time meet an alteration to starboard which he expected them to make. They did come round to starboard, placing him 3,000 yards off track, but he was able to set up a deliberate attack and scored hits on the heavy cruiser *Bolzano* and the light cruiser *Muzio Attendolo*, both of which suffered such damage that they took no further part in Italy's war. These were Mars' last torpedoes and he returned to base. Amidst congratulations for redressing some of the Royal Navy's heavy losses, he was not asked to account for disobeying orders.[22]

'Pedestal' did not end the terrible shortages in Malta, but it did alleviate them sufficiently for the island to become once again an offensive base. More U-class boats joined the 10th Flotilla, together with one or two S-class, and with the island's Beaufort bomber force, resumed the attack on Axis supply lines across the central Mediterranean. In return, the German squadrons in Sicily inten-sified their air assaults on the island. The S-class *P247* (later *Saracen*), arriving by night to join the 10th Flotilla in September, was shown the way by the pyrotechnics of a raid in progress. The following morning she was guided by two minesweepers along a swept channel through mines laid by the enemy. She passed the entrance to Grand Harbour, opening the view of sheer fortress walls that stretched back through centuries of maritime command in peace and war, and the partly ruined buildings, towers and domes beyond, 'all white or pink and sand-yellow against the blue sky'.[23] She was cheered round Fort St Elmo by a group of Maltese children, entered Marsamxett harbour with the seamen lined smartly at attention on the fore casing, and turned into Lazaretto Creek where the blue-painted submarines were berthed, each at the end of a floating catwalk before the partly wrecked, colonnaded façade of the old Lazaretto building. Her first lieu-tenant, Edward Young, writing a decade later, could 'not remember anything quite like the Malta submarine base at this time'. Food was still miserably short; air raids occurred around the clock.

> We got a preliminary warning from the ringing of a cloistral hand bell, the signal for putting the smoke screen into action. Besides the smoke canisters along the shore, each submarine in harbour had one placed ready on the casing fore and aft. In a few minutes a dense white fog would spread over the creek and the submarine base ... Sometimes through a gap in the smokescreen we caught a glimpse of the air battle going on high over our heads ...[24]

William King, who had last looked in at Malta as commander of the T-class *Trusty*, returned to the base a month after Young arrived. *Trusty* had been the first British submarine transferred east after the Japanese assault; arriving at Singapore in the final days before its capitulation, King had departed on patrol undirected, and without intelligence, quite alone it seemed in a dissolving world. Withdrawn first to Surabaya, then to Ceylon with the only other British submarine in the east, the tropical patrols without air-conditioning had broken what remained of his health – 'After three years in a submarine I had forgotten what it was like to feel well.' He had been sent home to recover, thence to Malta to serve ashore as Staff Officer Submarines. He found amid starvation and misery a fierce morale among both the British and the Maltese, and mutual admiration, quite the opposite to the disintegration he had witnessed at Singapore. The talk was of little but food:

> No food. No spares. Incessant bombing. Submarines being repaired by half-starved Maltese workmen in inadequate shelters hand-scooped out of rock around the harbour. It was amazing that any base could function at all, much less continue delivering blows at the enemy ...[25]

He put the miracle down to 'Shrimp' Simpson, who had been improvising for so long 'and with extraordinary flair instilling heart into both weary sailors and hungry Maltese'.

The submarines did less well in this period than at any time since the very early months of 1941, perhaps because, as then, the new skippers had not got their eyes in, perhaps because of the new efficiency of the Italian escorts fitted with German asdic, or because some of the supply shipping was routed east for Tobruk. There was an exception in October when Simpson, who continued to set up ambushes whenever possible on Ultra intelligence, directed five boats to the south of Pantellaria to lie in wait for a Tripoli-bound convoy of four supply ships and a tanker. Unlike Dönitz's packs which were essentially reconnaissance lines to find convoys, and hence were directed to cover the widest area across shipping routes, Simpson's groups, when positioned on Ultra, were lined or staggered along the anticipated track of the target to attack in depth. In this case, he added in his signal that the destruction of the convoy could make all the difference to the North African campaign.[26]

The northernmost boat, Safari, was too far off track to see the convoy as it zigzagged southwards on the morning of 19 October. Ten miles to the south of her was the Utmost, formerly Cayley's command, now under Lt. John Coombe. He saw the convoy over the horizon, fired a desperate salvo at extreme range, which missed, then surfaced at grave risk in view of the escorting sea-planes to send a sighting report. As a result, Lt. Edward Stanley in Unbending, 10 miles to the south of him, was able to get into position to fire from only 1,000 yards, sinking one of the merchant-men and an escorting destroyer. Ten miles to the south of him, Mars in P42 had also been alerted. He found the escorts thoroughly stirred up, speeding on different courses, and above them hovering anti-submarine seaplanes. As he approached through rough seas, with the periscope sometimes thrust conspicuously high by the motion and difficulties with trim, he was sighted. A destroyer and a seaplane headed towards him, and he was forced to fire from long range on the swing. His last view through the periscope as he ordered the boat deep was 'of a seaplane in a steep bank with a full view of the pilot in his cockpit, and a dropping marker flare'.[27] Descending as the pulsing screws of the destroyer passed close above, he heard two distant thuds at the correct time and interval for hits – probably on the tanker, which however did not sink. He was then subjected to an accurate depth-charging which shattered over half the cells in the batteries and started a battery fire; he was fortunate to surface after dark and make his way back to base.

The tanker he had hit received further damage in an air attack that evening, and was later torpedoed by Lt. Thomas Barlow, in United, ordered up from a station off Tripoli. Finally Cdr. 'Ben' Bryant of the Safari, who had turned south when he realized he had missed the convoy and chased after dark on the surface, caught up before dawn and sank a 5,000-ton merchantman. However, the badly holed tanker and the two remaining merchant-men reached port that day.

Between them the 10th Flotilla and the 1st Flotilla boats, still operating from Beirut, and the aircraft operating from Malta and the Egyptian bases sank 25 per cent of the Axis supply tonnage during this period.[28] More significantly in strategic terms, aircraft from Egyptian bases – assisted by the Axis' shortage of fuel for escorts – forced the Italians, against Rommel's most urgent protests, to route convoys to Benghazi and Tripoli, respectively 800 and 1,300 miles to his rear. Even Tobruk, which was too small to handle more than a quarter of his monthly requirements at best, was 300 miles behind his lines. Moreover, the port and supply columns from it were as exposed to the British aircraft from Egypt as Grand Harbour, Valetta, had been to the Axis air fleet in Sicily, and suffered as heavily.

Meanwhile, the British and Commonwealth forces in Egypt, recently electrified by a charismatic new leader, General Bernard Montgomery, received large-scale reinforcements of men and *matériel*, including American Sherman tanks and 105-mm self-propelled assault guns, via the long haul around the Cape and up the Suez Canal. Rommel had realized that the gamble had failed after being checked at Alam Halfa, south of El Alamein, at the end of August. It was not that he lacked sufficient supplies, particularly of fuel, simply that he could not bring them up from his rear bases in sufficient quantity.[29]

Montgomery meanwhile was reading his messages to German Army headquarters in Rome in daily Ultra decrypts, and knew his troop strengths and dispositions and his many requirements as intimately as the German staff. On 23 October Montgomery struck; after masterly feints in the early stages, he launched massed Sherman tanks and self-propelled guns through the lines on 2 November, breaking Rommel's armour at El Aqqaqir. Thereafter, what remained of the *Panzerarmee Afrika* could only make a precipitate retreat by the way it had come. Meanwhile, in the night and early morning of 7/8 November, large Anglo-American forces under the supreme command of US General Dwight Eisenhower landed at the western end of the North African coastline in French Morocco and Algeria. The operation, named 'Torch', was designed in concert with Montgomery's advance from the east to drive the Axis from Africa.

The Mediterranean submarines had been reinforced before the invasion. Four 8th Flotilla boats from Gibraltar were ordered off Toulon with instructions to watch and report if the French fleet should sail to interfere with the landings on Vichy French colonial territory; when this did not happen they were repositioned off Italian bases. Others acted as navigation beacons and scouts off the landing beaches. The 1st Flotilla boats in the eastern Mediterranean were positioned to prevent Axis forces moving westwards from the Aegean, and some were loaned to the 10th Flotilla, which was positioned to cordon off the Italian fleet from the landings;

they were stationed in lines both north and south of the Strait of Messina, and off Cape St Vito at the north-west corner of Sicily.

Here, on the day after the landings, the Italian submarine *Granito*, on passage westwards on the surface, almost overran the position of *P247* (*Saracen*), whose commander, Lt. Michael Lumby, fired a full salvo at her from 800 yards; he confided to his first lieutenant, Young, that he could clearly see the smiling faces of the Italian officers on the bridge. Three of the torpedoes struck, blowing the submarine apart. Nothing of her or the smiling officers or the crew below remained as *P247* closed to search for survivors, only three seat lockers floating in a stain of oil.[30] The following morning Lt. J.S. Stevens of *P46* (later and appropriately named *Unruffled*), also in the line off Cape St Vito, hit and damaged a cruiser after penetrating her destroyer and seaplane screen.

The Italian battlefleet, short of fuel, did not emerge to challenge the Allied heavy forces covering the landings; a battle squadron sailed from Taranto up through the Strait of Messina to Naples but was missed at long range by the only boat near enough to the speeding ships.

'Torch' had caught the Axis high command by surprise, but on news of the landings Italian and German U-boats were concentrated against the Allied supply lines both inside and outside the Straits of Gibraltar. On 11 November, off Cape de Gata east of the Straits, OLt. Ernst-Ulrich Brüller in command of *U407* sank the 19,600-ton P & O liner, now troop transport, *Viceroy of India*. She was returning after landing troops and the loss of life was small as the great ship rolled over and the sea claimed the magnificent public rooms, the oak panelling and leaded windows, and spread across the promenade and sports decks. On the same day KLt. Joseph Röther in *U380* sank the 11,000-ton Dutch liner *Nieuw Zeeland*, while outside the Straits KLt. Hans Adolf Schweichel in *U173* sank a 9,300-ton transport and a destroyer and damaged another, larger transport. The following day the *Paukenschlag* boat, *U130*, still under Ernst Kals, sank three US transports totalling 34,400 tons – after they had landed their troops – and KLt. Werner Henke of *U515* sank a depot ship and a destroyer; but the most serious losses outside the Straits were the 20,100-ton liner *Warwick Castle*, torpedoed by KLt. Gustav Poel of *U413* on the 14th while she was returning after landing troops, and the 13,800-ton escort-carrier *Avenger*, victim of *U155* under KLt. Adolf Piening, who sank an 11,200-ton transport on the same day, the 15th. For the most part, though, the swarming U-boats and Italian submarines were forced under and neutralized or sunk.

From 7 to 19 November three Italian boats, including the *Granito*, and five U-boats were destroyed in the western Mediterranean, and two U-boats outside the Straits; a further four Italian submarines were sunk in December.[31] In addition the CO of *U572*, which had arrived off the Moroccan coast only a day after the landings started but accomplished nothing, was relieved of command and placed before a court martial for cowardice in the face of the enemy. Judged guilty and denied clemency by Dönitz, who decided an example had to be made, he was executed by firing squad.[32] On 21 December the beautiful 23,700-ton P & O liner *Strathallan* was sunk by KLt. Horst Hamm in *U562*. While these important individual ships were a great loss, the sinkings as a whole were minor in comparison with the scale of the landings and supply operations, and in relation to the destruction of submarines involved.

In the central Mediterranean meanwhile, during the week preceding the battle of El Alamein, the Malta Spitfires had beaten off massed air raids and destroyed 131 aircraft for the loss of 34 – of whose pilots 21 had survived.[33] The losses had been too high for the Axis command, which had at last given up the attempt to subjugate the island by air. The desperate shortages remained. The submarine 'Magic Carpet' service could neither bring in enough food for the population, nor sufficient aviation spirit, fuel and ammunition, and as the battle for North Africa shifted westwards four merchant ships which had sailed around Africa and up the Suez Canal were assembled in Alexandria harbour for a relief operation from the east codenamed 'Stoneage'. They left on 17 November with a strong cruiser and destroyer escort and fighter cover from the Egyptian bases, relieved as they neared Malta by Beaufighters, then Spitfires from the island. One cruiser was seriously damaged by air attack, but the merchantmen came through unscathed; they steamed into Grand Harbour on the 20th to triumphant martial music and the shouts and cheers of the population, waving and dancing in their excitement. For William King it was the most moving moment of the war; 'tears poured down the cheeks of stalwart naval officers'.[34]

The instinct was sound; it was indeed the saving of Malta, which had stood alone, suffering heavier, more sustained bombing and infinitely more severe privations than London in the Blitz, sustained only by pride, steadfast leadership and, as King noted, 'absolute courage ... and stoic good humour'.[35] More important, the whole balance of the war changed that month: El Alamein and 'Torch' had ensured the end of the Axis offensive in North Africa, as in the Pacific the defeat of the Japanese in the ferocious supply battles for Guadalcanal had signalled the end of conquest; and on the eastern front in Europe Soviet counter-attacks encircled von Paulus's Sixth Army in Stalingrad. It was the end of the desperate gambles on which Hitler, Mussolini and the Emperor Hirohito of Japan had embarked. They had staked all on a short war and had failed. While the leaders in their rational moments undoubtedly recognized this, and Hitler had begun to formulate his excuse that the German people had failed him, for the participants, those who survived, it would only be apparent in retrospect. For the moment, the struggle for the Mediterranean intensified.

From mid-November the Allied submarines had been directed to new positions off Tunis and Bizerta, where the Axis were pouring in reinforcements and supplies in destroyers and heavily escorted convoys running between minefields laid either side of the track. And the 8th Flotilla depot ship *Maidstone* had been moved from Gibraltar to Algiers to be nearer this focal point of the supply war. On 21 November all restrictions on sinking merchantmen in the Mediterranean were at last lifted, except for Turkish waters and a corridor between Spain and Algeria; otherwise any ship could be sunk on sight.

One of the 8th Flotilla boats ordered to the Narrows between Sicily and Tunisia to operate alongside the Malta submarines was the S-class *P228* (later *Splendid*) under Lt. Ian McGeoch. It will be recalled that before the war McGeoch had written a paper seeking to demonstrate the 'offensive value of the submarine'; he was also the 'Naval Officer' who had written to *The Times* that summer to suggest that the offensive value of British submarines be harnessed to 'cripple the Axis supply line to Libya'.[36] He had arrived at Gibraltar in October and made his first patrol off Toulon, thence off the Italian coast, where he had missed surfaced submarines at long range on two separate occasions, as he afterwards assumed by underestimating their speed, but had damaged a destroyer with his last torpedo and sunk an already damaged merchantman and a schooner by gunfire. On 8 December he was directed – on Ultra intelligence, of which of course he knew nothing at the time – to a patrol line off the Gulf of Tunis in the track of a convoy. It duly appeared precisely where forecast, two merchantmen abreast of one another, escorted by two destroyers and an aircraft. McGeoch headed for a position midway between the merchantmen, intending to fire a bow salvo at one, the stern torpedo at the other. The sun was bright, and although the sea was ruffled by a light breeze he went deep between periscope observations to lessen the chance of being seen by the aircraft. The pinging of asdic became clearly audible as the convoy approached, but the boat was not detected.

Rising to periscope depth three-quarters of a mile ahead of the merchantmen and between their tracks, he made final attack observations on the starboard column vessel, confirmed 12 knots speed with the fourth hand operating the fruit machine, ordered the periscope down and called for a director angle.

'DA green twelve, Sir – one thousand three hundred [yards range]!'

'Set me on!'

The control-room rating adjusted the angle of the periscope with the fore and aft line until the bearing pointer indicated 12° to starboard.

'Up periscope!'

McGeoch waited as the target ship closed the vertical centre graticule in his lens, firing the first torpedo somewhat before the bows reached the line and thus aiming a quarter of a ship's length ahead of her for a standard spread of three. But suddenly wondering if he might have misjudged her speed and anxious lest he miss ahead, he ordered the boat brought round to starboard and fired the next two individually, then a fourth, afterwards swinging the periscope round to aim the stern torpedo at the port column ship. Fifty seconds after the last of the bow torpedoes had left the tube he heard the thud of a hit. Ten minutes later, while creeping away below, expecting a counter-attack which never came, he felt a second, far more violent detonation shake the boat, and after it the asdic operator reported a series of smaller explosions. He felt sure he must have hit an ammunition supply ship, but when he returned to periscope depth he was mortified to see what he took to be the two merchantmen steaming away in the distance. It was not until after the war that he learned there had been three merchantmen in the convoy and he had indeed blown up a 5,000-ton ammunition carrier. Two other boats in the patrol line, Stevens' P46 (*Unruffled*) and Lt. John Bromage's P212 (later *Sahib*) each sank one of the other two.[37]

That night he was ordered into another patrol line in the track of a convoy which had sailed from Naples for Bizerta. Once again the ships appeared as expected, a single supply vessel escorted by two destroyers and four aircraft, but he was some way off their track. He made two full-speed submerged dashes to close the range, then fired a six-torpedo salvo at 2,500 yards as one of the escorting destroyers merged into a continuous line with his target.

He heard two thuds at the correct time for hits, then two more, after which the propeller sounds from both destroyer and supply ship ceased. He felt confident he had scored on both. In fact the supply ship *Ankara*, loaded with Tiger tanks, had sighted the tracks and evaded; only the destroyer had been hit, and had sunk.[38]

Ten miles to the south, Edward Young, on periscope watch in *P247* (*Saracen*), sweeping the horizon slowly, was startled to see a pillar of flame erupt over the edge of empty sea. He had no sooner called 'Captain in the control room!' than the detonation wave reached them, clanging dully on the plates of the pressure hull. Knowing that *P228* was to seaward of them, he and Lumby guessed it was McGeoch's doing. Some while later the masts and then the superstructures and hulls of the supply ship and its single escort appeared and Lumby set up an attack, firing a salvo of four torpedoes; all missed. Later, after McGeoch had reported his result, Simpson returned, 'Suggest you aim at the destroyer next time.'[39]

In the Mediterranean before the war McGeoch had, as noted, made a plea for training in night surface attack; he had also designed a night sight and had a prototype constructed in the depot ship workshops.[40] On his next patrol in the Bay of Naples he was confronted with the reality, an escorted supply ship approaching by night in the position to which he had been directed off the island of Ischia. The moon was behind thick cloud. He steered for the nearest wing destroyer with the submarine trimmed low, keeping her head towards the enemy to minimize her silhouette. His watch officer, writing under a psuedonym after the war, provided a vignette: 'The Captain crouched by the voice pipe and held the submarine close on her course as the destroyer came ahead, and then, sickeningly near, crossed the bow.'[41]

She passed about half a mile ahead, the gun's crew visible around the gun on her foredeck, a dim, blue glow at the end of her main yardarm, a shadowy figure walking towards the stern. The watch officer felt numb with apprehension, his stomach gripped as if by an iron band. Surely they must be seen. They were not, and as the destroyer passed McGeoch altered round to an attack course, increased to full speed and ran in ahead of a second destroyer to within 1,500 yards of the nearest large supply ship, when he fired a salvo of five torpedoes spread over two ships' lengths. Going deep, he heard one explosion at the correct time for a hit.

In his patrol report he recorded, 'The pattern 12040 night sight was used for the first time in action and was entirely satisfactory.'[42] But, of course, compared with the U-boats' night firing system of *Vorhaltrechner*, illumined UZO binoculars and angled torpedoes, the Admiralty system was primitive in the extreme and wasteful of torpedoes.

The ship he had damaged did not go down and he made a second attack, at times surfaced, at times submerged as the moon appeared from behind clouds, but it was not until after daylight next morning that he had the satisfaction of sinking her.

In this whole period of intense struggle after El Alamein and the 'Torch' landings, as the Axis poured in reinforcements and supplies through the narrow, protected funnel of sea to Tunisia, until April 1943, when his submarine was lost, McGeoch sank seven supply ships of a total 30,000 tons and one destroyer, damaged another destroyer and sank a schooner by gunfire. In the early months of 1941 as a relief CO at Malta, he had lost all confidence in his ability to carry out a successful attack and had asked Simpson for permission to re-qualify as a CO. Simpson had agreed. After sailing home and completing the course again, he had recovered his confidence; now in command of *P228* – from January 1943 HM Submarine *Splendid* – his score was the highest of any British CO over the same period. He was also one of the few who, not wishing to emphasize the 'private navy' character of the submarine service, nor make claims which might prove false later, did not fly the Jolly Roger on return to base.

On his penultimate patrol, before running into a German anti-submarine destroyer whose accurate pattern of depth-charges forced him to the surface out of control, he was conscious of becoming over-tired:

> Thinking about this later I felt that my total capacity to master events was a finite quantity; and although some of it was restored during each spell in harbour between patrols, there was an overall and cumulative loss – like a steel spring that when fully compressed and released, fails by an increasing amount over time, to return to its original shape. . .[43]

This accords with Lord Moran's experiences as a doctor during the trench fighting of the First World War: in *The Anatomy of Courage* he drew an analogy of a man's will power as a capital balance which he expended in action; after a time, when he had spent it all, he was finished.[44] William King had perhaps reached that point in Ceylon after three years in command. Now, in his shore posting at Malta, he had to watch the 10th Flotilla COs drawing heavily on their balances. Talking to one, he sensed he was at the end of his tether, but there was no relief to replace him and he was sent out for one more patrol, the last patrol before returning home that had proved fatal for Wanklyn and others. 'When a man is fighting against his own inner convictions that he is burned out, his leaders must sense it and act ... His ship did not return. Too late I realized that I had, like him, known it and felt powerless to speak.'[45]

Among those lost during this period were several serving on their second tour in the Mediterranean, including Lt.-Cdr. R.D. Cayley, last survivor of the top-scoring 10th Flotilla trio of 1941–2. His new command, the T-class *P311*, had been adapted to carry human torpedoes termed 'chariots'. These had been developed after de la Penne's success at Alexandria had shown the potential of such weapons against capital ships. Rejected pre-war designs had been disinterred and one of the Italian SLCs or 'pigs', salvaged by the Royal Navy after the operations against Gibraltar, had been used as a model; the resulting craft bore a strong resemblance to this machine. The body was the size and shape of a torpedo. The pilot or No. 1, clad in rubber diving suit, boots and helmet with oxygen breathing apparatus, sat astride behind a faired shield enclosing a joystick for steering and trim, controls for the electric motor, served by batteries, and a pump and compressed air equipment used for diving or surfacing. A box-shaped main ballast tank rose at his back. His No. 2 sat behind the tank, similarly enclosed in a diving suit; his task was to help in negotiating boom defences and anti-torpedo nets, and securing a detachable warhead forming the fore part of the weapon, to the target ship's hull. Behind him was another faired, box-like structure housing wire cutters, magnets and other equipment.

The original intention had been to employ chariots against the new German battleship, the *Tirpitz*, lying at Trondheim, Norway, and the Italian battlefleet at Taranto. The attack on the *Tirpitz* had proved abortive as the chariots broke away from their parent craft in a storm only 10 miles from their target up the Asenfiord. The attack on Taranto had been called off after the T-class *Traveller*, sent to reconnoitre the base for the operation, had failed to return, probably lost to one of the defensive minefields. Other targets had been selected; late in December the *Trooper* and *Thunderbolt*, carrying in total five chariots in closed cylinders attached to the fore and one to the after casing, sailed for Palermo, where two of the crews were successful, sinking a 3,300-ton light cruiser and badly damaging a large troop transport.[46] Cayley had sailed at the same time for Maddalena, northern Sardinia, carrying three chariots to operate against cruisers in the naval base. He never arrived. Probably he too ran into one of the defensive minefields.

His loss was another terrible blow for Simpson who had known him so well for so long. It was the fourth in as many weeks: in late November *Utmost*, in which Cayley had pioneered the route through the minefields of the Sicilian Narrows in July 1941, had been lost, probably to a mine, possibly to depth-charges from an Italian torpedo boat; next *Traveller* had failed to return, and on 12 December the S-class *P222* under Lt.-Cdr. A.J. Mackenzie, formerly CO of the *Ursula*, was sunk by an Italian torpedo boat in the Bay of Naples off Capri; finally Cayley, one of the 10th's original 'band of brothers', had failed to return. Simpson had for two years been the mentor, friend and confidant of the young officers he had sent out against the enemy. He had lived their successes and failures, had indulged their wild antics ashore, had observed them fray and had tried to judge their psychic state, waiting anxiously for each boat's return, too often 'a week over-due, presumed lost'. Now he was as depleted as any of them. Towards the end of January 1943 he was relieved by Captain George Phillips; in retrospect he realized he was spent and it had been time for him to go.

He left at the height of the struggle, feeling he was asking almost the impossible of the COs he sent through the minefields to operate in such confined waters against ships protected by more numerous, asdic-fitted escorts and aircraft. Over the next month, however, the success rate improved: in February, the best month for the submarines, over 40,000 tons were sunk at an average of three ships for every boat on patrol. By April, such was the Allied air, submarine and surface dominance of the Axis supply route, little over 20 per cent of the tonnage despatched arrived at its destination, and Dönitz offered U-boats loaded with drums of benzine as supply runners. By this time the Axis forces had been squeezed into the bridgehead around Tunis. Early in May the Allied armies burst through the lines behind advancing carpets of bombs, and mass surrenders followed; the North African campaign was over.

As in the land battle, so in the supply battle, air power had made victory possible. Aircraft had sunk 48 per cent of the total supply tonnage lost by the enemy since the turn of the year against 29 per cent sunk by all the Mediterranean submarines; half the aircraft victims had been in harbour, however, and the submarines had actually sunk more in the open sea, and very much more than the surface forces which were once more operating from Malta.[47]

To weigh the contribution of one arm against another is unhelp-

1. Interior of the wardroom of a British S-class submarine showing view forward through the bulkhead door into the galley and ERA's and petty officers' accommodation

2. The early U-boat aces: KLt. Günther Prien (*above, centre*) returns after a record patrol in July 1940 during which he rescued three Luftwaffe aircrew, here seen with him; (*below left*) KLt. Joachim Schepke after a successful patrol in September 1940 and (*below right*) among admiring crowds in Berlin after receiving the Knight's Cross

3. Grand Admiral Erich Raeder bestows the Knight's Cross on KLt. Otto Kretschmer, August 1940; note the British 'tommies' battledress abandoned in the retreat from France

4. Konteradmiral Karl Dönitz (*second left*) presents KLt. Wilhelm Schulz with the Knight's Cross for sinking over 100,000 tons, April 1941

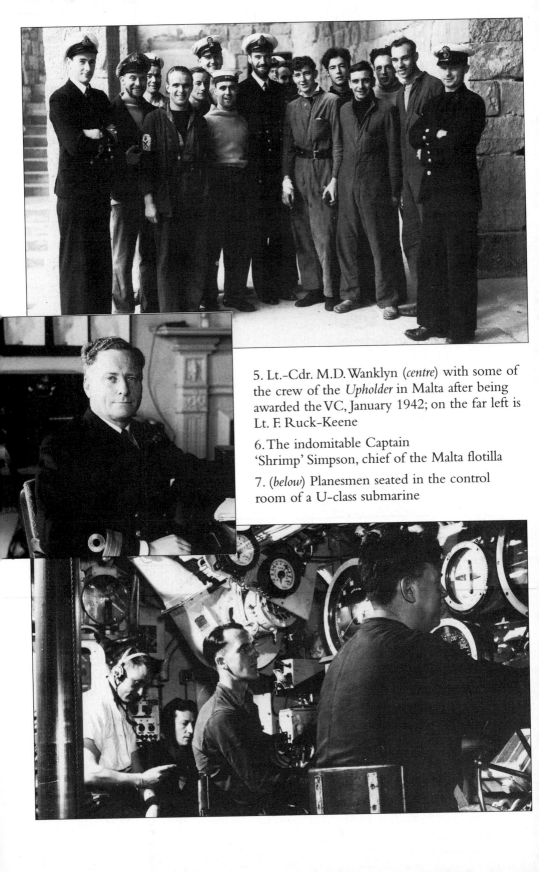

5. Lt.-Cdr. M.D. Wanklyn (*centre*) with some of the crew of the *Upholder* in Malta after being awarded the VC, January 1942; on the far left is Lt. F. Ruck-Keene

6. The indomitable Captain 'Shrimp' Simpson, chief of the Malta flotilla

7. (*below*) Planesmen seated in the control room of a U-class submarine

8. Lt.-Cdr. B.D. Cayley of the *Utmost* and (*right*) Lt.-Cdr. E.P. Tomkinson of *Urge*, together with Wanklyn the top scoring COs of the first phase of the Mediterranean war

9. Flotilla headquarters, the Old Lazaretto, with *Upholder* taking in stores alongside the wall

10. KLt. Günther Hessler brings the Type IXB *U107* in to Lorient, June 1941; note his thirteen victory pennants, totalling 86,699 tons, the highest patrol score of the war; (*below*) Hessler after being awarded the Knight's Cross

11. These astounding photographs of the capture by HMS *Bulldog* on 9 May 1941 of KLt. Julius Lemp's Type IXB *U110* — one of the best-kept secrets of the war — have only recently been donated to the Imperial War Museum; (*above*) the destroyer's armed whaler approaching *U110* and (*below*) a close-up of the U-boat after the Enigma cipher machine and cipher tables had been seized

12. KLt. Reinhard Hardegen takes the Type IXB *U123* from Lorient on 8 June 1941 for his first war patrol in command; note the 'wounded' medal insignia of the previous CO, Moehle, on the conning tower. The Type VIIC *U201* can be seen departing on her quarter

13. KLt. Hardegen receives the Knight's Cross after his return from the *Paukenschlag* operation off the US east coast in February 1942

14. KLt. Wolfgang Lüth returns to Lorient in *U43*, December 1941

15. Battle stations surface on *U25*

16. Lt. Richard O'Kane (*left*) and Lt.-Cdr. Dudley Morton on the bridge of US S/M *Wahoo* after Morton's historic first patrol as CO in January 1943

17. Cdr. Samuel Dealey, the 'destroyer killer'

18. Capt. John Cromwell, who chose to ride his submarine on her last dive rather than risk the Ultra secret to Japanese methods of torture

19. Two of Morton's victims as seen through *Wahoo's* periscope: (*above*) a Japanese destroyer in Wewak bay with her bows folded back by her bridge and (*below*) the troop transport *Buyo Maru*, whose survivors were afterwards massacred in the water

6-WAHOO-2

20. Downed aircrew being hauled aboard O'Kane's *Tang* on lifeguard patrol off the Japanese naval base at Truk, April 1943

21. A British X-craft midget submarine of the type that crippled the battleship *Tirpitz* in Norway in September 1943

22. The Japanese *I68* at speed. With her number changed to *I168*, under Lt.-Cdr. Yahachi Tanabe, she sank the carrier USS *Yorktown* on 6 June 1942

23. A U-boat sinking after attack by aircraft from a US escort carrier

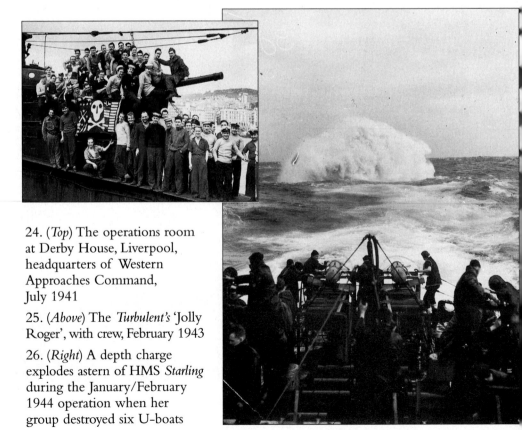

24. (*Top*) The operations room at Derby House, Liverpool, headquarters of Western Approaches Command, July 1941

25. (*Above*) The *Turbulent's* 'Jolly Roger', with crew, February 1943

26. (*Right*) A depth charge explodes astern of HMS *Starling* during the January/February 1944 operation when her group destroyed six U-boats

27. A Coastal Command pilot's view of a North Atlantic convoy

28. A U-boat is mortally damaged by aircraft depth charges. Two shocked crewmen can be seen sheltering beside the conning tower

29. The torpedo compartment in the bows of *I58* which sank the US heavy cruiser *Indianapolis* in July 1945

30. Japanese *Koryu* midget submarines prepared for the final defence of the homeland, here seen at Kure naval base after the Japanese surrender, August 1945

ful for a campaign that was as successful when all arms co-operated effectively as it was unsuccessful when this fundamental principle was neglected. Nonetheless, it is useful to ask how much more
effective the submarines would have been had the small U-class
boats of the 10th Flotilla been joined earlier in their epic assault
on the main Axis supply lines by the faster, more powerful T- and
few S-class boats of the 1st Flotilla at Alexandria. Sir Ian McGeoch
would not say so, but his claim to ask this question is second to
none; he has pointed out that the 1st Flotilla disposed of over
eighty torpedo tubes on average against the thirty or so of the 10th,
and that 'sinking caiques in the Aegean was not an economic use
of force' while troop and supply convoys were reaching Tripoli
unmolested by submarines.[48] With knowledge of convoy departure and arrival times from Ultra intelligence the 1st Flotilla boats
could have made effective use of their time on the main supply
lanes. Why they were only rarely used there is a question that has
not been studied. Ultimate responsibility lay with the Chiefs of
Staff, in particular the Naval Staff and the First Sea Lord. Operational control was exercised by the C-in-C Mediterranean, Admiral
Sir Andrew Cunningham, through his Captain Submarines at
Alexandria. It is here that the chief elements of the answer must
lie. Cunningham was a man of overpowering personality and pronounced conservative views who, like Admiral King in Washington, demanded perfection from his subordinates, and bullied or
dismissed them if he did not find it, and who did not understand
staff work. He also disliked submariners, although this may have
had more to do with their free and easy buccaneering image and
disregard for dress regulations, for which he was a purist, than
their effectiveness.[49] At all events, in common with most of his
contemporaries, he underestimated the submarine arm, viewing it
more as an extension of the surface fleet than a potent instrument
in its own right. For whatever reasons of personality or perception
the fact remains that, like the American submarine effort in the
Pacific, the British Mediterranean submarine campaign was for a
long period disjointed and unscientific, and failed to reach its
potential.

In the last months of the campaign in early 1943 six more boats
were lost, three from the 8th Flotilla at Algiers in February and
March. They included the *Turbulent* under the veteran and much
respected Cdr. J. W. Linton who, during two tours in the Mediterranean, had sunk over 90,000 tons of merchant shipping and one
destroyer. This last had been an unexpected bonus: attacking a
convoy of two supply ships at night from periscope depth the

previous June he had been detected by one of the escorts which had headed towards him at high speed intent on ramming. While he waited for the supply ships to steam on to his firing line the destroyer closed until, as he expressed it in his patrol report, at the moment he fired 'it looked revolting and occupied the entire periscope'. He went deep just in time, the enemy roaring directly overhead as the boat began to descend. Both supply ships were hit, but the final torpedo circled back, making an alarming noise as it neared the boat, then sped off and hit one of the destroyers.[50] On his ninth and last patrol in *Turbulent* before she was due home for a refit he attacked an escorted ship off Bastia, Corsica, and in the ensuing counter-attack his boat was sunk with all hands. Two months later his outstanding record and example were recognized by the award of a posthumous VC.

In April, one of the 1st Flotilla boats from Beirut was lost, and two more from the 8th, McGeoch's *Splendid*, and Bromage's *Sahib* which was similarly forced to the surface by depth-charge attack, and abandoned after the vents had been opened to scuttle her.

During all this time the decisive submarine battle was being fought in the Atlantic. In August 1942, after the US Navy organized a system of interlocking convoys up the east coast, Dönitz had returned a proportion of his boats to the main convoy lanes; now, since the balance of the war had shifted against the Axis everywhere else, the oceanic supply routes to Great Britain appeared the one area in which the western Allies were still vulnerable. The battle was approaching its climax.

Both sides had increased their forces vastly; thus far neither had been able to bring a decisive concentration to bear. In August 1942, at the start of this phase, U-boat production rose to 21 a month, total strength to 342 boats; yet of these, 59 were employed for training and a further 131 were on trials or working up in the Baltic. Of the 152 operational boats, Hitler tied up 23 in Norway against the threat of invasion, and a further 16 to help the Italians in the Mediterranean supply battle. Only 113 were available to Dönitz for the Atlantic; of these a third or more were generally refitting between patrols, a large proportion of the rest on passage out or home.[51] It did not leave many: at the beginning of August there were 49 boats – including six Italian submarines – in six separate patrol areas, but for the month as a whole the average number in the operational areas was 31.[52] It was too few to comb the expanse of the North Atlantic, particularly as Dönitz always sent groups further afield to probe weak spots and disperse the defences. Had it not been for the shutting out of Bletchley Park since the addition of the fourth rotor to the Enigma, and brilliant work by the *B-Dienst* cryptanalysts, he would not have found many convoys.

As for the Allies, by August the Royal and Royal Canadian Navies deployed over 150 destroyers for escort duty, almost 200 of the 'whale-catcher' corvettes, 30 rather larger, faster 'sloops' and the first few of a still larger type named 'frigates' which could make 20 knots. The routes to be protected had also increased though. Apart from the Japanese threat to shipping in the Pacific and Indian Oceans, the U-boats' range had been extended by replenishment from *Milchkühe* (Type XIV) submarines to the Caribbean – where they sank forty-one ships of over 200,000 tons in August; South American waters, where, believing Brazil was about to join the enemy alliance they made a pre-emptive strike and sank five Brazilian merchantmen – so precipitating her declaration; and South African waters. Convoys were also now being run 1,500 to 2,000 miles around the North Cape of Norway to Murmansk or Archangel to supply the Russians with arms and equipment; so close to German bases in Norway, these required a particularly strong destroyer escort. In addition, large numbers of destroyers had to be retained for the Home Fleet, which was on constant readiness against a break-out into the Atlantic by the *Tirpitz* or other German heavy units; the US carrier task forces in the Pacific also retained strong destroyer forces. As a result, convoys were still weakly protected, usually with six escorts or less, the majority corvettes that lacked sufficient speed in a night action to catch surfaced U-boats; and with so few escorts it had become accepted that they did not leave the convoy for long to hunt and destroy U-boats which had been forced under or chased away.

Scientific or naval historical analysis would have allowed far better protection with existing numbers of escorts, and reduced losses considerably. An 'Operational Analysis' unit had been started at the Admiralty in early 1942 by Professor P. M. S. Blackett, who had analysed operational problems for Anti-aircraft Command in 1940, and later for Coastal Command. Writing six years after the war, he suggested that his unit at the Admiralty had 'made a bad mistake in not realising as soon as the group was formed . . . the vital importance of working out a theory of the best size for a convoy'.[53] As it was, they did not focus on the problem until towards the end of 1942 when considering how to allocate shipbuilding resources between escort vessels and merchant ships. It soon became apparent that over the past two years convoys with nine escorts had suffered 25 per cent less losses than convoys with six escorts, and further analysis had revealed that each additional escort in service should save over two merchant ships a year. The conclusion had been obvious: provided the war lasted more than a year priority should be given to building escorts rather than replacing merchant tonnage.

During the investigations it was also discovered that large convoys had suffered relatively far less than small convoys; indeed they appeared to be twice as safe. This ran counter to the common-sense, profoundly unhistorical Admiralty view that large convoys were inherently dangerous; given the extreme shortage of escorts, forty ships was considered an optimum and sixty ships stipulated as an absolute maximum convoy size. Knowing it would be difficult to persuade them of error, Blackett's team looked for an explanation of their own findings. After intensive research, particularly into what captured U-boat men had told their interrogators, they found what would have been known from the beginning had a statistically researched staff history of the First World War U-boat campaign been written: that the chances of a convoy being discovered in the first place were practically the same whatever its size; that the chances of a U-boat penetrating the screen were inversely proportional to the number of escorts per mile of defended perimeter; and, vitally, that the number of merchant ships sunk for each U-boat that did penetrate the screen was the same whatever the size of the convoy 'simply because there were always more than enough targets'.[54] Had it been realized that escorts were a better investment than merchant ships, and that large convoys were far safer than small convoys, it is safe to say that there would scarcely have been a U-boat crisis after the first shock of pack attacks on the surface at night had been countered. This is not merely hindsight. The experience had been gained in the first war; moreover, the lessons could have been deduced theoretically from a statistical study of the naval wars of the past 300 years. Yet the intellectuals in the Royal Navy, no less than the 'gun club' admirals, had neglected this less glamorous aspect of their glorious tradition.

So far as North Atlantic convoys were concerned, a chief weakness remained the lack of air cover in the mid-Atlantic 'air gap' south and south-east of Greenland. The vital importance of aircraft, especially in forcing down shadowing U-boats, had of course been recognized for a long time, but remarkably little action had been taken. The first four escort carriers ordered from American yards in 1941 had been completed;[55] one was in commission; three were to become operational in the autumn of 1942, but they were deployed almost immediately to cover the 'Torch' convoys to the Mediterranean; they did not become available for the main Atlantic convoy routes until the following spring of 1943, by which time one, the *Avenger*, had been sunk by *U155*, and a second had blown up. Those merchant ships provided with a catapult and fighter aeroplane to give some protection against land-based aircraft were of no use for patrols around ocean convoys since the single fighter could only be launched once; after catapulting off, it could not land on the ship again. A captured German merchant ship had been converted into a stop-gap escort carrier with a flight deck the previous year, but it had been torpedoed by a U-boat at night while sailing apart from the convoy it was protecting. Why other merchant ships had not been converted in the same way to fill the time lapse before escort carriers became available is a mystery. In August 1942 six such merchant carriers – MAC ships – were ordered, but the congestion, mismanagement, out-of-date equipment and restrictive trade practices followed by workers in British shipyards were such that the first did not enter service until the following spring.[56]

British shipyard workers were not above striking despite the desperate situation of the country; this and the huge disparity between their wages and those of sailors fighting the enemy – or, in the event of the sailors' death, the amount paid to their dependants – were a source of bitterness. 'To sailors working under sub-human conditions for four shillings a day, wartime strikes seem a mixture of blackmail and pure treason,' Nicholas Monsarrat wrote in his wartime account of service in corvettes, and he described the black humour of the messdecks: bandying ideas of refusing to sail a convoy the last hundred miles unless a bonus were paid every man, or soldiers in north Africa demanding so much a mile for advancing, time and a half for retreats.[57] Alastair Mars noted that most submariners, having 'stood by' their boats during the final fitting-out period, had 'seen at first hand that even unskilled workers were being paid five times as much as themselves', yet frequently struck for more money.[58] William King records strikes holding up the completion of two of his submarines.[59]

A similar bitterness surfaces in the memoirs of US officers: Admiral Galantin quotes from a letter he wrote home at the height of the Pacific war while his submarine was refitting at the

Bethlehem Steel Yard, San Francisco: 'The power, the selfishness, the indifference, the lack of patriotism the Unions now show is nauseating. It is disheartening to see what contemptible selfishness we are fighting to preserve . . .'[60]

German shipyard problems were different. After Hitler's invasion of Russia, resistance movements had mushroomed in occupied France, and the Biscay shipyard workers, who had once been acknowledged as over 20 per cent more productive than their German counterparts,[61] had to be closely watched for acts of sabotage. When Cremer took *U333* out of La Pallice that summer of 1942 he found water pouring in during his first emergency dive. Examination revealed that a large bolt had been misplaced and the exhaust valve partially sawn through, the former probably, the latter certainly sabotage.[62]

More serious were acute shortages of labour and raw materials, particularly steel and copper. In January 1942, Hitler had accorded priority in armaments manufacture to the army in the east, and although German steel production had risen gradually through the following months to peak in September, the navy quota had fallen from about 180,000 tons a month to 120,000 tons by the summer.[63] Fortunately for Dönitz, the Naval Staff in Berlin had at last come round to his view that the U-boat campaign was the navy's decisive contribution to the war and it was necessary to put every effort into it before US shipbuilding could tip the scales against them.[64] The chief of the U-boat department in Berlin had also accepted Dönitz's arguments that 'only great numbers of U-boats can sever the supply lines across the Atlantic' and that 300 operational boats was the minimum number for an effective campaign.[65] Consequently, planned production had risen to twenty-five boats a month and, since building a Type IX cost approximately twice the man-hours needed for a Type VII boat, the proportion of Type IXs to Type VIIs had been reduced. As it was expressed: 'Inasmuch as the chief problem of the U-boat war today is finding the enemy, two boats in the Atlantic are double the value of one boat irrespective of their size.'[66]

Despite building more of the smaller types and stopping work on surface warships, tankers and supply vessels, the steel and labour shortages prevented the construction department meeting its target of twenty-five boats a month, and during the late summer and autumn of 1942 losses of over ten boats a month further slowed the rate of increase; by this time the question of finding and training crew for the new boats had also become a major problem.

For the Allies, the shortage of surface escorts and the lack of escort carriers or converted merchantmen with flight decks which could fly off planes to patrol around their own convoys to put down shadowing boats was compounded by the desperate shortage of long-range land-based aircraft to fill the North Atlantic 'air gap'. Coastal Command had only one squadron of long-range, one of very long-range Liberators, in total twenty-eight long-range aircraft. This was not because of a general shortage, but entirely because Bomber Command continued somehow to win every argument.

The Admiralty and Coastal Command had renewed their urgent pleas for long-range aircraft in 1942.[67] The Air Staff had responded by citing shortfalls in the supply of the new centimetric radar, and arguing that they could not transfer bombers to long-range reconnaissance without radar as this would be 'a dispersion of our bombing resources'; it was their 'considered view' that they could make a much greater contribution to the defeat of the U-boats by continuing to bomb the industrial areas of German cities.[68] Their optimistic predictions were passed to the Admiralty's Operational Research unit now established under Professor Blackett. By using the known results of German bombing on British cities rather than the reports from neutral capitals on which the airmen had based their estimates, Blackett punctured the calculations and showed that the proposed offensive was unlikely to reduce German production by even 1 per cent.[69]

The Air Staff were on thin ice: attempts at precision bombing on specific industrial targets had been abandoned long ago, since when it had become clear that the force lacked the navigational or bomb-aiming equipment even to produce the expected results from 'area bombing'. This had been established in an analysis carried out in August 1941 under the auspices of Churchill's close adviser, Lord Cherwell (Professor Frederick Lindemann). The analysis had shown that on average only one in three aircrews claiming to have dropped bombs within 5 miles of their target had actually done so. The proportion varied with the target; on Biscay ports the average was two in three, over German cities generally one in four, but over the heavily protected, smoke-laden industrial heart of the Ruhr only seven in a hundred air crews came within 5 miles of their target.[70] With internal doubts about the strategy and external criticism of their predictions the Air Staff changed tack: instead of destroying factories and killing industrial workers – since Blackett had shown that they would achieve a mortality rate little over half that claimed by German road accidents – they made their aim the destruction of morale by de-housing industrial workers.

A paper arguing this new case was passed to Professor Blackett in April. Although his own method of prediction had been used this time, he was able to show that the figures had been extrapolated so crudely that the effects of the proposed offensive had been exaggerated by a factor of five to one. His analysis was disregarded.[71] The policy of bombing German working-class housing to lower morale was adopted; British Lancaster bombers, the only aircraft comparable to the American long-range Liberators, were fitted for the offensive as they came out of production, and on the night of 30 May the first 1,000-bomber raid took off for Cologne; three nights later Essen was the target. The irresponsibility of the policy was revealed by post-war analysis: the error in prediction had not been five to one as Blackett had suggested, but ten to one.[72] And German production had risen steadily until almost the end of the war.

In truth, there had been no reasoned basis for the policy; it had been dictated by the belligerent prejudice of Churchill, his advisers, Lord Cherwell – who before the war had advised against the development of radar – the former air force chief, Lord Trenchard, and the dominant 'bombing' group in the Air Staff, whose tunnel vision was most notably expressed by the new chief of Bomber Command, Air Marshal Sir Arthur Harris. The failure of the Admiralty to make a reasoned case did not help their cause. They had diluted the urgency of the argument for long-range aircraft for Coastal Command by mixing it with issues of naval command of bombers operating over the sea and naval training for Coastal Command aircrews.[73] Above all, they had failed to point out the idiocy and profound historical ignorance of the bombers' claim that strafing German cities was 'offensive' while protecting convoys was 'defensive'. Churchill's mistake – as ultimately it was – derived not from the need to make a hard choice between options of outstanding importance, as Hitler was having to do between tanks, guns and aircraft for the east or U-boats for the west, but rather from blood reasoning and the semantics of 'offence' over 'defence'. It would only have taken forty long-range aircraft, preferably but not in the first instance necessarily fitted with centimetric radar, to close the air gap south of Greenland and so make the U-boats' task on the principal supply routes from America practically impossible.[74] Instead, the aircraft were thrown into blundering and costly mass raids whose sole achievement was to wind up the ratchet of mutual hatred; this would rebound on merchant sailors and later on aircrew who had the misfortune to come down among the enraged population. By comparison with this epic misjudgement, Admiral King's failure off the east coast of America and the US Bureau of Ordnance's refusal to contemplate errors in torpedo design seem temporary oversights.

Aside from this shortage of long-range aircraft, the western Allies by mid-1942 possessed all the scientific tools to render U-boat attacks on convoys, if not impossible, then at least so costly as to be ruled out, although delays in production had meant that a great number of warships and aircraft were still not equipped with them. Most of the inventions have been mentioned. High-frequency direction-finders (HF/DF or Huff Duff), which could fix even the shortest U-boat transmission as a point of light on a fluorescent screen, were now standard on many Royal, though not Canadian, Navy destroyers, and on a number of vessels termed rescue ships which were now sailed with convoys especially to relieve the escorts of the task of picking up survivors from torpedoed ships. The sets alerted escort commanders to shadowing U-boats. There was no means – apart from cross bearings from other ship-borne or shore DF stations – of gauging the range of the transmitting boat and thus, until more escorts were fitted with Huff Duff, seldom any certainty that a boat was shadowing the particular convoy; nonetheless, experienced operators could make good guesses based on the strength and clarity of the signal, and escorts could be sent out to hunt along the bearing of the transmitting boat to force it under and cause it to lose the convoy, or to hunt and destroy it.

The naval version of centimetric radar, Type 271, was now fitted in most Royal Navy escorts and its greater range and definition were, in the words of the Anti-Submarine Warfare Division, 'giving A/S ships steadily increasing confidence in their ability to defeat U-boats on the surface at night'.[75] The reconnaissance aircraft version, ASVIII, was not yet in service due to the priority that had been given to Bomber Command's navigational version and to the British radio industry's inability to cope with the more advanced components; these had to be manufactured in America. Nevertheless, aircraft fitted with metric ASVII radar were now effective U-boat killers.

Much of their new efficiency was the result of operational research work that Professor E. J. Williams had carried out in Blackett's unit at Coastal Command in 1941. Hitherto, aircraft depth-charges had been set to 100 feet, since on average a plane was sighted by a U-boat two minutes before it could arrive in position to attack, and in that time a U-boat could dive to 100 feet. During analysis of past attacks Williams spotted the fallacy in the premise: if the aircraft were sighted two minutes before she could drop her charges, by the time she attacked, the U-boat had been invisible for so long that the attack was likely to be inaccurate; if, however, the aircraft caught the U-boat by surprise and managed to attack through cloud, fog or darkness while she was on the surface or submerging, great accuracy was achieved, but the charge would detonate 100 feet beneath her, doing little damage. By altering the setting of aircraft depth-charges to 25 feet for the latter type of attack, and ignoring the former, Coastal Command achieved at a stroke a vastly more effective weapon system.[76]

Another simple improvement brought about by Blackett and Williams was to paint Coastal Command aircraft white to make them less visible against the sky by day or night. Calculations suggested that white aircraft would catch U-boats on the surface 30 per cent more often than dark ones. No direct proof of this could be established after the change since a number of other improvements complicated analysis, but the operational research team was confident that the new colour made a contribution to the greater rate of U-boat sinkings by aircraft in the second half of 1942.[77]

One of the more important innovations introduced was a powerful searchlight named after its inventor, Squadron Leader Humphrey Leigh, which was fitted to the nose of Coastal Command aircraft to illuminate U-boats on the surface during the final stage of a night-time approach by radar. The first squadron to be fitted had been employed in June 1942, patrolling the U-boats' exit and entry routes across Biscay. It had come as a shocking surprise to those watch officers and lookouts whose boats were detected, who found themselves suddenly lit up out of the night by an aircraft already low on their tail in its attack run whose approach had not been heard because of the clamour of their own diesels. Hitherto, all boats had made the passage of the Bay on the surface at night, submerging by day when, to quote Dönitz's war diary for 11 June, Biscay was 'the playground of British aircraft.'[78] Before the end of the month he had ordered all boats to transit the Bay submerged by day and night. It made for slow progress which could add as much as five days to the voyage to the operational areas.

Seeking a more permanent solution, he renewed earlier pleas for aircraft to defend the Bay against British incursions; tackling Göring at Luftwaffe headquarters on 1 July, he put the point that having achieved complete security for the boats in port beneath their bomb-proof shelters, he now found them vulnerable on passage on the surface both by day and night. Göring allocated twenty-four more Junkers 88C long-range fighters to Atlantic Air

Command.[79] Not only was this too few, but the aircraft could neither intercept by night nor match the Beaufighters which Coastal Command sent over by day.

Dönitz's despair comes through in his war diary entry for 21 August:

> the numerical strengthening of enemy flights, the appearance of a wide variety of aircraft types, the fitting of the aircraft with an excellent location device against U-boats have rendered U-boat operations in the eastern Atlantic very much more difficult ... the daily enemy reconnaissance extends to 20°W and has forced a movement of U-boat dispositions far into the middle of the Atlantic, since discovery of these dispositions would lead to convoys being routed around them. Besides the daily air reconnaissance, the presence of some especially long-range aircraft types which are deployed as convoy escorts has come to light. Already air escorts have flown with convoys under attack by U-boats at a distance approaching 800 miles from English bases and the motherland. As the war diary entry of 20.7 shows, this has greatly impeded U-boat operations, making them in some instances no longer worthwhile. This increasing difficulty of operations must lead, with corresponding further development, to high, insupportable losses, a decline in success and thus to a decline in the prospects of success for the U-boat war as a whole.
>
> In view of this situation I must once more demand the use of the only aircraft which has the range and fighting power to combat the enemy aircraft, the He 177 in Biscay and in the Atlantic against convoys.[80]

This was as much a pipe-dream as his earlier hopes for effective Luftwaffe co-operation. Göring and the aircraft industry were fully stretched by the war in the east, in the Mediterranean and over the cities of the Reich. And in fact the four-engined He 177 never achieved its expected range or speed, and was so prone to technical faults it was christened by aircrew the *Reichs Feuerzeug*, or cigarette lighter.

Dönitz ended his 21 August entry in defiant vein: convoy operations in the Atlantic were still possible. All COs and crews gave the same impression: 'Despite the heaviest depth-charging attacks and little success, a resolute, confident mood, unbroken through unshakeable faith in victory.'

This was not always the impression captured U-boat men gave their British interrogators. A report on the survivors of *U131*, *U134* and *U574*, which had been forced to the surface by depth-charges in December 1941 while trying to attack a homeward-bound convoy from Gibraltar, stated that a number expressed doubts about the ultimate success of the U-boat campaign. Moreover: 'there is no doubt that large numbers of them speak with loathing of their service in U-boats, which they find very different from what, from propaganda, they had been led to expect. Some said they would never have joined the U-boat arm if they had known what active service was going to be like.'[81]

The certainty in victory that had marked those captured in 1940 was missing, as was enthusiasm for the service. A young lieutenant named Peter Hansen, posted to U-boats at this time without option, wrote in a letter long after the war:

> I don't actually recall any U-boatmen, certainly after 1942, who liked the war and were enthusiastic about it. I am talking about experienced people at the front, not headquarters staff or people in the training establishments or the Propaganda Companies. Fatalistic is the only appropriate way to describe the mood of the crews of the front boats. It certainly was no longer any question of being or becoming again victorious, but solely or somehow to survive, nothing more, nothing less.[82]

There were of course exceptions, especially among younger officers who had not yet seen active service in the Atlantic and who believed the propaganda of National Socialism and final victory.[83] But after three years of war the 'old salts', like the captain of Lothar-Günther Buchheim's classic fiction, *Das Boot*, expressed their scepticism of propaganda and the 'teeth-gritters who practised martial expressions in front of the mirror' with studied irony, understatement and a pretended complete sang-froid.[84] The figure of this splendid captain is based largely on KLt. Heinrich Lehmann-Willenbrock, CO of *U96* in which Buchheim made a war patrol in late 1941.

Dönitz's war diary comments on 'a resolute, confident mood' and 'unshakeable faith in victory' should probably be read as expressions of his own convictions. Throughout his career he had pursued his goals with fanatic determination and emotional commitment, shutting out contrary views and disregarding any impediments to the current aim; this was indeed a great part of his undoubted strength as a leader. Since the Nazi system exaggerated the normal tendency for facts and opinions to be polished as they ascended the chain of command, he was usually told what he wanted to hear, especially, one perceptive former U-boat officer has commented, as 'he was very slow in judging people upon their ability . . . yes-men and ass-kissers could often fool him, at least for a period of time', and 'he instinctively disliked the outspoken man'.[85] There were few enough of these. Even in the élite U-boat arm, men did not express critical or pessimistic views for fear of Party informers. The same officer stated, 'One only actually said things when talking with one other person whom one knew well enough.'

If the general mood in the service was more realistic than confident, morale remained good, preserved by the high U-boat allowances, the good life in the rest camps between patrols, above all by the status U-boat men enjoyed as a *corps d'élite*. Yet even more important, as in all submarine services, it was a matter of shared trials and trust in individual COs and officers: a U-boat's crew that had survived several patrols with few changes was in truth a 'band of brothers'. An officer of that time explained: 'For most crews it did not matter so much what decorations the captain had, but that he was a lucky chap and looked after his crew. Then they would put up gladly with a lot of hardships and problems.'[86]

The loss and damage to boats on transit across Biscay was at least partially solved for a time, not by the Luftwaffe, but by the provision of a simple radar detector. The first models fitted in August 1942 were crude wooden crosses holding a diamond-shaped wooden frame wound with an aerial which led down to a receiver in the control room. The apparatus picked up radar pulses on the 1.4 to 1.8 metre wavelength band to a distance of almost 20 miles from the emitting set, and gave out a warning whistle or hum, or by other accounts a 'beeping tone'. It was a French device presented to Dönitz by the Vichy French premier, Admiral François Darlan, who hated the British, more especially for the Royal Navy's actions against French ships after the armistice in 1940.[87] Termed from its construction the 'Biscay Cross', this *Funkmessbeobachtungsgerät*, officially designated FuMB 2 'Honduras', was secured in a fitting abaft the bridge when the U-boat surfaced and thereafter rotated by hand by one of the bridge watch. Before the boat submerged it had to be lifted out, partially dismantled and sent down through the hatches, a process that took the fine edge off emergency dives. Herbert Werner describes the 'cross' on his boat being thrown down to the control room and the bridge watch falling down on top of it one by one, smashing it to pieces during an alarm dive by night.[88] On this occasion it had not operated out to its theoretical range since bombs dropped close to the boat inside a minute from the first warning beep. The apparatus was soon repaired, and when the boat surfaced, swayed up through the hatches and secured again in its fitting.

This rough device was replaced in the autumn of 1942 by a metal dipole aerial named after its principal manufacturer as the 'Metox 600'. It was quite as cumbersome to hand down the hatches before diving, but had the great advantage of being able to detect radar pulses up to 80 miles from the emitting set;[89] in theory this did away with the need for emergency dives, and in practice restored a feeling of security in darkness which allowed boats to make much of their former rate of progress across the Bay.[90]

Once in contact with a convoy U-boats might now face a new weapon which was being fitted to destroyers: called the 'Hedgehog' after its appearance, it was a system which lobbed 65lb. bombs, each armed with 35lbs. of high explosive, 230 yards ahead of the firing ship, thus while in asdic contact before the blind period. Previously U-boat COs under depth-charge attack had been able to sidestep a pattern during the final 200 yards when the asdic operator lost contact and before the launching parties on the after deck had released the charges over the stern or down chutes. The new system, which spread the bombs 12 feet apart in an elliptical pattern 100 feet across, could be fired to fall on the precise bearing of the asdic echo. Each bomb was fitted with a contact fuse armed by water pressure, without a depth component; it either hit with a fatal detonation or dropped past without causing any damage, however close. The first destroyers had been fitted in January 1942, but there were production and teething problems, and it was not for some months that this potentially lethal weapon scored its first kill.[91]

Of more immediate significance in the convoy battles was a new tactical school set up to train escort commanders. Up to the beginning of 1942 commanders, officers and asdic operators had been trained to hunt individual U-boats in 'Attack Teacher Houses' simulating an escort at sea, and ships' companies had been put through a vigorous four-week work-up at a sea training establishment at Tobermory in the Inner Hebrides, run by Vice-Admiral Gilbert Stephenson, who more than earned his soubriquet the 'Terror of Tobermory'. Afterwards, ships joined an escort group to work up as a team under their group commander. There had been no group tactical training, however, and no authorized tactical doctrine based on accumulated experience or study of previous convoy battles; each commander in action responded to the perceived threat as it developed.

The first set evolution for an escort group appears to have been established towards the end of 1941 by Cdr. F. J. Walker. Before the war Walker had commanded the Anti-Submarine Warfare School, HMS *Osprey*, an unregarded backwater, and had then been 'passed over' for promotion to captain; although top of his class and King's Gold Medallist at the Royal Naval College, Dartmouth, he had been unsuited to the ceremonial peacetime navy. After the outbreak of war he had made repeated requests to go to sea and finally, in September 1941, was appointed to command the sloop *Stork*, as senior officer of the 36th Escort Group. After working up he issued group operational instructions to his ships – one other sloop and seven corvettes – emphasizing that the safe arrival of their convoys was to be achieved by destroying, rather than simply putting down, any U-boats which attacked; officers were 'to act instantly without waiting for orders' immediately a U-boat was detected. And in the event of a successful U-boat attack by night, he laid down an operation to be performed by all escorts together on receipt of the code word 'Buttercup' – his name for his wife. This was a formalization of the manoeuvre evolved soon after the first surprise night surface attacks: all escorts were to turn outwards, increasing to full speed and firing starshell to illuminate the entire area around the convoy, so forcing the U-boat or boats to submerge; for 'once submerged, the destruction of the submarine is considerably simplified'.[92]

He ordered 'Buttercup' for the first time in the early hours of 19 December 1941 while escorting a homeward convoy from Gibraltar through U-boats that Dönitz had directed across the track. His group, reinforced by three destroyers and the merchant aircraft carrier *Audacity* converted from a German prize, *Hannover*, had already accounted for *U131* and *U434*; now one of the additional destroyers sighted a surfaced U-boat on her quarter coming up into the convoy from astern. In the excitement she reported 'Submarine in sight!' without indicating where, and turned to attack. Walker, who could not see the destroyer in the dark, ordered her to fire a flare to indicate her position, but before she could do so she was hit by a torpedo and exploded in a high sheet of flame. Walker turned his sloop towards her blazing hulk and ordered 'Buttercup!'

KLt. Dietrich Gengelbach of *U574*, who had fired the fatal torpedoes, dived, whether because of the massed starshell rising or the sight of the *Stork* bearing down on him is not clear, but he was soon detected by Walker's asdic operator and blown to the surface by an accurate pattern of ten depth-charges. There followed a chase during which Gengelbach turned three complete circles inside the sloop, but Walker finally closed and overran him, completing his boat's destruction with depth-charges at the shallowest setting as it emerged from under the sloop's stern.[93] The few who miraculously survived this shocking experience were rescued and joined the survivors from *U131* and *U434*. It was from among these men that British interrogators were to learn how 'large numbers' loathed their service in U-boats.[94]

The U-boat attacks continued, and on the night of the 21st

Walker again ordered 'Buttercup!' This was the occasion on which the *Audacity*, whose commander was senior to Walker and was zigzagging independently to starboard of the convoy, was torpedoed and sunk. A little later a surfaced U-boat was sighted to port of the port columns; she was attacked, forced down and hunted for an hour before all trace of her disappeared from the asdics, when she was rightly adjudged sunk. This had been *U567*, commanded by the ace KLt. Engelbert Endrass, formerly Prien's first watch officer, who had fired the salvo which sank the *Royal Oak* in Scapa Flow. By this date, after two years of war without sufficient rest periods, he had become a bundle of nerves.[95] The 'old salts' believed he should have been relieved as a 'front boat' CO and transferred to a shore or training command; they blamed his loss on the staff who had sent him to sea because, so they believed, Dönitz wanted sinking figures, and it was the veterans who produced these.

The following day a Coastal Command Liberator appeared and patrolled over the convoy, which arrived home without further loss. In all, the escorts had destroyed four U-boats for the loss of the converted merchant carrier *Audacity*, one destroyer and two merchantmen. For Dönitz this was an unacceptable 'exchange rate' – quite apart from the loss of one of his favourite aces;[96] and it had indicated that U-boats could be held off and destroyed by a well-trained and numerous escort, aided by aircraft. Whether the actions had also proved the value of 'Operation Buttercup' is questionable: on both occasions Walker employed the manoeuvre, the majority of escorts steamed off in the wrong direction, and on the second occasion the boat destroyed, Endrass's *U567*, was not the one causing the alarm. Nonetheless, Walker believed 'Buttercup' had proved itself and reported accordingly to the Commander-in-Chief Western Approaches and the Director of Anti-Submarine Warfare at the Admiralty; as a result in early 1942 the manoeuvre was issued for the guidance of all escorts of Western Approaches Command.

In the meantime, an officer had been selected to evolve anti-U-boat tactics and train escort-group commanders in the conduct of actions. This was Captain Gilbert Roberts, a gunnery officer with a fine analytical brain who had served two years on the staff of the Tactical School at Portsmouth before being struck down by tuberculosis and invalided out of the service. His time at the Tactical School had begun in 1935, the year Hitler unveiled the revived U-boat arm, yet the problems studied there had concerned the British versus the Japanese battlefleet on 'Jutland' lines; submarines had scarcely been mentioned, the protection of convoys never. In his second year, under a new director, the emphasis on line of battle had lessened and modern problems of carrier actions, night fighting, shadowing and actions between dissimilar forces had been played out. Roberts had enjoyed every moment, showing an obvious flair for the work; he was an inspired choice to study anti-U-boat tactics, but why it had taken so long to create the post is a mystery. Roberts' biographer states that the idea originated with Admiral Usborne, a naval aide to Churchill. Before he took up the post Roberts was briefed by Usborne, and taken to see Churchill. The Prime Minister told him to find out what was happening in the Atlantic, and 'Find ways of getting the convoys through and sinking the U-boats!'[97] This had been immediately prior to Pearl Harbor and Dönitz's switch from the Atlantic convoy routes to the US east coast.

After arrival at Derby House, Liverpool, in early January 1942 Roberts questioned as many escort commanders as possible and analysed reports of convoy battles, including Walker's recent series of actions. It did not take him long to deduce that a favourite U-boat tactic at night, the most dangerous time for pack attacks, was to infiltrate the convoys from astern on the surface, fire and withdraw by the same route. Using wooden models to represent merchantmen and escorts, Roberts then worked out a manoeuvre to counter this form of attack on a plotting floor he had had laid out in an empty block allocated to him adjacent to the Derby House headquarters. This involved the escorts turning and racing back to form a line abreast astern of the convoy, then following behind it, sweeping with asdic, as he described it 'trawling' for the U-boat or boats as they withdrew. He demonstrated the manoeuvre to the C-in-C, Admiral Sir Percy Noble, who had greeted his arrival some weeks earlier with scarcely disguised scepticism. Noble was impressed, and asked what he proposed to call it.

'Raspberry, Sir!' Roberts replied, explaining that a Wren assistant had called it a 'raspberry to Hitler'.[98] So 'Operation Raspberry' was born and, like 'Buttercup', it was promulgated to the escort groups.

In March Roberts opened a tactical school running courses for escort commanders, their first lieutenants and navigators. They sat at tables around the edge of the plotting floor, prevented from seeing the full area by canvas screens with apertures which could be adapted to permit a view only of the area appropriate to their escort. A team of Wrens moved the models representing the convoy and escorts up the squared floor while Roberts or his deputy commanded the unseen U-boats and advised players of asdic or radar contacts, sightings, sinkings and other incidents; after each of these the players had two minutes to make up their minds what to do and write their instructions as to alterations of course and speed on chits, which they passed via a letter box in the view screen to the Wren moving their escort. In the wash-up after the 'game' they were able to see for the first time where the U-boat had actually been, analyse their mistakes and learn whether or not they had made a kill.

Besides providing invaluable training week after week for escort commanders and officers, the courses became catalysts for new manoeuvres as recent Atlantic experience was analysed by Roberts in the plotting room. Thus 'Operation Raspberry' was followed by 'Pineapple' – for a boat detected ahead of the convoy; 'Beta Search' and 'Step-aside' – for U-boats which dived when they sighted an escort making for them – and a series of other evolutions and searches. Coastal Command officers also attended the courses, with the result that each service began to understand the difficulties the others faced; closer tactical co-operation followed naturally.

So it was that in the summer and autumn of 1942, at the end of the third year of war, the Royal Navy was at last focused as sharply on the struggle against U-boats as it had been on battle-fleet action. The necessary detection apparatus, weapons, operational analysis and training establishments were to hand. It only needed industry to supply centimetric radar sets, US industry to supply escort carriers and more long-range aircraft, and the game was up for Dönitz's U-boats, which remained in essentials unchanged from the start of the war, their sole, reactive, innovation being the Metox 600 radar detector.

The Royal Canadian Navy, which had been expanded hugely from a tiny pre-war establishment to take over convoys west of what was now termed the 'Change of Operational Control' or 'Chop' line on the 26th meridian, created its own escort simulator for teaching night tactics at this time; and the US Navy, which had set up an operations analysis group in March, issued a manual for escort-group tactics in July, following it in August with more comprehensive instructions for convoy defence and anti-submarine search and attack tactics.

For Dönitz, after his return to the attack on the North Atlantic convoy routes in August 1942, the chief threat appeared to be from Allied aircraft. Had the British Air Staff been able to read his war diary entries and submissions to Berlin they might possibly have reconsidered their attitude. On 3 September he described how the air escort of a convoy being shadowed by his boats 450 miles south of Iceland, 800 miles from Great Britain, had been strengthened on the evening of 1 September:

> This led to the boats being systematically forced under water, so losing contact [with the convoy] in the evening twilight, and thereby to the complete frustration of the prospects for all boats during the first four moonless hours of the night. The enemy used the loss of contact cleverly to make a sharp leg [*Zack*], so that contact could not be regained until 0300 and the boats of the group were unable to get near the convoy . . . The operation had to be broken off on the morning of the 2nd since gaining position ahead by day did not appear possible in face of the strength of the expected enemy air cover [and] on the other hand because poor visibility rendered aircraft with radar too great a danger. Altogether on 1 September three boats were more or less heavily bombed.
>
> . . . from observation of [the enemy's] development in the air the BdU [Dönitz] foresees with the gravest concern the day when the same unfavourable situation of air cover over convoys extends to almost all areas of the North Atlantic – the chief battleground of the U-boats. Without suitable countermeasures that would signify an unendurable reduction of the prospects for U-boats.[99]

Six days later he made another impassioned plea to Berlin for the new four-engined He 177 that he believed was about to come into service. He listed five recent instances of U-boat groups with favourable prospects against convoys being forced to break off their attacks on the appearance of enemy aircraft, and pointed out that He 177s, had they been deployed to support the groups, could have scattered the enemy planes, thereby aiding the U-boats' operations, and also contributed their own sinkings by bombing. This was theoretically sound, but it betrayed ignorance of the technical problems besetting these aircraft.[100]

Given the decisive effect of the U-boat war on the conduct of the war as a whole, he went on, it was necessary to employ every means available which could help the U-boats 'in their difficult, costly struggle'. In fact, losses had been tabulated at the end of the previous month as 105 out of 304 U-boats commissioned since the start of the war, 2,600 officers and men killed or missing, and a further 1,148 prisoners of war.[101] Heavy by comparison with the submarine arms of the other powers, these were a tithe of the losses he was to preside over in the years to come. In his view, he continued, it was 'unconditionally necessary that the only aircraft suitable for this purpose, the He 177, is made available as soon as possible'.[102]

The same day he sent a suggestion to Berlin that rockets under development at Peenemunde should be adapted for U-boats as anti-destroyer weapons. His agitation at the growing difficulty of his war and the lack of support he was receiving from other arms is very apparent:

> The U-boat arm today completes the third year of continuous battle missions. It has remained through all the changing events of the war ever the chief weapon of German naval warfare, in the first line because its characteristics allow it not only to engage the enemy successfully, but also to exist in the face of forces superior in numbers and strength. If all resources are not deployed in the first line to maintain the battle strength of the U-boats at the highest possible level the danger must be recognized that one day the U-boat will be crushed by the [Allied] defence and eliminated [ausgeschaltet wird].
>
> The German naval leadership would thereby have the sole weapon which it can deploy against the great sea powers struck from its hand . . .[103]

And he made another plea for the weapons departments in Berlin to co-operate in an examination of ways to improve U-boat armaments. By this he no doubt meant weapons to enable U-boats to tackle convoy escorts, both air and surface.

The scale of the task facing Dönitz was perhaps the prime cause of his anxiety. Forecasts of enemy shipbuilding in 1943 indicated that it would be necessary to sink about 1 million tons a month to keep pace with Allied, particularly of course American, ship-building, and 1.3 million tons to have a decisive effect on Allied capacity. It will be recalled that six months earlier, on 15 May 1942, Dönitz had reported to Hitler that it would be necessary to sink 700,000 tons a month at the maximum, but that US ship-building forecasts were probably exaggerated, in which case they would only need to sink 400,000–500,000 tons a month. However, the sinkings from January to August 1942 during the 'golden time' off the US east coast had averaged only 400,000 tons a month – actually an underestimate – and it seemed to the Berlin staff questionable whether a sinking rate of over a million tons a month could be maintained. This should surely have seemed an understatement to Dönitz after his agonized war diary entries. However, there is no sign, apart from the vehemence of his submissions, that the colossal monthly sinkings demanded by the US merchant ship construction programme caused him to revise his concept of the 'tonnage war'.

The Berlin staff certainly questioned it: 'Can a war-decisive influence be brought to bear in the trade war by sinkings alone, irrespective of where and whether [ships are] laden or unladen, or must specified tonnage in specified areas be sunk to achieve this goal?'[104]

What was meant was the interdiction of supplies for Great Britain by transferring 'the centre of gravity of the trade war to the South Atlantic, North Sea and incoming British traffic' – in other words, to the Western Approaches. The decision as to whether to move to such a 'supply war' from 'tonnage war', the staff concluded, would depend on the judgement that the U-boat arm made of future prospects of success. With the figures available to Dönitz and the trend that he clearly foresaw of enemy counter-measures growing to a point at which his boats would be 'crushed and eliminated', he could not rationally have expected to be able to sink over a million tons a month. Neither, of course, could he have sent his boats to the North Sea and Western Approaches, where aircraft patrols would have caused unsustainable losses. Since he was an unquenchable optimist who had never allowed impediments to stand in his way, he continued to maintain that ships had to be sunk where it could be done most easily and cheaply, and placed his hopes in great increases in the number of operational boats, Luftwaffe aid and new weapons to meet the Allied countermeasures.

It was unfortunate for the U-boat arm that, at this decisive juncture after it had become clear that the race against time and enemy shipbuilding capacity was irretrievably lost, Dönitz was not on speaking terms with Raeder. The Navy chief was a reserved, somewhat inarticulate, conservative and rather sensitive man with a vast area of responsibility extending from the North Cape of Norway, the Baltic, and the north and west coasts of Europe to the Mediterranean and the Black Sea; Dönitz's extraordinarily focused vision, lack of tact and continual interference far beyond his operational responsibilities had brought about a complete rupture between them. Yet Raeder felt unable to relieve him of his post: the reputation of the U-boatmen and their dynamic chief had been so inflated by propaganda that Dönitz's removal would have had a negative effect on morale, and more important perhaps, it would have been hard to explain at Führer headquarters. Hitler and those about him understood little of naval warfare, but the U-boats were the one offensive weapon they now had against the western Allies.

Because of this rift all communication between Berlin and U-boat Command in Paris was by teletype; if a personal conversation were absolutely necessary it was made by proxy between the chiefs of staff, Eberhard Godt for Dönitz, Konteradmiral Erich Schulte-Mönting, a very diplomatic officer, for Raeder. It was an intolerable situation, yet Raeder was forced to tolerate it; in the words of one officer who saw this at first hand: 'With Erich Raeder, the first priority was always to shield the Navy from any negative publicity and to defend its independence [from the Nazis at Führer headquarters] and what little influence it had.'[105]

Dönitz was never quick at grasping situations, but as he came to realize the strength of his personal position he began to exploit it. It was here, in the impasse in relations at the top, that irrationality entered U-boat operations.

In his strategy of dispersal to keep the enemy guessing and stretch their defences Dönitz had despatched a group of four Type IX boats and a *Milchkuh* to the waters off South Africa in August 1942. In order to achieve surprise the boats, named *Gruppe Eisbär* (Polar Bear), had been instructed not to attack any targets below 5°S until they reached the operational area off Capetown, focal point for traffic to and from the Middle and Far East. Just before this cut-off point, a little south of the Equator, one of the boats, *U156* under KK Werner Hartenstein, came upon the 19,700-ton former Cunard liner, *Laconia*. It was the evening of 12 September. Hartenstein attacked after sunset and put his first torpedo into the liner's starboard side at mid-length, wrecking the engine room and causing her to list and settle. He closed as lifeboats were filled and lowered, to his great surprise hearing Italian cries for help coming from men who had leaped into the water from the decks. Pulling some of these aboard, he learned that the ship was carrying hundreds of Italian prisoners of war from the desert campaign. In fact she had embarked nearly 1,800 Italians at Suez, together with their guards, Poles who had volunteered in Russia to fight in the so-called Anders Army for the Allies. She also carried wounded Allied servicemen, RAF personnel and British officials from the Middle East with their wives and families; including crew the total ship's complement was about 3,250 persons.

Hartenstein, appalled at consigning so many Axis soldiers to death by drowning, began a rescue operation and reported to U-boat Command, requesting instructions. In Paris Dönitz was roused from his bed; after discussing the remarkable situation with his staff, he signalled the other *Eisbär* boats to join Hartenstein's rescue operation and then informed the Naval Staff in Berlin. Raeder approved his action and began negotiations with the Vichy

French to send ships from Dakar, in French West Africa, to take the survivors from the U-boats.

Hartenstein, meanwhile, his boat crowded with over 200 extra people including 21 British, sent out messages in English clear text, giving his position and promising not to attack any ships that came to the rescue provided they did not attack him. Peter Hansen, who knew Hartenstein and discussed the affair with him later, has remarked that these 'expectations were outdated and unrealistic by then'.[106] The messages were picked up by two British steamers in the area and passed to the British naval authorities at Freetown, Sierra Leone. Scenting a trap, they took no action.

Hartenstein spent that day, 13 September, shepherding survivors on to rafts and into lifeboats, periodically taking the wounded and women and children aboard U156 for medical treatment, food and shelter. From Berlin, after agreement had been reached with the French, the incident was reported to Hitler's naval adjutant, *Kapitän* Jesko von Puttkamer, at the Führer's advanced headquarters in the Ukraine. When Hitler was told that afternoon, he instructed Puttkamer to summon Dönitz to report on the U-boat war as soon as possible – the choice of date was his. In the meantime Putterkamer was to tell him that he did not wish the Capetown operation to be compromised or the boats exposed to danger.

Two days later, on 15 September, Hartensein was joined by KLt. Erich Würdemann in U506 and KK Harro Schacht in U507. The survivors, both Italian and British, were distributed between the three boats and they set course for the rendezvous position agreed with the French. Next morning Hartenstein, on his own with four lifeboats in tow and additional survivors on his casing, saw a US aircraft approaching; he showed a two-metre square Red Cross flag and attempted to signal by lamp, unsuccessfully it seemed. The pilot nevertheless took in the situation and circled away again, calling his control at a new US Army Air Force base on Ascension Island for instructions. His query was passed up the line to the base commander, who in turn tried to call Washington; unable to get through, he was forced to make the decision himself. Militarily it was the only one possible; it was passed to the aircraft concisely: 'Sink sub!'

The pilot, Lt. James Harden, on his first overseas patrol, returned and attempted to fulfil the order, only succeeding on his first three runs in overturning a lifeboat as it was being cast off and killing a number of Italian survivors. On his next run he dropped two depth-charges, one of which seemed to explode directly beneath

U156's control room, sending a column of water over the conning tower, starting leaks and damaging both periscopes. Hartenstein, having put the survivors from the casing into the water near the boats, dived. Harden, on his next run, saw the upturned bottom of the lifeboat, and believed he had sunk the submarine, reporting this on his return to Ascension Island.

Hartenstein's signal detailing the attack only reached U-boat Command at eleven that night. Another staff discussion took place, which Dönitz in his memoirs described as *temperament-voll* – passionate. The staff apparently argued that the rescue operation was unjustifiable, but Dönitz was determined to finish what he had started and eventually, according to his own account, closed the argument with the words, 'I cannot put the people in the water now; I shall carry on.'[107] Whether or not he said 'people' he meant 'Italians', and instructions were sent to the boats ordering them to keep only the Italians aboard and proceed to the rendezvous with the French ships. In his war diary he commented that it was impossible to understand Hartenstein's belief that the sight of a Red Cross flag and the rescue measures would deter the enemy from attack; he assumed he must have been influenced by the sight of hundreds of survivors fighting for their lives.[108] The tally of those who finally reached Dakar alive was about 800 Britons, 450 Italians and 120 Poles.

Dönitz's own view was set out in orders to all COs the following evening, 17 September – after *U506* had also come under attack from the same aircraft piloted by Harden, but had managed to dive in time:

> All attempts to rescue members of ships sunk, therefore also fishing out swimmers and putting them into lifeboats, righting capsized lifeboats, handing out provisions and water, have to cease. Rescue contradicts the most fundamental [*primitivisten*] demands of war for the annihilation of enemy ships and crews.
> ... Be hard. Think of the fact that the enemy in his bombing attacks on German towns has no regard for women and children.[109]

He followed this up at some date that month or the next – unrecorded in the war diary – with another order to all COs categorizing the 'so-called rescue ship' which sailed with most convoys as a valuable target in view of 'the desired destruction of the steamers' crews'.[110]

These two orders, together with some verbal testimony, were used by the British prosecution at the Nuremberg trials after the war to support their case that Dönitz had ordered the killing of survivors from torpedoed ships. The phrases which aroused the suspicion were, of course, in the 'Laconia order', 'the most fundamental demands of war for the annihilation of enemy ships and crews', and in the 'Rescue ship order', 'the desired destruction of the steamers' crews'. However, only one proven case could be cited of a U-boat CO deliberately killing survivors. In contrast, and as these pages have shown, there were innumerable instances of COs showing great humanity, amongst them, of course, Hartenstein himself.

German records show that at the time Dönitz issued these orders the treatment of survivors was under discussion by the Naval Staff in Berlin; the spur, perhaps, was Hitler's wish to have survivors eliminated. In early January, he had told the Japanese Ambassador that however many ships the Americans built they would have difficulty manning them; for this reason he would have to give the order that 'since foreign seamen cannot be taken prisoner, and in most cases this is not possible on the open sea, the U-boats are to surface after torpedoing and shoot up the lifeboats'.[111] The Ambassador had agreed and said that the Japanese would be forced to use the same methods, as of course many had. When Hitler first put the proposition to Raeder is not recorded, but the question had come up in May when Raeder and Dönitz had reported to him at Führer headquarters; during his exposition of new weapons for U-boats Dönitz had pointed out the great advantage of a new Abstand, or non-contact (magnetic) pistol under development for torpedoes: 'in consequence of the very rapid sinking of the torpedoed ship the crew will no longer be able to be rescued. This greater loss of ships' crews will doubtless aggravate the manning difficulties for the great American shipbuilding programme.'[112]

In early September, reports of British destroyers machine-gunning survivors of the minelayer Ulm, which they had sunk 150 miles east of Bear Island on the route of the Arctic convoys to Russia, had caused Hitler to erupt: 'An eye for an eye and a tooth for a tooth. We must straightway declare that from now on parachuting airmen will be fired on and our U-boats will shell the survivors of ships regardless of whether they are soldiers or civilians, women or children.'[113]

Raeder had immediately set up an investigation into the Ulm case and previous incidents of a similar nature. A preliminary report had been drafted in the International Law, Propaganda and Politics section of the Naval Staff by 14 September, thus two days before Hartenstein was bombed while towing the Laconia's lifeboats. It listed twelve cases of German survivors being, as it appeared, deliberately shot in the water, the first three during destroyer actions in Narvik in the Norwegian campaign in 1940, the remainder during the battle for Crete in May 1941 when it was reported that German crews and troops from transports destroyed by surface forces had been picked out by searchlights and machine-gunned in the water; in one case a British submarine was cited.[114] Oddly, the carnage caused by Miers among the caiques in July 1941 was not listed.

Dönitz, accompanied by Raeder and other admirals, including the chief of the U-boat section of the Naval Staff, reported to Hitler at the Chancellery in Berlin on 28 September. The official record of the meeting indicates that Hitler opened by expressing great appreciation for the performance of the U-boat arm. He then passed to the shipbuilding programme announced by the Americans, which he considered propaganda, impossible to realize in practice; even if they did manage to launch the projected number of hulls, they would still want for engines, auxiliary machinery and, above all, men to man the vessels. At this point he remarked: 'how disadvantageous it is if large portions of the crews from vessels which have been sunk are always in a position to go to sea again in new ships'.[115] Next Dönitz outlined the situation in the Battle of the Atlantic, passing on to the technical developments necessary, the most important of which was an increase in the underwater speed of the boats; this would be fulfilled, he said, by the types under development by Professor Walter. Afterwards he pressed again for He 177s to dispute Allied air command in the Atlantic. It was Raeder this time who pointed to the development of the *Abstand* pistol for torpedoes and the increased loss of life to be expected from the more rapid sinking which would result.[116]

Probably more was said on this topic than found its way into the official record. What emerges from the whole series of discussions, Naval Staff papers and indeed Dönitz's 'Laconia' and 'Rescue ship' orders is that Hitler had at some earlier date proposed the annihilation of surviving enemy crews for the dual purpose of reducing the pool of men available to man the new ships sliding down US slipways and deterring sailors from serving. Raeder and Dönitz had objected on the practical grounds that such an order would undermine U-boat morale: officers and men would react against shooting defenceless people in the water and would assume that the enemy would mete out the same treatment to them in reprisal if the positions were reversed.[117] Perhaps the arguments were rehearsed again at this conference of 28 September; perhaps Dönitz convinced Hitler that the ambiguities in his orders calling for the destruction of ships and crews were as far as it was possible to go in written orders which might find their way into enemy hands. At all events, there is no record of Hitler, or indeed Raeder or Dönitz, ever returning to the theme.[118]

On moral and international legal grounds it would be difficult to differentiate these discussions about annihilating shipwrecked survivors from those mentioned earlier between Churchill, his advisers and the Air Staff on area-bombing to kill, de-house and break the morale of the German working-class population – except perhaps that the British offensive was likely to affect women and children more directly, and was in the event carried out.

Dönitz, like Hitler and the rest of the German leadership, certainly made the connection. This is clear from the final section of the 'Laconia' order in which he enjoined COs to be hard and bear in mind that the enemy bombers had no regard for women and children. According to the affidavit and Nuremberg testimony of OLt. Peter Heisig, he made the same point to officers of the 2nd U-boat Training Division at this date, late September or early October 1942. Heisig, then an Oberfähnrich, or senior midshipman, heard a speech Dönitz gave to the course during which he was asked about a recent newspaper article on US shipbuilding. Dönitz replied that the Allies were having considerable manning difficulties and that the stage had been reached when total war had to be waged at sea: in order to make it impossible for the Allies to man their new tonnage, crews, like the ships themselves, were targets for U-boats. If anyone considered these tactics harsh they should remember that their wives and families at home were being bombed.

Afterwards Heisig discussed these remarks with others, for Dönitz had not expressed himself clearly; all came to the conclusion that he had meant fire should be opened on survivors. On another occasion Heisig spoke about the matter to one of his senior officers, who advised that 'if possible only officers should be on the bridge ready to annihilate shipwrecked sailors should the possibility arise'.[119]

Further testimony on Dönitz's policy in this area was given at the Nuremberg trials by KK Karl-Heinz Moehle, chief of the 5th U-Flotilla at Kiel, who gave final briefings to COs sailing from that port. Concerned at the lack of clarity in Dönitz's 'Laconia' orders, he sought guidance from a staff officer at U-boat Command, KLt. Herbert Kuppisch. Why he was content to take the word of an officer junior to himself, indeed number six on the staff, when he had access to the Chief of Staff, Godt, or Dönitz himself, was never made clear; a cynical explanation would be that by the time he gave his testimony Kuppisch had been lost at sea, but Godt and Dönitz were alive, the latter on trial for his life. Moehle's motive for testifying was that he feared that otherwise he might be put on trial himself.

Kuppisch, Moehle said, had explained the order by means of two examples: the first was a U-boat outward-bound in Biscay, which had come across survivors from a British aircraft in a rubber dinghy; unable to take them aboard, the U-boat CO had made a wide circle around them and continued on his mission. When he subsequently reported this at his debriefing, he was reproached by Dönitz's staff for not attacking the airmen, since they would have been rescued by British patrols within twenty-four hours and returned to anti-U-boat operations in new aircraft. This referred to OLt. Hans Kandler of U386, although it appears that his reprimand was actually for not taking the men aboard as prisoners.

The second example concerned U-boats working off the US east coast during the first half of the year. Because of their proximity to land, the greater part of the crews of the torpedoed ships had been rescued, an 'extremely regrettable' circumstance since the enemy merchant fleet consisted of crews as well as tonnage, and these crews were then available to man newly built ships.

Moehle repeated the two examples to COs who asked him about the interpretation of these orders; few did, he said, and he always added, 'However U-boat Command cannot give you such an order officially. Everybody has to handle this according to his own conscience.'[120] In that exemption Moehle encapsulated the essence of Dönitz's secret policy. The ambiguities are captured vividly in *Das Boot* by Lothar-Günther Buchheim; in the Bar Royal of the Hotel Majestic, La Baule, his fictional officers discuss the deliberate lack of clarity in the orders at length.

'He didn't say anything about machine-gunning men in the drink – or did he?'

'No, of course he didn't. He simply pointed out that crew losses would hit the British where it hurts ... everyone can read what he likes into that. Smart idea, I call it!'[121]

Despite Bletchley Park's continuing inability to break the four-rotor Enigma cipher, Rodger Winn in the Submarine Tracking Room correctly predicted the southward movement of the *Eisbär* boats. Shipping around the Cape was routed away from the land, and vessels calling at Capetown were escorted clear of the regular shipping lanes. The new routing proved fatal for the latest Orient liner, the 23,000-ton *Orcades*. Homeward-bound from Suez with British service personnel and families from the Middle East, her holds filled with oranges and other foodstuffs loaded at Capetown, she was steering a wide zigzag well to the south and west of her usual track from the Cape when, soon after 11.00 on 10 October, she was struck on the port side by three torpedoes, one right aft, two in the forward holds. Her commander, Captain Fox, finding that the ship, although settling, remained on an even keel, sent the passengers and most of the crew away in the boats, retaining a small nucleus of volunteers aboard to try and take her back to Capetown.

KLt. Carl Emmermann of *U172*, who had fired the salvo, remained observing the liner from periscope depth. When he saw her under way he set up another attack, this time from her starboard side, and hit her with three more torpedoes. She took an immediate heavy list to starboard. Captain Fox, recognizing the end, ordered his small party to abandon ship in the boats retained for the eventuality and, after throwing the weighted bag with the code-books from the bridge, he went below to check that all hands had received his order. Finally he clambered along the inclined deck to the poop and jumped off, hoping he would be seen from one of the boats. He swam some way to escape the suction when the vessel sank, then turned to float on his back. Lifted on succeeding swells, he saw his lovely ship lying right over on her beam ends, her main mast and after funnel touching the water. He had not glimpsed even the periscope of the U-boat that had hit her: 'Slowly the ship sank lower and lower . . . and disappeared beneath the waves. The Red Ensign was still flying as she sank. Something of me went down in that ship – call it what you will, but it was gone.'[122]

The *Eisbär* boats pressed round the Cape and up the east coast to the route between Durban and Capetown, sinking in all twenty-four ships of over 160,000 tons by the end of the month, marginally better than the actual results of the five *Paukenschlag* boats at the beginning of the year. In early November they were joined by a second wave that Dönitz had despatched in September. These boats were a larger, 1,600-ton modification of the Type IX, designated IXD2. Their increased displacement was accounted for chiefly by extra fuel tanks which gave them a prodigious range of almost 24,000 miles at 12 knots; they also had an improved top surface speed of rather over 19 knots. The most successful was *U181* under the ace KK Wolfgang Lüth, introduced earlier as CO of the Type II *U138* and the Type IXA *U43*.

Lüth had been born of German stock in the Baltic seaport of Riga, where his father owned a manufacturing business. As a Balt, Lüth strove to be more thoroughly German than those born in the Reich; he was certainly a most ardent Nazi, retaining absolute commitment to Hitler and the ideals proclaimed by the Party. The most obvious manifestation of this so far as his crew was concerned was his belief in the sanctity of marriage and the virtue of procreation; he preached on these themes to his men at every opportunity. His recent biographer, Jordan Vause, believes that Lüth's own marriage and children were 'the most significant, most sacred' part of his life, 'more significant than his commission, medals or sinkings'.[123] The corollary was hatred of indecency and promiscuity: he counselled married crew members to stay away from other women in port, and even followed his officers around to ensure that they did not stray. Aboard, he forbade the usual 'pin-ups', examined magazines and other reading matter in the crew's quarters for lewd passages, and did not allow profanity. He saw himself as father to his crew, and his wife ran a network of companionship and support for their wives and families. Officers often saw him in a different light. Peter Hansen likened his attitude towards his crew to that of a Baltic landowner towards his servants.[124]

His appearance seemed to match his character. Although only 29 he was bald on top with a fringe of hair around the sides and back of his head like a monk's tonsure; at sea the inevitable U-boatman's beard grew down his jawline, leaving gaunt, bare cheeks; his nose was prominent, his eyes a brooding blue. He was a distinctive, quiet man of volcanic passion when roused, yet for those who could tolerate his moralizing and patronizing treatment, interspersed with occasional storms when he acted the super-disciplinarian, he was a revered leader.[125]

There was no more severe test of leadership than the 7,500-mile voyage from Kiel northabout around Scotland to the Cape. Lüth fought boredom and the inevitable petty animosities aroused in the cramped quarters of the boat in the most imaginative way by organizing discussion groups, chess and card game tournaments, team quizzes, singing contests, tall story contests, classes in meteorology, engineering, philosophy and other subjects, talks by members of the crew with a special interest, and record requests played over the loudspeaker system, during which he would introduce selections from the great German composers with a few words to aid the men's appreciation. A ship's news-sheet with items from the radio news was typed and distributed, and he read news bulletins himself over the speakers and gave regular talks on German history and politics with an unequivocal Nazi gloss. Later, ashore, he would give a lecture on leadership in U-boats which would be so well regarded that it would be published and distributed as a model for U-boat officers to follow. In it he would assert that political talks were necessary to correct the 'passive philosophy' of a portion of the crew: 'On Sundays I sometimes dive and hold musters under water to tell them something about the Reich and the centuries' old struggle for it, and about some of the greatest men in our history. On the Führer's birthday I tell them something of his life and of my visit to Führer headquarters . . .'[126]

Of course, none of this would have counted had he been found wanting in action, especially under depth-charge attack, the ultimate test of a CO. But like Kretschmer, whose tonnage record he would come close to equalling, he had strong nerves and a cool head under pressure.

U181 reached the latitude of the Cape on 1 November after a passage of seven weeks, and Lüth turned east. Two days later he sank an 8,000-ton US ore carrier after missing with his first two torpedoes from the uncharacteristically long range of 2,500 yards. He passed on eastwards into the Indian Ocean, the following week sinking another three ships, bringing his personal total since the start of the war to over 200,000 tons. Two days later, in the early hours of 15 November, he received a signal that the Führer had awarded him the Oak Leaves to his Knight's Cross. By then *U181* had moved up the east coast to within 100 miles of Durban. At dawn the same day the bridge watch was surprised in high seas by a destroyer on anti-submarine patrol and made an emergency dive.

Asdic pulses rang through the hull, and the swish and rumble of propellers increased in volume as they went deep, but it was some time before the destroyer was sufficiently sure of the contact to drop her first depth-charge. She continued the attack throughout the morning. The boat, 160 metres (525 feet) below, shook and groaned as patterns of charges detonated close above. In the control room Lüth listened impassively to reports of leaks and minor damage. Those detailed to repairs padded in their socks over mattresses and blankets laid on the deck plates to muffle sound; hands off duty lay quietly in their bunks to preserve the air, sucking breaths in through potash cartridges which filtered the excess carbon dioxide. Shortly before midday Lüth had the impression that a second destroyer had joined the first. He was mistaken, but during the afternoon two corvettes arrived from Durban, and all three ships continued the hunt, attacking at intervals until nightfall. By this time the boat's bilges were full, and the crew were struggling for breath; nevertheless, Lüth waited until midnight to. make sure the hunters had really gone before ordering stations for surfacing. He recorded in the log, 'Boat and crew behaved well.'[127]

He had been given freedom to range the area at will, and when next day his radio operator intercepted a signal from Kapitän Hans Ibbeken of *U178* reporting that he had sunk two vessels off Lourenço Marques at the southern end of Portuguese East Africa, he headed north to join him. Over the following days he and the other *Eisbär* COs wrought such havoc off the approaches to Lourenço Marques and further up the coast that they forced the closure of this important neutral supply port for a time. Lüth made the largest killing, accounting for a further seven ships, the last four during the week of 23–30 November, all completed with sustained artillery barrages from his 105mm (4.1-inch) deck gun and 20mm AA gun – the barrel of his other AA gun having exploded at the first shots. On the final occasion, against an old 4,300-ton Greek steamer, *Cleanthis*, armed with four machine guns and a deck gun aft, he opened fire with the 105mm from 1½ miles' range after missing with a salvo of two torpedoes, and continued bombarding her for the next thirty minutes, long after the crew had abandoned ship. With the vessel ablaze and only one 105mm round left – such had been his expenditure on the previous three occasions – Lüth closed to 450 yards and had his gunlayer fire this last shell after careful aim at the stern below the waterline; at the same time he ordered the AA gun's crew to open up into the stern. Whether other crew members, who had been issued with machine guns at the start and ordered up on to the casing, were encouraged to loose off their weapons is not recorded, although it may be significant that the surviving crew of the steamer assumed from the mode of attack that they had been assaulted by a Japanese submarine which had the intention of killing them all. The *Cleanthis* sank after nearly an hour of point-blank bombardment from the AA gun, leaving several bodies floating.[128]

Among Buchheim's fictional officers discussing the ambiguities of Dönitz's orders about ships and crews in the Bar Royal, one was said to have solved the problem in his own way by shooting up the lifeboats – presumably before they were filled and lowered – and was thus able to maintain that while ensuring no survivors, he had never killed a man in cold blood.[129] Lüth had departed Kiel on 12 September before the '*Laconia*' or 'Rescue ship' orders had been issued, and although he must have received both on passage, he cannot have been briefed by Moehle on their interpretation. He was of course precisely the type of convinced Nazi who would not have needed much briefing to understand their gist, and he possessed just the sort of puritan, absolutist mind to execute the veiled injunction. Yet there seems no indication that he took any such action against his previous victims on the current cruise. Moreover, in his former command, *U43*, in May 1941, long before Dönitz had issued the orders, Lüth had destroyed an unarmed 500-ton sailing schooner with a similar artillery barrage, and continued firing into the burning wreck as it turned over on its side and sank. Plainly he had derived fierce satisfaction from the assault.[130] He was a man of moods. Perhaps, in the fifteenth week of the voyage, that is sufficient explanation.

Leaving the survivors of the *Cleanthis*, a dozen wounded among them, without a sign of recognition or remorse, Lüth set course southwards for the Cape, where he sank a 4,300-ton Panamanian ship on 2 December, bringing his tally for the cruise to 12 vessels totalling 57,500 tons. Now short of fuel he started homewards. He reached Bordeaux five weeks later. The other COs began their return passages at about the same time and, as Dönitz had sent the next long-range group to the waters off Brazil, shipping off the Cape and in the Indian Ocean enjoyed a respite.

During November the Allies had suffered the highest losses of any month of the war, 134 ships totalling 807,754 tons; the U-boats' contribution had been 730,000 tons, 130,000 tons of which had been accounted for by the Type IXs in the Indian Ocean. Dönitz was elated. His COs' reports suggested the total would 'probably exceed 900,000 tons', within a whisker of the million he needed to break even in the tonnage war; 'The time has come to regard these results in a true light', he wrote in his war diary.[131]

There were many reasons for this upturn after the pessimism of his September entries: the invasion and subsequent supply convoys for the Allied 'Torch' landings in North Africa had drawn off numbers of escorts from North Atlantic convoy routes, and made it impossible to extend the convoy system to and around the Cape; the first convoys between Durban and Capetown were not established until December. The completed escort carriers had also been deployed to protect the North African convoys, while others built to US order had been sent by Admiral King to the Pacific. Moreover, the escort groups remaining in the North Atlantic included several which still lacked Type 271 radar or Huff Duff; all lacked air cover in the mid-Atlantic 'air gap'; and since Bletchley Park was still unable to penetrate the U-boat cipher, evasive routing was based chiefly on DF plots of U-boat signals and Winn's remarkable insights into Dönitz's mind; too frequently, however, these were nullified by *B-Dienst*'s successes in breaking the convoy routing cipher. In addition, and despite losing almost 50 boats to other commands, principally Norway and the Mediterranean, Dönitz now controlled 160 boats from his Paris headquarters, and during November managed to keep an average of 95 at sea each day, 38 of them in the chosen operational areas.[132] By the end of the year the total number of boats in service had reached 393, and during January 1943 passed the 400 mark. Deducting those employed in training and trials, over 220 were available for operations, and of these Dönitz controlled 178 in the Atlantic.[133]

Nonetheless, sinking figures fell in December to 330,000 tons, under half the November figure. In part this was due to ferocious storms which hampered operations, at times making attack impossible, in part to the return of the long-range boats from the easy areas without convoys. Dönitz blamed the poor figures on the dispersal of his forces to combat the Allied North African landings. In a situation report of 19 December he cited the remark of one of his 'best and most experienced U-boat commanders' that in the western Mediterranean it was 'hardly possible to exist'. It was the same in the area outside the Straits of Gibraltar. The difference between the tonnage his boats had actually sunk in these difficult areas and that which would have been sunk had he been allowed to deploy them 'in the main theatre of the naval war' – meaning the North Atlantic – he estimated as 'at least 300,000 tons. Thus the enemy has gained a considerable amount of tonnage which he can use to strengthen the African front.'[134] He concluded:

> The tonnage war is the chief task of the U-boats, perhaps the U-boats' decisive contribution to the outcome of the war. It must therefore be conducted where the greatest successes can be gained with the least losses. It is necessary, in clear recognition of this position, categorically to draw the conclusion, namely to concentrate all forces it is in any way possible to muster on the chief task, knowingly accepting the gaps and disadvantages [this will leave] in other theatres.

Quite unbeknown to him, he was about to be given the power to realize this aim. Hitler had become increasingly dissatisfied with the surface navy, which consumed scarce raw materials and manpower he needed for the eastern front without, it seemed, contributing to the war; and Raeder was being undermined at Führer headquarters by the Minister for Armaments and Munitions, Albert Speer, Göring and others for their own reasons. When on the last night of 1942 British destroyers and two cruisers successfully defended one of the convoys bound for Russia in a brilliant series of actions against the pocket battleship *Lützow*, the heavy cruiser *Hipper*, and accompanying destroyers, Hitler erupted. Summoning Raeder, he lectured him for an hour and a half without pause on the twentieth-century history of the German surface fleet and the uselessness of the big ships which, he said, he had decided to scrap forthwith; the Naval Staff were to decide where the ships' guns should be mounted ashore, and to what extent the U-boat arm could be expanded with the resources thus released. Raeder had no option but to resign.

This was, perhaps, the predictable outcome of the deepening rift with Dönitz, whom Hitler predictably chose to succeed him. In a historical sense it was the predictable reaction of an essentially military power, as pressure mounted, to divert resources from the navy to vital land campaigns. In this case Hitler chose Dönitz because the U-boats, whose successes shone amid the darkening outlook elsewhere, were his sole means of striking at the western Allies; he also knew Dönitz believed that, given his head, he could decide the outcome of the war in the west.

8

Crisis for the U-boats

DÖNITZ TOOK OVER as C-in-C of the Navy (ObdM) on 30 January 1943, the tenth anniversary of Hitler's seizure of power. His first directive to his staff indicated the new focus:

1) It is a question of winning the war ...
2) The sea war is the U-boat war.
3) All has to be subordinated to this main goal ...[1]

To ensure this he retained command of the U-boat arm himself, combining the post of BdU with that of ObdM, and brought U-boat headquarters to Berlin, where the Hotel am Steinplatz, Charlottenburg, was taken over as accommodation. *Admiral* Hans-Georg von Friedeburg, who since the outbreak of war had been responsible for U-boat personnel, training, supply and administration, was kept in his post as Admiral Commanding U-boats, responsible for everything except operations, the everyday conduct of which Dönitz deputed to his own long-serving Chief of Staff, Godt, promoted *Konteradmiral* with the title of FdU – *Führer der U-boote*. This transfer, inevitable as it was, marked a further stage, begun with the move from Lorient to Paris, in distancing the officers and men of the boats from the headquarters staff and the person of their inspirational chief, whom they knew as '*der Löwe*' ('the lion'), or in mellow mood, '*Onkel Karl*'.

At first Dönitz intended to scrap the big ships, but he soon came round to the Naval Staff view that this would hand the Royal Navy a major bloodless victory and enable the immense resources tied up by the threat the great ships posed to be deployed on anti-U-boat operations. He had trouble convincing Hitler, but eventually won a reprieve for six months, after which the subject was not raised again. He was less successful in his attempts to gain more steel to increase the rate of production of U-boats. There were too many competing demands from the other services; it was not for some months, after handing over naval construction to Speer, that he was able to step up the U-boat programme significantly.

In retrospect it is plain that instead of continuing to strive for numbers, Dönitz would have done better in these first weeks of power to bend his enormous energy and drive to the development of a new type of boat with enhanced underwater speed, forgoing radical and thus more or less distant solutions such as Professor Walter's in favour of a type which could be produced quickly with existing technology. The Japanese had already done this: a prototype high underwater speed submarine, 'Type 71', had been built at the Kure navy yard as long ago as 1938, and had achieved submerged speeds above 20 knots over short distances in trials. It was not to be followed up with a production series until much later in the war.[2]

The need for a high underwater speed boat to regain the initiative had been obvious from at least the previous September when Dönitz had pointed it out to Hitler at the Chancellery. But, no doubt lulled by work on Professor Walter's prototypes and misled by the high November sinking figures, Dönitz's priority remained numbers of conventional boats.

From the other side, the November sinkings had provoked the western Allies into another of their periodic alarms about the Atlantic. A 'Germany first' policy, whereby the main threat, Germany, was to be defeated before Japan, had been agreed by both powers before the United States entered the war. This required the invasion of Continental Europe from the British Isles, and hence a concentration of American troops and munitions in Great Britain, and their continued replenishment and supply. It was this that Dönitz's tonnage campaign threatened; consequently when Roosevelt, Churchill and the Combined Chiefs of Staff met in Casablanca in January 1943 to hammer out future strategy, the defeat of the U-boats was, at least in theory, high on the agenda. In the event the means were scarcely discussed. The British First Sea Lord, Pound, was groggy and dying slowly of a brain tumour. Admiral King was plainly immersed in the struggle against Japan since Pacific operations were the prerogative of the US Navy, the US Army looking after all other theatres. It was left to Air Marshal Sir Charles Portal to suggest in the first Chiefs of Staff meeting that the defeat of the U-boats should receive first priority from Allied air power. King roused himself from silence to retort that in his view the Royal Air Force was doing very little towards bombing submarine construction yards and bases.[3]

The British, who found King stiff, stand-offish and, as Sir Ian Jacob expressed it in his diary, ever on the lookout for 'attempts to put something over on him', recognized that they had probably antagonized him by monopolizing the meeting; they had come to Casablanca very much better prepared than the Americans, who were indeed out of their depth with joint service planning, let alone combined planning with allies.[4] Consequently in the next, after-noon, session King was invited to expound on the Japanese theatre; as Jacob recorded, 'Our Chiefs felt ... that "Uncle Ernie" would take a less jaundiced view of the rest of the world if he had been able to shoot his line about the Pacific'.[5] King explained plans for taking the offensive against Japanese-held islands, provoking the British to express fears that the resources for both a Pacific offen-sive and the main thrust against Germany were not available. This only confirmed suspicions King harboured about the British: they would exploit the United States to defeat Hitler, then leave them to fight Japan alone while they rebuilt their empire. The British Chiefs tried to reassure him of their total commitment, but neither they nor Churchill could move him from the planned Pacific offen-sive. Nor, at the lower level of the Combined Staff Planners, could the British team shift King's sole planning representative, Admiral Cooke, from his view that, to quote Jacob again, 'the Pacific was a US theatre, and it was nobody else's business what was done there ... the US Navy had made their plans for 1943, and did not intend to alter them'.[6] Nor did they intend to alter the forces they had allocated. This inflexibility defeated the concept of either joint or combined planning; it certainly defeated the British idea that forces for the Pacific should be held to a minimum to ensure suffi-cient to defeat Germany. So far as the Atlantic battle was con-cerned it meant that escorts, escort carriers and specially adapted very long-range (VLR) Liberator aircraft would go to the Pacific rather than bring the anti-submarine forces in the main theatre up to decisive strength.

When it came to a discussion of the U-boat war King's main sug-gestion was that the Royal Air Force, instead of bombing German cities, should concentrate on the areas where the boats were built and their bases in France. It is likely that he was put up to this by Pound, with whom he was on good terms – possibly because the First Sea Lord was not intellectually threatening. Certainly the British Naval Staff had been pressing this idea since at least the previous October, and it had been floated at the Cabinet Anti-U-boat Warfare Committee, a body established in early November 1942 in response to the rising sinking figures as a successor to the Battle of the Atlantic Committee, which had lapsed in October 1941.[7] Had the idea been put up a year or more earlier while the U-boat bunkers were under construction results could have been achieved. Now it was too late. The Biscay submarine pens were impenetrable to any existing bomb, and concrete covers had also been built or were under construction over the building yards at

Kiel, Hamburg and Wilhelmshaven. The Air Staff had pointed this out, arguing that to achieve their object it would be necessary to devastate the adjacent towns and docks and that heavy French casualties around the Biscay bases might have unfavourable political repercussions. The project was shelved. It was raised again in early January by the Naval Staff; this time the Cabinet backed it, and on the night of 14 January, the date of the first two sittings of the Combined Chiefs at Casablanca, the first raid took place on the port area of Lorient – after its citizens had been warned by leaflet drops.

At Casablanca the final report was issued on 21 January. The defeat of the U-boats was to be the first charge on resources, and the U-boat building yards and Biscay bases were to be the primary objects for Allied bombing, with the recommendation that eighty VLR aircraft be found at once to close the 'Greenland air gap'.[8] Two days later Sir Arthur 'Bomber' Harris protested that the offensive against the U-boat building yards and Biscay bases was a waste of effort and could not reduce sinkings in the Atlantic. He was right but not heeded, an unfortunate reversal of the usual situation. Without waiting for analysis of the results at Lorient the bombing programme had already been extended to St Nazaire, supported by US daylight precision-bombing raids, which were also directed at Brest, La Pallice and Rennes. By 17 February intelligence revealed that while much of Lorient and St Nazaire was flattened, the U-boat pens were undamaged and U-boat operations remained unaffected, as did U-boat construction. Undeterred, the Admiralty managed to have the costly and counter-productive offensive continued on a reduced scale for another month.[9]

Meanwhile King, and it seems most others in positions of influence, ignored the recommendation to transfer VLR Liberators to plug the Atlantic air gap. King had over fifty Liberators either operating or about to become operational in the Pacific, none in his bases on the western Atlantic seaboard, and at least a further fifty were due for delivery to the Pacific. The US Army Air Force had two squadrons of a total of twenty-four Liberators working from the west of England over Biscay, but these were about to be transferred to Morocco to cover US supply convoys for North Africa. The British Air Staff, for their part, remained unwilling either to allow British Lancasters to be adapted by Coastal Command for long-range work or to forego Liberators coming from America for Bomber Command. Thus the one useful directive to emerge from Casablanca, so far as the Battle of the Atlantic was concerned, was disregarded.

There were many parties to this outcome, but, as with the earlier shambles off the US east coast, it can hardly be doubted that King bore the major responsibility. Before entering the first meeting of the Combined Chiefs, King had pointed out to his US colleagues that the United States had become the stronger power; it was up to them to show the way in determining the strategy of the war.[10] The United States was much the stronger in productive power; moreover King disposed all the resources necessary to turn the Atlantic battle. And as Cominch he was responsible for US Atlantic escort groups and naval and air bases, and the merchant ships and sailors – a large proportion of whom were American – they protected. Finally, he was responsible to Roosevelt for the naval side of US and Allied strategy in all oceans. Yet wedded to a Pacific plan evolved over decades at the Naval War College, he was not prepared even to discuss a diminution of resources for that theatre. Impervious to argument and as suspicious of his army colleagues as of his wily, imperialist allies, he lacked the understanding or perhaps the generosity of spirit to broaden his perspective.

In retrospect it is apparent that flexibility in the Pacific could have brought major dividends; if, instead of following the official orthodoxy, King had opened his mind laterally to the havoc Dönitz had wrought on Allied shipping, he might, as noted earlier, have organized his own magnificent submarine force for a concentrated assault on Japan's fragile communications. Had this been combined with a scaling down of the conventional Pacific offensive it would have allowed the release of sufficient resources, particularly very long-range Liberator aircraft, to the Atlantic to eliminate the U-boat threat at once; it might also have forced Japan's capitulation in short time with only minor losses long before the atomic bomb became necessary or indeed possible.

Hindsight, of course, allows such crystalline views free from the distractions, emotions and grinding choices of the moment. Yet that is precisely what the Casablanca Conference, held over ten days in a tranquil, neutral setting far from the pressures of daily business, was supposed to offer. Jacob recorded that outside the formal sessions the Americans and British 'met round the bar, went for walks down to the beach together, and sat about in each others' rooms in the evenings'.[11] Mutual understanding and respect ripened and future strategy was resolved more satisfactorily than perhaps in any grand alliance in history; yet the precondition for that strategy was the defeat of the U-boats. King failed to understand either the urgency or the detail of this problem, as he had failed to master the rather similar problem of the U-boats on the US coast the previous year. Admiral Pound, the British Naval Staff, the 'bombers' on the Air Staff and Churchill must take a large share of the responsibility, yet ultimately it was King who now commanded the necessary resources; he failed the test as he, and they, had earlier.[12]

The price was again to be paid by Allied sailors. It would have been higher but for another breakthrough by the cryptanalysts of the naval section at Bletchley Park. At the end of October 1942 a copy of a U-boat weather codebook had been recovered from *U559*, which had been sunk in the shallow waters off Port Said. The U-boats' regular short weather signals were still transmitted in a three-rotor cipher – a serious mistake by the German signals branch – and with the code in their hands the cryptanalysts were soon able to crack the daily settings of the three rotors used, after which it was apparently not difficult to discover the daily starting position for the fourth rotor. At all events, by 13 December Bletchley was reading U-boat signals again, and, by the beginning of January 1943, breaking into the settings so quickly that on some days the traffic was read in time to be of operational value.[13] A superimposed code for the geographical grid references in the messages still caused problems, however, and after every change in this additional 'address book' code, positions could only be deduced in co-operation with the Submarine Tracking Room by close study of DF bearings and contact reports; these deductions were not always correct.

At the time Bletchley began reading the four-rotor cipher, the Admiralty introduced changes in their own ciphers which shut out *B-Dienst* for a while. For a brief period, therefore, at the beginning of 1943, the Admiralty was able to use evasive routing, often on the strength of Ultra intelligence, which U-boat Command was unable to counter.[14]

There seems little doubt that this temporary cryptanalytical advantage to the Allies played a significant role, together with more violent Atlantic storms, in keeping January tonnage losses below even the December figure. This was the view of the Anti-Submarine Warfare Division, but they took little comfort:

> Evasive alterations of route were employed with success, but it should be appreciated that with the growth of the operational U-boat force and the consequently greater areas covered by their patrols – which sometimes appear to approach ubiquity – the use of this method is limited and may soon be outworn ... The potentially annihilating superiority which the enemy, given a favourable strategic situation, might bring to bear on a convoy unlucky enough to be caught early on a homeward journey and far away from effective air cover cannot be appreciated by reference to

any past experience, still less to the fortunate phase we have recently enjoyed.[15]

This referred, of course, to the air gap south of Greenland; they concluded, 'the critical phase of the U-boat war in the Atlantic cannot be long postponed'.

By February 1943 the number of U-boats had risen to 409; of 222 operational boats 178 were assigned to the Atlantic, and no less than 70 of these were on station, some in the central area across US convoy routes to the Mediterranean and traffic around the Cape, but the majority poised in two large groups at either edge of the North Atlantic air gap; eight others were attacking the east-bound convoy HX224 and seven were refuelling from *Milchkühe* U-boats stationed just south of the convoy routes.

Other boats were on their way to join the northern patrol lines; one was the Type VIIC *U230* commanded by KLt. Paul Siegmann. The first watch officer was Lt. Herbert Werner, who had made his first war patrol as a *Fähnrich* fresh from the Naval College in Paulssen's *U557* in the early summer of 1941, and who after the war was to write *Die Eisernen Särge*.

Heading westerly into one of the frequent gales of that winter of 1942–3, *U230* sliced through huge seas, taking advancing combers green over the bridge; ice-cold water slammed against the hunched, oil-skinned figures on watch, swirled and funnelled down the open hatch to sluice about the plates of the control room below. After the deluge, driving snow or sleet and frozen spray lashed the eye-masks the watch wore, threatening to tear them off, and whipped red the small areas of skin exposed beneath their sou'wester hats. Whilst they were secured by steel belts and harnesses from being washed or pitched overboard, below the hands were alternately pressed to the deck or their mattress by the violent motion, and then propelled upwards or sideways as the boat lurched down the next precipitous slope. Time merged into a blur of motion and fatigue. Sheer tiredness was perhaps the feature that impressed itself most on the memory of those who rode the Atlantic in U-boats at this period; thus Peter Hansen:

> If there is one overwhelming thing I remember from those war patrols, it is the fact that I seemed to be frequently so dead tired that I almost fell asleep standing on the bridge, and my back was so stiff and hurt so much that I could often hardly even rest, much less sleep after watchkeeping, which turned into a vicious circle . . .[16]

Godt had directed a group called *Pfeil* ('arrow') across the assumed route of the eastbound convoy following after HX224 in the middle of the air gap south-east of Greenland. In the early morning of 4 February one of this group, *U187* under KLt. Ralph Münnich, sighted ships. It was the slow convoy SC118. The escort was a British group of seven destroyers and corvettes under Cdr. F.B. Proudfoot RN together with another British destroyer, a Free French corvette and a US Coast Guard cutter, altogether ten warships to protect sixty-four merchantmen. The Coast Guard cutter and the rescue ship with the convoy, the *Toward*, were both fitted with Huff Duff, and at 10.46 that morning the latter picked up *U187*'s sighting signal to U-boat Command. Her radio message to Proudfoot – since even at this stage of the war the group was not equipped with radio telephones – was intercepted by the destroyer *Beverley*, whose commander anticipated Proudfoot's order to head out along the line of bearing. He sighted *U187* on the surface shortly before 11.00, kept her on his starboard bow to force her away from the track of the convoy and when she was clear increased to full speed and chased. High seas prevented his guns' crews from opening fire, but when the range had been reduced to 2 miles the boat dived. The *Beverley*'s asdic was temporarily out of action, but she was soon joined by another destroyer, *Vimy*, which obtained a contact on the submerged boat soon after noon. She attacked and after an hour and a half forced *U187* to the surface, where she listed and began sinking by the stern; the crew hurriedly abandoned her.[17]

Godt meanwhile had ordered the remainder of the *Pfeil* group and eight others including *U230* to the convoy. The first five arrived that afternoon and evening, but each of their sighting reports drew an escort or escorts out along the DF bearing and they were forced down and depth-charged; as a result all were left trailing and unable to work up into position to attack that night.

The same countermeasures by the escorts prevented any attacks the following night, although one straggler was sunk during the afternoon. By next morning, the 6th, three more escorts had joined from Iceland, all US vessels, and as the convoy moved into range of Coastal Command aircraft a Liberator appeared, followed by others throughout the day which swept the flanks and forced down any boats attempting to work ahead.

With thirteen escorts and air cover the convoy should now have been safe, but some boats managed to work up ahead after dark and during the early hours of the 7th *U402*, commanded by KLt. Siegfried Freiherr von Forstner, together with one, possibly two other boats, succeeded in penetrating the cordon in high seas and squalls. Siegmann, having driven *U230* at full speed towards the reported positions over the past two days, reached the scene at about this time and was guided to the convoy by the sound of explosions and the light of flames as von Forstner struck. Werner fetched the night-sight binoculars up from below and fixed them atop the UZO post. Shortly, the shape of two escorts emerged from the dark ahead and Siegmann altered to port to avoid their zigzag courses, coming round into the wind and driving through oncoming seas, intermittently lashed by snow squalls when visibility closed around the nearest ridges of water. After more than an hour the sky suddenly cleared and Siegmann saw more escorts looming up in silhouette to port. He altered away, leaving them astern. The low conning tower of the boat was indistinguishable against the tumult of waves, and he soon altered back towards the wind and the convoy, which was lit at that moment by another beacon of fire from a torpedo explosion.

Now inside the escort cordon, he pressed on until the indistinct shadows of the convoy's starboard column had grown into the shapes of ships. Werner, finding it impossible to steady his sights on target against the steep rolling motion of the boat, asked permission to fire two 'fan' shots, screaming to make himself heard above the gale. Siegmann nodded and came round slightly towards the nearest ships. Werner fired two salvos of two torpedoes each, angled apart and spread over several degrees, after which Siegmann brought the boat right round to allow a shot from the stern tube; the violence of the seas smashing into them on the new course made this impossible, but Werner had the fierce satisfaction of seeing a pillar of fire rise from one of the ships he had aimed at, the blast of the explosion rumbling above the sounds of the storm. He saw the ship's derricks outlined against flames aboard; above, distress signals and flares arched, cutting briefly into the darkness before they were swept away 'like sheets of burning fabric' in the wind.[18] From somewhere on the far side of the convoy he heard the explosion of a torpedo from one of the other boats.

After disengaging, Siegmann turned on to an easterly course to run with the wind and sea and ease the motion for the hands in the forward torpedo compartment, who were sliding reload 'eels, by means of endless chain slings, rails and loading carriages into the empty tubes. It was desperately strenuous, watchful work requiring the utmost vigilance in that narrow space where every movement was magnified by the distance from the boat's centre of gravity. Siegmann could not dive to allow them the tranquillity of the depths below the surface swell or he would lose the convoy.

He lost it nonetheless. The gale rose and, as the next dawn broke, all they could see briefly as the boat shook herself free at the summit of each moving ridge was an expanse of similar blown white peaks and green troughs marbled with trails of knitted foam. In such conditions it was impossible to continue searching, and Siegmann dived again, ordering her down to 140 metres (460 feet) to allow the crew a rest.[19]

Somehow they must have outrun the convoy, for that afternoon the sound man reported propeller noises and Siegmann ordered the boat up. Werner followed him through the hatch on to the bridge. Looking round as they secured their safety lines they were astonished to find themselves within 500 yards of a damaged escort, while in every direction there were merchantmen burying their bows, exposing rudders and turning screws, or rising to great seas which swept superstructure, lifeboats and funnels in sheets of spindrift. Werner imagined the horror which *U230*'s sudden appearance must be causing. But neither they nor the escort fighting the storm nearby could take any action. Torpedoes would not run in such towering breakers and guns could not be directed.

Siegmann took *U230* into the quiet depths again. Next day, the 8th, three aircraft patrolled around the convoy at all times, and although Godt exhorted the boats to attack it proved impossible; the following day he called off the operation. Altogether ten merchantmen had been sunk, six of them by von Forstner, who was awarded the Knight's Cross for his remarkable exploit; of the other nineteen U-boats which had been directed to the convoy, most had been subjected to attack by bombs or depth-charges; three, including *U187* which had first sighted the convoy, had been destroyed, and three so seriously damaged they had to return to base. Siegmann had been one of the few who had managed by luck or judgement to avoid a pounding.[20]

Neither side was pleased with the result: U-boat Command was dissatisfied that no boats had attacked during the first, usually most favourable night while the convoy was in the air gap; the Admiralty Anti-Submarine Warfare Division was equally dissatisfied that so many ships had been sunk after the convoy had been fought successfully through the most hazardous section of the air gap with the loss of only one straggler; moreover, at the time the ships had been lost, the convoy had been under the protection of over twice the average number of escorts. Analysis suggested the old lesson that escorts had to be trained as a group to be effective; the US commanders had not fully understood British practice, and without radio telephone, radio frequencies had frequently been overloaded with messages and jammed. The report concluded: 'the sort of things that went wrong ... can always be expected to go wrong when the escorts are made up of a miscellaneous collection of ships who have had no previous experience with each other'.[21]

B-Dienst, meanwhile, having switched the major part of its cryptanalysis effort to the new Admiralty codes, had broken them again and was not only reading convoy routing traffic but also the Admiralty's daily U-boat situation reports; these allowed Godt and the staff at U-boat Command to forecast the areas through which convoys were likely to be diverted. By contrast the naval crypt-analysts at Bletchley Park were running into more difficulties; they had failed to crack the settings on 8 February, and did not break them again until the 17th, after which they were to experience many more blank days, especially from 10 March onwards.[22] Thus, besides the increasing numbers of boats Dönitz and Godt were now deploying, they had a decided signals intelligence advan-tage. By the end of February three more Atlantic convoys had been intercepted, all westbound, and the last had suffered a worse maul-ing than SC118, losing 22 per cent of its original ships.

Among the Allied staff ashore, dissatisfaction with the divided operational control of the Atlantic battle which had evolved since the summer of 1941, together with alarm that the air gap remained despite the Casablanca recommendations, had led King to call representatives of all the national naval and air escort commands to a convoy conference. This convened in Washington for the first of many sessions on 1 March. The British solution would have been to bring the whole struggle against the U-boats under a single supreme authority had they not feared losing control of a battle vital to the survival of the nation if an American were appointed to supreme command. The Canadians, who had by far the greater share of escort groups in the western North Atlantic since US escorts had been drawn southwards for the troop and munitions convoys serving the Mediterranean theatre, were irritated that they came under the command of the American Admiral at Argentia, Newfoundland. King himself disliked mixed-nationality escort groups on principle – with some reason in the current state of mixed training and differing doctrine, as the defence of SC118 had demonstrated – and wanted to withdraw entirely from the North Atlantic to concentrate on those supply convoys to US forces in the Mediterranean which ran between New York or Norfolk, Virginia, and Casablanca or Gibraltar. He was against a unified Atlantic organization, no doubt because it would cut deeply into his own authority and US control; and he probably feared that the British, who had the greatest stake in the outcome of the battle, would claim the supreme command post.

Over the weeks King's concept was adopted: the North Atlantic routes between Great Britain and the North American seaboard from New York northwards were to be divided solely between the British and the Canadians, each responsible on their own side of a new 'Chop' line at 47°W; the US Navy was to control the central Atlantic convoys for the Mediterranean and the tanker convoys between Britain and the Dutch East Indies oil ports, and in addition provide one US escort-carrier group to operate under British control in the North Atlantic.

As a result of defining distinct national spheres King was able to reorganize all the diverse authorities within the US escort structure – the separate Sea Frontiers and air components, the Atlantic Escort Fleet, his own 'Convoy and Routing' under Captain Knowles in Washington – into a unified command, which he termed the Tenth Fleet. He named himself as commander but appointed a Chief of Staff, Rear-Admiral Francis Low, to run day-to-day operations. The Tenth Fleet Control Room, sited near King's office at Main Navy, Washington, was to provide in the US sector all that the British wanted for the Atlantic as a whole, a unified organization able to cut through most of the former inter-command problems, bureaucratic obstructions and authority disputes, and bring optimum resources to bear wherever indicated by the latest (internal) intelligence assessments. It also included sections to sponsor and co-ordinate the development of anti-submarine weapons and administer training programmes. After it became operational towards the end of May 1943, the Tenth Fleet was to prove as formidable as the previous US command structure had been flawed.[23]

The really pressing problem, however, recognized by everyone at the convoy conference, was how to provide the long-range and VLR aircraft to close the mid-Atlantic air gap. Once again inter-service and inter-theatre prejudice seemed set to block solutions. By this date King had seventy-one VLR Liberators on reconnaissance operations in the Pacific, yet none working on the US/Canadian side of the Atlantic, and none had been allotted to the Canadians; British Coastal Command still operated only nine VLR Liberators from Iceland and nine unadapted Liberators from Northern Ireland.[24] It seemed incredible to them that King could have so disregarded the Casablanca recommendation and indeed the primary strategy for the war as to employ his entire Liberator force on non-urgent missions in the Pacific; moreover, he maintained continuous and largely fruitless anti-submarine patrols over the Caribbean and Gulf Frontiers. These were regarded largely as training flights for pilots who might not have been equal to the fogs and storms off Newfoundland and Greenland. Yet that is where the convoys were beset by the U-boats.[25]

King continued to maintain that the only immediate way of closing the Atlantic air gap was by removing heavy bombers from other assignments; his staff concluded in a pre-conference paper: 'it seems that the only possibility is to divert these planes from the bombing of Germany'.[26] Neither the US Army Air Force, whose chiefs considered the navy responsible for all anti-submarine work, nor of course the 'bombers' on the British Air Staff would agree. In the light of current intelligence estimates, amply confirmed by post-war research, King was right. The bombing offensive over Germany and the French U-boat bases was costly, wasteful and virtually useless. Nevertheless, his own concentration on the Pacific at this crisis in the Atlantic was an equally costly, more dangerous and even less comprehensible misuse of air power.

While the conference was in progress during March 1943 the battle at sea reached a climax. Despite a record loss of 19 boats during February – 11 during the convoy battles – Godt was able to maintain a daily average of 116 boats at sea throughout March, almost 50 of them in the operational areas. This was made possible by stationing two *Milchkühe* tanker U-boats in mid-ocean south of the convoy routes, enabling the U-boats to make the equivalent of two war cruises without moving far from the fighting zone. In the Admiralty Submarine Tracking Room it seemed as if the 'potentially annihilating superiority' of the U-boat patrol lines forecast by the Anti-Submarine Warfare Division in January might be realized.[27]

At the beginning of the month, four groups comprising over forty boats were ranged astride the northern convoy routes, two at the western edge of the air gap north-east of Newfoundland, two at the eastern edge south-west of Iceland; another smaller group was positioned west of Gibraltar across the supply routes to the Mediterranean. In the north the two western groups were formed in patrol lines across the routes of two convoys whose instructions had been deciphered by *B-Dienst*, one westbound, one eastbound. The weather was stormy and thick, and both convoys passed through without being detected; but the following day, 6 March, a boat stationed to the rear of the more southerly line sighted the eastbound convoy, SC121, and reported. Immediately Godt directed seventeen boats from both groups towards it, forming them into a new pack named *Westmark*. Fog, driving snowstorms and huge seas had already caused ships and groups to break off and straggle behind the main body of the convoy; these fell easy victims as the U-boats pursued, and on the 8th Godt directed another ten boats to join the hunt.[28]

One was Siegmann's *U230*. He found the convoy that evening, homing in on beacon signals sent by one of the shadowing boats. There followed the same desperate hide-and-seek with escorts that he had experienced in the last battle, through curtains of sleet or snow alternating with clear periods when the moon emerged from torn clouds to reveal shapes of escorts, or at other times dark beads of merchantmen strung out at intervals along a bumping horizon. It was not until the following morning that he managed to break through the cordon into the stern of the convoy. Werner hit one laggard from close range, but Siegmann was unable to catch up with the others before daylight forced him to flee. That evening he broke through again on the surface and Werner torpedoed another ship, but once more they were chased off by escorts and this time lost the convoy.

Werner detected it next morning, 10 March, by the smell of smoke. Siegmann had gone below at dawn to catch some sleep. A few minutes after his nostrils had detected the first traces from the funnels, Werner saw through a sudden break in the weather a group of half a dozen ships pitching in a swathe of sunlight. He had just shouted down to call the captain to the bridge and the crew to battle stations when he heard the detonation of a torpedo from another, unseen U-boat – in fact *U221* under KLt. Hans Trojer, known in the fraternity from his heavy black beard and birthplace in Transylvania as Count Dracula. The ship that had been hit was evidently carrying explosives, for she began to erupt in a series of internal explosions, hurling debris high in every direction. Werner ducked under the shelter of the bridge plating as pieces of steel hurtled into the sea around the boat. When he was able to look up again, he saw two escorts which had appeared from behind the ships, and another astern, all heading for him at speed.

'Clear the bridge! *Ala-a-arm!*'

It was the end of Siegmann's operations against SC121. The escorts attacked with accurate patterns of depth-charges and held *U230* down at 200 metres (over 650 feet) for the rest of the day before they rejoined the convoy. By that time leaks in the packing around the propeller shafts had caused the boat to sink to the astonishing depth of 245 metres (over 800 feet) well below her test depth. Siegmann waited for two hours after the sounds above had faded before he surfaced. In the darkness there was nothing to be seen but foam streaking the seas. They had escaped.[29]

The following morning, as the convoy moved into the cover of aircraft from Iceland, Godt called off the attack. The battle had stretched over 800 miles; an average of fifteen U-boats had been engaged throughout; ten had reported hits; thirteen merchantmen had been sunk. Godt believed it would have been more but for the high winds and poor visibility, scarcely above 2 miles, often far less, and the early break-up of the convoy formation: 'Without a doubt there would have been greater prospects of success had the convoy remained intact as more than one ship could have been torpedoed in one attack ... None of the boats sustained serious damage.'[30]

Meanwhile, on 7 March another eastbound convoy, HX228, had been located by the more southerly of the groups south-west of Iceland, which stalked and attacked on the night of the 10th/11th, sinking four merchantmen. Next morning Cdr. A.A. Tait, RN, senior officer of a mixed British, Polish and Free French escort group, located U444, blew her to the surface and rammed her with his destroyer, Harvester. The collision left the destroyer so damaged she became a sitting target for U432 under KLt. Hermann Eckhardt, who sank her. One of three Free French corvettes, Aconit, had meanwhile finished off U444 with depth-charges; she started a hunt for the new boat and, gaining asdic contact within an hour, blew U432 to the surface with an accurate pattern of depth-charges and completed her destruction by ramming. The twenty-four survivors they rescued from the water said they had been eating, celebrating the success over the destroyer when they were attacked. 'I hope they appreciated their dessert of my ten grenades,' the French captain remarked in his report.[31]

Elsewhere in these first eleven days of March four other convoys were attacked, two bound for Gibraltar, one off Durban and one in the Arctic; from these a total of twenty merchantmen were sunk.

Godt had already formed another group of thirteen boats named, almost certainly by Dönitz, Raubgraf ('robber baron') at the edge of the air gap north-east of Newfoundland to intercept the next eastbound convoys from New York, the slow SC122 and the fast HX229, both of whose routing instructions had been deciphered by B-Dienst. In fact there were three convoys since the fast ships were split into two sections, HX229 and HX229A, travelling separately with their own escort groups. Had the operational research recommendations for large convoys been adopted by this time, as they were to be shortly, the seventy-five ships of the fast

convoy might have had eleven escorts; as it was HX229 was provided with five hastily assembled from different groups and
HX229A with six. It was to prove an unfortunate division of force,
for on 12 March Dönitz decided to gather all boats withdrawn
from the battles against the previous eastbound convoys to reinforce *Raubgraf* against the new convoys. They were formed into
two packs. Typically, he named them *Stürmer* and *Dränger* –
literally 'stormer' and 'driver' or 'thruster', but more probably
derived from the expression, *Sturm und Drang* ('storm and stress').
They were directed to form northerly–southerly patrol lines and
rake westwards.

Soon after noon next day, the 13th, one of the *Raubgraf* boats
north-east of Newfoundland sighted an incoming convoy and
reported. Godt ordered the rest of the group to attack, but in foul
weather they sank only one merchantman before the convoy
escaped. Captain Knowles's 'Convoy and Routing' division in
Washington had received no Enigma decrypts since 10 March, but
this action, during which several U-boats were detected and
attacked by escorts, revealed the position of the group right across
the track of the three outward convoys from New York. Knowles
reacted by diverting the leading two, SC122 and HX229, east to
pass south of the pack, and HX229A to a northerly course – after
rounding Newfoundland – to pass to the west of it. The convoy
instructions were intercepted by *B-Dienst*, and decrypts for SC122
and HX229, but not however HX229A, were on Godt's desk four
hours afterwards. He was still hoping the *Raubgraf* boats would
regain contact with the incoming convoy, and it was not until the
afternoon of the next day, the 14th, that he ordered the group to
break off and proceed south-easterly at full speed to form a line
across the tracks of the two convoys whose eastward diversion
courses he had been given. It was too late by then to form ahead;
in any case another gale had blown up, rendering sighting and
attack conditions impossible. Again for both sides it became a matter of survival against the elements.

The weather eased around midnight. The two convoys continued easterly, SC122 about 150 miles ahead and rather to the north
of HX229, the *Raubgraf* boats bearing down astern and the
Stürmer-Dränger lines approaching on a south-westerly course
across the track ahead. Had Bletchley Park not been blacked out
for the past five days the danger would have been apparent, and
a northerly diversion might have been expected from 'Convoy and
Routing'. As it was, the two separated groups of ships sailed on,
riding steep seas from the quarter, rolling, plunging, altering

course only at the times set for the zigzag they were executing.

First contact was made by *U653* under KLt. Gerhard Feiler. Directed to refuel from one of the *Milchkühe* stationed just south of the convoy routes, Feiler had broken from the *Raubgraf* group on a course that unwittingly took him straight into HX229; called to the bridge at 03.00 on the 16th, he found himself in the midst of ships. He dived at once, allowed the noises of engines and thudding propellers to pass overhead, then surfaced astern, reported and trailed, sending out beacon signals for the other boats every two hours.

At U-boat Command it was assumed he had found the leading convoy that the *Raubgraf* group was pursuing, SC122, and Godt directed all *Raubgraf* boats to it, together with ten of the approaching *Stürmer-Dränger* lines, closing up the rest behind to catch HX229, which he believed to be following. A few hours later, *B-Dienst* supplied a decrypt of the three-day-old signal ordering HX229A on to a northerly diversion. Still not realizing that the fast convoy had been split, Godt assumed this referred to HX229, which must, he thought, have eluded him; so he directed the second line of boats also to the convoy Feiler was shadowing. Thus all thirty-eight boats in the three North Atlantic groups headed for HX229 – which Godt believed was SC122 – and a further thirteen, either fresh from port or refuelling from *Milchkühe*, were directed to join them. It was the largest combination ever to be unleashed against a single convoy.[32]

Had they all arrived at the same time and been able to co-ordinate their attacks, they must of course have overwhelmed the escorts. This did not happen, for only the *Raubgraf* boats were close enough to reach the convoy that day; by dusk seven were in contact and *U615* under KLt. Ralph Kapitzky had taken over as shadower from *U653*, whom Godt directed to break off and refuel. The senior officer of the escort, Lt.-Cdr. G.J. Luther, RN, knew of the boats' presence; their signals had been picked up by his Huff Duff operator and he was expecting attack that night. One of his destroyers was missing: he had sent her out along the bearing of a U-boat signal that morning, and she had not returned. He was reduced to two destroyers and two corvettes. The seas were still high from the storms of the previous days, but the night was clear, lit by a nearly full moon from between low clouds.

The first boat to go in shortly before 20.00 that evening was *U603* under KLt. Hans Bertelsmann, who penetrated between the destroyer and the corvette on the starboard wing without being detected. He had four torpedoes remaining; three were of a new type called *Federapparat* (FAT) especially for use against convoys: they ran their set course for a predetermined distance, then executed a half turn and came back through the columns. Despite the increased chances that this type gave, Bertelsmann hit with only one of his salvo, perhaps because the convoy made a fortuitous alteration as he fired. Afterwards he dived beneath the starboard columns to escape astern as Luther ordered his escorts to execute a 'Raspberry' without starshell; the moon was bright enough to see by.

Throughout the rest of the night another five of the boats worked their way up the flanks of the convoy and came in at intervals singly. The corvette stationed on the port quarter sighted one in the path of the moon, forced her down and attacked but failed to inflict more than minor damage. The other boats all scored, hitting another seven ships. It was far from the annihilating concentration Dönitz and Godt had hoped for, indeed the single boats attacking at intervals would have been detected and chased off had there been sufficient well-equipped escorts. Of course there were not enough and several radar and asdic sets had suffered storm damage; moreover there was no rescue ship and, since Luther had made a decision beforehand that his own ships would make up the deficiency if necessary to prevent a collapse of morale among the merchant crews, the escorts spent much time on rescue work, leaving the convoy on occasions virtually undefended.

One of the last merchantmen to be hit was the 8,700-ton *Nariva*. Her second officer, Gwilym Williams, has left a record of his impressions of that night of explosions, emergency turns and pyrotechnics as ships from different parts of the convoy were hit and dropped astern in flames, painting the clouds with a ruddy glow. From some as they passed he saw men escaping the searing heat on deck by jumping into the sea where they must soon have frozen to death.

The *Nariva*'s turn came shortly before 03.00 on the 17th. Williams was standing on the wing of the bridge watching a ship to port sinking even as they passed her, when he saw the phosphorescent wake of a torpedo speeding towards the side below. He had no time even to call out before it hit and detonated with a shattering roar and vivid green flame that almost blinded him. The deck bucked beneath his feet as the ship was lifted bodily, then settled back, and suddenly he saw the hatch covers of No. 2 hatch on the fore deck below burst open, and smelled 'the stench of cordite filling the hot air as it mixed with the flames which shot up hundreds of feet into the air above us'. He ran across to switch on

the red light on the stay to indicate that the ship had been torpedoed. As he did so, he was doused by the water column thrown
up by the explosion falling to the deck about him.[33]

All hands were sent to their boat stations. Williams had just
reached his with his 'getaway' bag, previously prepared for this
ever-present eventuality, when he was shaken by another explosion from the column of ships to starboard. Dashing to the rail he
saw a fountain of water raised high over a 12,000-ton former whale
factory ship, *Southern Princess*, now carrying oil fuel. Within
moments she was ablaze from stem to stern and once again
Williams saw crewmen leap from the unbearable heat on deck into
the sea, already spreading with fire on oil leaking from the ruptured tanks. Returning from this ghastly sight to the men at his
boat he received the order from the captain to abandon ship. He
had no means of knowing, but the torpedoes which hit his own
ship and the *Southern Princess* both came from the same 'fan' fired
by *U600* under KLt. Bernhard Zurmüllen.

Later, after the convoy had passed, leaving his boat seemingly
alone in the vast Atlantic, he heard voices hailing them from the
dark, then saw the shape of one of the corvettes approaching.
Williams would never forget the 'wonderfully safe, hard feeling
that piece of grey steel afforded' as, having brought his boat
alongside, he was helped up by willing hands on deck.[34]

KLt. Manfred Kinzel of *U338* in the *Stürmer* line, making his
best speed through the seas south-westerly to join the attack, found
himself approaching a broad front of ships over 100 miles east of
where he expected to come upon them. He reported and then, having by chance slipped through undetected between the leading
escorts, attacked, hitting and sinking four merchantmen. At U-boat
Command initial puzzlement that his reported position should be
so far from that of the other attacking boats gave way gradually
to the realization that Kinzel had found another convoy, that it
must be the leading convoy, SC122, and that the other boats must
therefore have been attacking HX229. As Godt did not know the
exact position of all boats he now gave COs permission to act
against whichever convoy they found nearest. The reports of successes during the night, amounting to fourteen ships of 90,000 tons
and a further six damaged, had induced high spirits among the
staff, and he sent a general message in the style of Dönitz, then
in Italy.

'*Bravo! Dranbleiben! Weiter so!*' (Bravo! Keep at it! More of the
same!')

It was not to be. Both convoys had now reached the eastern edge

CRISIS FOR THE U-BOATS

of the air gap, and that morning, the 17th, a Coastal Command Liberator from Northern Ireland arrived over SC122 and forced Kinzel and two other COs who had found the convoy to submerge. At this extreme range the Liberator was not able to patrol for long, and after it left Kinzel surfaced, worked his way ahead again on the flank and carried out a submerged attack to claim his fifth victim. He was immediately detected by the escorts and subjected to sustained counter-attacks, which he survived by lying low at 200 metres (656 feet), a good way below the British depth-charge settings. Meanwhile HX229, without air cover, lost a further two ships to submerged attack.

During the afternoon, other Liberators from Northern Ireland reached both convoys and forced down the gathering boats so that by dusk, when the convoys made sharp course alterations, they lost touch. Contact was regained next day, and more ships were picked off from HX229, but as air cover increased, nearing Ireland, the boats were forced down continuously, several were damaged and one was sunk. On the morning of the 20th Godt called off the action.

Summarizing the four-day battle in the war diary, he noted that 'as in so many actions the surprise attacks on the first night were the most successful', after which, due to increasing activity from land-based aircraft, 'the boats had a very hard fight'. Nonetheless, 'Altogether 32 ships totalling 186,000 tons and one destroyer were sunk, and nine others hit. This is so far the best result obtained in a convoy battle, the more gratifying as almost 50 per cent of the boats took part in it.'[35]

The actual results were twenty-two ships lost from the two convoys, and no escorts sunk, far from the best results achieved in the long list of convoy battles since the autumn of 1940, and in terms of the number of boats deployed a poor sinking rate. However, the shock of the losses on the first night, 16/17 March, at last produced action. Roosevelt asked Admiral King where the US Liberators had been when all the ships had been sunk. The convoy conference in Washington was still in progress, and measures were soon agreed whereby over the following weeks the air gap would be closed by VLR Liberators sent to Iceland and Newfoundland. In addition, Churchill was persuaded by Admiral Horton, who had taken over as Commander-in-Chief Western Approaches in November 1942, to make destroyers and frigates available to form five support groups which could go to the aid of threatened convoys; this was made possible by discontinuing convoys to Russia.

While the four-day battle for SC122 and HX229 may be seen as the turning-point in the Atlantic battle when King and the Allied Chiefs of Staff were finally jolted into closing the air gap, the balance was already tipping against the U-boats, as the previous September Dönitz had predicted it would. One US and two British escort carriers were due to join Western Approaches Command that month; more were completing. Coastal Command aircraft were at last being fitted with centimetric ASVIII radar, whose more potent beams could not be detected by the U-boats' Metox sets; and once again boats crossing Biscay were surprised at night or out of low cloud by aircraft of which they had no warning, and were suffering damage, great delays and loss.

At Western Approaches Horton could feel the necessary material resources and training at last coming together; on 23 March he wrote to a friend, 'although the last week has been one of the blackest on the sea, so far as this job is concerned, I am really hopeful'.[36]

Dönitz was also hopeful. By the end of March, aggregate monthly sinkings had reached 779,533 tons (actually over-reported by over 150,000 tons), almost up to the November 1942 record. While recognizing the increasing difficulties his boats were experiencing from aircraft and 'the new location device', he still believed that with a supreme effort he could raise the monthly figure to a level that the Allies would find unacceptable. He issued guidelines for his staff in the form of twelve 'commandments' in which he again stressed that the tonnage war was of predominant importance.[37] And on 11 April, he told Hitler, who had awarded him the Oak Leaves to the Knight's Cross in recognition of the March triumph, that since many more U-boats were now needed to achieve the success of one boat in 1940, it was essential to increase U-boat building.[38] The new programme agreed was for twenty-seven boats a month, chiefly Type VII, rising to thirty a month through 1944. Here Dönitz was guilty of fatal over-optimism or, in the language of his period, of that National Socialist fanaticism which he demanded from his men; in another sense his response simply showed the disregard for obstacles in the way of his goals which he had exhibited throughout his career. For his tonnage war was essentially a matter of mathematics and the figures kept at U-boat Command and in the U-Boat division of the Naval Staff proved that it was now impossible to win with existing types of boat.

The key figure in these calculations was what was called the U-boat 'potential' – the tonnage sunk per U-boat per day at sea as computed on a monthly basis. In 1940, before effective British countermeasures, this figure had been in the region of 1,000 tons. During the second 'golden time' off the US east coast and Caribbean in the first half of 1942 the highest 'potential' achieved had been 438 tons, in June. Since the U-boats had returned to the North Atlantic it had dropped sharply to an average of around 250 tons, and even in the record month of November 1942 had only reached 329 tons. It had fallen further in January and February 1943 to 99 and 148 tons respectively, and risen to 230 tons in March. Then, as increased escorts and air cover produced their effects in April, it fell back again to 127 tons sunk per U-boat per day at sea, giving an average for the first four months of the year of 160 tons.[39] Even if this rate could be maintained, which was doubtful, it would take 325 U-boats to achieve sinkings of a million tons a month, almost a third again to sink the 1.3 million tons needed just to keep pace with Allied new building. On 1 April there were 207 boats in the Atlantic theatre out of a total number in service of 423.[40] An average of 15 boats were being lost a month; thus even with the enhanced building programme of 27 new boats a month, it would take ten months before the total in the Atlantic could reach 325, when it might be possible to sink just a million tons. But over this period a further 150 boats, and more importantly their increasingly scarce trained crews, would have been lost. And still the Allies would have been building more than he could sink.

The tonnage war was unwinnable. By refusing to acknowledge this mathematical certainty Dönitz not only condemned his young crews to a lethal struggle in boats whose technology had been mastered and rendered obsolescent by the enemy, but again lost precious time during which he might have focused his immense drive and energy on the development of more advanced types of boat which could compete.

In April, sinking figures fell to little over half the March total and the U-boat 'potential' dropped to 127 tons sunk per U-boat per day at sea. The Admiralty Anti-Submarine Warfare Division deduced from decrypts of the U-boats' messages to U-boat Command and the instructions and encouragement issued to the boats, once again being deciphered by Bletchley Park, that the will to attack was faltering. Their monthly report concluded:

Historians of the war are likely to single out the months of April and May 1943 as the critical period during which strength began to ebb away from the German U-boat offensive, not because of the low figure of shipping sunk ... but because for the first time the U-boats failed to press home their attacks on convoys when favourably situated to do so.[41]

Dönitz and Godt ascribed the disappointing results to new and inexperienced COs. Thus after the pursuit of HX234 from 21 to 25 April by nineteen boats at the outset during which only two ships were sunk, Godt explained 'the slight success' as due to the increasingly difficult conditions of convoy warfare, the shorter nights in the north, and the strong air protection the enemy now provided from Greenland and Iceland which allowed only night attack: 'It [the darkness] could not be exploited owing to the very unfavourable weather conditions in conjunction with the inexperience of the new commanders, who were not equal to the situation.'[42]

Early in May, Godt succeeded in bringing a potentially annihilating concentration of forty-one boats on to a westbound convoy, ONS5, north-east of Newfoundland. The escort was a superbly trained and highly experienced group under Cdr. Peter Gretton, RN. By the time the boats closed and attacked on the evening of 4 May, convoy formation had become scattered by a succession of gales, and Gretton himself, unable to refuel in the high seas, had been forced to take his destroyer back to St John's, Newfoundland. Another escort group of five destroyers had come out to reinforce the rest of his group, however, and when two of these were also forced back by fuel shortage, a third group was ordered out to the convoy from St John's. Meanwhile, Canadian aircraft forced two of the approaching boats under and sank one. Eight other boats penetrated after dark and sank six merchantmen, and the following day another four ships were sunk in submerged attacks; in the ensuing counter-attacks one U-boat was destroyed by depth-charges.

That evening, fifteen boats closed and were waiting to go in under cover of darkness when fog drifted up over the now calm sea, giving the radar-fitted escorts a decisive advantage. As the boats probed their way in on the surface they were met by gunfire from vessels they could not see; one was rammed and sunk, others depth-charged as they executed alarm dives; three were destroyed, five so heavily damaged they had to break off, and all the others reported damage. The following morning, Godt called off the action.

During the two days nine ships from the convoy and two stragglers had been sunk, one ship earlier, but six U-boats had been destroyed and five so seriously damaged they could only limp home; another boat had been destroyed by a Coastal Command aircraft ahead of the convoy earlier, and two had been lost in collision. To the Allies it seemed evident that no force could sustain such a rate of casualties, and the encounter was seen as a turning-point. For Dönitz and Godt, however, it was the fog that had robbed the boats of sure successes on the second night and led to the heavy losses. While acknowledging the difficulties now facing his men, Dönitz was determined they should be overcome. The final summing up of the battle against ONS5 in the war diary read:

> The enemy radar location device ... is together with enemy aircraft at present the worst enemy of the U-boat ... The location device is robbing the U-boat of its most important characteristic, its undetectability.
>
> The task of again providing the U-boat with apparatus to detect the enemy radar is being pursued with the utmost urgency by the responsible departments, as well as the task, seen as the chief and distant goal, of masking the U-boat against radar [with a radar-absorbent coating] ...
>
> Air escort, so far as it is conducted with great numbers of aircraft and in a great area around the convoy, has always led to the boats lagging hopelessly astern with no further prospects of success, especially with skilful co-operation between sea and air escorts ...
>
> AA armament is being strengthened as a countermeasure, but a solution can be considered satisfactory only when the boats' armament allows them to remain on the surface to fight it out with the planes, or at any rate when it is essential for the boats to remain on the surface to get ahead to make an attack despite enemy aircraft. AA U-boats are also to be tried out against aircraft in Biscay ... [as] losses and damage in this area have again sharply increased ...
>
> In summary it remains to be stated that the battle of the U-boats is at present harder than ever, but that all departments are working with all energy to ease the boats' struggle and to arm them with better weapons.[43]

Thus refitted, boats from the Biscay ports and new boats fresh from training in the Baltic were directed to join those remaining in the hunting ground south of Greenland in patrol lines extending 550 miles to catch the next two eastbound convoys. Bletchley's decrypts enabled both to be routed around the lines, but B-Dienst put U-boat Command back in the picture, and on 9 May *U359* picked up the fast convoy HX237. Within half an hour of her sighting report, an escort sent out along the Huff Duff bearing had forced her down and she lost contact. The convoy, which made a sharp zig to the north, was detected later that afternoon on *U186*'s hydrophones, and Godt directed the group of seven to form a line ahead of the new easterly course. However, a support group formed around the escort carrier HMS *Biter* had been sent to reinforce the escort and, as the convoy ran into the patrol on 11 May, both shore-based aircraft and those from the small carrier forced the boats under.

Godt directed them to take up new positions across the track to the eastwards. One was Siegmann's *U230*. Herbert Werner was on watch the following morning when, shortly after sunrise, he saw a smudge of smoke from a myriad funnels over the western horizon. As masts appeared over a wide front it became evident *U230* was lying directly in the convoy's track and Siegmann dived to periscope depth and ordered all tubes prepared for firing. Soon afterwards, the ships altered on to the north-easterly leg of a zig-zag. Siegmann was left cursing as he watched the starboard wing escorts steam obliquely past out of range, the thrashing of scores of propellers mixed with the beat of piston engines and the hum of turbines reverberating through the boat as the procession drew away.

Siegmann surfaced when the convoy was hull down below the north-eastern horizon and started eastwards to try and gain position ahead again before dusk, but the radio operator scarcely had time to send a contact report before the starboard lookout cried, 'Aircraft!' Werner saw a small, twin-engined plane approaching out of the sun.

'*Ala-a-arm*!' The lookouts leaped for the open hatch and tumbled down, Werner close behind, as the plane dived towards them. Four bombs exploded nearby as they descended, the shock waves jolting the boat, forcing her bows to a steeper angle. Werner wondered where such a small plane could have come from so far from any land. There seemed only one conclusion: the convoy had its own carrier.[44]

This was confirmed several times that day as Siegmann surfaced and attempted to push on eastwards only to be forced down time and again by the sudden appearance of a small plane. One of their comrades, *U89*, was hit by bombs from one and destroyed. Another was sunk by an escort, and the following morning, the 13th, yet another by combined air and sea escorts. Almost half their small group had been wiped out, and they had managed to sink only three stragglers from the convoy. Godt called the action off, writing in the war diary:

> Carrier aircraft were sighted in this convoy from the first day, and later even the carrier itself. These, together with land-based aircraft, greatly hindered the operation so that the action finally had to be broken off on account of the strength of the air escort . . .

In summary, it must be said that a greater success was not to be expected with this convoy, since today it is almost hopeless for such a small number of boats to fight a convoy which is escorted by a carrier.[45]

Meanwhile, another group of twenty-five boats had been directed to the slow convoy SC129; twelve had made contact during 12 May, but all were located and depth-charged, and by nightfall none were in touch. On the 13th the *Biter*'s support group, having beaten off the attacks on the fast convoy, was sent to reinforce SC129's escort. Again Godt was forced by the strength and apparent ubiquity of air and sea escorts to break off the action. Before that another two U-boats had been lost; only two stragglers had been sunk. Among the boats which had been bombed frequently and depth-charged several times to within an ace of destruction or exhaustion of their air supply was *U230*; she was now incapable of further operations. Siegmann was steering for a rendezvous with a *Milchkuh* to replenish with sufficient fuel to take him to Biscay.

Noting the unprecedented rate of detection of all boats which had reached the convoy, Godt suggested in the war diary that the enemy had perhaps developed 'a novel type of location apparatus of great capability'.[46] This appears to have been the closest U-boat Command ever came to divining the existence of Huff Duff afloat in Allied escorts. But the leap of imagination or analysis which might have suggested a connection between the rapidity of the boats' detection by the enemy and the sighting signals they sent to U-boat Command was never made. It was a significant failure. Of course, had the true nature of the 'novel type of location apparatus' been deduced it would have rendered the pack system in which Dönitz had trained his officers from the beginning as obsolete as the boats themselves now were.

Dönitz was in Italy as Hitler's emissary at the time of these convoy battles, attempting to stiffen the Axis partner in the face of crisis in North Africa. He returned on 14 May and, evidently deducing from the recent results that fighting spirit had declined, sent a message to all COs on the 15th. He admitted that the Allies were far ahead in radar detection, but assured them that all departments both in and outside the navy were working to improve U-boat weapons and equipment; he concluded:

I expect of you that you continue your determined struggle against the enemy, setting against his ruses and technical developments your ingenuity, ability and hard will to finish him off.

In the Mediterranean and Atlantic commanders have proved that even today the enemy has weak spots everywhere and that the enemy devices are in many cases not nearly so effective as they appear at first, if one is determined to achieve something despite all.

I believe I shall soon be able to give you better weapons for this hard struggle of yours.   Dönitz[47]

Two days later, *B-Dienst* supplied an Allied U-boat situation report and routing instructions taking the next eastbound convoys south of the patrol lines located in the report. Godt directed two groups of a total of twenty-one boats southwards across the diversion, and in the early hours of the 18th *U304* under OLt. Heinz Koch sighted the slow convoy SC130. The escort was the formidable group under Peter Gretton which had led the fight against forty-one boats concentrated on ONS5 early in the month. Koch reported and shadowed, and by the following morning had drawn nine other boats to the convoy, which made a sharp leg at dawn, leaving them trailing. As they tried to work up ahead on the surface a Coastal Command Liberator arrived. Sweeping up the flank she detected by radar *U954*, in which Dönitz's younger son, Peter, was serving as second watch officer; diving out of low cloud the aircraft straddled the boat with bombs close on either side. The detonations tore the tanks open and she went down with all hands.

The Liberator flew on, forcing another five boats into hasty dives and calling surface escorts to the scene; these destroyed one boat with depth-charges and severely damaged another. More aircraft and another escort group joined in the afternoon and three more boats were destroyed in sudden, fierce encounters, three so severely damaged they had to break off, and the rest forced under so that when SC130 made the usual alteration of course at dusk, contact was lost. It was picked up the following morning, 20 May, by hydrophones, but air cover was continuous and those boats surfacing to work up ahead were attacked at once from the clouds; one was destroyed. Godt called off the operation, noting in the war diary that air cover prevented the boats approaching the convoy, and again remarking on the potency of the enemy location apparatus and the reports made by several boats of efficient co-operation between the air and surface escorts.[48] *U92* had reported sinking a 6,500-ton freighter and hitting another, but in fact no ships had been hit. Five of the attacking boats had been lost.

In the past ten days ten U-boats had been sunk by air or surface escorts in North Atlantic convoy battles; elsewhere seven boats had been sunk, mainly by air patrols. In the same period that May, the majority of convoys had either been diverted successfully around Godt's patrol lines, or air cover had allowed their escorts to fight them through without casualty. Only two convoys had suffered losses amounting in total to five ships, all stragglers.[49] Even allowing for the few ships reported to U-boat Command as sunk which had not been hit, it should have been evident that the position Dönitz had foreseen the previous September when 'air cover extends to almost all areas of the North Atlantic' had been reached and did indeed 'signify an unendurable reduction of the prospects for U-boats'.[50]

This was not accepted: as Godt repositioned his groups on the 21st to intercept the next eastbound convoy, HX239, reported by *B-Dienst*, Dönitz sent another message to all COs. It may be interpreted as a sign of the strain he was under, aggravated perhaps by suppression of all emotion on the loss of his son – apparent to his staff – but it was by any standards an extraordinary signal, bearing no relation to the conditions reported from all recent convoy battles and detailed in the war diary summaries:

> If there is anyone who thinks that fighting convoys is no longer possible, he is a weakling and no real U-boat commander. The battle of the Atlantic gets harder, but it is the decisive battle of the war. Be aware of your high responsibilities and be clear that you must answer for your actions. Do your best with this convoy. We must destroy it. If the conditions for this appear favourable do not dive for aircraft, but fight them off. Disengage from destroyers if possible on the surface. Be hard, draw ahead and attack. I believe in you.   C-in-C[51]

The boats which closed on HX239 and a westbound convoy in the vicinity were forced down by aircraft from escort carriers with both convoys, reinforced by shore-based planes. How many may have tried to follow instructions to remain on the surface and fight them off is not clear, but two more boats were sunk, one by aircraft from USS *Bogue*, one by aircraft from HMS *Archer*, and on the 23rd Godt called the boats off. He noted: 'The convoy operation again showed clearly that it is at present not possible with available weapons to fight a convoy with a strong air escort . . .'[52]

In the month up to the 22nd thirty-one boats had reported themselves sinking or had failed to report or answer when called; it seemed two more had been lost in the recent operation, and none had been able to get near their targets. Dönitz at last bowed to arithmetic. Analyses of losses suggested that at least 60 per cent, probably more, had been sunk by aircraft, and he instructed Godt to withdraw the boats southwards to an area west of the Azores where they would not be in such danger from shore-based aircraft, and not to attack convoys 'except under specially favourable conditions, that is to say in the new moon period'. Why these should have been favourable when all reports indicated the potency of the enemy's location devices is not clear. The truth is Dönitz was constitutionally unable to admit he was beaten. The withdrawal was to be temporary only, until the boats could be made radar-proof and fitted with multiple AA guns which would allow them to fight off enemy aircraft. Withdrawal was not defeat, but tactical retreat:

> in order not to allow the U-boats to be beaten at a time when their weapons are inferior by incurring unnecessary losses while achieving very slight successes. It is, however, fully clear that the chief battle area of the U-boats lies in the North Atlantic, and that the battle there must be resumed with all hardness and determination as soon as the U-boats have been given the necessary weapons for this purpose . . .
> It is to be expected that after rearmament with quadruples [2cm AA guns], that is to say from the autumn, the battle in the Atlantic can be resumed in full measure.[53]

He sent another message to all COs to this effect, again admitting that the enemy was for the moment technically superior:

> Believe me, I have done and will continue to do everything to catch up with this enemy lead in countermeasures. Shortly the day will come when, with new and sharper weapons, you will be superior to your opponent and will be able to triumph over your worst enemies, the aircraft and the destroyer . . .
> Then we shall be victorious, my belief in our arm and in you tells me so. *Heil dem Führer!* Your C-in-C. Dönitz.[54]

It was not to be. It was the Allies who would grow ever stronger with ever sharper weapons and techniques that would render conventional U-boats, in Herbert Werner's term, mere 'iron coffins'. The day of massed pack attacks was over.

9

Victory in the Pacific

IN THE PACIFIC war, meanwhile, submarines still played a sub-
sidiary role. Japanese new building, principally large I-class boats,
had just kept pace with losses; these amounted by the end of May
1943 to twenty-eight sunk and two over-age boats retired. In the
same period thirty new submarines had been completed, maintaining operational strength at almost sixty boats.[1] Many, however,
were employed on supply and transport runs to garrisons isolated
from normal supply by US air power in the northern Solomons,
Papua and New Guinea, even in the Japanese-held islands in the
Aleutian chain in the far north. The few boats committed to offensive operations were dissipated on pointless diversionary bom-
bardments or directed to reconnaissance or ambush lines for the
war of attrition against capital units before the decisive fleet battle
which remained the Japanese Navy's goal. Since Japan had lost the
initiative and it was seldom known where US forces would strike,
these tactics were even less successful than they had been earlier.

At the same time, the number of US submarines had almost
doubled. Losses had been small, thirteen to the end of May 1943,
and sixty-six new fleet boats had been completed, over fifty of
these commissioned and sent to the Pacific.[2] They not only outnumbered the Japanese boats, particularly that fraction of the
Japanese force on offensive operations, but were also technologically far in advance. In addition to their superior torpedo fire-
control and air-conditioning systems – the latter so important in
the tropic seas of the South Pacific – and non-directional air warning radar which had been fitted from the early months of the war,
most US boats had by now been equipped with a new high-
definition centimetric radar similar to those which had played a
key part in defeating U-boat packs in the Atlantic. The first of
these SJ surface search sets had been tested operationally in the
Haddock in August 1942. Her CO had been able to discover
targets 6 miles distant by night, compute their course and speed,
and then run ahead to attack positions on the bow, an evolution
known in the US service as an 'end around'. Since his enthusiastic
report, SJ sets had been fitted in submarines as fast as industry
could produce them. They not only allowed COs to find targets

by night when they themselves could not be seen, but also enabled the fire-control party to plot target course and speed with an exactitude impossible by visual range and 'angle on the bow' observations. An idea of target size could also be gained from the height of the blip raised by the returning pulse on the radar's 'A-(oscillo)scope' screen. As neither Japanese submarines nor escorts had radar of any kind the SJ sets put US boats in a class of their own for fighting by night or in poor visibility. The new radar was also valuable for navigating among the many reefs and islands.

Against this potentially overwhelming superiority there remained one vital area in which US submarines remained far inferior to Japanese and indeed all others: their torpedoes. Eighteen months into the war, too many exploders still either went off prematurely or failed to detonate at all. This extraordinary state of affairs, known to every submarine CO and naturally observed with glee by the Japanese, owed much to the arrogance of experts at the torpedo department of the Bureau of Ordnance, and more perhaps to the in-fighting indulged by area commanders and department chiefs seeking to extend or protect their spheres of power. This was, of course, endemic in all armed services, but especially prevalent in the US Navy, which was run on more rigid lines of promotion by seniority than any other. The area submarine commanders and staffs were especially culpable. Rear-Admiral R.H. English at Pearl Harbor had devoted more energy to preserving the independence of his own sphere than to investigating the real concerns of his sea-going officers, or indeed co-operating with his opposite numbers in Australia. He had been killed in an air crash in January 1943 and Rear-Admiral Charles Lockwood, who had listened to his COs in the south-west Pacific, run his own torpedo tests and finally forced the torpedo establishment to admit their weapons ran deeper than set,[3] succeeded him as Comsubpac at Pearl Harbor. Lockwood's command at Perth/Fremantle had gone to Captain Ralph Christie, and his at Brisbane to Rear-Admiral James Fife.

Christie, who had overseen the development of the magnetic exploder before the war, defended it against all comers. Lockwood also defended it, believing earlier failures had been the result of torpedoes running deep, a fault which had been corrected. He was also influenced by the favourable opinions of the exploder held by his new star skipper, Lt.-Cdr. Dudley Morton.

Morton had burst into prominence early in 1943 in a brilliant first patrol as CO of *Wahoo*. He had taken her over at Brisbane in December 1942 after one patrol as a prospective commanding officer (PCO) with her first skipper, a perfectionist with a reputation as one of the service's most able approach officers, who had

worked the crew and fire-control party up to a pitch of precision, but who had appeared to Morton and his executive officer,
Lt. Richard O'Kane, to be too cautious in action. One historian
of the Pacific war who was stationed at Pearl Harbor at the time
has suggested that Morton might not have achieved his successes
without the previous 'meticulous and exacting' training the crew
had received from their first CO.[4] On the other hand, Edward L.
'Ned' Beach, who was also there, describes Morton as 'precise
by nature' and 'quick to denounce inefficiency if he thought it
existed'.[5]

There was no doubt about Morton's aggression and burning
desire to take the fight to the enemy, nor of O'Kane's. There can
have been few submarines led by such a vocally combative pair.
One of the junior officers has described Morton as 'constantly
joking, laughing or planning outrageous exploits against the enemy'
and O'Kane as equally garrulous, with 'reckless, aggressive talk',
so much so that it was natural to wonder whether it was just
talk.[6] Morton, whose pronounced Kentucky drawl had led to the
nickname 'Mush' – short for 'Mushmouth' – was described by the
same officer as 'built like a bear, and as playful as a cub'. He had
been an outstanding footballer at college. He talked and joked with
the enlisted men as freely as with the officers, and inspired them
with his own super-confidence. In turn they revered him.

Wahoo had departed Brisbane on 16 January 1943, Morton's
orders to patrol off Palau Island to the east of the Philippines, and
on the way to reconnoitre Wewak on the north coast of New
Guinea, where the Japanese were believed to have established a
supply base. Wewak did not appear on any of the charts provided,
nor in the New Guinea Sailing Directions, but a motor machinist's
mate aboard had a school atlas purchased in Brisbane which
marked the place. Using this as a guide the bay was located on the
small-scale chart and one of the officers who made a hobby of
photography improvised an enlargement of that area on the chart.
So provided, O'Kane, as in all US submarines both 'exec.' and
navigator, successfully brought the *Wahoo* to a position off the
anchorage. Despite the limitations of his chart Morton decided that
'reconnoitre' meant penetrate, and in the early hours of 24 January
he began the approach, submerging 2½ miles offshore.

The commander of the Brisbane submarines, Fife, had suggested
to Morton a reversal of the normal action stations of the two senior
officers whereby, instead of the skipper taking the periscope, the
exec. made all observations, reporting what he saw and leaving
the skipper free to evaluate the data coming in and generated by
the fire-control party, and thus better able to make cool judge-

ments on the developing situation. Morton had the imagination, self-confidence and faith in his exec. to adopt this procedure. So it was that O'Kane was at the periscope as they steered in. It was a long and testing passage; the water was glassy smooth as the morning sun climbed, forcing O'Kane to make only the briefest observations whenever patrol boats were picked up on the sound arrays. All auxiliary machinery, including air-conditioning fans and blowers, was shut down for silent running and the heat and humidity built up inexorably. Despite this, Morton seemed to relish the situation and the danger, as he certainly looked forward to finding the enemy; relaxed and joking, he created a mood that one officer described as resembling a 'fraternity raiding party'.[7]

It was not until after 13.00 that O'Kane sighted the masts of a warship against the dense trees of the shoreline. Morton closed. It proved to be a destroyer with a number of small submarines alongside. As O'Kane reported her at anchor Morton decided on a comparatively long shot from 3,000 yards so that he would still be in deep water when the alarm was raised. But as O'Kane looked through the periscope for the final observation before firing, he saw the destroyer had weighed and was steering towards them. Morton ordered 'Right full rudder! Port full ahead!' to swing the boat to starboard and bring the stern tubes to bear. However the next periscope observation revealed she had altered course and was heading to cross their bows as they swung. O'Kane steadied the vertical lens graticule on her foremast. 'Bearing – mark!'

The quartermaster watching the periscope bearing ring above his head called out the degrees.

O'Kane turned the range knob, aligning the masthead with the water line. 'Range – mark!'

The responses to the quiet calls were fed into the TDC against the curved side of the conning tower, and below in the control room a plot was started. Morton asked for an estimated speed, but the destroyer was still gathering way, and while the sound man counted her propeller revolutions O'Kane hazarded a guess, 15 knots. That was fed into the TDC. Morton had already ordered the forward tubes made ready and the depth set on the torpedoes for the shallow draft of the enemy.

'Stand by forward! Stand by one!' Morton turned to O'Kane for a final observation.

He steadied the scope. 'Bearing – mark!'

The quartermaster responded with the reading.

The officer operating the TDC called 'Set!' indicating that his display matched and that the firing solution was established and transmitting to the torpedoes.

'Fire one!'

'Fire one!' the chief quartermaster repeated and pressed his palm on the brass plunger of the firing key beneath the 'tube ready' light panel on the bulkhead.

They felt a slight shudder as the torpedo was launched, and pressure on their eardrums as the impelling compressed air was sucked back into the boat. The sound man reported the torpedo running hot and straight.

Two more were launched at 10-second intervals, angled to spread the salvo along the destroyer's track. Before the running time of the first had elapsed, though, O'Kane could see that three of the tell-tale lines of bubbles streaking the surface would all pass astern of the target. He had underestimated her speed. Morton ordered 20 knots set on the TDC and a fourth torpedo fired. By this time the destroyer's lookouts had seen the original tracks and she had begun to swing away.

O'Kane was about to lower the periscope, but Morton told him to keep it raised. He had determined to draw the destroyer towards him and fire straight down her track as she closed; whichever way she tried to evade she must swing her broadside across the torpedo's course. Such was the theory, and 'down the throat' shots had been attempted by US skippers before, but usually of necessity; this was probably the first time a skipper had enticed the enemy to charge by deliberately flaunting his periscope. Given the known failure rate of torpedoes, it was the height of recklessness. The destroyer swung from its evasive manoeuvre and headed straight for the submarine. O'Kane reported a zero angle on the bow and took her range at intervals as the image in his eyepiece grew larger. He could see sailors in white running to lookout positions on her fo'c'sle, atop the fore turret, climbing the mast, behind which black funnel smoke swept aft as she worked up to full speed. Those who may have wondered at O'Kane's rash, boastful talk in port had seen a transformation that morning; under this extreme pressure he remained 'calm, terse, and utterly cool ... a prime fighting machine'.[8] Morton waited until the range had come down to 1,200 yards, then fired the fifth tube. O'Kane watched the track run towards the destroyer's oncoming bows and miss narrowly down the side. Only one torpedo remained in the forward tubes. The tension was palpable.

At 800 yards Morton fired again. O'Kane felt a curious sense of relief and detachment as this final torpedo sped on its way, but he made a mental note to lower the 'scope if it missed lest the destroyer break it off as she charged overhead.[9] The yeoman in the conning tower recalled afterwards that he had had 'an almost uncontrollable desire to urinate'.[10] The line of bubbles was sighted by the destroyer's lookouts. She began to turn, heeling and opening her port side as her rudder was put hard over. The white line of the torpedo track advanced to meet it, intersecting at mid-length when a tremendous concussion jarred the boat, seeming to those away from the control party in the conning tower as if the first depth-charge had detonated close by; O'Kane saw a column of water rise from half way along the enemy's side and debris hurtling skywards. The suspense in the conning tower broke in an outburst of cheers and shouts of triumph.

Photographs of the broken wreck taken through the periscope were to provide sufficient proof of Morton's first 'kill', although the victim was salvaged later from the shallow bay. Meanwhile, as patrol boats neared and aircraft appeared overhead, Morton took the *Wahoo* down to 90 feet and headed back the way he had entered, using the sonar to warn him of reefs in the way. That night, outside the harbour, he broke out the medicinal brandy and had a measure passed to each man.

On the second morning after this episode, 26 January, *en route* for Palau, smoke was sighted on the horizon. *Wahoo's* bows were pointed straight for it so that the general direction of movement could be established, the standard practice in all navies. It became apparent the ships were heading easterly and Morton set an approach course at right angles to the direction in which they lay, diving as the masts and superstructures of two unescorted freighters appeared beneath the smoke over the rim of the horizon. O'Kane took the periscope. It proved a simple approach as the ships were steering a steady course without zigzagging, and two torpedoes from the stern tubes at each of them produced three satisfying thuds.

Morton swung the submarine to bring the bow tubes to bear, after which O'Kane raised the periscope again. To his surprise there were now three ships, one of which must have been obscured by the others. The third was a large transport whose decks were crowded with troops. Of the two they had hit, one was sinking, the other damaged but making way towards them. Morton ordered the bow torpedoes made ready to fire at the transport and the outer tube doors opened. O'Kane steadied his lens on the target; the officer at the TDC fed the angle into his machine using the speed and course for the original set-up; there was no time to track her. Morton ordered the first tube fired and then two more at 10-second intervals. The last two hit.

O'Kane now transferred his attention to the freighter damaged in the first attack, still steering slowly towards his periscope. Morton fired the fourth and fifth tubes at her, hitting with the last. Still she came on, intent on ramming, and he took the boat down hastily. Above, they could hear a bewildering clamour of explosions, tearing, cracking, creaking and bubbling sounds as the sea broke down compartments in the stricken hulls. After the tubes had been reloaded Morton came back to periscope depth. O'Kane found only two ships in sight, the troop transport stopped dead in the water and the damaged freighter which had tried to ram making away slowly; the other had sunk, leaving a patch of floating debris. He lined up the stationary transport at mid-length and Morton fired. The track lengthened straight for her, but the torpedo passed underneath without detonating. Morton fired again. This time a violent explosion raised a column of water at the point of aim and hurled fragments high. The ship's back was broken and, as the bow dipped, the figures on deck clad in olive green began leaping over the side while sailors started to launch boats and rafts.

Morton steered after the freighter but it soon became evident that despite her slow progress with two holes from torpedoes in her hull they would not catch her while submerged, and O'Kane picked up the masts of another ship beyond her over the horizon. Morton ordered *Wahoo* up to charge batteries and continue the chase on the surface. In the meantime, and quite possibly his first priority, he ordered the guns' crews to battle stations to deal with the survivors of the transport; they were crowded in lifeboats and rafts or floating in thick clusters in lifejackets. As with Miers and the German troops for Crete, Morton saw them as the enemy bound for New Guinea to fight his countrymen. No doubt, too, he had heard of the cruelties suffered by Allied survivors at Japanese hands. He had an 'overwhelming, biological hatred of the enemy', one of his officers wrote later,[11] and like Miers his blood ran high in action. The Japanese in the boats and in the water were to experience this over the next hour or more as 4-inch and 20mm rounds ripped through timbers and flesh and bone, and the sea stained red, attracting sharks. Morton appeared determined to kill every one of the thousands floating there. Again like Miers, he made no attempt in his subsequent report to hide the massacre.

Afterwards he resumed his chase of the crippled freighter, now joined by the other ship whose masts O'Kane had sighted, which proved to be a tanker. Making an end around on the surface at the limit of visibility to the tanker's mastheads with the periscope fully extended to gain extra height of eye, he circled into position ahead and submerged in their track as the sun was setting. He had only four stern torpedoes and three left in the bow tubes; he fired a salvo from the bow at the tanker, scoring one hit. By then it was too dark to see through the periscope and he surfaced to chase the freighter, surprised to find the damaged tanker keeping her company. After much manoeuvring he succeeded in hitting the tanker again with one of a salvo of two of his stern torpedoes. The spectacular results convinced him she was finished and he turned his attention to the freighter, which had altered away, firing wildly into the night with her deck gun and making wide changes of course that defied prediction. When he closed, her fire became so accurate he was forced to submerge. Finally, he saw a searchlight beam from a ship on the horizon which he assumed to be an escort sent out in answer to her radio signals. Anticipating the freighter would head towards it, he placed himself between the two and succeeded in hitting and sinking her with his last two stern torpedoes.

With all fish expended and orders to transfer *Wahoo* to Pearl Harbor at the end of the patrol he headed there, reporting by radio that in a 'ten-hour running gun and torpedo battle' he had destroyed 'an entire convoy of two freighters, one transport, one tanker'. He entered his new base on 7 February in corresponding style, with a broom lashed to the attack periscope to symbolize a clean sweep of the convoy, and eight small Japanese flags flying from the signal halyards for the eight ships sunk in *Wahoo*'s three patrols; one was a naval ensign with red stripes radiating from the central red ball for the destroyer at Wewak. Above them floated a pennant printed with the boat's slogan: 'Shoot the sunza bitches'. After the war Morton's patrol total of five ships of 32,000 tons was reduced to three of an aggregate 11,300 tons since the destroyer had been salvaged and the tanker had not gone down. The elusive freighter, although she could not be found in the records, was allowed at a reduced 4,000 tons, and the first freighter sunk was only 2,000 tons.[12]

Morton became an instant hero for the submarine arm, which needed such a figure. Lockwood christened *Wahoo* the 'one-boat wolf pack' and, most unusually, released the story of the patrol to the press. Normally, every aspect of US submarine warfare was kept secret to prevent the enemy gaining useful information; the submarine arm was known as 'the Silent Service'. One aspect of the patrol was not reported, or questioned in the staff endorsements on Morton's report: the massacre of the survivors from the transport. Morton was awarded the Navy Cross.

For his second patrol, Lockwood sent Morton into the Yellow Sea. Finding no targets when he entered in mid-March, Morton

pressed on deep into the northern shallows of the Dairen peninsula. There, among a stream of local junks and sampans, he
surprised a number of freighters and sank eight totalling by his
estimate over 36,000 tons, and damaged another. Since several of
his torpedoes detonated prematurely and at least one failed to
explode under the target, he despatched two of his victims by gunfire, exulting afterwards that anyone who hadn't been on a submarine's bridge at 'battle surface' on a clear, crisp morning with a
4-inch and three 20mm guns at rapid fire 'just ain't lived!'[13] After
the war his sinking estimate was revised downwards from Japanese
records to 20,000 tons despite the addition of the ship he reported
damaged, which had actually sunk, thus bringing his bag to nine.

Wahoo returned in April with a record hoist of little rising-sun
flags to an enthusiastic reception at the advanced base for the Pearl
Harbor submarines established on Midway Island. Such welcoming parties on the quay had been started as morale boosters and
were much appreciated by all coming back from the tension and
austerities of a long patrol in enemy waters. Unlike the Biscay
ports' receptions for returning U-boats there were no girls with
flowers and kisses. There were, however, besides the Squadron
staff and colleagues from other boats, crates of fruit laid out and
celery and lettuce, all the fresh greenery they had missed at sea,
ice-cream and cool drinks and accumulated mail from home. Ned
Beach recalled: 'It was not at all uncommon to see a bearded sailor,
pockets stuffed with apples and oranges, reading letter after letter
in quick succession and munching on a celery stalk ...'[14]

While refitting, the boat was passed over to a relief crew and
all hands lived ashore, the officers in the former Pan American Air-
ways Hotel, a single-storey timber building set among trees, the
men in barracks. They could swim in the lagoon, sunbathe on
palm-fringed white sand beaches all day, eat good, fresh food such
as they had not tasted for weeks; drink beer or Bourbon, which
were unknown aboard since submarines, like all US Navy ships,
were dry apart from a few bottles of spirits allotted the COs for
special occasions; and in the balmy evenings they would yarn, play
cards, look through old magazines and listen to records or the
radio. The one thing these young men missed from this Pacific
island idyll was the thing they craved most. But there were no girls
for more than a thousand miles. Admiral Galantin has described
this frustratingly wholesome life as making men eager to return to
sea; 'perhaps the next patrol would terminate in Australia, that
Shangri-la for submariners'.[15]

The priority targets for US submarines remained enemy capital units, despite the almost complete lack of success so far achieved against them, and as *Wahoo* became ready for sea again towards the end of April Lockwood sent her to the southern Kuriles on Ultra intelligence of a coming sortie by the Japanese fleet. When this failed to materialize, he diverted her across the track of a large seaplane tender on another signal deciphered by Frupac, now vastly expanded and housed in a specially constructed building near Nimitz's headquarters. The tender appeared as predicted and Morton ran in to an ideal attack position at 1,300 yards with O'Kane on the periscope and fired a salvo of three torpedoes. One hit but failed to sink her and she escaped. Directed on the basis of further Ultra intelligence to an escorted freighter, he ambushed the two vessels on 7 May and fired a salvo of six divided between them, sinking the freighter, but not her escort, which evaded. Another Ultra signal allowed him to intercept an escorted naval auxiliary the following day, but of the three torpedoes he fired, one detonated half way to the target, probably diverting the second, which missed, and the third hit, raising a small column of water up the auxiliary's side, but failing to explode. His rage was assuaged somewhat by his next interception, again Ultra-directed, when he sank a small tanker and an even smaller freighter. Finally, on 12 May, he expended his remaining torpedoes on two escorted freighters, damaging one but failing to sink her, although he heard the dull thud of a second hit which did not detonate properly; he believed at least one of the other torpedoes had also been a dud or erratic. He surfaced to finish her off with his guns, but she returned fire to such good effect that he was forced to submerge, and she escaped. He set course for Pearl Harbor in a violent mood, feeling certain that faulty torpedoes had cost him three ships. On his return on 21 May, still fired with anger, he marched in to Lockwood's office and denounced the torpedoes in blunt, outspoken language, detailing the premature detonations, erratic runners and duds which had cost him ships; and he continued to fume in hospital, where he received treatment for prostate trouble between patrols.[16]

The previous month the *Tunny* under Lt.-Cdr. John Scott had made a brave, tactically brilliant night attack on a carrier group heading for the major Japanese naval base at Truk at 18 knots. Using radar to manoeuvre on the surface between the columns until forced down by an escort at the last moment, Scott had launched his four stern torpedoes from 800 yards at the leading ship in the column to port, hearing four hits, and moments later his six bow tubes starting from 650 yards at a carrier in the column to starboard, hearing three hits before he went deep. It was one of the outstanding attacks of the war, perfectly combining audacity and judgement in the approach, followed by precision close-range firing, left and right. Scott and his crew had been jubilant, confident they had crippled and probably sunk at least one, possibly two carriers. Lockwood had been equally elated when he received the report. Next day, Frupac deciphered a signal from the port director at Truk reporting the arrival of all three carriers. They had scarcely been damaged. The seven 'hits' had been premature detonations.[17]

In early June, after Morton's furious denunciation of the torpedoes, *Trigger* under Lt.-Cdr. Roy Benson had a similar experience against the fleet carrier *Hiyo*, flagship of Admiral Mineichi Koga, new C-in-C of the Combined Fleet. For Yamamoto had been killed in April when an Ultra decrypt detailing his schedule for a tour of inspection of Bougainville in the northern Solomons had allowed US fighters to intercept and shoot down the aircraft in which he was travelling. *Trigger* was one of a group of submarines Lockwood stationed off Tokyo Bay on Ultra intelligence that Koga would return there from Truk with a powerful battle group. Koga's speed and zigzags took him safely through the ambush, but *Trigger* remained on station outside the bay, and in the late afternoon of 10 June, seven hours before she was due to begin her return passage, the officer on periscope watch sighted smoke in the bay and called the CO to the conning tower. Benson took the periscope and ordered the diving officer, Lt. Edward L. Beach, to plane the boat up 2 feet to raise the periscope and extend his range of vision, when he saw a large carrier coming out at speed with a destroyer on either bow. 'Men, this is the jackpot!' he announced, after the musical chimes of the general alarm.

The carrier approached, making wide alterations of course, the destroyers following a different zigzag pattern either side. The fire-control party established that her base course track passed close to the submarine. Writing after the war, Beach recalled his palms sweating, the flesh around his knees creeping as he listened from the control room to the terse exchanges above in the conning tower between Benson and the officer at the TDC.[18] Inside 3 miles the great carrier was heading to pass 500 yards to starboard as they steered north-easterly; she was due to make another zig before that. The escort on her starboard bow, steering independently, was approaching from port ahead. Raising the periscope Benson found she was heading directly for his lens: 'Near screen, angle on the bow zero. He will pass overhead ... Down periscope!'

The sound man reported bearings of the destroyer's propellers continuously. They remained constant. The fast beat could be heard throughout the boat, increasing in volume until the sounds rushed overhead like an express train, and then away. The Japanese were unaware of their presence below. Benson had the sound man focus on the heavier throb of the carrier's screws. These bearings opened to starboard; she had made her zig to the left, not as they had expected to the right. Periscope observations confirmed it and Benson swung the boat to starboard on to an easterly approach course and had the forward tubes made ready. Beach urged more speed for better control of depth with the planes when the torpedoes were launched.

Benson made his final periscope observations on the carrier, now to port, and fired the first torpedo with some 1,200 yards to run to its track. The other five forward torpedoes were launched in succession at 10-second intervals with an angular spread of 2°. Beach fought to keep the bows from lifting with the rapid release of weight.[19]

Aboard the *Hiyo*, the tracks were seen streaking a smooth sea over 1,000 yards off the bow; the captain ordered hard a-port. They began to swing, running up a flag hoist ordering the escorts to attack the submarine, when the sea erupted at the head of the third extending stripe which was still a long way off. The other tracks sped on, the first and second passing ahead as the carrier turned, but the next, from the fourth torpedo, swept into the bow wave; a tremendous detonation shook the ship, hurling a water column high over the flight deck. The fifth flew into the side half way between the bow and bridge, but those watching saw the head of the torpedo break off without exploding and slide astern in the wash. Seconds later the sixth and last torpedo streaked in directly under the bridge, detonating correctly, wrecking No. 1 boiler room and the bulkhead to No. 2 boiler room, and causing those on the decks above to stagger. Sea rushed in and leaked aft to No. 3 boiler room, extinguishing all fires, and without steam the great ship slowed to a stop.

In *Trigger* they counted four explosions as they went deep, and believed they must have sunk the carrier, the first US submarine to accomplish such a feat. Elation soon gave way to apprehension as the destroyers came overhead and began an accurate counter-attack. Knocked off their feet, men clutched at anything solid to support themselves as the boat rocked in a storm of close explosions. Beach describes heavy steel bulkheads squeezed in by the giant blows before springing out again, deck plates and gratings jumping from their seatings, pipelines vibrating to set up discordant humming noises in the closed compartments: 'The whole hull rings and shudders, whips and shakes itself, bounces sideways, up and down.'[20] With the air-conditioning closed down for silent running the temperature rose above 120°F. Men glistened with sweat in the emergency lighting; bulkheads and decks shone with condensation; sea water dribbled in through valve seatings and propeller shaft stuffings. The pumps could not be started without giving away their position to the hunters above; water had to be transferred to the bilges quietly by passing buckets. Carrying such excess weight and squeezed by the pressure into a smaller volume, the boat, creaking and groaning, sank far below the test depth. Bow and stern hydroplane motors had been shut down and the planesmen struggled to control the planes manually, fighting for each breath in the stale atmosphere, for they had been submerged since dawn. Such was the effort involved, they were relieved every five minutes.

Benson eventually eluded the destroyers and was able to increase speed sufficiently to arrest the submarine's descent, later surfacing under cover of darkness and blowing sweet night air through all compartments. *Trigger* had received such damage, however, that after returning to Pearl Harbor she was out of action for two months refitting. Before her return on 22 June Lockwood had learned from Frupac that the carrier had not sunk but had been towed back into dock in Yokosuka, and that only one torpedo had done serious damage.

The experiences of Scott, Morton, and now Benson convinced Lockwood that magnetic exploders, whatever their advantages when they performed correctly, cost too many lost targets, and on 24 June Nimitz issued an order that they were to be deactivated; in future torpedoes were to be primed for detonation on contact only. Christie at Fremantle in the south-west Pacific command did not follow suit. It will be recalled that he had overseen the original development of the magnetic exploder. He entered in his diary that Lockwood, while 'agin' the torpedoes, bragged about the tonnage his boats sank.[21] Japanese *Maru* (merchant) shipping was indeed being sunk, although not so much of it as the force commanders believed: post-war analysis was to halve the tonnage they had credited to their COs. It may be that the overestimates of sinkings, combined with the absence of a clear goal such as Dönitz had always set himself and the divided operational command, contributed to the unbelievable apathy shown towards the complaints of COs in the front line by all in authority from squadron staff up. Despite the increased numbers of boats and the priceless advantage of SJ surface search radar, the true sinking rate of Pearl Harbor and Australian-based submarines combined still averaged under 100,000 tons a month; it had only recently climbed above the 65,000 tons a month that Japanese shipbuilders were producing, and Japanese tanker tonnage had actually increased since the start of the war. On the same day that Nimitz issued the order to deactivate magnetic exploders, Lockwood brought out an 'Operation Plan' giving higher target priority to tankers than freighters; analysis had shown that loss of oil would have a greater effect on the Japanese war economy than the loss of other materials.[22] At Fremantle Christie had received orders to give priority to the tanker traffic carrying oil from Borneo and Sumatra to the Japanese advanced base at Truk in the Caroline Islands.

The success rate of Lockwood's submarines was not improved by the abandonment of magnetic detonation. Instead, the number of torpedo failures seemed if anything to rise. The most telling example was provided by Lt.-Cdr. Lawrence 'Dan' Daspit of the *Tinosa* on patrol off Truk. Directed by Ultra to the track of a 19,000-ton tanker converted from a whale-factory ship, he found her on 24 July and, submerging ahead of her, fired a salvo of four torpedoes. He saw two hit and raise water splashes up her side at mid-length, but no sign of an explosion or damage. As she turned away to escape he fired another two torpedoes. Both hit, one detonating violently right aft and causing her to settle by the stern and slow to a halt. With this helpless, motionless target Daspit closed to a prime position under 900 yards off her port beam and fired the first of his stern torpedoes, watching the track run straight to the point of aim at mid-length. It raised one of the harmless fountains he had observed from the first salvo; again there was no discernible damage. He fired a second stern torpedo with the same result. He dared not surface for a gun action since the tanker was armed with deck and machine guns and had been blazing away at the torpedo tracks and his periscope, and a submarine was more vulnerable to a well-placed shot than a surface vessel. Instead, he carried out what amounted to a trial of his remaining torpedoes in near perfect test conditions. He had each carefully examined before reloading, fired aimed single shots and watched the tracks through the periscope. All hit; all raised splashes without exploding; one careered off after hitting under the angle of the stern and porpoised up out of the water before disappearing. He kept the last torpedo for inspection at the Navy Yard, and set course for Pearl Harbor. In all he had counted eleven certain duds.

Lockwood found his report incredible, but finally had to accept that the contact exploder was faulty. He had the firing mechanism of *Tinosa*'s last torpedo taken apart for examination, and when no fault could be discovered ordered test firings with live torpedoes at the vertical cliffs of a nearby island. The first detonated perfectly, but the second failed. It was salvaged at some hazard. On examination it was found that the metal guides for the firing pin had been so contorted by the impact against the rock that instead of directing the pin to the fulminate detonator, they had retarded its action. Lockwood then set up tests ashore, dropping torpedoes with dummy warheads fitted with real contact exploders from a 90-foot crane on to a steel plate. The results confirmed that on impact at right angles the firing pin guides bent out of shape before the pin reached the fulminate cap. If the steel plate was angled at 45°, however, the guides were less affected and the pin fired the detonator in about 50 per cent of cases. He ordered his torpedo staff to redesign and manufacture a firing mechanism robust enough to survive impact, and in the meantime instructed boats at sea to set up their attacks for acutely angled shots, the reverse of all their training.

He reported his findings to the Bureau of Ordnance, who made tests of their own and came to similar conclusions. While striving to design an effective firing mechanism, the Bureau advised setting torpedoes to run at a slower speed to lessen the force of impact, and using slower, 30-knot electric torpedoes, designated Mark XVIII, which were now being supplied in small quantities. Development work on a torpedo powered by electricity, which thus left no trail of exhaust bubbles to warn the target of its approach or indicate the position of the firing submarine, had been carried on intermittently for years. The capture of *U570* equipped with electric torpedoes in late summer 1941 and the salvage of other unexploded torpedoes from the U-boat onslaught on the US east coast in early 1942 had provided working models, and Admiral King had supplied the impetus for results. There were still many problems with the new type though. COs generally distrusted them.

Such was the position on 16 September when Lt.-Cdr. Ignatius 'Pete' Galantin brought his new command, *Halibut*, in to the submarine base at Pearl Harbor after a patrol off the main Japanese islands of Honshu and Hokkaido. The base band greeted the boat with 'Happy days are here again', and directly she had tied up and the gangplank was secure Lockwood walked aboard. He welcomed Galantin back, spoke to the officers and men drawn up on deck in his usual breezy style, and then went below to the wardroom, where Galantin, like so many previous COs, described the appalling performance of his torpedoes. Three had hit without exploding; four he had tracked to the target, which they had passed under, but he had been unable to observe the tracks of the others because of sea conditions. Only one had hit with a normal explosion.

'I think we finally know what's wrong, Pete,' Lockwood said. 'By the time you go out again, we should have the fix.'[23]

As at Midway, a relief crew took over the *Halibut* for refitting while Galantin and his men recovered from the patrol in the luxury of the Royal Hawaiian Hotel, Waikiki Beach, taken over by the navy as a rest centre for returning submariners. The officers had one floor, the men another. Galantin, as skipper, had a large corner suite whose windows looked out over palms to the beach and the lines of incoming rollers towards Diamond Head. The simple act of standing under the shower and letting cold water play over his face, and run into his open mouth and down his body was the purest pleasure. As at Midway there were no duties; for two weeks the crew could catch up on sleep, eat fresh food, swim, exercise muscles long constrained aboard, sunbathe and refresh their spirits in the Hawaiian evenings. Clothes and hair lost 'that submarine stench, that not so subtle essence of diesel oil, battery gas, body odours and sweat'.[24]

Six days before Galantin had brought *Halibut* in to Pearl Harbor Morton had departed in *Wahoo* for the Sea of Japan. It was to be his second incursion. Lockwood had despatched three submarines to pioneer this hitherto untapped area at the end of June. They had cruised in on the surface through La Pérouse Strait north of Hokkaido on the night of 4 July, but despite finding much traffic steering steady courses with bright navigation lights, results had been meagre, a mere four *Marus* sunk of an aggregate 21,000 tons – in fact, according to post-war research, three totalling just 5,500 tons.[25] Morton had entered with a second group sent in August. 'Dick' O'Kane had been posted to a new boat fitting out, and the new exec. had lacked experience. Nevertheless Morton had nursed the extravagant aim of firing a single torpedo at each target he sighted and so sinking at least fifteen ships. When, after three days inside the Sea of Japan, eight single torpedoes and a double salvo had all missed, except for one which had proved a dud, he had signalled Lockwood roundly damning the torpedoes and asking permission to return to Pearl Harbor to reload. Lockwood had agreed. Now he was on his way back with a fresh supply of torpedoes, all thoroughly inspected, about half of them the new electric Mark XVIII. He was acccompanied by the *Sawfish*, also carrying a mixed armament of conventional and electric torpedoes. Morton entered first in the way that had become accepted, through La Pérouse Strait on the surface by night. Before sailing and while undergoing his usual hospital treatment for prostate trouble, he had asked for intelligence on the large train ferries between Japan and Korea that plied the Tsushima–Kaikyo Channel at the southern entrance to the sea. And when, on 5 October, the Japanese announced that one of these ferries had been sunk with great loss of life, it was evident at Lockwood's headquarters that Morton had struck.[26] Nothing was heard of *Wahoo* or Morton again.

After the war, research from Japanese sources revealed another three ships that he must have sunk – since the *Sawfish* had experienced a maddening series of erratic torpedoes and duds which robbed her of any success. The records also revealed much Japanese anti-submarine activity around the Straits of Tsushima and, on 11 October, the date Morton had been due to leave the Sea, a depth-charge attack by an aircraft patrolling La Pérouse Strait; this is accounted the most likely cause of *Wahoo*'s end. Morton's loss caused as much shock in the US submarine arm as had that of Prien in the German or Wanklyn in the British service. Like them he had been an inspiration. He was credited with sinking seventeen ships totalling 100,000 tons during his comparatively brief, meteoric command of *Wahoo*, and was posthumously awarded a fourth Navy Cross. After the war his score was amended to nineteen ships of a total 55,000 tons, still sufficient to maintain him in third place among the US top scorers in terms of numbers of ships sunk.[27]

On 9 October, far to the south in the Makassar Strait between Borneo and Celebes, a new submarine, *Puffer*, under Lt.-Cdr. Marvin Jensen set a record for submerged endurance that would not be broken by any US submarine during the Second World War. Jensen had scored two hits on a tanker, failing to sink her, and was running in for a second attack when he was forced down by an accompanying escort. He went deep, expecting her to leave after a while, as Japanese escorts usually did; instead she remained above holding him with sonar, and that evening she was joined by another anti-submarine vessel. Rigged for silent running with auxiliary machinery including air-conditioning shut down, the temperature inside *Puffer* rose to 125°F. The crew spread CO_2 absorbent and released oxygen from oxygen bottles into the compartment at intervals, but nothing could be done about the heat. Ned Beach has described a similar ordeal at depth in *Trigger*: 'You simply sweat and eat salt tablets. Your clothes and shoes are soaked. The decks and bulkheads are slippery and literally alive with water. The humidity is exactly 100 per cent.'[28]

That night Jensen and his exec. lost control of *Puffer*'s crew. Drained by the insupportable heat and depleted atmosphere, several of those off duty lying on their bunks to conserve air vented their anguish in outbursts against fate and the submarine service, relapsing afterwards into a sullen torpor from which they refused to rise for their watches. Essential stations had to be manned by volunteers. The following afternoon, with the escorts still hovering above, Jensen took an informal poll of whether or not to surface and fight it out with the gun; many were past caring, but a majority preferred to remain deep. That evening the options were plainer: to surface or to succumb to the increasingly toxic air in the boat. Jensen gave the order to surface and, although the escort showed on radar, he was able to outrun her and escape in the dark. *Puffer* had been submerged for fifteen minutes short of thirty-eight hours. Her record was to be surpassed, so far as is known, only by *U358* by a margin of a few minutes the following year, and by the Japanese *I174*, *I44* and no doubt others which did not survive to record the experience.[29]

Meanwhile, at Pearl Harbor the *Halibut* had been refitted and prepared for sea. First in early October she was to run tests on torpedoes fitted with contact exploders modified at the Navy Yard workshops. Galantin sailed to the small Hawaiian island of Kahoolawe, whose vertical cliffs had been used for the first trials, and positioning himself 1,000 yards offshore, fired six of the torpedoes with a zero gyro angle to strike the rock at 90°. All detonated perfectly. The next failed, but the success percentage was taken as evidence of the reliability of the modified firing mechanism.[30] So it was to prove. At last the Pearl Harbor Command, at least, had a weapon cured of the three major faults of deep running and inconsistent magnetic and contact detonation which had plagued COs for almost two years. A period of increasing success was about to begin.

In Europe, the weakest of the Axis partners had capitulated. Mussolini had fallen and a new Italian government had signed an armistice, announced on 8 September 1943 shortly before major Allied landings on the Italian mainland in Salerno Bay. Hitler had been anticipating 'betrayal', and German forces acted swiftly to disarm their former ally and take possession of the country. The measures for taking over the navy were not so successful; the greater part of the Italian fleet escaped to the Allies, including thirty-four of their surviving forty-four submarines.

The war record of the Italian boats had been disappointing. As has been seen, the larger submarines sent to work with U-boats in the Atlantic had been found wanting in convoy operations. A few had prospered briefly against independent shipping off the Caribbean and South America in early 1942, and since that period two COs in particular had distinguished themselves, Lt.-Cdr. Carlo di Cossato of the *Tazzoli*, who had sunk fifteen merchantmen, and Lt.-Cdr. Gianfranco Gazzana Priaroggia, who had sunk eleven aggregating over 90,000 tons, ten while in command of the *Da Vinci*, the top-scoring Italian submarine of the war, indeed of all time: seventeen merchantmen of a total 120,200 tons were recorded to her account. Both aces had subsequently been lost with their boats; both had been honoured by Hitler with the Knight's Cross.

A third Italian, Lt.-Cdr. Enzo Grossi of the *Barbarigo*, had been awarded the Knight's Cross after claiming two US battleships. He was credited with sinking both and accorded hero status, but post-war research revealed that the first 'battleship' on 20 May 1942 was a light cruiser and neither her crew nor others in her group were aware that they had been attacked. The second 'battleship' on 6 October 1942 was HM corvette *Petunia*. A single torpedo had underrun her keel, but she suffered no damage.[31]

Over the whole period of the war the thirty-two Italian submarines sent into the Atlantic had accounted for only 109 ships of an aggregate under 600,000 tons, less than a comparable force of U-boats had sunk in the two months of May and June 1941 alone. Sixteen of the Italian boats had been lost.[32] After the war Dönitz's first staff officer, FK Günther Hessler, told his British interrogator that the Italian boats were 'very bad, and he himself would not take one to sea'.[33] Finally, in the spring of 1943, seven of those remaining at Betacom had been converted to carry cargo from the Far East through the Allied blockade. None had completed a round voyage before the armistice.

The record of the larger number of Italian submarines retained in the Mediterranean had been worse, a mere fifteen merchantmen and ten small warships sunk. The reasons for their failure were similar to those applying to the Japanese submarine force; they had been used chiefly as adjuncts to the fleet in reconnaissance or in attempted ambushes of British forces. Without signals intelligence and lacking radar, they had seldom found themselves in a position to attack. And later many had been used for supply runs to garrisons in North Africa.

There had, in any case, been few merchantmen to prey on until the 'Torch' landings; afterwards, Allied supply shipping had been so heavily escorted they had been unable to close. Their high point, and the only brief time they exerted a significant influence on the Mediterranean campaign, had come earlier in the group action against the 'Pedestal' supply convoy to Malta in August 1942, when they had sunk one cruiser and damaged two others, as well as the tanker *Ohio* and other merchantmen. Apart from this – and participation in the human torpedo attack which had grounded the two remaining battleships of the British Mediterranean fleet – their record compared very unfavourably with that of the sixty-two U-boats which entered the Mediterranean and accounted for a battleship, two aircraft-carriers, three cruisers, twelve destroyers, a submarine tender and nearly half a million tons of merchant shipping.[34] Moreover, Italian losses had been heavy in comparison to results, eighty-four boats in all.

British Mediterranean submarines had lost their major role with the end of the North African campaign. In total the three flotillas had sunk nearly a million tons of Axis shipping; the 10th Flotilla alone had sunk over half a million tons.[35] If not decisive, it had been a vital and splendid defiance, and the threat posed had caused Hitler to order the diversion of U-boats from the Atlantic to the Mediterranean, significantly affecting Dönitz's 'tonnage' campaign. Those inclined to accept Dönitz's claim that with 300 U-boats he could have cut British Atlantic communications and so decided the war in the west, must also accept that if the British Admiralty had built sufficient submarines and concentrated them across the Axis supply lines to North Africa they could very quickly have snuffed out the desert campaign. Less than a dozen of the small U-class boats provided with Ultra intelligence, and aided by the 1st and 8th Flotillas, had shown what might have been accomplished with an adequate and concentrated force. But neither Dönitz nor the British Mediterranean flotillas received enough boats until too late.

After the invasion of mainland Italy operations moved northwards, and in early December 1943 the 10th Flotilla moved from its now historic home at the Old Lazaretto, Manoel Island, to the island of Maddalena off the north-eastern corner of Sardinia, to shorten the distance to the new chief patrol area off the southern French ports. It was a cheerless base; barren, scrub-covered rocks earned it the sobriquet of 'the Mediterranean Scapa Flow'. Officers lived four or five to a small room in what had been the Italian detention barracks, most of the other buildings by the dockside having been flattened by Allied bombs. The men slung hammocks in stone stables as damp as the boats they had left. Fresh food was lacking; beer was rationed to a bottle a week in the canteen, the only alternative a sickly local vino. Officers enjoyed whisky or gin, and when entertained by the US officers of a patrol boat squadron based nearby, a lethal fruit juice cocktail based on 90 per cent proof alcohol bled from torpedo fuel. It was a far cry from the Pacific or Australian paradises enjoyed by US submariners between patrols or the U-boatmen's rest camps on the Biscay coast, indeed 'life ashore was so dull and uncomfortable', Captain John Coote, then a lieutenant in *Untiring*, recorded long afterwards, 'that the ship's company ... all cried out to be sent off to sea again'.[36]

There were fewer substantial targets than there had been when the 10th Flotilla had fought virtually alone from the bombed-out ruins of Malta, and conditions at sea were as hazardous; indeed the asdic-fitted German escorts they now met were a good deal more dangerous than Italian escorts then. Yet they found victims, mostly small, on the coastal supply routes. The top-scoring CO in this final period before the flotilla was disbanded in September 1944 was Lt. George Hunt of the *Ultor*, like his famous predecessor, David Wanklyn, a reserved, retiring man. He established an unrivalled reputation for accuracy, achieving 32 hits from 68 torpedoes fired – 47 per cent – and destroyed a higher number of vessels than any other British submarine CO during the war: 20 ships and 8 small craft. Of his aggregate 43,000 tons sunk – considerably smaller than Wanklyn's – a high proportion were supply tankers. His much-respected predecessor among the flotilla's high scorers, John Stevens of *Unruffled*, had returned home just before the move to Maddalena showing 21 bars or stars to the Jolly Roger, representing over 35,000 tons.

Meanwhile, in September 1943, as the Allies began the fight up Italy against German forces, Dönitz had been sending U-boats armed with new, but largely untested weapons to renew the struggle against convoys, as he had promised when he withdrew from the North Atlantic at the end of May. The British Admiralty had been as concerned with three German heavy ships – *Tirpitz*, *Scharnhorst* and *Lützow* – all based in Altenfiord, just below the North Cape of Norway. The main strength of the British Home Fleet had been sent to the Mediterranean for the Italian campaign and the remaining force, augmented by a single US light carrier, was insufficient either to cover supply convoys to Russia, which had been discontinued, or to be sure of preventing a break-out by the German ships to wreak havoc on the Atlantic convoy routes. The *Tirpitz* alone outmatched any single British battleship in speed and armament. 'Chariots', the Admiralty version of Italian human torpedoes, had failed to reach her in Trondheim the previous October, and Altenfiord was out of range for effective air attack. Now preparations had matured for an attempt with midget submarines.

Plans for small submarines capable of penetrating net defences to attack capital ships in harbour had been proposed since before the first war; Max Horton had been a particular advocate. In 1940, as Vice-Admiral, Submarines, Horton had learned of a prototype midget being developed privately by a retired submariner, Cdr. Cromwell Varley, on the Hamble River in Hampshire. He had rushed down to see the work in progress, convinced Varley that time was of the essence and arranged for him to have official assistance. Nevertheless, it was March 1942 before the craft was launched. She was a complete submarine in miniature although without conning tower or torpedoes; she was to be armed instead with crescent-shaped 'side-cargoes' either side containing time-fused high explosive charges for dropping to the sea bed under the target ship. By this time, the successful Italian human torpedo attack on the *Queen Elizabeth* and *Valiant*, and the presence of fast German capital units in Norwegian harbours had added urgency to the project, and after trials the design had been modified by the Director of Naval Construction, and a series of six boats laid down in the strictest secrecy. They were termed 'X-craft'. Varley's prototype had been designated X3 since X1 and X2 had previously been used for different types. Another prototype was designated X4 and the production series were given the numbers 5 to 10.

They were smaller than the Japanese Type A midgets, some 51 feet against 78 feet in length overall, but unlike them had a diesel for surface cruising and recharging batteries as well as the electric motor for submerged running; in consequence they lacked the astonishing speed of the Japanese craft; they could make just over 6 knots on the surface, about 5 submerged. They were of course designed for a completely different task, the stealthy penetration of enemy harbours rather than fleet action on the high seas.

Inside, they were extraordinarily cramped. The pressure hull was a mere 5 feet 6 inches in diameter at mid-length, tapering at either end, and since a deck was raised 6 inches from the bottom it was impossible to stand upright anywhere. A forward compartment housed fuel tanks and batteries, an after compartment the engine and motor. A four-man crew had their stations in the mid-length control room, the CO at a central periscope position within reach of each of the others: these were the first lieutenant seated aft of him at the hydroplane, pump and motor controls, an engineer rating seated forward of him at the steering, and a diver, who had access through a small opening closed by a watertight door into a so-called 'wet and dry' (W & D) room between the control room and the forward compartment. When this small room was flooded he could open a hatch above and emerge from the craft to cut nets or move obstructions.

X-craft were never regarded as suicide weapons. It was obvious, however, that the crews would face unusual dangers, and so they had been carefully selected from the submarine branch or hand-picked from young officers who answered a call for volunteers for 'special service'. Training had begun with X3 and X4 in the remote, fiord-like Loch Striven opening into the Firth of Clyde, continuing both there and in Loch Cairnbawn on the north-west corner of Scotland as the series craft X5 to X10 were completed in the spring of 1943. It had been too late by then for the operation, codenamed 'Source', to go ahead immediately because of the shortening periods of darkness in the high latitudes of Altenfiord. So training continued throughout the summer, the crews exercising repeatedly against all obstacles they were expected to meet. By September, when the six operational craft were joined in Loch Cairnbawn by six S- and T-class submarines that were to tow them to Norway, they had reached a peak of efficiency and confidence in their weapon. The Rear-Admiral, Submarines, who inspected them prior to departure, wrote of them: 'like boys on the last day of term, their spirits ran so high'. He ascribed this not to 'youthful daredevilry', but to the conviction that they and their boats were capable of surmounting all difficulties and hazards. He went on: 'It was in this spirit that they went out into the night in their tiny craft to face a thousand miles of rough seas before they reached their objective, which itself, to their knowledge, was protected by every conceivable device which could ensure their destruction . . .'[37]

The submarines, each with an X-craft in tow, departed from Loch Cairnbawn between 11 and 12 September. They had almost 1,500 miles and eight days to go before D-day and the midgets were manned by passage crews of three; the full crews who would take over for the operation sailed in the relative comfort of the parent submarines. The small craft, trimmed down by the bows in order to follow some 40 feet below the depth maintained by the towing submarines, required constant attention on the planes and pumps, besides general maintenance; and while the parent submarines proceeded on the surface at night, the midgets remained submerged, only coming up every six hours or so for brief periods to renew the air. It was numbingly cold and demanding work. Two craft parted their tows – *X8* surfaced and was recovered later, but became unmanageable and was finally scuttled; *X9* simply disappeared and was not seen again.

Meanwhile, Spitfires fitted for photography had been flown to an airfield near Murmansk in north Russia and, on 14 September, their reconnaissance confirmed that the *Tirpitz* and *Scharnhorst* were in Kaafiord at the head of Altenfiord, the *Lützow* in Langefiord in the same complex, all at their normal protected berths enclosed by antisubmarine and anti-torpedo net defences. Details of the photographic reconnaissance were signalled to the parent submarines together with final orders: *X5*, *X6* and *X7* were to attack the *Tirpitz*, *X9* and *X10* the *Scharnhorst*, and *X8* the *Lützow*; it was only later that the loss of *X8* and *X9* became known at the Admiralty.

The weather worsened as the boats entered the Arctic Circle, but eased sufficiently as they reached the slipping points for the operational crews to change places with the thoroughly exhausted passage crews. On the evening of the 20th the four surviving midgets steered towards minefields guarding the approaches to Altenfiord, *X5* under Lt. H. Henty-Creer, *X6* under Lt. D. Cameron, *X7* under Lt. B.C.G. Place and *X10* under an Australian Reserve officer, Lt. K.R. Hudspeth. All passed safely through the mines; the three former craft continued in to the sound leading to Altenfiord, but *X10* had developed a number of faults and Hudspeth took her to a small inlet in the island of Stjernoy across the mouth of the fiord to hide away and make repairs. During the day of the 21st, while the crew attempted to correct numerous electrical and mechanical defects, the other three craft succeeded in making their way separately past the island and into Altenfiord. Despite water leaking into *X6*'s periscope, misting the lens with condensation, and difficulties in trimming the tiny boats in layers of fresher water, they evaded detection from passing traffic and that evening hid among the Brattholm islands at the head of the fiord, where it branched into Kaafiord. There they charged batteries, ate and rested before the attack on the morrow. *X10*, meanwhile, had left the Stjernoy inlet and followed into Altenfiord. Her repairs were not satisfactory and more faults developed on the way: leaks above the main switchboard caused further electrical failures and after they reached the Brattholm group in the early hours of the 22nd the periscope hoisting motor burned out.

By this time the other boats had started on the final leg towards Kaafiord, although the movements of X5 will never be known with certainty since none of her crew survived. Place in X7 set off shortly after midnight. Three hours later he was through the boom and net defences across the entrance, but in diving afterwards to evade a patrol boat he found his craft snared in anti-torpedo netting about a deserted mooring, formerly for the *Lützow*. He spent much time blowing and filling his tanks and using his motor before he could shake free. Cameron in X6 started about an hour after him. His periscope lens was still misted; as he wrote afterwards, he 'might as well have had a beer bottle'.[38] He succeeded nonetheless in making his way to the net across the entrance, and surfaced astern of a coaster, following her through as the gate was opened. It was 04.45 by then, and bright morning, but his audacity paid off: neither the flush casing of his craft, scarcely above water, nor the diesel exhaust or turbulence were spotted in the wake of the small vessel. Through the mist over the lens he made out the great sunlit shape of the *Tirpitz* and other ships against the land in the west, and set course for her, diving to 60 feet so that he could strip his periscope down and try to cure the leak. In this he failed; to add to his difficulties the periscope hoisting motor brake burned out and when he rose to con the craft on the last half mile of the approach, not only was his lens blurred, but he had also to control the brake manually when raising or lowering the periscope. He scraped under the bows of a moored destroyer and shortly afterwards turned sharply to miss the mooring buoy of a tanker which he had nearly run into.

Unbeknown to him as he closed the double curtain of anti-torpedo netting surrounding the *Tirpitz*, Place in X7, having worked free from the nets around the *Lützow*'s deserted berth, was only five minutes, or under 150 yards astern of him. And somewhere astern of both was Henty-Creer in X5. Cameron penetrated the net barrier by following a picket boat in as the gate was opened; moments later he ran aground. He was already near the surface, and in working free he broke above water briefly. A lookout on the great ship reported the dark, submarine-like shape as it slid under again, but no immediate action was taken. Could it have been a porpoise?

X7 had now reached the net barrier 100 yards off the *Tirpitz*'s port bow and just to the left of the small gate, since closed, through which Cameron had entered. Place dived to 75 feet to pass under, but was surprised to find the bows caught in the net. He blew tanks and went astern on the motor, freeing the boat but rising to the surface broadside on to the line of buoys holding the net. He dived again, this time going down to 95 feet in an effort to work underneath, but again found himself ensnared.

He had not been seen as he bobbed up outside the net, probably because all attention aboard *Tirpitz* was on *X6*, which had run into a submerged rock about 100 yards off the port beam and been forced to the surface again. This time there was no doubt about what she was, and the alarm was raised. She dived immediately and Cameron set a course blindly for the battleship, the gyro compass having been knocked out by the grounding. After some minutes he ran into an obstruction which he assumed was anti-torpedo netting on the far side of the berth. He surfaced, but found himself close under the battleship's port bow with grenades exploding and rifle and machine-gun fire hammering the casing. Going astern on the motor until the hydroplane guard caught the ship's side, he ordered the release of both charges, then scuttled the craft and abandoned her. He came out last.

Place had meanwhile worked *X7* free from her second encounter with the *Tirpitz*'s anti-torpedo nets and, much to his surprise, found himself inside; in blowing and filling and using his motor, he had probably passed underneath both curtains. Steering for the battleship at 40 feet, he ran obliquely into her port bilge below B turret, at which point he must have been very close to Cameron as he dropped *X6*'s charges. Sliding under the great ship's keel, he ordered the starboard charge released, then turned and motored 200 feet towards the stern, where he dropped the port charge, as he estimated, under X turret aft. It was between 07.25 and 07.30. The charges from both boats had been set to explode an hour after release. He doubled back along his track, emerged from the shadow of the great ship and at 07.40 hit the anti-torpedo net again, this time sliding out over the top, hearing machine-gun bullets ringing on the casing as he did so. Once outside he vented tanks and went to the bottom at 120 feet. Whether, in the meantime, Henty-Creer had also succeeded in penetrating the nets and depositing his charges is not known.

Aboard the *Tirpitz* surprise was complete. Cameron and his crew were taken from the water by a picket boat and resuscitated aboard with hot coffee and schnapps; divers were sent over the side, watertight doors closed and the ship prepared for sea. The intention to move from the berth seems to have been changed after *X7* was sighted escaping over the net; instead the starboard bow line was hauled in and the port line slackened to shift the ship from the position where *X6* had gone down. The four prisoners were about to be interrogated when, at 08.12, rather less than the hour set on the time fuses, the ship was lifted bodily by two thunderous explosions, the first just clear of the port side aft, the second a fraction of a second later 60 yards from the port bow. All hands were hurled flat on deck and the ship took an immediate list to port, after which the guns' crews began firing wildly at phantom submarines, some hitting their own ships, and the prisoners were threatened with pistols to try and force them to reveal the number of midgets in the attack.

Meanwhile, Place in X7, having escaped from the nets enclosing the battleship, had found himself somehow ensnared again as he moved away. The shock waves from the explosions blew his craft free, but wrecked the compass and depth gauges and rendered her unmanageable. After breaking surface several times, and coming under fire from the Tirpitz's light batteries on each occasion, it became evident she would have to be abandoned. Place came up alongside a moored gunnery target float and climbed out on to the casing to wave a white sweater in surrender, when the craft began to sink beneath him. He stepped up on to the float. The first lieutenant pulled the hatch down quickly and X7 slid beneath the surface. On the bottom, vents were opened to flood for escape with the Davis escape gear, but she filled so agonizingly slowly that only the diver eventually made it to the surface, literally at his last gasp. Long before that, shortly after she went down, X5 had been sighted from the Tirpitz 600 yards off the starboard bow, her periscope high. She was subjected to a barrage of fire from main and secondary armament which sank her, so it appeared to the Germans and, to the prisoners from X6 watching from the quarterdeck. A destroyer then dropped depth-charges over the spot where she had disappeared. This is assumed to have been the end of X5, Henty-Creer and his crew. Nothing was seen of them again.

The damage to the Tirpitz caused by the single 2-ton charge Place had released, as he thought under X turret aft, but in all probability beneath the engine room just forward of the turret complex, was crippling: all three main turbines were disabled, together with generators and electrical equipment, the port rudder, rangefinders and A and C (X in British terminology) turrets. She was out of action for six months, as a direct result of which the supply convoys to Russia were restarted and British fleet strategy became freer. It was the most significant blow ever struck by small underwater craft, for the even greater strategic success which might have followed from the Italian human torpedo strike in Alexandria harbour had never been realized. The cost was three 35-ton midgets and six very courageous young men, exactly half the number who had set out on the mission. The survivors, respected by the German officers and crew for their feat, all received gallantry awards, Cameron and Place the VC. Henty-Creer and his crew should surely have been similarly honoured. But none lived to tell their story.[39] Horton, whose original enthusiasm and drive had been so strikingly vindicated, wrote to his successor in command of submarines of the crews' 'gallantry . . . unsurpassed in the history of the submarine service'.[40] The official Admiralty communiqué commended their 'persistent daring and endurance . . . unique even in the annals of the Royal Navy'.[41]

Of the three craft assigned to the two other heavy ships, two had of course been lost on passage, while X10 had had so many defects by the time she reached the head of Altenfiord that she had been in no condition to attack: besides the burnt-out periscope hoisting motor, which obliged Hudspeth to lash the periscope at a suitable height and hang a knife nearby in case it became necessary to lower it, the gyro compass was wandering and the magnetic compass light had flooded and was out of action. Hudspeth decided that they were bound to be seen if they made an attempt, and as this could prejudice the other craft's chances, he had lain low and waited, listening to the explosions which signified success and the subsequent gunfire and depth-charges before retiring that night by the way he had come, naturally very dejected. Had he but known it, his assigned target, the Scharnhorst, had left for exercises before the attack; and had he tried to enter Kaafiord after the other three had stirred it to a frenzy he would have been fortunate to have accomplished anything other than an addition to the death toll. He was able, eventually, to make a rendezvous with one of the parent submarines, and a passage crew was put aboard his craft. Before they reached Scotland, however, an order came to scuttle her as a gale was imminent, and the last of the midgets went to the bottom.[42] After the debriefings, Rear-Admiral, Submarines, commended Hudspeth for his qualities of leadership and 'good judgement in coming to his decision to abandon the attack'.[43]

The operation against the Tirpitz coincided with the U-boats' new offensive in the North Atlantic. Dönitz had concentrated a group of twenty-one boats in mid-Atlantic south of the convoy lanes and preserving strict radio silence. On 16 September he ordered them northwards on B-Dienst intelligence to form a long patrol line across the track of a slow westbound convoy, ONS18. In the Submarine Tracking Room Rodger Winn had suspected that the mute boats somewhere in the Atlantic might portend Dönitz's return to the northern convoy routes; the signal, deciphered by Bletchley Park on the 18th, confirmed the suspicion. Although the co-ordinates of position had been disguised, Dönitz's phraseology left no doubt: operations were to be resumed 'in the main battle area' and would constitute 'the decisive struggle for the German race'; Dönitz had also reminded COs of their new weapons and instructed them to remain undetected until the last moment, and then to 'decimate the escorts . . . and denude the convoy'.[44] The warning had been clear. The 9th Escort Group was diverted from Biscay to reinforce ONS18's escort, additional long-range air cover was requested from Coastal Command, and the convoy and a fast convoy, ON202, which was catching up almost on the same track, were both directed to alter course north-westerly.

The new weapons in which Dönitz placed his faith were both offensive and defensive. In the first category was an acoustic torpedo designated T5 and known as the *Zaunkönig* (wren). Work had begun even before the rebuilding of the U-boat arm in 1935 on a torpedo that would home in on propeller noises. A prototype, with sound sensors in the nose connected to the rudder so that the torpedo would steer towards the side whose sensor was picking up the loudest noise, had been tested in 1940, and an operational model, T4, had scored some successes as early as March 1942. The *Zaunkönig* was an improved version with a higher speed and combined magnetic and contact exploder, and was envisaged primarily as an anti-escort weapon; it could pick up the propeller noises of an average escort at 300 metres (328 yards). Sea trials had been conducted in the Baltic since April, firing at all ranges out to 3,000 metres (3,280 yards) and from as little as 5° off the target's track. The first eighty of the production model had been rushed through in August and supplied to a proportion of the boats sent out to reopen the Atlantic campaign. Dönitz had every confidence they would indeed 'decimate the escorts'.[45] The boats also carried a number of anti-convoy FAT torpedoes which could be set to run back and forth through the columns.[46]

The defensive weapons were for use against aircraft. In the three months from June to August, since the retreat from the North Atlantic, sixty out of seventy-nine boats lost had been destroyed by aircraft, nineteen of them by aircraft patrols over the entry and exit routes to the Biscay bases. In an increasing number of cases reported by the boats which survived air attacks the Metox radar detector had given no warning. Herbert Werner records being forced by aircraft into innumerable dives by night as *U230* returned through Biscay that May. The first the bridge watch ever learned of danger was a bright white light low in the sky, usually astern or on the quarter, increasing rapidly in size and brilliance until the bridge was as light as day. The plane would roar overhead and away, the light switched off, and four bombs would erupt shockingly close in the darkness, shaking the boat, jarring and deafening the watch. Far too late, they would dive.[47] This was of course the lethal combination of ASVIII radar, whose 9.7-centimetre pulse was too short for the Metox to detect, and the Leigh Light. Dönitz's reaction had been to increase the anti-aircraft armament of the boats and send them out in groups for mutual defence to transit the Bay on the surface. There can scarcely have been a worse AA-gun platform than a U-boat in the Atlantic, however, and the experiment only resulted in increased damage to the surfaced boats. By mid-June the instructions had been reversed: boats were again to proceed singly through the Bay submerged by night and day, and only surfacing to recharge batteries.[48]

It had then appeared that Metox sets were giving no warning because Allied aircraft were homing in, not on radar but on emissions from the Metox itself, an idea planted by a captured pilot during his interrogation. It was not true, but on 14 August Dönitz had banned the use of the sets altogether in all sea areas 'as it is believed that the enemy makes use of the [Metox] receiver radiation to approach the U-boat ...'[49] Rushed research to produce a warning device free from radiation had resulted in the *Wellenanzeiger* or *Wanz G1*, like the Metox generally better known by the name of its manufacturer, Hagenuk. A few of the boats returning to the Atlantic were fitted with Hagenuk; they were to learn that it was of no more use than the Metox: it searched the frequencies automatically, but only between 1.3 and 1.9 metres, and consequently could not detect the centimetric radars now fitted to a majority of Allied escorts and aircraft.

All boats were equipped with a more numerous anti-aircraft armament consisting of twin 20mm guns on the circular deck abaft the bridge and a quadruple 20mm mounting on a second lower platform added aft of this. Their effective range, however, was no more than about 1,000 yards, not sufficient to stop aircraft before they could deliver their bombs, for the long-range Coastal Command planes were now heavily armoured. Dönitz was pressing for a heavier 37mm piece.[50] Meanwhile it was found that the hastily added lower AA-gun platform, which naturally affected the weight distribution, slowed alarm dives and caused steering difficulties when the boats were submerged. In consequence, to reduce weight, practically all Type VIIs had their 88mm (3.5-inch) deck guns removed. There were now few opportunities for surface action in any case.

Thus inadequately equipped either to evade or fight aircraft, now their most dangerous enemy, the boats cut northwards through high seas to take positions in a patrol line south-west of Iceland designated Group Leuthen. Their instructions were to dive if they saw ships or aircraft but, when they received the order to attack, to run in on the surface ready to engage enemy aircraft and use *Zaunkönig* torpedoes against the surface escorts.

The first loss came in the early morning of 19 September when a Royal Canadian Air Force Liberator returning to Iceland sighted *U341* 160 miles north of the slow westbound convoy ONS18 and made a successful attack. By the early hours of the following morning, the 20th, the fast convoy ON202 had caught up to within 30 miles north-east of ONS18, when the latter was sighted by *U270* under KLt. Paul-Friedrich Otto. An hour later came the order for the group to attack. The patrol line was so extended that few were in position, but Otto crippled the frigate *Lagan* with a *Zaunkönig* which detonated in her wake, blowing off her propellers, and two merchantmen were sunk. By this time the 9th Escort Group had joined and that morning Liberators from Iceland appeared overhead, forcing down boats working around the flanks on the surface and sinking *U338* with an aerial acoustic torpedo called Fido, a new weapon working on the same principle as the *Zaunkönig*.

By noon the two convoys were running side by side and Horton at Derby House ordered them to join. This eventually created a broad front of fifty-six merchantmen protected by the escorts of three groups, seventeen vessels all told, and in the air Swordfish planes from a merchantman converted with a flight deck into a merchant aircraft carrier, or MAC ship, sailing with ONS18, and Liberators from Iceland. The U-boats were unable to close and two were damaged and forced to retire. In attacks that evening, however, the pack claimed two more escorts with *Zaunkönig* torpedoes, a Canadian destroyer and a corvette, which both sank. Their crews were rescued by the frigate *Itchen*. Dense fog closed in early on the 21st and continued for most of the 22nd, preventing further attacks, but the pack remained in touch by sound and the destroyer *Keppel*, homing in with Huff Duff along the bearing of signals from one of the shadowers, *U229*, surprised her on the surface and rammed and sank her. The boats succeeded in keeping in touch and that night the *Itchen*, carrying the survivors from the other two escorts, was sunk by a *Zaunkönig* from *U666* under KLt.

Herbert Engel. In the early hours of the 23rd four more merchant-men were sunk, but with daylight the massed convoy, now inside 600 miles from Newfoundland, was met by Canadian aircraft, and Godt called off the operation.

Dönitz was delighted with the results as reported. The COs who had taken part in the initial attacks in the early morning of the 20th had claimed seven destroyers – as they termed all escorts – sunk and three probably sunk from fifteen *Zaunkönig* torpedoes fired, and only five misses.[51] From the attacks on the final night and early morning they claimed a further five, thus altogether twelve escorts sunk and three probables, together with nine merchant-men, over the four days. Dönitz recorded 'a complete success' in his war diary: 'the new weapons proved themselves in every respect . . . It remains to be seen how the convoy war in the North Atlantic develops after installation of the 3.7 cm [AA guns] and after the co-operation of [our] own air[craft].'[52] Actually none of the reported hits on the escorts had been observed. The *Zaunkönig* had such a short arming distance, only 400 metres (437 yards), that in order to ensure the torpedoes' sound sensors could not home in on the boats' own propeller noises COs were instructed to go down to 60 metres (196 feet) after firing from a bow tube, or cut all engine noise if firing from a stern tube. In practice most COs went deep and so had no opportunity of witnessing the results of their shooting; and they evidently made the most optimistic interpreta-tions of subsequent sounds from above. The true figures were three escorts sunk, one damaged, and six merchantmen of an aggregate 36,400 tons sunk for the loss of one U-boat in the patrol line, two more during the attacks, and three so seriously damaged as to have to return to base.

Godt re-formed the remaining boats with others arriving in the area into another group of twenty-one named *Rossbach* towards the end of September and directed them across the track of the next two westbound convoys. Both were diverted successfully on Ultra decrypts, and on 4 and 5 October aircraft from Iceland sank three of the boats. The remaining eighteen were directed to an eastbound convoy with a strong escort and air cover. They succeeded in sink-ing a Polish destroyer with a *Zaunkönig*, but the screen was not penetrated and three more were lost to air attack. Again Godt re-formed the survivors and new arrivals into another group, *Schlieffen*, and threw them into the path of convoys reported by B-Dienst on the 15th, instructing them to remain on the surface to beat off aircraft rather than lose the convoy.[53] Six boats were lost; only one merchantman, a straggler, was sunk.

Meanwhile, to the southward, aircraft from US escort carrier groups mopped up the net of *Milchkühe* whose fuel and supplies were sustaining the boats; only one escaped, and she was moved far to the south-west out of the area. By the end of October, the euphoria after the apparent early success of the *Zaunkönig* had entirely evaporated. The extent of Allied air cover and the mortal danger to which boats exposed themselves if they remained on the surface to try and beat off armoured aircraft with their 20mm guns had rendered convoy attacks impossible, at least by day.[54] Over the month as a whole, twenty-six U-boats had been lost, twenty of them to aircraft, nearly all in the North Atlantic. In return twelve merchantmen aggregating 56,000 tons had been sunk in the theatre, all either independents or stragglers. They represented a minute fraction of well over a thousand ships which had been convoyed safely, and less than a tenth of the tonnage of Liberty ships completed each month in US yards. Moreover, the exchange rate was little over half a merchantman for every U-boat lost, and over all theatres of operation it was still less than one merchantman per U-boat sunk. The U-boat 'potential' had dropped to a point not worth calculating.

The one gleam of light seized on by German propaganda was the return on 10 October of Wolfgang Lüth after a record voyage of twenty-seven weeks in the Indian Ocean. He had departed Bordeaux with the 'cruiser' Type IXD2 *U181* on 23 March. His first sinking on 11 April off the west coast of Africa brought his personal score to over 200,000 tons, and on the 16th he received a signal from Führer headquarters informing him he had been awarded the Knight's Cross with Oak Leaves and Swords; he was the fourth ace to be so honoured after Otto Kretschmer, Erich Topp and Reinhard Suhren. Proceeding around the Cape, he then sank two more merchantmen sailing independently before refuelling from a tanker, *Charlotte Schliemann*, and replenishing with mainly Japanese provisions, meanwhile allowing his men aboard her for the luxury of a shower. He continued northwards and sank another five independents off Madagascar, the last the 10,500-ton British freighter *Clan Macarthur* on 11 August. Surfacing after she went down, he took wounded from one of her lifeboats aboard the submarine for first aid, and after returning them promised he would signal Mauritius with the lifeboats' position when he had moved a safe distance away – as he did.[55]

Sinking the *Clan Macarthur* had brought his total to over 250,000 tons – adjusted by post-war research to 225,713 tons – and raised him to second highest-scoring ace after Otto Kretschmer.[56]

He received another signal from Führer headquarters; this time it was the Knight's Cross with Oak Leaves, Swords and Diamonds, the Reich's highest military honour. It had been bestowed only six times before; he was the first naval recipient. He broke out the medicinal brandy and bottles of beer to allow the crew to celebrate, and after a rendezvous to pick up code-books for the next period from another Type IXD2 entering the area, began his return passage, rounding the Cape westwards on 2 September and putting in to Bordeaux again on 10 October, two weeks short of seven months from the day he had set out. It was his last war patrol. He flew forty-eight small white victory pennants from his periscope for the ships he had sunk in his various commands since the beginning of the war.

Perhaps more remarkable had been his success in preserving the morale, health and fighting efficiency of his men in the confined quarters of the submarine over such a protracted voyage. One of these told Lüth's biographer, Jordan Vause, 'When you've been at sea that long you can't walk more than a couple of hundred metres before you have to stop and massage your legs.'[57] The lecture Lüth was to give naval officers two months later on leadership was acknowleged as both a practical and a spiritual guide from a CO who had proved his precepts in the most arduous conditions over the longest period imaginable; it was printed and adopted as a standard text in training classes. There was much in it of value about defeating the monotony of patrol with competitions and educational programmes. There was also much in line with the political mood as the Reich braced itself for increasingly desperate battles for existence. This was perhaps its chief merit in Dönitz's eyes. There were other opinions about the sermonizing, Nazi tone of the message, as of the man, principally among the 'old salts' in the front line. The captain of Buchheim's *Das Boot* had a constitutional aversion to Nazi propaganda; discussion of politics was taboo in his wardroom, and 'even in private conversation the captain promptly put paid to any serious discussion with a sardonic curl of the lip . . .'[58]

Lüth's own propaganda value was exploited in newsreels, in the press and on the radio when he travelled to Führer headquarters towards the end of October to receive the Oak Leaves, Swords and Diamonds of supreme distinction from Hitler personally. Their brilliance reflected on the U-boat arm itself, momentarily concealing the impasse it had reached. Lüth had been fortunate. He had scored his early successes before centimetric radar and the recent great extension of air power over the North Atlantic convoys, and indeed into the Bay of Biscay, and his later ones against ships sailing independently off southern Africa and Madagascar, where anti-submarine activity was far less intense. His good fortune would outlast the war by just a week. At midnight on 13 May 1945, as Commandant of the Navy cadet school at Flensburg-Mürwik, he failed to respond to the challenge of one of his guards and was shot dead.

Five 'cruiser' U-boats had remained in the Indian Ocean after Lüth left, patrolling singly off the East African coast and Ceylon and off the entrance to the Red Sea and Persian Gulf, using the Japanese naval bases at Penang and Singapore to resupply and refit. One had since been lost to aircraft attack, but together with eight Japanese submarines, chiefly large I-class boats, they had taken a marginally larger toll of Allied tonnage than all the boats stationed in the Atlantic together;[59] it was still an insignificant proportion of Allied resources and new building.

Despite self-evident failure in either the tonnage, or the supply war Dönitz was determined to continue the U-boat campaign. Remembering the armada of anti-submarine forces which he had seen in Gibraltar roads at the end of the First World War, he had expressed his opinion to Hitler at the Berghof above Berchtesgaden on 31 May 1943 after his first withdrawal from the North Atlantic.

'The U-boat war must be continued even if the goal can no longer be obtained, because the enemy forces it absorbs are extraordinarily large. Jellicoe in his book quoted the considerable quantity of forces which the U-boats [by] themselves tied up in the world war . . .'[60]

At this point Hitler interrupted: 'There is absolutely no question of abandoning the U-boat war. The Atlantic is my western approaches [Vorfeld], and even if I have to fight there on the defensive, that is better than defending myself first on the coasts of Europe.' He went on to agree with Dönitz that the magnitude of enemy forces tied up by the U-boat war was such that he could not permit their release.[61]

This then was the immediate rationale for continuing the struggle with a type of submarine and a tactic that had been rendered ineffective by Allied advances in radar and weaponry. But Dönitz had not wished simply to continue; he had intended to increase production of these virtually obsolescent craft from a rate of thirty a month to forty. When, that 31 May, he produced the figures of shipyard workers and crews needed for the expanded programme, Hitler pointed out that he did not have these men when the other military needs of the Reich were taken into account. Dönitz responded by warning him that a cessation or relaxation of the U-boat war would allow the enemy to hurl all his material strength against Europe, and the coastal supply routes for vital raw materials would also be endangered. Whereupon Hitler agreed to his programme.[62]

It is not clear why Dönitz stepped up production of conventional boats to such an extent, or indeed at all. It was evident that only a new type altogether could regain the initiative in the Atlantic, one with a high underwater speed to enable it to run ahead of convoys even when forced down by aircraft, and to outmanoeuvre comparatively slow frigates, sloops and corvettes while still submerged. Such a boat had already been designed. Professor Walter's advanced prototypes driven by closed-circuit turbines powered by hydrogen peroxide had run into too many difficulties for immediate production, but construction plans for an ocean-going Walter boat had inspired a director of naval construction in the U-department, Marine Bau Rat Oelfken, to devise a similarly streamlined and faired but conventionally powered submarine which could be produced at once with existing technology. To gain the required high submerged speed he had proposed three times the normal battery capacity to be contained in a second cylinder beneath the main hull, giving the boat a figure-of-eight cross section. He had presented working plans to Dönitz on 19 June. Immediately enthusiastic, Dönitz had decided to incorporate the class, to be designated Type XXI, in the existing building programme in place of Type IXs. The plans for a small Walter submarine had been similarly modified with extra battery capacity into a 230-ton coastal boat and incorporated into the programme as Type XXIII.[63] On 13 August, Dönitz decided on a complete switch of future production to these two new classes, termed collectively *Elektro* boats, but with the proviso that current production of conventional boats was neither to be interrupted, nor slowed down; this was in case teething problems delayed the *Elektro* boats. Of these it was the 1,600-ton ocean-going Type XXI with a designed underwater speed of 18 knots for one and a half hours, 12 to 14 knots for ten hours, and capable under a separate silent 'creeping' motor of 500 miles at 2 to 3 knots, in which he was principally interested.

In July he had entrusted naval production to Albert Speer. The *Elektro* boats were to be prefabricated in eight sections at different inland factories after the American method, the sections to be despatched to the north German shipyards to be welded together and fitted out under concrete, bomb-proof shelters. This was to increase speed of production and disperse manufacture to make it less vulnerable to disruption from Allied bombing. Such was the priority Dönitz accorded these *Elektro* boats that he had agreed to production starting without testing prototypes first, an abomination to his naval constructors, already incensed at having their responsibilities handed to the Minister for Armaments and Munitions. For his part, Speer handed detailed responsibility for production of the *Elektro* boats to Dr Otto Merker, a former car manufacturer. Thus it was that the high officers of the *Kriegsmarine* who, more than most naval and military hierarchies, considered themselves superior to civilians, finally enlisted civilian expertise. Had they done so earlier, as the Royal and United States Navies had, the maritime war must have taken a longer and more dangerous course for the Allies.

After arranging matters with Speer, Dönitz had enthused to Hitler about the new *Elektro* boats; they would render all enemy anti-submarine measures ineffective since, he asserted, the construction of escorts was based on the low underwater speed of U-boats. 'The goal must be for sinkings to keep pace with [enemy] new construction, and this will be achieved when the new boat has arrived.'[64]

Other projects to reduce the effectiveness of radar-fitted aircraft were under way. German scientists had discovered with astonishment the wavelength of the new radars from a set salvaged from a crashed bomber, and the Naval Communication Experimental section in co-operation with Telefunken had developed a detector known as 'Naxos' (or 'Timor') which registered pulses between 8 and 12 cm. The first boats were fitted with Naxos in September and October 1943, but the apparatus proved to have a range of no more than 5 miles and was prone to electrical failure. Boats continued to be surprised by night. It would not be until the early spring of 1944, when an improved centimetric receiver termed the *Fliege* came into operation, that COs would feel confident they would not be surprised on the surface. Shortly after the *Fliege*, which had a detection range of over 12 miles (20 km) and indicated the bearing of the emitting set, came the *Mücke*, which could detect the even shorter 2 to 4cm wavelength of the latest US Navy radar.[65]

Dönitz was as excited about a compound under development by the chemical complex I.G. Farben which, he had been assured, would absorb 100 per cent of radar waves and so render boats which had been coated with it invisible on any sets. This was never, however, to fulfil the hopes placed in it.

The proposed 37mm anti-aircraft gun has been mentioned. The first boats were fitted with single 37mm mountings in place of the quadruple 20mm in November 1943; however, it would not be long before Allied aircraft were mounting even heavier cannon to outrange them. Probably the most important development was a hinged air mast called a *Schnorchel* which could be raised above the surface to allow the main diesel engines to suck air in and expel exhaust gases while the boat was submerged. This would allow boats to recharge batteries without exposing themselves on the surface, even to make speeds up to perhaps 8 knots submerged in calm conditions on the main engines. The first boats would be fitted with *Schnorchels* in early 1944.

All these measures were defensive. Equipping the boats with effective radar would have had both defensive and offensive potential, but here German science was far behind the Allies. A few sets adapted from surface ships' gunnery radar had been fitted to Type IX boats in early 1942 with antennae fixed on the fore plating of the conning tower, thus requiring the submarine to be pointed in the direction of search or, for an all-round search, to be turned right around through 360°. Since the effective range was found to be under 3½ miles (5.5 km), less than good night visual range, the apparatus, which took up precious space in the control room, was obviously useless. A modified version with an antenna atop an extending mast which could be rotated manually had proved no more effective.

In August 1943, after much urging from Dönitz, an adaptation of a new Luftwaffe 56cm set was tested on *U743* in the Baltic and proved successful at ranges from 2 to a maximum of 10 kilometres (1 to 6¼ miles). Although vastly inferior to the performance of the latest Allied sets – or indeed to the range of the boats' own hydrophone arrays which could detect single ships up to 20 kilometres (12½ miles) and convoys to 100 kilometres (62 miles) – this *Funkmessortungsgerät* (FuMO)–61, termed Hohentwiel U, seemed to promise at least some search and defensive potential, and on 25 October it was ordered as standard equipment for all boats.[66] Delays due to the bombing of the manufacturers in Berlin were to hold up production; and by the following autumn, when a substantial number of boats had been fitted, Allied air supremacy had rendered the device practically superfluous. It is seldom mentioned in U-boat memoirs.

None of the belated measures being taken by the U-boat technical departments could return to the existing boats the surface mobility and hence tactical effectiveness that they had lost. This could only be restored by the *Elektro* boats when they came into service. Speer gave these top production priority. Meanwhile Dönitz, despite the defeats of October, continued to search for ways of fighting the vital North Atlantic convoys. He ordered boats to proceed submerged by day to prevent the Allies detecting them and so re-routing convoys around them, surfacing only at night, and divided them into smaller groups. When this failed to produce contacts he divided them still further into groups of three, one boat in each group stationed in advance in the direction the convoys were expected, to report increased air activity to the others; and realizing 'more clearly that the enemy aircraft are superior to our defences', he ordered boats not to pursue convoys by day if the air escort were strong.[67] When this system, too, failed to produce contacts he again withdrew from the North Atlantic – and in mid-November moved the boats down to the convoy lanes to and from Gibraltar where he would have the co-operation of the Luftwaffe. Still they failed to make contact. Finally, on 7 January 1944, he admitted defeat for his pack tactics and disposed all boats individually. As it was put in the war diary:

> this marked the end of the method used hitherto to pick up convoys – by patrol or reconnaissance line ... Convoy operations proved the enemy was able to discover the extent of our dispositions ... and avoid them so cleverly that it was suspected for some time that he had broken into our ciphers. It was only realized for certain that he gained accurate knowledge of our dispositions from radar when the range of enemy radar sets became known.[68]

It was of course not radar so much as Bletchley Park and Rodger Winn that enabled the Allies to re-route convoys so successfully. Meanwhile, noise-making 'foxers' had been introduced as part of the escorts' defence against the *Zaunkönig*: towed a long way astern from either quarter, the foxers made a humming, rattling or screeching noise on the same frequency as the escorts' propellers but considerably louder, so enticing the acoustic torpedoes towards them and away from their target. They were unhandy, restricted the towing ship's speed to 15 knots, interfered with asdic/sonar and were audible at a greater distance than ships' propellers. They were not popular with escort commanders. Captain F.J. Walker of 'Operation Buttercup', now established as one of the Royal Navy's most effective U-boat hunters, preferred to rely on detecting the U-boat before it could attack, then reducing to under 8 knots or increasing to near full speed to alter the sound frequency of his propellers out of the range which activated the *Zaunkönig's* sensors. It was also possible, since the torpedo homed in astern, to countermine the warhead by dropping a depth-charge with a shallow setting; naturally this depended on timely detection and very rapid response.

Walker owed recent successes in part to his command of a support rather than an escort group; whether patrolling the U-boat approaches to Biscay or reinforcing a convoy's escort, once he found a boat he could hunt it to destruction without having to break off to protect merchantmen. Like similar groups of Admiral King's Tenth Fleet operating in the lower latitudes of the North Atlantic, his 2nd Support Group was a hunter-killer force. And given this freedom to concentrate on the quarry, time was inevitably on the side of the surface warships, for the U-boat could not hold out indefinitely below. The creation of support groups had been made possible chiefly by the greater number of escorts available as ships from earlier building programmes on both sides of the Atlantic were completed.

Thus, in addition to armoured Liberators and other aircraft equipped with long-range, high-definition centimetric radar now covering every part of the Atlantic convoy routes, and planes from escort carriers and MAC ships with convoys, U-boats had to contend with specialized hunting groups from which, once detected, there was seldom hope of escape. From the feared grey wolves of the oceans they had become the harried prey.

Walker had perfected two lethal methods of destroying them: 'Operation Plaster' involved two or three sloops of the group advancing up the track of the boat below, dropping charges at five-second intervals usually set to the extreme depths between 500 and 800 feet at which COs now sought to hide.[69] On other occasions, when asdic contact was particularly good or 'Operation Plaster' had failed to bring up oil, debris and the mutilated remains of those who had experienced this terrifying moving barrage, Walker would mount a 'creeping' attack. His sloop *Starling* would follow the U-boat, maintaining asdic contact from about 1,000 yards astern of her, meanwhile directing another of his sloops ahead of him along the line of bearing at very slow speed and not using her asdic; when she reached a position just ahead of the U-boat – to allow for the time the charges would take to fall to the set depth – Walker would give the order by radio telephone to start the attack. The charges would be dropped in pairs at intervals of about nine seconds. This method eliminated the blind period in the last 200 yards of an asdic approach and gave the U-boat CO no opportunity to evade since he only heard the regular 'pinging' from the directing ship's asdic well astern. No survivors of this devastating tactic, which was promulgated by the Admiralty and adopted as a standard form of attack, ever returned to warn their comrades.

Walker made his most successful cruise in late January and February 1944 in the western approaches to the British Isles and south to Finisterre. In a period of twenty-seven days his 2nd Support Group destroyed six U-boats with 'Plaster' or 'creeping' attacks, while escort groups in the same area sank a further five for the loss of only one straggler from a convoy. The final success went to a U-boat, however, when OLt. Hans Kurt von Bremen of *U764* blew off the stern of one of Walker's sloops with a *Zaunkönig*; she sank under tow home. It was a quite unacceptable exchange rate, nonetheless. On return to Liverpool the 2nd Support Group received a tumultuous reception all the way up the River Mersey. Bands played the *Starling's* signature tune, 'A hunting we will go!' Thousands lined the sides of ships in port to raise their caps and cheer. After they had tied up, Walker's wife came aboard. 'Isn't it funny?' he said to her. 'All this fuss and ceremony and I'm still just the same old Johnny they didn't think it worthwhile to promote.'[70]

Walker's secrets were his methodical training of the group and a personal commitment which kept him on the bridge for days at a time without respite, and which contributed before the end of the war to his early death from cerebral thrombosis. Nothing would convince his officers that he had not died from sheer overstrain.

In the Biscay bases, meanwhile, wardroom walls spread with photographs of those who had not returned from patrol. Their places at table were filled by ever younger officers and COs, many from the surface fleet, trained more hurriedly and lacking the experience their predecessors had won as junior officers on many war patrols. There were no aces to emulate and vie with; these had been lost or promoted or posted ashore to await the new *Elektro* boats. When Dönitz came to inspect the flotillas he no longer spoke of success, only containment; they were pinning down some two million of the enemy in escorts and shipbuilding and munitions works, he told them. They had to keep at sea even if they never sank a ship. When boats departed there were no bands to send them on their way now; other crews gathered to wave their comrades farewell, wondering if they would see them again. And when their own time came: 'we just drank a glass of champagne in silence and shook hands, trying not to look each other in the eyes. We got pretty tough, but it shook us all the same. Operation suicide

... though nobody made much of it. Heroics are for people who have never known the real thing.'[71]

Thus Heinz Schaeffer, then CO of *U997*, writing soon after the end of the war. Another survivor, Peter Cremer, wrote of this period, when he commanded *U333*, that he had discovered once and for all what courage meant: for a fighting man who had suffered wounds and pain and barely survived, who knew that death was not only possible but probable, to carry on required real courage.[72]

The war diary at U-boat Command leaves a similar impression:

despite the harshness of the battle the bearing of commanders and crews remains above all praise: although aware of heavy losses, although ... constantly pursued and weary, the U-boat man remains undaunted. Hard on himself, resigned to a hard fate, hating the enemy, believing in his arms and victory, he continues the unequal struggle.[73]

One of those who continued the struggle with no hope of winning the glory of former aces, little even of surviving, so short was the life expectancy in U-boats now, was KLt. Rolf Manke, CO of the Type VIIC *U358*. A calm and deliberate 29-year-old, possessed of common sense and humour, he had been posted to U-boats from the naval air arm. He was fortunate in having an exceptionally able chief engineer, OLt. (Ing.) Fritjof Wiebe, who had saved the boat on at least one occasion under attack by bringing her up dynamically with perfect trim and use of the hydroplanes – thus not giving away the boat's position by blowing tanks – and escaping from waiting destroyers under motor with just the bridge above water.

Manke sailed on his fifth war patrol from St Nazaire on 14 February 1944 to the same area of the western approaches to the British Isles in which Walker's 2nd Support Group had scored its successes earlier in the month. He was detected by asdic from the frigate *Garlies* of the 1st Escort Group on the morning of the 29th (a leap year) and was immediately subjected to a hedgehog salvo followed by creeping depth-charge attacks from two other frigates of the group. He evaded these at great depth for twelve hours, and at dusk, after another hedgehog salvo, the attacks were called off. The frigates waited, maintaining asdic contact, expecting him to surface after the moon set in the early hours of 1 March. Manke did not oblige. Consequently mass creeping attacks, Walker's 'Operation Plaster', were recommenced shortly before 08.00. Manke continued to evade skilfully throughout the morning. In the afternoon the weather deteriorated, and with it asdic conditions.

Two of the group's four frigates broke off to refuel and take on more depth-charges – 530 had been expended thus far – the other two frigates maintaining contact despite the worsening weather.

At some time before 19.30 that evening, after thirty-eight hours submerged and with the carbon dioxide build-up in the boat approaching danger levels, Manke told Wiebe to take her up and had a *Zaunkönig* prepared for launching. As the engineer brought the boat dynamically towards the surface Manke gave the order to fire on sound bearings of the nearest warship. At 19.29 the torpedo homed in and detonated on the stern of the frigate *Gould*, which started to sink. About four minutes later *U358*'s conning tower broke surface 1,500 yards ahead of the second frigate, *Affleck*. Manke threw open the hatch and, after the first gale of foul air had escaped, climbed to the bridge. The superstructure had been spotted, however, and the *Affleck* opened fire. Manke was killed and few of the crew managed to escape from below before the boat was despatched with a depth-charge at shallow setting. Since the *Affleck* picked up survivors from the *Gould* first, only one of Manke's crew survived to tell the story of the longest continuous U-boat hunt of the war, one that ended in magnificent defiance and the loss of one of the hunters.[74] As the official British historian, Stephen Roskill, put it: 'Tribute must be paid to the enemy's endurance, and the fact that he had fought to the end, rather than surface and surrender.'[75]

That month also saw the only proven war crime to stain the U-boat arm in the war. KLt. Heinz Eck had taken his first U-command, the new 'cruiser' Type IXD2 *U852*, from Kiel on 18 January 1944 with orders to round the Cape and enter the Indian Ocean. According to a British officer who saw much of him later, he was a young man 'of considerable charm, tall and handsome', who was idolized by his crew.[76] He was also inexperienced, having only transferred to U-boats from command of a minesweeper in May 1942. Prior to departure he had been briefed by Godt's first staff officer, F.K. Günther Hessler, and the first staff officer operations, KLt. Adalbert Schnee at U-boat headquarters, now moved to a specially built compound named Koralle in open country near Eberswalde 20 miles north-east of Berlin. They had warned him of the highly dangerous conditions in the North Atlantic, where he should proceed submerged by day, only surfacing in the dark; and in the South Atlantic of the especially strong air cover between Ascension Island and Freetown, Sierra Leone, augmented by US escort-carrier hunter-killer groups. Four Type IXD2 boats with very experienced COs had been lost in this area in the past few months. He should avoid anything that would attract the enemy's attention to his boat.[77]

Returning to Kiel he had received a final briefing from his flotilla commander, K.K. Karl-Heinz Moehle. It will be recalled that Moehle was the officer who had been concerned at the lack of clarity in Dönitz's 'Laconia' order, particularly that the rescue of survivors contradicted 'the most fundamental demands of war for the annihilation of enemy ships and crews'.[78] It is not known whether he explained this order to Eck by means of the two examples he claimed he had been given at U-boat Command by Herbert Kuppisch – who had since been lost in command of U847, one of the Type IXD2s destroyed in the South Atlantic. All that is clear is that both the 'Laconia' order and the 'Rescue ship' order with its phrase about 'the desired destruction of the steamers' crews' – which Dönitz had repeated over Godt's signature only three months previously, on 7 October 1943 – were both contained in the standing-order book aboard U852.[79] Testifying at his trial, Eck was to state that before sailing he had been told that Hartenstein, after sinking the Laconia, had been bombed by enemy aircraft while rescuing survivors including women and children, and flying a red cross, thus illustrating that for the enemy 'military reasons take precedence over humane reasons'.[80]

After sailing up the Norwegian coast and northabout around Scotland into the North Atlantic, U852 made slow progress, submerged for much of the time, only surfacing at night to recharge batteries and refresh the boat. It was not until 13 March, almost two months after leaving Kiel, that she reached the Equator. She was then midway between Freetown, Sierra Leone, 550 miles to the north, and Ascension Island, 500 miles to the south, precisely the area Eck had been warned was most dangerous. That afternoon he sighted a fair-sized freighter – the 4,700-ton Greek tramp Peleus under charter to the British Ministry of War Transport. He shadowed until it was dark and then attacked with two torpedoes armed with magnetic pistols. Their explosions broke the ship apart; what remained of her sank beneath clouds of steam and smoke in just two minutes. Hearing whistles and shouts and seeing lights, Eck closed and had the ship's third officer and a sailor hauled up from a raft for questioning. When satisfied, he allowed them back aboard the raft and steered away.

It was at this point, it may be assumed, that he decided to dispose of the survivors, for he had machine guns, machine pistols and hand grenades passed up to the bridge, and then turned back towards the scene. At his trial he said he had determined to destroy all pieces of wreckage and rafts. Since the wreckage and rafts were of wood and could not be disposed of by small-arms fire, the explanation was rejected by the court. His reasoning will never be known. His lack of experience must have been a factor, and on that account he was surely influenced by the briefings he received, either at U-boat Command or at Kiel. He always denied acting under superior or secret orders; all those accused with him stated that they had understood he was carrying secret orders.

By the time he approached the scene again, two rafts carrying survivors had been lashed together, and the ship's chief officer was attempting to round up other survivors from the water. Eck or his chief engineer, KLt. (Ing.) Hans Lenz, who spoke English, instructed the chief officer to bring his raft closer. As he attempted to do so Eck gave the order to fire. The second watch officer, Lt. August Hoffmann, the doctor, *Stabsarzt* Walter Weisspfennig, and a 19-year-old leading seaman on the bridge, Wolfgang Schwender, began firing machine guns at the raft while someone shone the signal lamp to illuminate it. The engineer Lenz had protested to Eck about the order, but when Schwender's machine gun seized up, compelling him to clear the blockage, Lenz took it from him and began firing too. His explanation at the trial for this remarkable about-face was that he considered Schwender 'bad', apparently because he had fathered an illegitimate child, and if the survivors were to be killed, he, Schwender was not fit to do it.[81]

Eck cruised among the wreckage from raft to raft for five hours while these officers fired or lobbed grenades; he did not leave the scene and resume his course for the Cape until shortly before 01.00 on the 14th. At his trial he explained that he had been under the impression that unless he sank all the rafts his boat was lost. In fact they did not sink. The only effect of his action was to delay his passage and slaughter survivors; sharks, scenting blood, had gathered and were tearing at the dead and the wounded in the water.

By this time the mood among the crew below was, as he described it at the trial, 'depressed'. He went down to the control room and spoke to them over the loudspeaker system, explaining that he had made the decision to destroy the remains (*Überreste*) with a heavy heart, but 'If we are influenced by too much sympathy we must also think of our wives and children who die as the victims of air attack at home.'[82] It will be recalled that this was the precise justification Dönitz had used in his 'Laconia' order.

On 1 April, off Capetown, Eck sank his second victim, the 5,270-ton British steamer *Dahomian*, before continuing into the

Indian Ocean. On 2 May, high up the East African coast off Somalia, he was surprised on the surface by a Royal Air Force bomber which caused so much damage to the boat that he was forced to run her aground and set demolition charges. He and the surviving crew members were captured. Meanwhile, three of four members of the crew of the *Peleus* who had survived the slaughter on the rafts, one at least by feigning death, had been picked up by a passing ship. Their statements were taken in London, and after the war Eck, Hoffmann, Lenz, Weisspfennig and Schwender were tried as war criminals. None denied the facts. Eck's defence was that he had attempted to destroy all traces of wreckage in order to preserve his boat; the others pleaded they had only obeyed the CO's orders. Yet a German court after the first war, confronted with a similar case of a U-boat's crew firing on survivors, had ruled out 'superior orders' as a defence for an obviously criminal act. Eck, Hoffmann and the doctor, Weisspfennig, were sentenced to death and on 30 November 1945 – not six weeks after the start of the trial – were taken to Lüneberg Heath, tied to posts and shot by a British army firing squad; the other two were sentenced to long terms in prison, of which they eventually served only six years each.

In court Eck had made as good an impression on the judge, Major A. Melford Stevenson, KC, as he had on the British officer quoted previously. 'His courage and dignity were impressive,' Stevenson said afterwards. 'Of all those in that Court it is his personality that survives in my memory. It was clear he'd lost his head.'[83]

There is another explanation. It will be recalled that a one-time *Oberfähnrich*, Peter Heisig, testified at the Nuremberg trials – just after Eck's trial – that he had formed the impression during one of Dönitz's speeches to a training class that Dönitz was advocating 'total war' at sea in which crews as well as ships were targets. Discussing it afterwards with others, Heisig had found that all had come to the same conclusion, that fire should be opened on survivors, and one of his senior officers had advised 'if possible only officers should be on the bridge ready to annihilate shipwrecked sailors should the possibility arise'.[84] Heisig, who had since served as 1WO of *U877*, had become a prisoner of war when the boat was sunk in the North Atlantic in December 1944. While still in captivity he heard of the trial of *U852*'s officers and came forward to assist Eck's 2WO, Hoffmann, who was a former classmate. After the trial, on 20 November, he was flown from London to Nuremberg without being informed of the verdicts or sentences, and on the 27th he made a formal affidavit, used later as evidence for the prosecution against Dönitz.[85] Three days afterwards, Eck, Hoffmann and Weisspfennig were executed. It seems that Heisig's evidence was deliberately withheld from the trial of U852's officers. If so, the reason was surely that the British prosecutors were after bigger game, Dönitz himself. On the day Heisig was flown to Nuremberg, a British officer who claimed to be acting for Dönitz's defence interrogated Eck where he was being held in Altona prison and asked him whether he had ever received direct orders from Dönitz to shoot at shipwrecked survivors. 'No,' Eck replied.

'Have you ever heard that orders had been issued either by Dönitz himself or in his name that survivors from wrecks or anything which might be held to save such survivors should be shot at?'

'Only now when I was in London did I hear through the British authorities that such orders really did exist.'[86]

It is probable that Eck and his officers were victims of the deliberate ambiguity of Dönitz's orders and admonitions about the crews of merchant ships. Among the thousands in the U-boat arm who went loyally to their deaths Eck, for all the horror of his action against the defenceless survivors of the Peleus, has a poignant place.

As Dönitz withdrew for the second and final time from the North Atlantic convoy routes, US submarines in the Pacific, supplied at last with reliable torpedoes and enjoying the priceless advantage of surface search radar, began making real inroads into the stock of Japanese shipping. September 1943 had seen a record thirty-one merchantmen totalling 135,000 tons sunk by Pacific and Australian-based submarines; in November submarines set another record of forty-seven Marus aggregating 228,000 tons,[87] while sinkings from all causes that month amounted to 320,000 tons,[88] a rate of loss the Japanese could not afford for long. By the end of the year their merchant fleet had been reduced to under 5 million tons, a million tons below minimum requirements for supplying the extended empire and war economy.[89]

The situation was analogous to that which Great Britain had faced during the U-boat 'happy time' in the first half of 1941.[90] It will be recalled that British planners then, extrapolating sinking figures to the end of the year, predicted supply shortfalls which in their analysis could only be avoided by 'a reduction in the rate of loss'. Japanese planners had reached the same conclusion: it had been agreed at a conference at the end of September that shipping losses had to be cut to under 1 million tons a year – approximately half the current rate. This required above all more escorts. Here was the dilemma, for the Naval Staff and the C-in-C, Admiral Koga, still had their eyes fixed on the 'decisive battle' and wanted carriers, aircraft, destroyers and more submarines – the latter both for supply and to whittle down the US fleet before the battle. There was insufficient capacity to meet all these demands and build the 360 escorts deemed necessary. The eventual compromise resulted in a programme for forty escorts, Type A or *Kaibō-kans*, similar to frigates of 19½ knots.[91] In view of the ever-increasing US submarine force this was much too few, much too late.

The Japanese problem was insoluble: already the first products of Roosevelt's 1940 'Two Ocean Navy' programme had tilted the Pacific balance. Nimitz had a surface force more formidable than the Imperial Navy at the height of its power. A further dozen carriers were completing; more were to follow down the ways. For anti-submarine protection he had eight escort carriers and radar- and hedgehog-equipped destroyers and destroyer escorts, all well trained, as they were proving, in tactics honed by the battle against the U-boats in the Atlantic. Above all, US forces had overwhelming superiority in the air in terms of quantity, quality and production potential. Victory in any decisive battle was as much a mirage for Japan as was the hope of stemming merchant shipping losses, for the US submarine force was now over 150 strong and increasing at the rate of 6 boats a month. This was recognized at the upper levels of the two services and in the highest tier of government. In August, the Emperor Hirohito had called for exhaustive, independent studies of prospects in the war from the operations and intelligence departments of both Army and Navy General Staffs. The results were conveyed to his chief civilian adviser on 19 November, who imparted them to the Emperor on the 24th. They were unanimously pessimistic. The Naval Staff concluded that Japan had lost the war irretrievably and would be forced to give up all territories and islands she had acquired since 1880. The Army study was even more pessimistic, fearing the nation itself might be decimated.[92]

Great Britain, it will be recalled, had been rescued from her somewhat similar position in early 1941, certainly in respect of the attrition of merchant shipping, chiefly by the shift of German resources eastwards in the Russian campaign, and US aid and subsequently a formal alliance. Japan had no such geopolitical prospects. Overwhelming American power was about to be unleashed against her defensive perimeter of islands, and her one ally, Germany, was too hard-pressed to contemplate helping her.

Surrender was, however, out of the question. The nation had been indoctrinated too well in the martial values of the samurai; too much patriotic capital had been invested in the ethic of victory or suicide; the empire was too large; too many hundreds of thousands had already died for the Emperor. If he were to capitulate now it would appear that the sacrifice had been vain and that he was failing his people. To preserve his divine power and that of the cabal around the throne it was necessary that the struggle continue. Millions more would have to die until, in utter war weariness, the people could be persuaded that they had failed their Emperor; then he might surrender to spare them further suffering. Thus, while army and navy chiefs planned defence to the death, a so-called 'peace faction' was formed under a former prime minister of the princely family to lay a false trail to bamboozle the American conquerors and preserve the power of the throne after eventual surrender.[93]

In tactical terms, Great Britain's deliverance from the U-boat threat to her merchant shipping had been due chiefly to radar. Japan could not hope for similar relief, indeed radar worked against her. The primitive apparatus she had begun to develop in 1941 was not yet operational and would not in any case begin to match the centimetric sets fitted in new US submarines. These could pick up large ships out to 30,000 yards or more, far beyond the horizon, presenting them as points of luminescence on a 'plan position indicator' (PPI) screen instead of the earlier A-scope; the PPI provided a picture of all vessels within range, spread out in their relative positions as if on a chart. Their range and bearing could be read off rapidly for use in plotting course, speed and pattern of zigizag without recourse to approximations of 'angle on the bow' and estimated speed from visual observations. Thus, away from air patrols, US submarines could remain on the surface even in daylight and make an 'end around' below the horizon in perfect confidence of their target's rate and direction of progress, and submerge ahead to carry out a standard attack.

On dark nights radar plotting gave greater advantages over an enemy without radar. Having detected a target or convoy, a submarine could shadow while plotting the base course, time the alterations of course for the zigzag, and also determine which of the luminous 'pips' on the screen were escorts. Ned Beach has described how they would then select an approach based on the direction of the moon or a dark land mass or cloud, the formation of ships and the position of the escorts, and begin the attack run as the enemy completed a zig, or sometimes in anticipation of the next zig. Whether closing fast or slowly, all four diesels would be put on line and they would run in on a 'long swoop' calculated to show minimum silhouette while passing astern of the nearest escort: 'it was pretty heady stuff, with radar information coming in steadily, the plotting parties regularly announcing development of the situation, our fire control group tense as bowstrings, ready for unexpected changes . . .'[94]

They tried to come within a mile, ideally 1,000 yards, of the targets before firing; and once all 'fish' were on their way, would attempt to retire without alerting the enemy and so provoking an alteration of course which might nullify their calculations.

With such advanced weapon systems, technologically superior to the defence, and with intelligence from decrypts of what US codebreakers termed the 'Maru code' detailing convoy routes and schedules,[95] it is abundantly clear that a concentrated campaign against merchant shipping could have cut off Japan from her southern sources of supply and crippled her war effort in a relatively short time and, as suggested earlier, at a relatively low human cost. Clear as it is in retrospect, Nimitz's and MacArthur's staff were intent on their own plans for direct assaults, and Lockwood and Christie complied. Moreover, although tankers had been moved up the order of target priority, Washington still placed capital ships at the head of the list. This appears the more perverse since no Japanese capital ship had been sunk by submarine in two years of war; indeed the only major Japanese warship sunk by any submarine had been the cruiser Kako, despatched by the S44 in August 1942.

At Nimitz's daily conferences Lockwood provided the submarine force input, tying his command tactically into the C-in-C's plans; thus submarines continued to be used as they had been from the start, in reconnaissance for the fleet, in patrols off Japanese fleet bases and island targets, and in the new tasks of weather-reporting, photo-reconnaissance of potential invasion beaches and 'lifeguarding' – rescuing downed aircrew from the sea off carrier strike targets. This proved particularly valuable for morale and conserving trained pilots. In the south-west Pacific area MacArthur continued to demand submarines for special tasks. In both theatres the campaign against merchant shipping was pursued almost by default after military requirements had been met, and boats on patrol were still diverted on Ultra intelligence against fast and elusive enemy task forces. There was no Dönitz to argue for an all-out tonnage war on the slowest and easiest targets in the most profitable areas. This is the more surprising since the tonnage credited to submarines should have suggested that the Japanese merchant fleet had been reduced to about half its pre-war size.

The much smaller, yet increasing volume actually sunk had, as mentioned, been sufficient to alarm the Japanese, and in November 1943 the haphazard system of local escort commands was consolidated under Admiral Koshiro Oikawa into a single organization named the Combined or Grand Escort Fleet with headquarters in Tokyo. That it had taken almost two years of war for the Japanese to take the protection of merchant shipping seriously is a comment on the ineffectiveness of the US submarine commands, in particular their arthritic reaction to the torpedo failures at the root of the problem, as much as on the uncoordinated Japanese command structure and fixation on decisive battle. But still the best destroyers and the most ambitious destroyer commanders remained with the fleet; Oikawa could glean only fifteen older destroyers, a few *Kaibō-kans* entering service from earlier programmes and an insufficient number of sub-chasers, coast defence vessels, patrol boats, converted minesweepers and trawlers which had been attached to local escort groups. All lacked radar and there was no escort doctrine, nor a rigorous training programme such as Allied navies found essential to weld individual vessels into a team; in any case shortage of escorts meant they could not be spared from operational duties.

There was also a shortage of officers to act as convoy commodores, and older, retired naval captains were recalled to lead the merchantmen, with mixed, often unsatisfactory results. Communications were a particularly weak point, both between ships and between headquarters ashore and escort commanders. In December additional aircraft were provided for the 901st Air Flotilla, formed specifically for patrol and escort for convoys, but problems of communication between escorts and aircraft were not solved; messages had to be routed through the aircraft's base.[96] This was in marked contrast to the easy radio telephone links between ships in Allied escort groups, and between US aircraft and submarines on lifeguard duty, another symptom of the huge gap in electronic and communications technology that had opened between US and Japanese forces since the attack on Pearl Harbor. The Japanese had scarcely moved forward while US industry, aided by British scientific input, had raced ahead.

Another sign of the technology gap was to appear in the spring of 1944 when the first Japanese escorts were fitted with radar detectors; like those initially employed in German U-boats, these were simple warning devices unable to hint at bearing or range of the source of the emissions.[97] Radar itself was not to be provided for escorts until towards the end of 1944, and then it barely reached the standard of the earliest Allied sets and there were constant problems with components. A post-war US technical mission concluded that in the field of radio, radar and sonar, Japan had been a victim of her own sense of power and superiority. Specifically, success in the pre-Pacific war operations in China had 'convinced them of the superiority of their equipment'; it was only after their drive south into the tropics that reports had begun to indicate the need for specialized component design, tropicalization and better performance overall:

> Thus in the summer and fall of 1943, Japanese engineers began the study of component design to meet the conditions existing in the field. By the end of the war no equipment to meet the new requirements had yet been produced ... components while well made, closely resembled those available to amateur radio in the United States in the early and middle 1930s.[98]

The shortfall in numbers of escorts and in doctrine, training, communications and radar detection equipment resulted quite often, to judge from post-war interrogation of Japanese escort officers, in utter confusion.[99] Meanwhile, conversions had been ordered of a seaplane carrier and five N.Y.K. passenger liners into escort carriers; the first were already in service but were employed ferrying aircraft to Truk, Rabaul and other advanced bases. When in early 1944 they began sailing with important convoys, US submarines picked them out as priority targets and few survived long.

Similarly, lack of radar or radar detectors fatally handicapped Japanese submarines; they had become as vulnerable to aircraft and hunter-killer groups as the U-boats in the Atlantic; and since Japanese signals intelligence could not provide advance warning of US movements and targets, they could not even be placed defensively in their favourite 'ambush' lines. When, on 19 November, Nimitz began his offensive with strikes on Makin and Tarawa islands in the Gilberts chain – 'Operation Galvanic' – Vice-Admiral Takeo Takagi, who had just succeeded Marquis Komatsu in command of the Sixth (Submarine) Fleet, ordered one RO-class and eight I-class boats to the area. However, he shifted them so often in reaction to enemy moves or in efforts to create the impression of greater numbers he exposed them to attack on the surface and caused total confusion – so it appeared to Lt.-Cdr. Nobukiyo Nambu of I174, one of only three of the boats to survive the mission.[100]

That she did so was a miracle. After an emergency dive for the bright searchlight of an approaching aircraft Nambu surfaced, only to sight the bow wave of a destroyer approaching at speed. He went under again, the bridge watch, as in all large Japanese submarines, sliding down a metal pole like firemen to the control room. The subsequent depth-charge attack knocked out the electric power, and to maintain trim and prevent flooding chain gangs shifted water from compartments in drums. Next day, at the limit of submerged endurance, Nambu was forced to surface to fight it out, but had barely opened the hatch and assembled the bridge watch before an aircraft forced him down again. After a while he came up but the aircraft was still there. He was fortunate to escape in a rain squall.

When he eventually reached base, he reported to Vice-Admiral Takagi that it was suicide for submarines without radar and unable to remain submerged for longer than forty hours to operate in the vicinity of US anti-submarine forces. Takagi replied that even if boats failed to return they were nonetheless playing their part – an echo of Dönitz's rationale to the U-boat arm.[101]

The only submarine to score a success against the Gilberts invasion forces was *I175* under Lt.-Cdr. Sunao Tabata. Heading for Makin Island in the early morning of 24 November, he sighted the escort carrier *Liscome Bay* and succeeded in closing undetected and firing a salvo, one torpedo of which hit and detonated the bomb magazines. She erupted in violent explosions and sank in little over twenty minutes with heavy loss of life. She was one of only five warships of importance sunk by Japanese submarines in the whole of 1943; the others were three destroyers and the submarine *Corvina*, sunk by *I176* while patrolling off the naval base at Truk on 16 November – the only US submarine to be sunk by a Japanese, submarine during the war. Those boats assigned to commerce raiding sank forty-two Allied merchantmen aggregating 254,900 tons over the year, almost half in the Indian Ocean. In return, twenty-seven submarines had been lost, and although thirty-seven new boats were completed in Japanese yards during the year, it was a very poor exchange rate.[102]

US submarine losses were far lower. Before Nimitz's offensive in November the three submarine commands had lost only four fleet boats each. From the largest force at Pearl Harbor three had almost certainly been the victims of minefields north-east of the main Japanese island, Honshu,[103] while *Wahoo*, as suggested, had probably been caught by an aircraft while coming out of the Sea of Japan. Meanwhile, new boats from home had increased the force to such an extent that by October Lockwood had been able to experiment with wolfpacks. This was in response to a directive from Admiral King in Washington. If King was influenced by Dönitz's tactics, then being tested for the final time, this was not how Lockwood's system was planned. Instead of huge groups spread by signal from headquarters ashore in reconnaissance lines to detect convoys, then home in on beacon signals from a shadowing boat, the US pack was a tight group of three boats under the tactical command of a group leader embarked in one of them. Since they were often directed to targets by Subpac headquarters on Ultra intelligence, the purpose of forming the packs seems to have been to achieve co-ordinated attacks to split and draw off escorts as much as to find targets in the first place.

Although mooted before the war, group tactics had not been adopted in the US service largely because of inadequate communications and the danger of collision or friendly-fire disasters. Short-range 'talk between ships' (TBS) radio telephones as now employed in US and Allied escort groups and a system of signalling with radar pulses seemed to have solved the communications problem, but anxiety about confusion and friendly fire remained. Thus, instead of free-for-all, simultaneous attacks to swamp the defence with as many boats as possible, as Dönitz had intended from the first, and frequently achieved, the tactics devised by Lockwood's staff, principally a genial giant, Captain John 'Babe' Brown, who had led the first group of three submarines into the Sea of Japan in July 1943, called for a formal pattern of successive attacks. Two of the group would stand off on either flank of the convoy as the first attack boat ran in, fired and then dropped astern to 'trail' and reload, ready to pick up damaged ships and stragglers, while one of the flankers ran in. It was hoped that ships trying to escape her attack would turn towards the opposite flanker, still standing off. Such was the theory. Brown had established a training programme which came to be termed 'Convoy College'; it began on the open-air dance-floor of the submarine officers' mess at Pearl Harbor, a polished black-and-white chequered space surrounded by palms. Like Captain Gilbert Roberts's tactical school in Liverpool, each of the three boats' fire-control parties would occupy one corner of the floor behind a screen, the COs manoeuvring their 'submarines' on the basis of signals received until after 'contact', when they were permitted brief glimpses of targets moved over the chequered floor by Brown and his assistants from the fourth corner. After tactical games, the group would go to sea and practise dummy runs on US convoys approaching the Hawaiian islands.[104]

Despite the excellence of the boats' radar, and hence, provided the radar had been properly calibrated, the accuracy of their plotting once in contact, difficulties in communication and co-ordinating navigational positions when chasing proved too great. Seldom knowing precisely where their consorts were, the COs of the first packs failed to achieve the set-piece manoeuvres in which they had been trained, and it was felt that equal or better results could have been gained by boats patrolling separately. It was also felt that the group leader embarked was superfluous and it would be more effective, if packs were to be continued, to adopt Dönitz's method of shore control. This had been ruled out in planning in order to keep signals to a minimum. Lockwood continued to reject the idea for that reason. In Australia, meanwhile, Christie and Fife had not organized formal packs, but both directed boats in adjacent patrol areas to co-operate when it seemed appropriate.

Since the 'Maru code' had been broken in early 1943, the previous somewhat informal liaison between the codebreakers and submarine headquarters had been established on a regular basis. At Pearl Harbor Lockwood's operations officer, Cdr. Richard Voge, would take himself to the Combat Intelligence unit of Frupac each morning at about nine with a chart on which he had plotted estimated positions of all his boats on patrol. While he read through the decrypts accumulated in the previous twenty-four hours, the tracks and routes of all Japanese convoys known to be at sea would be added to his chart. In addition, a direct line bypassing all telephone exchanges had been set up between Combat Intelligence and the operations room at Subpac headquarters, through which immediate information was passed, particularly signals from Japanese ships reporting they had been attacked by submarine, and in the other direction reports from US submarines after they had attacked. In this way both intelligence and operations kept themselves up to the minute, and an officer was on duty at both ends of this highly confidential line twenty-four hours a day.

'There were nights', wrote Cdr. W.J. Holmes, the principal intelligence liaison with the submarine staff from the beginning, 'when nearly every American submarine in the central Pacific was working on the basis of information derived from cryptanalysis.'[105] The same might, of course, have been said of U-boats in the Atlantic during the long periods when B-Dienst was on top form. The difference in the Pacific was that Japanese cryptanalysts had not cracked US naval ciphers and hence never knew where submarines were being directed. Moreover, Japanese DF information was considered too secret to be disseminated, and so convoys were seldom re-routed on up-to-the-minute information. Each month Japanese signals intelligence drew up an elaborate chart of where US submarines *had* been. The best the escort commands could do with this 'statistical analysis' was to try and predict where enemy submarines were likely to be.[106] It appears that signals sent by Japanese ships under attack or hit by submarines were also treated as secret, or the staff system was so dislocated that warnings of enemy activity were not sent to relevant escort commands. Ships and convoys often sailed straight into areas where other ships had just been sunk.

Prior to Nimitz's 'Galvanic' offensive against the Gilberts, Lockwood despatched several submarines to patrol off the Japanese naval base at Truk. They were not organized as a wolfpack, but he sent Cdr. John Cromwell – who was to receive his promotion to captain during the patrol – to form a pack and co-ordinate attacks should Japanese forces sortie in response to the invasion. Cromwell was one of Lockwood's divisional commanders; as such he stood watches in the operations room and had taken calls on the confidential line to Combat Intelligence. He knew all there was to know about Ultra as applied to submarine dispositions, and the plans for 'Operation Galvanic'. He was also an old friend of Holmes, and a few days before departing he went shopping with Holmes's wife for Christmas presents for his family, leaving them with her to mail at the appropriate time while he was away. On 5 November he sailed in the *Sculpin* under Cdr. Fred Connaway; after topping up with fuel two days later at Johnston atoll, Connaway set course for his assigned billet between the atolls of Oroluk and Ponape east of Truk.

On the 16th a signal in the *Maru* code detailing a convoy due to sail eastwards from Truk to the Marshall Islands was decrypted at Frupac and Holmes passed the information on the confidential line to Voge in the operations room at Subpac; that night Voge had a signal sent to Connaway, directing him to intercept the convoy. He did so two nights later by radar, and made an end around at full power, submerging at dawn on the 19th and setting up an attack. His periscope was seen, however, and the convoy zigged towards him, forcing him deep. When he judged the ships had passed over the horizon he surfaced, intending to make another end around, but found a destroyer waiting behind for him only 3 miles away. He went deep again, subjected to a depth-charge attack as he descended. This time he remained under for several hours until at about midday he ordered the boat brought up to periscope depth. As she rose, the depth gauge jammed at 125 feet and the diving officer unwittingly planed her up above the surface.

The destroyer, still waiting, attacked before he could regain depth, and shallow charges rocked the boat in a storm of explosions so close that they distorted the pressure hull, disabled the planes and steering gear, and started leaks. Deciding that the only hope lay in coming up and fighting it out with the gun, Connaway ordered the tanks blown and the crew to battle surface stations.

The destroyer was close and hit her with her first salvoes, killing Connaway on the bridge, the gunnery officer on deck by the gun, and the exec. in the conning tower, and shattering the main induction for the diesels. With no hope of escape, the submarine's senior surviving officer, Lt. G.E. Brown, gave orders to scuttle and abandon ship. Cromwell, knowing Japanese methods of interrogation, said he knew too much; he would stay with the ship. After the surviving crew had donned lifejackets and jumped into the sea, and the vents had been opened, Cromwell and one junior officer, perhaps preferring death to the notorious cruelty of the enemy, together with ten crew men and the dead, rode *Sculpin* down for her last dive.[107]

That afternoon the destroyer *Yamagumo*, having picked up forty-two survivors and thrown one who was seriously wounded back into the sea, reported sinking a submarine. The message was decrypted at Frupac and passed to Combat Intelligence, thence to Subpac operations. Little attention was paid. Although the position given was close to where *Sculpin* should have met the Japanese convoy, Japanese escorts usually claimed success after attacking. Some concern was felt nonetheless when *Sculpin* failed to report, and it increased after Lockwood ordered Cromwell to form a pack with two other boats on the 29th, for no rendezvous orders were transmitted to the other two. She was not heard from again. When Holmes's wife posted Cromwell's Christmas presents to his family, Holmes himself was certain his friend was dead, although *Sculpin* was not officially posted missing presumed lost until 30 December. After the war, when the facts of Cromwell's decision became known from survivors, he was awarded the Congressional Medal of Honor.

The first award of this supreme distinction in the submarine service had been made earlier that year to Cdr. Howard Gilmore of the *Growler*, also posthumously, also after a gun fight. Closing what he believed to be a patrol vessel at battle surface stations on 7 February, Gilmore had misread her course and collided at speed. *Growler* rolled over almost on her beam ends with the violence of the impact, and as they parted the enemy swept the bridge with machine-gun fire, killing the assistant officer of the deck and a lookout and wounding Gilmore. Shouting 'Clear the bridge!' he watched the surviving members of the watch scramble below, then as the exec. waited for him to follow, he roared, 'Take her down!' After appreciable hesitation the order was obeyed. Gilmore was left to float off as the boat submerged. *Growler* survived and was to make another six patrols and claim nine vessels including a destroyer, a frigate and two tankers before she was lost in November 1944. Gilmore's last order, 'Take her down!' entered submarine service lore as, over a century earlier, the wounded Captain Lawrence of the frigate *Chesapeake* had entered US naval legend with his exhortation, 'Don't give up the ship!'

After *Sculpin's* loss her forty-one survivors were taken to Truk where they were interrogated for ten days in the Japanese manner with prisoners. They were then embarked for Japan on two escort carriers, *Chuyo* and *Unyo*, returning home with the light carrier *Zuiho* and escorts after ferrying aircraft to the base. A signal detailing their route was decrypted at Frupac at the end of November and Holmes, on duty in Combat Intelligence, left a message in the daily 'book' for Voge's attention during his morning visit. Voge alerted three submarines along the track, *Skate* off Truk, *Gunnel* off the island of Iwo Jima, and *Sailfish* off the main Japanese island, Honshu. The first two missed the fast-moving targets, and as the force neared Honshu on the night of 3 December a typhoon raged; sheets of rain and crests of immense seas were swept by winds up to 50 knots.

A few miles ahead of the carriers and their escorting heavy cruisers and destroyers, the *Sailfish* under Lt.-Cdr. R.E.M. Ward rode the surface tumult. The officer of the deck and lookouts, secured to the bridge rails with canvas safety belts, were physically exhausted, buffeted, bruised, and soaked through. Their faces stung, their eyes smarted, their vision, even when the boat rose momentarily clear of the seething water, was limited by screens of rain and driven spray to the next sheer wall advancing upon them. Below, in the red lighting of the conning tower, the radar watchkeeper braced himself against the gyrations and stared at green fluorescent clutter on the screen, straining to discern permanent echoes amongst the sea return. He thought he had one. The pip hardened and brightened as the beam swept through it, and beyond were another two, three. He called, 'Captain to the conn! Radar contact!'

Ward, wearing red goggles to preserve his night vision, hauled himself quickly up the ladder and steadied himself to peer at the screen while the fire-control party, provided with a bearing and range to the nearest target, 9,000 yards distant, began the plot. Ward ordered flank speed and gave the helmsman a course to close. As the four diesels worked up to full power *Sailfish* began to slide through rather than over the tumultuous seas. What had been extreme discomfort for the bridge watch became a torment of alternating flood and flailing wind and spume. An effective lookout was impossible, as was a standard night surface attack. Ward ordered diving stations and took her down to 40 feet. As yet there was no night periscope with built-in radar; the decision to develop such a refined instrument combining optics and electronics in a single standard periscope tube was only made that month and the tested product was not ready for operational use until November 1944;[108] nonetheless, by riding at 40 feet the radar antenna was well above what in normal conditions would have been the surface, and Ward closed by radar. At 00.12, when the screen showed the nearest large target distant 2,100 yards, he fired a salvo from his four bow tubes.

The Japanese force, which had been warned of a submarine in the area, had been zigzagging at 18 knots, but as the storm intensified the danger was discounted, and shortly after midnight the zigzag had been abandoned. Minutes later the *Chuyo* was hit by a torpedo. Another torpedo may have been detonated by the tumbling sea for Ward heard what he believed were two hits as he went deep to avoid an escort which had been only 400 yards from him when he fired. That any torpedo had maintained its set depth and course in such conditions was testimony to the new reliability of the standard Mark XIV.

He reloaded in the quiet below. When he came up shortly before 02.00 the typhoon still howled and high, wild slopes rose on every hand, but he was able to pick up the Japanese force again on radar. One of the larger pips was separated from the rest and moving more slowly. He closed this one at his best speed on the surface, scarcely 12 knots, and shortly before 06.00, as the dark began to give way to the first hint of dawn, he was only 2 miles off. He continued to close as the eastern sky lightened until at 3,100 yards he felt he could wait no longer and fired a second salvo from the bow tubes, again by radar plot. Counting the seconds, he saw a great flash of fire split the horizon in the direction of the unseen target, and heard two hits. Whatever she was, the ship began firing wildly and he dived to reload.

The *Chuyo* was stopped completely by this second attack. The *Unyo* was ordered to her assistance and the destroyers, which had become separated, were instructed to combine to neutralize the submarine. It was hard enough for them to find the crippled carrier, and Ward, after reloading again and rising to periscope depth, was able to make slow progress towards her, impeded only by the difficulties of maintaining depth below the volatile surface. At 09.00 he fired his third salvo at the carrier, which he had at last seen, heaving with no way on. The range was 1,700 yards and intervening seas blocked his view as detonations from the salvo completed her destruction. The sonar operator reported tremendous breaking-up noises through the hydrophones. Ward could not possibly have known it, but twenty-one of the forty-one survivors of the *Sculpin* were lost with the Japanese crew as she sank.

The remaining twenty members of the *Sculpin's* men were landed from the *Unyo* when she made port and taken to a navy prison camp at Ofuna 10 miles south of Yokohama for further interrogation, whence they were sent to work in copper mines at Ashio. After the war, starving and emaciated, they were liberated and were able to provide the hitherto unknown details of the loss of their submarine.

In the meantime, Ward suffered heavy damage in a surprise attack from the air, but made extemporary repairs and afterwards sank two *Marus* before returning to Pearl Harbor. Lockwood greeted him warmly. The *Chuyo* had been an escort carrier conversion from a 20,000-ton liner, nonetheless a carrier, and the first to be sunk by a US submarine. She was also the first major warship to be sunk by a fleet submarine (it will be recalled that the cruiser *Kako* had been sunk by the *S44*). Lockwood commended Ward for 'one of the most outstanding patrols of the war';[109] he was decorated with the Navy Cross and the *Sailfish* received the President's Unit Citation. Equal admiration was expressed in Japan. An analysis of the attack on the *Chuyo* was circulated to Japanese submarine officers as an example of what could be achieved with courage, persistence and skill.[110] It does not detract from Ward's extraordinary feat over more than nine hours in extreme conditions to note that it would have been beyond any Japanese CO since none had the benefit of radar; Ward had not actually seen his target until about an hour before he hit her with his final salvo.

The third formal wolfpack consisting of the *Tullibee*, *Haddock* and *Halibut* departed Pearl Harbor on 14 December 1943, the first two showing a new grey profile, the result of camouflage experiments carried out by a Naval Reserve artist sent to the Pacific in the summer. *Halibut* under Galantin retained the all-black paintwork with which the submarine service had started the war. Galantin was soon to become a convert to the new colour scheme –

under which decks and horizontal surfaces viewed from above remained black – for he found the others sighted his boat first when they met at sea.[111] *Halibut* also rode somewhat higher than the other two, a portion of whose main ballast tanks had been converted to carry oil fuel, allowing them 24,000 extra gallons – 50 tons – for the passage to the patrol area, and hence longer endurance in the war zone. Once a fuel ballast tank was empty its fuel lines would be blanked off by the engineers, the air lines reconnected and the flood and vent valves unlocked. Most fleet submarines were to be converted to this system.

After the comments of the leaders of the first two packs, no separate group commander was embarked; the senior skipper, Lt.-Cdr. Charles Brindupke of the *Tullibee* was in tactical command. However, the over-formal attack tactics had not been abandoned; the three skippers and their fire-control parties had been through Convoy College and a two-day exercise at sea against a US convoy. They were eager to test their skills in action and outdo their predecessors. It was not to be, in large part because warships remained the magnet; the group patrol area was in the Marianas close to an advanced base at Saipan and on the warship route between Japan and the major base at Truk; moreover they were to be directed by Ultra intelligence against warship targets.

After topping up with fuel at Midway the group steered westwards on the surface, meeting gales and violent head seas which restricted them to 5 knots and made life miserable, especially for the many youngsters on their first patrols. Buckets for sick were wedged in control rooms and conning towers; the sleeping quarters began to smell of 'salt water, sweat and vomit and unwashed bodies'.[112] One of *Tullibee's* lookouts had his binoculars jammed into his midriff with such violence when he was forced by a wave against his confining guard rail that he died after being carried below.

When Christmas came, messrooms and wardrooms were hung with decorations; the smell of roast turkey from the galleys mixed with the less enticing odours. One of *Halibut's* junior officers, who had broken all regulations by smuggling a bottle of sparkling wine aboard, produced it in the wardroom. After opening it and drinking a toast to 'loved ones now far distant', Galantin punished the offender by restricting him to the ship for the next thirty days. Later, the chief of the boat disguised as Santa Claus distributed presents provided and gift-wrapped by the ladies of Honolulu.

The first Ultra came on 2 January 1944 after the weather had abated. Brindupke disposed the boats at 6-mile intervals across the track of an I-class submarine. It appeared on schedule making 15 knots on a steady course, but the wakes of the Mark XIV torpedoes Brindupke fired from 3,000 yards were spotted by the bridge watch in time for her to evade and then dive. The following week, having come across nothing more, Brindupke called a conference aboard *Tullibee*. The three submarines met at the assigned rendezvous and closed to allow Galantin and Lt.-Cdr. John Roach of the *Haddock* to be taken off in a rubber dinghy to the *Tullibee*. There they conferred on future search strategy over charts laid out on the wardroom table – the first such mid-ocean conference by any US submarine commanders, indeed the first time any COs had left their boats at sea.

On the new patrol patterns Galantin sighted the giant battleship *Yamato* over the horizon and brought in the other two prepared for a co-ordinated attack, but at dusk, before they could close, the battleship made a radical alteration of course and disappeared. Later Roach sighted a force of two carriers. They approached so rapidly he was forced to dive before he could raise contact with the others, and he made a lone attack, firing at the larger carrier but missing and instead hitting the smaller *Unyo* with two torpedoes. Although severely damaged, she was able to limp in to Saipan. *Halibut* was now running low on fuel and Brindupke released Galantin while he and Roach watched Saipan for the *Unyo* to emerge. Brindupke sank a small net tender, but anti-submarine activity was so heavy that the *Unyo* was able to come out undetected towards the end of the month and make it safely home under tow. As Galantin had no success either, the pack which had started with such hopes returned with the lowest score of any to date, one tender of 500 tons, although of course the escort carrier had been severely damaged.

Despite the disappointing showing by the pack, January 1944 was a record month: the submarines sank fifty-three *Marus* totalling over 280,000 tons and three small warships; Japanese shipping losses from all causes amounted to over 350,000 tons,[113] a figure portending disaster. The commander of the Grand Escort Fleet, Admiral Oikawa, had earlier proposed defending shipping on the main route to the south by laying an immense minefield from southern Japan along the Nansei Shoto chain of islands to Formosa and routing all shipping to Singapore and the Dutch Indies inside the barrier. Now his plan was approved. The field was begun in February.

Meanwhile, Lockwood had spread six submarines in patrols off Truk prior to the next phase of Nimitz's advance, the invasion of the islands in the Marshalls group. The boats' primary mission was to detect Japanese forces emerging from the base; they were instructed to report before attacking – although the former undoubtedly precluded the latter. Admiral Koga gave them no opportunity. Intent on preserving his fleet for the final battle further westwards, where he would have the support of more extensive shore-based air forces, he declined to contest the landings, instead retiring homewards. The Marshalls were secured by the first week in February and Lockwood gave instructions for the establishment of an advanced base at Kwajalein and a rest camp for submariners between patrols on a nearby island. Next, in preparation for a carrier air strike planned on Truk itself, he re-deployed his boats, together with three from Fife's Brisbane command, in an arc to the west of the island, hoping to catch shipping fleeing from the anchorage; he also placed two closer in on lifeguard duty, now standard practice.

Stationed in the arc directly west of Truk was a new boat, *Tang*, first command of Morton's former exec., 'Dick' O'Kane, who had been posted to her prior to *Wahoo*'s last, fatal patrol. O'Kane's hunger to engage the enemy, tempered in action by a cool brain and steady nerve, have been described. Morton had called him the bravest man he had ever met. His aggression had been enhanced, if that were possible, by the loss of his former skipper and shipmates in the *Wahoo*; according to Ned Beach, he had a mission to avenge them.[114] He was also extremely competent: Galantin, who had served with him before the war, was to describe him long afterwards as an 'innovative non-conformist' and 'the best man to leave to his own devices in the shipyard when something had to be done in a hurry'.[115] Beach refers to his insistence on perfection. Added to these qualities was the priceless experience he had gained under Morton's command. These attributes, aided by the more reliable torpedoes and the excellence of the new radar, were to raise him to the top-scoring US submarine CO of the war in terms of numbers of ships sunk. He took little time to establish himself.

On 17 February, after the carrier strike on Truk which devastated the base's air squadrons and naval auxiliaries and merchantmen in the harbour – though not submarines since they dived – he detected a convoy by radar and that night in a submerged attack sank his first *Maru*. It could be said he had already sunk many since he had been at the periscope in all Morton's attacks. Several other skippers followed Morton's practice, but O'Kane was more conventional in this respect and made his own attack observations.

Next, directed to the west of Saipan, he picked up another

convoy after a carrier strike on the island on 22 February, closed at night and sank two more freighters from close range in surface attacks. US submarines were now fitted with torpedo-bearing transmitters (TBTs) for night surface attack similar to the UZO-posts on German U-boats. Ordinary watch-keeping binoculars slotted into the fixture; the observer, when on target, pressed a button and the bearing was read off in the conning tower below. It was not as refined as the UZO apparatus, but nor was it so necessary since during a radar approach it was little more than a check on radar bearings. It could become important, however, if an escort which was not being plotted by radar interfered in the action. O'Kane found another convoy on the 24th and sank two more freighters by night, the second in a submerged attack from 500 yards. Typically, he described the explosions from three torpedoes as 'wonderful, throwing japs [sic] and other debris above the belching smoke'.[116] On return from this patrol he flew five small rising-sun pennants and claimed 42,000 tons in total, an estimate that was to be halved in post-war analysis.

During February 1944, US submarines as a whole sank over 250,000 tons of merchant shipping, slightly more than the January total, but when sinkings from carrier aircraft and other forces were added the aggregate was higher than that of January, coming to over 500,000 tons.[117] Admiral Oikawa of the Grand Escort Fleet, thoroughly alarmed by the figures, held back ships in port and began forming larger convoys organized in set formations; hitherto individual convoy commanders had devised their own methods of sailing and screening.[118]

Submarines were the main threat to shipping in home waters and the routes south, and Oikawa planned to sweep convoy lanes 20 miles wide with aircraft fitted with a new submarine detector termed Jikitanchiki, a device which could locate boats over 400 feet below the surface by the disturbance their metal mass caused in the earth's magnetic field. In this development Japanese scientists were scarcely behind the Americans, whose magnetic airborne detector (MAD) had recently become operational. On first detecting a magnetic anomaly, the Jikitanchiki automatically dropped a slick of coloured aluminium, at the same time alerting the pilot with a red light. The pilot flew on until, passing out of the magnetic disturbance, the apparatus dropped another slick, after which he flew back to make a second pass at right angles to his initial course and half way between the two slicks on the water. During this pass the apparatus dropped two more differently coloured slicks at the perimeter of the magnetic disturbance. The submarine was deemed to be at the centre of the triangle formed by the first two slicks and the last one. However, allowance had to be made for the drift of the aluminium between aircraft and water according to altitude and speed; this was done with a table. A single aircraft could complete the process in about fifteen minutes; two could track a submerged submarine, although this was extremely rare due to a shortage of planes and the amount of training time required.

The *Jikitanchiki* apparatus was to undergo gradual improvement until an expert pilot flying very low, 40 feet above the waves, could locate submarines down to 800 feet;[119] this was way below the depth at which most fleet submarines would collapse and was at the extreme limit of the latest *Balao* class, whose operating depth had been increased to 400 feet – one of the best-kept secrets of the Pacific war. A submarine's theoretical point of collapse was about twice the operating depth, which in the case of existing boats was 300 feet.[120] Once a submarine was located, the pilot would drop a depth bomb and mark the spot with a floating flare, then attempt to alert a surface vessel visually; as mentioned, the problems with air-to-ship or ship-to-ship radio communications were never solved.

There were not enough aircraft fitted with magnetic detectors, nor sufficient fuel for Oikawa's plan for swept routes to be realized; it would in any case have been an extravagantly inefficient use of resources. Instead these specialized planes either swept ahead of important convoys or were ordered up if a submarine were reported, when they confined their hunt to that submarine.

Another ingenious airborne device which was tried out by the Japanese at this time was a torpedo designed to be dropped 200 metres ahead of a submerged submarine, when it was supposed to spiral downwards in decreasing circles. It proved a failure – unsurprisingly, since it was armed with a contact exploder – and was soon abandoned. Patrol and escort aircraft relied on 550 lb. bombs adapted from standard aerial bombs and time-fused to detonate after sinking 265, 150 or 40 feet, the latter for use against submarines near a convoy at periscope depth or those which had just submerged after being sighted on the surface. It was calculated that they had to detonate within 40 feet to be certain of sinking a submarine. Smaller planes carried 130 lb. bombs which needed to score a direct hit.

The real disadvantage suffered by the Japanese escort forces was their lack of radar. Surface escorts were about to be equipped with radar detectors, but escort and patrol planes of the 901st Naval Air

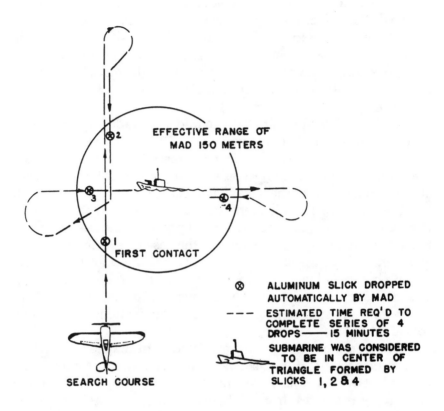

Track flown by MAD-equipped plane after initial submarine contact

Flotilla were not fitted until the end of the year, and as mentioned the detectors were non-directional and could do no more than give a general alert. Radar itself was not available for escorts until the autumn of 1944, and it was the end of that year before most were equipped. It was then not equal to visual observation in daylight; aircraft used it only at night.[121]

Despite these shortcomings, the merchant shipping lost to US submarines fell by over half in March to 121,000 tons, and further to 98,000 tons in April. This was due in part to Oikawa's measures for fewer, larger convoys, hence to the numbers of ships held in port while they were gathered, but mainly to Lockwood's and Christie's support for fleet operations, now extending from the Palaus to the Marianas as Nimitz co-operated with MacArthur in a two-pronged advance towards Japan. And the lure of the great fleet units remained, not only for Lockwood's and Christie's staffs, but also for the submarine COs themselves. John Scott of the *Tunny*, who had made the brilliant attack on three fleet carriers from between the columns the previous year, only to be betrayed by torpedo prematures, allowed a string of freighters out of Palau on 29 March without attacking – strictly against orders. A carrier strike was due on the 30th and he anticipated the emergence of capital ships which had been based there since the strike on Truk. Koga's flagship, the giant *Musashi*, obliged that evening of the 29th. Scott closed to within 2,000 yards and launched a six-torpedo salvo beneath her screen of destroyers. The tracks were spotted from one of these and warnings passed by flag hoists and signal lamp which gave the great ship time to swing. She sustained only one damaging but not disabling hit right forward in the chain locker and was repaired inside three weeks.

After Palau the carrier forces struck Woleai 600 miles to the east. The *Harder* under Cdr. Samuel Dealey, on patrol off the island, was called in to rescue a downed airman. Finding him on the beach, Dealey lay to close off the reef while volunteers went in with a rubber dinghy, paying out a line secured aboard as they worked through breakers over the coral to the smooth water beyond. Above, naval aircraft swooped back and forth to restrain the Japanese ashore and subdue their fire. This brazen rescue, which was completed successfully without loss, became celebrated in submarine lore.

Two weeks later, a destroyer came to hunt the *Harder*. Instead of evading, Dealey approached her and, like Morton earlier, remained at periscope depth as the enemy, locating him with sonar, ran in to attack. He allowed the range to close to 900 yards, then fired a salvo 'down the throat' which caught her as she slewed with full rudder across the track. Rent by explosions, her smoking remains sank in minutes, depth-charges, already armed, exploding beneath the survivors in the water. Dealey's report, 'Range 900 yards. Commenced firing. Expended four torpedoes and one Jap destroyer',[122] also entered submarine service legend.

Another of more than twenty submarines tied to US fleet movements was O'Kane's *Tang*. After patrolling off the Palaus, O'Kane was directed to lifeguard duty for a second carrier strike on Truk at the end of April. Despite chafing at the mission, he performed with his customary dash and rescued twenty-two of the twenty-eight American airmen recovered from the sea. For much of the time he was within range of guns ashore and relied on naval planes both to spot the downed aircrew and quell Japanese fire, such was the efficiency of US air–submarine VHF radio telephone communication.

During the operations in the Marshalls at the beginning of February, Japanese documents captured in Kwajalein had alerted Frupac to Oikawa's new minefields. Lockwood would not send his boats through the barrage until safe routes had been found, and was consequently denied the fruitful area of the East China Sea. This left him with more submarines than convoy routes to patrol – despite the numbers he was deploying in support of the fleet – a problem which he and Voge solved first by resurrecting wolfpacks, and then in mid-April by instituting a rotating patrol plan. Groups of boats were sent to patrol areas subdivided into several sections from inshore to offshore, active to inactive, and were required to change from one to another every five days or so, avoiding the possibility of attack from one of their own by following defined safety lanes as they moved. In this way it was intended that each boat would share equally in dangers, opportunities and quiet periods while the group as a whole would cover all areas from the waters off Japan to the Luzon Strait. Further south, the Fremantle force, now thirty strong, patrolled especially the tanker routes from Borneo and ranged the South China Sea up to Saigon and Hong Kong. In January 1944 Christie had most reluctantly ordered his skippers to deactivate magnetic exploders, although it was not until March after more action test failures that he finally conceded defeat and made the ban permanent.

For his new wolfpacks, Lockwood re-established the practice of sending a senior officer as tactical commander to ride in one of the submarines of the group, no doubt because the COs of boats could not be expected to handle their own approach and guide two others in the very formal tactics of 'attack boat/trailer' and two 'flankers' with which he persisted, and in which all groups were trained. Dönitz, who had dispensed with tactical commanders very early in the war, chiefly because of communication difficulties when a boat was forced under, had never been tempted to reintroduce them since he had never envisaged set-piece actions.

Results from the first two packs sent to the Luzon Strait were disappointingly patchy. The first sank seven ships totalling over 35,000 tons from two convoys, the second sank one escort and damaged a freighter and a tanker from four convoys. The point was brought home once again that the quality of COs was all-important in submarine warfare: one skipper from the second pack was relieved of command for poor performance. There must be a suspicion, however, that the tactics themselves contributed to the low hitting rate. For with the US cryptanalytical advantage, finding convoys was not usually the major difficulty, as it had been for Dönitz. Once in contact, Japanese escorts, while unable to communicate efficiently between themselves, were able to listen in to the radio telephone dialogues between the US submarines as they sought to gain their set positions. Hence convoy commanders could and did make radical alterations which upset manoeuvres, leaving 'flankers' on the wrong quarter and 'attack' boats trailing.[123] This and the very deliberate system of attack, one submarine at a time, nullified the advantages of surprise and the opportunities for creating confusion and overwhelming the escorts. At night especially, the radar-equipped US fleet submarines had greater advantages over Japanese escorts than Dönitz's U-boats had had over British escorts in the 1940–1 period before radar. Individual US commanders proved the point, notably Lt.-Cdr. Walter Griffith of the Fremantle-based *Bowfin*, who the previous December had caused havoc among two Japanese convoys reminiscent of Kretschmer's nocturnal firework displays. Other individual COs were also to prove it in future. But in the early pack actions this technological superiority was almost neutralized by ultra-cautious co-ordinated tactics. In theory and results achieved, Lockwood could have learned from Dönitz's attack philosophy so faithfully followed by his ace COs: 'In the first line attack, always keep attacking; do not allow yourself to be shaken off . . . search again in the general direction of the convoy to regain touch, advance again! Attack!'[124]

Voge salted his duties in the operations room at Subpac Command with the invention of blackly humorous codenames: patrol areas were designated 'Hit Parade', '*Maru*'s Morgue', 'Convoy College' and the like, wolfpacks by combative alliterations composed with the CO's name. In May 'Blair's Blasters', comprising *Shark II*, *Pintado* and *Pilotfish* under the tactical command of Captain Leon Blair riding in *Pintado*, were sent to the area northwest of the Bonin Islands to interdict troop and supply convoys from Japan reinforcing Saipan and neighbouring garrisons – obvious targets for the next phase of Nimitz's advance, which had already been softened up by carrier strikes.

Several lone submarines patrolling the area had intercepted troop convoys on Ultra intelligence. As 'Blair's Blasters' arrived towards the end of May one of these, *Silversides*, coached them on to a small northbound convoy she was trailing. Blair took over and positioned the boats on either flank whereupon *Silversides* ran in to fire her last two torpedoes. Both missed and the convoy altered course radically, throwing the other boats out of position. That night they made end arounds and the following early morning, 1 June, Blair's command boat, *Pintado*, under Lt.-Cdr. Bernard Clarey, ran in and sank a medium-sized freighter. Blair then directed the pack to a Saipan-bound, and hence more important, convoy which *Silversides* had found on her way home. Japanese aircraft of the 901st Naval Air Flotilla prevented them closing, but they ran across a second Japan-bound convoy, and Lt.-Cdr. Edward Blakely in *Shark II* attacked and sank a small freighter. Trailing this convoy northwards, they crossed yet another southbound, their fourth convoy in as many days, and Blair, again deeming this the more important target, transferred the pack to it.

This convoy, which had departed Tokyo Bay on 30 May for Saipan, comprised seven *Marus*, three larger ones of 5,600–7,000 tons carrying between them 7,200 troops and 22 tanks, and four smaller ships of 3,000 tons each. They were protected by three submarine chasers and a torpedo boat, testimony to Oikawa's desperate shortage of escorts, for it was an important convoy carrying aviation fuel as well as troops. It also says much for the dislocation between Japanese intelligence and routing, or perhaps the inadequate communications, that despite the activities of *Silversides* and Blair's boats so many convoys had run straight into the pack – this one after a circuitous route south-west, south and finally south-east towards Iwo Jima, where aircraft of the 901st Air Flotilla were based. By the early afternoon of 4 June, the day after the first sighting, Blair had managed to position *Pilotfish* ahead, and *Pintado* and *Shark II* on either flank of the convoy, and he ordered the attack to begin. The escort leader, Cdr. Tadao Kuwahara of the Naval Reserve, had heard the frequent orders and responses passing between the boats and when his lookouts reported a periscope ahead – it must be assumed, since he did not detail the action in his post-war interrogation – he ordered a course alteration which left *Pilotfish* and *Pintado* trailing, but took the convoy over the other flanker, *Shark II*.[125] Blakely seized his opportunity and sank one of the transports, which took 11 tanks down with her and left 2,800 soldiers struggling in the water. The pack worked ahead again that night.

Why Blair did not stage a surface attack is not clear; the submarine-chaser escorts lacked radar and were 4 knots slower than the US submarines. Instead, having gained position ahead by the following morning, Blair prepared another set-piece attack which was delivered in the afternoon and followed the previous day's pattern: Kuwahara again altered towards Shark II and Blakely sank a small freighter and a second transport carrying 11 tanks and 3,300 troops. Repeating the tactics on the third day, 6 June, Blair found his own boat in a position to attack and Clarey hit a small freighter converted to carry aviation fuel which exploded in searing pyrotechnics. In the resulting confusion he was able to make a second attack about an hour later, and sank the third and final troop transport. Blair continued trailing the remaining two small freighters and escorts, but Lockwood called him off next day on Spruance's instructions to clear the area and deploy submarines for the assault on Saipan and Guam.[126]

The four-day action had proved that the premise of co-ordinated tactics as evolved on the submarine officers' dance-floor at Pearl Harbor could be made to work: the convoy had altered away from an attack towards one or other of the flankers during each of the engagements. However, in view of the prime night-time advantage the submarines enjoyed with radar and the comparative weakness of the escort, it remains open to question whether the results achieved were any better than might have been gained from each boat acting independently, running in whenever in position to do so and continually harrying the escorts. As it turned out, only one submarine at a time was ever in position to attack successfully and Pilotfish did not fire a single torpedo. Whatever may be said of the tactics, the decision to transfer to the southbound convoy was correct: whilst 80 per cent of the troops from the transports were picked up by escorts and eventually landed at Saipan, their weapons and equipment were lost, together with the tanks, and it is doubtful if they did much more than add to the appalling death toll as the island was invaded and overrun.

By this stage US anti-submarine technology had rendered Japanese submarines practically powerless. Like the U-boats in the Atlantic, they found themselves harried mercilessly; it had become a question of survival rather than attack or even reconnaissance.

During the ranging movements of US carrier forces through the Gilberts, Marshalls, and Carolines, towards the Palaus – and now the Marianas – they had provided no intelligence and had sunk only one warship of importance, the escort carrier *Liscome Bay*. It was hardly surprising: besides technological superiority and abundance, especially in the air, the Americans held the strategic initiative and there were simply not enough submarines to stretch across every route they might take, especially as a third of the Japanese boats were engaged on transport and supply missions to island garrisons isolated by US advances. This was a futile misapplication since it was recognized that submarines could not provide more than 10 per cent of the garrisons' requirements at best. Now, with the defeat of the U-boats in the Atlantic allowing the deployment of more US hunter-killer groups in the Pacific, the life expectancy for Japanese submarine crews was falling to that of their German counterparts. Already, during the first four months of 1944, nineteen Japanese boats had been lost, a quarter of the strength at the beginning of the year, four of them on supply or transport runs. May and June were to see the rate of loss double.[127]

The C-in-C of the Combined Fleet, Admiral Koga, had been killed in an air crash in late March; his successor, Admiral Soemu Toyoda, taking over in early May, had seen the time ripening for the decisive fleet battle as US forces pressed westwards, and had issued Operation Plan A – 'A-Go' – for luring the American carriers into the western corner of the Pacific bounded by New Guinea and the Philippines, where shore-based aircraft could redress the numerical odds against his reconstituted carrier force. This he concentrated with the major units of the fleet at the island of Tawi Tawi between the southern Philippines and Borneo, close to the oil ports. The submarines were accorded their usual functions of preliminary reconnaissance and ambush. The Sixth Fleet commander, Takagi, who had withdrawn his headquarters to Kure on Hiroshima Bay since the carrier strikes had devastated Truk's defences, directed his mainly large I-class boats to patrol sectors in the Marshalls and eastern Carolines. The 7th Submarine Squadron of medium RO boats, still based at Truk, was directed to form a reconnaissance line designated 'NA', stretching north-east from 130 to 300 miles from the Admiralty Islands off New Guinea across the waters south of the Carolines, where it was anticipated, and hoped, that the US fleet would advance for an attack on Palau or the southern Philippines. It is interesting that several of the boats of both groups were also to make supply runs, or were diverted from supply runs.[128] The submarines began departing their bases as they were ready from 9 May onwards, encouraged as they began to arrive at their positions by a Nelsonic injunction from Toyoda: since the fate of the empire hung on the coming battle, 'Each man must vow to do his duty, and all must strive mightily to attain certain success in the battle.'[129]

On 16 May, the *I176* on a transport run from Truk to Buka at the top of the Solomons chain was sunk by a US destroyer division called up by a patrol plane. Japanese radio operators in the area followed the action by listening in to the group's communications and their report went back to Sixth Fleet headquarters. The following day, Japanese radio intelligence intercepted another sighting report by a patrol plane, this time of a submarine in or near its position in the 'NA' line. Takagi reacted immediately, moving the whole line 60 miles south-eastwards by radio signal and allotting new positions for each of the boats. This in turn was picked up by US radio intelligence, and in two days of intense work at Frupac the co-ordinates of position had been deciphered and passed to Cincpac headquarters; there the officer responsible for independent anti-submarine operations, a recent appointment, instructed a hunter-killer group of three new destroyer escorts based in the Solomons to attack the line.[130]

The group under Cdr. Hamilton Hains in the *George* was hunting a submarine running in supplies from Truk to the bypassed garrison at Buin, Bougainville Island. In the early afternoon of 19 May this boat, *I16*, was detected with sonar by the *England* under Lt.-Cdr. W.B. Pendleton, who ran in and attacked with hedgehog ahead-thrown projectiles, scoring two hits with his second salvo and three with his fifth. A minute later an explosion below the stern lifted his ship so violently that all hands were knocked flat on deck. Oil and debris rose to the surface of the sea, and human remains which were soon attacked by sharks. The first hedgehog kill in the Pacific had been three months before, the victim *I175* which had sunk the *Liscome Bay*.

The group now moved north-westwards to the northernmost point of the repositioned 'NA' line, and in the early morning of the 22nd located a submarine on the surface charging batteries. It dived as they approached and the *George* ran in to make the first attack. There was no result and Pendleton, whose sonar operator also had contact, moved in, scoring almost immediately with a hedgehog salvo which caused the boat, *RO106*, to blow up.

Moving south-west next day, the 23rd, the group caught the second boat in the line, *RO104*, also on the surface. Both the *George* and the third ship, *Raby*, attacked after she had dived, but without success. Hains called Pendleton in, who hit and destroyed the boat with his second hedgehog salvo. The group then moved southwards down the line, picking up their third surfaced submarine by radar in the early hours of the 24th: *RO116*, fourth from the northern end of the line. She dived as they closed within 4 miles, but *England*'s sonar operator located her and Pendleton's first hedgehog salvo hit; again gruesome debris shot to the surface in the disturbance caused by the underwater explosions. Next day the group was ordered to refuel while an escort-carrier group took over the hunt. However, on the way south-westwards, at 23.00 on the 26th, all three destroyer escorts picked up yet another surfaced submarine on their radar screens: *RO108*, stationed at the southern end of the line. She dived as they approached and Hains ordered *Raby* to attack; she lost contact and once again it was Pendleton's *England* which located and then destroyed the boat with hedgehogs.

After replenishing with fuel and projectiles, the group returned to the 'NA' line and on the 29th joined the carrier group. Next day one of the latter's destroyers located a submerged submarine by sonar: *RO105*, third from the northern end of the line, which had retained her position despite losing her southern and her two northern consorts. The *George* and *Raby* attacked, but the Japanese CO evaded throughout the night and the early dawn of the 31st, when another destroyer from the carrier group joined them. Finally Pendleton, who had been ordered to stand clear during these attacks, was called upon. The *England* ran in, fixed the boat below on sonar and fired her hedgehog; seconds later the sea ahead erupted with the effects of a tremendous deep explosion. *RO105* was the *England*'s sixth victim in under a fortnight, a phenomenal performance, even exceeding the combined operations of Walker's 2nd Support Group which had destroyed six U-boats in the Atlantic earlier in the year.[131] The US historian of the naval war, Samuel Morison, wrote that much credit for the *England*'s success was due to the executive officer, Lt. J.A. Williamson, of the Reserve. It is certain that the calibration of sonar and hedgehog, and the training and co-ordination between these positions and the bridge must have been exceptional to achieve such a percentage of direct hits. From Washington Admiral King signalled, 'There'll always be an *England* in the United States Navy!'[132] The ship had been named after an ensign killed during the surprise attack on Pearl Harbor.

The rolling up of a large portion of Takagi's 'NA' line with hedgehog salvoes of deadly accuracy highlights the technological superiority of the US over Japanese anti-submarine forces by this time. It was underscored a few days later when Japanese destroyers attacked Samuel Dealey in *Harder* – it will be recalled that Dealey had 'expended' one of their kind in April.

In the dispositions for Spruance's assault on the Marianas Dealey had been assigned to patrol off the Combined Fleet anchorage at Tawi Tawi. He had also been instructed to take off a group of Australian intelligence officers from the neighbouring coast of north-eastern Borneo. He was proceeding on this mission between Tawi Tawi and the island of Sibutu on the night of 6 June when a small convoy was picked up by radar. He ordered flank speed to make an end around on the surface, but the submarine was sighted from one of two escorting destroyers as the moon emerged from behind cloud. The destroyer turned towards him and he altered away and ran. Then, as the enemy's superior speed brought her nearer, he dived to periscope depth, swung to port on full rudder and had the stern torpedoes readied. The fire-control party slipped swiftly into their routine as he called out observations on the enemy creaming down the broadening wake they had left on the surface. Dealey had a sharp mind; he had passed out of the Naval College first in his class in Mathematics. In action he was possessed by what Ned Beach has termed 'precise ferocity'.[133] When the destroyer had closed to 1,100 yards, less than four minutes since they had dived, he gave the order to fire. The torpedo officer at the TDC started the count, spacing the torpedoes at 5-second intervals. Shortly after the last one left the tube the boat was rocked by a close detonation, then another. Dealey at the periscope watched as the destroyer, struck forward and at mid-length, started to go down. Her stern rose high; depth-charges rolled down the sloping deck into flames enveloping the bridge, exploding in peals of thunder and lighting thick clouds of smoke and steam. In two minutes the torn remains had disappeared beneath the surface.

Dealey came up and chased in the direction of the convoy, but in the moonlight he was sighted by the second destroyer and again forced to dive. This one zigzagged towards him and he missed with a bow salvo of six torpedoes, taking the boat deep immediately afterwards. Subjected to depth-charge attack and held under for several hours, he lost the convoy. The following morning, while submerged, a third destroyer appeared, evidently called up by a patrol plane. He steered towards her until at 3,000 yards it appeared his periscope was sighted, for she turned and headed for him, like the previous destroyer weaving from side to side on her approach. He let her close to 650 yards, calling his final periscope observations and giving the order to fire as she reached the end of a starboard leg and swung to port. He watched as the tracks sped to meet her, calling 'Check fire!' before the fourth torpedo was launched. The order was barely out of his mouth when the tremendous pressure wave and thud of the first torpedo detonating was felt as much as heard by the whole crew; two more detonations followed, and shortly afterwards a 'terrific explosion' which Dealey assumed to be the magazine going up. Inside a minute from the first hit at mid-length she had gone.[134]

There was little time for exultation; another set of fast screws heralded the approach of yet another destroyer, and Dealey took the boat deep. They counted seventeen depth-charges exploding above, but none close, and he was able to come up to periscope depth again in less than four hours. Later in the day, while he was resting, more destroyers appeared, obviously from the fleet anchorage, until there were eight hunting in a line. The odds were too great. He lay low, coming up again after dark and resuming his course to the rendezvous on the coast of Borneo.

He picked up the Australians and returned to the patrol area off the fleet anchorage, where in the evening of 9 June two destroyers were sighted ahead. The sun had just set; it was too light for a surface attack, so he submerged and made a cautious approach as the two steamed nearer in line of bearing. When the foremost had reached 1,000 yards, her stern overlapping the other's bows in his sights so that the two made a single, continuous target, he fired a salvo of four torpedoes. Watching, he saw the track of the first pass ahead, but the second and third hit the leading ship; the fourth ran astern of her and went on to hit her consort. Moments after the detonations and pillars of water and flame he saw beneath the smoke billowing from the leader, now inside a quarter of a mile distant, a mighty explosion, whose blast rocked the submarine, and shortly after it the blinding flash of a similarly devastating eruption from beneath the bridge of the second ship. Soon there was nothing to be seen of either. Both he and his exec. were convinced both ships went down, but it emerged from post-war research that only one sank.[135]

The following afternoon, *Harder* was at periscope watch off the fleet anchorage when increased activity and smoke, and the appearance of more aircraft above, suggested some large movement about to take place. Presently a force of two battleships, several cruisers and escorting destroyers could be seen emerging. Dealey correctly identified the nearest battleship, hull down 8 miles distant, as one of the giant *Yamato* class. At the same time his periscope, or perhaps the shadow of the submarine beneath the water, was spotted by one of the patrolling planes and he saw a destroyer peeling off from the screen to head for his position as marked by a smoke flare dropped from the plane. He turned the submarine's bow towards her as she raced for him under a thick banner of black smoke, and had the torpedoes set for a zero gyro angle for a salvo 'down the throat'.

It has been said that the probable consequences of being caught at shallow depth in the event of torpedo failures or missing altogether rendered this tactic little short of Russian roulette. Indeed Morton's use of the technique has been described as 'the height of recklessness'. That, however, had been at a time of more or less constant torpedo failure. Certainly it required a high order of nerve and steady judgement, but it appears from the record that missing seldom proved fatal. Dealey had already missed on this patrol. He missed again now – although detonations and pro-longed rumbling and bursting noises as he went deep with full rud-der immediately after loosing the last torpedo convinced all hands he had hit twice and claimed another 'tin can', as enemy escorts were termed. After the war, however, Japanese records failed to disclose any destroyer sunk at this time. While deep, the *Harder* took a terrible beating, Dealey thought from a second destroyer whose screws had been picked up on sound before he fired. He marvelled that the submarine could survive 'such a terrific pound-ing and jolting around' with only minor damage, and the Australian passengers wished fervently that they were back in the Borneo jungle or indeed anywhere else.[136]

Dealey and Morton were by no means the only US COs to employ 'down the throat' shots at escorts; it had become an estab-lished technique for the bolder spirits. Earlier that year Lt.-Cdr. William Post of the *Gudgeon* had attempted it twice in one day against destroyers coming at him from a screen around the damaged escort carrier *Unyo*. He had fired at the first from 900 yards, at the second from 800 yards, missing on both occasions. Assuming a destroyer charging at 25 knots and a salvo of four torpedoes commenced at 800 yards' range and fired at 5-second intervals, the enemy would be on top of the submarine's firing position in 45 seconds. However, his sonar would be inoperable at that speed. And since US fleet boats employed a splashless discharge, sucking the expelling compressed air back into the boat, the destroyer captain would have to judge where to drop his charges by an estimate of where he had last seen the periscope or by the beginning of the air bubble torpedo tracks if they were still visible. Moreover, he would almost certainly have had to swing his ship to comb the oncoming tracks and would probably come in on a different angle. It may be that far from Russian roulette, the 'down the throat' tactic was a case of attack being the best form of defence. For once deep, the submarine had lost the initiative and was vulnerable either to sonar location and attack or, like the aptly-named *Puffer*, to being held down until the air was exhausted. It was perhaps not so dangerous as it undoubtedly appeared through the magnifying lens of a periscope. Post had written after his experiences that he had often wondered about the consequences of missing with 'down the throat' shots at a destroyer: 'Glad to report it's not much worse than a routine working over.'[137]

That night Dealey surfaced to count the force left in the anchorage, reporting the numbers and the sailing of the battle group by radio, after which he was 'rotated' to a less exciting sector of the patrol area while the *Redfin* relieved him off Tawi Tawi. It was as well. Latterly Dealey had had to dig deep into his reserves of will. On one occasion his exec. had found him apparently in a state of mild shock, unable to make a decision, and he seemed to have become 'quite casual about Japanese anti-submarine measures'.[138] It was his fifth patrol in *Harder*.

The patrol ensured Dealey's place in US submarine legend, and his name remains an inspiration to this day. The five destroyers with which he was credited – and it is not altogether certain that he did not sink five since Japanese records were notoriously incomplete – together with the one sunk on his previous patrol earned him the title 'the destroyer killer'. His force commander, Christie, who headed a large reception committee on his return to an advanced base at Darwin, northern Australia, and then took passage with him back to Fremantle and put him up at his residence, endorsed his patrol report with the words 'epoch making'.[139] It was indeed as phenomenal as Pendleton's feat in the *England*; it had also required more sustained nerve. And like David Wanklyn, Engelbert Endrass and so many high-scoring aces in all services who had driven themselves to the limit but were unaware of it, indeed had the bit between their teeth, he insisted, according to Christie, on making another patrol.

Dealey sailed again in August in command of a wolfpack off the Philippines. In the early hours of the 22nd off Manila Bay he and Lt.-Cdr. Chester Nimitz (son of the Admiral) in *Haddo*, attacked and sank three *Kaibō-kans*, Dealey claiming two, Nimitz one.

They moved northwards and the next day Nimitz missed a destroyer with a 'down the throat' salvo, but sank a second. Believing the damaged destroyer had been towed in to Dasol Bay below the entrance to Lingayen Gulf, Dealey steered there and waited with another of his group outside. It was here the following morning, 24 August, that the enemy caught him. A destroyer and a minesweeper converted for anti-submarine work with sonar and depth-charges appeared from inside the Bay. The destroyer turned back, but the minesweeper came on, her sonar pinging. Locating the *Harder* in the shallows she attacked at 07.28 with fifteen depth-charges. After the eruptions oil and debris from the interior of the boat rose to the surface. The loss of Sam Dealey and *Harder* came as a profound shock to the submarine service as a whole, as numbing as Morton's loss the previous year. He was eventually awarded the Congressional Medal of Honor, received by his widow.

In the meantime on 8 and 9 June, Spruance's 5th Fleet, headed by seven fleet and eight light carriers, concentrated in the Marshalls and steamed west for the assault on the Japanese bases in the Marianas, principally Saipan and Guam. Neither the fleet nor the armada carrying the invasion forces were sighted by the few Sixth Fleet submarines Takagi had disposed on reconnaissance. On the 11th the carriers launched the first strikes on the Marianas, and by the 13th had gained complete control of the air over the islands. By this time Toyoda and the Japanese Naval Staff realized the attacks were a main assault, not a feint, and the signal was given for 'Operation A' which was to lead to the decisive fleet battle. Vice-Admiral Jisabura Ozawa, in command of the First Mobile Fleet of five fleet and four light carriers with battleships, cruisers and screening destroyers, began moving from Tawi Tawi that morning. The *Redfin*, which had relieved *Harder* on patrol off the anchorage, saw them going, but was unable to close. In any case, instructions were to report first. Such was the air and surface activity that he was unable to come up and get off his report until that evening.

Ozawa steamed northwards up the Sulu Sea, thence weaving through the Philippine islands to emerge into the Philippine Sea from San Bernardino Strait south of Luzon on 15 June. There he was picked up by another submarine, *Flying Fish*, which trailed as he headed eastwards, reporting after dark. The same evening the *Seahorse*, 180 miles further south and 200 miles east, sighted a battle squadron steering northwards, reported and trailed. This was the force headed by the *Yamato* and *Musashi* which Dealey had seen departing Tawi Tawi on the 10th; it was to join Ozawa's fleet for the decisive battle.

The invasion of Saipan had begun that morning; by nightfall

20,000 men had stormed ashore. Admiral Takagi had transferred Sixth Fleet headquarters from Kure to Saipan some time previously and since the start of the air attacks he had been attempting to re-form his submarines in patrol lines to the east of the islands across the American line of advance. Now he sent them another general signal reminding them of their duty:

> This is the crucial time when the decisive battle which is imminent will directly determine victory or defeat for the empire. We must work for the preservation of the empire, displaying the full strength of our submarines which kill without fail when they attack, with all hands sacrificing themselves boldly.[140]

So difficult were his communications under the US assault that the next day, the 16th, the commander of Submarine Squadron 7 at Truk, Rear-Admiral Noboru Owada, took over temporary command of the whole submarine force. Owada immediately sent a message enjoining COs to make attacking the enemy the primary objective without staying in fixed stations, and on the 17th ordered the boats to circle the island of Rota, south of Saipan, in an anti-clockwise direction. When they had expended all their torpedoes they were to take position in specified sectors around the island to report enemy movements.[141] But such was the scale of anti-submarine effort surrounding the assult and invasion forces that few of the twenty boats which had been ordered to the area were able to reach attack positions; still fewer survived.

On the 16th, the new 600-ton *RO114* off Guam south of Rota reported firing at an *Iowa*-class battleship which, she observed, exploded with great violence and sank, a report that seemed to be confirmed by the Japanese 754th Guard Unit on Guam. No American ship was aware of being attacked and none was damaged or sunk. That night the submarine itself was detected by two destroyers 700 miles south-west of Saipan and depth-charged to destruction. On the same day, the even newer 600-ton *RO117* was caught on the surface and sunk by a patrolling island-based Liberator 350 miles south-east of Saipan after she had reported sighting a carrier task force. The previous day, *RO44*, one of the few boats not ordered to the patrols off Saipan, had been sunk in hedgehog attacks by a destroyer escort in the Marshalls.

Some idea of the hazards faced by the Japanese submarines and the impossible conditions aboard them can be gleaned from the log and reports of *RO115*. She was singled out in an extended staff analysis after the campaign as an example of what could be achieved with perseverance and fighting spirit, for it was believed she had sunk a carrier:

The captain and the whole crew, even after having been spotted and bombed by enemy aircraft, burned with a desire to meet the enemy. Bearing up under difficult conditions with the temperature 36° [97°F] in the conning tower and 45° [113°F] in the motor room, and an internal pressure of 940 mm, they dashed into the centre of the enemy task force. Cruising at periscope depth from beginning to end, they gained success in a desperate fight which lasted about six hours.[142]

The boat had arrived 50 miles west of Guam on 19 June, having completed a transport run to Wewak, a patrol off Palau and a reconnaissance off New Guinea before receiving the orders to proceed with all speed to the Marianas. Although a new boat, her cooling system was defective and by then all hands, drained with heat fatigue, had reached breaking point. The message that they were moving towards the decisive battle on which the fate of the empire hung had miraculously restored vitality. Attacked repeatedly by patrol planes on the morning of the 19th, they had continued at periscope depth, sighting a battle group in the early afternoon and numerous carrier groups which passed them by as they manoeuvred for position. Shortly before sunset a group they had sighted earlier in the afternoon was seen approaching again. They turned towards it, observing anti-aircraft fire peppering the sky as if the group were under attack from their own planes, and twenty minutes after sunset were able to close within 1,100 yards of a *Wasp*-class carrier and unleash a salvo of four torpedoes at 3-second intervals. Going down immediately to 250 feet, the CO was unable to see the result, which he recorded in the log as 'uncertain'.[143]

For the next three hours *RO115* was subjected to a 'neutralizing' attack by three destroyers and she did not surface until 23.23, some two hours after the propeller sounds had faded. The submarine staff, clutching at straws, married this report to a radio message intercepted at about 19.00 by signals intelligence, and concluded the carrier had 'sunk beyond doubt'.[144] No US carrier was hit by torpedoes, nor any other warship. The same day *I184*, which had been ordered to break off a supply mission and rush to Saipan, was sunk by an escort carrier's Avenger aircraft 20 miles south-east of Guam. Three days later, her sister *I185* was detected by escorts screening a group of transports and sunk by depth-charge attack.

From the 24th to the 26th, *I184*, *I185*, *RO36*, *RO42*, *RO44*, *RO111*, *RO117* and *RO114* were called from submarine command but did not answer.[145] The following day Owada signalled four fresh submarines he had ordered to the Marianas to 'be careful of attacks in that area on dark nights when visibility is poor'.[146]

During May nine boats had been lost, five on the 'NA' patrol line; in June ten were lost, mainly in the Marianas; in July a further seven were to be destroyed, including three of the original I-class boats in the Marianas and two of the fresh boats sent to join them. Successes like the sinking of the *Wasp*-class carrier and the *Iowa*-class battleship appeared to balance this sacrifice, but these were mythical; in the conditions the mission had been suicidal and entirely vain.

Admiral Takagi died in the same manner. Two I-class boats had been directed to evacuate him and the headquarters staff from Saipan, but neither had been able to penetrate the patrols, and on 2 July he ordered all further attempts abandoned. Four days later, as organized resistance to the US invasion collapsed, he sent a message that he and his staff would make a *banzai* attack against the enemy. The same day the naval base commander, Admiral Nagumo, who had led the *Kido Butai* in its days of glory, sat at the mouth of one of the many caves in the cliffs and slit his abdomen in the formal act of *seppuku*, whereby a man of honour 'proved his sincerity' before passing to the next world. That night, it must be assumed, Takagi and his staff joined the starving remnants of the island garrison when they made a suicidal charge at the US lines. Nothing more was heard from him.

By contrast with the failure of the Japanese boats in 'Operation A', Lockwood's and Christie's submarines, deployed in much the same strength, twenty-eight in all, made a major contribution. *Redfin, Flying Fish* and *Seahorse* had, as noted, reported the emergence of Japanese forces from outside the range of reconnaissance aircraft; they had been unable to maintain contact and thus did not report the junction of Ozawa's fleet which occurred in the late afternoon of 16 June. Nevertheless, their initial signals had alerted Spruance to the coming battle. He had postponed the planned invasion of Guam and concentrated his fleet west of the islands, so between Ozawa and his own transports and supply train. On the 17th, the new submarine *Cavalla*, under Lt.-Cdr. Herman Kossler, made radar contact with a fast force, reported and attempted to follow. She lost them, but on the strength of Kossler's report Lockwood moved four of twelve submarines stationed north of the Palaus across the Japanese line of advance to more southerly stations north and north-west of the island of Ulithi in the western Carolines.

The following afternoon, 18 June, Ozawa's reconnaissance planes, which had greater range than their US counterparts, located Spruance's fleet. They fixed him again early in the morning of the 19th, and at 07.30 – as 300 miles to the east *RO115* was beginning her eventful day off Guam – the Japanese admiral ordered the first wave of strike aircraft launched. By a blend of extraordinary chance and good judgement on Lockwood's part, one of the submarines he had moved after *Cavalla*'s report lay almost directly in the track of Ozawa's flagship, *Taiho*, latest and largest of the Japanese carriers, as she turned south-easterly to fly off her planes. This was the *Albacore* under Lt.-Cdr. James Blanchard. Rising to periscope depth shortly before 08.00, having been forced deep repeatedly by patrol planes, he found himself in the path of the Japanese force. The first carrier he sighted was almost past him, but a few minutes later a second emerged from funnel smoke and masts on the horizon, showing only a 10° starboard angle on the bow. He swung right and started an approach; the orders had been changed by this time to attack first, report later. As he raised the periscope to make the final observations at 08.08 it was found that the light on the TDC indicating a correct firing solution was out. The carrier was well inside 3 miles' range, travelling at 27 knots, and it was too late to shift to the 'Is-Was' for another solution. He ordered his observations cranked into the computer and began a salvo of six spread widely along the track, going deep as aircraft and destroyers wheeled towards him. Before the depth-charges started falling he heard two detonations. One was caused by a pilot who had spotted the torpedo tracks after taking off from the carrier and crashed his plane ahead of one of them in a heroic suicide attempt to protect the ship. The other was a hit which tore open the *Taiho*'s aviation fuel tanks and jammed the forward aircraft elevator. It was soon apparent that the ship herself was in no danger and Ozawa sped on. However, the officer deputed to damage control, attempting to disperse the petrol fumes from the ruptured tanks, spread them through the ship, creating a potent explosive mixture in some compartments which went off that afternoon, raising the flight deck and blasting out side plating; by 16.00 the 31,000-ton flagship had disappeared.

Ozawa had lost his first carrier two hours earlier. Kossler in the *Cavalla*, having abandoned the pursuit he had begun on the night of the 17th and since been forced under for considerable periods by patrol planes, had come up to periscope depth shortly before 11.00. He found two cruisers, and a carrier flying off aircraft and screened by destroyers which were approaching fast. He came round to starboard towards the carrier's track and at 11.18 fired a bow salvo of six torpedoes at 1,200 yards. The first three – by Japanese accounts, four – hit, starting fires which ignited incendiary material and ammunition on the decks and turned the ship into an exploding firework display. Within less than three hours she had sunk. This was the *Shokaku*, the first fleet as opposed to escort carrier ever sunk by a US submarine; the *Taiho*, two hours later, was the second.

Meanwhile the Japanese strike aircraft had been decimated by Spruance's fighters. Concentrated on radar data high above the incoming waves of Japanese planes, they swooped down in what the pilots were to describe as 'the Marianas' turkey shoot'. By the end of the day Ozawa had scarcely a hundred planes remaining, and the US fleet had suffered only minor damage. The following afternoon Spruance received his first sighting report of Ozawa's force from a reconnaissance plane, and the first US strike was launched. The dive-bombers and torpedo bombers, covered by eighty-five Hellcat fighters, arrived over the targets and pressed home a deadly attack which sank the fleet carrier *Hiyo* and two fleet tankers, and seriously damaged the remaining fleet carriers, *Zuikaku* – to which Ozawa had transferred his flag – and *Junyo*, as well as two light carriers, a battleship and a cruiser. Ozawa, left with only sixty-one aircraft, nonetheless ordered preparations for a night attack on the US fleet. The C-in-C Combined Fleet, Soemu Toyoda, countermanded the order and instructed him to withdraw.[147] He headed north-westerly, missing 'Blair's Blasters' whom Lockwood had positioned to cover a northerly retreat towards Japan.

So ended the Battle of the Philippine Sea. For the second time Japanese carrier aircraft had been practically wiped out, and with them a second generation of not so thoroughly trained pilots. The Japanese submarine force had been halved. US submarines, on the other hand, had played a major role without loss in both their reconnaissance and their attack functions. It was the first time any nation's submarines had participated effectively in a fleet action. Moreover, during the same period those not engaged had made further inroads into Japanese merchant tonnage. In May submarines had sunk fifty-four *Marus* totalling 236,000 tons, in June forty-four of 190,000 tons. And, in addition to the two fleet carriers sunk in the Philippine Sea, a further fifteen warships had been sunk by submarines during the two-month period.

In the immediate aftermath of the battle, on 21 June, the captain of the light carrier *Chiyoda*, formerly an ADC to the Emperor Hirohito, sent a message to an admiral of his acquaintance, hoping it would be forwarded to the Emperor, as it was: 'No longer can we hope to sink the numerically superior enemy aircraft carriers by conventional attack methods. I urge the immediate organisation of special attack units to carry out crash-dive tactics.'[148]

Officers on the Naval General Staff had reached similar conclusions. The time for conventional operations was past. A human torpedo named *kaiten*, essentially a Type 93 standard 24-inch diameter torpedo with a hollow compartment at mid-length for a seated, fully enclosed pilot, provided with steering and depth controls, a gyro compass and a short periscope, had been developed by two young midget-submarine officers in collaboration with the torpedo design department. This suicide weapon to be carried by I-class submarines was now hastened into production.[149]

10

The End

THERE WAS A certain symmetry between the Pacific and the Atlantic campaigns, provided in large measure by the immense growth of American armed power. On 6 June 1944, as Spruance's carriers sortied from their anchorage in the Marshalls, to be followed by the Joint Expeditionary Force for the invasion of the Marianas, a comparable armada from the ports of southern England launched Allied troops on the beaches of Normandy. Like the Japanese naval high command before the Battle of the Philippine Sea, Dönitz viewed the outcome of this campaign as decisive: if the Allies could be thrown back into the Channel, large German forces held in the west to meet the invasion could be transferred east to halt and turn the Russian advance. This would enhance the prospects of a split between the Soviet and Anglo-Saxon Allies, on which Hitler now placed all hopes for a successful outcome; for his own aims, the Baltic would remain a safe training area for the U-boats; and time would be won to complete sufficient of the new, high-underwater speed *Elektro* boats to wrest command of the North Atlantic convoy routes and so bring 'war decisive' pressure to bear on the western Allies.[1]

Already in April two of the new coastal Type XXIII boats had been launched by Deutsche Werft, Hamburg; in May the first of the 1,600-ton ocean-going Type XXIs had gone down the ways at Blohm & Voss, Hamburg; two more were scheduled for June and two for July, after which the production tempo would rise to six a month before the end of the year. This was the goal on which his gaze was fixed; this and knowledge of the enemy resources tied up by convoy protection had enabled him to hold his course over the past calamitous year for the U-boat arm.[2] Since he had insisted to Hitler at the end of May 1943 that the U-boat war must be continued – and Hitler had agreed there was no question of abandoning it[3] – 239 boats had been lost. Over the whole of 1943 and the first five months of 1944 the figure was 341, an average of over 20 boats a month. More important, 20,000 officers and men had failed to return from patrol.

The rate of production of new boats had been marginally higher than the rate of loss. From 400 in commission at the beginning of 1943, the figure had by June 1944 risen to 448, including 5 ex-Italian boats.[4] The 20,000 men who had gone down or been captured by the enemy had been replaced by scouring the surface fleet. Both the age and the level of experience of crews had fallen alarmingly. Herbert Werner, attending a course for prospective commanding officers in Gotenhafen earlier that year had found only one beside himself from the U-boat arm. None of the others had even been on a submarine war patrol. Entirely lacking the seasoning that only action could provide, the instinctive feeling for when to make an alarm dive, when to fight it out on the surface, when and how to manoeuvre under depth-charge attack, when to play possum, he thought they 'stood almost no chance of survival, and neither did their crews'.[5]

Morale remained surprisingly good. Peter Hansen has described the attitude as 'fatalistic' from at least 1942, yet inherent German martial virtues combined with very skilful 'total war' propaganda and a whispering campaign about devastating new 'secret weapons' – among them, of course, the Type XXIs and XXIIIs which were to revolutionize submarine warfare – prevented a relapse into pessimism. Neither Dönitz nor the U-boat staff were unaware of the scale of the sacrifice they demanded. This is apparent from the number of justifications entered in the war diary for not abandoning the U-boat campaign: once it had been allowed to cease it would be impossible to pick it up again; to 'parry with the enemy' was a 'tactical, technical and above all psychological necessity'; to give up would release great numbers of Allied aircraft for the bombing campaign against German cities and a large number of destroyers and other light craft to prey on coastal shipping; the same applied to the Allied aircraft and ship-construction industries. As for the U-boat men themselves:

> the task of conducting a war to tie down the enemy has been especially difficult . . . The chances of success [sinkings] are now only slight; on the other hand, the prospects of not returning from a patrol are very great. In the last few months only 70 per cent of the boats that sailed per month returned from patrols. That the crews managed at all in this last year of heaviest loss and smaller success, and came through unimpaired in their morale and will to fight and attack is marvellous proof of soldierly courage, proof of the quality of the human material involved, a reward for thorough training and a result of the determination of the U-boat arm.[6]

That this was not just a hopeful view from the top was to be proved by the outstanding, if vain, efforts of U-boats sent out against the invasion forces in the Channel.

Dönitz had held back two groups to contest the anticipated

assault: in the Biscay ports Group *Landwirt* comprised forty-nine Type VIIC boats, thirty-five of which were ready for operations, the great majority divided between Brest and St Nazaire; the other group, *Mitte*, of twenty-one boats was held in central and southern Norwegian ports in case the attack were launched via Scandinavia. These numbers are misleading. Recent operations had shown that U-boats not fitted with the air-breathing mast termed the *Schnorchel* could not live in waters patrolled by anti-submarine forces, but *Schnorchel* production had been disrupted by bombing to such an extent that only five of Group *Mitte* and eight of Group *Landwirt* were fitted with it, seven of these in Brest, one in Lorient. They were the only boats that had a chance of penetrating the air and surface screen the Allies were bound to throw around their invasion forces.

The situation for all boats was clarified in the starkest terms by a series of decrees Dönitz had issued that spring. Believing as he did that the decision of the war hinged on the outcome of the coming invasion, he had exhorted the men of the *Kriegsmarine* manning the coastal defences and the destroyers, torpedo boats, fast patrol boats and U-boats who would be in the forefront of the battle to commit themselves to the uttermost without regard for the odds or preservation of their vessel; and he had warned of the consequences of failure to do so:

> The soldier who does not commit himself to the last and fulfil his duty to the uttermost, I will disgrace and destroy with shame.[7]

On 27 March he had promulgated what appeared to be suicide instructions to COs:

> Every commander must be clear that upon him (when the enemy invades), more than at any other time, the future of the German *Volk* rests, and I demand from each commander that he, without regard to otherwise valid caution [*Vorsichtmassnahmen*], keeps only one goal before his eyes and in his heart: attack – close – sink! [*Angriff – ran–versenken!*][8]

As a result of questions and objections about the decree reaching his staff, on 1 April he superseded it with another, headed 'Reckless Attack!':

> Every enemy vessel taking part in the landing, even if it only carries half a hundred soldiers or one tank, is a target which demands the full mission of the U-boat. It is to be attacked even if this carries the risk of the loss of one's own boat.
>
> If it is a question of approaching the enemy invasion fleet no regard is to be paid to dangers such as flat water or possible mine barriers or any other considerations. Every man and weapon of the enemy destroyed

before landing reduces the enemy's prospects of success. The boat that causes the enemy losses in the invasion has fulfilled its highest task and justified its existence, even if it is lost.[9]

The overall chief of the Biscay U-boats, FdU West, was *Kapitän* Hans Rösing. His headquarters were at Angers on the Maine and Loire rivers above Nantes and St Nazaire – a building specially constructed to accommodate U-boat Command, but Dönitz had been promoted to Berlin before it was complete. On 10 May Dönitz visited Navy Group Headquarters West in Paris to review preparations for countering the invasion. Rösing attended and was inspired by Dönitz's confidence that the invasion forces would be defeated on the coast before they could establish themselves ashore; he was known for repeating Dönitz's every assertion about final victory as 'His Master's Voice'. The same month Rösing toured his Biscay bases to brief the U-boat COs on their responsibilities in the coming battle. Few of those who heard him survived the months ahead, but of the fifteen captains gathered from the 1st and 9th Flotillas at Brest, two have left published accounts. The recollections of OLt. Karl Heinz Marbach of *U953*, one of the boats fitted with *Schnorchel*, formed the basis of a chapter in a 1952 book by Dr Harald Busch, formerly of the Propaganda Kompanie. In this Rösing is described as explaining Dönitz's April decree in terms of total commitment: 'Once we [the COs] could do no more, then we should at least ram [a vessel of] the invasion fleet, be it only the smallest dinghy!'[10] Herbert Werner, by then an *Oberleutnant* in command of *U415*, which was not equipped with a *Schnorchel*, wrote later in *Iron Coffins* that Rösing told them to attack the invasion fleet 'with the final objective of destroying the enemy ships by ramming'. The words, he recalled, were greeted with a deathly silence. 'Was suicide the purpose for which we had been trained for so long?'[11] These accounts of the so-called 'Ramm Befehl' drew intense fire from Dönitz's supporters, who insisted he had never ordered suicide attack; yet the words attributed to Rösing were scarcely more extreme than the actual texts of Dönitz's decrees, which can be seen today in the archives.

All Group *Landwirt* boats were held in port at six hours' notice through that early summer of 1944, the crews denied passes into the towns, although the COs at Brest, Werner recorded, spent much time at the flotilla resort at Le Treshier with girls employed at last, and despite Nazi ideology, for naval administrative duties. 'We never talked about the invasion, but we thought about it incessantly, and of our death.'[12]

No reconnaissance lines were established in the Channel to give warning of invasion since it would have been wasteful to hazard and undoubtedly lose some of the few boats available for attack; they would in any case have been forced under before they could sight or report the fleet. And since the Allies had air supremacy and had knocked out much of the coastal radar no other warnings were given. The Allies achieved complete strategic and tactical surprise, as the Americans had in the Marianas. Dönitz was on holiday in the Black Forest when the assault and landing craft hit the beaches.

The first reports of parachute landings came in at 01.30 on 6 June, followed between 02.00 and 03.00 by reports of large invasion forces from the sea. At 03.10 Group *Landwirt* was brought to instant readiness, at 03.43 Group *Mitte* likewise, and at 03.52 five *Schnorchel*-fitted boats heading into the Atlantic were ordered to make for western France with all possible speed. Dönitz was awakened with the news that the enemy was landing in Seine Bay, and at 08.00, when it appeared to the naval staff at least that the main invasion had begun, the seven *Schnorchel* boats at Brest were ordered out. After Dönitz arrived at 11.15 the whole of Group *Landwirt* was ordered into the Channel; the entry in the war diary concluded: 'For boats without *Schnorchel* this means the last operation.'[13]

Allied measures to prevent U-boats approaching the invasion fleet were more comprehensive than the U-boat staff had contemplated. Minefields had been laid across the approaches to Brest, west of Ushant and around the North Brittany coast, and 350 specialized anti-submarine aircraft had been organized to cover the entire area of the western Channel from the Cherbourg peninsula out around Biscay into the south-western approaches in patrols so scheduled that no area of sea would be left unobserved for more than half an hour. The operation was aptly named 'Cork'. An aircraft locating a U-boat would attack immediately, then mark the position and report, upon which reserve, so-called 'rover' planes would relieve it and call up naval support groups and air strike forces while the original aircraft returned to its scheduled patrol. Nine support groups and three escort carriers in the western Channel and western approaches provided a density of surface anti-submarine forces of about fifteen escorts every 100 miles. Further surface and air escorts were allocated to the flanks of the invasion force itself in case any U-boat should penetrate 'Cork'. A Submarine Tracking Room had been established at Plymouth to correlate all intelligence.[14]

The orders issuing from U-boat Command outside Berlin were

changed several times in the hours after Dönitz's arrival, reflecting the uncertainty and confusion there, as elsewhere. As finally established, only the eight *Schnorchel* boats were directed to the main invasion transport area south of the Isle of Wight. The seven non-*Schnorchel* boats at Brest were instructed to sail at midnight and proceed on the surface at full speed to the English coast between Land's End – the extreme western tip of Cornwall – and Start Point, near Plymouth, Devon. The nineteen non-*Schnorchel* boats at the other Biscay ports were to establish a reconnaissance line along the 200-metre [roughly 100-fathom] line down the Biscay coast in case other landings were planned there.

Air attacks on the *Schnorchel* boats began almost as soon as they put to sea, forcing them to dive and make the passage submerged, thus reducing their speed to 6 or 7 knots at best; in practice they only made 30 to 40 miles a day. For the crews it was tense and debilitating. Trim had to be perfectly maintained so that the *Schnorchel* head valve did not submerge, hence movement through the boat was restricted; before moving any distance forward or aft a man had to obtain permission. If a wave washed over the *Schnorchel* head or the boat dipped below the correct depth the valve closed automatically and the diesels sucked air from the interior of the boat, lowering the pressure sharply and causing intense pain in the ears; sometimes exhaust gases were forced back inside, half-suffocating the engine-room hands; in any case there was generally a slow leakage of exhaust into the boat, building up carbon monoxide, poisoning the atmosphere and causing headaches.

The eight non-*Schnorchel* boats sailed in a group line ahead when they left the shelter of their concrete bunker that night, and attempted to beat off the first air attack in the early hours of the 7th with their combined anti-aircraft guns. Herbert Werner has described the continuous chirping and screaming from the radar detectors before the attack, the close sound of aero engines and sudden eruptions of tracer fire, fountains illuminated by flares rising from the sea, boats ahead weaving to escape bombs as their own guns answered. A plane was hit and, catching fire, streaked in flames into the sea; *U413*, caught by a stick of bombs, slowed and settled in the water.[15]

Ali Cremer, who took *U333* from La Pallice to a position in the Biscay reconnaissance line, also left a record of that night when he was forced to dive so continually that he had to surface by day to recharge batteries and replenish the compressed air used during the countless times they had blown tanks to come up after each descent. Detected as he rose above the surface, he was attacked immediately and was fortunate to escape with only shell holes in the casing and conning tower and a vivid memory of the faces of the aircrew through a glass cockpit as the plane roared by less than 100 feet away. Three depth-charges failed to drop free from the aircraft; the other three straddled but were not close enough to damage the boat.[16]

Others were not so fortunate. In the first two nights three *Landwirt* boats and one returning from Atlantic patrol were sunk and six so damaged they had to return to base.[17] Werner's *U415* was one of the latter. Depth-charges from an aircraft had lifted the boat bodily, hurling all hands to the deck, putting the diesels out of action and jamming the rudder hard a-starboard. As she slewed to a stop two more planes had come in, one after the other from either bow, guns blazing, sweeping the decks and superstructure, and dropping further charges, whose explosions, close alongside the ballast tanks, again lifted and tossed the boat. In the silence afterwards a flare floating nearby lit the punctured plating of the conning tower, a member of the gun's crew lying scalped by a shell, others wounded. Werner's face streamed blood from head wounds caused by splinters. Below he found a shambles, but somehow the engineer patched her up for a shallow dive and he set course homewards on the one electric motor still operational, steering manually by magnetic compass. Caught by the tide the boat was almost swept up on the rocks of Ushant, but escaped as the tide turned and eventually limped back in to Brest, where Werner found that two of his fellow skippers who had set out with him for the English coast without *Schnorchel*s had preceded him.[18] By then two more of their colleagues had been lost.

Six surviving *Schnorchel* boats were still making an excruciatingly slow, disagreeable and dangerous passage eastwards along the north coast of Brittany, five more from the Atlantic were making an equally painful approach towards the Channel, and the five *Schnorchel* boats from Group *Mitte* in southern Norway were beginning a passage northabout around Scotland to join them. Of the first wave of boats from Brest, two reached St Peter Port in the German-controlled Channel Island of Guernsey on the 13th and 14th, thus a week after the landings began, with batteries exhausted. After sailing with partially recharged batteries one was so badly damaged by a surface support group that she turned back for Biscay, and a week later the other, evidently unable to penetrate the main invasion shipping routes, was sunk by a destroyer off Portland. A third had already decided to return; she was sunk by a 'Cork' air patrol off Ushant. On the same day, the

15th, the only successes were scored: *U764* under OLt. Hans Kurt von Bremen sank a Royal Navy frigate with a *Zaunkönig* off Portland, but was damaged in the counter-attacks and forced to put back, and *U162*, the single *Landwirt* boat to reach the main landing area, sank a 1,500-ton US tank landing craft. Her skipper, 23-year-old OLt. Hermann Stuckmann, was forced by the subsequent activity to lie low for three days, after which he found and attacked two US battleships of the bombarding force, but missed. With all torpedoes now spent, he too began the arduous passage back to Brest. For his outstanding devotion Stuckmann was awarded the Knight's Cross, surely as richly deserved as those won by the tonnage aces in the years of glory. He did not survive long: on 2 August he was caught attempting to return to La Pallice by a surface support group and went down with his boat.[19]

Of the subsequent waves of *Schnorchel* boats entering the Channel, *U767* under OLt. (Reserve) F. Dankleft sank a Royal Navy frigate off Land's End, but was subsequently caught and destroyed by a support group, as were two others before reaching the central area. Of those that did so, *U988* under OLt. Erich Dobberstein torpedoed and sank a corvette, but was detected by a patrolling Liberator two nights later while schnorchelling and destroyed by an escort group called to the scene; another was so hunted by surface forces that she retired, damaged, into Boulogne. The only substantial success of the campaign was scored by *U984* under KLt. Heinz Siedler. Having recharged batteries in St Peter Port, he escaped numerous attacks, finally torpedoing one of his hunters, and four days later off Selsey Bill, to the east of the Isle of Wight, torpedoed four Liberty ships in a troop convoy; three were beached and lost; only one survived. Siedler made Brest five days later and was awarded the Knight's Cross, but like Stuckmann he did not survive his next patrol in the Channel. By the end of June two further boats had struggled to the central shipping focus and another six were creeping towards it.

Thus over these first crucial weeks when the Allies had to funnel sufficient troops and armour into the beachhead to resist a counter-attack by the German divisions held in France for the purpose, the U-boats had been literally overwhelmed by the forces massed to prevent them reaching the transports, as indeed had the German light surface forces. The U-boat arm had suffered more grievous losses and damage without exerting any effect upon the landings, except in the sense of tying up vast numbers of aircraft and surface warships. Dönitz had conceded that the invasion was a success as early as 10 June.[20] Had the skippers attempted to fulfil his decrees to the letter they would have suffered even greater losses with no gain. None did. None were shamed. They had done their best in impossible conditions, as the U-boat staff fully realized. Explanations for Dönitz's 'suicide' orders must be sought in the hysterical atmosphere at Führer headquarters, where he spent much time, and in his own extreme personality. On the rational assessment that most skippers made, it was the height of folly to sacrifice what would be the scarcest resource of all for the new miracle *Elektro* U-boats, the trained officers and experienced crews.

Late in 1943 Dönitz had established a Small Battle Units Force – *Kleinkampfmittel Verband*, or 'K Force' – under a particularly imaginative and forceful staff officer, Vice-Admiral Helmuth Heye, whom he charged with the development and production of human torpedoes, midget submarines and explosive devices with which to attack an invasion fleet. None of these was ready by June, but in early July the first devices named *Neger* ('negro') were launched against the left flank of the invasion from Trouville at the mouth of the Seine opposite Le Havre. They were modified torpedoes with a compartment for a pilot wearing breathing apparatus and enclosed in a perspex dome. A real torpedo was slung below and aimed by aligning an upstanding fore sight on the craft travelling just below the surface with graduations around the pilot's dome projecting above the surface. They were simple, indeed crude machines, with a maximum speed of 4 knots; they sank three minesweepers and damaged a destroyer beyond repair, but proved extremely vulnerable. From the twenty-one which set out on 9 July none returned. They were in reality suicide weapons. A subsequent development called *Marder* ('marten') could dive to 30 metres (100 feet) to escape attack, but these proved scarcely less vulnerable when they went into action against the shipping off Normandy by night in August. They were accompanied by radio-controlled explosive motor boats termed *Linsen* and their guiding craft, and fast patrol – *Schnell* – boats armed with a new long-range circling torpedo. A destroyer, a trawler and a landing craft were sunk, but of fifty-eight *Marder* taking part only twelve survived.

Of various one- and two-man midget submarines under development, none was produced in time for action against the invasion, nor were any as formidable as the midgets Japan was developing and laying down at this time for the defence of the home islands. The Type XXVIIB or *Seehund* ('seal') two-man submarine of 12 tons' surface displacement was probably the most effective of Heye's craft; he expressed that opinion after the war.[21] Yet it could only make 6 knots at best under the water against the 18 to

19 knots of the much larger Japanese midgets. It was perhaps better suited for a stealthy approach – like the British X-craft on which many of its features were modelled – since the small hull was extremely difficult to locate by asdic and at slow speed the motor and propeller noise was impossible to detect. A British submarine expert has suggested that the Allied defences might have been swamped and the transports and landing craft have suffered disastrously if large numbers of *Seehund* had made co-ordinated attacks.[22] That is no different from Dönitz's claim that he could have won the Atlantic battle with 300 U-boats at the start. The truth is that he had begun the Small Battle Units, like the *Elektro* U-boats, too late; on this occasion it was his sole responsibility. With his gaze fixed on the offensive in the Atlantic, he had been caught out by the sudden turn in the war and had no effective units in place for defence against invasion.

At the beginning of July U-boat Command ceased sending even *Schnorchel*-fitted boats against the invasion transports since there had been no reports from those in the Channel. However, when two of them returned to Brest, proving that it was just possible to survive, the operation was continued. It was futile, or worse: successes were negligible, and six more *Schnorchel* boats were lost in the Channel that month, three in August, all to surface forces. By then the Biscay bases were under threat from the landward side as US troops under General Omar Bradley swept westwards. Dönitz had already begun to transfer U-boats from Brest and Lorient south to La Pallice and Bordeaux. By the end of August even these bases had been abandoned and all surviving boats were heading for Norway. The Channel operation was abandoned at the same time. It had been a costly three months: all told since the beginning of June eighty-four U-boats had been lost, nineteen of them in the English Channel, sixteen in Biscay.[23]

In the Pacific, meanwhile, US submarines were unleashing their potential against Japanese merchant shipping. Sufficient had now been learned of Oikawa's great mine barrier to plot safe routes through, and on 20 June, as Ozawa's beaten fleet retired from the Philippine Sea, *Tang*, *Tinosa* and *Sealion II* had penetrated the East China Sea. They were not a formal pack, but met four nights later south-west of Kyushu, southernmost of the Japanese home islands, to co-ordinate activities. Next night O'Kane in *Tang* detected a convoy and called the other two; they were too far away to reach the scene and he went in alone on the surface, ghosting at slow speed, bows towards the nearest of a screen of escorts to present the smallest silhouette while his fire-control party below set up an attack on the merchantmen beyond by radar ranges and bearings. Reaching the firing position, O'Kane unleashed a full salvo of six torpedoes and saw two hit a freighter, two more hit a tanker, which ignited before he was forced down by escorts.

Over the following weeks he sank another six *Marus*, and *Tinosa* and *Sealion II* sank six between them – none, however, in co-ordinated attacks. After the war Japanese records showed that O'Kane had actually hit and sunk four merchantmen in his first attack, raising his six-torpedo salvo to the most destructive from any US submarine in the war in terms of numbers of victims and taking his patrol into first place for numbers of ships sunk, just above Morton's second patrol in *Wahoo*. O'Kane had, of course, been at the periscope for those nine sinkings as well.[24]

To the south, in the Luzon Strait, Lt-Cdr. Slade Cutter in *Seahorse* was sealing a reputation as the most consistent scorer in Lockwood's force. Working in a wolfpack with *Bang* and *Growler*, he sank four ships, which brought his total to nineteen *Marus* of 72,000 tons in all, and placed him just above Morton, whose nineteen sinkings had totalled 55,000 tons – although the figures credited at the time were much higher for both. It was, as Lockwood expressed it in his endorsement, Cutler's 'fourth successive brilliantly conducted patrol',[25] also his last: exhausted, he asked for leave to see his family, after which he was posted to a new boat under construction. His total sinkings would only be overtaken by O'Kane.

Three other wolfpacks worked the Luzon Strait that July, the most successful the 'Mickey Finns', *Piranha*, *Thresher* and *Guardfish* under Cdr. W. 'Mickey' O'Regan, riding in the latter. Directed by Ultra to a southbound convoy, each of the three shared in a total of six *Marus* sunk in a night surface action on the 26th, the best pack attack thus far, and they returned to base with a total bag of eight ships aggregating 40,000 tons. 'Wilkin's Wildcats' led by Cdr. Warren Wilkin from *Tilefish* scored only damage to merchant ships but ambushed and sank *I29* on Ultra intelligence. The third pack, named 'Park's Pirates' after Cdr. Lew Park who rode in Cdr. Lawson 'Red' Ramage's *Parche*, suffered weeks of bad weather and frustration, compounded for two of the pack when the third member picked up and attacked a convoy in the early hours of 30 July, without success, and sending such confusing signals they could not find the action. Later that morning convoy smoke was sighted from one of these two, *Steelhead* under Lt-Cdr. David

Whelchel. He trailed, despite patrolling aircraft, and that night succeeded in bringing up Ramage's command boat, *Parche*. He then ran in to attack, observing hits on a freighter and a tanker, which burst into flame.

When he withdrew to reload, Ramage went in on the surface at full speed, curving between two escorts but finding himself closer to the merchantmen within the screen than he expected as they made an emergency turn towards him. He swung past the first too close to fire, turned to open the range, then launched two bow torpedoes at her and two from the stern tubes at another freighter. The second salvo hit, starting fires. Both merchantmen and escorts had opened fire on the submarine, now visible in the light from the blazing ships augmented by flares but Ramage, determined to continue the battle on the surface, sent the bridge watch below and, retaining only a volunteer on the target bearing transmitter, rounded on the convoy again.

For the next forty minutes he ran amok, conning *Parche* like a torpedo boat, turning at speed from escorts or merchantmen which attempted to ram while he bored in to attack the now disorganized columns. It was perhaps the wildest mêlée of the Pacific submarine war. The night was split by flashes of gunfire, tracer arced towards the twisting submarine, shells ripped the air nearby, fountains sprang from the sea, flame and water columns rose from ships hit by torpedoes. Ramage, lifted by the exhilaration of action, fired another fifteen torpedoes before eventually withdrawing. Afterwards Whelchel came in again and fired two more salvoes, observing hits on another two ships before he was forced deep and depth-charged. It was a perfect example of a loosely co-ordinated attack relying on individual initiative rather than formal tactics, reminiscent of the first U-boat night surface attacks and similarly overwhelming for the escorts; yet the results were not as good as they had seemed to the participants in the heat of battle. Post-war analysis revealed five merchantmen sunk, two each to Whelchel and Ramage, one shared between them. In terms of tonnage it was the most successful attack thus far: the five totalled over 39,000 tons, some 10,000 tons more than the six *Marus* sunk by the 'Mickey Finns' earlier in the month. For the epic onslaught Ramage was awarded a Congressional Medal of Honor, the third submariner to be so distinguished, the only one so far to have survived to receive it.

The first formal wolfpack from Fremantle was operating in the South China Sea during this period, the three boats under the tactical command of the senior skipper rather than an additional senior officer. Directed by Christie from Ultra intelligence, they found and attacked several convoys, returning with a score of five *Marus* and one light cruiser sunk, some 36,000 tons in all.

To the west of Christie's operational sphere British submarines based on the depot ships *Adamant* and *Maidstone* at Trincomalee, Ceylon, patrolled the Malacca Strait almost as far as Singapore, up the west coast of Siam and the Bay of Bengal. The force had been built up since the Italian armistice with new or refitted T- and S-class boats now equipped with air-conditioning for the tropic seas, radar – although not the superb surface search sets fitted to the US fleet boats – and main ballast tanks converted to carry extra fuel. They remained a different species to the American submarines. William King, in the east again in command of *Telemachus*, has described his first sight of one of these, 'streamlined, shark-nosed', ripping easily past him at a cruising speed of 17 knots; '*Telemachus* goggled.'[26] Remembering the emotionally charged times when he had missed his prey for lack of surface speed, King felt as if he had brought a little Model T Ford to compete with Rolls-Royces.

Lt.-Cdr. Edward Young of the Royal Naval Volunteer Reserve, in command of *Storm*, had similar feelings when posted to Fremantle. The crew accommodation of a US submarine he was shown around made him feel 'downright ashamed' of the conditions in which his own sailors and stokers had to exist at sea. And he found it galling to compare the latest centimetric radar on the US boat with his own 'somewhat out-dated aircraft warning set'.[27]

The British boats had the dangerous advantage with their lesser periscope depth of being able to operate in shallower waters. Their chief targets were the small craft the Japanese were now using to supply their army in Burma, but there were also tankers from the refineries at Medan and Belewan in north-eastern Sumatra and occasional warships and Japanese and German submarines from Penang operating against Indian Ocean commerce.

One of these was sighted from *Telemachus* shortly after she had dived in the first light of 17 July; it was heading south-east through the narrow One Fathom Bank Channel in the Malacca Strait where King had been waiting for days. He hurried to the control room to take the periscope: 'I saw a sea mirror-calm, metal still. The fingers of mist half-dispersed were moving in the morning sun. My heart tightened as out of a curl of fog there burst a large Japanese U-boat . . . going top speed for home on the surface.'[28]

He was unable to observe her bow wave for an estimate of speed since he dared not raise the periscope far above the surface, which was so calm he 'could see flies floating on the water'. Instead he had *Jane's Fighting Ships* turned up to find the best speed of *Kaigun*-class submarines: 19 knots. Judging her plates foul with marine growth after her patrol, he allowed her 18. She was in fact *I166* with a theoretical top speed of just over 20 knots. *Telemachus* hung silent and motionless at 32 feet as she approached on a steady course which would bring her inside a mile range. The intent hush inside the boat and the stillness of the morning were such that for King, cautiously raising the periscope at intervals, the action had a dream-like quality. He could hear men breathing as they waited.

'Stand by to fire numbers one, two, three, four, five, six tubes!'

Pins were pulled by each tube in the bow and valves turned. He ordered the periscope up for the final observation, controlling its height above the surface with the briefest finger signals to the leading hand working the hydraulic control lever, and commenced firing individually aimed shots spread from a quarter of a length ahead to half a length astern of the submarine at roughly 4-second intervals. A minute and a half after the first torpedo left the tube a tremendous explosion shook the boat, but by that time the first lieutenant had lost control of trim and King was unable to see the result as *Telemachus*'s bows, having briefly broached the surface, plunged downwards. It turned out they had been supplied with torpedoes with a new, heavier 'Torpex' warhead but not the necessary new weight data. King felt sure the enemy must have sunk, but dared not surface to look for the tell-tale oil and debris; it was only later that Ultra intelligence confirmed *I166* had gone down.[29]

After moving away for some days, King returned to the scene of his triumph to find two submarine chasers waiting for him. He was fortunate to survive their attack and only escaped by bumping silently at minimum speed along the side of the shallow channel just beneath the surface while the enemy lay listening in the middle. 'Did we sweat! All machines, fans and air conditioning had to be switched off. Sixty men lay or sat at their work while the humid heat increased to an appalling moist mist. Our hair stood on end and itched, and our skins burst out into the red spots of prickly heat.'[30]

During this tense period the first lieutenant handed King a message he had just decoded. It described the sinking of a Dutch merchantman, *Tjisilak*, in the Indian Ocean by the Japanese submarine *I8* under Cdr. Tatsunoke Ariizumi, and the subsequent murder of ninety-eight survivors with swords and spanners wielded as clubs on the submarine's deck. The story had come from two witnesses left for dead in a lifeboat and subsequently rescued. King prayed the submarine concerned was the one they had blown up.

I166 was the third Penang-based submarine sunk by British patrols in the Malacca Strait: the previous December Lt.-Cdr. Mervyn Wingfield in *Taurus* had sunk *I34*, and in February Lt.-Cdr. L.W.A. Bennington in *Tally Ho* had despatched a 1,100-ton ex-Italian boat taken over by the Germans and renamed *U.IT23*. On his previous patrol Bennington had sunk a Japanese light cruiser. Apart from these successes and damage to another light cruiser, substantial targets were so scarce that British submarines had achieved little: in the first six months of 1944 they sank only eight sizeable *Marus* totalling 16,000 tons.[31]

By contrast, in the same period, Lockwood's and Christie's forces sank over a million tons of merchant shipping and 125,000 tons of warships, much of the latter in June during the Philippine Sea campaign.[32] This rate of attrition continued through July when the Japanese lost a further 220,000 tons of merchant shipping to US submarines, finally persuading the naval staff in Washington that Japan could be strangled by a blockade of her sea routes. Admiral King proposed the capture of Formosa and the establishment there and on the neighbouring China coast of bases from which the Japanese home islands could be cut off from their southern sources of supply, in particular oil. It was a surgical alternative to the conventional strategy of invading islands and annihilating garrisons along the 'two roads to Japan', but MacArthur was intent on fulfilling a promise he had made when forced out of the Philippines that he would return. That he might return at less cost, but with less personal glory, after Japan's economic sinews had been cut was not a concept he was prepared to consider; and since Nimitz and Spruance were doubtful about the logistics of invading Formosa from the Marianas, MacArthur's arguments were accepted by the Joint Chiefs of Staff.[33]

This continued failure by Roosevelt's strategists to comprehend the fragility of Japan's economic lifelines almost certainly prolonged the war and, in the words of the submarine historian, Clay Blair, 'committed the United States to tens of thousands of unnecessary casualties'.[34] That the attrition of Japanese merchant shipping continued during the late summer and autumn at an increasing rate was due to increasing numbers of US submarines, together with the establishment of an advanced fuelling and repair base at Saipan, considerably shortening the time to the operational areas.

Two of the most productive of these were the 'choke points' of the Formosa and Luzon Straits, the latter christened 'Convoy

College'. Since the demarcation between the Pearl Harbor and Fremantle spheres still ran through 'Convoy College', the line was shifted 90 miles further south to give Lockwood's numerically stronger force an unimpeded run of the area, now the chief battle-ground in the commerce war. Had Admiral King's plan been adopted, the Japanese anti-submarine surface and air forces based at Takao, southern Formosa, would have been deprived of their bases, and overwhelming US air power established in their place could have completed the severance of Japanese shipping lanes in a short time.

On 3 August the Japanese reacted to the steady loss of their shipping by placing the Grand Escort Fleet under the Combined Fleet. It was intended that the resources of the fleet would thereby be made available to strengthen convoy escorts. Given the Japanese naval predilection for decisive battle and indifference to such unheroic operations as the protection of merchant shipping, it was inevitable that the reverse would occur. The fall of Saipan and defeat in the Philippine Sea had made it clear to Admiral Toyoda and his planners that the war was irretrievably lost, but in accordance with the samurai ethic they intended to stage a glorious suicide ride with the great ships in which they would 'bloom as flowers of death', a purpose they concealed from the crews under the codename for the coming action, 'Sho-[victory-]1'.[35] Thus the best destroyers would be retained for the fleet and the best pilots and aircraft drained from escort duty to fill the huge gaps in fleet air squadrons. Captain Atsushi Oi, who served on the staff of the Grand Escort Fleet from its inception, understated the position when he told his American interrogator after the war that incorporation into the Combined Fleet had not improved their situation. He went on:

during the [US] carrier attacks on Formosa in October 1944 [Japanese] aircraft suitable for scouting and anti-submarine patrol were practically eliminated. Prior to the organisational change in August these aircraft for anti-submarine patrol were for the exclusive use of the Grand Escort Fleet and could not be used in offensive operations by the Combined Fleet.[36]

But in truth there were no measures the Japanese could have taken to compensate for the superiority of US radar, hence for the US submarines' decisive advantages over escorts during night surface action. In September the new chief of the Grand Escort Fleet, Admiral Naokuni Nomura, who had succeeded Oikawa as the organization passed under Toyoda's supreme command, issued orders that in danger areas convoys were to proceed only by day, hiding at night in suitable anchorages along the coasts and islands.[37]

Japanese submarines, which had suffered further severe losses in the Marianas in July, were all recalled during August to be fitted with radar, and the large I-class boats were adapted for carrying human torpedoes – *kaitens* – on deck. Some were ordered out in September as US carrier air strikes on Japanese bases in the Palaus, the western Carolines and the Philippines heralded MacArthur's coming assault on the Philippines; two were lost without any success in their scouting or attack roles, together with one of a new 1,700-ton class designed specifically for carrying supplies and troops to isolated garrisons. On 17 October, as it became apparent that the anticipated US invasion of the Philippines was imminent, Toyoda issued orders for 'Sho-1'; training with *kaitens* was suspended and Vice-Admiral Shigeyoshi Miwa, who had succeeded Takagi in command of the Sixth (Submarine) Fleet, ordered out all available submarines, fourteen in all, to form two scouting lines east of the Philippines. They arrived too late to sight the invasion forces which landed troops on the shores of Leyte, central Philippines, on the morning of the 19th.

The following night Toyoda's main force, headed by a fleet carrier, three light carriers and two battleships converted with flight decks over their after sections, sortied from the Sea of Japan under Vice-Admiral Ozawa. The 1st Striking Force of battleships, including the giant *Yamato* and *Musashi*, and heavy cruisers under Vice-Admiral Takeo Kurita, had left Lingga roads north of Singapore two days previously, and the following evening, the 21st, a smaller squadron of cruisers named the 2nd Striking Force, under Vice-Admiral Shima, sailed from the Pescadores off the west coast of Formosa. Toyoda's 'Sho-1' plan was simple in concept but, in the Japanese naval tradition, complex in detail. Ozawa's carriers had few aircraft; most, together with their trained pilots – and too many aircraft of the Grand Escort Fleet – had been lost attempting to defend Formosan bases from US air strikes earlier that month. Ozawa's carrier force was therefore to be little more than a decoy to lure the US fleet under Admiral William Halsey away to the north while the 1st and 2nd Striking Forces, the former split into a main body under Kurita and a smaller force under Vice-Admiral Nishimura, were to fall on the transports off the invasion beaches in the Gulf of Leyte, Kurita from the north by way of the San Bernadino Strait, Shima and Nishimura from the south by way of Suriago Strait. On the 23rd, as the four separate forces steered their diverse courses for Leyte, Miwa ordered all submarines to close Samar, the island north of the Gulf of Leyte, and concentrate 60 miles off the coast to attack enemy task forces or transports, pressing home their attacks at any cost.[38]

Lockwood and Christie, meanwhile, had disposed submarines to report Japanese fleet movements, although they sent none to the east of the Philippines, where US anti-submarine forces would treat all contacts as hostile. Lockwood's patrols off southern Japan missed Ozawa, but Shima's cruisers from the Pescadores were detected by three submarines during their transit of 'Convoy College' south of Formosa; they were reported and attacked by Sea Dragon, without success.

Kurita's main battleship force was detected by one of Christie's packs, Darter and Dace under Darter's skipper, Cdr. David McClintock, while steaming north-east up the Palawan Passage north of Borneo. The pack had been active in this area for a week and had sunk two tankers and damaged a further 20,000 tons, yet Kurita steered straight for them on a steady course at 15 knots. Darter's radar picked him up shortly after midnight, on the 22nd/23rd, after which both submarines tracked, pulling ahead to submerge and attack just before dawn, McClintock taking the port column, Lt.-Cdr. Bladen Claggett in Dace the starboard. McClintock fired first, launching six torpedoes at the leading cruiser, in fact Kurita's flagship Atago, and then swinging to fire his stern tubes at the second in the line. Four of the first salvo hit Atago, detonating with heavy explosions as he was making his final observations for the second salvo at what proved to be the cruiser Takeo. Two of these hit. He ordered the boat deep and, swinging the periscope back to the first target, saw her settling by the bows, issuing bright flames and smoke. As destroyers sped in dropping depth-charges indiscriminately she sank. Meanwhile Claggett, identifying the leading ship of the starboard column as a cruiser, fired all his bow tubes at what he believed was a battleship astern of her, scoring four hits. She was actually the cruiser Maya. She too quickly sank.

Kurita, who later transferred his flag to the Yamato from the destroyer which took him from the Atago, continued on his way towards Mindoro in the Philippines, where he was picked up on radar and reported by Angler and Guitarro of Christie's force. The badly damaged Takeo, meanwhile, remained where she had been hit under the protection of destroyers, which detected McClintock and prevented him closing. Surfacing that night, he and Claggett agreed on a co-ordinated attack whereby Darter would come in on the surface and draw off the screen to leave the way clear for Dace from the opposite direction. However, in making his way around the enemy, McClintock, who was working on a de'd reckoning position twenty-four hours old, grounded on a shoal at speed and drove up high and dry. All attempts to get off proved unsuccessful, so he had codes and all secret material and instruments destroyed and demolition charges set, then transferred his crew to the *Dace*. Over the following days, while the *Takeo* limped home, several American submarines were directed to finish off *Darter* and attempted to do so with shell fire, but she proved indestructible and remained high up on the shoal for the duration of the war, and long after.

The reports of Shima's and Kurita's movements alerted Halsey – who had already received notice from radio intelligence that the Japanese forces were emerging – but the submarines, which were of course excluded from the eastern side of the Philippines, took no further part in the series of actions that took place off Leyte and Samar on the 24th. It may be, however, as the British naval historian Stephen Roskill has suggested, that the brilliant combined attack by *Darter* and *Dace*, during which Kurita had his flagship struck from under him, contributed to his loss of nerve at a critical juncture in the battle. On the morning of the 25th Halsey was lured northwards as Ozawa intended, leaving Kurita's way in to the Gulf of Leyte clear, but instead of entering and devastating the assembled transports, he withdrew to re-form his force, then retired, thus losing 'the greatest opportunity to come the way of the Japanese navy since Pearl Harbor'.[39]

US submarines came into action again in the closing stages in the evening of the 25th. Lockwood had moved two wolfpacks in the Luzon Strait into Ozawa's path as he retired northwards with the remains of a battered carrier force. One group, *Tuna*, *Haddock* and Galantin's *Halibut*, were combing south in line abreast 30 miles apart when the radio operators began picking up cryptic exchanges between US dive-bomber crews attacking Ozawa's ships. Presently smoke was sighted and above it the bursts of a heavy anti-aircraft barrage whose rapid concussions could be heard. Then at 17.42 the pagoda-like foremast of a battleship rose above the horizon directly ahead of the easternmost boat, *Halibut*, at a radar range of 31,000 yards. Galantin dived in case the battleship had an equally powerful radar or could detect his own radar pulses, and set up for a submerged attack.

An hour later the battleship, evidently damaged since she was only making 15 knots, had approached inside 2½ miles, but then she altered to starboard, forcing Galantin to fire at once despite the comparatively long torpedo run of 3,400 yards. He launched a full bow salvo spread over the length of the target and went deep. After 3 minutes and 14 seconds they heard the explosion of the first torpedo, then four more at intervals, followed by other explosions and breaking-up noises over the next half hour. Surfacing in the moonlight shortly before 20.00, Galantin sighted a mound 'strongly resembling the hull of a large, capsizing ship', but as he closed it disappeared from view and from the radar screen at the same time.[40] He was certain he had 'fulfilled every submariner's dream', the sinking of a battleship. Spirits in the boat soared and he broke out the two bottles of beer per man that US submarines were now permitted to carry. Later that evening a member of the other wolfpack, *Jallao*, sank one of Ozawa's light cruisers, and the next day a third pack intercepted the group but was unable to get in an attack. Alas, after Galantin's return he learned that the only two battleships in Ozawa's force, the hybrid battleship-carriers, had made port. Lockwood credited him with a heavy cruiser, but post-war research suggested his victim had actually been a destroyer.

So ended the second battle of the Philippine Sea, usually known as the Battle of Leyte Gulf, one of the most complete victories in naval history: Ozawa lost his four carriers to fleet air strikes, Kurita the giant battleship *Musashi* and another three heavy cruisers, Nishimura his only two battleships and a heavy cruiser. Shima with his lighter force had simply withdrawn. Halsey lost only one light fleet carrier, two escort carriers and some smaller vessels, although a number of fleet and escort carriers suffered extensive damage and casualties from suicide pilots crashing their aircraft into their targets as primed incendiary bombs in the first planned kamikaze offensive. One escort carrier had gone down as a result of kamikaze damage; another, the *Santee*, was on fire from a kamikaze when she was struck by a torpedo from *I56* under Lt.-Cdr. Morinaga, the only one of the Japanese submarines off Samar to penetrate the escorts and score. Morinaga reported sinking the carrier, but the *Santee* was able to extinguish fires, control flooding and steam off. One I-class boat was sunk on the 24th; another eight remained off the invasion area while the medium RO-class boats returned home. Over the following weeks the I-class boats on station reported sinking three carriers, two destroyers, six transports and damaging a battleship; their actual successes were one anti-aircraft cruiser damaged, one destroyer escort sunk. The price they paid was heavy: only two of the eight returned from patrol; most were destroyed by the specialized anti-submarine escorts, several in attacks with hedgehogs, a weapon of which the Japanese were unaware.

Although the Japanese boats were equipped with radar, the sets were obsolete by US standards and liable to frequent faults, and the technicians were poorly trained. As a result most COs seem not to have used them except in poor visibility and only for brief periods. While the air search sets seem to have given adequate warning of planes, the principal surface enemies, small escort vessels, could only be picked up at about 4 miles, and some COs reported not being able to detect small ships at all.[41] By contrast it is notable that all the US sighting reports and attacks on Japanese forces in the Leyte campaign were triggered by radar detection, usually at great ranges beyond the horizon. The same now applied to the war against merchant convoys and transports, which was taken to new heights that month: altogether seventy *Marus* totalling over 300,000 tons were sunk by submarines; a further forty-seven, chiefly ships carrying supplies and reinforcements to the Philippines, were sunk by aircraft.[42]

October was also a record month for US submarine losses, five in all, almost as many as had been sunk in the whole of 1942. Only two of these – or three if the *Salmon* is included, as will appear – were directly due to enemy action, one by mine, one by depth-charge attack. Of the others one was almost certainly the victim of friendly fire: a US aircraft and destroyer escort hunting for a Japanese submarine – *RO41* – which had sunk an escort off Morotai, south of the Philippines, believed they had located her and, although in an area scheduled for US submarine operations, attacked. The victim, *Seawolf*, evidently tried to send out sonar recognition signals, for the destroyer picked up dots and dashes, but in a garbled form. After firing her hedgehog she reported seeing a large air bubble, followed by a small amount of debris.[43] Another boat, *Darter*, was lost, as described, by stranding in the Palawan Passage while trying to work around the damaged cruiser *Takeo*; and the same night in the Formosa Strait, *Tang* was hit by one of her own torpedoes.

It was O'Kane's fifth patrol in command. He had already despatched five small freighters and damaged others in night sur-face mêlées from extraordinarily close range inside their escorts. That night he picked up another convoy bound southwards on radar. He manoeuvred inshore, as he had done for a convoy the previous night, then slipped in slowly from ahead between the escorts until he was within 300 yards of the leading merchantmen and between their columns, when he fired two bow torpedoes at one, swung and launched three from the stern at another.[44] They hit, starting fires. Other merchantmen began shooting and the escorts wheeled in towards the submarine silhouetted against the flames. O'Kane fired a salvo at one escort which appeared from behind a blazing ship and saw it rent by explosions as he made away from the scene at full speed. Post-war research did not substantiate his impression that it sank. After reloading his last two torpedoes he circled and came in again on the landward side, setting up on a damaged ship stopped in the water. The first torpedo ran straight, leaving a phosphorescent trace in the sea, and a cheer rang through the compartments as the second and last left its tube – now they would turn for home. It porpoised up ahead though and started a tight circle, again visible from the phosphorescence stirred beneath the surface. O'Kane yelled down the hatch, 'All ahead emergency! Right full rudder!' and as the trail continued the circle, heading back towards the submarine, 'Left full rudder!' in a vain attempt to swing the stern clear. The torpedo struck aft, detonating violently and opening up the ballast tanks and the after compartments, which flooded, pulling the stern down, as he described it later 'much as you would drop a pendulum suspended in a horizontal position'.[45] He shouted to the startled telephone talker staring up from the conning tower, 'Shut the hatch!' But water was pouring in before he could do so. O'Kane and eight others from the bridge and one from the conning tower found themselves in the sea as the submarine sank beneath them.

By morning only O'Kane and three others were alive, together with another five who had managed to leave the submarine 180 feet down on the bottom through the escape hatch from the forward compartment and had survived the subsequent ascent with breathing apparatus known as Momsen Lungs. They were fished up by a Japanese escort and severely beaten. O'Kane said afterwards that when he and his men realized the 'clubbings and kickings were being administered by the burned, mutilated survivors of our own handiwork, we found we could take it with less prejudice'.[46] They spent the rest of the war in Japanese prison camps. O'Kane was credited with thirty-one sinkings totalling nearly 228,000 tons over his five patrols in command of *Tang* – reduced by post-war research to twenty-four of 93,800 tons, but still sufficient to leave him the highest-scoring American CO of the war in terms of numbers of ships. He was awarded the Congressional Medal of Honor.

The US submarine force suffered far fewer losses than the Japanese force or indeed that of any other major belligerent – fifty-two all told during the course of the war, forty-five of which were fleet boats. Only forty-three have been put down to enemy action, an average of less than one a month. The reasons have much to do with Japanese neglect of shipping protection until too late, the subsequent squandering in particular of air escorts in fleet combat operations, and their chronic shortage of surface escorts. As in the British case in the early years, this generally precluded escorts remaining behind over a submarine which had been forced down and hunting it to death. On the American side, fleet submarines, while not able to dive so deep as U-boats, were ruggedly built and capable of absorbing tremendous punishment. The pre-war system of testing and adapting individual pieces of machinery and components such as battery cells for shock, together with a series of tests in the winter of 1940-1 when three *Tambor*-class submarines were subjected to actual depth-charge explosions at sea from ranges closing eventually to 100 feet, and during the war detailed analysis of damage suffered in action, followed by the introduction of structural modifications, allowed survival under often ferocious beatings.[47]

Ned Beach has described the experience in *Trigger* in graphic detail: 'Her heavy steel sides buckle in and out, her cork insulation breaks off in great chunks and flies about. Lockers are shaken open and the contents spewed all over everything.'[48]

Some men prayed secretly under such poundings, Beach noted; others, with a more fatalistic concept of life and death, felt 'a sort of masochistic pleasure'; all watched covertly to see how others were taking it; and, as in every service, the skipper's demeanour was all important.[49] Previous experience did not inoculate anyone against fear. Beach, like everyone else who came through the ordeal, made no attempt afterwards to disguise it. As exec. during one close attack he climbed into his bunk deliberately to demonstrate unconcern to the others in the wardroom. 'I turned my head to the bulkhead so that no one would see my eyelids quiver, and forced myself to lie still.' The beat of the enemy propellers carried plainly through the hull plates close by:

SWISHSWISHSWISHSWISHSWISH, drop you bastard . . . drop and be goddamned to hell! SWISHSWISHSWISHSWISHSWISHSWISHSWISH-SWISHSWISH click click click! Here they come here they come here they come here they come! WHAM! WHAM! WHAM![50]

On 30 October, *Trigger* started a chain of events that led to one of the worst beatings any US submarine survived. Operating as part of a pack with *Sterlet* and *Salmon* south of Kyushu, she torpedoed but failed to sink a 10,000-ton tanker. *Salmon* under Lt.-Cdr. Harley Nauman went in next and fired a salvo at the damaged ship, which was guarded by four escorts. Three of the salvo broached the surface, revealing the submarine's position, which was also betrayed by squealing propeller shafts as Nauman turned hard left and took her deep. All four escorts thrashed towards her and, accurately pinpointing her position, dropped four patterns of six to eight charges each, the first two patterns exploding with thunderous detonations close above the engine room and after end of the submarine as she descended through 310 feet. Nauman reported: 'The Conning Tower vibrated up and down so violently that I thought the ship was going to shake herself apart. I remember bending my knees to ease the shock.'[51]

Small fixtures were torn off seatings and propelled about the compartments, together with unattached gear, creating 'an appreciable missile hazard to personnel in some areas' during the whiplash contortions to which the submarine was subjected. The after torpedo room hatch was blown completely open and only back-up blanking plates across the hatch opening – an innovation resulting from previous reports of hatches momentarily lifting from their seatings during close depth-charging – saved the compartment from immediate flooding. As it was, the diesel engine air induction piping collapsed and flooded, three hatch trunks flooded and all main engine exhaust valves started leaking, as did the upper conning-tower hatch and the stuffing boxes for both periscopes. The vent of No. 7 fuel/ballast tank was ruptured, permitting sea water to displace 7,000 gallons of the lighter oil fuel and, most serious, the valves were torn from the fuel ballast tank riser inboard vent lines, allowing sea water to stream at high pressure into both engine rooms. The after hydroplanes had been jammed at hard a-dive, and with the weight of water coming in and the downward pressure waves from the third and fourth patterns of charges bursting above, depth control was lost and the submarine sank rapidly to 400 feet. Fortunately the electric motors had not been affected. Emergency full ahead was rung up, auxiliary tanks pumped and, with the bow planes set to rise, the descent was checked and the submarine brought up to 300 feet. No sooner was the speed eased, however, than she started down, soon going off the gauge at 450 feet and sinking to about 500 feet, twice her operating depth, before she could be checked with emergency full speed. She was brought up to 150 feet, but again as soon as emergency revolutions were reduced she started sinking and this time no action could stop her descent; she fell to something over

600 feet. At this depth the deformation of the pressure hull where it was squeezed inwards between the frames was 2 inches in the worst-affected areas, as measured afterwards.[52]

With batteries much depleted from the sustained high speed and the water in the engine room up to the level of the main motor casing and rising, Nauman had no option but to blow tanks and attempt to fight it out on the surface. It was 20.30, seventeen minutes after the first patterns of charges had stricken the submarine, when he gave the order to surface. She came up and floated with decks awash and a 15° list to starboard. There was no possibility of diving again since most of the high-pressure air which would be needed to blow tanks to bring her up afterwards had escaped through internal leaks and damaged external vents. The escorts could be seen in the moonlight 3½ miles away, fortunately distracted by the large oil slick from No. 7 tank, and still dropping occasional depth-charges. This gave Nauman's crew vital minutes to make repairs, plug leaks, start main engines, correct the list and blow tanks to increase freeboard. At 21.00, by which time only two main engines had been put on line, one of the escorts spotted the submarine, illuminated her with a searchlight and opened fire, without however making much attempt to close the range without the others' support. The sights of *Salmon*'s deck gun had been shattered and one of the loading numbers had to coach the trainer on target as they replied with deliberate shots. By 21.15 the engineers had succeeded in putting a third main engine on line, but they were defeated by the fourth. Nauman, restricted to a top speed of 16 knots, could only conduct an evasive, circling action without being able to outrun the four enemy vessels who were now manoeuvring round him in line ahead, firing, fortunately ineffectually, with deck and machine guns. The unequal contest continued for another three hours until Nauman charged and broke through the enemy line towards a rain squall he had spotted beyond. His boldness paid off and he was able to hide and escape in the squall.

The following night, in answer to his call for assistance, he was joined by the other two of his pack and another submarine in the area, who escorted him back to Saipan; there *Salmon* was temporarily patched up for passage back to the United States, but her damage was subsequently found to be so extensive she was scrapped as a constructive war loss.[53]

Galantin suffered a similar hammering the following month while *Halibut* was operating with a wolfpack in 'Convoy College'. It was shortly after noon on 14 November, a bright Pacific day;

he was at periscope depth and had just fired a salvo of four torpedoes at a large freighter in a northbound convoy. He heard two explosions, then became aware of 'a loud, fast buzzing noise' unlike anything he had experienced before.[54] The sound was reported by hands both forward and aft as passing over them four times, or circling, although Galantin heard it only once, 'a low-pitched buzzing, increasing in loudness and then decreasing for an estimated total of 40 seconds'. As it faded there was a heavy explosion close to port. Wondering if this were some new anti-submarine weapon, he took the boat deep, using the negative, 'down express' tank and full speed. Reaching 325 feet another four explosions sounded above, not however 'the characteristic "click-brr-roomp-woosh" of depth-charges', and the depth-charge indicator lights lit for detonations close to starboard. He crept away, rigged for silent running, all watertight doors closed for depth-charge attack until seventeen minutes later another close explosion shook the boat, shattering glasses and gauges, and cracking the cork lining of the hull as the plates were pressed inwards. In the silence afterwards they could hear the rapid chirping of sonar pulses indicating the enemy had sonar contact, then a pattern of close charges burst just above, sounding to men in the forward compartments like 'a thousand sledgehammers pounding the hull' and sending the submarine into violent contortions 'as if she was a giant fish trying to shake off a hook', pressing her down another 100 feet to 420 feet.[55] In the control room Galantin had the impression of a greenish glow, a phenomenon other skippers had reported, but he had never experienced before; he was momentarily stunned, wondering if this was the way it would end.

The interior was a shambles of broken fittings and glass, cork and paint flakes, the contents of lockers, drawers and the pantries strewn over the decks, oil and water leaking from glands and ruptured piping. In the torpedo compartment forward, deck plates had been dislodged and men hurled into the bilges, and valves had spun open admitting sea water. After the initial shock Galantin asked the diving officer to try and ease her up to 350 feet. Reports of damage began to come in to the control room; the hands, still appearing dazed, responded to orders quietly as if at drill. The sonar apparatus had been knocked out, but from the silence above it appeared the escorts had left to return to the convoy. So it proved, and after dark Galantin surfaced and recharged batteries and expelled the hot, foul air from below that had caused their eyes to smart and heads to ache. Later he was able to call a submarine from another pack operating in the Strait, which escorted him back to

Saipan at 12 knots. An inspection there revealed the pressure hull dished in between the frames as *Salmon*'s had been to a depth of 2 inches in the worst-affected area by the forward deck gun. The gun itself showed signs of a very close explosion: the paint was burned off the barrel, the bronze breech cover split, the trunnions blown apart. Galantin speculated that perhaps the gun had saved them.

In Saipan he learned the cause of the mysterious noise that had preceded the first explosion. The CO of another of their pack had observed large flying boats circling continuously ahead of and over the convoy during *Halibut*'s attack. Since it was possible to hear very low-flying aircraft from a submarine at periscope depth, they concluded that this was what had been heard, and Galantin realized he had been the victim of *Jikitanchiki*, the Japanese magnetic anomaly detector.[56] After returning to Pearl Harbor a Board of Inspection judged the *Halibut*'s pressure hull so distorted that she was unsafe to dive, her damage too extensive to repair, and like *Salmon*, she became a constructive loss.

Damage on such a scale was exceptional, although three more submarines were lost in November, two probably to depth-charge attack, one to a mine. In general the wolfpacks, now commanded by their senior skipper without a tactical commander, ruled the seas from the former Dutch Indies to Japan, terrifying Japanese merchant seamen, numbers of whom tried to jump ship in port, and forcing convoys on circuitous routes close inshore, sheltering by night. The Luzon Strait in particular had become 'the devils' sea'.[57]

In the late summer and autumn losses had run at over 200,000 tons a month; in October, despite the diversion of submarines to the Leyte operations and supply of the many guerrilla bands operating in the Philippines, Lockwood's and Christie's forces sank a record seventy *Marus* totalling over 300,000 tons; a further forty-seven were sunk by aircraft. The figures fell in November and further still in December, but this was a measure of the dearth of shipping remaining to Japan: her stock had been cut by half to something over 2½ million tons, quite inadequate to sustain the economy. By the end of the year US submarines, and to an increasing extent aircraft, were exerting an effective blockade, choking supplies of oil, raw materials and food to a fraction of the levels Japan needed for survival. Already defeated militarily in the air, on the sea and in her defensive perimeter of islands, she was now in an economic stranglehold.[58]

In addition to the merchant shipping sunk, US submarines had completed the destruction of the escort carriers converted from liners: on a black, rainy night in August Cdr. Henry Munson in *Rasher* had sunk the *Taiyo* escorting an important southbound convoy of tankers through 'Convoy College', and in two forays into the disorganized columns afterwards had claimed another four ships, bringing his total to five of altogether 52,600 tons, a patrol tonnage record only to be exceeded by one other skipper.[59] In September Lt.-Cdr. Eugene Flukey of *Barb* sank the *Unyo*, again in a night surface attack in 'Convoy College'; coming in on radar, he lined her up with an overlap on a large tanker, firing three torpedoes at each in a single bow salvo and hearing two hits on the tanker, three on the carrier, a record salvo which sank both ships for a total 31,000 tons. Flukey was to head the list of US COs in terms of total tonnage sunk – as corrected after the war 95,360 tons to O'Kane's 93,824 tons.[60] He was awarded the Congressional Medal of Honor.

In November Lt.-Cdr. Gordon Underwood in *Spadefish* sank the *Shinyo* on her first escort mission with infantry transports from Manchuria to the Philippines. The same month submarines delivered two of their heaviest blows on the Imperial fleet: in the early hours of the 21st Lt.-Cdr. Eli Reich in *Sealion* sank the 31,000-ton battleship *Kongo* in the East China Sea, the only battleship sunk by a submarine during the Pacific war; and a week later Lt.-Cdr. Joseph Enright in *Archerfish* mortally wounded the 60,000-ton *Shinano*, sister of the giant battleships *Yamato* and *Musashi*, but converted on the stocks into a carrier. She had sailed from Tokyo Bay the previous night in order to escape US bombing raids, and was not quite complete; in particular, several pumps and watertight doors had not been fitted. Enright, on patrol outside the Bay, picked her up on radar and trailed, urging extra revolutions from his engineer as the great ship sped southwards. Only her zigzags allowed him to stay in touch, but at 03.00 on the 29th she altered towards him. He dived and sixteen minutes later was able to fire six torpedoes from an ideal position with 1,500 yards to run. Four hit. It should not have been sufficient to sink a capital ship of her size and internal subdivision, but the new crew was undrilled, some watertight doors were missing, others leaked, and dockyard workers aboard to complete her panicked. She sank a few hours later.

Finally, in December, Lt.-Cdr. Louis McGregor of the *Redfish* damaged the escort carrier *Junyo* so badly that she never sailed again, and ten days later, on the 19th, he sank the light carrier *Unryu*. The counter-attack by the screening destroyers was so accurate *Redfish* suffered the same degree of damage as had

Salmon and *Halibut*, and she was lucky to survive. In fact no US submarines were lost that month.

Thus in the third year of the Pacific war the American force fulfilled its potential. Besides the obvious factor of increasing war experience, this was largely due to superiority over the enemy at night, Ultra intelligence and growing numbers, over 150 fleet boats by the end of the year. It is notable, however, that the rate of sinking achieved, one and a half *Marus* for every submarine in the operational area, was no higher than in 1943;[61] and as in all navies, for every high-scoring CO there was another who seldom or never hit. In September and October, the high point of the campaign against merchant shipping when almost three-quarters of a million tons were destroyed, 42 out of the 113 war patrols returned no sinkings.[62]

In the desperate closing stages of the war, Japan resorted to suicide weapons. She had no option. With her air forces and navy overwhelmed, and supplies of oil and materials to rebuild them cut to a trickle, she could only turn to the weapons of the weak or surrender. The latter was psychologically impossible. Her people had been taught to believe that they were divinely ordained to rule the world; recently they had been misled by their government about the defeats suffered by their forces and kept in ignorance of the impossible material odds against them. They could not have considered surrender. The Emperor and governing circles were no doubt as much the victims of their creed and code as those they ruled; they called for sacrifice in a cause they knew rationally was lost and, unready as a group for the shame of surrender, clung to hopes more unreal than those on which they had launched the war.

The development of the human torpedo named *kaiten* has been mentioned.[63] The name was compounded from the Japanese for 'sky' and 'change' and carried the connotation of a mystical turn in the fortunes of the war, perfectly mirroring the Emperor's hopes. The success of the kamikaze pilots in the Gulf of Leyte, and the adulation they received, had excited the young naval officers already training with *kaitens* at a secret island base, Otsujima, in the Inland Sea off Honshu. It was hoped that they could attack the invasion supply ships and transports off Leyte. There were production difficulties however, and the first operational unit of twelve *kaitens* carried by three mother submarines was not formed until early November, by which time the opportunity had passed. The advanced US anchorages at Ulithi in the western Carolines and the Kossel Channel in the Palau group were chosen as targets instead after aerial reconnaissance had shown concentrations of shipping at both.

Vice-Admiral Miwa inspected the twelve young officer pilots at their base on 7 November, reminded them in a speech of the glorious deeds of the kamikaze pilots, and presented each with a short ceremonial *seppuku*, or *hara kiri* sword. They were indeed embarked on a suicide mission, for although Miwa had insisted on an ejection apparatus in each cockpit to allow the pilot to escape when nearing his target, its use was never seriously envisaged – and would hardly have saved the pilot in any case.

The senior pilot of this first group to go into action was Lt. Sekio Nishina, co-inventor of the weapon; he carried in his pocket a photograph of his fellow inventor, Lt. Hiroshi Kuroki, who had drowned during the rigorous, and often fatal, training and trials programme. Next day the pilots boarded the mother submarines, the long-range B1 scouting types *I36* and *I37* with aircraft-hangars and deck guns removed to make space on deck for the *kaitens*, and the new C2, scarcely modified from the earlier C1 attack type, *I47*, also with her deck gun removed. As the submarines sailed, other crews and spectators cheered the pilots, each standing on his *kaiten*, a white towel *haitchi matchi* of purity bound around his forehead, brandishing his short sword, each perhaps filled with the vision of taking a US capital ship and a thousand barbarian sailors with him into the spirit world, earning with his deed an enduring place amongst the ancestral warrior heroes.

For most the reality was sadly anti-climactic. *I37* was detected before she reached her slipping point off Palau, hunted by two destroyer escorts and blown up with hedgehogs in the depths. The other two submarines arrived close off Ulithi on 19 November and made a reconnaissance of the anchorage to assist the pilots in their navigation and choice of targets. The *kaitens* were launched in the early hours of the 20th, four from *I47*, only one from *I36*, the other three having developed faults. The submarine COs waited, hearing a heavy detonation about an hour after the last *kaiten* had left, followed by other explosions, and they observed a tall pillar of flame and smoke inside the lagoon. This came from a fleet oiler loaded with aviation fuel, which had blown up when hit by one *kaiten*. The other *kaitens* were all destroyed before they could reach a target, one by ramming in the entrance channel, others by depth-charge or gunfire.

After the submarines returned to the Sixth Fleet base at Kure at the end of the month Miwa convened a meeting aboard his flagship to evaluate results. Aerial reconnaissance before the action and the submarines' own observations when they arrived on the 19th were compared with another aerial reconnaissance afterwards on the 23rd, and the skippers' reports of what they had heard and seen on the morning of the action. It was concluded that one aircraft-carrier had been sunk by the much admired Lt. Nishina, and three battleships altogether by the other *kaiten* pilots.[64] This was only a slightly exaggerated example of the optimistic way in which enemy losses had been assessed in the Japanese navy from the beginning. It stemmed perhaps from the nature of feared command hierarchies wherein each level reports what it believes the next above wishes to hear, perhaps from overconfidence after success in previous wars or maybe in this instance simply from the desire for good news for the navy and some hope after repeated disasters. Or was it pure propaganda? Certainly the great success supposed to have been scored by Nishina and the others was announced to the next batches of *kaiten* pilots under training, moving them to wild outbursts of shouting and cheering; one of them described after the war how it had inspired him to dream that 'I, too, would send a carrier to the bottom of the sea!'[65]

Vignettes of the next *kaiten* operation, aimed at six different US anchorages to strike uncertainty into the enemy and undermine his will, have been provided by the skipper of one of the parent submarines, Cdr. Mochitsura Hashimoto of *I58*. By this time, such had been the losses, only five others from his class of fifteen at the Naval College Submarine Course had survived; they commanded the other five I-class boats of what was termed the 'Kongo' unit. *I58* and two others left Kure on 29 December for the *kaiten* base, where the craft were loaded and secured on deck. After a ceremonial send-off by Miwa the submarines were cheered out to sea by an accompanying flotilla of small craft from whose masts flags and banners flew inscribed with the *kaiten* pilots' names and praise for their courage and patriotism; below, the crowded occupants chanted the pilots' names in unison repeatedly while the young men thus applauded stood on their craft on the submarines' decks, brows bound in white, brandishing their ceremonial swords in response.

Two of the pilots on *I58* were officers who ate in the wardroom with Hashimoto's officers, two were volunteers from the ranks who messed with the petty officers. They had no duties apart from maintaining their craft and spent much time playing chess together. Hashimoto found it painful to think he would send them out to certain death, but reflected that the numbers of those not returning were increasing so fast in all services that sooner or later their fate was inevitable in any case.[66]

Hashimoto's destination was Apra harbour, Guam. He arrived in the area on 6 January 1945 and waited some distance off, diving when air patrols appeared and spending much time submerged until the date fixed for the simultaneous attacks, passing up several merchant ship transports so as not to reveal his presence. Receiving confirmatory orders from Miwa on the 10th, he moved in the following evening, inviting all the pilots to a last meal in the wardroom and toasting their success. Surfacing shortly before 22.00 about 11 miles off the harbour entrance, he received a message with the disappointing results of an air reconnaissance from two days before: twenty large and forty small transports in Apra harbour, together with four floating docks. He advised the pilots to select the largest loaded transports and tried to console them with the hope that a carrier might have come in since the report.

Two of the *kaitens* could be entered from the hull of the submarine through flooding chambers whose upper hatches connected via flexible tubes to hatches on the underside of the pilots' cockpits; two could only be entered from on deck when the submarine was on the surface. Since Hashimoto did not intend to approach the launching point off the harbour on the surface, these two pilots had to take their places before he submerged for the final run in. They climbed to the bridge in white uniform shorts and tunics to report, standing in silence for a while, their faces indistinguishable in the darkness. One asked him which of the constellations visible between clouds was the Southern Cross. The question took Hashimoto by surprise, and not being able to find the group, he asked the navigator, who said it was not showing yet, but would soon appear in the south-east. The pilots said, 'We embark,' shook Hashimoto by the hand and climbed down to board their *kaitens* through the upper cockpit hatch.

He dived and steered in towards the entrance until 02.00 on the morning of the 12th, when he instructed the other two pilots, the young officers, to enter their craft; before they did so he showed them the lights of Apra through the periscope. 'Even now', he wrote long after the war, 'the composure of the two men remains fixed in my mind.'[67] At about 03.00 the pilots launched themselves one by one from the submarine after the final clamps had been released from inside, the officers crying 'Three cheers for the Emperor!' into the telephone connection with the control room just before the line was broken by their departure. Hashimoto steered some way out to sea before surfacing at 04.30 to observe the results of their attacks, but he was forced down by an air patrol and could neither see nor hear anything.

That night, while the young men's frugal belongings were being prepared for despatch to their families, he was shown two notes the pilots had written before departing. They manifested powerful feelings for 'Great Japan, the land of the Gods' for whom they were offering their lives as a sacrifice, confident in final victory. 'Only twenty-two years of life and it is now just like a dream. The meaning of life will be shown today ...'[68]

Whatever undue moral and psychological pressure was exerted to induce young men to 'volunteer' as kamikaze pilots[69] – and no doubt similar pressures were soon to be exerted by the navy to obtain recruits for increasing numbers of suicide units – it seems from these farewell notes that the first waves of volunteers for human torpedoes were filled with idealism. It was not surprising, of course, since the ancient samurai code adopted for the armed services taught that willingness to die was the supreme consummation of loyalty to the Emperor and love of country.

On the morning that Hashimoto's four pilots set off on their final ride towards Apra harbour, twelve other *kaitens* were launched from three 'Kongo' submarines variously off Hollandia, New Guinea, Kossol Passage in the Palaus and Ulithi; one of the 'Kongo' boats ordered to the Admiralty Islands had been attacked and so damaged that she had been forced to return to base; another, delayed by mechanical faults, was sunk by US escorts off Yap before she reached her launching position.

After the COs of the four submarines that had reached their targets had returned and been debriefed it was concluded from explosions that they reported hearing that as many as eighteen ships had been sunk, including a battleship, carriers, a cruiser, transports and a fleet oiler.[70] This was probably pure propaganda. A summary of submarine operations prepared at the end of the war by the staff of the Japanese Navy Ministry stated merely: 'there were no certain results reported ... However it is believed that in view of the amount of training of the pilots and the capabilities of the *Kaiten*, some successes were scored.'[71]

In reality there were none. Nor were there any successes from subsequent *kaiten* operations against US invasion forces off Iwo Jima in February and March or Okinawa in April. US anti-submarine defences were in most cases too tight for the mother submarines even to reach their launching points, and six more of these large, specially converted boats were lost. Finally conceding that the weapon might not be effective against defended anchorages, Miwa tried employing *kaitens* against US supply shipping in the open sea, recording between May and the end of the war one *Idaho*-class battleship hit and sunk, and hits on a carrier, a destroyer, a patrol boat, a tanker, three transports and ten ships in convoy.[72] The reality was possible damage to two transports and the certain sinking of the destroyer escort *Underhill* by a *kaiten* launched from *I53* on 24 July.

In theory the human torpedo, with a top speed of 30 knots over 25,000 yards and high manoeuvrability should have allowed the pilot to hit any target, whether at anchor or under way, with great precision. In practice the pilot had to slow down considerably to come up to periscope depth to make observations, and as with the German *Neger* and *Marder*, the smoother the sea and more helpful the conditions for observations and estimates of a target's course and speed, the easier it was for the enemy to spot his wake or the feather of water from his periscope. Conversely, rough seas which hid his approach rendered periscope observations and estimates extremely difficult if not impossible. At all events, against an alert enemy the weapon proved very much less effective than conventional aimed torpedoes.[73] It is probable that the super-optimistic trend of staff assessments of enemy losses concealed this: *kaitens* were built in great numbers up until the end of the war for the coming defence of the Japanese home islands, and hundreds of young men, many from the universities, were trained as pilots. It is in this final expansion of the suicide programme that doubts must arise about the methods of recruiting 'volunteers'. Yet it was but a part of the ultimate fanaticism imposed on the nation by the military code and Pharisaical ruling circle.

The same spirit of resistance to the death prevailed in Germany, squeezed between the Soviets advancing from the east and the Anglo-Americans from the west. The decisive battle had been decisively lost in Normandy, yet Dönitz continued to call for fanatic resistance and to send out both conventional U-boats and Heye's Small Battle Units against Allied shipping in the Channel and the North Sea, and on the oceans. Neither U-boat crews, nor the very young pilots of the *Marder, Molch, Biber, Seehund* and other midget submersibles were recruited or celebrated as volunteers for suicide, but their chances of survival were little different from those of the members of Japanese suicide units. The German midgets had been rushed through design and production too rapidly and were intended for coastal defence. At sea the young crews, relying on primitive navigational instruments, lost themselves or foundered if they were not sighted and destroyed by escorts; the great majority never returned; a few were recovered fast asleep from exhaustion in their tiny craft. As Godt admitted to British interrogators later, they were regarded as 'expendable'.[74] Of the U-boats, 112 had been destroyed between June 1944 and the end of the year – including the 35 lost in the Channel and Biscay in the operations against the invasion forces – and a further 27 had been scuttled in French ports or destroyed by bombing in harbour. The rate of loss continued in 1945. The life expectancy for U-boats on patrol was now no more than two to two and a half months.[75] As Dönitz reported to Hitler on 7 April, the enemy had massed anti-submarine forces in home waters, and once a U-boat revealed her position by attacking, 'such a concentrated defence action sets in that the boat is often lost'.[76]

The exceptions to this were provided by a very few of the new Type XXIII coastal U-boats. Speer had given the *Elektro* submarines absolute production priority in the new year. By then over ninety of the 1,600-ton ocean-going Type XXI had already been launched from yards in Hamburg, Bremen and Danzig, over forty of the 230-ton Type XXIII from yards in Hamburg and Kiel, and numbers of both classes had been fitted out and commissioned. The smaller boats, simpler in concept, had become operational first: in February the first Type XXIII had departed for patrol, and in March and April six more were transferred to Norwegian bases, Stavanger and Kristiansund, from where they had operated against shipping on the English and Scottish east coast. With a beam of under 10 feet and very quiet 'creeping' electric motors with rubber-belt drives to the shaft, they proved exceptionally difficult to detect and sank five merchantmen without loss. However, their restricted range and weak armament of only two torpedoes each without reloads meant they would not make a decisive impact. For this Dönitz and Godt, and indeed Hitler, looked to the ocean-going Type XXIs.

The Allies had obtained details of these from the early summer of 1944 through decrypts of messages sent to Tokyo by the Japanese naval attaché in Berlin, and had since been able to follow production of the three yards involved by aerial reconnaissance. In early October, after the naval attaché had sent a report recounting a visit to the Schichau yard in Danzig, the decrypt had been annotated by the Admiralty Naval Intelligence Division:

The present situation [of Type XXI U-boats], including all three yards, as far as it is known from aerial reconnaissance and Special Intelligence, is as follows:

On Slips	Fitting Out	Commissioned
37 U/boats	13 U/boats	11 U/boats[77]

The performance details as they had emerged from these Japanese reports were close to those actually achieved: a top surface speed of 18 knots – although only 15½ knots was attained – a top submerged speed of 17 knots for short bursts of little over an hour (24 miles) obtained by battery power three times that of conventional U-boats, and the ability to recharge batteries whilst submerged by making use of an extendable ventilating shaft, the *Schnorchel*. Experiments to test the likely effects of Allied countermeasures had been made and suggested that the boats 'could easily evade depth charge attack by reason of their high underwater speed and an increase in their permissible depth to 135 metres [443 feet]'. The naval attaché had given his opinion that the Type XXI was an 'epoch-making U-boat', a judgement fully endorsed by Allied naval intelligence.[78]

The programme had been slowed by mass air raids on German industry and communications, especially the breaching of canals along which the great prefabricated sections of the boats were floated to the shipyards at Bremen and Hamburg for final assembly. Nonetheless, the number of new boats completed and in training and on trials by January 1945 had roused the Admiralty to warn the Chiefs of Staff of a possible offensive on the Atlantic convoy routes in February or March, during which 'losses might even surpass those suffered in spring 1943'.[79] In consequence the transfer of 300 escorts to the Pacific was postponed, air minelaying in the Baltic and southern Norwegian U-boat training and transit areas was stepped up, and a portion of the mass bombing effort on Germany was transferred to the Type XXI assembly yards in Bremen and Hamburg and the Norwegian operational bases.

Dönitz had indeed planned a March offensive with Type XXIs but the cumulative effects of the Allied bombing and minelaying, together with hold-ups in the production of hydraulic machinery, which replaced manpower for reloading torpedoes in Type XXIs, set back his plans. And by March they were doomed: the Red Army had taken Danzig; the western Allies had crossed the Rhine and were close enough to the north German ports to mount devastating bombing raids which destroyed completed boats and further dislocated fitting out and training. Dönitz did not give up. Whether in conference with Hitler or speaking to the officers and men of the *Kriegsmarine* on tours of inspection, or sending U-boat officers out on patrol, he maintained an air of imperturbable confidence, always returning to the theme of the new *Elektro* boats and the remarkable things they would do.[80] In speeches to officers he invariably referred to unnamed political advisers – in reality Hitler himself – who had assured him that the Soviet–Anglo-American

Alliance was about to break up, after which they could look forward to a deal with the western powers.

Meanwhile he continued the conventional U-boat war in the shallow seas around Great Britain with Type VIIs, the few operational Type XXIIIs and *Seehund* (Type XXVIIB), and in the far oceans with 'cruiser' Type IXs. That March, thirty-seven boats departed Norwegian bases on war patrol, schnorchelling for the most part, and twenty-eight new or refitted boats from the north German ports took their place, including the first operational Type XXI, *U2511* commanded by Godt's former first staff officer, operations, KK Adalbert Schnee. Those boats on patrol in British waters sank ten merchantmen of 45,000 tons during the month, but fifteen boats failed to return; another was sunk off the north American seaboard, two were lost to mines in the Baltic and fourteen were destroyed in bombing raids on Hamburg.[81]

At the end of March there were 61 boats at sea out of a record total fleet which had topped 460 during the month, including the new types. During April, 44 more boats departed the Norwegian bases for war patrols, including Schnee's Type XXI, while 35 new boats from north Germany took their place. Dönitz's intention remained to keep up the struggle and tie down enemy naval and air forces, so preventing their use on offensive missions into waters still controlled by the *Kriegsmarine*, until he could take the offensive with Type XXIs. It was a forlorn hope; the only rational chance left to Germany was the last-minute split between Stalin and the western Allies that Hitler anticipated. This did not occur. On 25 April, units of the Soviet and US armies met at Torgau on the Elbe, splitting Germany in two. Dönitz had already evacuated his headquarters from outside Berlin to Plön, 15 miles south-east of Kiel, charged by Hitler with the defence of the northern half of the country, and it was there at the end of the month, after Hitler's suicide in Berlin, that he received the astounding news that he had been chosen by the Führer as his successor.[82]

On 2 May, having moved his headquarters further north to the Navy Cadet School at Mürwik, near Flensburg by the Danish border, to distance himself from a British spearhead which had crossed the Elbe and driven eastwards to the Baltic coast, he despatched *Generaladmiral* von Friedeburg to attempt to open negotiations for local surrender with the western Allies. Von Friedeburg returned the following evening with terms for unconditional surrender and the handing over of all war material intact. Clinging to a hope that this might provoke a split between Stalin and the west, Dönitz sent him back to sign the terms on the 4th and ordered all ships and submarines at sea to cease hostilities and return to base forthwith to surrender. To his favourite U-boat arm he addressed a special message:

My U-boat men!

Six years of war lie behind us. You have fought like lions. A crushing material superiority has forced us into a narrow area. A continuation of our fight from the remaining base is no longer possible.

U-boat men! Undefeated and spotless you lay down your arms after a heroic battle without equal. We remember in deep respect our fallen comrades, who have sealed with death their loyalty to Führer and Fatherland.

Comrades! Preserve your U-boat spirit, with which you have fought courageously, stubbornly and imperturbably through the years for the good of the Fatherland.

Long live Germany! Your *Gr.Admiral*[83]

After his recent exhortations and decrees about fighting to the end, this came as a bombshell; many COs refused to believe the message was genuine and wondered if the enemy had somehow broken into the code and faked it. Only eight obeyed at once, among them Adalbert Schnee. Thus far Schnee had evaded hunter-killer groups without difficulty on passage to his patrol area in the Atlantic. Now north of the Faeroes, he sighted a cruiser escorted by destroyers and, penetrating the screen at depth, made a dummy submerged attack on the cruiser from 500 yards without being detected. He was well below periscope depth, but could have fired his bow salvo of six torpedoes since Type XXIs, conceived as true submarines to operate almost permanently submerged, could fire from 50 metres (164 feet) down, using hydrophones for bearing, asdic for range. Whether this would have proved any more effective than US attempts early in the Pacific war to fire entirely on sonar observations is problematical. Certainly against fast-moving targets the inexactitude of hydrophone bearings would have proved critical. With acoustic torpedoes this would not have mattered, of course. Convoys were to be the targets, however, and it was intended to furnish the Type XXIs with improved FAT zigzagging torpedoes known as LUT – *Lagenunabhängiger* (literally 'position-irrespective') *Torpedo*.

Whether these new ocean-going U-boats, cruising underwater with *Schnorchels* coated with radar absorbent material, attacking with zigzag torpedoes from depth on sound plots without exposing their periscopes, reloading hydraulically within five minutes for a second and even a third attack after a further twenty minutes while remaining under a convoy, escaping still submerged at speeds only matched among the escorts by destroyers, or creeping away under a special silent-running motor virtually impossible to detect on hydrophones,[84] would have rendered current anti-submarine methods as ineffective as Dönitz predicted and Allied specialists feared – and subsequent historians have since debated – is a question that can never be answered. The techniques were new. At the least they would have taken time to perfect. Dönitz had simply run out of time. Moreover the Allies, besides deploying magnetic airborne detectors which could seek out submarines in the depths, and 'sonar buoys' which could record their passage, had a devastating new weapon in the 'squid' which threw depth-charges ahead, rather than contact bombs. The argument is as idle as Dönitz's claim that he could have won the Battle of the Atlantic with 300 U-boats at the beginning.

Schnee did not fire his torpedoes, but retired, still undetected, and made for Bergen. Meanwhile, that evening a delegation of U-boat officers from Flensburg sought out Dönitz for clarification of his order to surrender their boats. They simply could not comprehend it. The surrender of the German fleet after the First World War and its humiliating ride to internment in Scapa Flow had been such a shock to naval pride that it was an article of faith it would never happen again. Throughout their careers German naval officers had had it drummed into them they must never surrender their ship. Moreover, there had long been a standing order that ships and U-boats would be scuttled, preferably in deep water, or otherwise destroyed on receipt of a code word *Regenbogen* ('rainbow').

The delegation was met by Dönitz's adjutant, KK Walter Lüdde-Neurath, who told them they could not see the *Grossadmiral* since he was sleeping. The officers insisted and, when Lüdde-Neurath continued to deny them access, became very angry. He shouted above the clamour that the *Grossadmiral* now had the responsibility for the entire population, not just the navy. He needed this breathing space with the west to get as many refugees as possible from the clutches of the Soviets in the east. They pointed out that U-boats were useless for rescuing refugees, and asked how they could possibly surrender their boats; it was contrary to all standing orders. Lüdde-Neurath replied that the *Grossadmiral* was very conscious of this, but it was essential for the sake of the refugees.

'However,' he added, 'if I were a commander of a U-boat I know what I would do in the circumstances.'[85]

This was enough. The officers dispersed and in no time the word *Regenbogen* spread by telephone and word of mouth through Flensburg and Kiel. Before morning over 100 boats, including many Type XXIs, had been scuttled or otherwise wrecked. Many others, particularly in Hamburg and the Baltic ports threatened by enemy advance, had been scuttled during the previous days. By no means all were destroyed, however; as the terms von Friedeburg signed came into effect on the 5th many were obediently surrendered, as were most of those at sea after Dönitz was forced into capitulation to all Allied powers on 8 May. The final figures were 156 surrendered, 221 scuttled; and another 83 had been destroyed since the beginning of April, 38 of them on patrol, 29 in US Army Air Force or RAF bombing raids on the yards and bases, 22 during a last-minute dash from the north German ports to Norway.

In all during the war, 790 U-boats had been sunk or destroyed – excluding those scuttled or surrendered at the end – out of a total 1,162 built.[86] More staggering still, of 40,600 officers and men who had passed through U-boat training between 1934 and the end of the war – about 500 of whom had been weeded out as unsuitable – 30,246 were killed or died of wounds, a possibly unique percentage in the annals of warfare, and a further 5,338 rescued from sinking U-boats had become prisoners of war.[87]

Dönitz's supporters, very numerous among surviving U-boat officers, suggest that the heroism and scale of sacrifice recalling epics from the classical world were due to the Admiral's inspiring leadership. His critics maintain that, while this was undoubtedly true in the early days, from the time he moved U-boat Command from Kerneval to Paris, he became progressively more remote, and that finally he sent men to their deaths in obsolescent machines for no valid military reason; further that loyalty was maintained at the end by the threat of transfer to punishment battalions on the Russian front and terror imposed by the naval field police and harsh naval courts instructed by Dönitz to root out dissenters and what he termed 'intellectual weaklings'. There are hints of this in British interrogations of U-boat men, who frequently expressed loathing for their service. And there were savage court-martial sentences.

The fearful example Dönitz had made of the CO of *U572* for lack of aggression against the US 'Torch' invasion shipping at the end of 1942 has been mentioned.[88] There had been other cases: perhaps the worst was that of OLt. Oskar Kusch. A quiet, serious man and a convinced Catholic, Kusch had been unable to gain a university post before the war because police and Gestapo reports from his home town recorded that when two youth movements to which he had belonged were merged compulsorily into the *Hitler Jugend*, he had refused to transfer and made remarks critical of the Nazi party. He had, nonetheless, been accepted by the navy as an officer candidate in April 1937. Transferring to the

U-boat arm during the war, he had served as a watch officer on operational boats until in early 1943, after taking the commanding officers' course, he had been posted as CO to the Type IX *U154* in Lorient. He took her out on 20 March for the Caribbean, returning on 6 July after sinking an 8,100-ton tanker, damaging two other ships from the same convoy totalling 15,500 tons, and destroying two trawlers.

When he sailed again on 2 October he had a new 1WO, OLt. (Reserve) Dr Ulrich Abel, an ardent and overweening Nazi. During the patrol Abel became critical of what he perceived as Kusch's lack of aggression and on *U154*'s return to Lorient on 20 December 1943 with no successes to her credit he persuaded the LI, the 2WO and two *Fähnriche* watch officer trainees to join him in a formal complaint against Kusch to the FdU West, Rösing. The *Fähnriche* subsequently retracted their statements; the 2WO claimed Abel had exerted undue pressure on him and the LI weakened his statement under examination to such an extent that it was excluded from further proceedings. Rösing nevertheless instituted a court martial. Abel's accusation that Kusch had been hesitant in attack and had not approached close enough to the enemy to fire could not be substantiated, and the issue narrowed to whether Kusch had faith in the Führer and belief in victory. Lapses in either were punishable by death under the law against *Wehrkraft Zersetzung*, literally undermining military strength. The clinching point here was that Kusch had ordered the statutory picture of the Führer, issued to all U-boats at the fitting-out yard, to be removed from the bulkhead with the remark, 'There will be no idolatry here!' He was found guilty under the law and sentenced to be reduced to the ranks and shot.

The disturbance this provoked among the officers in the French bases when the news leaked caused Rösing to transfer Kusch to Kiel. The officers there were no less stirred up by the sentence and delegations led by KLt. Gustav-Adolf Janssen, former CO of *U151*, *U37* and *U103*, appealed for Kusch's life to von Friedeburg, who passed the matter to Dönitz in Berlin. Despite the strong representations Dönitz refused to consider commuting the sentence, or even to examine Kusch's file, but merely confirmed the court's decision by telephone and a brief teletype. At 06.30 on 12 May 1944 Kusch was placed before a firing squad at the shooting gallery of the 2nd U-Flotilla at Kiel-Holtenau and the presiding judge, whose name was blacked out in the subsequent record, read the sentence to him and asked if he had anything to say. '*Nein!*' he replied. The ten-man squad was formed up at five paces and brought to the aim. At 06.32 they were given the order to fire, and at 06.34 the medical officer in attendance, whose name was also blacked out in the record, pronounced Kusch dead. The details of time and the response, *'Nein'*, were hand-written on a prepared execution form, suggesting that Kusch's was no uncommon end.[89]

His denouncer had predeceased him by a few days. Promoted to command *U193*, Abel was on his way into the Atlantic across Biscay on 28 April when his boat was caught by a Coastal Command patrol and sunk with all hands.

Towards the end, as the Reich collapsed, Dönitz's decrees against 'weaklings' had grown ever more savage and the naval field police, known as *Kettenhunde* (chain dogs) from the chains of office they wore around their necks, had responded with summary executions, usually by hanging.[90] Herbert Werner has described one hellish episode a day before the formal end of the war when the U-boat crews in Cristiansand, Norway, were paraded before a makeshift scaffold by the recently appointed chief of the 15th U-Flotilla, KK Ernst Mengersen, to witness such an exemplary punishment. The three victims, whose crime had been to drink with Norwegians celebrating the end of hostilities, struggled so much they finally had to be despatched by gunshot at close range.[91]

While officers and men fortunate enough to have been posted to the new *Elektro* boats could look forward to turning the tables on the enemy, for those like Werner still serving on conventional boats, and the majority of ratings who had lived at sea much as miners in a deep mine, under constant artificial light with seldom a glimpse of sun or sky, whose knowledge of outside events had been limited to what was vouchsafed by their COs, whose repetitive tasks had been to pull levers and turn handwheels when ordered to do so, who had not known the precise chances of their survival but who had seen so many of their contemporaries sail on patrols from which they never returned, the end of hostilities came as blessed relief. Werner wrote: 'An unknown tranquillity took possession of me as I realized that I had survived. My death in an iron coffin, a verdict of long standing, was finally suspended. The truth was so beautiful that it seemed to be a dream.'[92]

However, it is also true that a British Admiralty mission to Flensburg later in the month found no sign of demoralization among the German armed forces; in particular, it reported the morale of the U-boat crews as 'extremely high'.[93]

Captain Gilbert Roberts, who was sent to inspect the U-boats and interview the leadership, was particularly impressed with the 'sleek, streamlined' form of the Type XXIs. Godt revealed to him that 'methods of attacking in packs by Type XXI had not yet been worked out and would not have been until a number had done war cruises and their sea qualities were known.'[94]

It also became clear to Roberts that Type XXIs were only a stop-gap for Godt and Dönitz until they could put ocean-going Walter Type XXVI prototypes into production. These 1,500-ton boats were provided with conventional diesel engines and electric motors for cruising as well as Walter closed-cycle turbines for short bursts of up to 23 knots under water to gain bearing for attack, and escape afterwards. Roberts suggested that such high underwater speeds would give off a great deal of hydrophone effect (HE). Godt agreed, but said much work had been done on this and, based on trials, the Type XXVI would make no more HE at 8 to 9 knots than a conventional U-boat at 3 to 4 knots.[95] It was an academic question: production models could not have been expected before 1946 at the earliest.

The Japanese turned to similar classes of high-underwater speed submarines at the end, and for the same reason: as explained to the US Naval Technical Mission after the war, 'radar had rendered surface operations of diminishing practicability and demanded that emphasis be placed on submerged performance'.[96] Large numbers of 400-ton coastal boats designated *HA201* were projected for the defence of the home islands, and even larger numbers of a 1,300-ton ocean-going class *I201* Type ST (*sen taka*, or submarine, high speed) for offensive missions. Both types were developed from the pre-war experimental high-underwater speed prototype *No. 71*. Like the German *Elektro* boats, they relied on vastly increased battery capacity, streamlined shape and recessed external fittings for their high submerged speeds, and both types were prefabricated in sections for rapid production and welded together at assembly yards.

The small *HA201s* carried two torpedoes like the German Type XXIIIs and had a similar underwater speed of 13 knots, against the Type XXIII's 12½ knots. The ocean-going *I201s* achieved virtually the same underwater speed as the German Type XXIs, 16.3 to 17 knots on trials, but had a bow salvo of only four torpedoes and half the number of reloads. Like the German *Elektro* boats they were overtaken by the end of hostilities. They had been started too late and Japanese industry was not equal to the large programmes planned. The first of only three of the ocean-going type to be completed was not fitted out until February 1945, the first of ten of the coastal type by May. None made an operational cruise.

Meanwhile two monster aircraft-carrying submarines, *I400* and

I401, had been completed. Started as early as 1942 to launch surprise air raids on US cities, by 1945 the target had been changed to the Panama Canal locks in order to obstruct the transfer of US ships from the Atlantic to the Pacific. A further boat in the class, *I402*, had been converted on the stocks to an oil-tanker submarine to break the US blockade. They were 400 feet long with a surface displacement of 5,200 tons, the largest submarines built anywhere in the world to that date, and carried three seaplanes in a 102-foot long cylindrical hangar on deck; an 85-foot catapult track led from the hangar – closed by a hydraulically operated door – to the bows.[97] They were a fantastical concept, a metaphor for the unreality of Japanese naval vision. By the time they had worked up and completed with aircraft their target had been changed again to the Ulithi anchorage, where it was hoped more immediate damage could be done by sinking US aircraft-carriers. They sailed on this mission, together with two rather smaller, equally new aircraft-carrying submarines, *I13* and *I14*, of 3,600 tons, but the war ended just before the attack scheduled for 17 August. They returned to Japan flying the black flag of surrender, and the force commander, Captain Tatsunosuke Ariizumi, riding in *I401*, shot himself as they entered Tokyo Bay. No doubt ashamed of Japan's capitulation, he was also a war criminal. Besides presiding over the massacre of survivors from the Dutch merchantman *Tjisilak*, while in command of *I8* in the Indian Ocean, he had ordered the murder of sixty of the crew of the US merchantman *Jean Nicolet* after torpedoing her in the same area.

It is ironic but hardly surprising that the only real success Japanese submarines achieved in the final weeks of the war was in a conventional torpedo attack by a conventional submarine, Hashimoto's *I58*. It will be recalled that Hashimoto had launched an unsuccessful *kaiten* attack on Apra harbour, Guam, in January. He had since made a voyage with *kaitens* to attack US communications on the open sea, equally unsuccessfully, and was on his third cruise with *kaitens*, patrolling the Guam–Leyte route in the Philippine Sea when, on 29 July, the US heavy cruiser *Indianapolis* ran practically straight down his throat. He sighted her directly he surfaced at 23.05. Silhouetted against the path of the moon, she appeared through his binoculars like a surfaced submarine with a high midship section. He went down to periscope depth – 19 metres (62 feet) – called the crew to action stations and ordered 'Firing Method six!' – prepare to fire six torpedoes. He also ordered the pilot of *kaiten* No. 6 to man his craft, and a few minutes later the pilot of No. 5 *kaiten*. His submarine was now fitted to carry six *kaitens* all of which could be entered from the interior while submerged.

The cruiser was unescorted. Despite the moonlight which enabled Hashimoto to see her clearly through his night periscope, and despite reports of submarine activity in the area, she had abandoned her zigzag shortly after sunset. Steering towards him at just under 16 knots, she presented his fire-control party with the simplest problem, and at 23.26, as she came within 1,600 yards, he commenced firing a salvo of six torpedoes spread at 3° with a lead, or director, angle of 28°. He observed one hit forward which started a fire under the forward turret, then a second, followed after some minutes by a bright flash at mid-length and a series of internal explosions, four or five of which were louder than torpedo hits. She slowed and stopped, settling rapidly, although Hashimoto, who was making away from the scene at speed on the surface to avoid counter-attack from aircraft which might be in the vicinity, did not see her as finally she went down.[98] Meanwhile he recalled his disappointed *kaiten* pilots who had been clamouring to be allowed to attack.

The cruiser's distress signal was not picked up, but Hashimoto's report fifteen minutes after midnight, 'Sank definite one *Idaho*-class battleship', was intercepted by US signals intelligence, and the decrypt was passed to Cincpac headquarters, now on Guam, at 17.00 that day, 30 July. It was discounted as another optimistic Japanese report; and there were no *Idaho*-class battleships in the area. It was not until 2 August when survivors from the cruiser were sighted by a patrolling aircraft that rescue operations began, by which time nearly 600 had died of exposure; of the ship's company of 1,199 only 316 were saved.

For this single substantial success, and the earlier sinking by *kaiten* of the destroyer escort *Underhill*, another twenty-seven Japanese submarines had been lost since the start of the year, their sinkings shared almost equally between surface escorts, escort carrier or other aircraft, and US submarines. The *Batfish* under Cdr. J.K. Fyfe had destroyed three in four days. All were RO-class boats on transport runs evacuating aircrews from the northern Philippines to Takao, Formosa. The first went down on the night of 9 February. Fyfe was patrolling the Babuyan Channel off the north coast of Luzon when intermittent interference on the radar screen revealed another set working in the vicinity, yet the vessel carrying it was not showing up. Fyfe, reasoning that it must be a submarine, went to 'battle stations, torpedo'. Using the radar in brief sweeps he established that the other's emanations were moving northwards, and he made an end around, eventually gaining a solid 'pip' on the screen at 11,000 yards. Once ahead he closed at slow speed, allowing the range to come down to 1,800 yards before firing four electric torpedoes on radar data; the enemy was still invisible from the bridge. All missed and it became apparent from the plot that she had just increased speed to 14 knots. Yet, despite the shimmering interference, she seemed unaware of *Batfish's* presence.

Fyfe made another end around, then closed, keeping bows-on to the unsuspecting enemy to present the smallest silhouette until he made out a darker smudge of darkness which solidified gradually at about 1,000 yards into the shape of a Japanese conning tower broadside on. He gave the order to fire. The first torpedo failed to leave the tube, but ejected at a second attempt; it was followed at intervals by two more. Seconds later, the shadowy shape of the enemy was erased in a searing fireball shooting upwards as the crash and pressure wave of the detonation hit the bridge watch. At the same time the green fluorescent 'pip' on the radar screen expanded, flashing at the edges, then shrank and disappeared. Delighted cries broke out, 'We got him!'[99]

There were no survivors from what had been *RO115*, the boat whose captain and crew had been commended for their persistence and ardour under continuous attack during the operations around Saipan the previous summer. The next night Fyfe detected *RO112* in the same way, and hunted and destroyed her in a similar manner. Two nights later, 12 February, he destroyed *RO113*, again in a radar approach. Nothing better illustrated the superiority of US radar and the dangerously ineffective performance of the Japanese sets than the loss of these three submarines.

By the final months of the war the Sixth (Submarine) Fleet, commanded from May 1945 by Vice-Admiral Tadashige Daigo in place of Miwa, had practically ceased to exist, certainly so far as conventional submarines were concerned. Only three survived, Hashimoto's *I58*, the modern C3 attack type *I53*, both converted to carry *kaitens*, and the medium *RO50*. Apart from these, there were three of the new high-underwater speed *I201* class, which had just come into service, together with seven of their high-speed *HA201* coastal counterparts, the two monster aircraft-carrying *I400* class, their tanker sister – which had not made a voyage – and one of the new 3,600-ton aircraft-carrying submarines. Otherwise there were only five ancient training boats adapted for *kaitens* and various midgets, and in the southern area six ex-German or Italian boats taken over at the end of the war in Europe. The powerful, highly specialized submarines with which Japan had entered the war and which she continued to build over the subsequent three years, and their confident élite of officers and men, from whom so much had been expected, had been eliminated as a coherent force.

The Japanese merchant marine had been similarly decimated, leaving few torpedo targets for over 170 US fleet submarines now in the Pacific commands or a force of British boats operating with them. In September the previous year the British 8th Flotilla of seven S-class, three Ts and four Dutch submarines working out of Trincomalee, Ceylon, had been transferred to Christie's command in Fremantle. In March 1945 the 4th Flotilla of eleven T-class boats had joined them from Trincomalee – leaving only one flotilla of mainly S-class submarines working from Ceylon – and in April Rear-Admiral James Fife, who had succeeded Christie in the South-West Pacific Command, moved the 4th Flotilla up to an advanced base he had established at Subic Bay, near Manila Bay in the Philippines.

Increasingly both US and British submarines had turned themselves into submersible gunboats operating against coasters, motor schooners, sampans and a variety of local craft which the Japanese were using to break the blockade and supply isolated garrisons and their army in Burma, even to bring oil in barrels to the home islands. Alastair Mars, in command of *Thule* at the time, has described how COs amassed as many machine guns, grenades and other arms as they could in port from whatever source so that when they chased or surfaced for gun action with coasters and small craft their bridges bristled with barrels.[100] A code of practice had been built up whereby native crew members were rescued if possible and transferred to the nearest land, and while there were of course exceptions, it is apparent from accounts of wounded Indonesians, Malays and other local seamen cared for in Allied submarines that in this bitter campaign of attrition humanity usually prevailed. One 8th Flotilla skipper with a reputation for creating havoc with the gun, Edward Young, in command of *Storm*, sank eleven small craft without killing a soul.[101]

One of the few US submarines to find worthwhile targets at this time was the *Tirante*, a brand new vessel under Lt.-Cdr. George Street, with Ned Beach transferred from *Trigger* as his exec. He sailed from Pearl Harbor in early March 1945 to patrol in the East China and Yellow Seas, and towards the end of the month *Trigger* under a new CO was instructed to join him for co-ordinated operations. When they called her *Trigger* did not reply, and it became apparent after a time that she had been lost. Meanwhile Street, working close inshore, sank two sizeable *Marus* and an escort, and survived a dangerously close and sustained depth-charge attack.

Finally, in the early hours of 14 April, after scouring a series of empty bays and roadsteads in the Yellow Sea, and with only six torpedoes remaining, he found a group of ships in an anchorage on the north shore of Quelpart (Cheju do) Island, south of Korea. The water was scarcely 10 fathoms, too shallow to dive; Street ghosted in on the surface, setting up on the largest target with Beach on the TBT night binoculars and ranges provided by radar, and hit her with a salvo of two torpedoes, whose detonations set off spectacular explosions, suggesting she was carrying ammunition. Before the escorts could get under way he hit one of them with a second salvo, causing equally spectacular pyrotechnics as her magazine blew up. Her bows and stern reared high either side of a blinding sheet of flame enveloping her mid-length. With his last two torpedoes he hit a second escort, then turned and steered for the open sea, evading two more escorts by now under way. One of these approached within half a mile. Street's special battle stations lookout watch of four experienced sailors selected for steadiness and night vision were ready with 40mm (1½-inch) guns on the bridge, but the Japanese did not sight the low shape of the submarine.[102]

Tirante's sinkings during this first patrol, as corrected after the war, amounted to six ships totalling 12,621 tons, placing Street among the top half dozen COs in terms of numbers sunk in a single patrol.[103] For his resolve in seeking out the enemy in their coastal hideouts he joined the select band of submarine COs awarded the Congressional Medal of Honor.

Lockwood, meanwhile, who had moved his headquarters to the advanced base at Apra, Guam, had been working on a scheme to re-enter the Sea of Japan with submarines to strike at the last regular shipping supplying Japan from the mainland. He had been deterred from doing so before by a combination of more active patrols and deep minefields laid across La Pérouse Strait, the entry and exit channel for the earlier incursions. The development of an improved frequency-modulated or FM sonar so sensitive that it could detect individual mines at up to 700 yards had promised a solution to the problem. After satisfying himself in extended trials and training through the spring of 1945 that the apparatus worked, he despatched a group of nine boats to the southern entrance to the Inland Sea towards the end of May. Termed collectively the 'Hell Cats', they were subdivided into three wolfpacks known by the names of their senior COs – 'Hydeman's Hep Cats', 'Pierce's Pole Cats', 'Risser's Bob Cats'.

To lead the mission, since Nimitz had turned down his own request to do so, Lockwood had chosen a comparative newcomer

to active war patrols, Cdr. Earl Hydeman of *Sea Dog*. The plan
was for the packs to dive under the minefields guarding the Strait
of Tsushima, then each to make its way to widely separated patrol
areas off northern Honshu, central Honshu and Korea. When all
were in place operations would commence on the same day.

Hydeman led his own pack through first on 4 June at depths of
150 feet or more without locating any mines, though not without
great tension during the passage. On the following day, Cdr.
George Pierce took the 'Pole Cats' through, the crew of one boat
suffering the unnerving experience of hearing a mine mooring cable
scrape down the length of the hull; fairing wires had been stretched
over the external fittings of all the submarines and she cleared
without snagging the cable and drawing the mine down on to her.
Finally, on 6 June, Cdr. Robert Risser led the 'Bob Cats' through;
again one of the crews experienced the heart-stopping scraping
sounds as a mooring cable ground along their side. Safely through,
the packs dispersed to their areas and began operations on the
evening of 9 June, surprising ships sailing independently without
escorts and, over the next fortnight, sinking twenty-seven sizeable
merchantmen totalling over 50,000 tons and the *I122*. It was one
of the most rewarding group attacks of the war, marred only by
the loss of *Bonefish* under Cdr. Lawrence Edge, one of Pierce's
pack working off central Honshu.

Edge, who had sunk one large transport and a medium-sized
freighter, had made a rendezvous with Pierce on the morning of
18 June near Sada Island off the west coast of Honshu above
Toyama Bay and asked permission to conduct a submerged daylight patrol in the bay. Pierce agreed, and Edge had departed
southwards. He was detected by a patrol craft off the northern
cape of the peninsula enclosing the bay and sunk during prolonged
depth-charge attacks.

On 24 June, all submarines with the exception of *Bonefish* met
inside La Pérouse Strait; shortly before midnight they went to 'battle stations, gun' and formed in two columns to race out on the
surface at 18 knots, while way to the south, off Tsushima, another
of Lockwood's submarines shelled the island of Hirado to mislead
the Japanese into watching that exit. In the event, thick fog
descended over La Pérouse and the 'Hell Cats' escaped without
challenge, to their immense surprise.

Having proved it could be done, Lockwood sent further submarines in singly, tightening the naval and air grip around Japan's
supply lines.

In these dying weeks of the war the British submarines working in the Pacific were very much the poor cousins, with some boats still lacking efficient air-conditioning, condemning their crews to the torments of prickly heat, 'crabs', other skin complaints, heat stroke and exhaustion in the tropic conditions. Nonetheless, they scored two signal successes. The first was by a 4th Flotilla boat at Fremantle, the *Trenchant* under Cdr. (later Vice-Admiral Sir) Arthur 'Baldy' Hezlet, a veteran survivor of the glory days of the 'Fighting 10th' with Wanklyn, Tomkinson and Cayley at Malta. On patrol in the Java Sea in early June, Hezlet intercepted a report from the US submarine *Blueback* that the Japanese heavy cruiser *Ashigara* had entered Batavia, western Java. Anticipating that the cruiser would return to her base at Singapore via the narrow strait between Sumatra and the offlying island of Banka, he requested permission to lie in wait there. Fife agreed.

Heziet formed an extempore 'pack', as British Far Eastern submarines sometimes did, by attaching Lt. G.S. Clarabut in the *Stygian* to his enterprise. Clarabut was on patrol outside a minefield laid by one of the Dutch submarines across the main northern exit to the strait between a shoal named the Klippen and the shallows off Banka. Leaving him outside the minefield, Hezlet dived inside. In the early hours of the following morning, 8 June, while on the surface, he picked up a signal from the *Blueback* that the *Ashigara* and a destroyer had departed Batavia northbound. Soon afterwards he sighted a destroyer approaching, which also spotted him and opened fire. He evaded successfully in the dark, and at dawn both he and Clarabut dived. Later in the morning the destroyer appeared again, evidently searching for him in the shallows on the Sumatran side of the Klippen shoal – the opposite side to the minefield, where there was a narrow but navigable channel about a mile wide. As the destroyer passed northwards into the *Stygian*'s sector Clarabut attacked, but missed. The destroyer counter-attacked with depth-charges and was still hunting the *Stygian* when, shortly before noon, Hezlet sighted the *Ashigara* steering northwards, hugging the Sumatran side of the strait. He had expected she might do so after seeing where the destroyer was searching and had moved towards that side. She came on at 15 knots, steering a straight course confined by the shallows, and as she closed to 4,700 yards Hezlet commenced an eight-torpedo salvo, spacing them along her side. The wakes fanning towards her were sighted aboard the cruiser, but she could neither turn away without running aground, nor increase speed in time to evade; she turned towards and five hit. Riven and blazing, she fought back, firing at the *Trenchant*'s periscope as Hezlet swung and launched his stern torpedoes. They missed, but inside half an hour the large ship, the last operational heavy cruiser in the Japanese fleet, turned over and sank.

If Hezlet's self-appointed task was eased by lack of an air escort for the cruiser and Clarabut's timely diversion drawing off the sole surface escort, it was nonetheless a brilliantly conceived and executed attack. Hezlet, who had sunk the Type IXD *U859* off Penang the previous year, was decorated personally by Fife with the United States Legion of Merit, degree of commander.[104]

The next British success was scored by midgets of the type that had immobilized the *Tirpitz*, now marginally improved and designated XE-craft. The most useful addition they had received for the Far East was internal air-conditioning and dehumidifying apparatus. When the first six arrived in the Pacific aboard their depot ship in July 1945 Nimitz was against employing them. In the American mind they were classed as 'suicide' craft, and he wanted nothing to do with the concept. The CO of the small flotilla, designated the 14th, pleaded with the C-in-C of the British fleet, which had joined the Americans for the final round against Japan, and then with Fife at Subic Bay, without success. The crews, who were as eager for action as *kaiten* pilots – although decidedly not with a view to immortality through self-immolation – were utterly despondent. At the last moment it was realized that there were two tasks for which their craft would be ideal: cutting the underwater telephone cables between Singapore, Saigon, Hong Kong and Tokyo, and striking two heavy cruisers, *Takao* and *Myoko*, lying high up the Johore Strait bounding the northern shore of Singapore Island. Although both cruisers were damaged, their broadsides might threaten a projected Allied invasion of Malaya.

The missions were planned for the last day of July. On the 26th Clarabut's *Stygian* towing *XE3*, and the *Spark* from the same flotilla towing *XE1*, departed for Singapore. Arriving in the Strait to the east of the island on the 30th, the operational crews took over from the passage crews and late that evening both midgets began their run-in to their targets 40 miles distant. They completed the first part in the open sea on the surface then, steering up the Johore Strait, departed the main channel and passed through mined areas in order to avoid suspected hydrophone listening posts, diving and lying on the shallow bottom when traffic passed. Lt. I.E. Fraser, RNR, in command of *XE3* made the faster passage and by 10.30 the following day, the 31st, had located the gate in the net defences to the anchorage; finding it open, he crept through at dead slow, necessarily close to the guard ship and praying that no one aboard her was looking downwards through the clear water.

Passing her safely, he rose to periscope depth to continue, at noon sighting the heavy pagoda-like bridge and foremast structure of the *Takao*, still under repair from the damage inflicted by the *Darter* before the Battle of Leyte Gulf. The water became so shallow as he approached, making the final run-in blind, that his keel scraped the sea bed, and after clanking against the cruiser's hull he found she was almost aground and he could not manoeuvre his craft beneath. Passing down her side, he eventually found a section at mid-length where he could just squeeze under her, but even here there was so little water that the diver, Leading Seaman J.J. 'Mick' Magennis, who was to attach limpet mines stored in a container in place of the port explosive charge, or 'side cargo', could not open his hatch fully. Determined not to be beaten, he deflated his breathing apparatus, exhaled to the full extent of his lungs and forced himself through the narrow opening, in the process tearing a small hole in his apparatus, through which a continuous stream of bubbles escaped. Undeterred, despite the possibility of an alert lookout seeing the bubbles, he began trying to attach the limpets, but found the cruiser's bottom so foul he had to scrape off barnacles first. In half an hour of swimming and scraping he arranged six limpets in a line stretching 45 feet along the keel. He returned to the craft and squeezed back through the partially open hatch in a state of exhaustion, his hands lacerated by the crustaceans. Fraser ordered the release of the starboard 'side cargo' and tried to get away. This was difficult since the tide had been falling, and when he eventually succeeded, practically broaching the surface as they shot clear, it was discovered that the empty limpet container had not dropped off and was making the craft unmanageable. Magennis volunteered to go out again and release it, after which Fraser was able to set course back down the strait.

XE1, meanwhile, had been held up by patrol craft, and her CO, finding it was too late to reach the *Myoko* and return before the *XE3*'s charges went off, also made for the *Takao*, 2 miles the nearer, and dropped his side cargo close alongside, then withdrew. At 21.30 the cruiser was lifted by a series of explosions which tore a 60-foot hole in her bottom, causing her to flood and settle, and putting her guns and rangefinders out of action, finally finishing her active career. Earlier the same day, close off the coast of Indo-China and further north off Hong Kong, the telephone cables between Singapore, Saigon, Hong Kong and Tokyo had been grapnelled up and cut by *XE4* and *XE5*. All four crews were safely recovered and were later decorated for bravery, both Fraser and Magennis of *XE3* receiving the VC.[105]

Dramatic as these final exploits of the Royal Navy's submarine service were, in strategic terms the most spectacular success in this last period of the war was the stranglehold obtained on Japanese merchant shipping by the US submarine commands and air forces, in particular by a mass aerial minelaying campaign termed 'Operation Starvation' which had begun towards the end of March to seal Japan's ports.

Japan was now cut off, not only from her southern conquests but also from mainland Asia. Her oil and aviation fuel tanks were dry, industry extemporizing from day to day, trains running intermittently, her people subsisting on average on under 1,700 calories a day. How long she could have sustained the siege, and mass bombing of her cities, how many more casualties the Emperor's circle would have deemed necessary before Hirohito could admit his people had failed him and might be released from their suffering, will never be known. Preparations were in train to repulse the anticipated invasion of the sacred homeland. *Kaitens* and midget submarines were assembled at strategic points, obsolescent aircraft hidden in forest airstrips and thousands of young men put under training for suicide missions under the sea or in the air. Trenches were dug along the beaches, pointed stakes driven in to impale the barbarians, and sharpened bamboo spears distributed to local villagers. Propaganda evoked the defeat of the invading hordes of Kublai Khan in AD 1280 by samurai aided by the kamikaze typhoon, and asserted that the American invaders were being lured to land on Kyushu, where they too would be destroyed 'at one stroke'.[106]

Meanwhile, a special group of US Army Air Force B29 pilots practised dropping atomic bombs over Japanese cities. The decision had been taken in Washington to force surrender with this latest triumph of technology in order to save an estimated million and a half Allied casualties, perhaps many more, in an invasion of the Japanese islands, together with tens of thousands of Allied prisoners of war who might be executed or simply allowed to starve to death. It would also save the Japanese nation from the suicidal frenzy which had descended on it. On the morning of 6 August the first uranium-235 bomb, Thin Boy, was dropped over Hiroshima, southern Honshu; bursting 1,500 feet above the city the fireball wiped out over 60,000 people in an instant, burnt and irradiated many thousands more and raised a firestorm which reduced the centre of the city to ashes. Three days later a second, plutonium, bomb, Fat Boy, was dropped over Nagasaki, Kyushu. The results were as awesome. These two demonstrations and the prospect of Tokyo and the Imperial circle being similarly liquidated in a twinkling released the scales of myth, hope, anxiety and duplicity blocking government decisions on peace. At last Hirohito insisted that they surrender for the sake of national survival.

Hashimoto was on the bridge of *I58* on 15 August, returning to base, when his radio operator appeared beside him and asked him to come below. The man looked so sad Hashimoto thought he was about to burst into tears. In the wardroom he was shown the cause – an Imperial edict announcing the end of hostilities and immediate surrender. Although he knew of the devastation of Hiroshima and Nagasaki, Hashimoto was stunned. In this his reaction was no different from that of the crowds in every Japanese city who had heard the Emperor's broadcast earlier in the day, and wept with humiliation and despair. He told the radio man to destroy the message; it might only be a press story.

On arrival at Kure two days later it was immediately clear there had been no mistake, and he read the Emperor's message to the crew assembled on the after casing; then he went ashore to report to his division commander on the valiant deeds of his *kaiten* warriors who 'had not survived to suffer the indignity of defeat'.[107]

Ned Beach was in the Sea of Japan when the message came through announcing the end of hostilities. For well over three years he had served as junior, and then executive officer on war patrols; finally, from *Tirante* he had been given his own command, *Piper*. He had departed Guam with her on 5 August and penetrated the barrier across Tsushima Strait into the Inland Sea on the 13th, the last to do so, hearing the bell-like ringing of the FM sonar indicating mines, seeing their image on the sonar's cathode screen and, as he tried to steer through a gap, scraping a mooring cable until he swung the stern clear with emergency helm and engine orders. Two days later *Piper* was submerged, the radar antenna poking above the surface, when he received the signal from Nimitz to cease offensive operations. A wild cheer rang through the submarine. Beach's own feelings were more complex, and while he tried to join in the elation of his officers and men, he found himself inwardly deeply despondent. He retired to his small cabin and sat on the bunk in darkness behind the curtain until, after surfacing that night, he paced the deck endlessly, thinking of *Trigger* and of colleagues who had not made it. 'We had won the war. It was over – finished – and somehow I had had the incredible luck to be spared. But what little divided those of us who were allowed to see this day from those who were not ...?'[108]

For nearly four years his mind had rejected feelings that he might not survive; as he paced alone under a clear night sky with the dark waters of the Inland Sea lapping the ballast tanks below, these feelings from his subconscious rose to torment him.

William King had similar reactions. His war had been longer. He had been in command of *Snapper* at the outbreak of hostilities in September 1939; he ended it in command of *Telemachus* on his way home from Fremantle. Now peace had come he should have been able to ease up and 'sleep the true sleep a captain never knows in time of war'; instead he felt more restless and overwrought than ever, and paced up and down the small iron deck of his submarine before retiring. '"The captain don't know 'ow ter take things easy", said a sailor's voice. The position of my little cabin had always forced me to listen in on the men and they all knew it. It was not the first time they said things on purpose for me to hear.'[109]

Figures of shipping losses are notoriously difficult to agree, but in round terms US submarines, starting very slowly with only ¾ million tons to their credit in the whole of 1942, sank over the course of the war 1,300 *Marus* – excluding small coasters and native craft – totalling rather over 5¼ million tons, only ¾ million tons less than the total tonnage with which Japan had entered the war. US carrier- and shore-based aircraft sank a further 750 *Marus* of over 2½ million tons, chiefly towards the end after the submarines had broken the back of Japanese shipping.[110] Finally, as recounted, the few convoys still running were sneaking around the coast close inshore where they hoped submarines would not venture, and holing up in creeks overnight.

Dönitz's U-boats had sunk twice as many merchantmen over the course of the European war, almost 2,500 of an aggregate 13 million tons in the North and South Atlantic alone.[111] Of course there had been more U-boats and a greater volume of targets over a longer period of time. Great Britain survived because of her success in attaching neutral shipping and seamen to her cause, especially the shipping and shipbuilding capacity of the United States.

In doing so she appeared to confirm Alfred Thayer Mahan's doctrine that *guerre de course* was impotent in the face of battlefleet 'command'. For Dönitz's U-boat campaign had been the ultimate exercise in commerce-raiding without main fleet or, for the most part, air support. Yet, as in the first war, it had been a close-run thing, turning, it seemed, on Hitler's decision to drive east before he had finished off his western foe. There is no certainty, however,

that Great Britain could not have redirected her obsessed air marshals to the threat by sea and concentrated her naval and merchant
shipping resources more effectively to defeat Dönitz's aims if Hitler
had not struck east in June 1941, no certainty indeed that Stalin
would not soon have forced Hitler to turn east in any case.

The US victory also confirmed Mahan's doctrine. It had been a
classic case of the battlefleet, represented now by carrier air forces,
winning such 'command of the sea' that she had been able to throw
a close blockade around the island empire. No matter that the
instruments of blockade had been the new underwater and air
craft; Japan's position at the end, cut off from all but pennyloads
of supplies, her industries and what remained of her navy and air
forces running down for want of fuel, her people on the verge of
starvation, had been essentially the same as that of Germany at
the end of the first war after the Royal Navy's 'hunger blockade',
or that of France at the end of almost any of her late eighteenth-
century and her revolutionary wars with Great Britain, cut off
from overseas trade and supplies by British squadrons riding the
storms off Ushant.

Aside from naval historical theory, it is evident that in both the
Atlantic and the Pacific campaign the Allies had decisive technological advantages: first was centimetric radar, a British invention made available by the manufacturing power of the US radio
industry. Radar in escorts and aircraft defeated the U-boats in the
Atlantic and Japanese submarines in the Pacific. Radar on US submarines defeated Japanese escorts in the Pacific. And whilst Ultra
decrypts, Huff Duff and VHF radio telephone communications
were all powerful contributors without which, no doubt, victory
would have been more costly and taken longer, radar was crucial.

In the older technologies, the German U-boat was supreme. Its
periscopes and night-attack optics were far superior to anything in
the US or British services, its torpedo fire-control system was more
effective even than the US TDC, and it could dive far deeper than
any other type of submarine in the world. Finally, in the new Type
XXI and prototype XXVI Germany was taking the submersible
torpedo boat which fought the war into new, almost truly submarine dimensions.

Of the force commanders, two stand out above the rest: Dönitz,
for his clear focus on the tonnage war, iron determination and
inspiring leadership, until towards the end he was betrayed by
these very strengths and led to betray his beloved U-boat men by
sending them to die in obsolescent machines. At the other end of
the scale stood 'Shrimp' Simpson of the 'Fighting 10th' at Malta

whose spirit, warm-hearted leadership and refusal to give in helped write a famous chapter in the twilight story or swan song of the former grand mistress of the seas. The most disastrous failure was surely Christie at Fremantle who contributed to perhaps the most notorious scandal to afflict any service in the war when he backed his own magnetic exploder against his COs and torpedo officers, undermining their confidence and probably helping to prolong the Pacific war. His was not the only faulty judgement on the US side. Admiral King eventually realized how vulnerable Japan was to submarine blockade, but failed to argue the case with sufficient conviction even to win over his own admirals.

The British Naval Staff under Pound lacked clarity or sufficient force in argument with Churchill, who was allowed to follow his instincts; these ran in parallel with the certainties of Sir Arthur Harris, high priest of what was euphemistically termed 'area bombing'. As a result, for the second time in twenty-five years U-boats were allowed to bring Great Britian within an ace of defeat. It was unnecessary, unscientific and foolish, and with hindsight can be seen to have stained Britain's and Churchill's own otherwise proud escutcheon.

On the other hand, the very young men who fought in submarines pursued their hard and dangerous trade honourably and – with certain notorious exceptions, several of whom have been mentioned in these pages – showed great humanity towards their victims. That U-boat officers were not lacking in chivalry, especially in the early years, was obscured for propaganda purposes. Several, though by no means all, of the most celebrated COs of all the major belligerents have been mentioned; it would be invidious to make comparisons for they operated in such different craft with different levels of technology under differing conditions. It is impossible even to compare U-boat skippers from different periods: Kretschmer, for instance, the highest-scoring submarine CO on any side in the war, with Rolf Manke, who appears in no lists of aces. He had the bad luck to rise to command after the U-boat had been mastered, and in five patrols sank only three ships totalling 12,500 tons, and damaged another. But he gave his enemies the longest continuous hunt in the Atlantic war and took a frigate with him when finally he was hounded to death.

The submarine arms of the Axis powers suffered a higher proportion of losses than any other branch of their nation's forces. The US service, which lost 50 submarines to enemy action, friendly fire or circling torpedoes, fewer than any other major belligerent, suffered 3,505 officers and men killed at sea.[112] While this was a tenth of the loss taken by the U-boat arm, it represented 16 per cent of the officers, 13 per cent of the men in the force.[113] From the 74 submarines of the Royal Navy which failed to return from patrol, 3,144 officers and men died, and a further 360 were taken prisoner, a total equalling the personnel strength of the arm at the outbreak of war.[114]

In September 1945, a month after the end of the Pacific war, Admiral Nimitz said at a press conference, 'Battleships are the ships of yesterday, aircraft carriers are the ships of today, but submarines are going to be the ships of tomorrow.' At the time it was a remarkable prediction. But it is doubtful if even Nimitz foresaw the total domination that would be exercised by the nuclear-powered submarine that emerged ten years later. This was the first true submarine, as opposed to the submersible warships that fought in both world wars; armed with nuclear weapons, it rules not merely the oceans of the world, but the world itself, and makes international conflict of the type described in this book unthinkable and indeed impossible. Let the final words, therefore, be with Captain Edward L. Beach USN, whose career spanned this historic transformation. As a young man he made twelve operational patrols in the Pacific, taking part in the sinking of twenty-seven enemy ships and damage to a dozen more, surviving close depth-charge attacks and earning seven decorations for valour, including the Navy Cross, second only to the Congressional Medal of Honor. Subsequently, in 1960 he commanded the US Submarine *Triton* on her epoch-making underwater circumnavigation of the world:

> The history of man is now totally in thrall to the extraordinary science he has developed. World War Two saw the last of the old species of land and naval warfare in which the fate of nations hung upon the ability of a few fearless men to rise above the shocking disruption of mind and terror of painful annihilation by drowning, suffocation, burning or scalding, to do their duty in spite of it all. Those days are past, but in future years their stories will become legends on a par with the Knights of the Round Table, the Spanish Armada and the Battle of Trafalgar. So long as ships travel the high seas, they will be remembered.[115]

CHRONOLOGY

1939

August
19–29   German U-boats depart to take up waiting stations around the British Isles and in the Atlantic

September
1   Hitler invades Poland
3   Great Britain and France declare war on Germany
Naval blockade of Germany declared
21.42 *U30* (Lemp) sinks SS *Athenia*; 118 passengers and crew lost
6   Coastal convoys started by Admiralty
7   First ocean convoys started by Admiralty
17   *U29* (Schuhart) sinks aircraft-carrier HMS *Courageous*
23   Hitler approves Raeder's recommendation that merchant ships sending radio messages when stopped by U-boats should be sunk
30   Hitler approves withdrawal of Prize Regulations for attacks on merchant ships in the North Sea

October
2   Hitler allows attack on darkened ships off British and French coasts
4   Hitler cancels Prize Regulations in waters out to 15°W
14   *U47* (Prien) sinks battleship HMS *Royal Oak* inside Scapa Flow base
Dönitz promoted to BDU
U-boats successfully directed to a convoy; the first pack attack, although by two U-boats only
17   U-boats given permission to attack without warning all ships identified as hostile
24   German government issues warning that safety of neutral ships can no longer be taken for granted off the British Isles and French coast
31   U-boat officers losing confidence in torpedoes; at least 30 per cent are duds

November
17   U-boats given freedom to attack passenger liners if clearly identified as hostile; thus a state of unrestricted U-boat war exists
Dönitz issues orders countermanding Prize Regulations: 'Rescue no one ... have no care for the ship's boats ...'

	Atlantic	Mediterranean
1940		
February		
24	Schultze (*U48*) returns with total sinkings of 114,000 t.; the first ace to be awarded Knight's Cross for sinking over 100,000 t.	
March		
	Dönitz withdraws U-boats from Atlantic and repositions them for the invasion of Norway	
April		
9	German invasion of Denmark and Norway. Great Britain launches counter-invasion. Admiralty lifts Prize Regulations for submarines operating off the coasts of Denmark and Norway	
10–19	U-boat COs report constant torpedo failures against British warships and invasion transports	
19	Dönitz withdraw all U-boats from Norway because of torpedo failures	
May		
9	German forces invade France	
15	*U37* (Oehrn) sails for Atlantic to test torpedoes with new exploders	
June		
		Old O-, P-, R-class submarines brought back from Far East in anticipation of Italy's entry into war, and based on Alexandria and Malta
9	*U37* (Oehrn) returns flying 10 victory pennants totalling 43,000 t.; Dönitz resumes Atlantic campaign	
10		Mussolini declares war on Great Britain and France
		British 1st Submarine Flotilla of 12 boats, divided between Alexandria and Malta, loses 3 Malta-based submarines in first week
14	US Congress authorizes 11 per cent increase in US Navy, including extra 21,000 t. of submarines	

22　France signs armistice with Germany, conceding German occupation of Channel and Atlantic coasts

24　France signs armistice with Italy

Despite fewer operational U-boats (29) than at the outbreak of war, sinkings in June amount to 58 ships/ 284,100 t.; sinkings from all arms 140 ships/585,000 t., the worst month of the war for Admiralty, reminiscent of the First World War

July

7　U30 (Lemp) first U-boat to use Biscay port Lorient for resupply

19　Roosevelt pushes through expansion of US Navy, 'two-ocean Navy Act', including an additional 70,000 t. for submarines

Admiralty lifts Prize Regulations for submarines within 30 miles of Libyan coast and for Italian shipping within 30 miles of Italian coast

August

2　Lorient becomes first fully operational U-boat base on Biscay coast

Admiralty responds to establishment of Biscay bases for U-boats (Lorient, Brest, La Pallice, St Nazaire) by routing shipping via North Channel, north of Ireland instead of SW approaches

15　German government declares 'Blockade area' around British Isles

17　Dönitz passes order for 'unrestricted' warfare to U-boats

29　Dönitz moves U-boat Command to Paris

September

7-10　First effective U-boat wolfpack action against convoy (SC2)

During month U-boats sink a record 59 ships/295,300 t.; sinkings from all arms 100 ships/448,600 t.

12　Italian Army in Libya (Graziani) makes lightning advance 100 miles into Egypt, halting at Sidi Barrani

Atlantic

October

Night surface attacks on convoys by wolfpacks of U-boats take Admiralty by surprise; during month U-boats set a new record, sinking 63 ships/352,400 t.; sinkings from all arms 103 ships/443,000 t. Admiralty fitting Type 286 ($1\frac{1}{2}$ m. wavelength) radar to escorts as rapidly as possible

November

4   Kretschmer (*U99*) becomes first ace to sink over 200,000 t. shipping, and is awarded Oak Leaves to Knight's Cross

11   Dönitz moves U-boat Command to Kerneval, below Lorient, Biscay

Wild Atlantic weather reduces U-boats' successes

December

Wild weather continues to hamper U-boats in Atlantic

1941

January

Mediterranean

28   Italy declares war on Greece and invades. British and Commonwealth troops from Egypt occupy Crete and establish advance base at Suda Bay to support Greece

4   First U-class submarine arrives at Malta

9   British Army of the Nile (Wavell) takes Italian position at Sidi Barrani and begins lightning drive west into Libya

Luftwaffe *Fliegerkorps* X, specialized in attacking shipping, arrives in Sicily to reinforce Regia Aeronautica. Onslaught on Malta begins. Malta's 15 Hurricane fighters overwhelmed

8th Submarine Flotilla formed at Gibraltar

10   Simpson takes over Malta submarines
22   Wavell takes Tobruk, reducing Italian Army to a single
      supply port, Tripoli

February

5   Admiralty lifts Prize Regulations in Mediterranean south
      of Malta as *Deutsches Afrika Korps* (Rommel) is
      moved from Italy to stiffen Italian Army in Libya
6   Wavell takes Benghazi
10   Wavell takes El Agheila
21   Rommel arrives in Tripoli

      Dönitz sends out U-boats on 'spring offensive' in North
      Atlantic

March

8   *U47* (Prien) lost
11   Roosevelt's 'Lease-Lend' Act to supply Great Britain with
      arms is passed; 50 First World War destroyers
      transferred to RN. USA becomes the arsenal for war
      against Hitler

      US 'Atlantic Fleet Support Group' formed; US air bases
      established in Greenland and Bermuda
17   *U100* (Schepke) and *U99* (Kretschmer) lost. The end of
      the first 'Happy time' for U-boats as the Atlantic
      battle becomes harder
19   'Battle of the Atlantic Committee' convenes for the first
      time, Churchill in the chair

April

      Construction of bomb-proof U-boat pens at Biscay bases

      Trials of first centrimetric radar (Type 271) at RN
      Signals School

5   Axis front stabilized at Sirte. British and Commonwealth
      troops sent to Greece from North Africa

      Deutsches Africa Korps and supplies transported to
      Libya with little loss

25   Rommel attacks British position at El Agheila

4   Rommel takes Benghazi
6   German forces attack Greece; British and
      Commonwealth forces in Greece withdraw

14   Rommel makes lightning advance and crosses Egyptian
      border, bypassing Tobruk

Atlantic

April

18 Roosevelt extends Pan-American Security Zone eastwards from 60°W to 26°W

First RN escort groups based at Reykjavik, Iceland, to extend convoy protection westwards

Admiralty sea trials of HF/DF (Huff Duff)

May

7 German weather ship, *München*, captured and June Enigma cipher tables found aboard her

9 *U110* (Lemp) capured by HMS *Bulldog*; Enigma cipher machine, cipher tables and secret charts found aboard and sent to Bletchley Park

15 US Navy establishes base at Argentia, Newfoundland

24 *Bismarck* sinks HMS *Hood* in North Atlantic

27 Home Fleet force sinks *Bismarck*

June

Bletchley Park reading U-boat Enigma cipher with aid of tables from *München* and *U110*

Eastbound convoys escorted all the way across the Atlantic for the first time

U-boats attacking in mid-Atlantic out of range of aircraft

22 German armies launch attack on Russia; the centre of gravity of German war effort moves eastwards

Mediterranean

By the end of the month 45,000 British and Commonwealth troops have been evacuated from Greece to Crete

Fliegerkorps X withdrawn from Sicily for forthcoming German invasion of Russia; easing of bombing offensive against Malta

20-30 German paratroop attacks force British and Commonwealth evacuation of Crete; heavy British naval losses

Bletchley Park breaks into Italian Naval cipher

23   First 'Ultra' to Alexandria and Malta

30   Simpson promoted Captain

31   Axis forces in Libya named *Panzerarmee Afrika*

Hitler offers Mussolini 20 U-boats to assist him in the Mediterranean

Malta submarines designated 10th Flotilla, although still under Captain Submarines at Alexandria

A monthly average of over 500,000 t. of shipping is being sunk by all Axis arms, submarines, aircraft, mines, surface raiders. Admiralty Intelligence predict a further 5 mil. t. sunk by the end of the year

July

4   Westbound convoys also escorted all the way across the Atlantic

AOC-in-C Coastal Command writes to Chief of Air Staff urging Bomber Command to smash U-boat pens under construction at Biscay bases; reply: there is no justification for a 'defensive strategy'; we must look for winning as opposed to not 'losing the war'

7   US Marine Brigade relieves British garrison at Reykjavik, Iceland

August

9   Churchill and Roosevelt meet at Argentia, Newfoundland, and agree Atlantic Charter

27   U570 (Rahmlow) surrenders to Coastal Command Hudson aircraft

September

4   U652 misses USS *Greer* with torpedoes and is herself attacked by the *Greer*, the first war action of the US Navy

5   AOC-in-C Coastal Command writes to Air Ministry repeating request for Bomber Command to smash U-boat pens while still under construction; the request is again turned down

Atlantic

September

11 Roosevelt characterizes the German U-boat campaign as 'piracy on the high seas'

27 The first of H.J. Kaiser's 'Liberty ships' is launched
The first wave of U-boats leave Biscay bases for the Mediterranean

October

First escorts fitted with effective HF/DF
Depth tests on captured U570 reveal that U-boats can dive well below 200 m. (over 650 feet)

17 U568 (Preuss) damages USS Kearney; first US war casualties

31 U522 (Topp) sinks USS Reuben James; first US warship loss; 115 crew lost

November

7 Revision of US Neutrality Act allows US merchant ships into war zones. 'By 7 November the US Navy was in the war' (US Chief of Naval Operations, Stark)
Second wave of U-boats leave Biscay bases for Mediterranean

December

Mediterranean

9 Chief of German Naval Staff, Rome, reports to Berlin that submarines are the most dangerous weapons in the Mediterranean, especially those at Malta

18 Upholder (Wanklyn) sinks 19,500-t. troop transports Neptunia and Oceania, bound for Tripoli

9 First wave of U-boats transit Straits of Gibraltar into the Mediterranean

9 Force K cruisers and destroyers sink an entire convoy of 7 Axis supply ships bound for Tripoli

13 U81 (Guggenberger) sinks aircraft-carrier HMS Ark Royal

24 Force K sinks a second Axis supply convoy

25 U331 (v. Tiesenhausen) sinks battleship HMS Barham
During the month Axis supplies to Panzerarmee Afrika fall to disastrous 30,000 t., the first serious interruption to the Axis supply lines

4 Rommel orders retreat of Panzerarmee Afrika

5 Hitler orders Fliegerkorps X to annihilate Malta

Atlantic

11 Hitler declares war on USA

21 *U751* (Bigalk) sinks first merchant aircraft-carrier coversion, HMS *Audacity*

1942
January
First RN escorts fitted with hedgehog ahead-throwing mortars, but this potentially lethal anti-U-boat weapon will be dogged by teething and training problems for 18 months
Majority of escort groups now supplied with US (lease-lend) radio telephones (TBS)

13 Operation *Paukenschlag* begins on east coast of USA

Mediterranean

19 Italian human torpedoes cripple the battleships *Queen Elizabeth* and *Valiant* in Alexandria harbour; the end, for the time being, of the British Mediterranean battlefleet

Round-the-clock bombing of Malta
Rommel stabilizes retreat at El Agheila, Gulf of Sirte
Italian anti-submarine forces now equipped with German asdic

29 Rommel advances and re-takes Benghazi

Pacific

7 Japanese carrier bombers and torpedo planes attack US battlefleet in Pearl Harbor. Simultaneous Japanese attacks on Hong Kong, Philippines, Siam, Malaya

10 British Far East battle squadron, *Prince of Wales* and *Repulse*, sunk by Japanese land-based bombers and torpedo planes

21 Main Japanese invasion of Philippines begins at Lingayan Bay, Luzon
US Manila-based submarines fall back on Surabaya, Java

2 Japanese take Manila, Philippines

	Atlantic	Mediterranean	Pacific
February			
1	Fourth rotor added to U-boat Enigma cipher machine; Bletchley Park is shut out; *B-Dienst* is reading 80 per cent of British naval cipher		
15			Singapore surrenders Japanese seize oilfields Sumatra, and Batavia occupied
18–19	U-boats begin campaign in Gulf of Mexico and Caribbean		
27			Battle of Java Sea confirms Japanese naval command US Asiatic Fleet submarines withdraw to Fremantle, West Australia
March			
		Bombing of Malta intensifies; Simpson orders all submarines to bottom during daylight	
8			Third US submarine flotilla established at Brisbane, eastern Australia (Christie) Japanese occupy Rangoon
16			Komatsu succeeds Shimizu as chief of 6th (Submarine) Fleet
28	British Commando raid on St Nazaire		
30	Dönitz withdraws U-boat Command from Kerneval to Paris		
April			
1	Adm. Andrews institutes partial convoy by day along US east coast		
14		*Upholder* (Wanklyn) lost	
15		Malta awarded the George Cross for valour	

26   Japanese invasion force departs Truk base for Port Moresby, New Guinea
Japanese 8th Submarine Sqdn. (Ishizaki) sails for Indian Ocean and Australia

3   Japanese occupy Tulagi, Solomon Islands

7–9   Battle of Coral Sea; the first check to the Japanese advance

14   English relieves Withers as Comsubpac, Pearl Harbor; Lockwood relieves Wilkes as Comsubsowespac, Fremantle

30   Japanese midget submarine (Akeida) damages battleship HMS *Ramillies* in Diego Suarez harbour, Madagascar

31   Japanese midget submarines enter Sydney harbour, Australia, but their attack fails

---

22   Simpson decides to evacuate the Malta submarines
Malta submarines begin to leave for Alexandria

Reinforcements have brought *Panzerarmee Afrika* up to 3 German, 7 Italian divisions

May

1   First 1,000-bomber air raid on Cologne

10   Heavy Axis losses in air battle over Malta after Spitfire reinforcements flown in

Full convoy system established on US east coast

26   Rommel begins second advance for Egypt and the Suez Canal

	Atlantic	Mediterranean	Pacific
June	First four Coastal Command aircraft fitted with radar (ASVII, 1½ m. wavelength) and Leigh Light work over U-boat entry and exit routes in Biscay, causing surprise and damage	Hitler cancels planned invasion of Malta in favour of taking Suez Canal	
1			Japanese change 5-digit naval code; Japanese 8th Submarine Sqdn. to Indian Ocean for commerce raiding
4			Naval Battle of Midway; decisive reverse for Japan; 4 aircraft-carriers lost from *Kido Butai*
6			I168 (Tanabi) sinks damaged carrier USS *Yorktown*; Lockwood conducts tests on Mark XIV torpedoes, finding that they run 11 feet deeper than set
22		Rommel takes Tobruk; British 1st and remains of 10th Submarine Flotillas withdraw from Alexandria to Haifa and Beirut	
24	Dönitz orders U-boats to transit Biscay submerged day and night		Advanced base for Pearl Harbor submarines established at Midway; US Bureau of Ordnance tests confirm Lockwood's findings that torpedoes run 10 feet deeper than set
July			
4		Rommel's advance halted before El Alamein	
5	ASVII-fitted Coastal Command aircraft sinks *U502* on her return from successful Caribbean patrol; the first sinking in the Coastal Command 'Bay offensive'		
19	Dönitz withdraws U-boats from US east coast to North Atlantic convoy routes in mid-Atlantic 'air gap'		

US coastal convoy system extended to Caribbean and Gulf of Mexico

Type 271 centrimetric radar now fitted in majority of RN escorts; U-boats trimmed low can be detected up to 5,000 yards

August

U-boats working in North Atlantic, off West Africa and Brazil/Venezuela

First U-boats fitted with FuMB 2 'Biscay Cross' radar detector, which gives effective warning of ASVII-fitted aircraft

16-17 *U507* (Schacht) sinks 5 Brazilian merchant ships

22 Brazil declares war on Germany Group (*Eisbär*) of four Type IX U-boats depart for operations off South Africa

Most RN escort groups have at least one vessel fitted with HF/DF (FH3 or FH4) able to distinguish between distant transmissions reflected from ionosphere and those from a near source within 15 miles; RCN escort groups not equipped to the same extent

22 Simpson returns to Malta; the 10th Submarine Flotilla is rebuilt

10-14 Operation Pedestal to supply Malta

11 *U73* (Rosenbaum) sinks aircraft-carrier HMS *Eagle*

Montgomery appointed to command British and Commonwealth (8th) Army in Egypt

30-7 Sept. Rommel attempts further advance, but is checked at Alum Halfa

Japanese change 5-digit naval code again; US code-breakers shut out

7 US 1st Marine Division lands on Guadalcanal, Solomons

9 Naval Battle of Savo Island; Japanese defeat US cruiser force

10 *S44* (Moore) sinks IJN heavy cruiser *Kako*; the first major warship sunk by a US submarine

Decision to replace S-class submarines at Brisbane with fleet submarines from Fremantle

Both US and Japanese submarines drawn from commerce warfare into Solomons campaign

Haddock (Taylor) tests new centimetric SJ search radar on war patrol; very positive report

Atlantic	Mediterranean	Pacific
September		
12	U156 (Hartenstein) sinks troop transport *Laconia* and begins rescue operation		
15			I19 (Kinashi) sinks aircraft-carrier USS *Wasp*, and damages battleship USS *North Carolina* with single salvo in Solomons
17	Dönitz sends 'Laconia' order to all boats, 'Rescue contradicts the most fundamental demands of war for the annihilation of ships and crews'; he subsequently sends the 'Rescue ship' order containing the phrase, 'the desired destruction of the steamers' crews'		
	Dönitz sends second wave of Type IX U-boats to South African waters		
October		
	Group *Eisbär* U-boats active off South Africa; main concentration of U-boats in North Atlantic mid-ocean 'air gap'		
23		Montgomery lauches offensive at El Alamein, forcing Rommel into second precipitate retreat	
26-27			Naval Battle of Santa Cruz; Japanese victorious
30		U559 sunk off Port Said; her weather cipher tables found and sent to Bletchley Park	

November

4 First meeting of Anti U-boat Committee, chaired by Churchill

7/8 Allied 'Torch' invasion of French Morocco and Algeria
FdU Mediterranean orders all U-boats to close Morocco
8th Submarine Flotilla depot ship moves from Gibraltar to Algiers

8 Dönitz orders all U-boats between Biscay and Cape Verde to close Morocco

15 U515 (Piening) sinks escort carrier HMS *Avenger*

16 Hirohito decrees that submarines are to be used to supply troops on Guadalcanal

20 'Stoneage' convoy lifts the siege of Malta

21 All Prize Regulations lifted for British submarines in Mediterranean

30 Naval Battle of Tassafaronga; Yamamoto gives up attempts to re-take Guadalcanal

U-boats achieve highest monthly sinkings of the war: 119 ships/730,000 t.; total sinkings from all arms 134 ships/807,754 t.

December

13 Bletchley Park breaks into U-boat 4-rotor cipher with aid of tables from U559
Majority of Allied escorts now fitted with HF/DF; over 100 escorts fitted with hedgehog ahead-throwing mortar
U-boat sinkings during the month fall to 60 ships/330,800 t.; sinkings from all causes to 73 ships/348,900 t.

First Solomons supply run by submarine I176 from Bougainville to Guadalcanal

	Atlantic	Mediterranean	Pacific
	1943		
	January		
14–21	Casablanca Conference; Roosevelt, Churchill and Joint Chiefs of Staff agree that the defeat of the U-boats is first priority, but no effective measures follow		
2			Japanese driven from Papua, New Guinea. Lockwood succeeds English (killed in an air crash) as Comsubpac, Pearl Harbor; Christie succeeds Lockwood at Fremantle; Fife succeeds Christie at Brisbane
14	Bomber Command (18 months too late) begins mass air raids on Biscay U-boat bases; the U-boat pens remain undamaged		
23		Simpson relieved at Malta by Phillips. Montgomery takes Tripoli	
29		Montgomery advances into Tunisia	Loss of *I1* off Guadalcanal; tables found by divers assist US code-breakers to break back into Japanese 5-digit code
30	Dönitz promoted C-in-C *Kriegsmarine*; he resolves to concentrate all efforts on the U-boat war		
	February		
7			*Wahoo* (Morton) arrives at Pearl Harbor after Morton's first war patrol flying a broom and 8 victory pennants. Japanese evacuate Guadalcanal. Two US submarine sqdns. transferred from Brisbane to Pearl Harbor
	U-boats are concentrated in North Atlantic 'air gap'. Centimetric ASVIII radar fitted in Coastal Command aircraft; 2 U-boats sunk in renewed Coastal Command 'Bay offensive' over Biscay transit routes		

March

1 Adm. King convenes Convoy
Conference in Washington
First escort-carrier group
organized around USS *Bogue*

16–19 Total of 41 U-boats directed
against convoys HX229,
SC122 in the North Atlantic
'air gap'; 22 merchant ships
sunk

Dönitz is awarded the Oak Leaves
to the Knight's Cross for the
success

Adm. King is at last spurred to
send Liberators to Iceland and
Newfoundland to close the 'air
gap'

Horton establishes 5 support
groups to reinforce threatened
escort groups in the North
Atlantic

U-boats achieve 2nd highest
monthly sinking total of 108
ships/627,380 t.; losses from
all causes 120 ships/693,390 t.

April

Refuelling escorts at sea is now
general

11 Dönitz presses Hitler for
expanded construction
programme of 27 rising to 30
U-boats/month

2 Battle of Bismarck Sea; over
3,000 Japanese troops bound
for Lae, New Guinea, lost

US code-breakers work back into
Japanese 5-digit code

Pacific

18 Yamamoto killed in air crash; Koga succeeds him as C-in-C Combined Fleet IJN

21 Morton (*Wahoo*) denounces Mark XIV torpedo to Lockwood

Mediterranean

Allied air and submarine dominance of Axis supply routes is such that only 20 per cent of supplies are arriving at Tunis and Bizerta

7 Allies take Tunis and Bizerta

13 Axis armies in North Africa surrender

17–26 First Allied convoy through Mediterranean since 1941

Atlantic

April

The Atlantic 'air gap' is gradually closed by VLR Liberators and escort-carriers

Admiralty Anti-Submarine Warfare Division reports: 'Historians are likely to single out April and May 1943 as the critical period when strength began to ebb away from the U-boat offensive'

May

RN and RCN take over North Atlantic convoy routes, dividing responsibility either side of new 'CHOP' line 47°W. USN takes over central Atlantic convoy routes

Adm. King organizes all US anti-submarine divisions and forces into the Tenth Fleet

23 31 U-boats lost so far in the month; Dönitz withdraws the boats from the North Atlantic to the Azores to escape air reconnaissance and attack

Coastal Command 'Bay offensive' with ASVIII centimetric radar-fitted aircraft accounts for 6 U-boats in Biscay

31   Hitler agrees Dönitz's expanded programme for the construction of 40 U-boats/month

June

19   Dönitz again orders U-boats to transit the Bay of Biscay submerged day and night

Dönitz approves plans for Type XXIII and Type XXI *Elektro* high-underwater speed U-boats

July

Dönitz entrusts naval construction to Speer (Min. for Arms & Armaments)

Intensification of Coastal Command 'Bay offensive' accounts for 11 U-boats in transit across Biscay

Hedgehog in surface escorts begins to fulfil its potential; during final 6 months of 1943 it will achieve a success rate of 8.2 per cent against 3.7 per cent for conventional depth-charge attack

4   First three US submarines penetrate Sea of Japan by La Pérouse Strait; commence attacks on 7th

10   Allies invade Sicily

24   Nimitz orders magnetic torpedo exploders deactivated; Christie at Fremantle refuses to follow suit

24   *Tinosa* (Daspit) experiences 11 duds from 12 torpedoes fired. It is clear that something is wrong with the contact exploder as well as the magnetic exploder

	Atlantic	Mediterranean	Pacific
August			
	German scientists discover that a radar salvaged from a crashed RAF bomber works on centimetric wavelength		Adm. King orders Christie to make tankers top priority for his submarines
9	Lüth awarded Diamonds, Swords and Oak Leaves to Knight's Cross, the first U-boat CO to be so honoured		
13	Dönitz switches construction programme to Type XXI and Type XXIII Elektro high-underwater speed U-boats in place of conventional boats Dönitz signals all boats to discontinue use of radar detectors		Lockwood tests contact exploders and finds them wanting; he orders dockyard to produce efficient contact exploders
			New electric Mark XVIII torpedo being supplied for US submarines
September			
	The first ahead-throwing depth charge mortars, Squid, fitted in RN frigates. Due to teething and training problems the first success will not be for 9 months		
3		Allies invade mainland Italy	
8		Italy signs armistice with Allies. German forces in Italy seize control and continue defence of country	
9		Allies land at Salerno, below Naples	

1 Lockwood sends out first formal
   wolfpack of 3 submarines
   under a senior officer (Momsen)
   Halibut (Galantin) conducts firing
   tests which confirm reliability
   of modified contact torpedo
   exploders; after nearly two
   years of war the Pearl Harbor
   submarines now have an
   efficient torpedo

11 *Wahoo* (Morton) lost coming out
   of Sea of Japan

   Advanced base for Brisbane
   submarines established at Milne
   Bay, south-eastern tip of New
   Guinea
   Takagi succeeds Komatsu as chief
   of Japanese 6th (Submarine)
   Fleet

20–23 First U-boat pack attacks in
   renewed North Atlantic
   offensive; *Zaunkönig* acoustic
   torpedoes sink 3 escorts; 6
   merchant ships sunk

22 *X6* (Cameron), *X7* (Place) midget
   submarines put battleship
   Tirpitz out of action

October

2 First U-boats fitted with 'Naxos'
   radar detectors for centimetric
   radar, but the range is too short

7 Dönitz repeats 'Rescue ship' order
   to all boats first sent in
   Sept./October 1942

November

16 Ubiquity of air cover in North
   Atlantic forces Dönitz to
   withdraw for second and final
   time from North Atlantic
   convoy routes

Atlantic

November

22 Heavy bombing on Berlin destroys much of *Seekriegsleitung* building; Dönitz moves naval high command to 'Koralle', 20 miles north-east of Berlin

December

1944

January

7 Dönitz finally abandons pack tactics and disposes U-boats individually

Mediterranean

10th Flotilla moves from Malta to Maddalena, Sardinia

Pacific

Japanese Combined Escort Fleet formed under Oikawa

19-20 Nimitz advances against Gilbert Islands; Tarawa and Makin atolls stormed

24 *I175* (Tabata) sinks escort carrier USS *Liscome Bay*

Hirohito receives naval and military staff assessments that Japan has irretrievably lost the war

3 *Sailfish* (Ward) sinks escort-carrier *Chuyo*, the first carrier sunk by a US submarine

By year's end the Japanese merchant fleet is reduced to 5 mil. t., a million tons below minimum requirements

20 Christie at Fremantle finally orders his submarines to deactivate magnetic exploders
US submarines sink record 56 ships/295,000 t.; record 355,000 t. sunk by all arms

Oikawa begins great mine barrier from Kyushu to Formosa to protect shipping inside
Advanced base for Pearl Harbor submarines established at Kwajalein
5 First Japanese submarine sunk by hedgehog, I175
17 US forces take Eniwetok
29 US landings Admiralty Islands
Monthly sinkings by US submarines 56 ships/264,000 t., over 500,000 t. sunk by all arms

Japanese begin construction of I201-class of high-underwater speed submarines
Oikawa forms larger convoys in set formations
12 US Joint Chiefs of Staff directive on 'two roads to Japan', Nimitz in the north, MacArthur in the south

22 Allied landings at Anzio, 25 miles south of Rome

February
5 First U-boat fitted with air-breathing *Schnorchel*, *U264*, departs St Nazaire on war patrol

19 *U264* sunk by 2nd Escort Group (Walker)

March
'Fliege' and 'Mücke' radar detectors at last give U-boats adequate warning of centimetric radar emissions

Atlantic	Mediterranean	Pacific
April		
1 Dönitz promulgates 'Reckless Attack' order to Group Landwirt U-boats held back in Biscay ports to oppose the anticipated Allied invasion of Europe		**2** First Japanese escorts fitted with (non-directional) radar detectors
3 Fleet Air Arm raid damages *Tirpitz* in Altenfiord		
17 First Type XXIII coastal *Elektro* high-underwater speed U-boat launched, Hamburg		**5** Koga killed in air crash; Toyoda succeeds as C-in-C Combined Fleet IJN
		9 Japanese submarines sail to NA line in Operation A to lure the US fleet for decisive battle in south-west corner of Pacific Takagi, having withdrawn 6th (Submarine) Fleet HQ from Truk, establishes himself at Saipan, Marianas
May		**22-31** USS *England* destroys 5 RO-class submarines in NA line (and previously *I16*) with hedgehog
North Atlantic practically clear of U-boats		A total of 9 Japanese submarines lost during the month
12 First Type XXI ocean-going *Elektro* high-underwater speed U-boat launched, Hamburg		

June

1   Only 34 U-boats have so far been fitted with *Schnorchel*; only 8 of these are in the counter-invasion Group Landwirt in the Biscay bases

4   Allies enter Rome

6   Allies invade Normandy. Dönitz orders Group Landwirt out to attack invasion fleet

6–9   *Harder* (Dealey) sinks 4 Japanese destroyers in single patrol

8–9   US invasion fleet sails for Marianas

13   Toyoda orders Operation A for the decisive fleet battle

15   US forces invade Saipan, Marianas

19–20   Decisive US victory at Battle of Philippine Sea

19   *Cavalla* (Kossler) sinks Japanese carrier, *Shokaku*; the first fleet carrier sunk by a US submarine *Albacore* (Blanchard) sinks Adm. Ozawa's flagship, carrier *Taiho* Total of 10 Japanese submarines lost in the month

Total of 13 U-boats lost in the Channel or Biscay opposing invasion

July

6   Takagi and staff killed on Saipan

13   Miwa succeeds as chief of 6th (Submarine) Fleet

21   US landings on Guam Total of 7 Japanese submarines lost during the month; an average 200,000 t. Japanese merchant shipping being sunk each month

31   First U-boat destroyed by Squid ahead-thrown depth-charges, *U333* Total of 9 U-boats lost in the Channel or Biscay opposing the invasion forces

Pacific

1 Japanese resistance in the Marianas ends

3 Japanese Combined Escort Fleet absorbed into Toyoda's Combined Fleet; Nomura succeeds Oikawa as chief of escort fleet

10 Adm. King proposes blockading Japan by invasion of Formosa astride the 'choke points' for supplies from the south; Joint Chiefs of Staff turn down the proposal

18 *Rasher* (Munsen) sinks Japanese escort-carrier *Taiyo*

24 *Harder* (Dealey) lost

Japanese shipping losses are so high that convoys travel by day and hide in anchorages by night

Japanese escorts at last being fitted with (relatively inefficient) radar

Mediterranean

15 Allied landings in the South of France

Atlantic

August

U-boats leave Biscay ports for Norwegian bases as US land forces close

Total of 14 U-boats lost in the Channel or Biscay opposing invasion forces; 8 scuttled or scrapped in Biscay ports; 12 lost in other theatres

September

The last U-boats leave southern Biscay ports for Norwegian bases

15   US forces invade Palaus and
     Morotai
16   *Barb* (Flukey) sinks Japanese
     escort-carrier *Unyo*
     British 8th Submarine Flotilla
     transferred from Ceylon to
     Fremantle under Christie

17   Toyoda orders Operation 'Sho-1'
     for fleet suicide ride to 'bloom
     as flowers of death'
20   US landings in Leyte Gulf,
     Philippines
20-25 Naval Battle of Leyte Gulf;
     decisive Japanese defeat; first
     Japanese kamikaze air attacks
23   *Darter* (McClintock) sinks Adm.
     Kurita's flagship, heavy cruiser
     Atago; *Dace* (Claggett) sinks
     heavy cruiser *Maya*

8   First *kaiten* human torpedo unit
     (*Kikimizu*) departs for
     operations against US
     advanced bases and
     anchorages in Palaus and
     western Carolines
17   *Spadefish* (Underwood) sinks
     Japanese escort-carrier *Shinyo*

15   Germans withdraw from Greece
     Allies enter Athens

October
12   *Tirpitz* sunk by RAF Bomber
     Command in Tromso

November
     All U-boats now fitted with
     Schnorchel

Atlantic	Mediterranean	Pacific
		20 *Kaitens* sink 1 tanker in first operation at Ulithi
		21 *Sealion* (Reich) sinks Japanese battleship *Kongo*, the only battleship sunk in the Pacific by submarine
		29 *Archerfish* (Enright) sinks Japanese carrier *Shinano*
		19 *Redfish* (McGregor) sinks Japanese escort-carrier *Unryu* Japanese merchant shipping reduced to under 2 mil. t., barely sufficient for food supplies
December Dönitz intensifies U-boat campaign in British coastal waters with *Schnorchel*-fitted boats and *Seehund* midgets During the final 6 months of the year hedgehog proves lethal, achieving 35 per cent success rate against 5.6 per cent for conventional depth-charge attack		9 US forces invade Luzon, Philippines
1945 **January** First operational Type XXIII *Elektro* U-boat sails for Norway 39 U-boats on operations in British coastal waters		12 Second *kaiten* human torpedo 'Kongo' unit scores no successes at Guam, Ulithi and elsewhere

February

First Type XXIII coastal *Elektro* U-boat departs on operational patrol

51 U-boats in British coastal waters

4 US forces enter Manila
16 First US air strikes on Japan
19 US forces invade Iwo Jima

March

First operational Type XXI ocean-going *Elektro* U-boat departs Kiel for Norway, *U2511* (Schnee)

53 U-boats in British coastal waters

British 4th Submarine Flotilla from Ceylon joins 8th Flotilla at Fremantle

April

7 Dönitz promulgates 'No capitulation' decree

12 Hitler commands Dönitz to establish a command post in northern Germany

30 First Type XXI *U2511* (Schnee) departs Bergen on war patrol

Hitler commits suicide in Berlin, naming Dönitz as his successor

Squid ahead-thrown depth-charges achieve 40 per cent success rate against conventional U-boats, against 26 per cent for hedgehog and 7 per cent for conventional depth-charge attacks. However no Type XXIII U-boats are destroyed

1 US forces invade Okinawa

Fife succeeds Christie at Fremantle and transfers British 4th Flotilla to US advanced submarine base at Subic Bay, Philippines

Japan is blockaded by sea; the only targets for US and RN submarines are small craft

Atlantic	Mediterranean	Pacific
May	**May**	
5 Montgomery accepts armistice in north German area; Dönitz orders U-boats to surrender	2 German surrender in Italy	
8 Dönitz authorizes unconditional surrender of Germany		
		June
		4–6 Three US submarine wolfpacks enter the Sea of Japan through mine barrier across Tsushima Strait
		9 HMS Trenchant (Hezlet) sinks Japanese heavy cruiser Ashigara
		21 Resistance on Okinawa ends
		July
		29 I58 (Hashimoto) sinks heavy cruiser USS Indianapolis
		August
		6 First atom bomb dropped over Hiroshima
		8 Russia declares war on Japan
		9 Second atom bomb dropped over Nagasaki
		14 Japanese government surrenders

APPENDICES

Appendix A

Representative submarine classes, Great Britain

	S Class	T Class	U Class
Standard surface displacement (tons)	715	1,090	540
Length overall (feet & inches)	217'	275'	191'
Maximum beam (feet & inches)	23' 9"	26' 7"	16'
Surface/underwater speed (knots)	$14\frac{1}{2}$/9	$15\frac{1}{4}$/$8\frac{1}{2}$	$11\frac{1}{4}$/9
Range at 10 knots (miles)	6,000	8,000	3,800
Torpedo tubes	6 bow, 1 stern	10 bow (later 8 bow, 3 stern)	4 bow
Reload torpedoes	6	6	4
Guns	1 × 3", 1 × 20mm AA	1 × 4", 1 × .303" mg.	1 × 3"
Diving depth (feet)	300–350	300	200
Complement	48	56–61	31

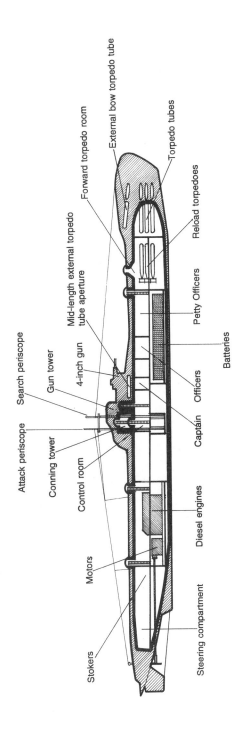

BRITISH T-CLASS SUBMARINE

External bow torpedo tube

Forward torpedo room

Torpedo tubes

Reload torpedoes

Mid-length external torpedo tube aperture

Petty Officers

Search periscope

Gun tower

4-inch gun

Batteries

Attack periscope

Conning tower

Control room

Officers

Captain

Diesel engines

Motors

Stokers

Steering compartment

Representative submarine classes, United States of America

	S class	'Fleet'	
		Tambor class (1939)	Balao class (1942)
Standard surface displacement (tons)	854	1,475	1,525
Length overall (feet & inches)	219' 5"	307' 3"	311' 9"
Maximum beam (feet & inches)	20' 8"	27' 3"	27' 3"
Surface/underwater speed (knots)	13/11	$20/8\frac{3}{4}$	$20\frac{1}{4}/8\frac{3}{4}$
Range at 10 knots (miles)	8,000	11,000	11,000
Torpedo tubes	4 bow	6 bow, 4 stern	6 bow, 4 stern
Reload torpedoes	8	14	14
Guns	1 × 4"	1 × 3"	1 × 4" (or 5")
Diving depth (feet)	200	250	400
Complement	42	60–79	80

UNITED STATES FLEET SUBMARINE

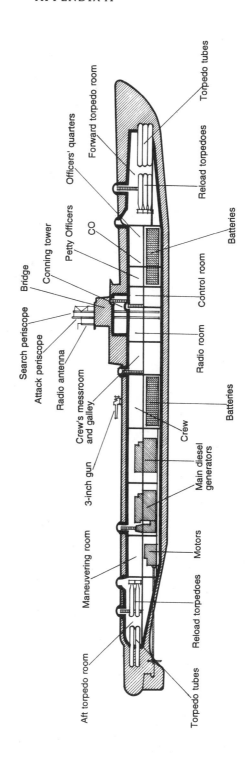

Representative submarine classes, Japan

	KS Type RO100 class	K6 Type RO35 class	B1 Scouting Type I15 class
Standard surface displacement (tons)	525	960	2,200
Length overall (feet & inches)	199' 8"	264'	356' 7"
Maximum beam (feet & inches)	19' 8"	23'	30' 6"
Surface/underwater speed (knots)	14/8	$19\frac{3}{4}/8$	$23\frac{1}{2}/8$
Range (miles)	5,260 at 12 kn	13,000 at 12 kn	14,000 at 16 kn (over 30,000 at 10 knots)
Torpedo tubes	4 bow	4 bow	6 bow
Reload torpedoes	4	6	11
Guns	1 × 3"	1 × 3", 2 × 25mm	1 × 5.5", 2 × 25mmm
Diving depth (feet)	250	260	325
Float plane	–	–	1
Complement	38	61	94

JAPANESE TYPE B1 SCOUTING SUBMARINE

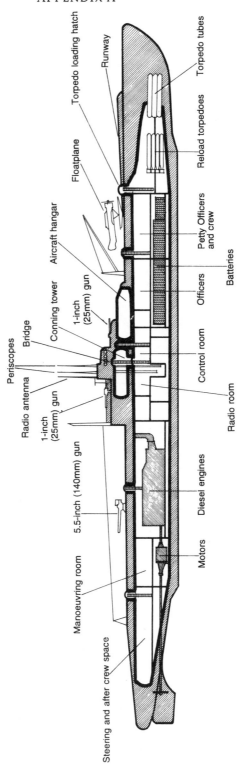

Torpedo loading hatch

Runway

Torpedo tubes

Reload torpedoes

Floatplane

Aircraft hangar

Petty Officers and crew

Conning tower

Batteries

Bridge

1-inch (25mm) gun

Officers

Periscopes

Control room

Radio antenna

Radio room

1-inch (25mm) gun

5.5-inch (140mm) gun

Diesel engines

Manoeuvring room

Motors

Steering and after crew space

Representative submarine classes, Germany

	Type VIIC (1940)	Type IXA	Type IXD₂ (1942)
Standard surface displacement (tons)	760	1,032	1,616
Length overall (feet & inches)	220' 2"	251'	287' 6"
Maximum beam (feet & inches)	20' 4"	21' 4"	24' 7"
Surface/underwater speed (knots)	$17/7\frac{1}{2}$	$18/7\frac{1}{2}$	19/7
Range at 10 knots (miles)	8,500	11,500	31,500
Torpedo tubes	4 bow, 1 stern	4 bow, 2 stern	4 bow, 2 stern
Reload torpedoes	9	16	16
Guns (all AA guns augmented later)	1 × 3.5", 2 × 20mm	1 × 4.1", 1 × 37mm, 1 × 20mm	
Diving depth (in practice far greater)	400	400	400
Complement	44	48	57

GERMAN TYPE VIIC U-BOAT

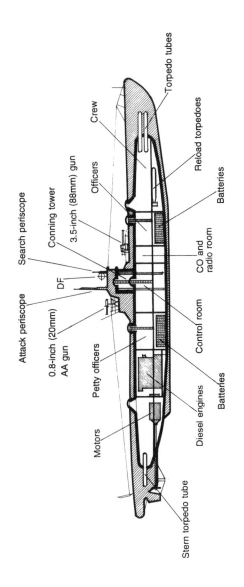

Search periscope

Conning tower

3.5-inch (88mm) gun

Attack periscope

0.8-inch (20mm)
AA gun

DF

Petty officers

Motors

Diesel engines

Control room

Batteries

Crew

Officers

CO and
radio room

Torpedo tubes

Reload torpedoes

Batteries

Stern torpedo tube

Appendix B

The Axis powers' fast underwater submarines, 1944-5

	German Type XXIII	*Japanese STS Type HA201 class*	*German Type XXI*	*Japanese ST Type I201 class*
Surface displacement (tons)	234	376	1,621	1,070
Surface/underwater speed (knots)	12/13	$10\frac{1}{2}$/13	$15\frac{1}{2}$/17	$15\frac{3}{4}$/17
Length overall (feet & inches)	113' 10"	173' 10"	251' 7"	259' 2"
Maximum beam (feet & inches)	9' 10"	13' 1"	21' 7"	19'
Range (miles)	1,350 at $9\frac{3}{4}$ kn	3,000 at 10 kn	11,150 at 12 kn	8,000 at 11 kn
Torpedo tubes	2 bow	2 bow	6 bow	4 bow
Reload torpedoes	–	2	17	6
Guns	–	1 × 7.7mm mg.	2 × twin 30mm AA	2 × 25mm AA
Complement	14	26	58	31

Appendix C

The German Type XXI *Elektro* U-boat

Extracts from the report of Captain G.H. Roberts RN after inspecting two Type XXI U-boats and interviewing U-boat Command staff in May 1945. The first Type XXI was scuttled in Flensburg harbour.

2. . . . The conning tower was on two decks and large, but slim and beautifully streamlined. The whole hull was absolutely sleek with internal main ballast tanks and all fittings faired.
3. The conning tower structure is unique. Instead of there being a proper open deck to the conning tower with a bulwark around [the bridge], my impression was that the conning tower was completely domed over and then holes had been cut in the top for various purposes.

    On the bridge, comfort, mobility for personnel, and facility for communications had all been sacrificed for streamlining . . .
4. The two 30mm mountings were without guns. One is mounted at each end of the conning tower and both are very well streamlined when trained fore and aft. These mountings are power worked. Access to these mountings for the crew of two in each is by a tortuous access from the conning tower under the 'top'.
5. The upper conning tower contains all the attack apparatus and steering gear . . .
6. The Schnorkel [sic] was, as in the Type XXIII, a double tube design, but larger. It is raised by power, a rod passing through the pressure hull to worm gear in the lower deck of the conning tower under the after gun mounting.

The second Type XXI U-boat was alongside at Kiel:

3. The torpedo compartment was enormous, and contained six tubes in two banks, all fitted for L.U.T. firing. There was a calculating box for angling and setting distance run and zigzag of the torpedo shots, and this was between the tubes. Settings on the torpedoes were done by flexible drive to the torpedo inside the tube.

    One torpedo rested in the ready racks, of which there were two per tube, and two racks on the deck, showing that 26 torpedoes could be carried . . .

Interview with Rear-Admiral Godt on 23 May:

Godt said that the projected methods of attack in packs by the Type XXI had not yet been worked out, and they would not have been until a number of Type XXI U-boats had done an individual and successful war cruise. After that, and when the sea qualities were known to the crews, he would have considered pack methods. He said there was one difficulty which would have had to be much improved [sic]. It would be intended that the Type XXI would not surface to attack by pack methods, and therefore that inter U-boat communications would have to be vastly improved. They had no underwater W/T, only the periscope W/T aerial, and from the point of view of communications between U-boats at periscope depth, this method was most unsatisfactory.

Interview with FK Hessler, 1st staff officer, U-boat Command on 24 May:

Hessler was quite definite that it was better to approach the convoy, and carry out screen penetration bow on to the convoy at silent speed because that kept his boat presenting the minimum asdic target for the least possible time.

He then stated that with the Type XXI, attack would be far easier. By the U-boat's asdic and with very good hydrophones, this U-boat would know exactly where he was at any given moment. He said that screen penetration by day, if there was no [temperature] layer (and in Type XXI they were all fitted with a type of Bathythermograph), he would penetrate at 50m. [164 feet], and fire at that depth. But if there *was* a layer, he would penetrate the screen by the normal method at periscope depth. If detected he could be below the layer before he was depth charged.

From his statements it appeared obvious that the projected pack attack by Type XXI [when communication difficulties had been solved] would have been by day with a number of U-boats operating at periscope depth.

REFERENCES AND NOTES

The following abbreviations have been used in the references:

A/S Reports   British Admiralty monthly Anti-Submarine Reports, Nav. Lib., MOD (now in PRO)
BA/MA   Bundesarchiv Militärarchiv, Freiburg, Germany
BdU KTB   Flag Officer U-boats war diary, Nav. Lib.
FdU KTB   Flag Officer U-boats war diary (before Dönitz was promoted BdU)
Führer Vorträge   C-in-C *Kriegsmarine* (ObdM) reports and discussions with the Führer
IMT   International Military Tribunal: evidence and documents presented at the Trials of the Major War Criminals, pub. Nuremberg 1948; English language ed.
IWM   Imperial War Museum, Lambeth Rd., London
MGM   *Militärgeschichtliche Mitteilungen* (mil. journal)
MM   *The Mariner's Mirror*
Nav. Lib.   Ministry of Defence Library, London, Naval Section
NR   *The Naval Review*
PG number   Classification given to German naval files captured by the British at the end of Second World War
PRO   Public Record Office, Kew, London
1/Skl. KTB   German Naval Staff war diary
USNIP   *United States Naval Institute Proceedings*
USNTM   US Naval Technical Mission to Japan
USSBS   US Strategic Bombing Survey (Pacific)

Books and journals listed in the Bibliography are referred to by author's name only, unless there are two or more titles by the same author, in which case the author's name is followed by a key word or words for identification.

Prelude

1. *U30* torpedo log, 3.9.39.
2. British account from PRO ADM 1 9760; ADM 199 140; Slader, pp. 20–1; German account, private information from a survivor of *U30*, who does not wish to be named; *U30* torpedo log.

Chapter 1: Submarines and Submariners

1. W.S. Sims, *The Victory at Sea*, Murray, 1920, p. 9; cited A.J. Marder, *From the Dreadnought to Scapa Flow*, OUP, 1969, iv, p. 148.
2. 1st Sea Ld. to 1st Ld., 27.4.17; cited H. Newbolt, *Naval Operations*, Longmans, 1931, v, p. 23.
3. Ibid., p. 24.
4. A.T. Mahan, *The Influence of Sea Power upon the French Revolution and Empire, 1793–1812*, Boston, 1894, ii, p. 217.
5. See Marder, op. cit. ref. 1 above, p. 101.
6. Dönitz, *Leben*, p. 127.
7. See Shelford, pp. 106–7.

8. Cited Coote, pp. 175–6.
9. Galantin, p. 8.
10. V. Adm. Sir Ian McGeoch to author, 21.10.92.

Chapter 2: Towards the Second World War

1. Capt. H.G.T. Padfield RN to author, 15.2.93.
2. V. Adm. Sir Ian McGeoch to author, 21.10.92; & see McGeoch, *Affair*, p. 89.
3. King, p. 25.
4. Cited Waters, 'ASW', p. 132.
5. *Hansard*, 5.11.37.
6. Waters, 'ASW', p. 130.
7. S.W. Roskill, *Naval Policy Between the Wars*, Collins, 1968, i, p. 536; cited Terraine, p. 177.
8. Gretton, p. 20.
9. Lt. I.L.M. McGeoch, 'The Offensive Value of the Modern Submarine', 1938, unpub.
10. Dönitz, *U-bootswaffe*.
11. Barnett, pp. 45–6.
12. See Nav. Staff History, *The Second World War; the Defeat of the Enemy Attack on Shipping, 1939-1945*, i, chap 1; cited H.P. Willmott, 'The Admiralty and the Western Approaches', in Howarth & Law, p. 180.
13. H.P. Willmott, in ibid., p. 181.
14. Ibid.
15. Kennedy, p. 279. Kennedy's chapter 'The Years of Decay (1919–1939)', pp. 267–98, provides the best account of the desperate situation facing the British Admiralty in these years.
16. P.W. Gretton reviewing Ld. Hill Norton, *Sea Power*, NR, April 1982, p. 134.
17. Alden, pp. 18–19, 36–7.
18. Barnett, pp. 479–80.
19. G. Weir, *Contributions to Naval History*, Nav. Hist. Center, Washington DC, No. 3, p. 112; cited to author Capt. E.L. Beach USN.
20. Galantin, p. 17; & see Blair, p. 199.
21. See Bergamini, pp. 402, 772–3, 777; S. Howarth, 'Isoroku Yamamoto', in Howarth, pp. 109, 113.
22. USNTM S-17, p. 46.
23. 'The Report' in ibid., p. 9.
24. Adm. S. Fukutome, 'Conclusion', in Hashimoto, p. 178.
25. Interrogation Adm. S. Fukutome, USSBS, ii, p. 530.
26. USNTM S-17, p. 11.
27. Hashimoto, pp. 33–4.
28. USNTM S-17, p. 24.
29. See Ienaga, pp. 139–40; Bergamini, pp. 764ff.
30. Cited S. Howarth, 'Isoroku Yamamoto', in Howarth, p. 114; & see Willmott, p. 33.
31. See Ienaga, pp. 46–8.
32. Willmott, p. 15.
33. Ibid., pp. 15–17.
34. Interrogation Capt. A. Oi IJN, USSBS, ii, p. 440.
35. Interrogation Cdr. K. Sogawa IJN, ibid., p. 441.
36. Ienaga, pp. 19ff.
37. Ibid., p. 52.
38. Ibid., p. 53.
39. USNTM S-17, 'Conclusion', p. 11.
40. Saville, pp. 17–20, 39; & see Polmar & Carpenter, pp. 89, 91.
41. Saville, p. 302.

42. Ibid., pp. 230–41, 285.
43. Ibid., pp. 432–4.
44. Rössler, p. 98.
45. Saville, pp. 576–7; Stern, p. 13; Rössler, p. 101.
46. K.Adm. W. Gladisch; see Padfield, pp. 102, 119–20.
47. Kap.z.S. K. Dönitz, 'Organisation der U-Bootswaffe', 21.9.35, B.Nr.Gkdos 65, PG 3443; cited ibid., p. 152.
48. Rössler, pp. 103–4.
49. See for inst. Schaeffer, pp. 66ff; Werner, pp. 26–7, 30; Stern, pp. 92–3.
50. Adm. Foerster, Beurteilung, 1.11.36; PG 31044; cited Padfield, p. 155.
51. Kap.z.S. V. Oehrn to author, 31.5.82.
52. See for inst. KLt. Wassner; cited Rössler, p. 121.
53. See Padfield, p. 164.
54. Dönitz, 10 Jahre, p. 18.
55. FK H. Heye, Denkschrift, 1a 1Skl., 25.10.38, BA/MA Box 39, PG 34181; cited Salewski, iii, pp. 27ff.
56. See Rössler, pp. 112–16.
57. Kap.z.S. K.Dönitz, 'Bericht über FdU Kriegspiel, 1939', 13.4.39; cited Padfield, p. 174.
58. Dönitz, U-Bootswaffe, pp. 68–9.
59. See Mallmann Showell, Swastika, pp. 60–2; Mallmann Showell, U-Bt Cd., pp. 134–5.
60. W. Fürbringer, 'Welche Entwicklungs-Aufgaben und welche operativen Vorbereitungen müssen heute zur Führung eines U-Boots-Handelskrieges gegen England in alle erste Linie gestellt werden', 17.5.39; PG 33390; cited Padfield, pp. 179–80; see also Rössler, p. 120.
61. FdU to K.Adm. Schniewind, 23.5.39; PG 33390; cited Padfield, pp. 180–1.
62. See Rusbridger, pp. 21–2: she took two and a half minutes to submerge.
63. Ibid., pp. 62, 184ff.
64. Meeting at Friedrichshaven, 20–21.6.39; see A. Santoni, 'The Italian Submarine Campaign', in Howarth & Law, p. 323.
65. See Cocchia, pp. 156ff.
66. See Compton-Hall, Underwater, pp. 56, 127–31; Kalapini, 'Convoys to Murmansk', NR, Oct. 1957, pp. 424ff.

Chapter 3: War

1. On 1.9.39 Dönitz had 17 Type II in the N. Sea; 16 Type VII on station in the Atlantic; 5 Type IX off Spain; the other boats were retained for training; & see U-boat staff chart of patrol areas for 7.9.39.
2. FdU KTB, 21.8.39.
3. Ibid., 26.8.39.
4. Ibid., 31.8.39.
5. Ibid., 3.9.39.
6. 'Gedanken über der Einsatz der deutschen U-Bootswaffe', dated 'Anfang September'; PG 33970; & see Padfield, pp. 190–1; Roskill, i, pp. 103–4.
7. FdU KTB, 4.9.39.
8. See German b'casts in PRO ADM 199 140; & for inst. E.H. Lehmann, Wie Sie Lügen, Nibelungen, Berlin, 1939, pp. 29–30.
9. See A/S Reports, Sept. 1939–June 1940, p. 8; & Lane, p. 17.
10. See D. van der Vat, 'Günther Prien', in Howarth, pp. 396–7.
11. See FdU KTB, 7.9.39.
12. See ibid., 16.9.39, 27.9.39; Slader, p. 23; Roskill, i, p. 68.
13. FdU KTB, 7.9.39.
14. Ibid., 15.9.39.
15. Ibid., 18.9.39.

16. Slader, p. 24.
17. FdU KTB, 18.9.39.
18. Ibid., 24.9.39.
19. Ibid., 18.9.39.
20. Information from survivor from U30's crew.
21. FdU KTB, 27.9.39.
22. See Roskill, i, p. 615.
23. J. Hansen-Nootbar to author, July 1982.
24. FdU KTB, 28.9.39.
25. v. Puttkamer, p. 24.
26. Frank, p. 31.
27. Description from Prien's log, cited Terraine, p. 222; & G. Prien, *Mein Weg Nach Scapa Flow*, Berlin, 1941, transl. as *I Sank the Royal Oak*, London, 1954; cited D. van der Vat, in Howarth, p. 400.
28. Prien, cited D. van der Vat, ibid.
29. W. Shirer, *Berlin Diary*, Hamish Hamilton, 1941, p. 190.
30. A/S Reports, Nov. 1939, p. 52.
31. IMT, Doc 642-D, v. 35, p. 270.
32. J.H. Casson, Nov. 1939; PRO ADM 199 2130; cited Lane, p. 240.
33. See Lane, ibid.
34. FdU KTB, 1.10.39.
35. BdU KTB, 31.10.39.
36. Ibid., 21.1.40.
37. Ibid.
38. Ibid.
39. A/S Reports, Jan.–Feb. 1940, p. 8.
40. BdU KTB, 9.2.40.
41. A/S Reports, Jan.–Feb. 1940, p. 12; but see Roskill, i, p. 106, where the number sunk from convoys is stated as 12, and a further 5 stragglers from convoys.
42. A/S Reports, Jan.–Feb. 1940, p. 13.
43. S.W. Roskill, *Naval Policy*, op. cit. chap. 2 ref. 7, ii, p. 135; cited Terraine, p. 252.
44. See King, pp. 34–5.
45. See Compton-Hall, *Underwater*, p. 88.
46. Standing Order No. 151, probably Nov. 1939; IMT Doc 642-D, v. 35, p. 266.
47. Compton-Hall, *Underwater*, p. 88.
48. King, pp. 33ff.
49. D.V. Peyton-Ward, *The Royal Air Force in the Maritime War*, AHB/II/117, p. 1; cited Terraine, p. 248; & see Roskill, i, pp. 37–8, 104–5, 107.
50. D.V. Peyton-Ward, op. cit. ref. 49 above, p. 48 footnote; cited Terraine, p. 248; but see Roskill, i, p. 599, listing two sunk by air escort.
51. Roskill, i, pp. 135–6.
52. Lipscomb, pp. 122–3; King, pp. 44–5.
53. King, p. 45.
54. Adm. P. Ruck-Keene, cited Chalmers, p. 93.
55. See Hinsley, *Br. Intelligence*, i, p. 124.
56. Mars, pp. 67–8; & *HM Submarines*, pp. 19–20, embellished by first-hand accounts of depth-charge attack from other submarines.
57. Mars, pp. 70–1; King, p. 56.
58. King, p. 57.
59. Ibid.
60. Kahn, p. 212.
61. Lipscomb, pp. 131–2.
62. King, pp. 59ff.
63. Ibid., pp. 66ff.

64. BdU KTB 10–19.4.40; & Prien's log; cited Terraine, p. 236.
65. BdU KTB, 19.4.40.
66. Ibid., 17.4.40.
67. Ibid., 19.4.40.
68. Ibid.
69. Ibid., 30.4.40.
70. Hezlet, p. 127.
71. Roskill, i, p. 164.
72. BdU KTB, 15.5.40.
73. See Stern, pp. 79ff; Mallmann Showell, *U-Bt Cd.*, pp. 25ff.
74. BdU KTB, 15.5.40.
75. See Terraine, pp. 239–41.

Chapter 4: Wolfpacks

1. Young, pp. 33ff.
2. See Kahn, p. 212; J. Rohwer, 'The Operational Use of Ultra in the Battle of the Atlantic', Medlicott Symposium, Edinburgh, 1.11.85; cited Terraine, p. 258.
3. King, p. 76.
4. Mars, pp. 81–3; Chapman, p. 118; see also Hezlet, p. 139; Roskill, i, p. 306.
5. Mars, p. 82.
6. Mallmann Showell, *U-Bt Cd.*, pp. 30–1.
7. BdU KTB, 12.6.40.
8. A/S Reports, July & August 1940, p. 7.
9. BdU KTB, 17.8.40.
10. Cited B. Herzog, 'Admiral Otto Kretschmer', in Howarth, p. 383.
11. Ibid., p. 386.
12. Ibid., p. 385.
13. See p. 48.
14. BdU KTB, 26.7.40.
15. Ibid., 2.9.40.
16. Ibid., 9.9.40.
17. See Vause, pp. 55–60.
18. BdU KTB, 22.9.40.
19. Log *U99*, cited Terraine, p. 268; Compton-Hall, p. 100.
20. BdU KTB, 19.10.40.
21. Ibid., 20.10.40.
22. A/S Reports, Nov. 1940, p. 25.
23. BdU KTB, 20.10.40.
24. Ibid.
25. See ibid., 30.9.40.
26. See A. Santoni, op. cit. chap. 2 ref. 64, p. 336.
27. BdU KTB, 1.11.40.
28. Cited Vause, p. 48.
29. W. Kaeding; cited Gannon, p. 49.
30. W. Lüth, *Boot Greift Wieder An*, p. 147; cited Vause, p. 48.
31. A/S Reports, Nov. 1940, p. 39.
32. Ibid., Oct. 1940, pp. 7–8.
33. Ibid., pp. 11–12.
34. Ibid., Nov. 1940, pp. 7–8.
35. Ibid., p. 15.
36. C. Barnett, *The Audit of War*, pp. 168–73; cited Terraine, p. 284.
37. P.B.[eesley], 'Op. Intell. Centre', p. 315; Kahn, pp. 98, 119–20.
38. P.B., op. cit. ref. 37 above, p. 318.
39. BdU KTB, 4.12.40.

40. Ibid.
41. Buchheim, *U-BT War*, 'Storm' section.
42. Monsarrat, pp. 44–5.
43. A/S Reports, Nov. 1940, p. 11; Dec. 1940, p. 6.
44. See Gannon, pp. 29–30; P. Hansen to author, 26.5.92, 1.2.90.
45. P. Hansen to author, 1.2.90.
46. Buchheim, *Boat*, p. 23.
47. A/S Reports, Nov. 1940, p. 47; Dec. 1940, p. 6.
48. R.A. Smith's account, in PRO ADM 199 2136; cited Lane, p. 237.
49. A/S Reports, March 1941, p. 23.
50. Terraine, p. 314; D. van der Vat, 'Günther Prien', in Howarth, p. 403.
51. *U110* log, 00.22, 16.3.41; cited Kahn, p. 10.
52. A/S Reports, April 1941, p. 42; B. Herzog, 'Admiral Otto Kretschmer', in Howarth, p. 390.
53. A/S Reports, April 1941, p. 37.
54. Adm. O. Kretschmer to P. Mallmann Showell; cited Mallmann Showell, *U-Bt Cd.*, p. 62.
55. *U37* log.
56. A/S Reports, April 1941, p. 42.
57. Ibid., p. 46.
58. Ibid., p. 45.
59. W.J.R. Gardner, 'An Allied Perspective', in Howarth & Law, p. 523.
60. 6.3.41; Roskill, i, p. 609.
61. Lt.-Gen. Sir Ian Jacob to author, 21.3.93.
62. See P.B., op. cit. ref. 37 above, pp. 314ff; Terraine, pp. 304–5; Kahn, pp. 406f.
63. BdU KTB, 18.4.41.
64. See Kahn, pp. 32–3, 285ff.
65. A/S Reports, Jan. 1941, p. 36.
66. See Kahn, pp. 155–9; Hinsley, *Br. Intelligence*, i, pp. 336–7.
67. 'The Last Cruise of *U99*'; A/S Reports, April 1941, p. 42.
68. Cdr. (D) 3rd Escort Group to Capt. (D), Greenock, 13.5.41; PRO ADM 1/11133, f. 32.
69. British version in 'Second and Last Cruise of "U110"', in A/S Reports, June 1941, p. 32; PRO ADM 199 2058; German version P. Hansen to author, 12.8.94.
70. '"U110's" War Correspondent', in A/S Reports, June 1941, p. 36; PRO ADM 199 2058.
71. 'Sinking of "U110"', in ibid., p. 33.
72. Ibid.
73. Kahn, p. 163.
74. Ibid., p. 162.
75. Snr. Offcr. 3rd Escort Group to Capt. (D), Greenock, 10.5.41, in 'Capture of *U110*', PRO ADM 1/11133, f. 10.
76. That is, J. Rohwer, P. Mallmann Showell & Anglo-Saxon authors who have obtained information from German U-boat veterans, for inst. J. Vause, M. Gannon; also P. Hansen to author, 1.2.90.
77. Sub.-Lt. D.E. Balme to CO *Bulldog*, 11.5.41, p. 1; PRO ADM 1/11133, f. 13.
78. Cdr. 3rd Escort Group to Capt. (D), Greenock, 13.5.41, 'Interrogation of prisoners from *U110*', in ibid., f. 26.
79. See Hinsley, *Br. Intelligence*, i, pp. 337–8, ii, p. 163; Kahn, pp. 169–85; Lewin, pp. 205–7.
80. Sub.-Lt. D.E. Balme, op. cit. ref. 77 above, p. 3.
81. Cdr. 3rd Escort Group, op. cit. ref. 78 above, f. 26; A/S Reports, June 1941, 'Crew of "U110"', pp. 34–5; PRO ADM 199 2058.
82. In fact tiered bunks only in officers' and petty officers' spaces.
83. Sub.-Lt. D.E. Balme, op. cit. ref. 77 above, p. 3.

Chapter 5: Mediterranean Centre

1. See Hezlet, p. 140; Hinsley, Br. Intelligence, i, p. 388.
2. Hinsley, Br. Intelligence, ii, pp. 22, 283.
3. Mars, p. 132.
4. See Allaway, pp. 80-1.
5. Ibid., pp. 87-9.
6. Capt. M.L.C. Crawford RN, Wanklyn's 1st Lt., to Allaway, 19.1.87; cited ibid., p. 89.
7. M.D. Wanklyn to P. Wanklyn, 10.5.41; cited ibid., p. 97.
8. Capt. C.P. Norman RN to Allaway, 1987; cited ibid., p. 38.
9. J. Wanklyn (widow) to Allaway; cited ibid., pp. 27-8.
10. Lt.-Cdr. R. Raikes to Allaway, 31.1.87; cited ibid., p. 25.
11. Mrs S. Danvers to Allaway; cited ibid., p. 43.
12. Ibid., p. 39.
13. Capt. M.L.C. Crawford RN to Allaway, 19.1.87; cited ibid., p. 105.
14. G. Curnall to Allaway; cited ibid., p. 106.
15. King, p. 95.
16. McGeoch, Affair, p. 43.
17. Mars, p. 130.
18. Mediterranean, 1943; cited in Compton-Hall, Underwater, p. 32.
19. Report cited Wingate, p. 75.
20. Kimmins' b'cast, BBC, 20.2.42; cited Allaway, p. 112.
21. Mars, p. 90.
22. A non-submarine officer on the Lieutenants' Course with Miers.
23. V. Adm. Sir H. Mackenzie; Chapman, p. 10.
24. Galantin, p. 49.
25. L. Kennedy, 'War Crimes'.
26. Galantin, p. 49.
27. Account from Chapman, pp. 25-7, 32, 34, 36-7, 40.
28. Ibid., p. 50.
29. Ibid., p. 55.
30. Capt. S.M. Raw RN to C-in-C; cited ibid., p. 57.
31. Ibid., p. 62; see also Torbay's log, cited L. Kennedy, 'War Crimes'.
32. Herr Ehlebracht report; cited S. O'Dwyer-Russell & P. Miller, 'The Torbay's Bloody Night', The Sunday Telegraph, 26.2.89; for Torbay's log, see L. Kennedy, 'War Crimes'; for Chapman's account see Chapman, pp. 65, 164-6.
33. Chapman, p. 67.
34. 1 Skl Teil C VIII 'Abschrift aus Schreiben der 1 Skl. 1a', 22792/42 g. Kds, p. 2, Berlin, 14.9.42; Nav. Lib.
35. King, p. 102.
36. V. Adm. M. Horton to Admiralty; cited L. Kennedy, 'War Crimes'.
37. Santoni, op. cit. chap. 2 ref. 64, pp. 336-8.
38. BdU KTB, 6.5.41.
39. Hinsley, Br. Intelligence, ii, pp. 147-8.
40. Roskill, i, p. 616.
41. Gwyer & Butler, Grand Strategy, iii Pt. 1, 1964, pp. 9-12; cited Hinsley, Br. Intelligence, ii, pp. 168-9.
42. See Barnett, pp. 256-7, 479-80.
43. Hinsley, Br. Intelligence, ii, p. 169.
44. Roosevelt, cited Cordell Hull to Joseph Kennedy, 30.8.39; cited Lash, p. 23.
45. Stimson, 10.4.41; cited ibid., p. 299.
46. Willmott, p. 8.
47. See Bergamini, pp. 797-8.
48. U93 KTB, 4.6.41.

49. BdU KTB, 20.6.41.
50. Ibid.
51. Ibid., 21.6.41.
52. Werner, p. 43.
53. See Terraine, pp. 349–50.
54. Werner, p. 32; description of convoy action ibid., pp. 28ff.
55. Hinsley, *Br. Intelligence*, ii, p. 33; see also R. Adm. Howard Johnston letter displayed in *Memorial International de la Bataille de L'Atlantique*, Pointe de Penhir, Camaret s.Mer, France, re sinking of *U651*.
56. See Bailey & Ryan, pp. 168–73.
57. Cited Lash, pp. 4, 7, 18.
58. BdU KTB, 1.11.41.
59. Ibid., 19.11.41.
60. See Kahn, pp. 206–7.
61. See p. 119 above; see Kahn, pp. 206–7.
62. Kap.z.S. H. Meckel, formerly A4, Signals Officer, on Dönitz's staff, to author, 24.6.91; and see J. Rohwer, 'The Wireless War', in Howarth & Law, pp. 410–12.
63. BdU KTB, 19.11.41.
64. See J. Rohwer, 'The Operational Use of Ultra in the Battle of the Atlantic', op. cit. chap. 4 ref. 2, p. 19; cited Terraine, pp. 400–1; & J. Rohwer, 'The Wireless War', in Howarth & Law pp. 411, 416–17, where the conclusion is somewhat modified. Rohwer estimates that 300 additional merchant ships totalling up to two million tons would have been sunk between June and December 1941 but for evasive routing on Ultra intelligence.
65. Hinsley, *Br. Intelligence*, ii, p. 283.
66. Simpson, p. 151.
67. C.F. Tuckwood to Allaway, 23.3.87; cited Allaway, p. 126.
68. Capt. M.L.C. Crawford RN to Allaway, 19.1.87; cited ibid., p. 127.
69. Capt. S.M. Raw RN to C-in-C; cited Allaway as PRO ADM 236 48.
70. Roskill, i, pp. 528, 537; v. Crefeld, pp. 189–90.
71. v. Crefeld, p. 190.
72. Chef OKW (Army High Cd,) to For. Min., 15.6.41; *Documents on German Foreign Policy* D, xii, No. 633; cited ibid., pp. 186–7.
73. v. Crefeld, pp. 187–90.
74. Wingate, pp. 84–5.
75. P.O. Kirk; cited Shelford, p. 144; see also Wingate, pp. 94–7.
76. Shelford, pp. 144–5.
77. Mars, p. 124.
78. Werner, p. 68.
79. See p. 50–1.
80. Simpson, p. 166.
81. See Hezlet, p. 145; Rohwer, 'The Operational Use of Ultra . . .', op. cit. chap. 4 ref. 2, p. 19; cited Terraine, pp. 400–1.
82. Wingate, p. 132.

Chapter 6: America at War

1. S. Fukutome, 'Hawaii Operation', *USNIP*, Dec. 1955, p. 1326.
2. Interrogation V. Adm. S. Fukutome, USSBS, ii, p. 530; & see S. Fukutome, 'Conclusion', in Hashimoto, p. 183.
3. See Bergamini, p. 894, note; Capt. E.L. Beach USN to author, 12.9.94.
4. See Roskill, i, pp. 564–7; Stephen, *Sea Battles*, pp. 106–14; Polmar & Carpenter, p. 18; HQ Army forces Far East . . . Japanese Monograph 105.
5. Cdr. S. Murray USN; cited Blair, p. 131.
6. Holmes, *Double-Edged*, p. 103.

7. See Holmes, *Undersea*, pp. 65–8; Blair, pp. 140–1.
8. Holmes, *Undersea*, p. 26.
9. From the account in ibid., pp. 22–3.
10. See Blair, p. 149.
11. Lt.-Cdr. A. Hurst USN, CO of *Permit*; cited Blair, p. 151.
12. See Blair, p. 55 and *passim*; and see p. 31.
13. Blair, pp. 901–3.
14. For Dutch submarines, see Mars, pp. 212–14; Holmes, *Undersea*, pp. 69–70; for probable sinking of *KXVII* by *I166*, see Rohwer.
15. See, for inst. *U.S. Submarine Losses*, p. 3.
16. Interrogation Cdr. K. Sogawa IJN; USSBS, ii, p. 441.
17. Interrogation Capt. A. Oi IJN, USSBS, ii, p. 440.
18. See D.W. Waters, 'Japan – Defeat', pp. 246–7.
19. Cited Buell, p. 52.
20. Morison, i, p. 115.
21. See for inst. Buell, pp. 105–6.
22. Diary, 19–23.1.43; cited Richardson, p. 166.
23. Morison, i, p. 115.
24. BdU KTB, 9.12.41.
25. FdU KTB, 1.10.39; see p. 66.
26. 1/Skl. KTB, 10.12.41; cited Gannon, p. 76.
27. See Gannon, pp. 77–81.
28. Ibid., pp. 128–30.
29. *U123* attack from Gannon, pp. 205–11; *Cyclops* details from Slader, p. 178.
30. U-boat Situation Report, 12.1.42; PRO ADM 225 15, 100820, No. OIC/S.1./57; cited Gannon, p. 211; Beesley, *Very Special*, p. 103.
31. Naval Message 121716, 12.1.42; cited Gannon, p. 212.
32. See Gannon, pp. 176–7.
33. R. Hardegen, *Auf Gefechtsstationen*, pp. 174–5; cited Gannon, p. 231.
34. Slader, p. 179; Gannon, pp. 233–4.
35. *U123* KTB, 25.1.42; cited Gannon, p. 286.
36. Slader, pp. 181–2.
37. *Cyclops*, 9,076 t.; *Norness*, 9,577 t.; *Coimbra*, 6,768 t.; *San Jose*, 1,932 t.; *Brazos*, 4,497 t.; *City of Atlanta*, 5,269 t.; *Ciltvaira*, 3,779 t.; *Culebra*, 3,044 t.; *Pan Norway*, 9,231 t.
38. *U123*, 9/53,173 t.; *U130*, 7/42,239 t.; *U109*, 5/33,733 t.; *U66*, 5/33,456 t.; *U125*, 1/5,666 t; verified post-war figures, & see Rohwer.
39. Navy spokesman quoted *NY Times*, 24.1.42; cited Gannon, pp. 267–9.
40. BdU KTB, 7.2.42.
41. See for inst. Roskill, ii, pp. 97–8, as an indication of British anger.
42. Terraine, p. 420; Roskill, ii, p. 100.
43. See Santoni, op. cit. chap. 2 ref. 64, p. 328.
44. See Kahn, p. 210.
45. See Gannon, p. 328.
46. Adm. Horne to Sec. of Navy, 18.3.46; cited Gannon, p. 457, note.
47. Gannon, pp. 375–7.
48. Cremer, p. 69.
49. Ibid., p. 71.
50. Ibid., p. 73.
51. BdU KTB, 17.5.42.
52. Terraine, p. 420.
53. BdU KTB, 15.4.42.
54. *Führer Vorträge*, 14.5.42.
55. BdU KTB, 1.5.42, 1.6.42.
56. Marshall to King, 19.6.42; cited Terraine, p. 422.

57. King to Marshall, 21.6.42; cited ibid., pp. 422–3.
58. See Beesley, *Very Special*, pp. 108–9.
59. See Buell, p. 298.
60. Gannon, p. 389.
61. This view is taken by Gannon, author of the latest study of the *Paukenschlag* operation; see esp. pp. 383–93, 413; see also Roskill's more diplomatic account, Roskill, ii, pp. 94–9. It is decidedly not shared by Prof. R.W. Love Jr.: see R.W. Love, 'Fleet Admiral Ernest J. King' in Howarth, pp. 89–92; & Love, ii, pp. 64ff; D.C. Allard in 'A United States Overview', Howarth & Law, pp. 568–70, inclines to Love's view, suggesting that King gave priority to the protection of trans-Atlantic troop convoys to Great Britain, and to the Pacific theatre. So he did, but the question is, why in early 1942 was it vital to transport American troops to Great Britain?
62. Cited Allaway, p. 162.
63. *Pegaso* log, 16.15–16.30, 14.4.42; cited Wingate, p. 176; Capt. Baron F. Acton to Allaway; Allaway, p. 163.
64. See Roskill, ii, p. 59; *HM Submarines*, p. 36; Lipscomb, p. 194.
65. V. Adm. Sir Arthur Hezlet to Allaway, 25.3.87; cited Allaway, p. 165.
66. R. Adm. G.W.G. Simpson to Mrs E. Wanklyn, 11.5.42; cited ibid., p. 166.
67. *HM Submarines*, p. 36.
68. Allaway, p. 166; Wingate, p. 176; Lipscomb, p. 194; all with different figures.
69. Simpson, p. 186.
70. McGeoch, *Affair*, p. 80.
71. *HM Submarines*, pp. 37–8; and account in Chapman, pp. 134–40.
72. Holmes, *Double-Edged*, p. 75.
73. See, however, S. Howarth's brilliant analysis of Yamamoto's mind, in 'Isoroku Yamamoto', in Howarth, pp. 119–25.
74. See Rohwer.
75. See Holmes, *Undersea*, p. 135; for US dispositions see Willmott, pp. 306–9; Blair, p. 236; and for US intelligence see Holmes, *Double-Edged*, pp. 89–92.
76. Stephen, *Sea Battles*, p. 167.
77. See Willmott, p. 347.
78. Y. Tanabe & J.D. Harrington, 'I sank the *Yorktown* at Midway', *USNIP*, May 1963, p. 62; cited Polmar & Carpenter, p. 25.
79. See Compton-Hall, *Monsters*, p. 140.
80. See for inst. the case of S.S. *Kwantung*, sunk by *I56*, Lt. K. Ohashi, 5.1.42; Slader, p. 5.
81. See Lane, p. 242.
82. Ienaga, p. 53; and for example of naval training, see Millott, pp. 7–8.
83. Holmes, *Undersea*, p. 150.
84. Galantin, p. 29.
85. R. Adm. C. Lockwood to R. Adm. R. Edwards; cited, undated, Blair, p. 274.

Chapter 7: The Turn of Fortune

1. See Bergamini, pp. 985–6, 989; & see the recently revealed diaries of Hirohito's younger brother, Prince Takamatsu.
2. Lt.-Cdr. J.R. Moore USN; cited Blair, p. 298.
3. Holmes, *Undersea*, p. 158.
4. See USNTM S-17; 'The Report', p. 15.
5. Polmar & Carpenter, p. 28.
6. D. Kurzman, *Left to Die; The Tragedy of USS Juneau*; brought to author's attention by Capt. E.L. Beach USN.
7. Bergamini, p. 1004.
8. Hashimoto, p. 61.

9. Ibid., pp. 60–3.
10. Bergamini, p. 1011.
11. See p. 37; cited S. Howarth, 'Isoroku Yamamoto', in Howarth, p. 114.
12. Cited ibid., p. 127.
13. Polmar & Carpenter, p. 29, without citing sources.
14. See Hashimoto, pp. 63–7.
15. Holmes, *Double-Edged*, pp. 108, 120, 124–5.
16. See USNTM S-17, pp. 13–14.
17. Douglas-Hamilton, pp. 58–61.
18. See Barnett, pp. 491ff.
19. *The Times*, London, 13.7.42.
20. Douglas-Hamilton, p. 94.
21. Mars, p. 149.
22. See ibid., pp. 149–55.
23. Young, p. 101.
24. Ibid.
25. King, p. 134.
26. Mars, p. 160.
27. Ibid., p. 162.
28. M. Gabriele, '*La Guerre des Convois entre l'Italie et l'Afrique du Nord*', in Comité d'histoire de la Deuxième Guerre Mondiale (ed.), *La Guerre en Méditerranée 1939–1945*, Paris, 1971, p. 287; Roskill, ii, p. 344.
29. See v. Crefeld, pp. 199–200.
30. See Young, pp. 104–5; Wingate, p. 237.
31. Roskill, ii, p. 336.
32. KLt. Heinz Hirsacker; private information. Many *Kriegsmarine* records, especially of courts martial, were destroyed in the final days of the war.
33. Douglas-Hamilton, p. 103.
34. King, p. 136.
35. Ibid., p. 133.
36. V. Adm. Sir Ian McGeoch to author, 18.9.94.
37. McGeoch, *Affair*, pp. 81–2.
38. Ibid. pp. 82–3.
39. Young, pp. 105–6; McGeoch, *Affair*, p. 83.
40. McGeoch, *Affair*, p. 90; & see p. 22 above.
41. J. Casing, *Submariners*, London, 1951, p. 21; cited McGeoch, *Affair*, p. 90.
42. McGeoch, p. 90.
43. Ibid., p. 101.
44. Ld. Moran, *The Anatomy of Courage*, Constable, 1945, pp. 63–4.
45. King, p. 136.
46. See Warren & Benson, pp. 100ff; Roskill, ii, p. 342.
47. See Hezlet, p. 153; Roskill, ii, p. 432.
48. V. Adm. Sir Ian McGeoch to author, 16.8.94.
49. See Stephen, *Admirals*, pp. 76ff, esp. pp. 82, 157.
50. *HM Submarines*, p. 59.
51. BdU KTB, 1.8.42.
52. Ibid., 1.9.42.
53. Blackett, p. 228.
54. Ibid., p. 232.
55. See p. 151.
56. See Barnett, pp. 574–5.
57. Monsarrat, p. 105.
58. Mars, p. 168.
59. King, pp. 92, 145.
60. Galantin, p. 201.

61. See Mallmann Showell, *U-Bt Cd.*, p. 32.
62. Cremer, pp. 95–6.
63. See Salewski, ii, pp. 623ff.
64. See ibid., pp. 439ff; BdU KTB, 21.6.42.
65. R. Adm. Lange (Skl. U 1a) *'Auswirkung der Arbeiterlage und des Rohstoffs-mangel auf die Führung des U-bootskriegsführung'*, Berlin, 22.1.42. pp. 14, 19; 1 Skl. Teil C IV KTB; PG 32174.
66. Ibid., p. 27.
67. See p. 151.
68. See Roskill, ii, p. 82.
69. Blackett, pp. 223–5.
70. Hinsley, *Br. Intelligence*, ii, pp. 260–1.
71. See Blackett, pp. 223–6.
72. Ibid., p. 227.
73. See Roskill, ii, pp. 79–80.
74. See ibid., p. 89.
75. A/S Reports, April 1942, p. 9.
76. See Blackett, pp. 214–15, 235.
77. Ibid., pp. 216–17.
78. BdU KTB, 11.6.42.
79. Ibid., 2.7.42.
80. Ibid., 21.8.42.
81. A/S Reports, Feb. 1942, p. 42.
82. P. Hansen to author, 1.2.90.
83. See Buchheim, *Boat*, pp. 16ff; & see A/S Reports, Feb. 1942, p. 29, re survivors of *U95*: 'the first lieutenant was an extreme Nazi, unpleasant, bloodthirsty and confident that the invasion of Britain would be brutally and successfully accomplished.'
84. See Buchheim, *Boat*, pp. 13–16.
85. A former U-boat officer, who wishes to remain anonymous, to author, 2.5.91.
86. P. Hansen to author, 1.2.90.
87. F. Lynder to author, Nov. 1982.
88. Werner, p. 89; & see Cremer, p. 86; & A. Niestlé, 'German Technical and Electronic Development', in Howarth & Law, p. 442.
89. See Cremer, p. 116; Mallmann Showell, *Swastika*, p. 65.
90. See Roskill, ii, p. 205; & Niestlé op. cit. ref. 88 above, p. 442.
91. See Barnett, pp. 587–8.
92. See Robertson, pp. 37–9.
93. Ibid., pp. 51–4.
94. See pp. 283–4; A/S Reports, Feb. 1942, p. 42.
95. Buchheim, *Boat*, p. 19; and private information.
96. BdU KTB, 23.12.41.
97. Cited Williams, pp. 85–6.
98. Ibid., pp. 93–5.
99. BdU KTB, 3.9.42.
100. BdU to OKM (Navy High Cd.), *'Waffenentwicklung für U-Boote'*, 9.9.42; 1 Skl. Teil C IV KTB; PG 32174.
101. *'Aufstellung U-bootsverluste'*, 24.8.42; in ibid.
102. BdU to OKM, 9.9.42; op. cit. ref. 100 above.
103. Ibid.
104. Baumbach, *'Einfluss der Schiffsversenkungen'*, 9.9.42; Skl. 3 Abt. B Nr. 85/42 gKdos. Chefs; 1 Skl. Teil C IV KTB; PG 32174.
105. P. Hansen to author, 1.2.90.
106. Ibid.
107. Dönitz, *10 Jahre*, p. 253.

108. BdU KTB, 16.9.42.
109. IMT Doc. D-650, v. 35, pp. 304ff.
110. Atlantic Operation Order No. 56, 7.10.43, repeating an order of autumn 1942; IMT Doc. 663-D, v. 25, pp. 338ff.
111. IMT Doc. D-423, v. 5, p. 219.
112. *Führer Vorträge*, 14.5.42.
113. Trevor-Roper, p. 696.
114. See p. 148; '*Abschrift aus Schreiben* . . .' op. cit. chap. 5 ref. 34, p. 2.
115. *Führer Vorträge*, 28.8.42.
116. Ibid., p. 2.
117. See IMT, v. 13, p. 375; & Dönitz's testimony in IMT, v. 13, p. 368: 'I have never put my name to any order which could in the slightest degree lead to anything of the kind [attacks on survivors], *not even when it was proposed to me as a reprisal measure*' (author's italics).
118. Confirmed by Adm. K.-J. v. Puttkamer, Hitler's naval adjutant.
119. P. Heisig's testimony, IMT, v. 5, pp. 223ff, esp. pp. 226-7; see also P. Heisig's affidavit, 27.11.45; Doc. D-566, IMT, v. 35, pp. 360ff.
120. K.-H. Moehle's testimony, IMT, v. 5, pp. 231ff; see also K.-H. Moehle's affidavit; IMT Doc. 382-PS, v. 25, pp. 395ff.
121. Buchheim, *Boat*, pp. 24-6.
122. Capt. C. Fox, in Kerr, p. 69.
123. Vause, p. 71.
124. P. Hansen to author, 28.8.92; and see Vause, pp. 54, 73, 77, 148.
125. Vause, p. 148; & P. Hansen to author, 28.8.92.
126. Kap.z.S. W. Lüth, '*Menschenführung auf einem Unterseeboot*', lecture at Weimar, 17.12.43; cited Vause, p. 124.
127. Cited Vause. p. 134.
128. *U181* KTB, 30.11.42, 06.00, 06.55 entries; cited Vause, pp. 141-2.
129. See Buchheim, *Boat*, p. 25.
130. W. Lüth & C. Korth, *Boot Greift Wieder An*, Berlin 1944; *U43* KTB, and Vause interviews with former crew members of *U43*; all cited Vause, pp. 2-4, 90-1.
131. BdU KTB, 30.11.42.
132. Ibid., 1.11.42, 1.12.42.
133. Ibid., 1.1.43.
134. BdU Situation Report, 19.12.42, in ibid., 31.12.42.

Chapter 8: Crisis for the U-boats

1. 5.2.43; cited M. Salewski, '*Von Raeder zu Dönitz*' MGM 2/1973, p. 146.
2. See Polmar & Carpenter, pp. 100, 116.
3. Buell, p. 272.
4. See ibid., pp. 267ff; Richardson, pp. 158ff.
5. Richardson, p. 157.
6. Ibid.
7. See W.J.R. Gardner, 'An Allied Perspective', in Howarth & Law, pp. 522ff. The Anti-U-boat Warfare Committee proved far more effective than the 'Atlantic' Committee, and notably brought Operational Analysis as purveyed by Prof. P.M.S. Blackett to the higher direction of the war at sea.
8. Roskill, ii, p. 362.
9. See Hinsley, *Br. Intelligence*, ii, pp. 753-5; Roskill, ii, pp. 352-3.
10. Buell, p. 270.
11. Richardson, p. 165; & see Schofield, pp. 205ff.
12. Schofield describes Pound, during leisure time by the sea, attempting to persuade King to increase the number of US destroyers allocated to the Atlantic. Every time he raised the subject King stooped and 'carefully selecting a flat pebble from

the beach, he sent it skimming over the water.' It was the only reply Pound ever
received; Schofield, p. 206.

13. Hinsley, *Br. Intelligence*, ii, pp. 552, 750–1.
14. Ibid., p. 553.
15. A/S Reports, Jan. 1943, p. 3.
16. P. Hansen to author, 26.5.92.
17. See Syrett, pp. 48–50.
18. Werner, p. 92. In fact the single ship *U230* sank was the 2,800-ton British SS
    Egyptian.
19. Werner, p. 93.
20. Syrett, p. 58; Roskill, ii, p. 356; Terraine, pp. 530–1.
21. 'Analysis of U-boat Operations in the Vicinity of Convoy SC118, 4th–9th
    February 1943'; PRO ADM 199 2017; cited Syrett, p. 60.
22. See Hinsley, *Br. Intelligence*, ii, pp. 553–4.
23. See Buell, pp. 293–4; Love, pp. 110ff.
24. See Roskill, ii, p. 363, and map; S. W. Roskill, *The Navy at War 1939–1945*,
    Collins, 1960, p. 273; Middlebrook, p. 309 states that Adm. King had 112 VLR
    Liberators in the Pacific by March 1943.
25. See Roskill, ii, pp. 468–71. Of 10 U-boats sunk in the Gulf/Caribbean areas and
    off Brazil between July 1942 and May 1943, only three were sunk by air patrols;
    the others were sunk by sea or air escorts.
26. Cominch staff memo.; cited Middlebrook, pp. 311–12.
27. See p. 313.
28. BdU KTB, 10.3.43.
29. Werner, pp. 95–8.
30. BdU KTB, 10.3.43.
31. Lt. Levasseur FFN; account of the action from the permanent exhibition at the
    Memorial International de la Bataille de l'Atlantique, Pointe de Penhir, Camaret-
    s-Mer, France.
32. See Middlebrook, pp. 154–7.
33. McGeoch (ed.), '*Nariva*'; 'the recollections of Capt. Gwilym Williams', *NR* July
    1993, pp. 257–60; Oct. 1993, pp. 386–90.
34. Ibid., Oct. 1993, p. 390.
35. BdU KTB, 20.3.43.
36. V. Adm. Sir M. Horton to R. Adm. R.B. Darke, 23.3.43; cited Chalmers,
    p. 188.
37. 31.3.43 decree; cited Salewski, ii, p. 278.
38. *Führer Vorträge*, 11.4.43.
39. 1 Skl. Teil C IV KTB, 1942–43; PG 32174, Nav. Lib., Reel 41, Frs. 247, 248,
    296, 323, 347, 348, 373ff.
40. BdU KTB, 1.4.43.
41. A/S Reports, April 1943, p. 184.
42. BdU KTB, 25.4.43.
43. Ibid., 6.5.43, '*Abschlussbetrachtung Geleitzug 36*', i.e. ONS5.
44. Werner, p. 120.
45. BdU KTB, 13.5.43, '*Abschlussbetrachtung Geleitzug 38*', i.e. HX237.
46. BdU KTB, 14.5.43, '*Abschlussbetrachtung Geleitzug 39*', i.e. SC129.
47. BdU KTB, 15.5.43; BdU Gkdos 2555 A4.
48. BdU KTB, 20.5.43, '*Abschlussbetrachtung Geleitzug 41*', i.e. SC130.
49. See Roskill, ii, p. 471; Terraine, p. 600.
50. See p. 291; BdU KTB, 3.9.42.
51. BdU KTB, 21.5.43.
52. BdU KTB, 23.5.43, '*Schlussbetrachtung Geleitzug 42*', i.e. HX239.
53. Bdu KTB, 24.5.43.
54. Ibid., *Anlage 2 'Tagesbefehl'*.

Chapter 9: Victory in the Pacific

1. See Polmar & Carpenter, pp. 35, 101ff.
2. See Alden, pp. 224ff, 248ff.
3. See p. 245.
4. Holmes, *Secrets*, p. 202; Holmes, *Victory*, pp. 201–2.
5. Beach, p. 31.
6. George Grider; cited Blair, p. 381.
7. Grider; cited ibid., p. 382.
8. Grider; cited ibid., p. 383.
9. See Beach, p. 41.
10. Forest J. Sterling; cited Blair, p. 383.
11. Grider; cited Blair, p. 384.
12. See Blair, p. 386.
13. Cited Holmes, *Victory*, p. 216.
14. Beach, pp. 105–6.
15. Galantin, p. 50.
16. See Holmes, *Secrets*, p. 137.
17. See ibid., p. 134; Holmes, *Victory*, pp. 219–20.
18. Beach, pp. 59–60.
19. For courses, bearings etc., see Beach, pp. 60–1.
20. Ibid., p. 62.
21. Cited Blair, p. 431.
22. See Holmes, *Victory*, pp. 236–7.
23. Galantin, p. 88.
24. Ibid., p. 89.
25. Blair, p. 931.
26. Holmes, *Secrets*, p. 154.
27. See Blair, pp. 511, 984.
28. Beach, pp. 63–4.
29. See Holmes, *Victory*, p. 274; In March 1945 *I44* under Lt.-Cdr. Genbei Kawaguchi is said to have been submerged under repeated attack for 46 hours. On his return Kawaguchi was relieved of his command for not launching his *kaitens*; see Polmar & Carpenter, p. 57.
30. Galantin, p. 92.
31. Santoni, op. cit. chap. 2 ref. 64, pp. 329–32.
32. Ibid., pp. 328–9, 334.
33. Capt. G.H. Roberts RN, 'Report on a visit to Germany', May 1945; PRO ADM 1 17561.
34. See Rohwer; Hezlet, pp. 157–8.
35. See Hezlet, p. 160; Wingate, p. 367.
36. Coote, p. 88.
37. R. Adm. C.B. Barry; cited *HM Submarines*, p. 61.
38. Cited Compton-Hall, *Monsters*, p. 130.
39. See F. Walker & P. Mellor, *The Mystery of X5*, Kimber, 1988.
40. Chalmers, p. 134.
41. *HM Submarines*, p. 62.
42. Account of X-craft evolution and attack on *Tirpitz* chiefly from Warren & Benson, pp. 56–61, 147–98, 323–6; Roskill, iii Pt. 1, pp. 64–9; Compton-Hall, *Monsters*, pp. 119–34.
43. Cited Warren & Benson, p. 192.
44. See Beesley, *Very Special*, pp. 196–7; Terraine, p. 637.
45. See Stern, pp. 87–9.
46. Ibid., pp. 84–5.
47. See Werner, pp. 130–2.

48. BdU KTB, 14.6.43; cited Stern, p. 107.
49. BdU KTB, 14.8.43; cited ibid., p. 124.
50. See Stern, pp. 100–8; & see BdU KTB, 20.2.44, *Anlage: 'Entwicklung des Geleit-zugkampfes seit Mai 1943'*.
51. BdU KTB, 20.9.43; cited Stern, p. 88.
52. 1 Skl. Teil C IV KTB, 24.9.43; *'Geleitoperation Nr. 5 Zaunkönig; Schluss'*, signed Dönitz.
53. See BdU KTB, 20.2.44; *Anlage*, op. cit. ref. 50 above.
54. See ibid.
55. See Vause, pp. 176–9.
56. Kretschmer's adjusted total: 44 ships/266,629 tons; Lüth's adjusted total: 43 ships/225,713 tons.
57. Schmidt; cited Vause, p. 185.
58. Buchheim, *Boat*, pp. 102–3.
59. See Roskill, iii Pt. 1, p. 389.
60. *Führer Vorträge*, 31.5.43.
61. Ibid., pp. 8–9.
62. Ibid.; & for details of the new U-boat construction programme, see E. Rössler, 'U-boat Development and Building', in Howarth & Law, pp. 130ff.
63. See ibid., pp. 133–5; & A. Niestlé, 'German Technical and Electronic Development', in Howarth & Law, pp. 434–6; & Rössler, p. 216.
64. *Führer Vorträge*, 31.7.43, p. 7.
65. See A. Niestlé, op. cit. ref. 63 above, pp. 442–4.
66. Ibid., p. 447.
67. BdU KTB, 20.2.44; *Anlage*, op. cit. ref. 50 above.
68. Ibid.
69. See Chalmers, p. 165.
70. Ibid., p. 184.
71. Schaeffer, p. 128.
72. Cremer, p. 149.
73. BdU KTB, 1.3.44; *Anlage 'e'*; see also interrogation FK G. Hessler, 24.5.45: 'Morale in 1943 at BdU was very low indeed because of high casualties and other factors'; PRO ADM 1 17561.
74. Account from unpublished talk by P. Hansen, 'The Longest Depth Charge Pursuit of the Second World War . . . the Story of *U358*'. The sole survivor was *Matrosen Gefreiter* (Ldg. Seaman) Alfons Eckert.
75. Roskill, iii Pt. 1, p. 257.
76. Cited L. Kennedy, 'War Crimes', p. 55.
77. KLt. H. Eck's and KK A. Schnee's testimony at the trial; Cameron, pp. 48–9, 65; for FK G. Hessler also briefing Eck, P. Hansen to author, 1.2.90.
78. See p. 296 above.
79. See ibid.
80. Law Reports, *Peleus* Case, pp. 54–5.
81. Ibid., p. 84.
82. Ibid., pp. 54–9.
83. Cited L. Kennedy, 'War Crimes', p. 55.
84. See p. 299 above; IMT, v. 5, pp. 223ff, esp. pp. 226–7; & Heisig's affidavit, 27.11.45; ibid., v. 35, pp. 360ff.
85. P. Hansen, an observer at Eck's trial, to author, 1.2.90.
86. See Cameron, p. 139.
87. Morison, iii, p. 26.
88. Holmes, *Victory*, p. 272.
89. Ibid., p. 247; Blair, p. 552.
90. See p. 150 above.
91. Holmes, *Victory*, pp. 247–8; Fukui, plts. 69ff.

92. See Bergamini, pp. 65, 1047, 1053–4.
93. Ibid., pp. 66–9, 1055–6.
94. E. Beach, 'Radar', p. 54.
95. See Holmes, *Secrets*, p. 126.
96. Interrogation Capt. T. Abe IJN, staff officer escort forces; USSBS, ii, p. 488.
97. Interrogation Capt. A. Oi IJN, staff officer Combined Escort Fleet; ibid., i, p. 59.
98. USNTM E-17, p. 1.
99. See interrogations Capt. A. Oi IJN, Cdr. K. Sogawa IJN, Capt. T. Abe IJN; USSBS, ii. pp. 440–1, 485–8.
100. See Z. Orita & J. Harrington, *I-boat Captain*, Major Books, Calif., USA, 1976, pp. 185–6; cited Polmar & Carpenter, p. 36; & see USNTM S-17, pp. 7, 116.
101. See Hashimoto, pp. 105–6.
102. See *US Submarine Losses*, pp. 176–7; Polmar & Carpenter, p. 42; Roskill, iii Pt. 1, pp. 373–4.
103. See Holmes, *Secrets*, p. 155.
104. See Galantin, pp. 124–30; Blair, pp. 541–2.
105. Holmes, *Secrets*, p. 129.
106. Holmes, *Victory*, p. 329; interrogation Lt.-Cdr. N. Yatsui IJN, USSBS, i, p. 161.
107. Account from *US Submarine Losses*, pp. 70–1; Holmes, *Secrets*, pp. 148–9; Holmes, *Victory*, pp. 264–5; Blair, pp. 524–5.
108. Alden, p. 95.
109. Cited Blair, p. 529.
110. See Holmes, *Victory*, p. 279.
111. Galantin, p. 169; & see Alden, p. 88.
112. Galantin, p. 136.
113. Morison, viii, p. 26; Holmes, *Victory*, p. 286.
114. Beach, p. 134.
115. Galantin, p. 17.
116. Cited Blair, p. 573.
117. See Morison, viii, p. 26; Hezlet, p. 217.
118. Interrogation Lt.-Cdr. S. Yasumoto IJN; USSBS, i, pp. 184–5.
119. Interrogation Capt. S. Kamide IJN; USSBS, ii, pp. 309ff.
120. See Alden, pp. 56, 105. One of the best-kept secrets of the war was the change from mild steel to high tensile steel with the *Balao* class.
121. See interrogations Capt. A. Oi IJN, Lt.-Cdr. T. Okamotu IJN, Capt. S. Kamide IJN; USSBS, i, pp. 57–9, 197ff; ii, pp. 309f.
122. Morison, viii, p. 19.
123. See Interrogation Capt. T. Abe IJN, Ch. of Staff, Southern Expeditionary Fleet; USSBS, ii, p. 486.
124. BdU Standing Order No. 151, Nov. 1939; IMT, Doc 642-D, v. 35, p. 266.
125. See interrogation Cdr. T. Kuwahara IJNR, escort commander; USSBS, i, pp. 212–13.
126. Account from Morison viii, pp. 22–3; Holmes, *Victory*, pp. 326–8; Blair, pp. 643–4; interrogation Cdr. T. Kuwahara, op. cit. ref. 125 above.
127. Polmar & Carpenter, pp. 43–5; Roskill, iii Pt. 1, p. 374; 'Table of Losses of I.J.N. Submarines' in USNTM S-17, pp. 125ff.
128. See 'Battle Lessons of the Greater E. Asia War Operation "A" Submarine campaign', transl. in USNTM S-17, pp. 27ff, 34–6, 49–50; see Morison viii, pp. 215–23.
129. 20.5.44; USNTM S-17, p. 52.
130. See Holmes, *Secrets*, pp. 171–2.
131. See p. 377.
132. Cited Morison, viii, p. 228; this account from ibid., pp. 224–8.
133. Beach, p. 84.

134. Quote from Dealey's report, cited Blair, p. 638; & see Beach, pp. 90–2.
135. Beach, pp. 93–4; Holmes, *Victory*, p. 335.
136. Dealey's report, cited Beach, p. 98.
137. Cited Blair, p. 548.
138. Lt. F. Lynch; cited Blair, p. 717.
139. See Beach, pp. 98–9; Blair, p. 639.
140. Commander Advance Force Directive 150715, 15.6.44; USNTM S-17, p. 65.
141. 'Extract from Battle Lessons', Commander Sub. Sqdn 7; & 'Outline of Events in the Campaign'; ibid., pp. 38, 71–2.
142. Ibid., p. 38.
143. *RO115* log, 19.6.44; USNTM S-17, p. 122; & see ibid., pp. 92–3.
144. Ibid., p. 89.
145. Ibid., pp. 78–9.
146. Ibid., p. 80.
147. See K. Ikeda, 'Jisaburo Ozawa'; in Howarth, pp. 285–7.
148. Capt. E. Jo IJN to V. Adm. T. Onishi, 21.6.44; cited Bergamini, p. 1067.
149. See Polmar & Carpenter, p. 137; USNTM S-01-1, p. 29.

Chapter 10: The End

1. See Salewski, ii, pp. 408ff; see Dönitz to *Befehlshaber der Kriegsmarine* in *Schlussanspruche auf der Tagung in Weimar*, 17.12.43; cited ibid., p. 414.
2. See for inst. BdU KTB, 1.6.44, 'Summary'.
3. See p. 371; *Führer Vorträge*, 31.5.43.
4. BdU KTB, 1.1.43 & 1.6.44.
5. Werner, p. 191.
6. BdU KTB, 1.6.44.
7. To all groups; 1 Skl. 13321/44 g.v.10.4.44, KTB BV; BA/MA IIIM 1005/9; cited Salewski, ii, p. 415.
8. OKM 2 Skl. BdU op 1961 gkdos v. 27.3.44; KTB C IIb; BA/MA IIIM 1012/8; cited ibid.
9. Ibid., 11.4.44; cited ibid., pp. 415–16 apart from concluding sentences, which can be seen in BA/MA.
10. H. Busch, *So War Der U-Boot Krieg*, Deutscher Heimats Verlag, Oldendorf, 1952, 4th (revised) ed. Bielefeld, 1983, pp. 462–3.
11. Werner, pp. 213, 257.
12. Ibid., p. 214.
13. BdU KTB, 6.6.44. All times above from ibid.
14. Skinner, p. 183; & see Roskill, iii Pt. 2, pp. 17ff.
15. Werner, pp. 220–2.
16. Cremer, pp. 182–4.
17. PRO AIR 41 74; cited Skinner, p. 183; see Roskill, iii Pt. 2, p. 463.
18. Werner, pp. 221–7.
19. Skinner, pp. 187–8; Mallmann Showell, *U-Bt. Cd.*, p. 202; Roskill, iii Pt. 2, pp. 17ff.
20. 1 Skl. KTB A, 10.6.41.
21. Heye's views summarized by US Office of Naval Intelligence, March 1949; cited Compton-Hall, *Monsters*, p. 152.
22. Ibid., p. 144.
23. Roskill, iii Pt. 2, pp. 463–5; Skinner, pp. 186–90.
24. See Blair, pp. 683, 988.
25. Cited ibid., p. 676.
26. King, p. 161.
27. Young, p. 305.
28. King, p. 151.

29. See ibid., pp. 150–5.
30. Ibid., p. 158.
31. Roskill, iii Pt. 1, p. 351.
32. Morison, viii, p. 26.
33. See Buell, pp. 463ff, esp. p. 468.
34. Blair, p. 695; & see Bergamini, pp. 1074–5, 1090–1; & for the strategic controversy see Buell, pp. 463ff; Roskill, iii Pt. 2, p. 200, both of whom find the Leyte landings the better option.
35. R. Adm. Y. Nakawasa, Ch. Nav. Operations Staff, to Hirohito, 18.10.44; cited Bergamini, p. 1079.
36. Interrogation Capt. A. Oi IJN; USSBS, i, p. 58; & see interrogation R. Adm. S. Horuichi; ibid., ii, pp. 195–6; & see Holmes, Secrets, p. 190.
37. See interrogations Lt.-Cdr. S. Yasumoto, Cdr. M. Chihaya; ibid., i, pp. 190. 202.
38. 'Summary of Japanese Submarine Operations and Activities'; USNTM S-17, p. 119; & see Holmes, Victory, p. 390.
39. Roskill, iii Pt. 2, p. 223.
40. Galantin, p. 217; action described from ibid., pp. 212–18.
41. See USNTM S-17, Appendix IX, pp. 95–101; & 'Performance Data of Mark 2 Model 2 Radar, May 1944'; USNTM S-19, p. 18; & see Hashimoto, pp. 129–30, 137, 148, 161–2.
42. Holmes, Victory, p. 379; Hezlet, p. 219.
43. US Submarine Losses, p. 109.
44. That O'Kane was by no means the only CO doing this is shown by a diagram of an attack in early Sept. 1944 included in the interrogation report of escort commander, R. Adm. M. Matsuyama; USSBS, i, p. 232, Plate 57-2.
45. Cited Blair, p. 768.
46. Cited ibid.
47. See p. 29; see Alden, pp. 48–9, 82–3, 88–90.
48. Beach, p. 197.
49. Ibid., p. 145.
50. Ibid., pp. 250–1.
51. Cited Alden, Appendix 6, p. 236.
52. Ibid., pp. 237, 88.
53. Ibid., pp. 236–41.
54. Galantin, p. 230.
55. Ibid., p. 231.
56. Ibid., p. 247.
57. See interrogation Cdr. T. Kuwahara IJN; USSBS, i, p. 216.
58. See Blair, pp. 816–17; Hezlet, pp. 219–21; Holmes, Victory, p. 494.
59. Lt.-Cdr. J.F. Enright, Archerfish, who sank the 60,000-ton carrier Shinano; see Blair, p. 988.
60. Blair, p. 984.
61. Hezlet, p. 220.
62. Blair, pp. 953–66.
63. See p. 421.
64. USNTM S-17, p. 120; Polmar & Carpenter, pp. 51–2; Holmes, Victory, pp. 412–13.
65. Y. Yokota & J. Harrington, The Kaiten Weapon, Ballantine Books, N.Y., 1962, p. 53; cited Polmar & Carpenter, p. 52.
66. Hashimoto, p. 130.
67. Ibid., p. 134.
68. Lt. Ishikawa's note, cited ibid., p. 136.
69. See I. Rikikei & N. Tadoshi, The Divine Wind Special Attack Units, 1951; cited Ienaga, p. 183.

70. See Holmes, *Victory*, p. 432.
71. USNTM S-17, pp. 120-1.
72. Ibid., p. 122.
73. See R. Adm. B. McCandles, '*Kaiten* – Japan's Human Torpedoes', *USNIP*, July 1962, p. 120.
74. Interrogation Adm. E. Godt, 12.5.45; PRO ADM 1 17617.
75. Ibid.
76. *Führer Vorträge*, 7.4.45; see Roskill, iii Pt. 2, pp. 286, 291-2 for confirmation.
77. NID 12/SI/Tech/005, 8.10.44; cited Hinsley, *Br. Intelligence*, iii, p. 523.
78. NID 12/SI/Tech/003, 30.5.44; cited ibid., iii, p. 520.
79. Cited Roskill, iii Pt. 2, p. 289.
80. See for inst. Schaeffer, p. 146.
81. Roskill, iii Pt. 2, pp. 294-5, 301, 467.
82. See Padfield, pp. 407-10.
83. Cited Lüdde-Neurath, p. 131.
84. Niestlé, op. cit. chap. 9 ref. 63, p. 435.
85. Lüdde-Neurath, p. 67; & see Cremer, pp. 207-8; & private information.
86. Roskill, iii Pt. 2, p. 304 gives 784 U-boats lost; *US Submarine Losses*, pp. 158ff gives 796 lost.
87. Latest figures from U-Boot-Archiv, Cuxhaven-Altenbruch.
88. See p. 266.
89. The execution form is reproduced in full in Buchheim, *Zu Tode*, p. 173. The details of Kusch's career and court martial are from a former *Kriegsmarine* officer uniquely well placed to know them, but who wishes to remain anonymous. The court martial records were almost certainly destroyed towards the end of the war. See also E. Topp, 'Manning and Training the U-boat Fleet', in Howarth & Law, pp. 216-17, where some facts are wrong.
90. See Padfield, pp. 392-7; & see for inst. Dönitz's decree of 7.4.45: 'We soldiers of the *Kriegsmarine* . . . stand bold, hard and loyal as a rock of the resistance. A scoundrel who does not so behave must be hung and have a placard fastened to him: "Here hangs a traitor who by his low cowardice allows German women and children to die instead of protecting them like a man"'; SSD MBKO 661; Gltd. Plan 'Paula' Ost, IWM; cited Padfield, p. 392.
91. Werner, pp. 305-6. Werner concealed Mengersen's responsibility for these barbaric executions, worthy of the late Führer in whose name they were carried out, under the pseudonym Juergensen.
92. Ibid., p. 304.
93. PRO ADM 1 18222, pp. 1-2.
94. Report of Capt. G.H. Roberts RN on visit to Germany, May 1945, p. 3; PRO ADM 1 17561.
95. Ibid., p. 7; & see interrogation of Adm. E. Godt in PRO ADM 1 17617.
96. USNTM S-01-1, p. 10.
97. Ibid., pp. 14, 24; & Submarine Supplement II, S-01-7, pp. 20, 25-40.
98. USNTM S-17, Enclosure B, 'Sinking of USS *Indianapolis* by Japanese Submarine *I 58*', pp. 109-10; & see Holmes, *Victory*, pp. 474-5.
99. Chiefly from Beach, pp. 205-14; Holmes, *Victory*, pp. 428ff.
100. Mars, p. 221; & see Blair, p. 857.
101. Capt. L. Shadwell RN, cdg. 8th Sub. Flotilla, Fremantle, cited in *The Times*, London, 7.5.88. This *Times* report refers to an example of inhumanity by Lt. W. St. G. Anderson, CO of HM S/M *Trusty*, when sinking an Indonesian coaster on 25.11.44; the PRO file on this case has a 75-year closure order. For Edward Young's care for prisoners, see Mars, p. 220; Young, pp. 289ff.
102. Beach, pp. 256ff; Capt. E.L. Beach USN to author, 12.9.94.
103. See Blair, p. 988.
104. Chiefly from Mars, pp. 227-9; Holmes, *Victory*, pp. 445-6.

105. See Warren & Benson, pp. 297ff; Roskill, iii Pt. 2, pp. 376–7.
106. See Holmes, *Victory*, p. 476; Bergamini, pp. 73, 1102.
107. Hashimoto, pp. 173–4; & see Bergamini, pp. 119–20.
108. Beach, p. 273.
109. King, pp. 173–4.
110. See Blair, p. 878, and mthly patrol summaries *passim*; Roskill, iii Pt. 2, p. 369; Hezlet, p. 224.
111. See A. Thowsen, 'The Norwegian Merchant Navy in Allied War Transport', in Howarth & Law, p. 60; Roskill, iii Pt. 2, p. 305 gives total MN losses as 2,828 ships/14,687,231 tons.
112. T. Roscoe, *U.S. Submarine Operations in World War Two*, US Nav. Inst. Press, Anapolis, 1950.
113. *US Submarine Losses*, p. 1.
114. Figures from RN Submarine Museum, Gosport, Hampshire, England.
115. Capt. E.L. Beach USN to author, 12.9.94.

BIBLIOGRAPHY

Unpublished

Admiralty Anti-Submarine Warfare Division Monthly Reports; Naval Library, MOD, London (now in PRO)

Führer Vorträge Chief of Naval Staff reports to the Führer, in 1/Skl. KTB Teil CVII, see below

Kriegstagebücher (war diaries)

BdU KTB war diary, U-boat Command

1/Skl. KTB war diary German Naval War Staff, Operations Division

1/Skl. KTB Teil CIV war diary German Naval War Staff, U-boat Division

1/Skl. KTB Teil CVII deliberations of the Chief of Naval Staff and [his] reports to and discussions with the Führer

1/Skl. KTB Teil C VIII war diary German Naval War Staff, International Law, Propaganda, Politics Division

Lt. I.L.M. McGeoch, 'The Offensive Value of the Modern Submarine', 1938, revised 1939, but Admiralty refused permission to publish

Sub.-Lt. J.L. Stevens, RNR, Submarine Course notebook, 1943–44

Saville, A.W. *The Development of the German U-Boat Arm*, D. Phil. thesis, Univ. of Washington, 1963

Official Histories and Monographs

Admiralty, *His Majesty's Submarines*, HMSO, 1947

Law Reports of Trials of War Criminals, vol. I *Peleus Case*, HMSO, 1947

IMT (International Military tribunal), *Evidence and Documents presented at the Trials of the Major War Criminals*, Nuremberg, 1948 (English language ed.)

HQ [US] Army Forces Far East, Mil. Hist. section, Japanese Research Division, *General Summary of Naval Operations, Southern Force*, Japanese Monograph 105

Naval History Division: Office of the Chief of Naval Operations, *United States Submarine Losses World War II*, Washington, 1963

US Naval Technical Mission to Japan:
Ship & Related Targets – Japanese Submarine Operations, S-17, 1946
Japanese Submarine Equipment, S-19, 1946
Electronics Targets, Japanese Submarine and Ship-borne radar, E-01, 1945
Electronics Targets, Japanese Radio, Radar and Sonar Equipment, E-17, 1946
Characteristics of Japanese Naval Vessels:
　　Article I, Submarines, S-01-1, 1946
　　Article 6, Submarines, Supplement, I, S-01-6, 1946
　　Article 7, Submarines, Supplement, II, S-01-7, 1946
United States Strategic Bombing Survey (Pacific)

Journals

Beach, E.L., 'Radar and Submarines in World War II', *Defense Electronics*, Oct. 1979, pp. 48–56

B[eesley], P., 'The Operational Intelligence Centre, Naval Intelligence Division', *The Naval Review*, Oct. 1975, pp. 314–24

G.M.B., 'Radar development in the U.S. Navy 1922–1941', *The Naval Review*, Oct. 1975, pp. 324–7

—— 'Radio *versus* The U-boats', *The Naval Review*, Nov. 1946, pp. 362–6

Gardner, W.J.R., 'Prelude to Victory: The Battle of the Atlantic 1942–1943', *The Mariner's Mirror*, Aug. 1993, pp. 305–16

Gretton, P.W., 'Why don't we Learn from History?', *The Naval Review*, Jan. 1958, pp. 13–25

Kennedy, L., 'War Crimes on the Ocean', *Telegraph Magazine* (date unknown), pp. 16–20, 55–7

J.C.L. & P.W.G., 'Shipbuilding in the U.S.A.', *The Naval Review*, Aug. 1955, pp. 311–14

McGeoch, I. (ed.), 'The Sinking of RMS *Nariva* – 17 March 1943', *The Naval Review*, July 1993, pp. 257–60; Oct. 1993, pp. 386–90

G.W.N., 'The Development of the Royal Canadian Navy', *The Naval Review*, Nov. 1951, pp. 368–78

Parkes, O., 'Japan's War Time Navy', *The Naval Review*, Feb. 1952, pp. 47–63

Peattie, M.R., 'Akiyama Saneyuki and the Emergence of Modern Japanese Naval Doctrine', *US Naval Institute Proceedings*, Feb. 1977, pp. 60–9

Plumtree, R.W., 'Easy Questions Difficult Answers – the Subjugation of Japan', *The Naval Review*, Oct. 1990, pp. 356–66

Scott, M., 'Submarine Boarding Party', *The Naval Review*, Oct. 1989, pp. 387–8

Skinner, I., 'The Naval Threat on the Western Flank of Operation Neptune, June 1944', *The Mariner's Mirror*, May 1994, pp. 178–90

Syrett, D., 'German U-Boat Attacks on Convoy SC 118, 4 February to 14 February 1943', *American Neptune*, Spring 1984, pp. 48–60

Tailyour, P., 'The Submarine through the pages of *The Naval Review*', *The Naval Review*, 75th anniversary, 1988

Waters, D.W., 'ASW: The first 40 Years', *The Naval Review*, April 1986, pp. 128–34

—— 'The Science of Admiralty', *The Naval Review*, Oct. 1963, pp. 395–410; Jan. 1964, pp. 15–26; July 1964, pp. 291–309; Oct. 1964, pp. 423–37

—— 'Japan – Defeat through Blockade', *The Naval Review*, July 1988, pp. 246–7

Books

All books were published in London unless otherwise stated.

Akerman, P., *Encyclopaedia of British Submarines 1901–1955* (privately published), Chippenham, Wilts., 1989

Alden, J.D., *The Fleet Submarine in the U.S.Navy*, Arms & Armour Press, 1979

Allaway, J., *Hero of the Upholder: the Story of Lt. Cdr. M.D. Wanklyn VC DSO***, the Royal Navy's top Submarine Ace*, Airlife, Shrewsbury, England, 1991

Bailey, T.A., & Ryan, P.B., *Hitler vs. Roosevelt: the Undeclared Naval War*, The Free Press, Macmillan, NY, 1979

Barnett, C., *Engage the Enemy More Closely: The Royal Navy in the Second World War*, Hodder & Stoughton, 1991

Beach, E.L., *Submarine!*, Henry Holt, NY, 1952 (refs from Heinemann ed., 1953)

Beaver, P., *U-Boats in the Atlantic (World War 2 Photo Album No. 11)*, Patrick Stephens, Cambridge, 1979

Beesley, P., *Very Special Intelligence*, Hamish Hamilton, 1977

Bergamini, D., *Japan's Imperial Conspiracy*, Wm. Morrow, NY, 1971 (refs from Pocket Book ed., NY, 1972)

Blackett, P.M.S., *Studies of War; Nuclear and Conventional*, Oliver & Boyd, 1962

Blair, C. Jr., *Silent Victory: The U.S. Submarine War against Japan*, Lippincott, NY, 1975

Blake, R., & Louis, R. (eds.), *Churchill*, OUP, Oxford, 1993

Buchheim, L.-G., *The Boat*, Collins, 1974

———— *U-Boat War*, Collins, 1978

———— *Zu Tode Gesiegt*, Bertelsmann, Munich, 1988

Buell, T.B., *Master of Sea Power: A Biography of Fleet Admiral Ernest J. King*, Little Brown, Boston, 1980

Cameron, J. (ed.), *Trial of Heinz Eck, August Hoffmann . . . The Peleus Trial*, Wm. Hodge, 1948

Chalmers, W.S., *Max Horton and the Western Approaches*, Hodder & Stoughton, 1954

Chapman, P., *Submarine Torbay*, Hale, 1989

Cocchia, A., *The Hunters and the Hunted*, US Nav. Inst. Press, Annapolis, 1958

Compton-Hall, R., *The Underwater War 1939–45*, Blandford Press, Poole, 1982

———— *Submarine Warfare: Monsters & Midgets*, Blandford Press, Poole, 1985

Corbett, J., & Newbolt, H., *Naval Operations*, Longman, 1920–31

Crefeld, M. van, *Supplying War: Logistics from Wallenstein to Patton*, CUP, Cambridge, 1977

Cremer, P., *U-Boat Commander: A Periscope View of the Battle of the Atlantic*, Bodley Head, 1984

Dönitz, K., *Die U-Bootswaffe*, Mittler, Berlin, 1939

———— *10 Jahre und 20 Tage*, Athenäum, Frankfurt, 1958

———— *Deutsche Strategie zur See im zweiten Weltkrieg*, Bernard & Graefe, Munich, 1969

———— *Mein Wechselvolles Leben*, Musterschmidt, Göttingen, 1975

Douglas-Hamilton, J., *The Air Battle for Malta*, Airlife, Shrewsbury, England, 1981

Dülffer, J., *Weimar, Hitler und die Marine*, Droste, Düsseldorf, 1973

Frank, W., *The Sea Wolves*, George Mann, Maidstone, 1953

Fukui, S., *The Japanese Navy at the End of World War 2*, We, Old Greenwich, Conn., 1970

Galantin, I.J., *Take Her Deep! A Submarine against Japan in World War II*, Unwin Hyman, 1988

Gannon, M., *Operation Drumbeat*, Harper & Row, NY, 1990

Haraszti, E.H., *Treaty-Breakers or Realpolitiker? The Anglo-German Naval Agreement of June 1935*, Harald Boldt, Boppard am Rhein, 1974

Hashimoto, M., *Sunk: The Story of the Japanese Submarine Fleet*, Cassell, 1954

Herzog, B., *60 Jahre Deutsche Uboote, 1906–1966*, Lehmann, Munich, 1980

Herzog, B., & Schomaekers, G., *Ritter der Tiefe, Graue Wölfe*, Welsermühl, Munich, 1976

Hezlet, A., *The Submarine and Sea Power*, Peter Davies, 1967

Hinsley, F.H., & Stripp, A., *Codebreakers; The Inside Story of Bletchley Park*, OUP, Oxford, 1993

Hinsley, F.H., Thomas, E.E. et al., *British Intelligence in the Second World War; Its Influence on Strategy and Operations*, HMSO, 1979–88

Holmes, W.J., *Undersea Victory: The Influence of Submarine Operations on the War in the Pacific*, Doubleday, NY, 1966

———— *Double-edged Secrets: U.S. Naval Intelligence Operations in the Pacific during World War II*, US Nav. Inst. Press, Annapolis, 1979

Howarth, S. (ed.), *Men of War: Great Naval Leaders of World War II*, Weidenfeld & Nicolson, 1992

Howarth, S., & Law, D. (eds.), *The Battle of the Atlantic 1939–1945: The 50th Anniversary International Naval Conference*, Greenhill Books/Nav. Inst. Press, 1994

Ienaga, S., *The Pacific War: World War II and the Japanese, 1931–1945*, Pantheon Books, NY, 1978

Kahn, D., *Seizing the Enigma*, Souvenir Press, 1991

Kemp, P.J., *The T-Class Submarine; The Classic British Design*, Arms & Armour, 1990

Kennedy, P.M., *The Rise and Fall of British Naval Mastery*, Allen Lane, 1976

Kerr, J. Lennox, *Touching the Adventures of Merchantmen in the Second World War*, Harrap, 1953

King, W., *The Stick and the Stars*, Hutchinson, 1958

Lane, T., *The Merchant Seaman's War*, Manchester Univ. Press, Manchester, 1990

Lash, J.P., *Roosevelt and Churchill 1939–1941: The Partnership that Saved the West*, Norton, NY, 1976

Lenton, H.J., *German Warships of the Second World War*, Macdonald & Janes, 1975

Lewin, R., *Ultra Goes to War*, Grafton, 1988

Lipscomb, F.W., *The British Submarine*, Adam & Charles Black, 1954

Love, R.W. Jr., *History of the U.S. Navy 1942–1991*, Stackpole Books, Harrisburg, Pa., 1992

Lüdde-Neurath, W., *Regierung Dönitz*, Musterschmidt, Göttingen, 1953

Mars, A., *British Submarines at War 1939–1945*, Kimber, 1971

McGeoch, I., *An Affair of Chances*, Imperial War Museum, 1991

Middlebrook, M., *Convoy: The Battle for Convoys SC 122 and HX 229*, Allen Lane, 1976

Millot, B., *Divine Thunder; The Life and Death of the Kamikazes*, Macdonald, 1971

Monsarrat, N., *Three Corvettes*, Cassell, 1945

Morison, S.E., *History of United States Naval Operations in World War 2*, Little Brown, Boston, 1947–62

Padfield, P., *Dönitz; The Last Führer*, Gollancz, 1984

Peillard, L., *Geschichte des U-Boot Krieges 1939–1945*, Wilhelm Heyne, Munich, 1974

Polmar, N., & Carpenter, D.B., *Submarines of the Imperial Japanese Navy 1904–1945*, Conway Maritime Press, 1986

Puttkamer, K.-J. v., *Die Unheimliche See*, Berlin, 1952

Richardson, C., *From Churchill's Secret Circle to the BBC; The Biography of Lt. General Sir Ian Jacob*, Brasseys, 1991

Robertson, T., *Walker, R.N.*, Evans Brothers, 1956

Rohwer, J., *Axis Submarine Successes 1939–1945*, US Naval Inst. Press, Annapolis, 1983

Roskill, S.W., *The War at Sea 1939–1945*, HMSO, 1954–61

Rössler, E., *The U-Boat; The Evolution and Technical History of German Submarines*, Arms & Armour, 1981

Rusbridger, J., *Who Sank Surcouf? The Truth about the Disappearance of the Pride of the French Navy*, Century, 1991

Saleswski, M., *Die Deutsche Seekriegsleitung 1939–45*, Bernard & Graefe, Munich, 1970–5

Schaeffer, H., *U-boat 977*, Kimber, 1952

Schofield, B.B., *British Sea Power*, Batsford, 1967

Shelford, W.O., *Subsunk; the Story of Submarine Escape*, Harrap, 1960

Showell, P. Mallmann, *U-Boats under the Swastika*, Ian Allen, 1973

—— *U-Boat Command and the Battle of the Atlantic*, Conway Maritime Press, 1989

Simpson, G.W.G., *Periscope View*, Macmillan, 1972

Slader, J., *The Red Duster at War*, Kimber, 1988

Stephen, M., *Sea Battles in Close-up*, Ian Allen, 1988

—— *The Fighting Admirals*, Leo Cooper, 1991

Stern, R.C., *Type VII U-boats*, Arms & Armour, 1991

Terraine, J., *Business in Great Waters; The U-Boat Wars 1916–1945*, Leo Cooper, 1989

Trevor-Roper, H. (ed.), *Hitler's Table Talk*, Weidenfeld, 1953

Vause, J., *U-Boat Ace: the Story of Wolfgang Lüth*, Airlife, Shrewsbury, England, 1992

Warren, C.E.T., & Benson, J., *Above us the Waves: The Story of Midget Submarines and Human Torpedoes*, Harrap, 1953

Werner, H.A., *Iron Coffins: A Personal Account of the German U-boat Battles of World War II*, Arthur Barker, 1970

Williams, M., *Captain Gilbert Roberts R.N. and the Anti U-Boat School*, Cassell, 1979
Williamson, G., *Aces of the Reich*, Arms & Armour, 1989
Willmott, H.P., *The Barrier and the Javelin; Japanese and Allied Pacific Strategies February–June 1942*, US Nav. Inst. Press, Annapolis, 1983
Wingate, J., *The Fighting Tenth; The Tenth Submarine Flotilla and the Siege of Malta*, Leo Cooper, 1971
Young, E., *One of Our Submarines*, Hart-Davis, 1952

SELECT INDEX

Submarine flotillas are indexed only by their base port; officers' ranks are those they held when first introduced in the text; operations, weapons, equipment, strategy, tactics are listed under two main headings: Anti-Submarine Warfare and Submarine; authors mentioned in the text are generally omitted; submarines, warships and merchantmen are indexed by nationality after the general index.